ISBN 978-0-331-94676-5
PIBN 11043660

APPENDIXES A, B, AND C

INDIANS OF THE UNITED STATES

HEARINGS

BEFORE THE

COMMITTEE ON INDIAN AFFAIRS

HOUSE OF REPRESENTATIVES

SIXTY-SIXTH CONGRESS
FIRST SESSION

ON

THE CONDITION OF VARIOUS TRIBES OF INDIANS

ACT OF JUNE 30, 1919

HOMER P. SNYDER, New York, *Chairman*.

PHILIP P. CAMPBELL, Kansas.
ROYAL C. JOHNSON, South Dakota.
JOHN A. ELSTON, California.
FREDERICK W. DALLINGER, Massachusetts.
BENIGNO C. HERNANDEZ, New Mexico.
MARION E. RHODES, Missouri.
JAMES H. SINCLAIR, North Dakota.
CLIFFORD E. RANDALL, Wisconsin.
ALBERT W. JEFFERIS, Nebraska.
R. CLINT COLE, Ohio.
JOHN REBER, Pennsylvania.
M. CLYDE KELLY, Pennsylvania.
CHARLES D. CARTER, Oklahoma.
CARL HAYDEN, Arizona.
WILLIAM J. SEARS, Florida.
JOHN N. TILLMAN, Arkansas.
HARRY L. GANDY, South Dakota.
WILLIAM W. HASTINGS, Oklahoma.
ZEBULON B. WEAVER, North Carolina.
RICHARD F. McKINIRY, New York.

(IN TWO VOLUMES)

VOL. 2—APPENDIXES

WASHINGTON
GOVERNMENT PRINTING OFFICE
1919

APPENDIX A

REPORT ON THE

SAN CARLOS IRRIGATION PROJECT AND THE HISTORY OF IRRIGATION ALONG THE GILA RIVER

SAN CARLOS IRRIGATION PROJECT.

DEPARTMENT OF THE INTERIOR,
UNITED STATES INDIAN SERVICE (IRRIGATION),
Los Angeles, Calif., November 1, 1915.

COMMISSIONER OF INDIAN AFFAIRS,
Washington, D. C.

(Through Mr. W. M. Reed, chief engineer.)

SIR: The following report on the status of the available water supply, and the estimated cost of the proposed San Carlos irrigation project on the Gila River, Ariz., is respectfully submitted.

This investigation was undertaken in accordance with an authority from the Secretary of the Interior, No. 120603, dated November 8, 1913, and was continued in compliance with an item in the Indian appropriation act approved August 1, 1914, providing for investigations in connection with the San Carlos irrigation project. The initial authority provided as follows:

For all purposes necessary for proper conduct of surveys, observations, and examinations to determine the extent of water rights in and to the normal and flood flow of the Gila River, Ariz., in connection with the old Indian ditches on the Gila River reservation and others, remaining available for appropriation and use under the legal theory of prior appropriations and use and for preparation of maps, plans, drawings, specifications, and such other records as may be necessary to determine said water rights and the feasibility of any new irrigation project for Indian lands.

The item of the Indian appropriation act, above referred to, provided for an investigation recommended by the Board of Engineer officers of the United States Army. That part of the act relating to this matter reads as follows:

For investigations recommendsd by the Board of Engineer officers of the United States Army as set forth in paragraph two hundred and seventeen of their report to the Secretary of War on February fourteenth, nineteen hundred and fourteen, House Document number seven hundred and ninety-one, sixty-third Congress, second session, and report as to the supply of the legally available water, acreage available for irrigation. and titles thereto, the maximum and minimum estimated cost of the San Carlos irrigation project, including dam and necessary canals, ditches, and laterals, with recommendation and reasons therefor, and the probable cost of adjudication of water rights along the Gila River necessary thereto, and to take the steps necessary to prevent the vesting of any water rights in addition to those, if any, now existing until further action by Congress, $50,000.

In compliance with this act the investigations were continued under authority No. 80303, dated September 8, 1914, issued by the Secretary of the Interior, which provided:

For all purposes necessary for continuing the conduct of surveys, observations, examinations, and investigations to determine the extent of water

APPENDIX A

REPORT ON THE

SAN CARLOS IRRIGATION PROJECT AND THE HISTORY OF IRRIGATION ALONG THE GILA RIVER

rights in and to the normal and flood flow of the Gila River, in Arizona, in connection with the old Indian ditches on the Gila River reservation, and others remaining available for appropriation and use under the legal theory of prior appropriation and use, and for the preparation of maps, drawings, specifications, and such other records as may be necessary to determine said water rights, and the feasibility of the San Carlos project.

SCOPE OF INVESTIGATION.

This investigation, as directed in the above act, was undertaken primarily for the purpose of securing data relative to the existing water rights along the Gila River to assist in the determination of the quantity of water legally available for the proposed San Carlos irrigation project. The report also includes an estimate of the maximum and minimum cost of the project, as called for in the act.

EARLIER INVESTIGATIONS.

The investigation of the water resources of the Gila watershed, with a view of increasing, through storage, the amount of water available for irrigation, was first considered by the United States in 1896, in consequence of the diminishing supply of water available to the Pima Indians on the Gila River Indian Reservation. Since that date several additional investigations have been made by the United States Geological Survey, the United States Reclamation Service, and the United States Indian Service, all under the direction of the Interior Department.

The need of an additional water supply in the vicinity of Florence and Casa Grande has been the means of interesting in the matter several irrigation companies and private persons, and as a result investigations have been conducted and reports prepared by several eminent irrigation engineers, among them Mr. J. H. Quinton and Mr. James D. Schuyler.

Finally, under section 2 of the act approved August 24, 1912, by which appropriations were made for the current and contingent expenses of the Bureau of Indian Affairs, Congress directed that a board of United States Army Engineers investigate and report on the question. The findings of this board were submitted under date of February 14, 1914, in a report entitled "Report to the Secretary of War of a board of Engineer officers, United States Army, under Indian appropriation act of August 24, 1912, on the San Carlos irrigation project, Arizona."

The results of the investigation by the Army board are summarized in their findings and conclusions, which are contained in pages 62 to 65 of their report, and from which the following paragraphs are quoted:

PRACTICABILITY AND ADVISABILITY OF PROJECT.

202. The board finds that the San Carlos irrigation project is entirely feasible from physical considerations.

203. The advisability of the project, as before stated, will depend on its cost as compared with the benefits to result from it.

204. The cost of the project per acre will depend upon the number of acres that can be taken under the project, and this upon the quantity of water physically and legally available.

205. The board has pointed out that the following uncertainties exist as to the water supply legally available:

(*a*) It is not known whether the run-off at San Carlos as determined by the board will continue to be available or whether additional diversions above that point will be made.

(*b*) It is not known whether all of the water that can be taken into the main canal will be available for lands under the project or whether a part of it will have to be delivered free to lands not entered under the project.

(*c*) It is not known whether a part of the water that might be taken into the main canal may not have to be left in the river to satisfy rights below the reservation.

206. Until these uncertainties are cleared up, either by an adjudication or by competent legal opinion, as Congress may determine, it would be inadvisable for the United States to proceed with this project. In the following discussion, therefore, it is assumed that all of the above questions are settled in favor of the project, so that the existing run-off at San Carlos is available for use under the project.

RECOMMENDATIONS.

217. The board recommends:

(*a*) That the San Carlos irrigation project, as described in this report, be adopted and carried out by the United States, provided it shall appear, either as the result of an adjudication or of competent legal opinion, as Congress may elect, that the legally available water supply is sufficiently close to that assumed in this report to make the cost of the project not more than $75 per acre.

(*b*) That suit for an adjudication of water rights along the Gila River be immediately brought in the United States district court (the United States being a party to the suit) and that every other step be taken which will hasten an early adjudication.

(*c*) That such executive and legal steps be taken as may be necessary to prevent the vesting of any water rights in addition to those, if any, now existing.

(*d*) That in case the project is not undertaken until after an adjudication, a diversion dam on the reservation (par. 171) be constructed to improve irrigation condition on the Pima Reservation.

A summary of all prior investigations of the San Carlos project has been aptly set forth on pages 11 to 23, inclusive, of the Army board's report, and it is deemed unnecessary to repeat the information here.

The report of the Army board, while it covers the practicability of the San Carlos project as a whole, confines itself more particularly to the investigations of the feasibility of the construction of the proposed San Carlos Dam and impounding reservoir. Very little or nothing can be added to the natural data assembled in connection with this feature of the investigation. It may be remarked in passing, however, that the observations made in connection with the silt determination seem capable of more than one interpretation, and it is believed that the problem of desilting a reservoir of the magnitude of that proposed at San Carlos has not received its final solution. It is admitted that no better method can be suggested at this time and therefore the figures of the United States Army board have been used in the computation of the annual maintenance costs of the project.

The duty of water assumed by the Army board in determining the amount of land which it would be possible to irrigate by means of the proposed reservoir, and on which depends the reclamation charge per acre, appears to be inadequate in the light of all data assembled in the preparation of this present report.

Neither the time nor the funds available to the board for the preparation of its report were sufficient to warrant an investigation to determine the amount of water physically and legally available.

In the preparation of the data presented herein an effort has been made to determine the amount of water physically available and to assemble facts which will be of assistance in the determination of the amount of water legally available, and these studies, together with a new estimate of the cost of the project, from the body of the following report. For this reason it may be regarded as supplemental to the report of the United States Army Board, and no effort is made to include data published therein, references simply being made to that document.

NATURE OF PRESENT INVESTIGATION.

The work in connection with the present investigation includes the collection and study of data which may be divided into three separate headings, or subjects, namely (1) The amount of water physically available for the San Carlos project; (2) The amount of water legally available for the San Carlos project; and (3) An estimate of the cost of the San Carlos project.

The first subject, the amount of water physically available for the San Carlos project, involves a consideration of the data bearing upon the actual flow of the Gila River and its tributaries, the influence of seepage, evaporation, and return flows, and in general the hydrography, of the stream.

The second subject, the amount of water legally available, depends upon a determination of all the water rights along the stream. To obtain the requisite information respecting existing water rights, it was necessary to determine the past and present use of water along the Gila River and all of its tributaries, with the exception of the Salt River, the waters of which already have been adjudicated. This necessitated a careful survey of the land now under cultivation, as well as of that which was previously cultivated, and the collection of all data having a bearing on the past and present use of water. The data thus assembled constituted a history of irrigation along the Gila and its tributaries.

The third subject, the estimate of cost of the San Carlos project, involves the designing and estimating of cost of the storage dam and other irrigation works which make up the project, and includes the cost of maintenance, operation, and purchase of the necessary water rights.

References.—The following is a list of the more important reports which have been freely used by this service in assembling the accompanying data:

Water Supply and Irrigation Papers, United States Geological Survey:
No. 2. Irrigation near Phoenix, Ariz., by A. P. Davis.
No. 33. Storage of Water on Gila River, Ariz, by J. B. Lippincott.
No. 73. Water Storage on Salt River, Ariz., by A. P. Davis.
No. 104. The Underground Waters of Gila River Valley, by W. T. Lee.
No. 136. The Underground Waters of Salt River Valley, by W. T. Lee.
Office of Experiment Station, United States Department of Agriculture:
Bulletin No. 126. Concrete Lining as Applied to Irrigation Canals.
Bulletin No. 235. Irrigation in Arizona.
Reports of J. D. Schuyler, on San Carlos Project, 1900, and Water Supply and proposed Irrigation Works of Pinal Mutual Irrigation Co., of Florence.

Report of J. H. Quinton on San Carlos project, 1909, 1910, and 1912.

Report on Reservoir Sites on the Gila River and its Tributaries, by W. A. Parish.

Cooperative Irrigation Investigations in California:

Bulletin No. 1. California State Department of Engineering.

Report of Duty of Water, by Don H. Bark, printed in Report of Idaho State Engineer, 1914.

Surveys.—The Gila River watershed, with the exception of the Salt River Basin, was divided into six districts, conforming as nearly as practicable with natural geographical divisions, in order to facilitate the classification of the data collected. These districts are as follows:

District No. 1 (Duncan). This district extends from the Apache Box Canyon, about 10 miles east of Duncan, to the lowest irrigated district at Guthrie, and comprises what is known as the Duncan Valley.

District No. 2 (Solomonville-Safford). This district begins at the Brown ranch, at the head of the Solomonville-Safford Valley, and extends down to the San Carlos Box Canyon. The lands along the Gila and San Carlos Rivers, in the San Carlos Indian Reservation, are also included. This district is commonly called the Gila Valley.

District No. 3 (Florence-Casa Grande). This district includes all the lands in the Florence-Casa Grande Valley, beginning at the Double Buttes, near the lower end of the Gila Canyon, and extending along the river as far west as the east line of the Gila River Indian Reservation, and including the Casa Grande Valley to the south.

District No. 4 (Gila River Indian Reservation). This district embraces all the arable lands of the Gila River Indian Reservation.

District No. 5 (Lower Gila). This district covers generally the basin between the west line of the Gila River Indian Reservation and the confluence of the Gila with the Colorado River at Yuma.

District No. 6 (Upper Gila). This district comprises the headwaters of the Gila and its upper tributaries, the San Pedro, the San Carlos, the San Francisco Rivers, and, to a limited extent, Eagle Creek.

A topographic plane table survey, on a scale of 1,000 feet to the inch, with 5-foot contour intervals, was made of the irrigable land in districts Nos. 1 to 4, inclusive. Reconnaisance surveys were made of the irrigable areas in districts Nos. 5 and 6, constituting the region along the Gila to the west of the Gila River Indian Reservation, and the upper Gila and its tributaries. In both surveys, advantage was taken of existing maps, and when these were found sufficiently accurate, they were incorporated in this work.

The surveys in each district were tied together by means of a triangulation system covering the district. The separate triangulation systems were in turn tied to the triangulation system of the United States Geological Survey covering this portion of the United States. No effort was made to survey the canyon forming the course of the Gila between the several districts, and such data as appear on the general map of these areas have been procured from the maps of the General Land Office, and such railway surveys through the canyon as were accessible during the course of this investigation. Elevations were determined by a system of ordinary levels tied to the United States Geological Survey bench marks.

In this work a total area of approximately 549 square miles was covered by plane table.

The reconnaissance survey covered some 490 miles of traverse along the channels of the upper and lower Gila and its tributaries. In this work closed surveys were made only where it was otherwise impossible to determine the area of the irrigated land.

The field work was placed in charge of C. H. Southworth, who directed this portion of the investigation under the supervision of N. W. Irsfeld, engineer, United States Indian Service, and the writer.

The work was carried on for the most part by two field parties, although three parties were maintained in the field during a portion of the time.

The following instrument men at various times were in charge of survey parties: W. W. Lane, C. V. Taylor, A. C. Embshoff, H. G. Guiteras, Ralph A. Hamilton, O. W. Bauer, R. B. Griffith, W. G. Roche, and H. L. Rath, while Wallace Adams and W. A. Hughes, holding positions as rodmen, remained with the work throughout.

The reconnaissance surveys and investigations along the upper Gila and its tributaries were made by W. W. Lane; while similar work along the lower Gila was performed by C. H. Southworth and R. A. Hamilton.

Maps.—Tracings have been made of the planetable sheets of districts Nos. 1 to 4, and the area along the Gila near Winkelman, not included in these districts, which show the arable land in each township, on a scale of 1,000 feet to the inch, with a 5-foot contour interval. These maps show in detail the land at present irrigated, that previously irrigated, and that susceptible of irrigation from the present canal systems. They show also the complete canal systems, including field laterals. The various kinds of crops to which the land was planted during the seasons 1913–14 are designated. All roads, land fenced, and land lines are shown with sufficient accuracy to determine individual ownerships. These township maps have been combined to form maps of each district, on a scale of 2 inches to the mile. A map of the reconnaissance survey was prepared on the same scale of the area extending from the west line of the Gila River Indian Reservation to Gila Bend. These district maps have been combined with that of the United States General Land Office to form a key map of the Gila River watershed.

Prints of the various maps appear in part 3 of this report. The drafting required in the preparation of these maps was performed principally by H. L. Rath during the course of the survey, while H. P. Shaw, who held the position of draftsman in the office of the Indian Service, Los Angeles, also assisted in this work.

History of irrigation.—The history of the use of the waters of the Gila River for irrigation in the various districts was gathered from various sources. This work includes a detailed history of both present and past cultivation, covering all of the irrigated areas of the Gila Basin, exclusive of the Salt River and Santa Cruz watersheds.

Claims of appropriation blanks, similar to the forms used by the State engineers of Nevada, New Mexico, Oregon, and other States, were distributed to the various land owners. These forms consist simply of a series of questions covering the history of irrigation of the cultivated lands to be answered by the present owners.

Abstracts were prepared of the records on file in the different counties through which the Gila flows, and an examination made of several adjudication decrees, and various court manuscripts relating to the use and ownership of water. The ownership of the land under irrigation and the individual holdings under the various canals, were also ascertained.

In the case of the Gila River Indian Reservation early histories have been consulted, with a view of ascertaining the early use of the Gila River waters by the Prima Indians, and a careful search was made of the records at Sacaton and in Washington to determine the extent and continuity of such use.

From a careful examination of all data obtained as the result of the surveys and the various researches, an analysis of the history of irrigation under each ditch has been made for the several districts, and these analyses have been combined to show the history of the use of water for irrigation in that portion of the Gila River Basin under consideration.

In connection with this work an estimate has also been made of the probable future uses of the Gila water above the San Carlos reservoir site, based on the rights that are claimed to have already been initiated and which may develop into actual use, and also on the areas susceptible of economical irrigation.

The assembling of the historical data was carried on simultaneously with the surveys, Wallace Adams and W. A. Hughes being engaged on this division of the work, while John S. Layne was employed for several months in searching and abstracting court records, and in the examination of correspondence on file at the United States Indian superintendency at Sacaton.

Throughout the rather large expanse of territory over which the work has been carried, the residents of the various districts, with perhaps one exception, have been uniformly courteous, obliging, and of much assistance to the work. In the Solomonville Valley, some feeling antagonistic to the work was encountered; but this, it is believed, resulted from a wrong conception of the object of the investigation. As the work progressed, however, this unfriendly spirit gave way to more helpful and cooperative interest.

Water physically available.—The determination of the amount of water physically available for the proposed San Carlos Reservoir, independent of such legal rights as may be established, necessitated additional data respecting the amount actually flowing in the Gila and its several tributaries. The preparation and assembling of these data was performed under the supervision of the Water Resources Branch of the United States Geological Survey, that organization being better equipped and prepared for the work than this service. By a transfer of funds from this bureau to the Geological Survey, Mr. C. C. Jacob, district engineer of the Geological Survey, has been enabled to direct this portion of the investigation.

Seven gauging stations were installed under the direction of Mr. Jacob along the Gila and its tributaries at points suitable to the determination of a proper hydrograph of the entire stream system. The sites selected for this purpose were as follows:

1. Ten miles east of the New Mexico-Arizona State line, at the head of the Duncan Valley, mouth of Apache box.
2. On the Gila near Guthrie.

3. On the San Francisco at Clifton (installed previously).
4. On the Gila at Brown ranch, at head of Solomonville district.
5. On the Gila at San Carlos Dam site.
6. San Carlos at San Carlos.
7. Gila at Kelvin.
8. Gila at east line of Gila River Reservation.

Automatic gauges were installed at the above points and sufficient measurements made to interpret the gauge readings.

Unfortunately the gauge at station No. 5, at the San Carlos Dam site, was destroyed by the large flood occurring in December, 1914, and that at station No. 8, at the east end of the Gila River Reservation, was destroyed by flood in July, 1914. The flow during the intervals when the gauges were out has, however, been calculated from other data, so the record at each point is virtually continuous.

Frequent measurements were also made of the flow of the Gila at Florence and at the east line of the Gila Indian Reservation.

In connection with this work frequent direct measurements were made of all the canals diverting water from the Gila. In cases where no water was found in the canals, their capacity was computed by the method of cross sections and grades. All previous data respecting the flow of the Gila and its principal tributaries have been assembled and placed in convenient form for consideration.

An effort was made to determine the effect of diversion of the waters of the Gila by the upper canals on its flow near Florence, but unfortunately the period during which observations were conducted was one of unusual rainfall and the river was practically in constant flood, no trustworthy observations being possible. This information has been deduced by a different method, based on various logical assumptions that will be set forth in the body of this report.

Water legally available.—In the spring of 1913, and before this report was authorized, Mr. John F. Truesdell, special assistant to the Attorney General, had recommended that, in order to determine what steps, if any, should be taken to protect the water rights connected with the Gila River Indian Reservation, certain surveys and investigations of stream flow on the Gila River should be made. These investigations were promptly undertaken, and were later merged in the more extensive one demanded in connection with the San Carlos project.

Mr. Truesdell's original suggestions as to what facts should be obtained have been used in the larger work and he has been consulted from time to time about various phases of the investigation as it has been carried on.

He has pointed out that a determination of the amount of water legally available could be accurately made now by litigation, so far as the vested water rights are concerned, but that a suit would not be effective in determining the inchoate rights, or those that have been initiated but are not yet vested.

Accordingly, in this report no attempt is made to give an opinion upon the question of what water is, as a matter of law, available for the project, but the investigation was shaped under the guidance mentioned with a view to the gathering of information necessary for such an opinion. It is thought, therefore, that the facts obtained will be sufficient to permit of the forming of a dependable opinion as to the extent of the vested rights, and sufficient also to show fairly well what inchoate rights exist, their possible extent within wide limits, and what particular rights of this character it may be thought necessary to limit definitely before the project is undertaken.

For the reason that, as above stated, an adjudication suit does not seem to be a necessary prerequisite to a decision upon the building of the project and also because of the difficulty of estimating in advance the cost of a complicated lawsuit no attempt has been made to estimate the cost of such adjudication.

It is respectfully recommended, however, that a copy of this report be furnished to the Department of Justice so that any opinion that is desired may be obtained or any legal proceedings that may be deemed advisable can be instituted.

Estimated maximum and minimum cost, San Carlos project.—The preparation of the maximum and minimum estimates of the cost of the San Carlos project required the redesigning of the proposed storage dam, diversion dam, and distributing system, in the light of the additional data made available by the surveys and other data assembled in the preparation of this report.

Mr. H. V. Clotts, assistant engineer of this service, under the supervision of the writer, has prepared estimates of the maximum and minimum cost for a straight monolithic dam of the gravity type, having a maximum height of 200 feet, for the San Carlos project. This estimate includes the entire cost of spillways, outlets, and other work necessary for the proper operation of the reservoir. The dam provides for a spillway height of 180 feet above the bed of the Gila River, while the maximum flow line of the reservoir is at the 2,499.5-foot contour above sea level, or 11.5 feet above the spillways. The maximum capacity of the reservoir resulting from this arrangement would be 714,450 acre-feet, which is sufficient to permit a yearly draft of 300,000 acre-feet on a normal supply basis.

The maximum and minimum cost of the distribution system of the San Carlos project was prepared by Mr. C. H. Southworth, assisted by Mr. H. V. Clotts, under the writer's supervision.

This estimate also includes two diversion dams, located at Florence and Sacaton, respectively, necessary to divert the stored and flood waters in the Gila into the distribution canals.

This system provides for the irrigation of 45,000 acres of land in the region contiguous to Florence and 35,000 acres on the Gila River Indian Reservation, a total of 80,000 acres, under an assumed duty of water of 3-acre feet per acre per annum, an annual draft of 300,000-acre feet and adopting the silt determination figures as presented in the report of the United States Army Board.

DESCRIPTION OF GILA RIVER WATERSHED.

A description of the physiographic, geologic, climatic, and other physical conditions closely related to the use of water, is necessary to the proper understanding of the conditions governing irrigation in southern Arizona, and this information is briefly given herewith.

PHYSIOGRAPHY.

With the exception of the Colorado, the Gila is the most important river in Arizona, its watershed embracing practically the entire region south of the thirty-fifth parallel of latitude in that State, an area of approximately 72,000 square miles.

The sources of the Gila rise among the eastern spurs of the Mogollon Mountains in New Mexico, at an elevation of from 7,000 to 8,000 feet above sea level. This range forms the Continental Divide between the waters flowing into the Gulf of Mexico on the east and the Gulf of California on the west. Flowing in a generally southwesterly direction, the Gila enters Arizona at latitude 32° 40′ north, at an elevation of about 3,800 feet, and following a course westward across the entire State corresponding closely to the thirty-third parallel, finally joins the Colorado at Yuma, at an elevation of approximately 120 feet above sea level. The distance along the Gila from its source to its confluence with the Colorado is approximately 450 miles.

The principal tributaries entering the Gila between its source and its mouth, with the extent of the respective drainage areas, and the average elevation are shown in the following table:

	Drainage area.	Elevations.
	Square miles.	
Agua Frio	1,700	800- 3,000
Salt River	12,700	1,000-10,000
San Pedro	4,000	1,900- 5,000
San Carlos	1,200	2,400- 4,000
San Francisco	3,400	3,400- 7,000

Total area of Gila Basin (inclusive of tributaries) above San Carlos, 13,455 square miles.

In New Mexico the watershed is for the most part a high rolling plateau, passing through contracted canyons, which occasionally widen into narrow valleys, where small plots of ground are irrigated. About 7 miles east of the Arizona line the canyon broadens into the Duncan Valley. This valley is 30 miles long, with an average width of one-half mile, although its maximum width is 1½ miles.

About 10 miles above its lower extremity the valley is crossed by a lava ridge, through which the river has cut a gorge known locally as York Canyon. Below York Canyon the Duncan Valley again broadens out, but it is then gradually contracted by the long, stony ridges extending from mountains known as the Sierre de la Petihaya and the Sierra Nutanes.

The San Francisco River drains the latter range and enters the Gila from the north about 15 miles below York Canyon. A few miles farther west two other tributaries, Eagle and Bonita Creeks, enter from the same direction.

After leaving the Duncan Valley the Gila passes through a narrow box canyon for a distance of about 20 miles, after which it emerges into the Solomonville Valley. This valley terminates at the San Carlos Box Canyon, which, together with the lower or western portion of the valley, is included in the San Carlos Indian Reservation.

The Solomonville Valley is about 70 miles long, that portion which lies east of the San Carlos Reservation having a length of 40 miles and an average width of 2 miles, while the portion which lies within the San Carlos Reservation is 30 miles long and has an average width of 1½ miles.

San Simon Creek, a comparatively unimportant tributary, enters the Gila from the south, a short distance below the head of the Solomonville Valley, while near the lower end of the valley the San Carlos enters the Gila from the north.

About 7 miles below the mouth of the San Carlos the Gila enters the San Carlos Box Canyon, the upper end of which forms the San Carlos Dam site.

The San Carlos Box is one of a series of narrow canyons extending for a distance of 70 miles through the Santa Teresa, Tortilla, and other detached mountain ranges to the head of the Florence Valley. About midway of this distance the San Pedro River enters from the south, and several miles farther west an unimportant tributary, known as Mineral Creek, joins the Gila.

The Gila emerges from the mountains about 16 miles above Florence and enters the broad desert plain which extends from that point to the confluence of the Gila and Colorado Rivers at Yuma, a distance of 243 miles.

Detached mountain ranges, such as the Sacaton, Estrella, Salt River, Gila Bend, Mohawk, and others, rising abruptly from the valley floor, form imperfect topographical divisions or interruptions in the general plain of the desert.

The upper end of this valley embraces the land which may be irrigated from the proposed San Carlos Project. This area includes the irrigated land contiguous to Florence, known as the Florence Valley, and a portion of the irrigable land of the Gila River Indian Reservation, the east line of which is located 11 miles west of Florence. South of the Gila the east line of the reservation practically coincides with the eastern limits of the Sacaton Mountains, which form the division between the Gila and the Santa Cruz watersheds. This stream joins the Gila at the base of the Estrella Range, some 50 miles below Florence. The town of Casa Grande, located on the Southern Pacific Railroad, is within the Santa Cruz watershed and is the center of a large territory that may also be irrigated from the Gila River, the character of country between the two watersheds offering no serious obstacle to the construction of a suitable conduit. On the north the San Tan and Salt River Mountains form the division between the Gila and Salt River Basins. The latter stream is the most important tributary of the Gila and joins it near the western boundary of the Gila River Indian Reservation, which extends for a distance of 52 miles along the Gila River. A little more than a mile below the mouth of the Salt River the Gila is joined by the Agua Fria, which drains the region immediately to the west of the Salt River Basin.

The Hassayampa, the last tributary of any importance, enters the Gila from the north at a point 23 miles further west. A short distance below the Hassayampa the Gila makes a long bend to the south and west around the Gila Bend Mountains. West of Gila Bend there are more detached ranges of mountains, and the valley lands along the river alternate with the mountain areas in about equal proportions. These conditions are not such as to admit of tributary drainage basins of any magnitude. However, between the Hassayampa and the Colorado numerous small washes are found which contribute to the water supply of the Gila only during times of heavy rains.

GEOLOGY.

Considerable variation in geologic structure is to be expected in an area as large as the Gila River watershed. Unfortunately, as far as can be learned, the geology of this region has not as yet received the attention of a trained geologist.

The upper reaches of the rivers forming the Gila system drain the eastern portion of the great plateau occurring in western New Mexico and eastern Arizona.

This plateau, which is of sedimentary origin, has been covered throughout a large part of its area by lava flow, which has since been greatly eroded. From these high regions the Gila and its tributaries rapidly descend through a broken country, which has been subject to extensive volcanic action, until the river emerges into the lower desert region in the vicinity of Florence.

The area drained by the Gila and its tributaries west of Florence is characterized by broad, level valleys, separated by low, abrupt mountain ranges, usually of volcanic formation. The valleys were formed by a process of aggradation, in which the original topography has become so obliterated under immense deposits of presumably Pleistocene sands and gravels that only the higher ridges of what were once mountain ranges are visible.

As a consequence, of the topography of the Gila watershed the streams change from eroding agents in the mountains of the upper reaches and the intermediate valleys to aggrading agents in the desert region to the west. In the intermediate valleys it is apparent that in former times the character of the river has changed from an eroding to an aggrading agent.

This change was evidently due to volcanic action, since the sedimentary rocks in this region have been subject to considerable upheaval, while in the higher mountain regions, where the rivers have been continually eroding, very little displacement has taken place. Consequently it is seen that the upper reaches of the Gila and its principal tributaries have cut through the Tertiary gravels, conglomerates, and lavas, and to some extent the earlier formations; while further west the canyons are eroded through the tilted limestones and quartzites of the Carboniferous and even earlier areas, as well as the later formation and more recent lava flows.

The streams of the mountain region are characterized by deep canyons, which occasionally widen out into long, narrow valleys, the bottom of which have been filled by recent alluvial deposits. The intermediate valleys, namely, the Duncan and Solomonville Valleys, have been partially filled by large deposits of sand and clay, evidently belonging to the Pleistocene period. These earlier deposits have been partially eroded through, and again partly filled with recent alluvial sand and silt. It is the more recent valley fill that constitutes the land now suitable for cultivation.

Where the Gila or any one of its tributaries breaks through an intervening mountain range, an attractive dam site frequently results. This is notably the case where the canyon occurs just below the confluence of the main stream and one of its tributaries, which permits the use of basins of both streams for storage purposes. This condition exists on Salt River, where the Roosevelt Dam is located, immediately below the mouth of Tonto Creek, and also at the San Carlos dam site, which is located on the Gila, a short distance below the mouth of the San Carlos River.

Several other excellent dam sites are found along the Gila, both below and above the San Carlos Dam site; those below at the Buttes, at Riverside, and possibly at Sentinel; those above at Guthrie and Red Rock, on the Gila proper; and at Alma, on the San Francisco. The three sites above San Carlos may form a solution of the difficult silt problem, which now seems seriously to limit the life of the proposed San Carlos project. If the construction of these reservoirs would so regulate the flow of the Gila as to prevent destructive floods, which now invariably erode and carry down the river large sections of cultivated land, it seems that, while the silt problem would not be entirely solved, the life of the proposed reservoir might be increased to compare favorably with that at Roosevelt.

The area drained by the Gila and its tributaries west of Florence does not lend itself favorably to the construction of storage works, owing to the absence of reservoir sites and the great depth to bedrock, although one reservoir site, located near Gila Bend, has received considerable attention. This region is, however, admirably adapted to the storage of underground water in the voids of immense deposits of débris. It is safe to predict that considerable development may be expected in this section through pumping. Over a considerable portion of this area, however, the deposits are very deep, and the water-bearing gravels lie at too great a depth for economical pumping.

The rich alluvial bottoms of the valleys about Florence and the broad, fertile plains to the west only require the application of water to make them of great agricultural value.

CLIMATE.

The great difference in elevation existing in the Gila River watershed induces great climatic variations. Along the headwaters of the Gila, at elevations ranging from 5,000 to 7,000 feet, the climate is comparable to that of Virginia. The average maximum temperature is 100 degrees, the average minimum is —8 degrees.

In the Solomonville Valley, which includes San Carlos, and which is situated at an elevation of 2,000 to 3,000 feet, the average maximum temperature is 106 degrees, the average minimum temperature is 8 degrees, while the normal precipitation is 13 inches.

From Florence to the mouth of the Gila at Yuma the elevation drops from 1,500 feet to 140 feet above sea level, and true desert conditions prevail. Here the average maximum temperature is 113° F., the average minimum temperature is 21° F., while the normal annual precipitation does not exceed 10 inches. It is this section that is responsible for Arizona's reputation for intensely hot summers; rather unjustly so, however, as a temperature of 120° F. at Yuma, owing to the low humidity, is scarcely more uncomfortable than 90° F. at Washington. D. C.

Throughout the entire watershed radiation is very great and produces a wide range in temperature from day to night, averaging 30° F. in the upper region and 10° F. in the lower valley.

There are two wet seasons, one in summer (July and August), the other in winter (October to March), which are separated by much drier periods. The summer rainy season is characterized by frequent violent local showers, which are due to convectional atmospheric currents and are usually accompanied by severe electrical storms.

The winter is marked by steady, gentle rains and by snowstorms at elevations above 4,000 feet. The winter precipitations are due to general widespread cyclonic disturbances.

Rainfall records have been kept at a number of different points in the Gila Basin. These records have been published in several previous reports, notably in Water-Supply Paper No. 33, page 20, and in the more recent report of the Army board elsewhere referred to, published as House Document No. 791, Sixty-third Congress, second session.

The local summer storms give rise to and are frequently accompanied by heavy winds, but during the remainder of the year very little wind occurs. An average wind movement at Phoenix is given at 2.4[1] miles an hour.

The atmospheric humidity over the entire area is unusually low. According to United States Department of Agriculture Bulletin 235, page 17, "Relative humidities of less than 10 per cent are often recorded in June, the annual average for four years at Phoenix being 35 per cent."

Owing to the prevailing high normal temperatures and low humidity, evaporation even in the absence of wind is very rapid and must be taken into consideration on planning any irrigation project. But little observed data are available. Deductions must be drawn from results obtained in regions where similar conditions prevail. In the report of the Army board the conclusion has been made that the mean annual evaporation at San Carlos is 60 inches.

VEGETATION.

The great range in elevation encountered in the Gila watershed, and the consequent variation in climate and rainfall, bring about striking changes in vegetation.

The upper region, above the elevation of 5,500 feet, are clothed in a magnificent forest of pine, fir, spruce, and juniper. Below this elevation, to 3,000 feet, the mountain sides are blanketed with a dense thicket of brush, scrub oak, etc., while occasional groves of juniper are found. Below 3,000 feet the usual desert vegetation is in evidence, consisting of mesquite, paloverde, ironwood, greasewood, sage, and the several varieties of cactus. The stream courses of the upper regions are fringed with cottonwood, walnut, and willow. The lower Gila is bordered by dense mats of "water motes" and willow, while the uncultivated tracts of the valley land are generally covered with thick groves of mesquite.

---

[1] Arizona Sta. Bul. 20, p. 36, 37.

Formerly, during the late spring and early summer, practically the entire unforested area of the watershed was covered with a thick carpet of various wild grasses and alfilaria. This, owing to overgrazing or other causes, has largely disappeared, and is not now sufficient appreciably to retard the run-off. As a result, the run-off from the lower regions is rapid, and in some localities considerable erosion has taken place, contributing still more to the muddy waters of the Gila.

CROPS.

While a considerable variety of natural vegetation occurs in the different portions of the Gila watershed, no great variety of crops are grown in the irrigated districts along the Gila River, and, except in the extreme upper portion of the watershed, the irrigation season extends throughout the year when sufficient water is available. In general the climatic conditions are such that plants which are grown throughout the year must be able to stand excessive heat and must also be able to endure some frost. The principal plant of this nature is alfalfa, and ordinarily five crops per annum are cut, yielding a total of 4 to 8 tons per acre. Wherever sufficient water is available throughout the Gila River Basin, alfalfa is the staple product.

When two different kinds of products are planted during the year, the first or spring crop must be of a variety favored by a long, hot, growing season, while the second or fall crop must be able to withstand some frost. Ordinarily small grains, such as wheat, oats, and barley, are planted in the fall and harvested in the late spring, after which the ground is planted to corn, sorghum, cotton, watermelons, squash, or other hot-weather crops.

The yield of grain crops, under favorable conditions, varies from 1,900 to 2,500 pounds per acre for barley, while a wheat crop varies from 1,500 to 2,400 pounds per acre. Of the summer crops, Egyptian cotton yields from 400 to 1,000 pounds per acre, while the corn crop averages 1 ton to the acre.

Subtropical fruits, such as dates, olives, oranges and lemons, figs and pomegranates are successfully grown in the lower Gila valleys, while in the upper valleys the fruit trees are of the deciduous variety.

HYDROGRAPHY.

The topographic and physiographic conditions obtaining in the Gila watershed are so varied that general statements covering the stream as a whole are, as a rule, impossible.

The watershed forms a complete river system, and each tributary presents its own individual problem. The streams comprising the system are, in order, from the source of the Gila to its mouth, the Upper Gila, San Francisco, Eagle Creek, San Carlos, San Pedro, Santa Cruz, Salt River, Agua Frio, and Hassayampa.

Reference to the map No. 1 of the watershed, accompanying this report, shows that all but two of these tributaries (namely the Santa Cruz and San Pedro) enter the Gila from the north, and that the more important of them have their source in the high mountain region in the vicinity of Mounts Thomas and Ord, in eastern Arizona and western New Mexico, of the two streams entering from the south, the San Pedro only is of sufficient importance to warrant investigation.

The Salt River, Agua Frio, and Hassayampa join the Gila below the western limits of the Gila River Indian Reservation, and as the flow of the Salt River is largely controlled by the Salt River Reservoir, and the flow of the Agua Frio and Hassayampa are of minor importance, and have only an indirect bearing on the proposed San Carlos project, the study of these streams has not received the attention required on the upper tributaries.

The headwaters of the Gila and its principal tributaries are typical mountain streams, while the Gila throughout its lower course is a characteristic desert river flowing over a shifting sandy bed, except where it cuts through the mountains that separate the several valleys.

The Gila, owing to the occurrence of the two rainy seasons already mentioned, is subject to two annual flood periods. The winter flood is the longest, usually continuing from December to the 1st of May, and, owing to melting snows in the mountains, reaching its maximum in March. The summer flood extends from the 1st of July to the 1st of September, or nearly October, and is the result of heavy rainfall concentrated over small areas along the Gila and its tributaries.

The discharge of the Upper Gila and its tributaries is fairly uniform, owing to the retarding effect of snowfall, and the heavily forested areas through which they flow. This flow is, however, largely dissipated through evaporation and seepage losses, before the lower valleys are reached. The territory contiguous to the lower Gila is sparsely covered with vegetation, and much of the region, aside from the valley proper, is of a steep and rocky nature, offering favorable conditions for an exceptionally large and rapid run-off. As a result the flow of the lower Gila often diminishes to a negligible quantity during low water, while during rainy seasons it is subject to violent and erratic floods. The current during flood periods, as it follows the tortuous channel of the Gila, often impinges against the soft silt banks and washes away considerable areas of cultivated land, which is later deposited lower down the stream. The Gila also possesses a characteristic common among western streams of deepening its beds during flood periods. A deepening of the channel from 10 to 15 feet often occurs with a rise of only a few feet. It is this fact that renders maintenance of diversions and protection work along the Gila so difficult, as there appears to be no economical means of preventing undercutting.

As set forth in the accompanying Appendix A, irrigation was practiced by the Pimas, and possibly other tribes along the Gila and its tributaries, long before the coming of the white man. At that time a considerable area was irrigated by the Pimas in the vicinity of Sacaton. Irrigation was commenced by the whites in the vicinity of Florence, and later was extended to include the Solomonville, Safford, and the Duncan Valleys. The small amount of water available during the low-water season placed a definite limit on the amount of land it was practicable to irrigate, and in general the irrigation of additional land higher up the stream was made at the expense of that lower down. This shortage was seriously felt at Florence and by the Pima Indians on the Gila River Indian Reservation. Early efforts were made by the settlers to increase the low-water supply and the situation was investigated as early as 1894 by the United States Geological Survey.

The great value of water for irrigation, and the possibility of storage along the Gila, also attracted the attention of parties interested in the development of the region. Experienced engineers were engaged and several reports prepared, which contain valuable information respecting the flow of the Gila.

The United States Army board, in the report already referred to, assembled and collated the data from the several sources. Unfortunately, the records have not been continuous at any one point, and an effort was made to supply the missing information by means of various assumptions based on correlated data.

As stated above, the low-water flow in the lower valleys is considerably affected by losses through diversions for irrigation purposes along the upper reaches of the streams. The exact amount of such losses is difficult to determine, since there are several vital factors that must be taken into consideration which are more or less obscure, namely, seepage losses in the wide, sandy stream channel, evaporation, transpiration from plant growth, return water from the canals, and possible inflow from hidden springs and other sources. Data relating to these factors are of great importance in determining the amount of water legally available where conflicting interests exist along the course of a stream, such as the Gila. As previously stated, an investigation to obtain this information, as well as to determine the influence of the several tributaries on the flow of the Gila, was made by Mr. C. C. Jacob, district engineer of the Water Resources Branch of the Geological Survey, whose report appears in Appendix B.

The problem was attacked from a different angle by Mr. H. K. Palmer, of this service, who arrived at certain theoretical conclusions respecting the effect of the diversions along the upper Gila, on the low-water flow of the lower valley. His arguments are presented in Appendix B, accompanying this report. The conclusions are based on logical deductions respecting the effect of transpiration and evaporation losses on the amount of water diverted in the canals above the San Carlos Box Canyon, in the Solomonville-Safford Valley. No effort was made to include the diversion in Duncan Valley or on the upper tributaries, as the effect of these diversions on the low-water flow at Florence was involved and the information was insufficient to permit of a definite result.

While the conclusions are theoretical and are therefore necessarily subject to a wide interpretation, they appear to be reasonable, and at least give an idea of the low water conditions prevailing along the Gila before the coming of the whites.

Appendix B, accompanying this report, includes an analysis of all the assembled data. In the volume of maps accompanying this report are charts showing graphically the flow of the Gila at Florence and San Carlos, and by means of mass curves, the possibility of storage at the latter point.

The analysis shows that the average low-water flow of the Gila at San Carlos, exclusive of the amount diverted above that point for irrigation, is 82 feet per second. Including that amount, with the application of return flow increments and evaporation losses, it is probably 182 second-feet.

The minimum recorded run-off of the Gila River at San Carlos, exclusive of the amount diverted above that point for irrigation, occurred in 1902 and amounted to 99,936 acre-feet. The probable minimum run-off during that year, if none had been diverted above, amounts to 157,936 acre-feet.

The maximum recorded run-off at the same point occurred in 1905 and amounted to 1,011,082 acre-feet. The probable maximum run-off, if there had been no diversions, amounted to 1,069,082 acre-feet. The analysis further shows that during the years from 1899 to 1904 (inclusive), a period of low water prevailed, during which time the annual run-off did not exceed 194,529 acre-feet. Applying corrections for diversions, it did not exceed 252,529 acre-feet.

WATER PHYSICALLY AVAILABLE.

The determination of the amount of water physically available, on which depends the amount legally available for the proposed San Carlos Reservoir, involves a study of the hydrography of the basin. To definitely ascertain this would necessitate a continuous series of observations extending over a term of years. The time available for the investigations and the preparation and submission of this report precluded these observations, and advantage was taken of such records as have been made from time to time in the preparation of previous reports and the investigations made along the Gila by the Water Resources Branch of the United States Geological Survey.

The amount of water actually available for irrigation in the Gila River at the San Carlos dam site and at Florence was known to the Army board; as all the observations respecting the discharge of the Gila, except those made during the course of this investigation, received their careful consideration.

"Physically available" as here interpreted differs from "actually available" in so far as by "physically available" water is meant that amount which would flow past a given point in the event that no diversion were made above; or in other words, the full discharge of the watershed such as existed for instance at the Pima Reservation before irrigation by the whites was commenced.

To find the real effect of irrigation in the upper valleys, there should be records of the flow at various points along the river before irrigation was begun. Obviously such records do not exist, and consequently any determinations of this character must necessarily be based upon observations of the present flow and the theoretical interpretations of this data in connection with known facts relative to plant growth, evaporation, sepage, and other natural data.

The amount of water legally available, assuming there were illegal diversions, and taking no account of rights that have been initiated but have not been vested and the extent of which can only be estimated within wide limits, would lie between the upper and lower limits, respectively, of the amounts physically and actually available.

The run-off of the Gila is extremely variable. In the upper sections it is more or less constant, while in the lower reaches of the stream in times of flood the run-off is torrential.

The stream measurements also show that in the Solomonville-Safford Valley more water is diverted for irrigation than flows at the head of the valley and water rises between the lowest canal heading and the San Sarlos Dam site. At the time that the special investigation on the return water was made, 92 second-feet returned to the surface, of which 64 was used again for irrigation and 28 reached the dam site. Adding the evaporation from the sand surface in the river bed, which would amount to 67 second-feet in June, the total inflow from the river bed would be 159 second-feet. A further investigation shows that during most of the year the underground flow varies from 180 second-feet at low-water periods to between 300 and 400 second-feet during normal high water. From the canal measurements it appears that the total diversion in the Solomonville canals amounts to about 189,000 acre-feet per year. The latest measurements on transpiration and evaporation from soils show that the average crops and the canals should use 58,000 acre-feet, leaving 131,000 acre-feet to return to the river. This is equivalent to a continuous flow of 183 second-feet, leaving from 10 to 150 second-feet to enter the valley underground from the adjacent watershed.

The run-off from the San Carlos River is negligible during low-water periods. The run-off from the San Pedro is more erratic than from the Gila. It provides about 10 per cent of the flow at Kelvin. The measurements indicate that between the mouth of the canyon and Sacaton there is a loss of 110 second-feet by absorption in the sand and a transmission loss of 10 per cent of the remainder. In the case of a flood, following a drought when the water plane is lowered, the amount is greater than 110 second-feet. Fortunately, this occurs when there is abundance of water.

A comparison of conditions as they exist with the theoretical conditions as they existed before irrigation was practiced in the upper valleys, shows that a diversion of 225 second-feet at Solomonville and 50 second-feet at Florence will divert all of the stream which would normally have reached Sacaton, amounting to 183 second-feet at the latter point. Since most of the loss between Solomonville and Sacaton is constant, not depending on the state of the river, it is impossible to express it as a certian percentage of the flow at Solomonville; but for ordinary stages of the river it can be said that, after sufficient water is provided to supply the evaporation and seepage losses, which can be taken care of by the underflow, the transmission loss from Solomonville will be approximately 40 per cent, and from Kelvin 10 per cent. This subject is fully treated in Appendix B, and the figures in the following discussion are excerpts therefrom.

The two points along the Gila of greatest interest in this investigation are San Carlos, in connection with the proposed reservoir, and Florence, where the main diversion will be effected.

Water Actually Available.

The records of the run-off flow of the Gila River cover a comparatively brief period of 21 years, a length of time too short to admit of conclusive deductions or predictions as to the average or extreme flows which may be expected in the future.

The run-off records which have been compiled by the Army board and published on page 28 of their report cover a period of 18 years. Since the Army board report was written, the run-off records for the years 1913, 1914, and a portion of 1915 have become available, so that we now possess the advantage of a somewhat longer period on which to base our study of the flow of the Gila River. (See Appendix B.)

An examination of these run-off data shows at once that the flow of the Gila varies within rather wide limits, not only during any single year but from year to year as well. In the 21 years for which we have any records its is apparent that during 11 years the total flow was below the average, and that for 7 consecutive years of the 11, commencing with the year 1898, the flow was below the average continuously. The flow varies from 0 second-foot to 100,000 second-feet.

The minimum flow was in 1902, while the maximum flood of which we have record occurred in 1905. This flood lasted six days, but during that time the gauge at San Carlos was destroyed, and consequently no record of the actual discharge is available.

Since such a large proportion of the total run-off of the Gila occurs in times of flood, without storage only a proportion of it can be used for irrigation. Storage of a supply for one year is not sufficient, for usually two or three wet years are followed by four or five dry years, making storage for at least two or three years imperative.

The run-off data also shows that these extreme floods or flood periods occur at more or less regular intervals. If there is plotted a run-off curve of the flow of the Gila during the entire number of years for which records are available, it will be noted that the periods of extreme floods occur about every nine years; it is also noted that the periods of drought occur in similar cycles. For this reason the estimated amount of water available for irrigation when storage facilities are provided should be based on the amount available during one cycle, rather than on the amount available during any one particular year, and the capacity of any proposed reservoir should be sufficient to permit the same annual draft, from one period of wet years to the next. To permit the greatest possible use of the discharge from the watershed, the estimate of the draft from the reservoir should be based on the mean discharge of the cycle rather than on the minimum discharge, and other means provided to tide over a shortage, should one occur.

Climatically southern California is quite similar to Arizona respecting the general atmospheric disturbances that determine a wet or dry year. The California records indicate that the dry cycle was exceptional and not likely to occur again for 30 or 40 years.

During the 21 years of record one period of extraordinary drought will be noted, a period so dry that in order to provide against total failure of the water supply the allowable draft from the reservoir must necessarily be reduced somewhat below the mean or average flow.

The total run-off of the Gila River at San Carlos during the 21 years for which we have records amounts to 7,557,465 acre-feet, or a mean annual flow of 359,880. It should be remembered, however, that under any practicable storage project, even with a maximum draft, at least some of the above run-off would have been lost over the spillway.

The total amount of water passing San Carlos during the dry cycle extending from January, 1894, to June, 1904, amounted to 2,873,400 acre-feet. That passing during the wet cycle from June, 1904, to January, 1915, was 4,684,065 acre-feet. By combining the corresponding years of the two nine-year cycles a mean annual run-off for a nine-year cycle is obtained, which is given in the following table:

Mean annual run-off at San Carlos, 9-year cycle.

1895 1904	1896 1905	1897 1906	1898 1907	1899 1908	1900 1909	1901 1910	1902 1911	1903 1912
301,841	782,833	445,822	481,709	287,479	213,674	150,030	237,851	248,414

Total average, 349,906.

This table is given in graphical form on plate No. 65 of the volume of maps accompanying this report. The inclusion of the years 1913–14–15, which are wet years belonging to the cycle following, would increase the average annual discharge. They were not included, as there were no corresponding years, and the exclusion was on the side of conservatism.

With the run-off averaged in this manner, for the nine years there was an average flow of 349,960 acre-feet; the run-off for six of the nine years was less than the average, and for the three remaining years it was considerably greater than the average.

In estimating the amount of water that can be stored and made available for irrigation at San Carlos, two very important factors must be taken into consideration; they are the losses of water by evaporation and the amount of silt deposited in the reservoir.

The United States Army board investigated these factors thoroughly, and the findings are discussed in Appendix B. The board found that the mean annual net evaporation (total evaporation less rainfall) over a body of water at San Carlos amounted to 60 inches, and that the silt accumulation amounted to 1.1 per cent of the annual run-off. These figures have been used in the computation relating to the reservoir. No matter how great the capacity of the reservoir, sooner or later steps must be taken to remove this silt. Just when this will occur depends on the annual draft to which the reservoir is subjected and the dryness or wetness of the cycles of years.

In order to study the San Carlos Reservoir a number of different mass curves were plotted, assuming various heights of dams and using various drafts of water. In the volume of maps accompanying this report are shown two of these diagrams, No. 65 and No. 66.

The first diagram has been made up on a basis of nine-year period of mean flow. The evaporation loss was assumed at 60 inches per annum, which is the same as determined by the Army board, and it was treated as though the losses caused by evaporation were uniformly distributed throughout the year, since whatever variations might take place from month to month would make very little difference in the final result.

The calculations for the annual draft from the reservoir have been treated in a similar manner. It was found that by plotting the monthly drafts in per cent, as given by the Reclamation Service for the Salt River project, and which are shown on page 31 of the Army board report, the resultant curve for the year varied but little from the straight line representing constant draft. The mass curve used in this diagram was derived in the following manner: The entire run-off for the period from 1895 to 1912 was plotted on cross-section paper and traced, and then the tracing was moved back until the curves of the two water-supply cycles coincided as well as they would. The length of the cycle, as nearly as could be determined in this manner, was nine years, thus bringing the high-flood years of 1896–1905 together. Corresponding years were then averaged and a table of monthly and yearly run-offs was prepared, from which the nine-year mean-flow curve was plotted.

The following table, prepared from this mass curve, gives the requisite reservoir capacity under various annual drafts to provide storage facilities during the mean cycle.

Annual draft in acre-feet.	Reserve capacity required to carry over 9-year cycle.	Waste over spillway in acre-feet.
200,000	90,000	1,040,000
225,000	230,000	880,000
250,000	370,000	585,000
300,000	714,450	92,000
310,000	790,000	0

The above schedule indicates that, to prevent waste during the mean cycle, using an annual draft of 300,000 acre-feet, a reservoir with a capacity of 806,450 acre-feet is required.

Under all other conditions of draft and corresponding reservoir capacities a large amount of water would be wasted over the spillways during the cycle.

A topographic map of the reservoir site (contour interval 5 feet, scale 1,000 feet to the inch) was prepared during the course of this investigation. The capacity of the reservoir, for various depths, taken from this map, is shown in the following table:

Capacity and area of reservoir at various depths.

Contour.	Area.	Capacity.	Contour.	Area.	Capacity.
	Acres.	*Acre-feet.*		*Acres.*	*Acre-feet.*
2,308	0	0	2,428	5,191	183,605
2,318	17	85	2,438	6,230	240,710
2,328	41	375	2,448	7,380	308,760
2,338	84	1,000	2,458	8,698	389,150
2,348	210	2,470	2,468	10,148	483,380
2,358	488	5,960	2,478	11,433	591,285
2,368	934	13,070	2,488	13,200	714,450
2,378	1,549	25,485	2,498	14,872	854,810
2,388	2,195	44,205	2,508	16,153	1,009,935
2,398	3,475	98,795	2,528	18,109	1,352,555

A study of the mean cycle flow diagram shows that, with a reservoir capacity of 714,450 acre-feet, the reservoir would be adequate to supply 300,000 acre-feet per annum in addition to the evaporation loss. If the draft were limited to 275,000 acre-feet the reservoir would supply all land during a period of five years, when the actual flow would be a total of 125,000 acre-feet below the mean. A draft of 250,000 acre-feet would guarantee a steady flow against a period 24 per cent below normal. With the 300,000 acre-feet draft the reservoir overflows during the third year, but relatively only a small quantity of water is lost in this manner, whereas a large amount of water is lost by evaporation, the reservoir being nearly full during the greater part of the nine years. If 10-foot shutter gates were used on the spillway no water would overflow, but the gates would be of service principally to prolong the life of the reservoir.

It is seen from the diagram that to supply a draft of 250,000 acre-feet would require a minimum storage capacity of 370,000 acre-feet. With a dam 180 feet to spillways, figuring the inflow of silt at 1.1 per cent, this minimum storage capacity would be reached in 91 years. With a draft of 300,000 acre-feet silt would immediately begin to curtail the required storage capacity and desilting would have to start soon after the construction of the impounding dam.

The 10-foot shutter gates would prolong the life of the reservoir to the extent of the additional storage provided, which amounts to 139,950 acre-feet, or an increased life of 37 years.

Considering now the run-off of the Gila River as it actually occurred during the period of record, it is seen that the average flow is, as already mentioned, 359,880 acre-feet; if we leave out the two extremely high-flood periods of 1905 and 1914 the average flow for the remaining years was 305,000 acre-feet.

A behavior diagram, plate No. 66, showing the run-off as it actually occurred and the effect of various drafts is shown in the accompanying volume of maps. This diagram was constructed in the same manner as diagram plate No. 65. Evaporation and draft were considered as being constant. In diagram (Pl. No. 66), however, it is considered that the silt will be removed as soon as deposited. In order to use as many periods of records as available the year (1894) preceding the first year of the diagram for which no records are available has been assumed to have had the same run-off as the only previously recorded year, 1890.

A study of this diagram (No. 66) shows that, if an empty reservoir were assumed at the beginning of the period for which run-off is recorded, or January 1, 1894, and a 300,000 acre-feet draft had been demanded, a full water supply would have been available until about the end of January, 1902, but from this time on until August, 1904, the reservoir would have been empty and the only available water would have been the actual run-off during that period. For the balance of the year 1902 there would have been only 95,100 acre-feet run-off available or sufficient water, including 20 per cent canal losses, to irrigate a 3 acre-feet duty, 25,400 acres. During 1903 the run-off for the year, at the above duty would have been sufficient for the irrigation of 30,000 acres, or would have supplied an 80.000-acre project with only a little more than 1 acre-foot per acre. Beginning with the high water of August, 1904, and continuing on to the present date, it will be seen from the diagram that the reservoir with a 180-foot dam would have served to supply even more than a 300,000 acre-foot draft.

A further study of the diagram shows that a reservoir of a capacity of 714,450 acre-feet, with an annual draft of 300,000 acre-feet, would have been empty from January, 1902, to August, 1904.

During the remainder of the 21 years over which the records extend, the 300,000 acre-foot draft could have been maintained and during the period February, 1906, to April, 1908, 516,000 acre-feet of water would have been wasted over the spillways.

A reservoir with a capacity of 854,800 acre-feet, with the same annual draft, would have been empty from February, 1903, to August, 1904. From January, 1907, to March, 1908, 245,000 acre-feet of water would have been wasted over the spillways.

A reservoir of 854,800 acre-feet capacity with an annual draft of 225,000 acre-feet would have maintained this draft during the dry period, but a total of 63,000 acre-feet of water would have discharged over the spillway during the period of September, 1897, to August, 1898.

Figuring that the reservoir was full instead of empty at the beginning of the period mentioned, it will be seen from the diagram that, with a 180-foot dam, the reservoir would have supplied a full draft until about June, 1902, when the water supply would have been depleted. The assumption that the reservoir was full in the beginning makes but little difference in the results, since the excess of inflow over draft, in the case of the empty reservoir, was stored and used, whereas, in the case of the full reservoir the excess of inflow over draft was lost over the spillway.

For drafts less than 300,000 acre-feet, it is seen from the diagram, and as pointed out by the Army board, that the maximum draft to carry through the extremely dry period from 1900 to 1905 would be about 200,000 acre-feet. A study of the diagram for the second period, 1905 to 1915, shows that with a 180-foot dam there would have been a surplus during the lowest period of approximately 200,000 acre-feet. With a dam 190 feet to spillway, there would have been a surplus of about 300,000 acre-feet during the lowest period.

If we assume 1.1 per cent of the total flow as representing the amount of silt remaining in the reservoir, there would have been 83,132 acre-feet deposited during the 21 years of record or an average of 3,959 acre-feet per annum.

In order to study the effect of silt in the reservoir, discharge curves were run back from the low-water or empty reservoir points at the end of the nine-year period, until the maximum ordinate distance between the run-off curve and the discharge curve thus plotted was reached. If the spillway had ceased to flow at this maximum distance, the minimum capacity of the reservoir would be measured by the ordinate distance between the two curves at this point.

From the actual run-off diagram (plate No. 66), it is seen that in order to supply a 300,000-acre-foot draft during a period similar to the one from 1894 to 1902, assuming a dam 180 feet to spillway, a minimum reservoir capacity of 500,000 acre-feet would have to be maintained. During the period from 1904 to 1915 the flow was much more regular, and the minimum capacity curve shows that only about 400,000 acre-feet storage capacity would have been necessary for a 300,000-acre-foot draft.

Figuring on the basis of a 500,000-acre-foot minimum capacity to be maintained and with a dam 180 feet to spillway, desilting would have to begin after 54 years. With a dam 190 feet to spillway, or by use of the 10-foot shutter gates, the life of the project without desilting would be prolonged to 87 years.

On the normal-cycle assumption desilting would have to begin at once to accommodate an annual draft of 300,000 acre-feet, unless spillway gates were provided, in which case it could be deferred 37 years. For an annual draft of 225,000 acre-feet desilting would not be necessary, except during a period as dry as from 1895 to 1904, for 127 years, unless spillway gates were installed, in which case it could be deferred for 164 years. For a period as dry as from 1895 to 1904 desilting would have to begin at once for an annual draft of 225,000 acre-feet, if spillway gates are not installed. With spillway gates raising it to 190 feet, a draft of 300,000 acre-feet per year would be possible a little over half the time and 275,000 all of the time, if silt removal begins as soon as its accumulation becomes enough to make its removal economical.

On account of the necessity of storing two or three years' supply, a reservoir impounding 714,450 acre-feet with a dam 180 feet high to the crest of the spillway was chosen. The largest flood of which there are definite measurments (December, 1914) was used in determining the size of the spillway. To make sure that the spillway was large enough, the discharge was doubled. This flood could have passed a 300-foot spillway with a depth of 11½ feet. Placing 10-foot gates in the spillway would reduce the clear space to 240 feet and increase the depth of the water over the spillway to 14½ feet. Doubling the duration of the flood as well as its intensity increased the depth to 17 feet, so a dam 200 feet high over all should be sufficient. The use of the spillway gates will increase the capacity of the reservoir to 854,810 acre-feet.

Regardless as to whether we use a 200,000 acre-foot or a 300,000 acre-foot draft, the diagram shows plainly the necessity of providing ample hold over capacity, and it also appears that 500,000 acre-feet, as assumed by the Army Board, should be the minimum capacity of the reservoir.

To provide a reservoir of this capacity and at the same time to defer desilting operations for a reasonable length of time, a dam capable of storing water to the 190-foot contour would be the most suitable height. This capacity could be obtained by means of a dam having the same height, 180 feet to spillway, as recommended by the Army board, but with the addition of 10-foot shutter gates along the spillway.

ANNUAL DRAFT.

In the case of the San Carlos project, the quantity of water that may be considered the proper annual draft from the reservoir is a problem affecting the operation of the entire project, and may well be a subject upon which opinions might widely differ.

The Army board has based its calculations of the annual draft on the critically dry period; which means that there is a full water supply guaranteed to the lands during a period as dry as the driest on record. On account of the protracted dry period on which we have the records of the Gila run-off, the quantity of water to be delivered each year by the reservoir must be made correspondingly small and the assured draft from the reservoir must be made considerably less than the normal or average supply. While it is proposed to utilize as much of the overflow from the reservoir as is possible, yet the area of the land to come under the project must necessarly be small and a project based upon a minimum supply can not, under more favorable conditions, be expected to make the best uses of the normal supply.

By basing a project upon a draft representing more nearly the normal supply, we approach a more thorough utilization of the available supply, less losses by evaporation and overflow, and a larger area may be supplied under the project, but it is impossible to guarantee a full supply of water to this area during a period of extreme drought similar to the driest on record.

It should be remembered that the dry period of record to which we have already frequently referred, viz., from 1899 to 1904, was a remarkable one, not only on account of small amount of the run-off of the Gila River for the different years, but more so on account of the continued succession of dry years.

The full possibilities of the project would not be developed were it decided to limit the draft to the quantity of water necessary to insure against future deficiency in case of a repetition of the worst period of which we now have record. It is believed that the draft should be based upon an amount more nearly equal to the normal basis.

The Salt River project is operated on the normal-supply basis. It should be pointed out, however, that the Salt River project differs from the San Carlos in this respect, that under the San Carlos project all of the lands are assumed to have the same right to the water, whereas under the Salt River project certain lands, as provided for by the Kent decree, have a preferential right, and these preferred lands during years of shortage receive a full supply, while the remaining lands get only what is left, or must be supplied by means of pumps.

The Salt River project must also conform with the provisions of the reclamation act.

The Salt River project as recently recommended[1] is to embrace 195,000 acres. Seventy thousand acres of class A, or preferred, land are to be supplied with gravity or stored water and the remaining 125,000 acres to be supplied by gravity and stored water, supplemented by 30 pumps.

The mean anual run-off of the Salt River at Roosevelt for the period from 1889 to 1911 was 808,000 acre-feet, with a maximum flow of 3,260,000 acre-feet and a minimum flow of 154,000 acre-feet.[2] The duty of water as recommended by the present board of survey above referred to, was assumed at 4½ acre-feet at the point of diversion and 3.3 acre-feet on the land.

[1] Report of a board of survey convened by the Secretary of the Interior to consider the selection of lands to be included in the Salt River project, Arizona, consisting of F. W. Hanna, supervising engineer, Reclamation Service, and W. A. Farish and Frank H. Parker, representing the Water Users' Association. Report published Jan. 15, 1914.

[2] Eleventh Annual Report of Reclamation Service, p. 45.

While the difference between the mean and the minimum flow of the Salt River has been relatively greater than that recorded for the Gila, yet the protracted dry spell recorded for the Gila has been more severe than any similar period on the Salt. Basing these calculations on the critically dry period of record on the Salt River, but assuming that supplemental pumps were installed, the board of survey in their report show that the water supply for the lands under the Salt River project would have been less than the mean during 6 of the 25 years of record and that the greatest deficiency would have been about 60 per cent below the normal supply. With respect to the deficiency during the driest periods, it is believed that the San Carlos project, as outlined above, compares favorably with the Salt River project.

Considering all phases of the annual draft problem, it is believed that it would be better to reap the benefit of the normal water supply during a greater portion of the time and to assume the risk of failure in unusually dry years than to provide for a much more limited use of the water at all times in order to insure against possible droughts during exceptional years. As pointed out before, the period extending from January, 1902, to August, 1904, during which the reservoir would be empty, was one of exceptionally low precipitation over the West, and from records available at other points may not be reasonably expected to occur more frequently than once in 30 or 40 years.

The permissible annual draft of a practicable reservoir at San Carlos, based on our present knewledge, should therefore lie between 300,000 acre-feet as an upper and 250,000 acre-feet as a lower limit. A greater draft would not be permissible, while a smaller draft would fail to utilize the possibilities of the project. In so far as the annual draft is concerned, these two figures form the basis of the maximum and minimum cost of the project.

In the computation of the annual draft, the beneficial effect of the flow of the San Pedro has not thus far been considered. Sufficient measurements have not been taken to determine the flow of the San Pedro with any degree of certainty. The United States Army board assumed its discharge as one-tenth that of the Gila. The observations made during this investigation seem to indicate that the flow varies from one-fifth of the flow of the Gila River during low water to one-tenth during flood periods.

For lack of better information, the flow of the San Pedro has been assumed to be one-tenth of the flow of the Gila. The San Pedro discharges into the Gila about 42 miles above Florence, and its flow during flood periods would decrease the amount necessary to be drawn from the reservoir for irrigation, permitting a larger amount to be stored. The effect of this flow on the behavior of the reservoir is shown in the mass diagram, plate No. 72, in volume of maps, accompanying this report, and is based on an annual 5,000 acre-feet transmission loss in the river between the dam site and the point of diversion above Florence. The effect of adding the flow of the San Pedro is to shorten the empty reservoir period, so that instead of going dry February 1, 1902, the water supply would have held out under a 300,000 acre-foot draft until December 1, 1902. Consequently, by adding the flow of the San Pedro, the reservoir with a capacity of 714,450 and the above draft would have been dry from December 1,

1902, to August 1, 1904. With a capacity of 854,800 acre-feet, under the same conditions, it would have been dry from May 1, 1903, to August 1, 1904.

During the succeeding cycle, the effect of the San Pedro would have been nil, owing to the discharge of surplus water over the spillway. The above calculations have been based on the amount of water actually available. Similar calculations, using the amount physically available, show that the only effect of using the water now diverted for irrigation in the Solomonville Valley is to diminish the time the reservoir is empty during the extremely dry cycle. The mass diagram, just referred to, also shows the behavior of the reservoir, including the effect of the San Pedro River, and water now diverted in the Solomonville Valley.

The mass diagram showing the effect of diversions at Solomonville is based on an annual net loss of 58,000 acre-feet. This figure is explained later in Appendix B of this report. This diagram indicates that the 714,450 capacity reservoir with an annual draft of 300,000 acre-feet and with combined flow from Solomonville and the San Pedro would have been empty from March 1, 1904, to August 1, 1904. With a capacity of 854,800 acre-feet it would have contained 2,000 acre-feet on August 1, 1904, when the succeeding flood began. During the balance of the 21-year period the addition of the Solomonville diversion water or the San Pedro would have no appreciable effect, since the run-off without this supply was more than sufficient to meet the demands of the project.

History of Irrigation on Gila River.

Irrigation, an essential requirement of agricultural development in the Southwest, has been practiced along the Gila since prehistoric times. Remains of ditches and other unmistakable evidences of irrigation by an ancient race, which apparently reached a higher stage of civilization than the Indians known to the early settlers, are to be found at different places in the valleys of the Gila and its tributaries.

The Pima Indians, who may be descendants of these prehistoric irrigators, were irrigating a large area of land along the Gila when the first exploring Jesuits penetrated this territory during the middle of the sixteenth century.

While the Jesuits and their followers intermittently irrigated a limited area of land along the Santa Cruz, and possibly along the San Pedro (both tributaries of the Gila), yet no important irrigation other than that practiced by the Indians took place until some time after the American military occupation in the middle of the nineteenth century, when protection to the settlers and markets for the crops were afforded.

A small area of land was irrigated at this time, in connection with the overland stage stations. This stage line was established in 1857, and the route, after leaving Tucson, was through the Pima villages on the present Gila River Indian Reservation, cutting across the big bend of the Gila and touching the river again at the present Gila Bend station; thence continuing along the river to its confluence with the Colorado at Yuma. All of the land formerly cultivated in connection with these old stage towns, as well as the other older irrigated area on the lower Gila, has since been allowed to revert to the desert state.

Subsequent diversion of the waters of the Gila by the whites proceeded in a rather uniform manner up the stream. Irrigation in the Florence district started earlier than in the Solomonville Valley, while the first irrigation in the Duncan Valley took place at a later date than in the other districts lower down on the Gila.

The first irrigation in the Florence district was initiated by, and for the profit of, the early Indian agents of the reservation, just below and contiguous to the Florence district.

The pioneers of the next valley up the river, the Solomonville district, were Mexicans, who ventured into this uncivilized territory in the early seventies. Americans followed, and with the advent of the Mormon colonists a few years later rapid agricultural development took place.

In the Duncan district, as well as along the upper tributaries, the Mexicans made the earliest diversions. Irrigation here, however, had many disadvantages, adverse natural conditions together with remoteness from civilized centers or military protection considerably delaying later diversions of the waters of the Gila for irrigation.

The progress of irrigation along the Gila River since the American occupation has varied in the different districts. Coincident with the development and consequent diversions of the river waters in the valleys on the upper reaches of the stream, the water supply for the irrigated districts lower down soon began to suffer, and in the extreme lower valleys many acres of irrigated land were no longer cultivated. In the middle Gila districts the agricultural development was either stopped entirely or greatly retarded.

The present status of irrigation along the Gila is summarized in the following tabulations.

The areas shown were actually under irrigation by the use of ditches and pumps, taking water direct from the Gila River at the time (1914) of the survey made in connection with this investigation.

Principal districts.

	Acres.	Acres.
No. 1. Duncan Valley	6,268.5	
No. 2. Solomonville-Safford Valley	26,633.0	
No. 3. San Carlos Indian Reservation	1,000.5	
No. 3. Florence-Casa Grande Valley	7,563.4	
No. 4. Gila River Indian Reservation	14,356.0	
		55,821.4
No. 5. Lower Gila district (west of Pima Indian Reservation)		24,045.0
Winkelman section		335.0
Between districts Nos. 1 and 2		90.0
Between districts Nos. 2 and 3		27.0
No. 6. Extreme Upper Gila		3,621.0
Tributaries:		
San Pedro	6,860.0	
San Carlos	936.0	
Eagle Creek	563.0	
San Francisco	1,739.0	
San Francisco tributaries, Blue	211.0	
San Francisco tributaries, others	780.0	
		11,089.0
Total on Gila and tributaries		94,693.4

In addition to the foregoing areas under cultivation at the time of the survey the following acreages are found to have been previously irrigated:

No. 1. Duncan	125.3
No. 2. Solomonville-Safford	2,120.0
No. 3. San Carlos Reservation	1,202.0
No. 3. Florence-Casa Grande	12,217.7
No. 4. Gila River Indian Reservation	11,315.0
Total	26,980.2

No attempt was made to obtain complete data covering the previously irrigated areas on the lower Gila or on the tributaries.

It should be pointed out that these previously irrigated areas do not necessarily represent areas that have been cultivated contemporaneously with the lands under cultivation at the present time, since in many instances the present cultivated areas were not reclaimed until after the abandonment of the lands now classified as previously cultivated.

In the four principal irrigation districts along the Gila or the districts numbered 1, 2, 3, and 4 in this report there is a white population of 10,670. The total Indian population directly affected by diversions of the Gila River waters on the two reservations included in the above districts, according to the most recent census, is 4,580.

Leaving aside the Indian reservation lands and considering only the four districts mentioned above there are 1,584 different persons or interests who are the present owners of land which is now being irrigated or which has been previously irrigated by ditches diverting water from the Gila River.

In the territory covered by districts Nos. 5 and 6, or the lower Gila, the tributaries, and the extreme upper Gila, it is estimated that 3,000 persons are dependent upon the agricultural industry. The total population along the Gila River and its tributaries, not including the Salt River, supported directly or indirectly by the agricultural industry, amounts to approximately 18,000, or a little more than one-twelfth of the total population of the State of Arizona.

A brief description and history of irrigation in each of the irrigated districts along the Gila and its tributaries follows, the districts being reported upon in the numerical order shown in the table of areas under cultivation at the time of the survey.

IRRIGATION IN DUNCAN VALLEY, DISTRICT NO. 1.

The Duncan district embraces a narrow valley about 30 miles in length, the upper 7 miles of which lies in Grant County, N. Mex., while the remaining portion is in Greenlee County, Ariz., which was created from a part of Graham County in 1911.

The elevation of the river bed at the extreme upper end of the Duncan Valley is 3,800 feet, while at the extreme lower end it is 3,400 feet. The elevation of the Government bench mark at Duncan, near the center of the valley, is 3,643 feet.

The Arizona & New Mexico Railroad from Lordsburg to the mining towns of Clifton and Morenci traverses nearly the entire length of the valley.

Alfalfa, grain, and vegetables constitute the principal crops, and stock raising is also an important industry in this valley. The mountainous territory contiguous to the Duncan Valley has provided a large area of excellent cattle range. This range, which in past years has been overstocked, is still capable of feeding a large number of cattle. Part of the hay raised in the valley is fed to cattle during the winter, while the remaining portion is usually baled, and, like the vegetables and other produce, finds a ready market in the near-by mining towns of Clifton and Morenci.

The total population of the Duncan Valley amounts to 1,400 persons, depending directly or indirectly on the agricultural industry. Of this number 750 reside in the village of Duncan, after which the valley is named and which forms practically the only town in the district.

The farming class of the Duncan Valley consists of Americans and a few Mexicans. Many of the former landowners have sold out and left the country. In 1895 a colony of Mormons settled in the upper part of the valley near what is called Franklin Flat, and to them credit is due for agricultural development in that section.

Most of the farms are situated in the upper portion of the valley, extending from the vicinity of the town of Duncan to the Apache Box Canyon, which terminates the upper end of the valley. In that portion below Duncan the irrigated area is not continuous, and many small areas are irrigated by means of pumps.

Irrigation began relatively later in the Duncan Valley than in the other agricultural districts lower down on the Gila. The cultivated areas in this valley comprise a rather narrow strip of land along each bank of the river. This unfavorable natural condition, together with the hostile activities of the Apache Indians during the early history of this region, no doubt were factors largely responsible for the retardation of its development.

The historical analysis of irrigation in this valley, compiled from the data collected in this investigation, shows that the first irrigation in the Duncan district was on land now being served by the Sunset Canal and was carried on by means of a very small ditch constructed in 1876. The next oldest ditch is the Cosper, Martin & Wilson, and this ditch represents a consolidation of two ditches, the Cosper-Martin and the Wilson, the latter being the much older of the two, having been constructed in 1879. The irrigated area under these two ditches was limited, as it is estimated that in 1880 only 250 acres were being served by these two ditches.

From 1880 to 1890 a number of small canals and a few larger ones were constructed, in addition to the two older ditches, and in the latter year the estimated irrigated area was 1,469 acres. In 1900 the cultivated area had increased to 3,660 acres, and at the time (1914) when surveys were made in this valley in connection with the present investigation, 13 canals and 9 pumping plants served to irrigate 6,268.5 acres. The nine pumping plants, lifting water direct from the Gila River, supply water to irrigate a combined area of 146 acres, which is included in the foregoing area.

Of the present cultivated area 2,037.2 acres are situated within the State of New Mexico, and six of the principal canals of the Duncan Valley have their headings east of the New Mexico line, five of these canals irrigating land in that State.

Besides the 6,268.5 acres of irrigated area in this valley, there was found an additional area of 125.5 acres which gave evidence of having been previously irrigated.

Between Guthrie Canyon, which marks the lower end of the Duncan Valley, and the first diversion made for the Solomonville Valley, there are three small pumping plants irrigating a combined area of about 90 acres, near the mouth of the San Francisco River.

A majority of the ditches in this district are owned by mutual companies or corporations, and the stockholders, as a rule, are the owners of the land under the canal. The few ditches and pumping plants not under corporate ownership are held by individuals or on a partnership basis.

Of the 13 canals serving to irrigate land in the Duncan Valley, 10 have been incorporated, and 167 landowners under the different canals are holders of the outstanding stock. The other 3 canals, together with the 9 pumping plants, are owned by 15 persons, thus making a total of 182 persons directly interested in irrigation in the Duncan Valley. All but two of the above number are landowners under the canals. The water is not made appurtenant to the land, and the owner may use the water called for by his shares of stock as he may see fit. The water right represented by each share of stock, as a rule, is the pro rata of all the water available for distribution.

The Duncan district has been singularly free from litigation over water rights. A suit which promised the settlement of the relative rights to the use of the Gila waters, between the farmers of the Duncan Valley, and those of the Solomonville Valley, was started in 1912. This suit, which was known as the William A. Gillespie, of the Solomonville Valley, *v.* The Valley Canal Co. et al., of the Duncan Valley, was in the form of an injunction proceeding, and was filed in the superior court of Graham County in the spring of 1912. Answer was made by the attorneys for the defendants, and it appears the case was then allowed to drop, as it has not been called to trial.

With one or two exceptions the lands under the different ditches have been continuously arrigated since their initial irrigation. This irrigation has not been carried on continuously under the same ditch, but a great deal of land, especially the irrigated areas in New Mexico, has been served at various times by a number of small ditches. The ditches now in use, though higher and more permanent, are virtually the same as the canals formerly used, which were located closer to the river. The pumping plants which have been installed recently in this district, serve to irrigate some of the small tracts formerly covered by gravity ditches.

Herewith is given a tabulation summarizing both the results of the survey made in connection with this investigation, and also an historical analysis of the development of irrigation in this district.

The results of the survey have been shown in this tabulation, as well as in the tabulations for the other districts, under three-column headings, as follows: "Pres. cult.," or present cultivation; "P. C." or previous cultivation; and "N. C. (fenced)," or areas that have never been cultivated but which are fenced.

Under "Pres. Cult." are the areas which were found to be under actual cultivation at the time of this survey, in 1914, and which were irrigated from the several ditches taking water from the Gila River. Under "P. C." are the areas which showed unmistakeable evidence of previous cultivation but which were not being irrigated or cultivated at the time of the survey. As a rule these areas have been in a condition of disuse for some time and, broadly speaking, may be compared to the lands classified as "B" in the well-known Kent decree of the Salt River Valley Adjudication suit. Although a small amount of the "P. C." land may have been cultivated within the past two or three years, yet while this area was being cultivated other similar areas were being neglected, so that the relative areas given remain approximately the same.

Under "N. C. (Fenced)" are included the areas of land under ditches in service in 1914 which have been fenced and which, though irrigable, have never been irrigated and for which no appropriations of water have been made in the past. These lands may be compared to class C lands of the Kent decree.

The remainder of the tabulation is devoted to irrigation analyses or the development of irrigation under each canal, shown by five-year periods. The compilation of this analyses tabulation is the result of a consideration of all data collected during the investigation.

The history of irrigation under the various canals and other data concerning irrigation in the Duncan Valley are given in Appendix A.

Analysis of irrigation, Duncan Valley, N. Mex. and Ariz.

Name.	Date of construction.	Date of last use.	Area, by U. S. Indian Service survey.				Area, by U. S. Indian Service survey, 1914.			Areas irrigated in five-year periods as estimated from all available information.								
			New Mexico, present cultivation.	Arizona.														
				Cultivated.	Previous cultivation.	Never cultivated (fenced).	Cultivated.	Previous cultivation.	Never cultivated (fenced).	1876	1880	1885	1890	1895	1900	1905	1910	1914
			Acres.	*Acres.*	*Acres.*	*Acres.*	*Acres.*	*Acres.*	*Acres.*	*Acres.*	*Acres.*	*Acres.*	*Acres.*	*Acres.*	*Acres.*	*Acres.*	*Acres.*	*Acres.*
1. Sunset	1876	Not abandoned.	694.0				694.0			8	8	155	260	400	445.0	555.0	694.0	694.0
2. Cosper, Martin & Wilson.	1879	do.	483.5				488.5		0.5		242	242	242	242	242.0	436.0	474.0	483.5
3. Cosper & Windham.	1886	do.	514.8	126.7			641.5						157	235	415.0	545.0	610.0	641.5
4. Model	1892	do.	278.9	1,540.6	9.0	38.6	1,819.5	9.0	38.6					680	1,394.0	1,714.0	1,787.0	1,819.5
5. Shriver	1887	do.	66.0				66.0						66	66	66.0	66.0	66.0	66.0
6. Valley	1887	do.		1,220.5	46.5	100.0	1,220.5	46.5	100.0				196	335	460.0	590.0	1,140.0	1,220.5
7. Burtcher	1881	do.		163.5		2.3	163.5		2.3			150	150	150	163.5	163.5	163.5	163.5
8. Duncan Extension.	1887	do.		67.5			67.7						150	115	100.0	85.0	75.0	67.5
9. Black & McCloskey.	1897	do.		153.0			153.0					100	110	120	126.0	150.0	153.0	153.0
10. Colmenero	1890	do.		390.0			390.0						38	38	38.0	67.0	345.0	390.0
11. Sexton	1901	do.		75.5	19.0		75.5	19.0								70.1	75.5	75.5
12. Billingsley	1907	do.		82.0			82.0										82.0	82.0
13. York	1881	do.		265.0	29.0		265.0	29.0				25	85	155	177.0	177.0	265.0	265.0
PUMPING PLANTS.																		
14. McNair	1913	do.		11.5			11.5											11.5
15. Craufurd	1909	do.		33.0			33.0										23.0	33.0
16. Shade	1911	do.		6.0			6.0											6.0
17. Edwards & Cauthen.	1906	do.		18.5	5.5		18.5										15.0	18.5
18. Goolsby	1911	do.		10.0	16.5		10.0	16.5										10.0
19. Foote	1914	do.		7.0			7.0											7.0
20. Angle	1908	do.		15.0			15.0										7.0	15.0
21. Brown	1913	do.		11.0			11.0											11.0
22. Short	1885	do.		35.0		27.6	35.0		27.6			15	15	15	35.0	35.0	35.0	35.0
Total			2,037.2	4,231.3	125.5	294.0	6,268.5	125.5	294.0	8	250	687	1,469	2,551	3,661.5	4,653.6	6,010.0	6,268.5

IRRIGATION IN THE SOLOMONVILLE-SAFFORD VALLEY, DISTRICT NO. 2.

Like the Duncan Valley, the Solomonville-Safford district, known locally as the Gila Valley, is almost wholly inclosed by rugged mountain ranges. Along the north and west it is bounded by the Gila range, through which the Gila cuts at the Narrows, about 10 miles above Solomonville. Along the southwestern boundary it is inclosed by the Pinaleno Range and the Santa Teresa Mountains. The culminating peak of the Pinaleno Range is Mount Graham, which has an elevation of 10,200 feet, and which, until well along in the summer, retains the winter snows. The highest peak of the Santa Teresa is Turnbull Mountain, whose elevation is over 8,000 feet.

While, from a geographical standpoint, the irrigated areas in the Solomonville-Safford district and those along the Gila in the San Carlos Indian Reservation are in the same valley, yet the Solomonville-Safford Valley is commonly considered to comprise that portion of the valley east of the reservation line.

The lower or reservation portion of the valley is 30 miles long, is much narrower than the upper portion, and contains a much smaller irrigated area.

The upper extremity of the Solomonville-Safford Valley has an elevation of approximately 3,100 feet, and the elevation of the river bottom 70 miles below, at the Upper San Carlos Dam site, is 2,308 feet.

Graham County, which includes the entire Solomonville-Safford Valley, was created in 1881 from portions of Pima and Apache Counties. Apache County originally extended as far south as the Gila River, while Pima County embraced all the territory in Arizona lying south of the Gila, i. e., nearly all of the Gadsden purchase. The town of Safford was the first county seat which was moved to Solomonville in 1883.

Alfalfa, wheat, barley, and corn are the principal crops of this valley, sorghum and cotton are raised to a limited extent, the former crop being utilized for cattle feed. Fruit growing is receiving considerable attention, and while the early fruits, such as peaches, apricots, etc., are liable to destruction by late spring frost, the hardier varieties, such as apples, pears, etc., yield well.

Cattle raising is carried on to a less extent than in the Duncan Valley, but the dairying industry promises to receive more attention in the future.

Nearly the whole of the valley, not including the area within the San Carlos Reservation, is thickly settled. The more important towns are Solomonville, which, according to the last census, has a population of 595; Safford and Pima, both incorporated towns, with 929 and 500, respectively; and Thatcher, with 900 inhabitants. In 1910 the population of this valley, not including the Indians on the San Carlos Reservation, totaled 6,470. There is a larger proportion of Mexican farmers in this valley than in the Duncan Valley. Early in its history Mormons made settlements and cultivated certain sections of this valley, and to-day a majority of the landowners are followers of the Mormon faith.

In the Solomonville-Safford Valley there are 19 incorporated companies, owning and operating canals at the present time. Four of these canal companies have built and own extensions of the other canals. There are three other canals not incorporated which are held by individual owners. The total number of shareholders of the incorporated canal companies is 1,217, and the unincorporated canals are owned by five individuals.

Of the above stockholders owning interests in ditches, all but four are land owners or lessees under the different canals.

The Arizona Eastern Railroad, leaving the main line of the Southern Pacific at Bowie, traverses the valley and terminates at the mining town of Miami, a short distance beyond Glove. These two mining towns have a combined population of over 8,000, and provide ready markets for much of the produce of the valley.

The Solomonville-Safford district, like other valleys along the Gila, is the site of many prehistoric dwellings, and ancient irrigation systems. The first immigrations to this territory of which we have historical record were those of Mexicans, who established themselves at a place now known as Solomonville, but formerly called "Pueblo Viejo" (Old Town), because of the many ruined dwellings of its aboriginal inhabitants. In time this latter name was applied to the whole valley, and even to-day this section is often referred to as the valley of Pueblo Viejo. Later, in 1879, after I. S. Solomon had established a store and residence in this settlement, the name was changed to Solomonville, in honor of its pioneer business man and trader.

Soon after that time more Americans began to arrive, and in 1879 a colony of Mormons established themselves in the vicinity of Smithville, to undertake the development of that section.

The general history of irrigation in this district is the usual one of modest beginnings followed by gradual development. The early irrigation practiced by Mexicans at no time became very extensive, being limited generally to patches of corn planted in the more favorable places along the ditches and without regard to land lines. Land-office filings were rarely made, nor were other steps taken to obtain title to the land. These Mexicans, as was customary among the Americans who followed a little later, would form a partnership for the purpose of digging a ditch, then the several partners would stake out their respective claims along the ditch, the size of each partnership's claim being in proportion to his interest in the ditch. Later, these partnerships or societies would incorporate under the laws of the State to form the now existing canal companies.

In spite of many disadvantages under which the early settlers were compelled to labor, the agricultural development of the valley proceeded at a fair pace. Irrigation began in 1873, and prior to 1880 twelve different canals had already been completed or were in process of construction.

The oldest canal in the valley and second in point of size is known as the Montezuma. Other important canals are the Union, San Jose, Smithville, Nevada, and the Consolidated.

With the advent of the Mormon colonists in the early eighties, a more rapid development took place, and in 1890 approximately 16,000 acres were under cultivation and 19 canals had been constructed. At the time of the survey made in connection with this investigation in 1914 there were 18 ditches in the Solomonville-Safford Valley, which served actually to irrigate 26,633 acres of land, and an additional area of 2,120 acres was shown to have been previously irrigated.

The agricultural lands of the Solomonville-Safford Valley lie in rather a narrow tract or trough varying from 1 to 4 miles in width. The river course for the most part lies on the northern side of the valley, but throughout the greater portion of its length irrigation takes place on both sides of the river.

The numerous canals which have been constructed at different times all have their headings within a few miles of each other along the river. The canals whose diversions are on the same side of the river parallel each other for long distances across the irrigated lands. In many instances water from the upper ditch is flumed across the lower ditch and used on lands which could be better served by the lower ditch. Much trouble and waste of water has resulted from these conditions. Many ditch consolidations have taken place, and while the cultivated area has increased from year to year yet the number of ditches serving the land has decreased in recent years, and at the present time 18 canals are serving a larger area than was served by as many as 26 ditches or canals during former years. The diversion works have been constructed of brush and rock, a type which has always been in use. These works are destroyed by each flood, but during the low-water flow are capable of diverting all the water required.

Since about the year 1890 the dams built in connection with the canals at the upper end of the valley have been diverting all of the available surface water during the dry season, thus causing a shortage of supply at other diversions from the river lower down. This condition has led to litigation which finally resulted in the well-known suit of the Smithville Canal Co. *v.* Oregon Irrigation & Canal Co. et al. This suit, which was tried in 1905, involved all of the water users in the valley. Judgment was rendered in 1906 and the resulting decree was in effect an adjudication of the water rights of the Solomonville-Safford Valley. The proceedings which resulted in this decree may be found in the copy of the findings, judgment, and decree of this case which has been printed in volume 1, supplemental exhibits, accompanying this report. Much valuable information concerning irrigation in that district is also contained therein.

The court found in the above case that the entire acreage then under cultivation has been continuously irrigated from the time of reclamation to the date of the rendering of the decision. It was found that the incorporated canal companies were carrying the water for the benefit of the landowners and not for hire, and that the canals did not appropriate any water in their corporate capacity.

The several landowners under the various ditches, however, were not given separate priorities, and it was found that—

> The individual landowners and appropriations of water that is furnished under the management of each of the several ditches or canals herein referred to have surrendered to their cousers in that canal their priority, and the water that is taken from the river for the use of the land under the several canals has been, by the consent of the different landowners under each canal, delivered to the different tracts of land in accordance with the extent of the interest in the ditch or canal of each landowner, regardless of the acreage cultivated by the said landowners and regardless of the date when the said acreage was placed under cultivation.

The return of seepage flow in the river channels was also taken into consideration, it being held that:

The water supply is comprised of the volume that enters the river at that point, and the accretions thereto that rise from the underground and the return waters from the lands irrigated under the several canals and from other sources.

The duty of water was taken at one-half miner's inch continuous flow to the acre, or equivalent to 9.02 acre-feet per acre per year, and it was further held that the total amount of water in the river in ordinary seasons was equivalent to one-half miner's inch per acre for all the land thus irrigated, and that during part of the year the amount available was more than one-half miner's inch per acre, and that the distribution of the water was based upon the requirements of the land and upon the ability of the irrigators to use beneficially the various amounts designated.

The several parties who failed to maintain their water rights in the suit were stopped as against their coowners and users under the same canal from the assertion of their rights to priority as evidenced by the several appropriations and reclamations of land. But the users under each canal system having contended for their priorities as against each other canal system, or rival, as a ditch company or as an aggregation of individuals were held to be entitled as against such other canal or ditch or the users of water thereunder to their priorities, as shown by the acreage in cultivation and the different dates on which water applied thereto for irrigation purposes.

All of the water users in this valley, with the exception of those using water under the Gonzales or Lee Canal, contended for their rights, and all of the canals, with the exception of the Gonzales, were decreed a portion of the flow. The Gonzales has been using a small amount of water since the decree, in spite of the water commissioner appointed by the court to distribute the water as provided for in the decree.

The distribution of the flow of the river since the decree has been entirely under the direction of the water commissioner.

A table showing the irrigated areas in the Solomonville-Safford district similar to that of the Duncan district is submitted hereunder.

This tabulation is a résumé of the data obtained as a result of the survey in connection with the investigation, and from various other sources.

The areas under cultivation during the years prior to 1904 were obtained for the most part from the findings in the case of Smithville Canal Co. et al. *v.* Oregon Canal Co. et al., previously referred to.

A detailed history of irrigation under each canal of the Solomonville-Safford Valley is given in Appendix A. A copy of the adjudication decree and transcript of evidence and other matters pertaining to irrigation in the Solomonville-Safford Valley are to be found in the supplemental exhibits accompanying this report.

Name of canal.	Date of construction.	Date of last use.	Area by United States Indian Service survey, 1914.			Area by decree of 1905.	Areas by "Claims of appropriation," 1914.	Areas irrigated in five-year periods as estimated from available information.								
			Cultivated.	Previous cultivation.	Never cultivated (under fence).			1875	1880	1885	1890	1895	1900	1905	1910	1914
			Acres.	*Acres.*	*Acres.*	*Acres.*	*Acres.*	*Acres.*	*Acres.*	*Acres.*	*Acres.*	*Acres.*	*Acres.*	*Acres.*	*Acres.*	*Acres.*
1. Brown	1896		559.5	103.0	13.0	820	1,011.0		50	195	405	663	663	663	559.0	559.5
2. Sanchez	1893	1905														
3. Mejie	1877	1905														
4. Fournese	1891		230.5	11.0		260	200.0					260	260	260	230.5	230.5
5. San Jose	1874		3,595.7	62.5	152.5	3,000	3,834.0	300	1,200	1,900	2,050	2,250	2,500	3,000	3,329.1	3,595.7
6. Michelena	1873		382.5	5.7	40.0	450	510.0	35	205	275	295	320	387	387	383.0	382.5
7. Gonzales	1896		38.7	26.4	55.2		70.0									38.7
8. Lee	1898	1905														
9. Montezuma	1873		4,837.8	107.0	73.0	3,750	5,780.0	520	1,590	1,840	2,160	2,440	3,190	3,750	4,293.0	4,837.8
10. Union	1875		5,865.9	340.0	756.1	2,900	8,163.0	270	950	2,888	4,980	5,425	5,575	5,575	5,720.0	5,865.9
11. Sunflower	1873		241.2	15.1	0.5	400	4,425.0	25	160	200	250	290	300	300	240.0	241.2
12. Graham	1879		999.9	166.8	203.1	962	1,165.0		50	176	430	540	776	962	981.0	999.9
13. Central	1873	1905	(1)	(1)	(1)	2,675	(2)									
14. Oregon	1874		1,469.2	185.1	189.4	1,100	1,315.0	30	90	200	500	800	950	1,100	1,284.0	1,469.2
15. Smithville	1879		2,049.3	374.5	386.8	1,760	3,818.0		350	1,220	1,600	1,650	1,750	1,760	1,904.0	2,049.3
16. Bryce	1883		593.7	19.5	23.0	515	1,147.0			95	190	380	430	515	554.0	593.7
17. Dodge	1881		363.4	21.6	64.6	450	482.0			220	420	450	450	450	406.0	363.4
18. Nevada	1877		1,222.6	73.1	400.7	800	1,220.0		150	400	650	700	700	800	1,011.0	1,222.6
19. Curtis	1881		1,637.3	74.8	133.9	800	1,874.0			1,240	1,650	1,650	1,650	1,650	1,644.0	1,637.3
20. Kempton	1883	1895	(3)	(3)	(3)	850										
21. Reid	1884		(4)	(4)	(4)	100										
22. Thompson-Clanton	1875	1876	(4)	(4)	(4)	240										
23. Clevenger-Stienfield	1881	1895	(4)	(4)	(4)	500										
24. Fort Thomas	1895	1905				900										
25. Military	1895	1905				400										
26. Saline-Colvin-Jones	1897		93.3	4.3	41.1	36	173.0					30	36	36	65.0	93.3
27. Black & Rose-Porter	1898		11.5				11.5									11.5
28. Consolidated	1905		2,441.0	530.2	1,039.0		3,350.0		90	372	530	525	1,530	2,200	2,321.0	2,441.0
Total			26,633.0	2,120.0	3,572.0	23,668	38,548.5	1,180	4,895	11,221	16,110	18,373	21,146	23,408	24,635.6	26,633.0

[1] Included in Union. [2] See Union. [3] Included in Curtis. [4] Included in Consolidated.

IRRIGATION ON THE SAN CARLOS INDIAN RESERVATION.

A portion of the San Carlos Indian Reservation embraces the western section of the same general valley of which the Solomonville–Safford district constitutes the eastern portion, an on account of this geographical position this section has been included with the Solomonville–Safford Valley in district No. 2.

The San Carlos Indian Reservation, or, more correctly, the San Carlos addition to the White Mountain Indian Reservation, was set aside by an executive order of December 14, 1872.

The area of the San Carlos Indian Reservation, including mountain ranges and lowlands, is 1,834,240 acres. Of this area approximately 5,000 acres may be classified as valley land along the Gila River.

The total population of the San Carlo Reservation is 2,608, according to the annual report of the Commissioner of Indian Affairs for 1914.

The number of Indians in Graham County on the San Carlos Reservation, according to the last census (1904) was 483. Only those Indians living along the Gila River on the reservation would be included in the Graham County census.

Leaving aside the prehistoric irrigation and excepting a reported but otherwise unknown ditch constructed by military forces stationed at Old Camp Goodwin in 1870, no irrigation seems to have taken place in this portion of the Gila Basin prior to the establishment of the reservation. Col. Emory, who passed down the Gila in 1846, fails to mention any irrigation in his description of this particular district.

The Apache Indians were not inclined to agricultural pursuits. They lived largely by the chase, never remaining in the open country for any great length of time. That they cultivated small tracts of land in the vicinity of their out-of-the-way hiding places is undoubtedly true, but their agricultural activities were very limited, and may in nowise be compared with those of the Pimas or others of the Pueblo Indians. Bandolier says of the Apache:

> Scattered over an immense territory, abiding nowhere permanently, often penetrating into the ranges of the Pueblos and trespassing upon them while at the same time they roamed all around the territory at will, except where their kindred, the Navajos, held them at bay, the Apache created the impression of being powerful in numbers, while in fact they were but outlying bands of the Navajos, long separated or outcast from the mother stock, and dangerous alike through their great mobility and their superior skill in waylaying and hiding which their roving life imparted.

While the Apaches roamed over the general territory in which the San Carlos Reservation was located, they did not live nor farm there, but were concentrated on the reservation mainly by force. The well-known campaign of Gen. Crook resulted in the surrender of these Indians. Their confinement to the reservation, and several subsequent outbreaks are matters of history. All of the early irrigation on the reservation was initiated by and carried on under the supervision of the military or Indian authorities in charge. Troops were stationed at San Carlos as late as 1895, and several of the agents after this date were army officers.

By reference to the map, plate No. 4, it will be seen that the irrigable lands of the San Carlos Reservation, both along the Gila and the San Carlos Rivers, are composed of small, narrow parcels which are cut up and separated from each other by cross-drainage gulches of various sizes. Conditions, therefore, are very unfavorable for extensive cultivation, since this would necessitate several systems of continuous canals. Unfortunately the greater part of the land previously irrigated, together with a number of old canals, has been completely swept away by high water. These disastrous floods, frequent changes of reservation agents, outbreaks of Indian renegades, and other unfavorable conditions, have combined to hinder irrigation on a large scale.

Frequent attempts, which in some cases have proven successful, have been made to irrigate these parcels of land. Numerous ditches have been constructed from time to time, some of which were never used, others for one irrigation only, while still others remained in service for a time, but eventually nearly all finally fell into disuse.

Many of the old ditches have been completely washed away, while a large portion of the land under those still remaining has long since become part of the river bottom, and the boundaries of the original cultivation can not, of course, be exactly determined at the present time.

It may also be said that these various ditches represent merely changed diversions or places of appropriation of preceding ditches. Frequently these changes were necessitated because the land formerly irrigated was washed away or the ditch headings destroyed. Better location for return or seepage flows, disturbances by hostile Indians and appropriations by the whites higher up on the stream are some of the factors which determined the selection of the tracts to be irrigated.

In spite of these adverse conditions, which began soon after the establishment of the reservation, there has been under cultivation each year along the San Carlos and Gila Rivers a varying area of land.

An analysis of the irrigation along the Gila River on this reservation shows that the first irrigation took place in 1873, when about 100 acres were under cultivation. This area was increased to 500 acres by 1880; and in 1900, 2,000 acres were under cultivation. At the time of this investigation 1,000.5 acres were being irrigated with water from the Gila, and an additional area of 1,202 acres was shown to have been previously irrigated.

An analysis of irrigated areas in five-year periods similar to those obtained for the Duncan and Solomonville-Safford districts is given for this reservation.

Information concerning previous irrigation has been gathered largely from the reports of former Indian agents of the reservation, and from the older white inhabitants who are familiar with early conditions.

Very little satisfactory evidence could be obtained from the Indians themselves in regard to past irrigation on the reservation. The Indians worked on the ditches ordinarily only when they were paid to do so and they expected the Government to keep the ditches in repair.

In the accompanying tabulation it will be seen that the two canals of the Bylas district are now the only canals on the reservation diverting water from the Gila. It is considered that these ditches represent merely the diversions which formerly took place lower down on the river and that changes of the points of diversion of the water as well as its use for irrigation on different tracts of land involve no losses of priority even if the reservation were entitled to no water except that which had already been put to beneficial use.

A detailed description of irrigation on this reservation along the Gila is published in Appendix A.

Analysis of irrigation on Ga Riiver, San Carlos Reservation, Ariz.

Name of canal.	Date of construction.	Date of last use.	Area by United States Indian Service survey, 1914.			Areas irrigated in five-year periods as estimated from all available information.									
			Cultivated.	Previously cultivated.	Not cultivated.	1873	1875	1880	1885	1890	1895	1900	1905	1910	1914
			Acres.	Acres.	Acres.	Acres.	Acres.	Acres.	Acres.	Acres.	Acres.	Acres.	Acres.	Acres.	Acres.
1. Agency farm or Tonto	1873	1905	[1] 25.0	200		100	200	560							
2. Desalin	1875	1905		186		100	200	560							
3. Yuma or Mohave	1875	1905		171		100	200	560							
4. Eskiminzin or S. H. 1	1882	1905		218		100	200	560							
5. Government	1881	1905		92		100	200	560							
6. South side Dewey flat	(2)	1874		46		100	200	560							
7. North side Dewey flat	(2)	(2)		74		100	200	560							
8. Opposite Calva south side	(2)	(2)		41		100	200	560							
9. Opposite Calva north side	(2)	(2)				100	200	560							
10. Bylas (south)	1881		591.5						360	750	700	1,000		200	591.5
11. Coyotero	1882		409.0	174					200	700	550	1,000		200	409.0
Total			1,000.5	1,202		100	200	560	560	1,450	1,250	2,000		400	1,000.5
Total given by agents in annual reports						100	200	560	560	1,450	1,250	2,000		400	

[1] This land irrigated now by San Carlos River.

[2] Unknown.

WINKELMAN-BRANAMAN SECTION.

Below the San Carlos Indian Reservation in the Box Canyon, which extends almost to Winkelman, there are two small detached tracts of land, which are irrigated by the waters of the Gila.

The first, consisting of about 15 acres and situated about 1 mile above the mouth of Dripping Spring wash, is irrigated by means of a ditch diverting water from the river. The other patch is situated about 7 miles above Winkelman and 2 miles below Copper Canyon. It consists of 12 acres of land irrigated by water pumped direct from the river.

In past years several other small tracts have been cultivated in the more favorable portions of this Box Canyon, but damages by floods and other adverse conditions have resulted in their abandonment.

One mile above Winkelman the walls of the canyon diverge to form a narrow valley. This valley averages about 1 mile in width from foothill to foothill, and extends to a point 2 miles below Winkelman, where the river is again confined by low-lying hills, which open out occasionally to form a narrow strip or a small pocket containing an inconsiderable area of arable land. This condition prevails to a point within 3 miles of the town of Kelvin, where the river again enters a canyon, its channel occupying the entire bottom.

Irrigation in the Winkelman section began about 1880, and increased rapidly until the flood of 1895, which was unusually destructive. A large area of irrigated land was washed away at that time, and in some instances entire ranches were lost. A destructive flood occurred in 1905, and the flood of 1915 destroyed large areas of bottom land. Each of these floods also greatly damaged the ditches.

The Ray Consolidated Copper Co. has purchased practically all of the bottom land in the Winkelman section, and in 1911 began to run over this land tailings from its concentrating plant at Hayden. Most of the land in this section is now covered with these tailings.

In the Winkelman section there have been four ditches diverting water from the Gila, two located on each side of the river. Those on the north side, the Old Settlers and the Winkelman ditches, were abandoned in 1911, but the two ditches on the south side are still in use. There are also two ditches irrigating small areas below the tailings dump of the Hayden concentrator. These latter ditches receive their water supply from the tailings pond.

In the Branaman section, which is simply a lower continuation of the Winkelman section, there are two ditches which are now in operation and a number of pumping plants. In both sections there is a total area of 335 acres being irrigated by waters from the Gila River. In addition to this area there were 565 acres including the area covered by tailings, shown to have been previously cultivated.

Besides the above, there are 44 acres estimated under the old Branaman ditch on the south side of the river now cultivated by dry farming, while 83 acres additional are irrigated by water pumped from wells.

In view of the very adverse natural conditions under which irrigation must be carried on along this part of the Gila, and also because of the fact that the tailings deposits from the mills at Hayden have rendered useless most of the land previously irrigated and are now constantly encroaching on the lands still cultivated, it may be said that the area under irrigation in this section will diminish rather than increase, and it is believed that the relatively unimportant diversions which are made here would have no effect on the diversions further down the Gila.

Between the Winkelman section and the Florence-Casa Grande district, a distance of 18 miles, there are a few small patches of irrigated land. These patches are so small and in such imminent danger of destruction by floods that they need not be considered.

A tabulated summary of irrigation data for this section is to be found in Appendix A.

IRRIGATION IN THE FLORENCE-CASA GRANDE DISTRICT.

The Florence-Casa Grande district and the Gila River Indian Reservation lie in the same broad valley, which comprises an area of over 600 square miles and is surrounded by a series of relatively low mountain chains or spurs. To the east of the valley are situated the Tortilla Mountains, through which the river emerges some 15 miles above the town of Florence. On the north the valley is flanked by the Superstition Mountain, while to the west the Estrella and the Salt River Range converge and from the western limits of the valley. The south boundary of the valley is marked by a number of more or less detached low rolling mountainous ranges or spurs.

Near the center of this wide area is a more or less isolated mountain chain known as the Sacation Mountains. This low range marks the dividing line between the Gila River Indian Reservation and the Casa Grande section of the Florence-Casa Grande district.

All of the Florence-Casa Grande district, as well as the greater portion of the Gila River Indian Reservation, lies within the confines of Pinal County, Ariz. This county, of which Florence is the county seat, was created from a portion of Pima County in 1871.

The distance from the uppermost diversion of the Florence Valley to the east line of the Gila River Indian Reservation is 21 miles, and the length of the reservation along the Gila is 52 miles.

The elevation of the upper end of the Florence Valley is 1,600 feet, while at the junction of the Salt River and the Gila at the lower end of the reservation the elevation is 950.

Wheat and barley are the staple crops in the Florence district; alfalfa, corn, and vegetables are also raised. While the grains are the least profitable, yet they require the least water for irrigation, and this consideration is responsible for the selection of these particular crops.

Many kinds of semitropical fruits, such as dates, pomegranates, and olives, have been successfully grown in this valley, as well as the more common fruits—plums, prunes, cherries, pears, etc. However, fruit raising has been confined to small orchards in connection with individual farms.

The Florence-Casa Grande district is not as thickly settled as the Solomonville Valley, and the population has not increased in recent years. Florence, the principal town of this section, according to the last census, had a population of 807 persons. Casa Grande is situated

149700—19—VOL 2——4

on the main line of the Southern Pacific Railroad, has a population of about 500, and the population of the entire district totals 2,800. Florence is on the Phoenix-Winkelman branch of the Arizona Eastern Railroad.

Formerly many Mexicans had land interests in the Florence Valley, but during recent years much of the land has changed hands, and at the present time nearly all of the farmers in the Florence-Casa Grande Valley are Americans.

The irrigated lands in the Florence-Casa Grande Valley are held by 79 interests, while the land showing evidence of previous cultivation is held by 107 interests, not including those who may also own land being irrigated at present. The land which is being irrigated at present and which is situated within the area it is proposed to irrigate by the San Carlos project, is owned by 64 individuals or companies. The land previously irrigated and coming within the area proposed for the San Carlos project, is held by 56 separate interests or individuals who are not owners of land being irrigated at the present time.

Of the 9 ditches serving to irrigate land in the Florence-Casa Grande district, leaving aside the Florence Canal, only 1, the O. T. Canal, is owned by a canal company, and 22 individuals hold stock in this corporation. The 7 unincorporated canals, exclusive of the Florence Canal, are owned by 14 persons.

The Florence Canal has been owned at different times by several companies, all organized on the common-carrier basis. Through the various transactions and sheriff sales, the tax title to this property is finally vested in the San Carlos Canal and Irrigation Co. This company having acquired title through a quit claim deed from Mr. Fennemore, the latter being the most recent purchaser at a tax sale.

There are 138 landowners under the Florence Canal whose land is either being irrigated now or has been previously irrigated by waters from this canal. In the water-right suit known as George Lobb *v.* Peter Avenente, and which will be hereafter referred to, 267 persons were made party defendants.

Practically all of the land owners in the Florence-Casa Grande Valley, regardless of whether their lands had ever been irrigated or whether they held interests in the canals, were made defendants in the above action.

The first diversion of the water of the Gila River in the Florence District is found to have been made under the direction of Ammie M. White, who, in 1864, while acting as Indian agent and trader on the Gila River Reservation, took up land in the vicinity of Adamsville and sent Mexicans to that district to construct the first ditch. These Mexicans were also hired to build a house near the spot where the town of Adamsville was soon afterwards founded.

In a few years, Adamsville grew to be quite a flourishing village, and it is reported that on one occasion, in its early history, it lacked only a few votes of being chosen the capital of the Territory. With the establishment of the near-by town of Florence a few years later, Adamsville began to decline, and to-day nothing remains but the ruins of abandoned adobe houses.

The town of Florence was founded in 1869 by Levi Ruggles, who, like White, was an Indian agent for the Government. Ruggles, however, was not a resident agent, but administered affairs from Tucson.

Shortly after the construction of the White Ditch, other small ditches were excavated on both sides of the river and gradual agricultural development of the valley took place. Prior to the construction of the Florence Canal in 1887, 12 ditches were in more or less successful operation in this district, and these ditches were capable of irrigating approximately 6,000 acres.

Of these 12 small ditches, four were on the north side of the river and the remaining eight on the south side. Irrigation took place most extensively south of the river, and it was on this side that the town of Florence and Adamsville were located.

The Florence Canal was constructed for the purpose of irrigating lands on the south side of the river in the Florence District, which had been irrigated up to that time by the older canals, and also to reclaim some 15,000 or 20,000 acres of land to the southwest of Florence in the territory between that town and the town of Casa Grande.

Three private ditches, which were in service prior to the construction of the Florence Canal, were taken over by the owners of this latter canal, and such private water rights as were acquired were exchanged in the Florence Canal.

The ditches acquired by the company operating the Florence Canal were not immediately abandoned, but continued in use for some length of time, and when it was impossible to obtain water from these older canals as independent ditches, they were supplied by the Florence Canal. This also applied to certain canals which were not absorbed by the Florence Canal Co. It appears in almost every case that when water could not be obtained through the older and lower ditches, the land owners, by agreement or purchase of stock or sometimes as the result of litigation as hereafter referred to, would procure water for their lands from the Florence Canal.

The great volume of water diverted by the Florence Canal soon after its completion resulted in an insufficient supply for the canals having their headings lower down the river and which had not been taken over by the Florence Canal Co. The owners of these canals in 1896 instituted a suit against the Florence Canal Co., said suit being known as Brady et al. *v.* Florence Canal Co. et al. In the decree rendered in this case the court sustained the priority claims of the plaintiffs to the use of the waters of the Gila to the same extent as when the said waters were first appropriated or were used at the time of and prior to the construction of the Florence Canal. These plaintiffs were also granted the rights to convey their waters through the Florence Canal heading to irrigate their lands; provided that the plaintiffs should not have any priority to the use of the waters from the Florence Canal over and above any other users and consumers of water from the said canal, and that the plaintiffs, while not having to pay rentals for the use of said water, were to receive the water under such rules and regulations as the defendant should see fit to adopt.

This decree also stipulated the amount of water that should be provided by the Florence Canal to these several plaintiffs.

As a result of this suit and decree many of the water users, at least for a time, received water from the Florence Canal instead of from the older and smaller ditches.

A much later water-right suit, and one in which it is intended to adjudicate all the water rights in the Florence district, is case No. 2329, entitled George Lobb *v.* Peter Avenete et al. in the superior court, Pinal County, Ariz. The complaint in the above case was filed December 9, 1913, and the case opened June 10, 1914. To date all of the evidence has not been heard, and it is quite likely that six months or a year may elapse before judgment is rendered.

The Florence Canal Co., which was incorporated as a common carrier and not as a mutual organization, disposed of its water stock to the landowners and entrymen. This company, after a portion of their ditch had been constructed, also issued bonds, and with the money thus obtained built the Picacho Reservoir, and extended the canal to a total length of 50 miles.

Under this reservoir and canal a great deal of land was proved up under desert and homestead entries. At one time, about 1900, approximately 7,000 acres were irrigated under this canal, and the aggregate area irrigated at all times is upward of 15,000 acres.

Observations of the land, as well as evidence from other sources, would indicate that many tracts of land formerly irrigated by means of the Florence Canal were reclaimed and irrigated for patent purposes only and never produced beneficial crops. Other tracts were irrigated more or less indifferently for a few years and then abandoned.

The Florence Canal at the time when surveys were being made (1914), was being used to irrigate 3,531.5 acres.

Owing to the great quantities of silt carried by the waters of the Gila River, and the low grade upon which this ditch was constructed, the company was unable to keep the canal in full service. As a result of these conditions, the Florence Canal Co. was unable to meet the interest payments of the outstanding bonds, and, in default of these payments, the property was sold, in 1893, at a tax or sheriff's sale, and was bought in by the bondholders and other creditors of the company. These creditors organized a new company, called the Casa Grande Valley Canal Co., to operate the canal. After a period, or in 1900, this new corporation also defaulted on payments and its property, the Florence Canal, was again disposed of at a sheriff's sale.

As a result of several transactions, which took place during the interval from 1900 to 1904, the tax title to the Florence Canal was vested in John W. Sharpe. When Mr. Sharpe became the owner of the canal, he acquired the water rights appurtenant to the canal, and, to add to his holdings, he acquired, by purchase, other filings for the right to divert water from the Gila River, making, in all, total filings calling for the appropriation of 145,000 miner's inches, now vested in Sharpe.

On March 30, 1891, Mr. Sharpe made application to the land office for a canal right of way, and this right of way covered the location of the Florence Canal. This application was later transferred to the Pinal Water Co., in whose name it was approved by the land office in 1907, the Pinal Water Co. being organized to take over the interests of Mr. Sharpe, who was made president of the company.

In 1907, certain complaints were made against this company, to which the previous owners of the Florence Canal also were made party defendants, and, on December 15 of the same year (1907), a receiver was appointed and the canal has been operated in this manner until recently (October, 1914), when the receiver was dismissed by court order.

Mr. Sharpe et al. conveyed by means of a quitclaim deed, dated March 13, 1909, to Charles R. Sligh, all rights in the Florence Canal and Picacho Reservoir.

In 1913, the Florence Canal was again sold for taxes and, according to the sheriff's certificate of sale, the tax title to the Florence Canal was then vested in Mr. H. M. Fennemore. This last title was perfected by a tax deed executed by the sheriff, under date of May 28, 1914.

On July 29, 1914, Mr. Fennemore, by means of a quitclaim deed, transferred all his right, title, and interest in the Florence Canal to the San Carlos Canal and Irrigation Co., a corporation, and this company is now (November, 1915) operating the canal.

While the Florence Canal was never completely abandoned, yet, on account of the accumulation of silt, many acres of land which had been placed under cultivation were allowed to revert to the original desert state.

Several attempts have been made to rehabilitate the Florence Canal not only by the receiver, but also by the individuals owning land under the canal. In the past two or three years some success has been attained in this direction. While the ditch has never been thoroughly cleaned, it has always been kept sufficiently open to supply water to the few remaining farms which lie beyond the immediate vicinity of Florence.

Upon the failure of the Florence Canal to supply the demands of irrigators in the Florence district, many of the farmers whose lands were formerly served by the Florence Canal organized an independent canal company and in 1909 constructed what is now known as the Old Timers' (Farmers') Canal, which now irrigates their lands. Besides the Old Timers' Canal several other ditches have been constructed since the construction of the Florence Canal, chiefly on the north side of the river.

Several groups of landowners owning water rights under the Florence Canal have at various times organized irrigation companies on a mutual or cooperative basis, with the intention of taking over the old Florence Canal and putting it into serviceable condition. Three different companies have been organized for this purpose, which were incorporated in the following order: The Pinal Mutual, the Florence Irrigation Co., and the Pinal Mutual Irrigation Co.

The Pinal Mutual Irrigation Co., by contract, succeeded the Pinal Mutual and the Florence Irrigation Co. The Pinal Mutual Irrigation Co. also obtained an option on all the rights and interests of one Charles R. Sligh, who, as previously shown, held the tax title to the canal and had purchased a majority of the stock and bonds of the Casa Grande Valley Canal Co. before the latter company went into the hands of a receiver.

Water-right filings have been acquired by the Pinal Mutual Irrigation Co., and this company has done some construction work, locally known as "the rock cut," on a canal which is proposed to closely parallel the Florence Canal. An able report on this project was prepared in 1911 by the late James D. Schuyler.

In 1911 the Casa Grande Water Users Association was organized, principally by persons interested in the Casa Grande section of the Florence-Casa Grande Valley. After selling stock to homeseekers and others, this company, with the money thus obtained, began the construction of a large irrigation project.

The main canal of this project is located just above the old Florence Canal, and nearly all of the land proposed to be irrigated, some 70,000 acres, is practically the same land as was originally or formerly proposed to be irrigated by the Florence Canal. This Casa Grande Valley Canal was in course of construction until recently, when operations ceased after approximately 12 miles of the 25, the proposed length of the canal, had been completed.

Many recent desert entries were made under this canal, and stock subscriptions in this company have been submitted to the Land Office for final proof as evidence of the availability of water. An unfavorable report was made by a Carey Act inspector of the General Land Office, and the entrymen were notified that they would be allowed to make an affirmative showing. In the subsequent hearing the attention of the Land Office was directed to the water-right case of Lobb *v.* Avenete, which has heretofore been mentioned, and action by the Land Office has been suspended pending the outcome of the case referred to.

Since the failure of the Florence Canal project practically all of the irrigated area in the Florence-Casa Grande district has been confined to the territory in the vicinity of Florence. This area at present is served by nine canals, six of which are on the south side of the river, the other three on the north side.

The total area which is irrigated by the waters of the Gila River in the Florence-Casa Grande district, according to the survey made in the early part of 1914, amounted to 7,563.4 acres. In addition to this area, 12,217.7 acres were found to have been previously irrigated.

Of the above acreage, 7,008.1 acres of the area now under cultivation and 7,820.1 acres of the previously cultivated area are situated within the boundaries of the territory subject to irrigation under the San Carlos project, as proposed by the Army board and also as indorsed in this report.

The irrigated area tabulation which follows has been compiled from the results of the survey and investigation. The compilation of the analysis was rendered extremely difficult by the complicated sequence of the canals used to irrigate different areas in the vicinity of Florence. As has already been stated, the Florence section was originally irrigated by several small ditches, and afterwards a few of these ditches continued to operate, but were finally abandoned. With the failure of the Florence Canal to supply the necessary water, other ditches were taken out, and these ditches cover a portion of the area earliest irrigated.

In the analysis submitted efforts have been made to show under what particular canal and during what year the several areas were irrigated.

Much of the same condition obtains under the more recently constructed canal called the "O. T." Under this canal are lands which were formerly irrigated not only by the older ditches but also by the Florence Canal, so it may be seen that efforts to obtain the sequence of the irrigation of much of the land in the older irrigated districts were beset with difficulties.

A detailed description of irrigation under each of the canals in the Florence district, as well as other relevant data, is published in accompanying Appendix A.

IRRIGATION ON THE GILA RIVER RESERVATION.

The Gila River Indian Reservation, comprising 369,000 acres, occupies the lower portion of the Florence-Casa Grande Valley, and is situated partly in Pinal County and partly in Maricopa County. The present extent of the reservation, measured along the Gila River, is 52 miles in length, with an average width of about 12 miles.

The Arizona Eastern Railroad from Maricopa on the main line of the Southern Pacific to Phœnix, crosses the reservation near its central portion.

The first official Government notice taken of the Pimas was in 1859, when an appropriation of $10,000 was made by Congress to be used in the purchase of gifts for the Pima Indians, and an additional $1,000 was provided for a survey of their lands. The legislation concerning this survey was an act of February 28, 1859, which was included in the Indian appropriation act of the year ending June 30, 1860.

As a result of this legislation 64,000 acres of land was set aside by Executive order in 1859.

The original area selected for the reservation was close to the river and embraced all the lands then being cultivated by the Pimas.

Subsequent additions to the original reservation have been made from time to time, until at present the reservation contains 369,000 acres. Of this area over 110,000 acres are considered irrigable and 96,000 acres suitable for grazing, while the balance of the reservation land is principally mountainous.

A complete census of the Pimas in the territory aftrwards reserved for the Indians was made in 1858 by Lieut. Chapman, who was connected with the militia. The census, covering nine Pima villages and two Maricopa villages, giving a population of 4,117 Pimas and 518 Maricopas. The present Indian population on the reservation, according to the report of the Commissioner of Indian Affairs dated June 30, 1914, numbers 3,796 Pimas and 300 Maricopas.

Tentative allotments of 10 acres of land for each head of a family have been made of the greater portion of the irrigated lands on the reservation. These allotments have not been finally approved by the Government. Very few of the Indians on the reservation have attaind citizenship.

The climate in this section, as elsewhere in the Florence Valley, is adapted to diversified crops; the soil is exceedingly fertile, and the large amount of sediment deposited by the flood waters of the Gila keeps the land in a state of productiveness.

The Indians seem always to have known the fertilizing value of the silt-laden flood waters. They knew that the Gila River during its lower stages carried large quantities of alkali and salt; that their lands, to be rid of these injurious salts, must be frequently flooded and washed. The fact that the reservation lands have been irrigated for unknown centuries without any perceptible deterioration of the soil is striking proof of the knowledge which these primitive agriculturists possessed of these essential precautions.

It has long been a custom among the Pimas to plant their first crop to grain, which was harvested in June or July; the next or second crop to corn or beans. Annually a portion of each field would be planted to pumpkins, squash, and melons. Prior to the introduction of calico by the early traders, the Pimas grew quantities of cotton, which they spun and wove into rude clothing. That the Pimas produced crops largely in excess of their own needs and supplied quantities of wheat and other foodstuffs to travelers and to traders is a well-known fact.

The overland route from El Paso via Tucson to the Pacific coast, established in 1858, passed through the Pima villages on the reservation. The choice of this route was largely due to the productivity of the reservation as well as the protection afforded by the Pimas. They have always been friends of the whites and enemies of the Apaches. Besides the supplies furnished, they also rendered great assistance to the militia in the field campaign against the Apaches.

The broad, level valley of the Gila west of Florence, a large portion of which is now included within the boundaries of the Gila River Indian Reservation, has been irrigated for many centuries. This is evidenced by the remains of many prehistoric canals, traces of which can be observed for miles along both banks of the Gila. Whether the Pimas are descendants of the ancient irrigators is not certain, but it is known, through the reports and narratives of the early Spanish explorers, that the Pimas were living on this reservation as early as 1539, when the first Jesuit father penetrated to this territory.

Many Spanish explorers and missionaries visited this section of the country in the seventeenth and eighteenth centuries. In the report of the early Spanish padres much has been written concerning the industry and the agricultural activities of the Pimas. Early in the nineteenth century American beaver trappers reached this territory, and they were soon followed by the military. In 1848, through the treaty of Guadalupe Hidalgo, the territory north of the Gila was annexed to the United States; and in 1854, through the Gadsden Purchase, the area south of the Gila became the property of this Government.

The military occupation and the subsequent rush of gold seekers to California in the early fifties marked the coming of the whites in increasing numbers; and as early as 1870 this territory was being settled and farmed by the whites. These pioneers, as has been previously stated, depended largely upon the Pimas for supplies and forage, as well as protection from the intractable Apaches.

The first resident agent on the reservation was Ammie White, appointed in 1864. Prior to this time, beginning in 1857, Indian agents had been appointed for the whole Arizona superintendency, with headquarters in Tucson. The first agency buildings were constructed at Sacaton in 1870, and the first school among the Pimas was opened in 1871. With the settlement and consequent diversions of the water of the Gila by the settlers above the reservation, the water supply of the Pimas soon began to fail, and as early as 1870 the Indians were much concerned over the diminished flow at the reservation. Shortly after this, in 1872, several bands of the Pimas left the Gila River Reservation and went over to the Salt River.

When the Florence Canal was constructed in 1887, the water supply was still further diminished, and many Indians were reduced to a state of poverty and want.

None of the descriptions of the earlier explorers is sufficiently accurate to aid in determining the area the Pimas had under irrigation. The "folklore" and traditions of the Pimas themselves, which received attention during the compilation of data for this report, are also vague regarding this matter. The earliest accounts of the Spaniards as well as Indian traditions would point, however, to the conclusions that the Pimas in the earliest days of the Spanish exploration were distributed over a much larger territory than they occupied at the time of the American occupation, and that at a later period the Apaches, or perhaps Mexican slave hunters, caused them to confine their agricultural activities and their habitations within a smaller area.

The coming of the whites, with the consequent decrease in the water supply, caused the Indians to cease to cultivate many of their old fields and reclaim land at places favorable to the use of the return or seepage flow of the river. Peace with the Apaches, together with conformity to tribal customs and superstitions (tending to scatter the Pimas formerly banded together), are other causes responsible for the present rather widely scattered locations of the irigated districts. Obviously these changes, whether enforced or voluntary, have rendered exceedingly difficult the determination at this date of the area previously under cultivation at one time.

There is also evidence to show that the channel of the Gila formerly was considerably narower than at present. Destructive floods of recent and comparatively recent times have swept hundreds of acres of irrigated or previously irrigated lands down the river.

From the chart which follows and which has been compiled from all the evidence and data gathered during the progress of this investigation and survey, it is seen that prior to the coming of the whites the Indians on the Gila River Reservation were irrigating an estimated area of 13,000 acres, served by nine large ditches. The largest area cultivated at any one time (about 1885) was estimated at 15,800 acres. At the time (1914) of the survey in connection with this investigation, 15,627 acres were being cultivated, and this area was served by 21 different canals, including the Little Gila. Of this area 1,271 acres were irigated by a ditch diverting water from the Salt River, so that the total area at present under cultivation and using water from the Gila River amounts to 14,356 acres.

In addition to the above surveyed areas, 11,315 acres were found to have been previously irrigated, at one time and another.

In Appendix A is published a historical sketch of irrigation on the reservation, containing a number of references from the reports and narratives of the early Spanish and American explorers concerning irrigation by the Pimas. A detailed historical description of irrigation under each canal, together with statements from Indians themselves, is also given in the appendix.

Analysis of irrigation on the Gila River Reservation.

Canals.	Date of construction.	Date of last use.	Area by United States Indian Service, 1914.			Area from Hoskimous Gap survey, 1904.		Estimated maximum cultivated area at any time under ditch.	Prior to coming of whites.
			Cultivated.	Previous cultivation.	Irrigable areas.	Cultivated district.	Previous cultivation district.		
			Acres.	*Acres.*	*Acres.*	*Acres.*	*Acres.*	*Acres.*	*Acres.*
1. Padilla	1910		44		44			1,250	
2. North Blackwater	1866		941	310	1,794	1,456.1		1,450	
3. Island Ditch	1862		1,029	30	1,506	1,505.0		1,050	
4. Little Gila. Lands irrigated by Little Gila are shown under the following diversions therefrom: [3]									
5. Old Woman's Mouth	1881	1905		173	234	60.0	10.0	173	
6. Yaqui Ditch	1891		44	289	713	48.8		330	
7. Sacaton Flats	1872		899	384	1,567	1,105.2		1,100	
8. Cottonwood	1872		819	153	1,108	453.6	100.0	820	
9. Hendricks	1904		76		116			76	
10. Old Santan	1865		168	1,272	1,440		918.2	1,400	
11. New Mount Top	1866	1868		182	314			180	
12. Old Maricopa	1848	1870		244	387	(?)		250	
13. Ancient Stotonic	(3)	1880		590	705	(7,711.0)		600	600
14. Present Stotonic	(3)		1,559	810	2,864			2,400	2,400
15. Old Mount Top	(3)	1866		718	718			720	720
16. Cayau	1869	1880		235	270			235	
17. Santan (Indian)	1877		3,319	201	4,539	4,424.4	319.8	3,520	
18. Bapchil	(3)		1,937	936	2,873	(?)		3,600	3,600
19. Sratuka-Snaketown	(3)		354	1,273	1,744	(2,090.0)		2,100	2,100
20. Sranka-Alkali Camp	(3)		198	736	1,323	(1,052.0)		1,050	1,050
21. Bridlestood	(3)	1890	22	1,143	1,200		666.0	1,200	1,200
22. Ancient Maricopa	(3)	1880		386	386		743.0	750	750
23. Old Santa Cruz	1855	1875		400	400			500	500
24. Holden or Webb	1877		660	38	993	900.0		900	
25. Hoover	1873		954	20	990	827.0		954	
26. Thomas & Head	1877		726	138	1,112	786.0		860	
27. Cooperative	1900		594	390	1,590	315.0		600	
28. Walker	1903		13	45	686	29.0		48	
29. South Blackwater ("B" line United States)	1914	(14)			2,222				
30. Santan Flood Canal (United States)	1909	(15)			5,461				
31. Agency (United States), Little Gila	1914	(16)			560				
32. Casa Blanca (United States), Little Gila	1914–15	(17)			28,517				
33. Maricopa from Salt River [18]			1,271	219	1,945	1,323		1,300	
Total			15,627	11,315	69,761	26,845			12,920

Analysis of irrigation on the Gila River Reservation.

Canals.	Date of construction.	Date of last use.	Area by United States Indian Service, 1914.			Area from Hoskimons Gap survey, 1904.		Estimated maximum cultivated area at any time under ditch.	Prior to coming of whites.
			Cultivated.	Previous cultivation.	Irrigable areas.	Cultivated district.	Previous cultivation district.		
			Acres.	*Acres.*	*Acres.*	*Acres.*	*Acres.*	*Acres.*	*Acres.*
1. Padilla	1910		44		44			1,250	
2. North Blackwater	1866		941	310	1,794	1,456 1		1,450	
3. Island Ditch	1862		1,029	30	1,506	1,505.0		1,050	
4. Little Gila. Lands irrigated by Little Gila are shown under the following diversions therefrom: [3]									
5. Old Woman's Mouth	1881	1905		173	234	60.0	10.0	173	
6. Yaqui Ditch	1891		44	289	713	48.8		330	
7. Sacaton Flats	1872		899	384	1,567	1,105.2		1,100	
8. Cottonwood	1872		819	153	1,108	453.6	100.0	820	
9. Hendricks	1904		76		116			76	
10. Old Santan	1865		168	1,272	1,440		918.2	1,400	
11. New Mount Top	1866	1868		182	314			180	
12. Old Maricopa	1848	1870		244	387	(7)		250	
13. Ancient Stotonic	(3)	1880		590	705	(7,711.0)		600	600
14. Present Stotonic	(3)		1,559	810	2,864			2,400	2,400
15. Old Mount Top	(3)	1866		718	718			720	720
16. Cayau	1869	1880		235	270			235	
17. Santan (Indian)	1877		3,319	201	4,539	4,424.4	319.8	3,520	
18. Bapchil	(3)		1,937	936	2,873	(7)		3,600	3,600
19. Sratuka-Snaketown	(3)		354	1,273	1,744	(2,090.0)		2,100	2,100
20. Sranka-Alkali Camp	(3)		198	736	1,823	(1,052.0)		1,050	1,050
21. Bridlestood	(3)	1890	22	1,143	1,200		666.0	1,200	1,200
22. Ancient Maricopa	(3)	1880		386	386		743.0	750	750
23. Old Santa Cruz	1855	1875		400	400			500	800
24. Holden or Webb	1877		660	38	993	900.0		900	
25. Hoover	1873		954	20	990	827.0		954	
26. Thomas & Head	1877		726	138	1,112	786.0		860	
27. Cooperative	1900		594	390	1,590	315.0		600	
28. Walker	1903		13	45	686	29.0		48	
29. South Blackwater ("B" line United States)	1914	(14)			2,222				
30. Santan Flood Canal (United States)	1909	(15)			5,461				
31. Agency (United States), Little Gila	1914	(16)			560				
32. Casa Blanca (United States), Little Gila	1914–15	(17)			28,517				
33. Maricopa from Salt River [18]			1,271	219	1,945	1,323		1,300	
Total			15,627	11,315	69,761	26,845			12,920

Canals.	Areas irrigated in five-year periods as estimated from all available information.													
	1850	1855	1860	1865	1870	1875	1880	1885	1890	1895	1900	1905	1910	1914
	Acres.	*Acres.*	*Acres.*	*Acres.*	*Acres.*	*Acres.*	*Acres.*	*Acres.*	*Acres.*	*Acres.*	*Acres.*	*Acres.*	*Acres.*	*Acres.*
24. Holden or Webb							100	230	380	580	680	900	700	660
25. Hoover						100	350	450	550	650	750	830	900	954
26. Thomas & Head							90	240	390	540	690	780	750	236
27. Cooperative											100	315	600	594
28. Walker												29	48	13
29. South Blackwater ("B" line United States)														
30. Santan Flood Canal (United States)														
31. Agency (United States), Little Gila														
32. Casa Blanca (United States), Little Gila														
33. Maricopa from Salt River[1]														
Total	12,450	12,525	12,840	13,432	13,860	14,380	15,100	15,860	15,133	14,795	14,490	13,676	13,995	14,356

[1] 1,271 acres irrigated by Salt River not included.

Analysis of irrigation on the Gila River Reservation.

Canals.	Date of construction.	Date of last use.	Area by United States Indian Service, 1914.			Area from Hoskimons Gap survey, 1904.		Estimated maximum cultivated area at any time under ditch.	Prior to coming of whites.
			Cultivated.	Previous cultivation.	Irrigable areas.	Cultivated district.	Previous cultivation district.		
			Acres.	*Acres.*	*Acres.*	*Acres.*	*Acres.*	*Acres.*	*Acres.*
1. Padilla	1910		44		44			1,250	
2. North Blackwater	1866		941	310	1,794	1,456.1		1,450	
3. Island Ditch	1862		1,029	30	1,506	1,505.0		1,050	
4. Little Gila. Lands irrigated by Little Gila are shown under the following diversions therefrom:[3]									
5. Old Woman's Mouth	1881	1905		173	234	60.0	10.0	173	
6. Yaqui Ditch	1891		44	289	713	48.8		330	
7. Sacaton Flats	1872		899	384	1,567	1,105.2		1,100	
8. Cottonwood	1872		819	153	1,108	453.6	100.0	820	
9. Hendricks	1904		76		116			76	
10. Old Santan	1865		168	1,272	1,440		918.2	1,400	
11. New Mount Top	1866	1868		182	314			180	
12. Old Maricopa	1848	1870		244	387	[7]		250	
13. Ancient Stotonic	[3]	1880		590	705	(7,711.0)		600	600
14. Present Stotonic	[3]		1,559	810	2,864			2,400	2,400
15. Old Mount Top	[3]	1866		718	718			720	720
16. Cayau	1869	1880		235	270			235	
17. Santan (Indian)	1877		3,319	201	4,539	4,424.4	319.8	3,520	
18. Bapchil	[3]		1,937	936	2,873	[7]		3,600	3,600
19. Sratuka-Snaketown	[3]		354	1,273	1,744	(2,090.0)		2,100	2,100
20. Sranka-Alkali Camp	[3]		198	736	1,323	(1,052.0)		1,050	1,050
21. Bridlestood	[3]	1890	22	1,143	1,200		666.0	1,200	1,200
22. Ancient Maricopa	[3]	1880		386	386		743.0	750	750
23. Old Santa Cruz	1855	1875		400	400			500	500
24. Holden or Webb	1877		660	38	993	900.0		900	
25. Hoover	1873		954	20	990	827.0		954	
26. Thomas & Head	1877		726	138	1,112	786.0		860	
27. Cooperative	1900		594	390	1,590	315.0		600	
28. Walker	1903		13	45	686	29.0		48	
29. South Blackwater ("B" line United States)	1914	[14]			2,222				
30. Santan Flood Canal (United States)	1909	[15]			5,461				
31. Agency (United States), Little Gila	1914	[16]			560				
32. Casa Blanca (United States Little Gila	1914-15	[17]			28,517				
33. Maricopa from Salt River[18]			1,271	219	1,945	1,323		1,300	
Total			15,627	11,315	69,761	26,845			12,920

Canals.	Areas irrigated in five-year periods as estimated from all available information.													
	1850	1855	1860	1865	1870	1875	1880	1885	1890	1895	1900	1905	1910	1914
	Acres.	*Acres.*	*Acres.*	*Acres.*	*Acres.*	*Acres.*	*Acres.*	*Acres.*	*Acres.*	*Acres.*	*Acres.*	*Acres.*	*Acres.*	*Acres.*
1. Padilla														[1] 44
2. North Blackwater					400	600	1,250	1,000	930	950	950	950	950	941
3. Island Ditch				300	1,060	1,060	1,060	1,030	1,030	1,030	1,030	1,030	1,030	[2] 1,039
4. Little Gila. Lands irrigated by Little Gila are shown under the following diversions therefrom:[3]														
5. Old Woman's Mouth								70	173	170	150			
6. Yaqui Ditch										200	350	48	45	44
7. Sacaton Flats						600	1,100	1,100	1,100	1,100	1,100	900	900	[4] 899
8. Cottonwood						300	400	550	550	550	550	550	680	819
9. Hendricks								40	40	50	50	60	70	[5] 76
10. Old Santan					500	1,400	300	100	100	100	110	114	150	[6] 188
11. New Mount Top				182										
12. Old Maricopa	30	105	170	250	100									
13. Ancient Stotonic	600	600	600	600	600	560	600							([8])
14. Present Stotonic	2,400	2,400	2,400	2,400	2,400	2,300	2,300	2,200	2,000	1,800	1,600	1,400	1,400	1,559
15. Old Mount Top	720	720	720	500										
16. Cayau					100	235								
17. Santan (Indian)							1,100	3,000	3,220	3,300	3,400	3,520	3,400	3,319
18. Bapchil	3,600	3,600	3,600	3,600	3,300	3,000	2,850	2,600	2,450	2,200	1,950	1,700	1,800	[9] 1,937
19. Sratuka-Snaketown	2,100	2,100	2,100	2,100	1,900	1,700	1,700	1,700	1,300	900	500	350	350	354
20. Sranka-Alkali Camp	1,050	1,050	1,050	1,050	1,050	1,050	1,050	1,050	800	675	550	200	200	[10] 198
21. Bridlestood	1,200	1,200	1,200	1,200	1,200	1,000	750	500	100				22	[11] 22
22. Ancient Maricopa	750	750	750	750	750	325	100				([12])	([12])	([12])	([12])
23. Old Santa Cruz			250	500	500	150					([13])	([13])	([13])	([13])

[1] This ditch leased by Indians, capable of irrigation by Blackwater United States "B" line
[2] Area under Cayau included in North Blackwater, by Hoskmson.
[3] Old.
[4] Agency farm west to Santan Road included.
[5] Irrigated first by Morego Ditch.
[6] Since 1880 irrigated by Cottonwood and Agency project.
[7] Cultivated and previously cultivated.
[8] Changed heading to present Stotonic.
[9] 700 acres lost by floods under Bapchil.
[10] Approximately 100 acres estimated lost by flood.
[11] Present irrigation under Bridlestood from Snaketown Canal.
[12] Approximately 300 acres estimated loss by floods under Ancient Maricopa.
[13] 100 acres estimated lost by floods under Santa Cruz.
[14] Padilla, Old Woman's Mouth.
[15] Santan (Indian).
[16] Old Santan.
[17] Stotonic, Bapchil, Sranka.
[18] 1,271 acres irrigated by Salt River not included.

Canals.	Areas irrigated in five-year periods as estimated from all available information.													
	1850	1855	1860	1865	1870	1875	1880	1885	1890	1895	1900	1905	1910	1914
	Acres.	*Acres.*	*Acres.*	*Acres.*	*Acres.*	*Acres.*	*Acres.*	*Acres.*	*Acres.*	*Acres.*	*Acres.*	*Acres.*	*Acres.*	*Acres.*
24. Holden or Webb							100	230	380	580	680	900	700	660
25. Hoover						100	350	450	550	650	750	830	900	954
26. Thomas & Head							90	240	390	540	690	780	750	236
27. Cooperative											100	315	600	594
28. Walker												29	48	13
29. South Blackwater ("B" line United States)														
30. Santan Flood Canal (United States)														
31. Agency (United States), Little Gila														
32. Casa Blanca (United States), Little Gila														
33. Maricopa from Salt River[1]														
Total	12,450	12,525	12,840	13,432	13,860	14,380	15,100	15,860	15,133	14,795	14,490	13,676	13,995	14,356

[1] 1,271 acres irrigated by Salt River not included.

IRRIGATION WEST OF GILA RIVER RESERVATION.

That portion of the Gila basin beginning at the west line of the Gila River reservation and extending to Yuma, a distance of 170 miles, commonly is called the Lower Gila Valley.

From the Gila bend, 50 miles below the reservation, and extending throughout the remaining portion of the Gila's course, the Southern Pacific Railroad is located at a distance of 2 or 3 miles south of the river.

The altitude of this portion of the Gila basin is extremely low; the elevation at the west reservation line, which has been previously given, is 950 feet, while the river at Yuma is approximately 100 feet above sea level.

On account of these low elevations the temperatures are very high. The extreme summer heat, however, is somewhat modified by the accompanying low humidity.

The crops grown along this portion of the Gila are similar to those grown in the Florence Valley. Where sufficient water is to be had, as in the Buckeye Valley, alfalfa is the principal crop and oats, wheat, barley, sorghum, and corn are also grown. Cattle grazing and feeding is also an important industry in this section.

Further down the river, where water is scarce, the crops are largely confined to the grains. In this climate all warm, temperate, and many tropical fruits could be grown. Not much attention has been paid to fruit growing in this section, however, due undoubtedly to the occasional frosts in the upper districts and to the scarcity of water in districts lower down.

The irrigation systems on the Gila below the Gila River Reservation, taken in the order of their location down the river are: On the north side, the Buckeye, the Arlington, and the Enterprise; on the south side, the Joslin, the James Bent, the Papago, and the Antelope Valley. Of the above systems all but the latter, the Antelope, are above Gila Bend.

In the past irrigation systems have been constructed in the vicinity of Gila Bend; and below Gila Bend in the Dendora, the Palomis, the Antelope, the Mohawk, and the Redondo Valleys, these systems are no longer in use.

No towns of importance are supported by agricultural or other industries along this portion of the Gila. The town of Buckeye, situated in the district of that name, with a population of less than 500, is the only town worthy of the designation.

In the territory along the river, between the west boundary line of the Gila River Indian Reservation and the confluence of the Gila with the Colorado at Yuma, irrigation has been practiced more or less for a number of years.

The first irrigation in this district was coincident with the establishment and maintenance of the early overland stage stations. These stage stations were established as early as 1857, but the irrigation in connection with them was never extensive and was confined to the lower portion of the Gila Valley.

With the coming of the immigrant trains in the early seventies, this portion of the country received its share of settlers, and a gradual development took place until about 1885. At that time a veritable agricultural boom developed in this section, many wildcat or ill-advised ventures were launched, several large canals were dug, and thousands of dollars were spent without satisfactory results.

In a pamphlet published in 1892, from data collected in 1889 and prepared by the citizens' executive committee of Yuma County, the claim is made that in Yuma County along the Gila there were then existing or were in course of construction 10 canals, having an aggregate length of 120½ miles and capable of irrigating more than 81,000 acres.

A similar summary was made of the canals further up the Gila, in Maricopa County. The report of the officials of Maricopa County showed seven canals to be diverting water from the Gila below the Gila River Reservation.

Of the canals mentioned in the Numa County group only one is at present in use, and this one has been rehabilitated only recently. In the Maricopa County group three canals are still in operation.

The history of these canals shows that most of them were constructed with little regard to the water available, and that consequently, after brief attempts at cultivation, they gradually fell into a state of disuse.

Between the west line of the Gila River Reservation and Gila Bend, a distance of about 50 miles, there are at the present time seven ditches taking water from the Gila River. Between Gila Bend and the Gila confluence with the Colorado only one ditch, the Antelope, is at present diverting water from the Gila. This later ditch has been referred to above as a rehabilitated older ditch, in Yuma County.

The several irrigated areas served by these canals are located in the Buckeye, the Enterprise, the Gila Bend, and the Antelope districts, and the combined areas in these districts amounts to 24,045 acres. Of this area all but 1,100 acres are within the Gila Bend, the Enterprise and the Buckeye districts. Practically all of the cultivated land in these districts has been reclaimed within comparatively recent years, or since 1880, and the success of this irrigation has been due to utilization of the return of seepage flow. This return flow is used almost entirely for irrigation under the most successful canals, flood waters being used only for fertilizing purposes. Since the Roosevelt project has been in operation, or in the past five years, an increased return flow has been available for irrigation immediately west of the Gila River Reservation, and this increased flow has resulted in increased agricultural activities.

The older or first irrigated districts have been vacated owing, apparently, to failure of the water supply. Past experience in the older districts prove that irrigation projects in this portion of the Gila Basin depending upon the normal flow or flood waters are at best very uncertain ventures; and it may be safely said that further flood or surface-water diversions will not be attempted.

While it is true, if continuous in flow, the annual run-off of the Gila at Yuma would be sufficient to irrigate a large acreage of land, yet nearly all of this water comes down the river during floods, and ordinarily the water supply is so meager during the dry months as to preclude the possibility of success of irrigation which is dependent upon flood water alone.

It was learned during the progress of the investigation that the regulation and control of the Gila by a reservoir such as that proposed at San Carlos would meet with the approval of the majority of the present water users west of the Gila River Reservation. These owners advised that the flood waters of the Gila usually did more damage than good, and that, while their lands required some flood waters for fertilizing purposes they considered that in the event of the construction of a reservoir project on the Gila above them they would still receive sufficient flood waters to supply their needs from the various tributaries, such as the San Pedro, the Santa Cruz, the Verde, and from the several other lesser ones.

These landowners were also aware of the fact that increased irrigation on the Gila Reservation or at Florence would increase the return flow for irrigation west of the reservation, and they accordingly would be benefited thereby.

In view of the large amount of capital required for construction, and in view of the very questionable water supply legally available, it is reasonably certain that no storage pr ect involving a high dam and providing water for irrigation of the lands west of the Gila River Reservation will be constructed by private or corporate interests.

Below the confluence of the Gila and the Salt, the waters of the Salt River hold the same relation to the total available water supply for irrigation west of the reservation as do the waters of the upper Gila itself.

In the suit which adjudicated the water rights on the Salt River and resulted in the well-known Kent decree, the users of water below the confluence were not parties and their rights of course were not affected. In the adjudication suit known as the Nels Benson *v.* John Allison et al., which is still pending and which has for its object the adjudication of the relative rights of the Buckeye Canal, none of the parties diverting water from the Gila River on or above the Gila River Reservation were made parties to the action.

In views of the facts set forth above, the conclusion has been drawn that the present irrigation west of the Gila River Reservation on the Gila would not suffer in the event of the construction of a reservoir project such as the San Carlos project; and it is also considered that the present or possible future uses of Gila River water west of the reservation need not be taken into consideration in the determination of the amount of water legally available for the San Carlos project.

A more detailed description of irrigation on the Gila west of the Gila River Reservation is published in Appendix A.

Analysis of irrigation, Florence—Casa Grande district, Arizona.

Canals.	Date of construction.	Date of last use.	Areas by United States Indian Service, 1914.		Areas irrigated in five-year periods as estimated from all available information.											Remarks.
			Cultivated.	Previously cultivated.	1865	1870	1875	1880	1885	1890	1895	1900	1905	1910	1914	
			Acres.	*Acres.*	*Acres.*	*Acres.*	*Acres.*	*Acres.*	*Acres.*	*Acres.*	*Acres.*	*Acres.*	*Acres.*	*Acres.*	*Acres.*	
1. Florence {Outside of project			555.3	4,397.6						2,021	2,310	3,757	2,866	2,600	555.3	
1. Florence {Inside of project	1887		2,976.2	6,600.7						3,649	4,732	4,336	2,909	3,079	2,976.2	
Montezuma Canal	1875	1901						270	201	294						Transferred to Florence Canal 1893.
Holland Canal	1868	1891				315	315	805	485	180						Transferred to Florence Canal 1891.
Alamo Amarillo	1865	1905				22	22	64	104	11	11	11				Transferred to Florence Canal 1901.
2. McLellan Canal	1871		190.1	12.2			500	500	500	500	500	180	180	180	190.1	
3. Ah Lee Canal	1911		0.0	10.3											0.0	Irrigated in 1911, 15 acres. Not irrigated at time of survey, 1914.
4. Old Timers Canal	1910		1,938.8	180.9										1,122	1,938.8	
Florence Canal	1887									355	1,063	1,063	1,423	790		
Montezuma Canal	1875	1901					795	1,030	1,160	1,160	775	775				
Holland Canal	1868	1891				504	504	627	287	23						
Alamo Amarillo	1865	1905			20	635	60	83	423	433	433	430				
Brady & Chase	1866					300	300	300	300	300						
5. Chino, or Brady & Chase	1866		172.0	32.4		461	551	551	600	305	197	197	195	170	172.0	
6. Pierson-Nicholas Canal	1872		950.7	0.0			890	520	570	680	740	740	760	780	950.7	
7. Adamsville Canal	1865		384.5	0.0	200	520	520	520	520	520	300	300	300	319	384.5	This canal known as White & Sanford.
8. Price & Powell Canal	1909		317.4	0.0										360	317.4	
9. Padilla Canal	1910		78.4	219.2										100	78.4	
Walker Canal	1868	1894				160	320	320	320	320					0.0	Walker Canal abandoned in 1894. Again in use 1909, 100 acres, 44 acres irrigated by this canal on Indian Reservation, shown on reservation analysis.
10. Moore Canal	1838	1905	0.0	332.9						332	19	19	12	12	0.0	
11. Brash Canal	1876	1890	0.0	310.4				200	200						0.0	This land irrigated through the Ah Lee Canal from 1905.
12. Sharpe Canal	1889	1896	0.0	14.7						160	160				0.0	
13. Stiles & Mason Canal	1868	1893	0.0	106.4		500	675	675	675	660					0.0	
Total			7,563.4	12,217.7	220	3,417	4,952	5,965	6,345	11,903	11,230	11,808	8,645	9,512	7,563.4	

IRRIGATION ON THE TRIBUTARIES AND THE HEADWATERS OF THE GILA RIVER.

The irrigated lands along the tributaries and headwaters of the Gila are more or less detached. They constitute the floor of small valleys separated one from the other by narrow canyons or ravines, through which the watercourse has cut its way.

The altitudes of the various irrigated tracts along the different tributaries naturally vary within rather wide limits. On the extreme upper tributaries and on the headwaters of the Gila some irrigation is carried on at an elevation of over 5,000 feet, while at the mouth of the San Pedro, which is the lowest point of any of the tributaries taken into consideration in this report, the elevation is 1,910 feet.

Climatic conditions in this part of the country vary directly with the elevation. On the headwaters of all these tributaries, as well as on the upper watershed of the Gila itself, snow falls during the winter months, while the summer months are cool. The upper drainage area is fairlv well covered with pine trees and undergrowth.

The agricultural products from these lands are the same as produced on the lands along the Gila proper. Grains, alfalfa, vegetables, and some hardy fruits are the principal products. None of the irrigated districts along the tributaries or on the extreme upper Gila is thickly settled. As a rule the farms are small and have been taken up as homesteads. In some instances, on the San Pedro, the irrigated districts are owned entirely by cattle or land companies.

Farming along the tributaries and on the extreme upper Gila has met with varying degrees of success. Intensive cultivation has not been practiced and many of the farmers seem to be content with only a fair return from their lands.

The farming class along the tributaries and on the extreme upper Gila is made up of Americans and Mexicans. It is evident that the Americans are rapidly superseding the Mexicans, who as a rule were the original cultivators.

The ditches are owned either by individuals, or cooperatively by the several landholders under the canals. In a few instances the canal owners have organized canal companies, which have been incorporated. When the ditches are owned by several different persons, the water available in the ditch is apportioned in accordance with the interest maintained.

A brief history of irrigation on the tributaries and headwaters of the Gila follows. Each tributary is taken up in the order in which it empties into the Gila, proceeding upstream.

San Pedro River.—Leaving aside the Salt River, which has not been taken into consideration in this report, the San Pedro River is the most important tributary of the Gila.

As in the valleys along the Gila, irrigation on the San Pedro has been practiced since ancient times. Most of the earlier trails between Old Mexico and northern Arizona followed the San Pedro along the greater part of its course and, in the narratives of the

Spanish explorers frequent mention is made of the Indian rancherias along this stream.

In more recent years, probably during the early part of the nineteenth century, Mexicans irrigated small patches of land along the San Pedro and its tributaries. Most of this early irrigation was in the upper portion of the San Pedro watershed.

When the general territory, south of the Gila, was obtained from Mexico through the Gadsden Purchase in 1854, two old Spanish land grants on the upper portion of the San Pedro were recognized by this Government. These land grants cover much of the areas early irrigation along the San Pedro, and some of these tracts have been continuously irrigated to the present time.

Americans began to irrigate lands along the San Pedro in the early sixties. The number of new ditches and irrigated fields increased rapidly until the floods of 1894 and 1895 caused a setback to agricultural development. Since these floods the reclamation of new lands has been less rapid, and in the past 10 years the acreage of irrigated lands lost by floods or abandoned has about equaled the area reclaimed.

Until about 1860 the Indians maintained their rancherias along the San Pedro. Since that time, however, they have either been forced out or have voluntarily vacated their land, and at the present time only two Indian ditches, irrigating 20 acres, are diverting water from the San Pedro. On the Aravaipa, a tributary of the San Pedro, one Indian ditch serving 80 acres is being operated at the present time.

On the San Pedro River there are 46 ditches, serving a total of 6,860 acres of irrigated land. On the tributaries of the San Pedro there is, in addition to the above, a combined area of 750 acres irrigated at the present time.

San Carlos River.—The next tributary above the San Pedro is the San Carlos River. This stream is entirely within the San Carlos Indian Reservation.

The history of irrigation along the San Carlos has been similar to the history of the irrigation along the Gila within the San Carlos Reservation. No irrigation was practiced previous to the establishment of the reservation, and what agricultural development has taken place has resulted from the efforts of the Indian agents in charge.

The first irrigation was in 1875, and in 1880 it is estimated that more than 30 acres were under cultivation. In 1890 this area had been increased to 400 acres, and at the present time there are 936 acres irrigated from waters of the San Carlos, this area served by 24 ditches.

Eagle Creek.—Proceeding upstream along the Gila the next tributary of any importance is the small stream called Eagle Creek. This stream empties into the Gila about 16 miles above the Solomonville Valley.

Prehistoric as well as early Indian irrigation took place along this stream, and prior to the arrival of the first American settlers, in the eighties, a few Mexicans had taken up small farms at favorable locations along the stream.

The irrigable area along this stream is comparatively inaccessible, is confined to narrow patches, and many ditches are required to irrigate a comparatively small area.

There is no irrigation practiced by Indians on Eagle Creek or on the other upper tributaries. In the upper region most of the ranches are primarily cattle ranches, while lower down the irrigation is carried on by Mexican gardeners, who sell their produce to the nearby mining towns of Clifton and Morenci.

A large pumping plant, pumping directly from the river and from wells, which furnish a water supply to these mining towns, has been installed at a point on Eagle Creek, nearly due west of the town of Clifton.

A summatation of the irrigated areas along Eagle Cheek shows that, at the present time, 24 ditches are serving 563 acres of irrigated land.

San Francisco River.—Two miles above the confluence of Eagle Creek and the Gila River the important tributary, the San Francisco River joins the Gila.

The practice of irrigation along this stream antedates the coming of Americans. The first American settlers came in the early eighties, and for 10 or 15 years prior to that time Mexicans had taken up and cultivated small patches of land at different places along this stream.

There are seven more or less important irrigation districts along the San Francisco. In the district comprising the headwaters of this stream, known as the Alpine district, irrigation of the land is only necessary during small portions of the year, since the land is subirrigated. In the district near the mouth of the San Francisco, the Clifton district, nearly all of the diversions from the river are by means of pumps.

On the Blue River, which is the main tributary of the San Francisco, are many evidences of prehistoric irrigation, as well as caves of ancient cliff dwellers. As on the San Francisco, when Americans came into this region about 1885, they found a few Mexicans farming small areas along this stream.

The Blue River flows through a narrow canyon throughout its entire length, and a number of small tributaries or forks join the main stream. The irrigated areas are situated along the course of the main stream and on the tributaries.

The total irrigated area in the seven irrigated districts along the San Francisco amounts to 1,739 acres, while on the Blue and on the other tributaries of the San Francisco an additional area of 990 acres is being irrigated.

Irrigation on the extreme upper Gila.—For a distance of 50 miles upstream from the Duncan Valley, the country adjacent to the Gila continues mountainous in character, and the stream flows through a narrow canyon which frequently widens out, forming small valleys, and it is in these small valleys that the irrigated areas are situated.

The territory along the headwaters of the Gila was settled by Americans at about the same time as were the lands along the upper tributaries, or in the early eighties. For about 10 years prior to this Mexican ranchers had been carrying on some irrigation in this section, although only a small portion of the land at present under cultivation was originally reclaimed by Mexicans. With the advent of the American farmers, the arable areas were soon placed under irrigation, and as early as 1900 all of the land cultivated at the present time had been reclaimed.

There are three irrigation districts along the Gila above the Duncan Valley, and in these districts there are at the present time 18 ditches, which serve to irrigate 3,621 acres of land. This area does not include certain reported but otherwise unknown small irrigated tracts situated on the minor forks of the Gila headwaters.

A summation of the total irrigated area along the four tributaries and the upper Gila, comprising district No. 6, gives a total area of 14,710 acres.

A more detailed description of irrigation along the tributaries and on the extreme upper Gila is given in Appendix A.

Analysis of irrigation on Gila River, Ariz.

Districts.	Areas by United States Indian Service survey, 1914.		Prior to coming of white man.	Areas irrigated in five-year periods.														Remarks.
	Culti-vated.	Previ-ously culti-vated.		1850	1855	1860	1865	1870	1875	1880	1885	1890	1895	1900	1905	1910	1914	
	Acres.	*Acres.*	*Acres.*	*Acres.*	*Acres.*	*Acres.*	*Acres.*	*Acres.*	*Acres.*	*Acres.*	*Acres.*	*Acres.*	*Acres.*	*Acres.*	*Acres.*	*Acres.*	*Acres.*	
Duncan Valley District No. 1	6,268.5	125.5	....	......	......	......	......	......	......	250	3,485	1,364	2,326	4,316	4,341.1	6,002.5	6,268.5	2,037.2 acres cultivated in New Mexico.
Solomonville-Safford District No. 2.	26,633.0	2,120.0	....	......	......	......	......	......	1,180	4,895	11,221	16,110	18,373	21,146	23,408.0	24,635.6	26,633.0	
San Carlos Indian Reservation District No. 2.	1,000.5	1,202.0	....	......	......	......	......	......	200	560	560	1,450	1,250	2,000	....	400.0	1,000.5	All land in Bylas district.
Florence-Casa Grande District No. 3.	7,563.4	12,217.7	....	......	......	......	220	3,417	4,952	5,965	6,345	11,903	11,230	11,808	8,645.0	9,512.0	7,563.4	555.3 acres outside proposed project which are cultivated; 4,632.6 acres of previous cultivated land also outside proposed project.
Gila River Indian Reservation District No. 4.	14,356.0	11,315.0	12,920.0	12,450	12,525	12,840	13,432	13,860	14,330	15,100	15,860	14,133	14,795	14,490	13,676.0	13,995.0	14,356.0	

RELATIVE USES.

The following table is submitted for the purpose of showing the cultivated areas in the four principal districts or valleys along the Gila River. The figures shown therein are taken from the analyses which have been estimated for each district. These analyses by districts represents summary of the history of irrigation under each ditch of each district.

For reasons already given, it was concluded that the diversions from the Gila below the Pima Reservation and above the Duncan Valley, as well as those in the Winkelman district, need not be taken into account in determining the supply of water legally available for the San Carlos project. The diversions from the tributaries of the Gila likewise are deemed to have little bearing on this phase of the investigation. Accordingly no analyses have been made of the irrigation in these districts.

It will be seen from the accompanying table that the users lowest down on the streams were the earliest appropriators of water, and that subsequent irrigation proceeded in a regular manner upstream, so that the highest diversions are the most recent.

Probable Future Uses of Gila River Waters Above the San Carlos Dam Site in Addition to Present Uses.

From observations on the ground and from a consideration of all data collected, the following estimate has been made of what may be expected to be the probable future uses of Gila River waters in addition to the present use.

FUTURE IRRIGATION ON THE TRIBUTARIES AND HEADWATERS OF THE GILA.

On the San Pedro and on the San Carlos Rivers the water supply for the lands under cultivation at present is generally inadequate during the dry season, and unless storage or pumping is resorted to it is expected that the future uses of waters of these two rivers will not become greatly in excess of the uses now being made.

Irrigation by direct diversion on these streams is fraught with more or less risk, and the cost of maintaining irrigating systems is high.

As to the probability of reservoir projects being constructed on these tributaries, it may be said that in the case of the San Carlos the topographic conditions are such as to preclude this possibility. On the San Pedro, at a point near Charleston, above the Benson and St. David Valleys, the topographic conditions are favorable for a storage project. An investigation of this project was made by engineers of the Reclamation Service, and a report on this project was published in the third annual report of the Reclamation Service. The following is an excerpt from the summary of this report:

> The limited time during which measurements of the run-off from the storage basin above the proposed storage reservoir have been made renders an estimate of the dependable water supply largely an assumption. The increasing demands in Mexico for water incident to extensions and increasing mining operations should be carefully considered, since one-half or more of the drainage area of the San Pedro project is in Mexico. Also the rights of the Indians lower down on the Gila River should be considered before definitely determining the merits of this project.

Since the above report was written, no further action has been taken, except the installation of a gauge on the river at this point.

It is reasonable to expect that the possible future construction of this project rests entirely with the Government. It is not at all probable that private capital will undertake its construction.

The fact that the San Pedro discharges into the Gila below the San Carlos Dam site affects the San Carlos project only in so far as it is assumed that the flow contributed by the San Pedro will make up the losses by evaporation and seepage of the stored waters between the impounding dam and the first diversion dam. Considering the large volume of water which this river would contribute to the flow of the Gila during flood times, and that during such times the stored waters of the San Carlos project would be conserved, it is believed that the above assumption is a safe one, and it is further considered that the future uses of river water on the San Pedro will never be in sufficient amount to affect the flow of the San Pedro to the extent that the above assumption would not apply.

The present diversions from the San Pedro or the San Carlos Rivers have very little effect on the water supply of the diversions lower down on the Gila. The discharge of either of these streams is not large during dry seasons, and the greater part of the flow contributed to the Gila is during times of floods or when there is sufficient water in both rivers for all requirements.

On the upper tributaries and on the headwaters of the Gila the water supply is adequate, yet nearly all of the irrigable land is at present under cultivation. For the most part these lands are confined within narrow canyons, where they are always subject to flood damages; and in general it may be said that the area which may be reclaimed in the future will be offset by the losses due to flood erosion, and accordingly the total irrigated area will remain unchanged

The above general statement does not apply to certain portions of the irrigable lands along the San Francisco River, where it is expected that at least 1,500 acres will be irrigated in the near future, in addition to the area already cultivated. This increased area, it is expected, will be irrigated from the extensions of the present ditches and from larger uses of a storage project already constructed. This storage project is in the Luna Valley, situated in New Mexico on the upper reaches of the San Francisco River about 80 miles above its confluence with the Gila. The project consists of an earth impounding dam on the river, and the resulting reservoir is of sufficient capacity, supplementing the normal flow of the stream during the summer, to irrigate 1,000 acres. While this reservoir now serves to irrigate only 300 acres, it is estimated that there are 2,200 acres of irrigable land in the Luna Valley.

This reservoir project was constructed in 1892 by an irrigation company working under a State permit or franchise. It is said to be the intention of the company to enlarge their ditches and increase the acreage to the full limit of the available water supply.

Considering the increased acreage which it is believed will be irrigated under this reservoir in the near future, together with probably increased areas under possible extensions in other directions along the San Francisco River, it is estimated that at least 1,500 acres additional will be irrigated at a comparatively early date, or within the next 10 years.

FUTURE IRRIGATION IN THE DUNCAN VALLEY.

Under the present canals in this valley, there were at the time of this survey 125 acres of land previously cultivated, and 192 acres of land that had never been cultivated, but which is susceptible of irrigation. By extending the present canals, an additional area of 500 acres could be brought under cultivation.

A summation of the above areas gives 817 acres as the amount of land susceptible of irrigation under the present canals or their possible extensions. Practically all of the land which might be brought under irrigation by possible extensions of the present canals would be served by two canals. The Sunset and the Cosper & Windham, whose headings are in the State of New Mexico.

While no records were searched to ascertain what filings have been made in New Mexico, it is understood that applications or filings have been made to cover the appropriation of sufficient water for the irrigation of all land under these probable extensions.

Inasmuch as these canals divert their water near the head of the valley where the water supply is adequate, it is reasonable to predict that these extensions to the present canals will be constructed and that the area irrigated under the present canals may eventually reach the maximum of 816 acres, as already given, over and above the 6,268.5 acres under cultivation at the time of the survey.

Several different projects have been proposed and surveys made for the irrigation of 4,000 or 5,000 acres of land in the vicinity of Franklin Flat, which is a part of the Duncan Valley, situated above the present canals. The irrigation of this area would require, besides a diversion dam, a long and very expensive canal, and the advisability of this project is extremely questionable. With the exception of surveys, no work has been done on these projects, and any initiated rights may be considered to have elapsed for want of due diligence.

In the vicinity of York Flat and York Station, some additional land may be irrigated by means of pumps. Owing, however, to the relatively high position of this land with respect to the river it is not probable that gravity ditches can be used successfully.

FUTURE IRRIGATION IN THE SOLOMONVILLE-SAFFORD VALLEY.

The duty of water for irrigation in the Solomonville-Safford Valley, as fixed by the court in the decree already referred to, amounts to 9.02 acre-feet per acre per year. This amount of water is more than twice as much as actually required for the land, and by a more economical use of the water apportioned an area of land much greater than that indicated by the decree could be cultivated.

From complete discharge measurements made on 13 of the 18 canals of this valley during a period of one year, from April 1, 1914, to March 31, 1915, it is found that the total water diverted was 183,970 acre-feet. During the time when measurements were being made these canals were serving to irrigate a total area of 25,885 acres, or all but 748 acres of the entire cultivated acreage of the Solomonville-Safford Valley.

The actual duty of water as shown by the above figures which are based upon the measured discharge of the canals amounts to 7.1

acre-feet per acre, which is a higher duty of water than required by the decree, but a lower duty than obtains on the Salt River project.

In the case of the five small canals of the valley serving the balance of the cultivated land and upon which no water measurements were made, it is assumed that the duty of water would be the same as under the canals previously considered. Accordingly the quantity of water diverted by these small canals would amount to 5,311 acre-feet.

Combining the above figures, it is found that the total diversions by the canals of this valley during the yearly period referred to amounted to 189,285 acre-feet. This quantity of water perhaps does not represent the actual flow which was applied to the lands, since some of this water undoubtedly found its way back to the river or may even have entered other canals. It also should be pointed out that the figure given above may not properly be assumed to represent a single equivalent diversion for the irrigation of the entire valley, since it is known that the upper canals divert the entire flow during the dry season and that the canals lower down the valley derive their water supply from the return flow or seepage.

This return flow or increment has been made use of since the early history of the valley, and in the adjudication decree above referred to the utilization of this return flow was also provided for.

Suppose, for purposes of comparison, that the total flow of the canals in the valley for the year, aggregating 189,285 acre-feet (equivalent to a constant flow of 264 second-feet), was the amount diverted and afterwards applied to the land, and assuming for the duty of water 4.5 acre-feet per acre at the point of diversion, it follows that the above flow would irrigate approximately 42,000 acres.

Considering now the discharge measurements that have been made during the three most recent years of normal flow (1911, 1912, 1913) at the gauging stations—the one on the Gila at Guthrie, 20 miles above the Solomonville Valley, and the other on the San Francisco at Clifton—it is seen that during May and June the combined average flow of these two streams was about 90 second-feet. The combined average flow for the entire year period, as nearly as could be estimated from all data available, was approximately 310 second-feet.

The possible extent of the future irrigation in the Solomonville Valley, however, may not properly be based on the 310 second-foot flow, since this would depend on the assumption that all of the flow during normal years would be diverted by the canals of the Solomonville Valley. Taking the most favorable case of fairly regular flow, it is considered that possibly 60 per cent of the above flow, or 186 second-feet, would be available at the point where the first diversions are made for irrigation in the Solomonville Valley. This quantity of water, considered as the normal flow, is less than the total amount found to have been diverted by the canals for the valley during the year in which measurements were taken; but taking into consideration also the return flow and other increments the 186 second-feet of continuous flow at the head of the valley would represent a quantity of available water in excess of the amount found to have been actually diverted by the canals.

Assuming, however, 7,500 miner's inches, or 187.5 second-feet, as a basis for calculations and apportioning this flow to the new lands in somewhat the same manner as the decree mentioned apportions water among the existing ditches, but assuming the more reasonable and economical duty of water at 4.5 acre-feet per acre at the diversions, which is the duty recommended in this report for the estimate of the minimum cost of the San Carlos project, and which duty corresponds closely with the duty of water recently recommended and as found on the Salt River project, it follows that while most of the present canals in the valley could be supplied with sufficient water to irrigate all the lands under them, as well as all the land under possible extensions, yet several of the lower canals have more new land under their possible extensions than the water supply would suffice to irrigate.

It was found from the totals of the acreages estimated to be susceptible of irrigation under the different canals and their possible extensions that the maximum area subject to cultivation in the Solomonville-Safford Valley under the assumed conditions would amount to 35,100 acres, or nearly 9,000 acres over and above the area cultivated at the present time. This estimate is based upon the assumption previously stated and which it is thought would in a general way permit of the irrigation of the largest amount of new land. It may be mentioned also that it is not considered that this area could be used in its entirety for general farming, such as growing alfalfa or other crops which require irrigation throughout the year, but all of the land not suitable for such crops may be utilized for crops which can be grown during the flood season or when there is a water supply in excess of the demands of prior appropriators.

No irrigation projects other than some extensions of present canals are known to be under consideration for the irrigation of any extensive areas in the Solomonville Valley.

By means of the Enterprise Canal project, which was under consideration about 15 years ago, it was proposed to irrigate some 5,000 acres of land along and above the south border of the area cultivated at the present time. In 1900 several miles of the Enterprise Canal were at least partially constructed, and $3,000 or $4,000 was spent upon this work. No diversion dam was built and the water was never turned into the canal. Since the initial construction work on this canal in 1900 no further work has been done, and the project has apparently been abandoned.

Water filings have been made at different times covering the dam site and so-called reservoir location in the box canyon through which the river enters the upper end of the Solomonville Valley.

It has been proposed, by means of these projects, to store water and irrigate the lands in the Solomonville Valley. While it is possible that a favorable dam site exists at this point, yet the impounding area would be so small that the project is considered entirely unfeasible.

Numerous filings have likewise been made on the surplus flow of the Gila at the reservoir and dam site locations in the lower end of the Duncan Valley. The dam site locations include the Guthrie Dam and Reservoir site described by Mr. Lippincott in Water Supply Paper No. 33. Mr. Dal M. Potter has a filing at the present time covering this site, and has recently carried on some survey work in connection with this project.

It is believed that none of these reservoir projects will be constructed by private capital, and that the future irrigation in the Solomonville-Safford Valley may be expected to be confined to the areas previously mentioned under present canals or possible extensions.

FUTURE IRRIGATION ON THE SAN CARLOS RESERVATION.

The area of the land on this reservation irrigable from the Gila River and its tributary, the San Carlos, is small, and numerous considerations make it impossible to predict how much of it is likely to be irrigated.

The situation undoubtedly will be for many years entirely under the control of the Government, so the question of irrigating new lands will doubtless be considered with the San Carlos project in mind, as also will the interests of the Indians on the reservation be considered and protected if that project is undertaken.

For these reasons no attempt has been made to estimate the area that will be irrigated on the reservation in the future.

SUMMATION OF PROBABLE FUTURE USES ABOVE THE SAN CARLOS RESERVOIR.

The total maximum area of land which will probably be irrigated in the future is estimated at 11,500 acres over and above the actual area at present under cultivation. Approximately 9,000 acres of this area is located in the Solomonville Valley, 1,000 acres in the Duncan Valley, while the remaining 1,500 acres lie on the upper tributaries of the Gila.

It should be pointed out that the above estimate is based for the most part on the assumption that the increased area to be irrigated will result not so much upon the use of a greater portion of the total river flow, but rather upon an increased duty of the same quantity of water as used at the present time. It could not therefore be said that the future available supply for a reservoir at San Carlos would be affected in direct proportion to the increased uses of the waters of the Gila above the proposed reservoir site. The effect of the diversions in the Solomonville-Safford Valley on the flow of the Gila at San Carlos is discussed elsewhere in this report, under the heading of Water Physically Available.

FUTURE USES OF GILA RIVER WATERS BELOW THE SAN CARLOS RESERVOIR SITE.

As to the probable future uses of Gila River waters for irrigation in districts below the proposed San Carlos reservoir, it is generally conceded that, with present conditions continuing, no materially increased use of the waters of the Gila River can be expected.

Owing to the difficulties under which the water supply is at present available, it would be unreasonable to expect a large increase in the area under cultivation by further increasing the duty of water. Much of the high-water flow of the Gila is not available because of the temporary nature of the diversions. The repeated destruction of land, headworks, and canals by successive floods has been very detrimental to the agricultural development of these irrigation districts.

Water filings, calling for the appropriation and diversion of many thousands of miner's inches of the Gila's flow, to be used in these districts, have been made. Many of these filings have not been followed up by the construction of ditches or the doing of other work necessary to the making of valid appropriations.

In the Florence-Casa Grande district, the project of the Casa Grande Water Users' Association is the principal prospective diversion for which any considerable amount of construction work has been undertaken. The status and description of this project have been set forth elsewhere in this report.

Another project of much smaller magniture, which was recently undertaken (that is, since the investigation in this district had been completed), is known as the Aztec Mutual Canal Co. project. Construction work has been in progress on this ditch since the past summer, and at the time of the writing of this report, November, 1915, this project was rapidly nearing completion. This ditch is opposite Florence on the north side of the river, and follows practically the same location as the old well-known and plainly visible north-side prehistoric canal of the Florence Valley.

During recent years much work has also been done by the Government on irrigation works on the Gila River Reservation. While the several irrigation systems known as the Blackwater, the Agency, the Santan, and the Casa Blanca (described in Appendix A of this report), have been constructed or are in course of construction, primarily for the purpose of providing larger and more modern irrigation facilities to supplant the less efficient system previously in use by the Indians, yet these projects also contemplated a more extensive use of the Gila River flow.

The failure of the low-water or dry-season supply is, of course, more keenly felt on the reservation than in the Florence district. It may be safely stated, however, that no material agricultural development by the use of the waters of the Gila River can be expected to take place in the future, either on the reservation or in the Florence district or in the irrigation districts west of the reservation, until present conditions are changed either as a result of the construction of a suitable storage reservoir or by the installation of permanent diversion works.

COST OF PROJECT.

The two factors which limit the size of the proposed San Carlos irrigation project are, first, the permissible annual draft from the reservoir, and, second, the duty of water or the amount of water it is necessary to apply to the land to successfully produce growing crops.

These factors definitely limit the amount of land it is possible to irrigate, and on the values supplied to them depend the maximum and minimum reclamation charges per acre. The minimum reclamation charge per acre is produced by combining the maximum draft with the maximum duty of water, the maximum charge by taking the minimum draft with the minimum duty.

INTERPRETATION OF MEANING OF MAXIMUM AND MINIMUM COST.

The words maximum and minimum cost of the San Carlos irrigation project as found in the paragraph of the Indian appropriation act calling for a report on this subject are capable of at least two interpretations:

First, it may be assumed that the maximum and minimum cost of the project refers to the reclamation charge per acre, a maximum cost resulting from a conservative interpretation of all the natural data affecting the amount of land irrigated, especially the permissible annual draft from the reservoir and the duty or minimum amount of water required to produce a profitable crop. A minimum cost would arise from a more liberal interpretation of these natural data.

It is perfectly obvious that a rigid interpretation of the permissible annual draft and the application of a low duty of water would so limit the size of the project that the reclamation charge per acre would be higher, although the total cost of the project would be lower than the estimate based on a more liberal interpretation. A project where the reclamation charge per acre is low is known as an economical project irrespective of the total amount involved in its construction. On the other hand, when the charge is high, it is considered to be an expensive project.

Second, it may be assumed that the total cost of the project is meant and that the maximum and minimum cost will be based upon the difference in the methods or type of construction employed as well as upon the extent of the project contemplated.

Other assumptions might be made, but those mentioned are the most probable and comparative costs will be determined on such assumptions.

Throughout the investigation and in the design the successive stages of development have been based upon the assumption that practically all the run-off of the Gila River should be impounded and that a project of such size and extent be embraced which would utilize the water to the greatest practical advantage. This assumption has resulted in a plan which will be termed the minimum cost per acre.

The maximum cost per acre and the various alternations which follow are explained according to the above asumptions in their proper order.

The principal items which enter into the cost of the project under the various assumptions will be found worked out in detail and discussed more fully in Appendix D.

The study of questions pertaining to the source and amount of water; the run-off, rainfall, and evaporation; and the duty of water are thoroughly discussed in Appendix B and only the findings relevant to the discussion of the general project plan are enumerated here.

WATERSHED.

The Gila River, upon which the San Carlos irrigation project is located, has its source in western New Mexico at an elevation of 7,000 to 10,000 feet.

The principal tributaries are the San Francisco, San Carlos, and the San Pedro Rivers; and it is just below the mouth of the San

Carlos River that the most promising dam and reservoir site is located. This is known as the San Carlos Dam site.

The total area of the Gila River drainage basin above the proposed San Carlos Dam site is 13,455 square miles, with a mean annual rainfall of 12.87 inches (incomplete records, 1867–1899. See Water Supply Paper No. 33.

RUN-OFF AT SAN CARLOS.

The run-off records at the San Carlos Dam site are not very complete; that for 1905, 1,011,082 acre-feet being the maximum; and for 1902, 99,936 acre-feet being the minimum. The average from incomplete records (1890–1912), based upon a ratio of 90 per cent of the run-off at the Buttes, is 346,567 acre-feet (see p. 28, Army Board Report), while the average, as deduced from all records up to 1915, is 359,880 acre-feet.

LAND TO BE IRRIGATED.

The land which can be irrigated under this project lies along the Gila River, in the vicinity of Florence, where about 7,563 acres of private land are at present under cultivation, and in the Gila River Indian Reservation, where 14,356 acres are now under cultivation.

The selection of the Indian land was, of course, determined by the limits of the Indian reservation, due attention being given to the selection of the best land available.

The selection of the private land has necessarily been determined by the location of the tracts of land at present under cultivation and the importance of keeping the land in as compact a body as possible consistent with securing the best land.

DUTY OF WATER.

It seems to be the consensus of opinion that between 3 and 4 acre-feet of water per annum is required for successful irrigation under the conditions obtaining along the lower Gila.

Undoubtedly, by the employment of so-called intensive methods a higher duty of water could be employed, and it is known that a crop of grain can be produced with 1.5 acre-feet. But it is assumed that irrigation under the project will be carried on by the average farmer and Indian, who will practice diversified farming with only a moderate degree of efficiency. Under these conditions to insure success it will be necessary to supply water continuously during the irrigating season, and it would not be safe to assume the duty of water at more than 3 acre-feet per annum, applied to the land. This is borne out by the duty assigned to the neighboring Salt River project of 3.3 acre-feet per annum. A lower duty of water than 4 acre-feet, except in isolated instances, is uneconomic and tends to the waste of water.

The maximum and minimum duty of water may then . . assumed to be 3 and 4 acre-feet, respectively.

PROJECT PLAN.

In general, the project plan comprises the Gila River. about 7 miles below

River, from which the water will flow down the present natural river channel for a distance of about 70 miles to a point about 12 miles above Florence, where a diversion dam will be built. At the diversion dam the water is taken into the main distributing canal on the south side of the river.

Part of the water is to be used in the vicinity of Florence, part to be taken to the Blackwater, Sacaton Agency, and Casa Blanca districts of the Gila River Indian Reservation and part to be returned to the Gila River opposite Santan, and again diverted to the Santan district on the north side of the Gila River by a diversion dam to be built at this point. This diversion dam will also be used to divert flood water from the San Pedro and other tributaries of the Gila River, as well as the return flow from the Florence-Casa Grande irrigation district, both to the Santan district, on the north side, and to the Sacaton Agency and Casa Blanca districts, on the south side of the Gila River.

A small amount of water will be diverted on the north side of the Florence diversion dam for use on a tract of about 1,200 acres of private land on the north side of the river and about 12 miles below the dam.

SAN CARLOS RESERVOIR.

A complete analysis and study of the reservoir created by the San Carlos impounding dam will be found in Appendix B, in which the required capacity to conserve the run-off is determined, together with the required height of dam, the behavior of the reservoir under various drafts, the maximum annual draft, and the required capacity of spillways.

AREA AND CAPACITY.

It has been determined that with a dam 180 feet high to the crest of the spillway the area of the reservoir would be 13,200 acres, the capacity 714,450 acre-feet, and the length 16 miles, and that if the crest of the spillway were raised to the 190-foot level the area would be 14,790 acres and the capacity 854,800 acre-feet.

AMOUNT OF SILT.

No experiments were made to determine the percentage of silt, but assuming 1.1 per cent, as determined by the Army board, the annual deposit in the reservoir would be 3,959 acre-feet. It seems possible, as mentioned in the report of the United States Army board, that with the advance of engineering science some method will be devised to successfully handle the silt. With the present knowledge, it is known that a large portion of the silt can be prevented from entering the reservoir. This can be effected by controlling the flow of the Gila above San Carlos through the construction of a series of small reservoirs along the upper Gila and its tributaries, which would greatly diminish the annual damage from flood erosion. The retardation of the flow would also be assisted by the reforestation of the denuded area of the upper watershed and the limitation of the grazing privileges. The protection of the river banks would also assist in preventing erosion.

ANNUAL DRAFT.

In the analysis of the reservoir behavior it was shown that with a dam 180 feet high to spillway crest and considering that whole period of record (1894 to date), with an assumed annual draft of 300,000 acre-feet, a full supply would have been available until January, 1902. From that time until August, 1904, the only available water would have been the actual run-off; that is, about 80,000 acre-feet per year. From August, 1904, until the present time the same reservoir would have supplied more than 300,000 acre-feet per annum.

The maximum draft which could have been maintained during the extremely dry period of 1899 to 1904 would have been 225,000 acre-feet.

In this analysis the net evaporation was assumed to be 60 inches per year.

To supply 300,000 acre-feet per annum during a period similar to the one from 1894 to 1902, with a dam 180 feet to spillway, a minimum reservoir capacity of 500,000 acre-feet would have to be maintained and desilting would have to begin at the end of 54 years. If the spillway crest were raised to 190 feet, desilting would not have to begin until 90 years had elapsed.

It should be noted, however, that the dry period of 1899 to 1904 when a draft of 300,000 acre-feet would have emptied the reservoir, was a remarkable and probably exceptional one and that the full possibilities of the project would not be developed if the annual draft were limited to the quantity of water necessary to insure against a deficiency during a similar period which may recur only at rare intervals.

This is the argument for the assumption of a draft of 300,000 acre-feet per annum in determining the minimum cost per acre.

SAN PEDRO RIVER.

In this connection it is to be noted that no part of the flow of the San Pedro and other tributaries to the Gila below the San Carlos Dam has been considered to augment the supply of water to be used upon the land or to conserve the stored water in the reservoir except to offset the loss due to evaporation in the open channels.

There are not sufficient records available to determine the average run-off of the San Pedro River, but it is variously estimated at from 10 per cent to 25 per cent of that of the Gila River at San Carlos and, as the estimated channel loss between the impounding and diversion dams is only about 5,000 acre-feet, it is evident that there is a considerable excess flow in the San Pedro which can be used for irrigation to the effect of conserving the storage in the reservoir. It is partly in order to secure this advantage that the Santan diversion is to be built.

PLAN OF MINIMUM COST PER ACRE.

Under the plan involving the minimum cost per acre, it is proposed to irrigate about 45,000 acres of private land in the vicinity of Florence and 35,000 acres of Indian land on the reservation.

This 35,000 acres of Indian lands is in addition to the 5,000 acres already provided for by pumping plants in the Santan district on the reservation, giving the Indians a total of 40,000 acres of irrigated land, or 10 acres per capita. This estimate is based upon an annual draft at the reservoir of 300,000 acre-feet and upon a duty of 3 acre-feet applied to the land. It involves the use of lined main canals and assumed that the loss due to evaporation between the impounding and diversion dams will be made up by the flow of the San Pedro River and other tributaries which discharge into the Gila River between these limits.

ADVANTAGES OF LINED CANALS.

The distribution system as proposed in this estimate is designed so that water will be delivered to the highest point on each 160 acres. The main canal and the Pima and Picacho branches have been estimated with concrete lining, as by the use of lined main canals the losses in the distribution system as a whole will be about 20 per cent, while with unlined main canals the losses would be about 30 per cent. Under the latter assumption the total area of irrigated land would have to be reduced from 80,000 to 70,000 acres. The advantage of lined main canals is much more apparent when the cost of maintenance is considered, especially so as the water of the Gila River is so heavily laden with silt.

Under the plan involving the maximum cost per acre in which a very conservative estimate of the water available is assumed as well as a more conservative allowance for the duty of water, only 15,000 acres of private land can be irrigated in addition to the 35,000 acres of Indian land. This estimate is based upon an annual draft at the reservoir of 250,000 acre-feet and upon a duty of 4 acre-feet applied upon the land. In this case lined main canals are to be used and the loss between impounding and diversion dams is assumed to be balanced by the flow of the tributaries between the dams.

ITEMS OF CONSTRUCTION.

The various items of construction will be discussed, beginning with the San Carlos Dam.

SAN CARLOS DAM.

The San Carlos impounding dam is to be located at the upper end of the box canyon of the Gila River about 7 miles below San Carlos.

This site is at the lower end of the Solomonville Valley, which extends upsteam for a distance of about 70 miles.

SUBMERGED LANDS.

In this valley and within the area which would be submerged lies the San Carlos Apache Indian Agency, including the town of San Carlos, the Indian lands, roads, and houses, and a portion of the Arizona Eastern Railroad.

149700—19—VOL 2——6

FLOW DAMAGES.

The flow damages accruing to the project by reason of the construction of the San Carlos Dam and Reservoir have been discussed in Water-Supply Paper No. 33, page 22, and in the report of the Army board, page 146. The amounts as given in the latter report, with the exception of the item for new roads which is eliminated, are deemed to be substantially correct and amount to $857,970, of which $680,192 is for damages to the railroad and the balance for buildings and lands of the reservation. (See also Appendix C.)

PHYSICAL FEATURES OF DAM SITE.

The rock at the dam site is principally quartzite and quartzite sandstone.

Diamond-drill borings made by the United States Geological Survey, the United States Reclamation Service, and the Army board in 1899, 1903, and 1913, at two possible sites about 1,000 feet apart, show the depth to bedrock to be 74 feet at the lower site and 23 feet at the upper site, also that there are distinct lines of fault at the lower site, while at the upper site the strata are practically unbroken. At both sites the dip of the strata is downstream. The upper site has therefore been chosen.

ACCESSIBILITY.

The nearest railroad point is on the Arizona Eastern Railroad near Rice, and it would be necessary to construct about 10 miles of wagon road over rough mountainous country from the railroad to the dam.

DATA USED IN DESIGN.

The following data pertain to the San Carlos Dam:

Elevation of stream bed	feet	2,308
Elevation of spillway	do	2,488
Elevation of crest and roadway	do	2,508
Area of reservoir at elevation 2488	acres	13,200
Area of reservoir at elevation 2498	do	14,790
Capacity of reservoir at elevation 2488	feet	714,450
Capacity of reservoir at elevation 2498	do	854,800
Length of reservoir at elevation 2488	miles	16
Maximum depth of rock surface below low water	feet	23
Assumed depth of excavation into bedrock	do	10
Maximum height of dam	do	233
Length of dam on crest	do	542
Assumed weight of masonry per cubic foot	pounds	150
Assumed uplift, full water pressure at heel varying uniformly to zero at the toe.		
Weight of water per cubic foot	pounds	62.5
Wind pressure per square foot	do	50
Safe bearing on foundation, per square foot	tons	16
Area of Gila Basin above dam site	square miles	13,455
Mean annual rainfall on watershed	inches	12.87
Average run-off at dam site	acre feet	359,880
Maximum run-off at dam site	do	1,011,082

DESIGN OF DAM.

In the design of the dam it was decided to use the straight-plan gravity type with spillways, the crest to be used for a roadway, the dam to be constructed of cyclopean masonry and designed to resist water pressure to the crest, including uplift due to a full head of water at the heel, decreasing uniformly to zero at the toe. Also, wind pressure at 50 pounds per square foot.

In the design of the dam it was decided to limit the pressure on the foundation to 16 tons per square foot, the lines of resultant pressure to fall at all times within the middle third. Trial profiles were assumed and analyzed graphically to determine the proper dimensions for various heights of dam. The final profile was then checked mathematically and the maximum pressure found to be 15.5 tons per square foot in the case of the reservoir empty and with the wind blowing upstream. The factor of safety against overturning at any point is never less than 2. The angle of the line of resultant pressure with the vertical was determined to be 37°-43-¼, which makes the equivalent coefficient of friction 0.773. The coefficient of friction between planes of dressed masonry is about 0.65, hence considerable reliance must be placed upon the cohesion of the masonry, the roughness of the foundation, the projection of the foundation of the dam into the bedrock, and the convergency of the canyon walls, any one of which, however, would be sufficient to insure against sliding.

Cut-off wall.—A cut-off wall is to be placed under the dam near the upstream edge of the foundation to prevent, as far as possible, percolation under the dam.

Drainage tunnel.—A 4 by 6½ by 300 foot drainage tunnel is to be left in the dam 192 feet below the crest with 6-inch drain pipes 10 feet apart, extending from the floor of the tunnel vertically to the bottom of the downstream side of the cut-off wall to intercept and carry off any possible leakage from under the cut-off wall or through the masonry, thereby relieving the uplift pressure under the dam. The tunnel will be placed on a slight grade and drained by a 2-foot pipe leading to the downstream face of the dam.

Inspection gallery.—For the purpose of affording access to the valve chambers and to the drainage tunnel, a 4 by 6½ by 300 foot inclined inspection gallery on a slope of 2 vertical to 3 horizontal, with steps, is to be left in the dam. This gallery will be reached by an iron stairway on the downstream face of the dam.

Discharge valves.—For the control of the discharge, three 60-inch balanced valves are to be installed 70 feet, 125 feet, and 180 feet, respectively, from the top of the dam and the discharge will be carried by 60-inch cast-iron pipes passing directly through the dam.

Spillways.—In determining the capacity and size of the spillways the hydrograph of the December, 1914, flood was used, but with the discharge ordinates doubled. (See Appendix and accompanying diagrams.)

It was found that with a 300-foot clear spillway a depth of 11.5 feet over the crest will be required.

Assuming that 10-foot automatic gates are installed and the clear opening cut down to 240 feet by piers a depth of 14.5 feet will be required.

Owing to the topographic features at the dam site, it was decided to construct a spillway 150 feet in length at each end of the dam. The crest of the dam is made 20 feet above the crest of the spillway, thereby allowing a free board of 5.5 feet over the gates.

The dam is designed to resist pressure to the full height so that if required at any time the reservoir level could be safely raised to the full height of the dam, providing a reliable type of automatic gates was installed.

The excavation for the spillway will provide nearly enough rock for the construction of the dam and as more is needed it can be economically procured by extending the spillway excavation.

Spillway bridges.—As the crest of the dam is to be used for a roadway it will be necessary to provide two bridges across the spillway. Two 150-foot steel bridge spans will serve for this purpose.

Automatic gates.—To provide for the installation of automatic gates it would be necessary to put in piers, which would make the use of short-span concrete bridges desirable. The extra cost of such gates and bridges is included in the estimate.

Dimensions of dam.—The following dimensions for the dam have been derived:

	Feet.
Height of dam to crest above low water	200
Height of dam to spillway above low water	180
Length of dam on crest	542
Width of dam on crest	16
Maximum depth of bedrock below low water	23
Assumed depth of excavation into bedrock	10
Maximum height of dam	233
Maximum width of base	200

The dam is to be constructed of cyclopean masonry, using 1:2½:5 concrete and 30 per cent plums. The following quantities will then be required:

Quantities (see complete estimate in Appendix C).—The total excavation will be 296,060 cubic yards. The total masonry required is 286,230 cubic yards, requiring the following materials:

Cement	barrels	260,470
Plums	cubic yards	85,870
Crushed rock	do	183,200
Sand	do	91,600
Total amount of rock in place	do	246,170

Cost (see detailed estimate in Appendix C).—The estimated cost of the impounding dam complete, not including property damages, is $2,526,400, which, for a capacity of 854,400 acre-feet, makes the cost per acre-foot $2.96, or the cost per cubic yard of masonry $8.83. For comparison it may be noted that the cost of the Roosevelt Dam was $2.84 per acre-foot of storage and $10.68 per cubic yard of masonry.

FLORENCE DIVERSION DAM.

Site.—The site selected for the Florence diversion dam is about 12 miles above Florence, where the Gila River flows between rock walls about 400 feet apart.

While the rock banks afford a substantial foundation for the end structures, the bed rock drops to a great depth in the middle of the channel, so that it becomes imperative to use the Indian weir or floating types of dam. In this type, destructive percolation under the dam is overcome by constructing impervious concrete aprons of sufficient weight to balance the upward thrust of the water and, by the use of sheet piling.

At this site, it is found that a weir crest 8 feet above the stream bed will be sufficient to divert water into a canal the bottom of which will be at the same elevation as the bottom of the Florence Canal.

The location of the old Florence Canal is such that the proposed main canal would most economically follow practically the same grade and alignment. If it was decided to use an unlined main canal and the partially constructed canal of the Casa Grande Valley Water Users' Association could be had at its true value to the project, the diversion dam could be raised the necessary height of about 3 feet, and the water diverted into this canal when completed.

The additional cost of raising the dam to this level, including the extra cost of canal extensions, will be found under the item of costs.

Data.—The following data were used in the design of the Florence Diversion Dam:

	Feet.
Elevation of present bed of the Gila River	1,553
Elevation of proposed dam crest	1,561
Elevation of intake of Florence Canal	1,554.2
Elevation of H. W. L. 1914 flood and 1905 flood	1,562.7
Width of stream bed	355
Width of stream bed at H. W. L.	395.7
Approximate slope of river per mile	13.37
Probable depth of flood flow, including scour	13

The calculated flood flow of December, 1914, assuming the coefficient of roughness "n" by Kutter's formula equal to 0.018 was 103,300 second-feet. A maximum flood of 150,000 second-feet was used, however, in the design of the dam to conform with the assumption made in connection with the San Carlos Dam.

In the design of the dam it was found that a crest length of 440 feet was necessary.

This gives a unit discharge of 341 second-feet per linear foot of dam and a depth of 16 feet over the crest.

Design (*see Appendix C*).—The formulas of W. G. Bligh, author of The Practical Design of Irrigation Works and at one time chief engineer of the British irrigation projects in India, based upon his experience with existing Indian weirs, have been used to determine the length and thickness of the aprons and talus, and after due consideration the following dimensions were given the dam and the estimate of quantities made therefrom:

Dimensions.—The following are the principal dimensions:

	Feet.
Breadth of upstream apron	20
Breadth of downstream apron	50
Breadth of base of weir	15
Breadth of top of weir	6
Breadth of talus	230
Thickness of base at toe of weir	5
Thickness of upstream apron	1.5
Thickness of downstream apron	2.5 to 5
Thickness of talus	2.5 to 4
Curtain walls	2.5 by 6
Length of sheet piling	12

The weir and impervious aprons are to be constructed of 1:2½:5 concrete, using 40 per cent plumbs closely laid, especially in the aprons, the end structures to be of straight 1:2½:5 concrete, reinforced only in places of exceptional stress, the talus to be of large rock carefully placed and concreted, using small-sized crushed rock for the aggregate.

Headings.—On account of the great amount of silt carried by the Gila River, especial attention was given the design of the intake. The intake gates are to be set parallel with the direction of the river flow and flush with the bank training wall. The intake gates close upon a sill 4 feet above the bottom of the sluiceways. There are 4 sluiceway channels separated by low training walls 4 feet in height to facilitate sluicing during low water.

Sluice gates.—The total sluice-gate opening on the south side is 20 feet, on the north side 5 feet.

It is proposed to operate the intake or regulator gates by hydraulic jacks of a special type, placed within the dam so as to leave no obstruction to the river flow over the dam.

The principal diversion is to be on the south side of the river, and this heading is designed for a capacity of 1,000 second-feet which will be ample for the annual draft of 300,000 acre-feet.

On the north side, it is proposed to divert about 30 second-feet for use on land on that side of the river and the heading is designed accordingly.

Sand trap.—At a suitable point just below the intake it is proposed to increase the size of the channel for about 2,000 feet to form a sand trap. At the lower end of this channel sluice gates are to be placed, opening into a channel discharging back into the river so that the deposit of sand may be sluiced out when necessary.

Spillway.—A 300-foot rollway is provided in the sand-trap section and emergency gates placed in the canal head at the lower end of the sand trap to take care of any sudden rise in the river level.

Quantities.—The total excavation required for the dam, heading, and sand traps amounts to 60,920 cubic yards, of which 45,300 cubic yards are required for the sand traps alone.

The total concrete required is 9,178 cubic yards, and the talus requires 1,227 cubic yards.

Cost.—The total cost of the Florence Diversion Dam is estimated to be $142,622.

The cost of raising the dam 3 feet including the extra cost of canal extensions in case it was decided to use the Casa Grande Canal is estimated to be about $36,810.

SANTAN DIVERSION DAM.

Location.—The Santan Diversion Dam is to be located about 2 miles above Sacaton and will be used to divert flood water coming from the San Pedro and other tributaries of the Gila between the San Carlos Dam and this point to the Santan district, for which the Reclamation Service has already constructed canals and headings, on the north side of the river and to the Sacaton Agency and Casa Blanca districts on the south side of the river. It will also be used to divert to the Santan district the water turned into the Gila River just above this point from the Pima Canal.

Plans and estimates for this structure were submitted by this office in a report dated November 25, 1914. At that time it was proposed to build this dam with a superimposed bridge which is badly needed both by the Indians and the white people. The cost of the combined structures was shown to be only a small amount more than the cost of a dam alone. The bridge, however, is not deemed to be a proper charge against the San Carlos project and only the cost of the dam itself is therefore included in this estimate.

Type.—The dam will be of the same type as the Florence Dam with the exception that it is to be regarded more as a reinforced concrete structure than the one at Florence, which has very little reinforcement. This will not affect the cost to a great extent and will be an advanage if it is decided to build a superimposed bridge at any time.

Since the estimate was made for the Santan Diversion Dam, about 500 feet of the bank on the south side has washed out necessitating a longer structure by 150 feet than originally estimated. The cost of the additional length has been estimated and the amount added to the cost shown in that report.

Site.—The channel is now about 2,200 feet wide at the proposed site, which is the narrowest point in this vicinity.

The bank on the north side is a high rocky butte from which all the rock needed for the structure may be obtained.

The south bank is about 8 feet high and consists of the ordinary river sand and silt.

On account of the light nature of the soil on the south side and the consequent erosion of the bank, about 3,000 feet of bank protection has also been provided for in this estimate.

Data.—The following data are submitted in connection with this site.

	Feet.
Elevation of the bed of the river	1,286
Elevation of the proposed dam crest	1,289
Elevation of the deck of the present United States Reclamation Service heading	1,296
Elevation of the floor of the present United States Reclamation Service heading	1,284.6
Elevation of the riprap at the United States Reclamation Service heading	1,305
Elevation of the top of the south bank of the river	1,294
Approximate slope of the river bed	0.00173
Depth of flood water taken from high-water marks found by survey	7.1

Assuming "n" the coefficient of roughness in Kutter's formula, at 0.02, the discharge was calculated to be 134,580 second-feet. As in the case of the Florence Dam, the maximum flood was assumed to be 150,000 second-feet. This gives a depth of 7.8 feet over the crest.

Cost.—The total cost of the Santan Diversion Dam is estimated to be $173,599.

DISTRIBUTION SYSTEM.

While the cost of the impounding and diversion dams will be practically the same under the various assumptions previously mentioned, the cost of the distribution system will vary considerably with the area and location of the land to be irrigated.

Under the assumption involving the minimum cost per acre which has been used as the basis for calculations, a tentative distribution system was outlined and estimates made thereon.

This system includes the main canal, the Picacho branch and its distributors, and the canals in connection with the Santan Diversion Dam.

The main canal, with a capacity of 1,000 second-feet, extends from the Florence Diversion Dam along the south side of the Florence Valley for a distance of 15 miles, when it divides into two branches—the Picacho branch, with a capacity of 350 second-feet, continuing southwest for a distance of about 7 miles to the old Picacho Reservoir; the Pima branch, with a capacity of 500 second-feet, turning west extends 9.5 miles to the Gila River Indian Reservation, thence a distance of about 3.3 miles into the reservation, where it empties into the Little Gila, 4½ miles farther west; a part of the water will be diverted from the Little Gila through a canal 1.6 miles in length into the Gila River just above the proposed Santan Diversion Dam. The balance of the water will continue down the Little Gila 8 miles to the diversion for the Casa Blanca district, for which a canal 12 miles long will be required. A canal 1.7 miles long is also required to conduct flood water from the Santan Diversion Dam to the Little Gila for use in the Agency and Casa Blanca districts. The total length of these main canals is about 62.4 miles, including 12.3 miles of the Little Gila.

The main canal and the Picacho and Pima branches are to be lined with concrete 3 inches in thickness.

The diversion weir and head gates as well as the distributing system for the Sacaton Agency district have already been constructed, but the actual cost of construction should be charged against the San Carlos project.

In the Santan district the Reclamation Service and the Indian Service have already constructed a combined flood-water and pumping-plant irrigation system, and only the proportionate cost for the irrigation of 5,000 acres under the flood-water system should be charged to the San Carlos project.

In the Casa Blanca district work was started in 1914, and the total amount spent in this district should be charged to the San Carlos project.

Cost of distribution system (not including diversion dams).—The total estimated cost of the main canal, laterals, and sublaterals, including the work already done and chargeable to this project, will be, under the "minimum cost per acre" assumptions, $1,796,962, or $22.46 per acre.

This includes canal structures and all appurtenances necessary to deliver water to the highest point on each 160-acre tract.

SUMMARY OF CONSTRUCTION COSTS OF THE SAN CARLOS PROJECT.

The following summaries of costs under the interpretations of the meaning and minimum costs show the total cost as well as the costs per acre; the amount of the equal annual payments without interest and with 3 per cent compound interest:

Minimum construction cost of San Carlos project.—Assumed draft, 300,000 acre-feet; duty, 3 acre-feet; canal losses, 20 per cent; Indian land, 35,000 acres; private land, 45,000 acres.

Item	Amount
Impounding dam, including flow damages	$3,384,370.00
Florence Diversion Dam	142,622.00
Santan Diversion Dam	173,599.00
Main canal (lined)	675,400.00
Picacho branch (lined)	159,940.00
Pima branch (lined)	294,932.00
Florence Casa Grande distribution (unlined)	290,532.00
Reservation distribution	376,158.00
Total construction cost	5,497,533.00
Cost per acre	68.72
Assuming this amount to be paid in 20 equal payments without interest, each payment will be	3.44
With interest at 3 per cent, compounded annually, each equal payment will be	4.62
Adding the cost of water rights at $50 per acre for 21,919 acres (see p. 193), the total project will be	6,593,503.00
Cost per acre	82.42
Each of 20 equal annual payments without interest	4.12
Each of 20 equal annual payments with 3 per cent compound interest	5.53

Maximum cost San Carlos project.—Assumed draft 250,000 acre-feet; duty 4 acre-feet; canal losses 20 per cent.

Indian land, 35,000 acres; private land, 15,000 acres.

Item	Amount
Impounding dam, including flow damages	$3,384,370.00
Florence diversion dam	128,360.00
Santan diversion dam	173,599.00
Main canal (lined)	606,170.00
Prima canal (lined)	334,680.00
Florence-Casa Grande distribution (unlined)	84,240.00
Reservation distribution (unlined)	376,158.00
Total cost	5,087,577.00
Assuming this amount to be paid in 20 equal payments without interest each payment will be	5.09
With interest at 3 per cent compounded annually each annual payment will be	6.83
Adding the cost of water rights at $50 per acre for 21,919 acres the total project cost will be	6,183,527.00
Cost per acre	123.67
Each of 20 equal payments without interest	6.18
Each of 20 equal annual payments with 3 per cent compounded interest	8.29

Purchase of water rights.—It has already been shown that there are 14,356 acres of land on the reservation and 7,563 acres in the Florence-Casa Grande Valley which are now enjoying the use of the waters of the Gila River. In the event of the construction of the San Carlos project the water rights appurtenant to these lands must either be bought outright or a portion of the available water supply of the project would have to be distributed to satisfy them.

As to the 14,356 acres of Indian lands that are already irrigated, it can probably be safely assumed that the Government will include them in the project and merge the water rights appurtenant thereto in the water rights of the project as a whole. The only question is, whether it will compensate the Indians for these rights or include them in the project rights without compensation.

If they should be taken without compensation, it follows that the total money expenditure for the project would be less than what it would otherwise be by the value of these rights and also that the per acre cost would be correspondingly reduced. No reason for such a course is apparent, however, unless indeed the water rights attached to the lands of the whites would be contributed upon the same basis, which seems unlikely.

If compensation is made for the Indian water rights, the money cost of the project will be increased to that extent, but money for that purpose would not have to be appropriated if the total cost of irrigating the Indian lands were charged against the Indians and the Indians were then merely credited with the value of these water rights.

It is impossible to say just how the problem of purchasing the white water rights and including them in those of the project would work out, but it is thought that practically all of the lands to which they are now appurtenant would come into the project. If they did, and to the extent that they did, the Government could probably in like manner merely credit their owners upon the total charge against them for water rights under the project with the amount agreed to be paid by the Government for such rights, and thus save any appropriation for the purpose of purchasing them.

If these white rights are not contributed or purchased, water to satisfy them will have to be allowed to flow in the river, or compensating water for that purpose will have to be furnished from the reservoir. Just how much this would amount to it is hard to estimate accurately, but it is thought that it would come to enough to make it best to purchase the rights and merge them in the project if that can be done at a reasonable cost.

On account of the present insufficiency of the water supply for the land now being irrigated, it is considered that a water right in the territory affected by the San Carlos project entitles the owners to sufficient water for the irrigation of at least one grain crop. Taking this into consideration together with the value of the reclaimed land, it is assumed that a water right in this district is worth $50 per acre.

Considering that these water rights can be purchased somewhat near this basis, it is evident that by so doing the per-acre cost of the project would not be increased, as the total number of acres irrigated under the project would be correspondingly greater. Other considerations, such as the increased ease of dividing and distributing the water of the river, also make a purchase and merger desirable. The following table is based upon the purchase of both the Indian and white water rights, and the full irrigation acreage thereby permitted. The water rights are assumed to be purchasable at $50 per acre, and the project to be operated under the minimum cost plan.

Assumption	Total water-right acres purchased.	Total acres to come under project	Total cost water rights.	Total cost project.	Total cost per acre project land.
Purchase of both Indian and white water rights	21,919	80,000	$1,095,950	$6,593,503	$82.42
Purchase of Indian rights alone	14,356	72,437	717,800	6,215,333	85.80
Purchases full present irrigated area supplied free	....	58,081	....	5,497,533	94.65

This table plainly shows that the purchase of both Indian and white water rights is altogether the best plan and that, if need be, a considerably greater price than $50 per acre could be paid for these rights, rather than supply these lands with free water.

Claims to rights to water may be made on account of lands that have been irrigated at one time but which are no longer under cultivation, and also on account of new projects that have not reached the point of actual use of water. The extinguishment of some of these claims may be necessary and if so, it will further increase the reclamation charges as shown above.

Also no account has been taken of the "reserved rights," so-called, belonging to the reservation. These rights will be mentioned later.

Table of first costs and annual charges including water rights.

	Without interest.		3 per cent compound interest	
	Maximum.	Minimum.	Maximum.	Minimum.
Total cost	$6,183,527 00	$6,593,503 00	$6,183,527 00	$6,593,503 00
Cost per acre	123 67	82 42	123 67	82.42
Annual payment	6 18	4 12	8 29	5.53
Operation and maintenance	1.50	1.50	1.50	1.50
Total	7.68	5 62	9.79	7.03
Desilting	6.39	4.00	6 39	4.00
Operation and maintenance	1.50	1.50	1.50	1.50
Total	7.89	5.50	7.89	5.50
Annual payment	6 18	4.12	8.29	5.53
Operation and maintenance	1.50	1.50	1.50	1.50
Desilting	6 39	4.00	6 39	4.00
Total	14.07	9.62	16.18	11.03

ALTERNATIVE PROJECTS.

The foregoing costs are based upon the assumption that the San Carlos storage reservoir would be included in the project. If, however, the San Carlos Reservoir is no constructed in the immediate future, other means should be found to supply water for the lands belonging to the Pima Indians on the Gila River Indian Reservation.

This irrigation could be accomplished without the San Carlos Reservoir, either by the construction of the diversion dam on the reservation alone or by the construction of the two diversion dams at Florence and Santan and thereby irrigating in addition to the reservation lands a large acreage in the vicinity of Florence. Either projects would, however, be based upon a supply of water for one crop per year instead of a full supply basis.

The actual amount of water available during the 8 months between October and May, based upon the mean low water flow and a maximum diversion of 1,000 second-feet, is 193,400 acre-feet.

With unlined canals the percentage of loss in the distribution system would be the same as that assumed in the previous calculation, i. e., 30 per cent, leaving 135,380 acre-feet to apply upon the land.

It has been demonstrated that to successfully produce one crop of grain in the vicinity of Florence and the Gila Indian Reservation a duty of 1.5 acre-feet is required. On this basis a total of 90,000 acres of land could be irrigated.

With a view, however, to the eventual construction of the San Carlos Dam and the adoption of an 80,000-acre project with perennial irrigation, it is deemed wise to limit the area to that amount.

Under the two diversion dam scheme it will be necessary to adjucate the water rights appuratenant to the land now under irrigation in the vicinity of Florence and one the Gila Indian Reservation. The construction of the diversion dams and the distribution systems under this plan would not differ materially from that under the plan including the storage reservoir, as the canals were originally designed to carry the flood waters entering the Gila below the San Carlos.

The following costs have been determined to apply to the construction of the flood water diversion projects under these assumptions:

Two diversion dams.—Assumed draft 193,400 acre-feet; duty 1.5 acre-feet; canal losses 30 per cent for unlined canals.

Indian land to be irrigated 35,000 acres; private land 45,000 acres.

Florence diversion dam	$142,622.00
Santan diversion dam	173,599.00
Main canal (unlined)	461,692.00
Picacho branch (unlined)	56,056.00
Pima branch (unlined)	131,230.00
Florence-Casa Grande distribution (unlined)	290,532.00
Reservation distribution (unlined)	376,158.00
Total cost	1,631,889.00
Cost per acre	20.40

Two diversion dams with lined canals.—Assumption the same as above except that Main and Pima Canals are lined; losses 20 per cent.

Florence diversion dam	$142,622.00
Santan diversion dam	173,599.00
Main Canal (lined)	675,400.00
Pima Branch (lined)	294,032.00
Picacho branch (unlined)	56,056.00
Florence-Casa Grande distribution	290,532.00
Reservation distribution	376,158.00
Total cost	2,009,299.00
Cost per acre	25.11

The cost of the diversion dams and the necessary lined main canals alone is estimated to be $1,361,177. This amount distributed over the 80,000 acres would amount to $17.01 per acre, or confined to the 21,919 acres now irrigated the cost would be $62.10 per acre.

One diversion dam.—A one crop project for the reservation would have cost items as follows:

Santan diversion dam	$173,599.00
Reservation distribution system same as above less cost of connecting ditch from Little Gila	365,191.00
Total cost	538,790.00

Confined to 35,000 acres, cost per acre, $15.39.

Of the above amount $131,280 has already been expended and therefore in order to complete the system a further expenditure of $407,510 would be required.

Recapitulation.

The data collected in the compilation of the history of irrigation in the Gila River basin shows that irrigation was practiced during prehistoric times by the Pima Indians on the Gila River Indian Reservation, and has been continued by them on the same land until the present date. Irrigation was begun by the whites in the vicinity of Florence, and later on the Solomonville and Duncan Valleys, and along the upper tributaries.

The Gila River Indian Reservation therefore has the first rights to the waters of the Gila River and thus in general the priorities are earliest near Florence and diminish in point of time as the river is ascended.

The survey shows that a total of 7,563.4 acres of land are being irrigated in the vicinity of Florence, while 12,217.7 acres have been previously irrigated. Included in the latter area is a large body of land that has had sufficient water to effect proof under the desert-entry laws, but has never been actually cultivated. In the valley there is practically an unlimited acreage that could be irrigated if sufficient water were available. On the Gila River Indian Reservation there is a total of 14,356 acres now under irrigation from the flood waters of the Gila and 11,315 acres that have been irrigated but are not now irrigated. A part of the above acreage, amounting to 3,312 acres, is under the Santan pumping system, and in addition there are 1,271 acres irrigated by the waters of the Salt River.

The survey shows that a total of 42,170 acres of land is now being irrigated above the proposed San Carlos dam-site, of which 26,633 acres are located in the Solomonville-Safford Valley.

In these upper valleys there is a total of 3,447 acres which have been previously irrigated but are not now under cultivation, and a total of 11,500 acres which could be irrigated at a reasonable cost either by an extension of the present systems, or through economic diversion. This makes a grand total of 53,670 acres which is susceptible to irrigation. Of this acreage, 35,000 acres lie in the Solomonville-Safford Valley. Title to the land now under irrigation in the two upper valleys, exclusive of the San Carlos Indian Reservation, lies in 1,393 individuals, of whom 1,213 own land in the Solomonville-Safford Valley. Irrigation is accomplished by 31 canals and 9 pumping plants, and 18 of these canals are located in the Solomonville-Safford Valley. During the season of 1914–15 a total of 189,285 acre-feet of water was diverted in the Solomonville-Safford Valley. This places the duty of water at 7.1 acre-feet, as computed from the actual diversion.

The hydrographic investigation indicates that while the flow of the Gila varies widely from year to year, it seems to follow cycles of nine-year periods. A reservoir, to be of the greatest economic use, should supply hold-over storage capacity based upon the run-off for a complete cycle. The annual discharge of the Gila at the San Carlos dam-site based on nine-year cycles is estimated to be 350,000 acre-feet for the mean, 412,000 acre-feet for the maximum, and 281,-300 acre-feet for the minimum. The maximum annual discharge of which there is record amounts to 1,011,082 acre-feet; the minimum to 99,960 acre-feet. The estimated maximum flood at San Carlos amounted to approximately 100,000 second-feet and extended over a period of six days.

The reservoir drafts are based on a net evaporation of 60 inches per annum. A reservoir 190 feet in depth at the dam-site will have a storage capacity of 854,800 acre-feet. This reservoir will supply an annual draft of 300,000 acre-feet during the mean nine-year cycle, but during the least low-water period, with the assistance of the San Pedro, the flow of which is assumed to be 10 per cent of the Gila, it would have been dry for a period of 15 months. Without the assistance of the San Pedro it would have been dry for a period of 31 months. This is the most severe low-water period of which there is record, and it seems probable that it will not reoccur for 30 or 40 years. During the remaining period of the 21 years over which the records extend, this draft could have been maintained.

The reservoir, with the assistance of the San Pedro, would have supplied an annual draft of 250,000 acre-feet during the entire period.

On the assumption that all the water rights now active above the reservoir in the Solomonville-Safford Valley were eliminated and practically the entire river discharge were available for storage, the dryest period under the 300,000 acre-feet draft would have been reduced to four months. Under similar conditions the flow of the Gila at Florence would have been theoretically increased by 65 second-feet. If the water now diverted at Florence was also permitted to remain in the river the theoretical increase at the east line of the Gila River Indian Reservation would amount to 95 second-feet. The effects of the diversions above the Solomonville-Safford Valley have not been included, as it was impracticable from the data at hand to trace this effect through the several intervening valleys. It should be pointed out that these figures are hypothetical and are based upon various logical assumptions.

A reservoir of 854,800 acre-feet capacity would be created by the construction of a straight gravity type dam of cyclopean masonry at the head of the San Carlos box canyon. This dam would have a maximum height of 233 feet above the lowest point of the foundation, or 200 feet above the bed of the river. At the bed of the river the dam is 180 feet in width. The dam is provided with two spillways, having a clear width of 240 feet. The crest of the spillways is at an elevation of 180 feet above the bed of the river, and they are provided with automatic shutter gates to raise the elevation of the reservoir 10 feet. The flow line of the reservoir on this basis would be at the 2,498 contour above sea level. The dam is designed in accordance with modern engineering principles, and adequate factors of safety are provided throughout. In the calculations the elevation of the reservoir has been assumed to be level with the top of the dam, and full upward water pressure has been assumed to exist diminishing from the full amount at the heel to zero at the toe. The annual accumulation of silt deposit has been assumed to be 1.1 per cent of the volume of water entering the reservoir, in accordance with the determination of the United States Army Board of Engineers. This will amount to an average of 3,959 acre-feet per annum, and as the reservoir is not designed to provide for silt deposits, theoretically the effect of these deposits will be felt during the first dry period. In reality the effect would probably not be felt for the first

10 years, and under mean flow conditions desilting would not be absolutely essential until 45 years had elapsed.

The minimum amount of water required to produce a succession of crops during the year has been accepted as 3 acre-feet per annum applied to the land. The greatest amount that should be used without incurring waste is accepted as 4 acre-feet.

An annual draft of 300,000 acre-feet with a duty of water of 3 acre-feet will admit of the irrigation of 80,000 acres of land, allowing for transmission losses in the San Carlos Canyon and 20 per cent seepage losses in the canals. The above figures form the basis for the minimum reclamation charge per acre.

An annual draft of 250,000 acre-feet with a duty of water of 4 acre-feet would irrigate 50,000 acres of land. These figures form a basis for the maximum reclamation charge per acre.

The land included in the project comprises 35,000 acres of land on the Gila River Indian Reservation, and the balance (depending on the size of the project (in the vicinity of Florence—the latter in as compact a body as possible and embracing the land now under irrigation. In this connection it is assumed that 50,000 acres of irrigated land are required to meet the eventual needs of the Indians, but that water for 15,000 acres could be supplied from that available at Salt River and by pumping.

Diversion will be effected by two dams of the East Indian weir type, one located across the Gila above Florence, the second above Sacaton on the Gila River Indian Reservation. The weir of the Florence Dam is 8 feet in height and 440 feet long, the extreme width, omitting talus, is 70 feet. The weir of the Santan Dam is 3 feet high and 1,850 feet long. The extreme width, omitting talus slope, is 60 feet. The canal system comprises 35.8 miles of main canal and 193 miles of laterals, assuming an 80,000 acre project. On the basis of 50,000 acres under irrigation the total of the main canals is 28.4 miles, with a total of 160 miles of laterals. The system is planned to deliver water to the highest point of each 160-acre tract. The capacity of the main canal heading at Florence is 1,000 second-feet; of the two heading at Sacaton, 310 second-feet and 300 second-feet. It is planned to use the Little Gila as a part of the main canal system.

It is assumed that the average value of the water rights now appurtenant to the 21,919 acres of land now under irrigation in the vicinity of Florence and on the Gila River Indian Reservation is $50 per acre. This would amount to a total of $1,095,950 for the entire acreage.

The storage project, planned on a basis of an annual draft of 300,000 acre-feet to irrigate 80,000 acres of land with a duty of water of 3 acre-feet, will cost a total of $5,497,533, exclusive of water rights, and including these, $6,593,503. The construction charge on this basis will amount to $68.72 per acre. Including the purchase of water rights, the reclamation charge will be $82.42 per acre. These are the minimum construction and reclamation charges.

The project, based on an annual draft of 250,000 acre-feet to irrigate 50,000 acres of land with a duty of water of 4 acre-feet, will cost $5,087,577, exclusive of water rights; including these, $6,183,527. The construction charge on this basis amounts to $101.75 per acre, the total charge, including the purchase of water rights, to $123.67.

These figures are the maximum construction and reclamation charge per acre.

In consideration of the above plans it is deemed advisable that periods of repayment be extended over a period of 20 years.

The annual charges on the basis for an 80,000-acre and a 50,000-acre project are shown in the following table:

Table of first costs, including water rights and annual charges.

	Without interest.		3 percent compound interest.	
	Maximum.	Minimum.	Maximum.	Minimum
Total cost	$6,183,527 00	$6,593,503 00	$6,183,527.00	$6,593,503.00
Cost per acre	123 67	82.42	123.67	82.42
Annual payment	6 18	4.12	8.29	5.35
Operation and maintenance	1.50	1.50	1.50	1.50
Total	7.68	5.62	9.79	7.03
Desilting	6 39	4 00	6.39	4.00
Operation and maintenance	1.50	1.50	1.50	1.50
Total	7.89	5.50	7.89	5.50
Annual payment	6 18	4.12	8.29	5.53
Operation and maintenance	1.50	1 50	1.50	1.50
Desilting	6 39	4.00	6.39	4.00
Total	14.07	9.62	16.18	11.03

CONCLUSIONS.

The proposed San Carlos project is entirely practicable from a construction standpoint, and is eminently desirable in that it will develop agriculturally a large section of Arizona which is now unproductive, but it has some serious faults, of a physical and economic nature, that should receive careful consideration before any plan of reclamation is adopted.

The most serious physical objection to the construction of the proposed San Carlos project is that due to the large accumulation of silt that will be annually deposited in the storage basin by the water of the Gila River. This problem received careful consideration of the United States Army Board of Engineers, and no improvement can be suggested respecting the solution advised. Grave doubts are felt, however, respecting the success of this or any other method now known to engineering science in accomplishing the desilting of the San Carlos Reservoir.

The reservoir, with the maximum capacity of 854,000 acre-feet as at present designed, and assuming 300,000 acre-feet draft, provides no large excess capacity for silt accommodation. A dam designed to provide such excess capacity and to be moderately effective would probably increase the initial cost of the project to a prohibitive extent, and at best would only serve to postpone the evil day when desilting would be necessary. It is probable that the detrimental effect of silt deposits will not be felt during the first 8 or 10 years; after that desilting will have to take place in order to maintain the full capacity of the reservoir.

If desilting does not take place, the effect of the silt deposits will be seriously felt during the first period of dry years, and the reservoir will theoretically cease to serve its full purpose in 45 years.

It seems possible, as mentioned in the report of the United States Army Board of Engineers, that with the advance of engineering science some method will be devised to successfully handle the silt. With the present knowledge, it is known that a large portion of the silt can be prevented from entering the reservoir. This can be effected by controlling the flow of the Gila above San Carlos, through the construction of a series of small reservoirs along the upper Gila and its tributaries, which would also greatly diminish the annual damage from flood erosion. The retardation of the flow could also be assisted by the reforestation of the denuded area of the upper watershed and by the limitation of the grazing privileges. The protection of the river bank would also assist in preventing erosion.

An entire change of plan, which would include these smaller reservoirs as an integral rather than an auxiliary feature, advantage being taken of the storage facilities, to permit a corresponding reduction in the size of the San Carlos Reservoir, as now proposed, may make possible the devising of a more desirable project from several points of view, and one whose reclamation charge per acre may not be greatly in excess of the plan under consideration.

As to this, however, there is not sufficient data available at this time, upon which to base a definite opinion.

The most attractive plan so far considered for the San Carlos project is that presenting the minimum reclamation charge per acre. This is based on an annual draft from the reservoir of 300,000 acre-feet, enabling the irrigation of 80,000 acres of land, with a duty of water at 3 acre-feet per annum. To attempt to reduce this charge would be impracticable, for to increase the reservoir draft or increase the duty of water to supply a greater area would be extremely hazardous.

The annual draft of 300,000 acre-feet is based on the average discharge of the Gila River during a mean 9-year cycle and not on the least low-water cycle, and is open to the objection that during the latter cycle and including the flow from the San Pedro the reservoir would have been emptied during a period of 15 months. This could have been reduced to a period of four months through the storage of the water now diverted to supply the 26,633 acres of land irrigated in the Solomonville-Safford Valley above the proposed reservoir. In defense of this draft it may be stated that it could have been maintained during the remaining period of the 21 years over which the records extend, and being based on the mean discharge makes the greatest economic use of the run-off of the watershed.

The operation of the Salt River project is also based on a mean discharge, and is subject to the same criticism as the proposed San Carlos project, under the minimum reclamation charge plan. The water rights in the Salt River that existed before the building of the Roosevelt reservoir have been adjudicated and these rights become active during periods of extreme low water. Adjudication has not been accomplished along the lower Gila, and if the rights were purchased as suggested they would be extinguished.

It is possible that the situation could be relieved by reduced use of water when a low stage of the reservoir indicates that an extreme dry period is approaching, and the supply could be further increased by drawing on underground sources.

A reservoir of greater capacity than that sufficient to furnish an annual draft of 300,000 acre-feet, aside from the increased cost, is not advisable; for to be effective it would have to provide a hold-over storage for a period of 18 years or longer. During this long period of time its advantage would be largely nullified by additional evaporation losses.

It seems to be the consensus of opinion that between 3 and 4 acre-feet of water per annum is required for successful irrigation under the condition obtaining along the Gila. Undoubtedly by the employment of the so-called intensive method of farming a higher duty could be obtained, and it is known that a crop of grain can be produced with one and one-half acre-feet. But it is assumed that irrigation will be carried on under the proposed project by the average farmer and Indian, who will practice diversified farming with only a moderate degree of efficiency.

Under these conditions, to assure success with a high reclamation charge, it will be necessary to supply water continuously during the irrigation season, and it would not be safe to assume the duty of water higher than 3 acre-feet per annum, applied to the land. This is borne out by the amount of approximately 3.3 acre-feet applied to the land assigned to the neighboring Salt River project.

On the proposed San Carlos project the minimum reclamation charge is $82.42 per acre, including the purchase of water rights. This divided into 20 payments without interest amounts to an annual charge of $4.12 per acre. The operation and maintenance charge is estimated to be $1.50 per acre per annum, while the desilting charge, in accordance with the estimate per cubic yard proposed by the United States Army Board, will amount to $4 per acre. To maintain the reservoir at its maximum of efficiency, desilting will be required before 20 years have elapsed. Including operation, maintenance, and desilting charges, the annual cost would amount to $9.62 per acre. Exclusive of the desilting cost, the charges would amount to $5.62 per acre per annum.

The water rights now appurtenant to the land under irrigation near Florence and on the Gila River Indian Reservation must be taken care of in some way.

If owners will subscribe to the project the lands to which their rights are attached, upon the basis that similar lands came into the Salt River project, these lands will have a preferred right during periods of low water. If they will not subscribe, their water rights will either have to be purchased, in which case it is assumed that they would be merged in the general water supply for the project, or else they will have to be supplied from water left in the river for that purpose. In the latter case the acreage under the project will have to be reduced to correspond with the more limited water supply.

It is estimated that the purchase of these water rights will not increase the per acre cost of the project and that the advantages to be gained thereby make a purchase altogether the best solution of the problem.

In addition to the above, claims of rights to water may be made on account of lands that have been irrigated at one time, but which are no longer under cultivation, and also on account of new projects that have not reached the point of actual use of water. The extinguishment of any existing rights of this character may slightly increase the reclamation charge per acre.

In the foregoing estimates, as indeed so far throughout this report, no account has been taken of the water rights appertaining to the reservation as having been reserved to the United States by the recognition of the Indian title of occupancy and possession and the creation of the reservation, in so far as such rights exceed the water rights already used. This is because the policy of the Government in connection with these rights may be to take them into consideration only in fixing the sum that the Indians are to pay the Government for their share of the benefits of the project, and also because the Government has plenary power in the matter, so that, unlike rights outstanding on others, these rights can not be a source of difficulty.

To be a success the reclamation charge per acre on an irrigation project and the annual operation and maintenance expense should have such a relation to the value of the crops produced as will permit the average irrigator a fair return on his labor and money invested, under average-crop market conditions. Otherwise the dissatisfied rancher will eventually seek more profitable employment elsewhere and the land remain idle. The operation and maintenance charges remaining practically the same will fall more heavily on the remaining farmers, who in turn will be compelled to abandon the land and the project, and, if in corporate ownership, it will finally be forced into the hands of a receiver. This is the history of many irrigation projects when the charges have been too high, and it partly explains the failure of the organization previously formed to irrigate the lands in the vicinity of Florence by means of flood water.

The San Carlos project, having its foundation in the need of the Government to provide a means whereby the Indians can reach and maintain a standard of living consistent with the civilized state that they are inevitably coming to, is not a reclamation project pure and simple. In a reclamation project the question of practicability can be answered by determining whether or not the land, after the project is constructed, will yield enough more in dollars and cents to pay for the cost of construction and maintenance.

That is not wholly true here, however; if this question can be answered it will help to answer the broader one of whether the project is practicable and ought to be carried out, bearing in mind the needs of the Indians and the Government's obligation to them.

If the project is practicable as a reclamation project only, it certainly is practicable as a joint reclamation and Indian project. If it is not wholly practicable as a reclamation project alone it still may be practicable and advisable as a joint Indian and reclamation project, and whether it is so or not will depend somewhat at least upon how nearly advisable it would be to undertake to carry out the project if it had to stand upon its economic practicability as a simple reclamation project for white men.

Looked at on this basis, the broad question is, Will the cost of the proposed irrigation pay, will the lands produce enough more when irrigated under the project to pay for the cost of construction and the cost of maintenance, and for removal of silt, and all other costs and burdens involved?

To answer this question it must be known what the land is capable of producing if the project is not constructed, or, in other words, its true value under present conditions; the cost of the project, and the true value of the land after the project shall have been completed.

The cost of the construction of the project as well as the cost of maintenance can be calculated fairly readily, but the other elements are not so easy to estimate accurately.

The raw land that would be taken into the project has now a present-use value that is only nominal. It is worth for grazing or for the wood that is on it from $2 to $10 per acre. It also has a present market value in excess of its value based upon its present productiveness, due to the possibility of its being irrigated as a part of the San Carlos project or irrigated from the Gila River by direct flow without storage or irrigated by wells. This value is speculative and difficult to estimate accurately.

The true value of the land after the completion of the project is also hard to estimate accurately. It is fair to assume that the conditions and values would be not greatly unlike those that now prevail on the Salt River project. Their market values seem to have a wide range, and the true value or real worth of the land as based upon the value of what it can now be made to produce is hard to arrive at.

This is a question upon which, even in ordinary times, there is bound to be a great diversity of competent opinion. Under present circumstances, which include the uncertainties of all future values until the effects of the war are more fully developed, it is thought that the margin of safety that ought to be assumed would be so great as to turn the balance against the project.

With this view—that is, taking into consideration the impossibility of knowing that the land when fully reclaimed would be worth more than a sum that it could now be said with confidence was conservative, it is thought that that part of the project involving the construction of the reservoir ought to be deferred.

If the San Carlos Reservoir is not constructed in the immediate future some other means must be found to supply water for the irrigation of the lands belonging to the Pima Indians on the Gila River Indian Reservation.

The facts herein recited show that their rights in the waters of the Gila River antedate and it is believed are superior, legally and morally, to any and all of the rights of the whites.

While a strict insistence upon these rights as against those who may be now unlawfully interfering with them and the prevention of future encroachments would doubtless relieve the situation somewhat and prevent it from becoming worse, the prime need is a storage and adequate diversion facilities, and these can only be had by the building of somewhat expensive dams.

Assuming that the storage features must be deferred for the present the general end sought can in a measure be obtained by building simply the lower or both diversion dams contemplated as a part of the more extensive project that has been discussed. Under this plan, however, only one crop irrigation can be safely practiced, except on lands with the earlier priorities or on lands where pumping is economically practicable.

It is apparent from the present data that 190,000 acre-feet of water are available at the reservation or at Florence during the months of October to June, inclusive of a mean low-water year. During the same months of a mean high-water year 400,000 acre-feet are available. These figures are taken from average conditions and it is evident that during periods of protracted drought the supply would be greatly reduced. The one-crop irrigation in this case probably would be confined to the grains and it is assumed that a water supply of 1½ acre-feet per acre would be sufficient.

Accordingly with adequate diversion facilities and under average conditions flood water could be supplied on a one-crop basis to even a greater area than the maximum advocated for the completed San Carlos project; but with a view to the eventual construction of the reservoir it would be wise to limit the area to 80,000 acres.

With the lower dam alone flood water for irrigation on the reservation could be had by constructing the dam at a cost of $173,599 and extending the existing distributing system at a cost of $233,911. The existing system has already cost $131,280, so the total for the project would be $538,790, and this distributed over 35,000 acres of Indian lands would give a per-acre reclamation charge of $15.39. The diversion dam alone with just the necessary connecting ditch to the Little Gila would cost $181,200 and this sum distributed over the 35,000 acres would amount to $5.18 per acre. Such a project would be purely Indian, and would be wholly embraced within the reservation.

Under the plan involving the construction of two diversion dams, the one above Florence and the other on the reservation, the necessary distribution systems would not differ materially from that required by the proposed storage project, as the canals under that project were designed to accommodate the greatest practicable draft. in order to provide for the use of flood water entering below the San Carlos Reservation. The estimated construction cost of the diversion dams and distributing system, based on a project of 80,000 acres and lined main canals. amounts to $2,009,299. This places the reclamation charge at $25.11 per acre.

The cost of the diversion dams and main canal, without distributors, is estimated to be $1,361,177. This distributed over the 80,000 acres would amount to $17.01; or confined to the 21,919 acres now irrigated, the cost would be $62.10 per acre.

The larger project, calling for the construction of both diversion dams, would have the following advantages:

1. It is assumed that a cement-lined canal from the upper dam to the head of the present canal systems on the reservation would be built, and in that way the loss due to carrying the water in the sandy bed of the river between the upper dam and these canals during periods of low water would be largely prevented and therefore the Indians would get longer flows of irrigation water and also the irrigation of more land would be made possible.

2. There would be less difficulty in enforcing the Indians' priority during times of low water.

3. Land within the reservation lying above the lower dam, a part of which are now irrigated, could be served with flood water.

4. A large body of land outside of the reservation in the Florence-Casa Grande district could be brought under cultivation.

5. The lands now irrigated both on the reservation and around Florence would be given permanent and adequate diversion facilities which at present they lack.

RECOMMENDATIONS.

It is recommended that—

1. That part of the San Carlos project involving the construction of the San Carlos dam and reservoir be deferred.

2. The two diversion dams across the Gila River described in this report, one above Florence and the second above Sacaton, with the necessary feeder canals, be constructed in the immediate future.

3. The title to the San Carlos reservoir site and as far as practicable the title to the other reservoir sites along the Gila and its tributaires be retained by the United States.

4. The investigations to determine the effect of the irrigation in the Duncan and Solomonville Valleys upon the flow of the Gila at and near the Gila River Reservation be continued. This is important to enable the Government to properly protect the water rights of the reservation and those of the project here recommended.

5. To provide for the construction of the diversion dams and main canals, $1,361,177 be appropriated to remain available until the completion of the work.

Respectfully submitted.

C. R. OLBERG,
Superintendent of Irrigation.

DECEMBER 1, 1915.

Respectfully forwarded to the Commissioner of Indian Affairs. This the latest and most comprehensive report ever submitted on this subject.

It will be of great use in discussing this matter in the future and will be the groundwork for any adjudication of the water rights on the river system and will be of great assistance in protecting the rights of the Indians.

W. M. REED,
Chief Engineer.

THE HISTORY OF IRRIGATION ALONG THE GILA RIVER

BY

C. H. SOUTHWORTH

United States Indian Irrigation Service

CONTENTS.

HISTORY OF IRRIGATION ON THE GILA RIVER.

There is presented herewith, as Appendix A, a history of the irrigation under individual canals and other pertinent data regarding irrigation along the Gila River.

In the progress of the surveys and investigations in connection with this report, there has been assembled a large amount of valuable information, which accompanies the report in the form of exhibits constituting statements from landowners and Indians, copies of adjudication decrees, transcripts of evidence, abstracts of records, and various other compilations. While it is obviously impracticable to include these data in their entirety, the report and this appendix contain a résumé of all the information assembled.

On page 294 will be found a list of the exhibits which accompany this report.

In the following history the various districts will be discussed in the order of their relative priority, commencing with the Gila River Indian Reservation, the oldest irrigated district.

Gila River Indian Reservation (District No. 4).

The Gila River Reservation, like many other portions of the Southwest, has been inhabited from prehistoric times. Since the advent of the earliest white explorers, this ancient land of the Pueblos has attracted the attention of numerous travelers, scientists, and adventurers. In nearly every work that has been published concerning the history or the archæology of this territory, mention is made, at greater or lesser length, of the Pima Indians and their rancherias, or irrigated farms.

To review these various works, or to attempt to treat in detail the subject of irrigation by these Indians, would, in itself, require no small volume, and would, of course, be beyond the scope or the purpose of this report. Sufficient reference, however, will be given, in addition to a brief historical sketch of the region in general, to prove beyond question the early and prior appropriations of the waters of the Gila River by the Pima Indians.

Historical Sketch.

Well-defined evidences of prehistoric irrigation on the Gila River Reservation are to be found in a number of localities. The well known Casa Grande ruins, and the ancient canals thereby, are situated just beyond the eastern limits of the reservation, while within the boundaries of the reservation are found the lesser ruins of Casa Blanca, of Sweetwater, and of Snaketown.

That the inhabitants of these ancient ruins were agriculturists and appropriators of water for irrigation there can be no doubt. Some difference of opinion arises, however, as to the ancestral relationship between the present-day Pimas and these ancient races.

Mr. F. W. Fekes,[1] of the American Bureau of Ethnology, who made an extensive investigation of these old ruins and who appears to be a recognized authority on this subject, concludes that these ancient dwellers were the forbears of the present Pima Indians, and writes:

> In ancient times the whole drainage of the Gila and its tributaries from points where they leave the mountains as far west as Gila Bend was inhabited by an agricultural people in a homogeneous stage of culture. Throughout this region existed various divisions of a common stock. The Pima name Hohoken may be adopted to designate this ancestral stock to whom may be ascribed the erection of the Casas Grandes on the Gila. In the course of time a hostile portion bent on pillage came into this section from the East or West and drove the agriculturists out of their Casas Grandes or at least broke up the custom of building such structures. But although dispersed, the ancient householders were not exterminated. Some of them became refugees and migrated south into Mexico; some followed the course of the Verde and the Tonto into the northern mountains, but others, perhaps the majority, lost their former culture but still remained in the Gila Valley, becoming ancestors of the present Pimas, Papagoes, and Kwahadts. Those who went northward later built pueblos in the Little Colorado Valley. Their descendants later joined the Zuni and Hopi. That the earliest inhabitants were agriculturists is without question, and from their canal systems they were essentially agricultural, cultivating fields of even possibly beans, squashes, and the like. They raised cotton and utilized the fibers of agave and other plants in weaving.

Other authors take the view that the early dwellers were of a different race entirely, and that the Pimas, as many of their traditions[2] would indicate, came at a later time and either drove out the early inhabitants or simply occupied the country that the former race had abandoned.

Our earliest historical accounts of the Pimas and the territory in which they have lived for many past centuries are gathered from the old reports and narratives of the Spanish missionaries who ventured into this country as early as 1539.

Of the early explorers in Pimeria[3] Fray Marcas de Niza, chief of the Franciscan band of explorers, is credited[4] with having been

---

[1] Twenty-eighth Annual Report of the Bureau of Ethnology, pp. 153–156.

[2] "There is a strong belief among the Pimas that they came from the East. It is in that quarter that the abode of their dead is located. Their gods dwell there." (Russell: The Pima Indians; 26th Annual Report of the Bureau of American Ethnology.)

"Now, according to these traditions, it was the tribes now known as Pimas, Papagoes, Yumas, and Maricopas that invaded the land from some mystic underworld and overthrew the Vakahkkas and killed their inhabitants, and this is the most interesting part of these tales from a historic point of view. Fewkes and other ethnologists think the ancestors of the Pimas built the Casa Grande and other vakahk-kas, but I doubt this." (Aw-aw-tum Indian Nights: The Myths and Legends of the Pimas, by Wm. Lloyd, p. 912.)

[3] "The most northern part of the intendancy of Sonora bears the name of Pimeria on account of a numerous tribe of Pima Indians who inhabit it." (Humboldt's Political Essay of the Kingdom of New Spain. Translations from the original French by John Block, Vol. II, p. 298. Published in 1811.)

[4] Bancroft's History of Arizona, 1530–1888, p. 30.

NOTE.—Bancroft takes the position that Alvar Nurvaez, sole survivor of the Nurvaez expedition of 1528, and who brought back the wonderful tales of the seven cities of Cibola, which, by the way, were the goal of Fray Marcas, never entered Arizona, but that his route lay farther east. There seems also to be some question as to whether the Niza expedition was the first to enter the Gila Valley. Fray Juan de la Asumpcion is reputed to have entered in 1538, a year ahead of the Fray Marcas Band. See commentary on Juan de Asumpcion in On the Trail of a Spanish Pioneer, p. 505.

the first Spaniard to cross into what is now Arizona[1], or to be less specific, into the territory of the Pimas. His narrative[2] states that the route lay for five days through a fertile and irrigated valley, and Bancroft[3] states that this may reasonably be regarded as the Gila Valley in the vicinity of the Pima village. Fray Marcos described a ruin which is believed to be the well-known Casa Grande[4] and which afterwards became more definitely known through the explorations of the Jesuit Father Ensibo Francisco Kino, in 1864. During the century and a half which elapsed between the Niza expedition and other expeditions of the early sixteenth century and the visit of Kino, not much was written concerning this territory.

Near the close of the seventeenth century and during the period of 20 years which followed, Kino and his followers carried on numerous exploratory expeditions in the territory then known as "Pimeria Alta." In connection with Kino's visits, we know that on numerous occasions he visited the rancherias of the Pimas, baptized many of the inhabitants, and named two of the more important villages.[5]

Capt. Mange, with the military escort who accompanied Kino on many of his voyages, wrote a rather extensive diary of these trips, and while many rancherias of the Pimas are mentioned in these diaries, very little definite or detailed information is given.[6]

According to Fewkes,[7] this territory, subsequent to the time of Kino's espedition, was visited by the Jesuit Father Ignacio Kelley and Jacob Sidelmair in 1736–37. These missionaries left no record of their travels, and some uncertainty exists as to the route which they followed. About 1762 the missionary who wrote the anonymous Rudo Ensayo[8] entered this country. In his narrative he states that:

> Between these Casa Grandes the Pimas, called Gilenos, inhabit both banks of the Gila, occupying rancherias for 10 leagues farther down, which, as well as some islands, are fruitful and suitable for wheat, Indian corn, etc. So much cotton is raised, and so wanting in covetousness is the husbandman that after each crop is gathered in more remains in the fields than is to be had for a harvest here in Sonora.

---

[1] "There is reason to believe the name Arizona is of Pima origin and composed of two Pima words: Ari, meaning a maiden, and Zon, a valley, and having reference to the traditionary queen who once ruled all the Pimas." (Hamilton"s Resources of Arizona, p. 21.)

[2] Describremento de los Siete Cendadles in Pachico, Doc. III, p. 325–351.

[3] Bancroft's "History of Arizona and New Mexico," p. 391.

[4] Hinton, in his Handbook of Arizona, p. 406, cites that both the Niza and the Coronado expeditions may have followed the San Pedro to Benson, then passing through the present Dragoon Pass, they reached the Gila approximately at Solomonville, in which vicinity was the Chichilticalli, erroneously thought by Niza to be the present Casa Grande ruin.

Bandelier, who is probably the best authority on this subject (Archaeological Institute of America, vol. 5, pp. 93–106), gives considerable evidence to show that Fray Marcos's route lay farther to the east through the present White Mountain Reservation, and that the rancherias mentioned were on the San Pedro

[5] "Por Noviembre del mismo ano mil seisciento noventa y quatro emprendio nuevo viaje el parde Kino y penetro hasta el Rio Gila que dista como cuarenta y tres leguas del San Xavier del Bac, rumbo entre Porrienti y Norte. A la primera rancheria que encontro compuesto de gente Pima, le puso el nombre de Encarnacion y a la de otra cuatro leguas mas adelante el de San Andres. Estos puestos eataban poblados de gente afable y docil." (Historia del Nayarit, by El Parade Jose Ortega.)

[6] See page 357, Bancroft's History of Arizona and New Mexico, 1630–1888.

[7] 28th Annual Report Bureau of Ethnology, p. 928.

[8] Rudo Ensayo is a tract written by a Jesuit priest, name unknown, translated into English by Esebia Guiteras in 1863, and in this form published by American Catholic Historical Society in 1894, Vol. V, No. 2, pp. 109–264.

Among other missionaries who penetrated this region during the century following the visits of Kino, Padre Frances Garces,[1] who was stationed at San Xavier del Bac[2] and who made five trips into the Pima country in 1768–1776, gives some early accounts of the irrigation of the Pimas. Of Garces's first entrada in August, 1768, he writes that he traveled about 80 leagues west, north, and southwest from San Xavier among the Papago rancherias, including a very large one on the Gila River.[3]

On his second entrada he reached the Gila during October, 1770.[4]

Garces made three other entradas before 1776. On his last trip in 1775 he was accompanied by Padre Font, who wrote a detailed diary of the journey. The latter refers more specifically to the early irrigation of the Pimas than do most early writers, and in this connection may be quoted the following:

These milpas are inclosed by stakes, cultivated in sections, with five canals or draws, and are excessively clean. They are close by the town on the banks of the river, which is large only in the season of the freshets. At that time its water was so low that an Indian who entered and crossed it had the water but halfway up his leg. From what they have told me, this is the reason they had not yet made their sowing, for inasmuch as the river was too low the water could not enter the canals. They also told me that to remedy this need they were all anxious to come together for a council and had already thought of sinking many stakes and branches into the river to raise the water so that it might enter the drains; this industry on their part is a proof of their devotion to toil and shows that they are not restless and nomad like other races, for to maintain themselves in their towns with their fields they themselves have contrived to hold and control the river.[5]

Garces himself wrote less specifically about the agricultural development of the Pimas. However, he states that—

In all these pueblos they raise large crops of wheat, some of corn, cotton, calabashes, etc., to which end they have constructed good acequias.[6]

After the expulsion of the Jesuits in 1776 the missions suffered a gradual decline, and prior to the treaty of Guadalupe Hidalgo[7] in 1848, which ceded to the United States that portion of this territory north of the Gila, the Mexicans maintained a precarious possession of this section of their country.

Early in the nineteenth century the American beaver trapper began to pentrate this territory. If one may judge from the few

---

[1] On the Tral of a Spanish Pioneer, or the diary and itinerary of Francisco Garces, who was resident minister at San Xavier del Bac; translation by Elliot Coues, p. 926.

[2] Of San Xavier del Bac, the same author, p. 975, writes: "Bac was a rancheria of the Sobaipuri, a Pima tribe closely related to the Papagoes on the Rio Santa Cruz, 9 miles south of Tucson in the northeast corner of the Papago Reservation. This rancheria in Bac was certainly visited by Kino in 1697, and probably as early as 1692. The church of San Xavier (still standing) was begun in 1699. In 1751 (during the revolt which continued at intervals until late in 1753) it was plundered by the natives and abandoned, but was reoccupied two years later as a mission under the protection of the Tubac Presidio. Little is known of its history from Garces's time until 1828, when it was again practically abandoned as a mission."

[3] The name Gila first appeared in a report of 1630, being applied to a New Mexican province of Gila or Xila, where the river had its source. (Bancroft's History of Arizona and New Mexico, p. 164.) The Gila was previously known as the Rio del Nombre de Jesus, having been so named by Onate in 1604–5. (On the Trail of a Spanish Pioneer, vol. 2, p. 541.)

[4] Garces's Diary, p. 927: "October 20. Here natives of Pitac received him joyfully. Here he baptized 22 and was almost detained by force, but managed to break away and went on down the river (Gila), where there were good crops and many rancherias."

[5] Translation from the original manuscript, pp. 48–52; Russell, in 28th Annual Report, Bureau of Ethnology, p. 29.

[6] On the Trail of a Spanish Pioneer, p. 107, by Coues. Diary of Francisco Garces; date, Nov. 2, 1775.

[7] The Mexican War, beginning in 1846 and ending with the treaty of Guadalupe Hidalgo in 1848, gave to the United States all that territory north of the Gila and the Rio Grande. Through the Gadsden Purchase in 1854 the present area of the United States lying south of the Gila was acquired.

accounts that have been written by these explorers, beaver must have been very plentiful along the Gila and other streams of Pimeria Alta,[1] and if these statements are considered to be reliable, it is safe to assume that these streams rarely, if ever, became dry at that time.

Only a few of the early trappers left any written accounts of their voyages or observations, and each narrative they did write dealt chiefly with their various adventures and the profits incident to their occupation; very little space having been devoted to descriptions of the country through which they traveled.

More reliable and definite knowledge came with the era of American ownership and military occupation during the early forties. Gen. Kearney's troops passed through this section in 1846, and the report of a military reconnoissance by Lieut. Col. Emory, an attaché to Kearney's command, presents a very good description of the early irrigation of the Pimas.

Writing under the date of November 11, 1846, he states:

> The camp of my party was pitched on the side nearest town, and we saw the first of these people (the Pimas). They were perfectly frank and unsuspicious. Many would leave their packs in our camps for hours; theft seemed to be unknown among them. We were at once impressed with the beauty and order and disposition of the arrangements for irrigating and draining the land. To us it was a rare sight to be thrown in the midst of a large nation of what are termed wild Indians, surpassing many of the Christian nations in agriculture, little behind them in the arts, and immeasurably before them in honesty and virtue. On November 12 we traveled fifteen and a half miles and encamped on the dividing ground between the Pimas and Maricopas. For the whole distance we passed through cultivated grounds over a luxuriantly rich soil. The bed of the Gila opposite the village is said to be dry, the whole water being drawn off by the acquias of the Pimas for irrigation, but the ditches are larger than are necessary for this purpose, and the water which is not used returns to the bed of the river with little apparent diminution of its volume. (Report of a military reconnoissance made in 1846–47, by Lieut. Col. W. H. Emory; Mississippi to Pacific Ocean Survey Report, Ex. Doc. No. 78, 33 Cong., 2d sess.)

A still more detailed report and undoubtedly the best of the early writing concerning the Pimas and their irrigation is given by J. R. Bartlett, the American commissioner of the Mexican Boundary Survey, who passed down the Gila in 1852. Extracts from his diary of this trip are quoted.[2]

> The dryness of the river was produced by the water having been turned off by the Indians to irrigate their lands, for which the whole stream seemed barely sufficient. It is probable, however, that, with more economical management, it might be made to go much further.
>
> The valley or bottom land occupied by the Pimos and Coco-Maricopas extends about 15 miles along the south side of the Gila and is from 2 to 4 miles in width, nearly the whole being occupied by their villages and cultivated fields. The Pimos occupy the eastern portion. There is no dividing line between them, nor anything to distinguish the villages of one from the other. The whole of this plain is intersected by irrigating canals from the Gila, by which they are enabled to control the waters, and raise the most

---

[1] On the 29th we made our last encampment on this river (Gila). We set our traps for the last time and caught a beaver in each. On March 3 we trapped along down a small stream that empties into the Helay on the south side, having its bend in a southwestern direction. It being very remarkable for the number of its beaver, we gave it the name of Beaver River. At this place we collected 200 skins, etc. (P. 99, Personal Narratives of Pattie.)

[2] Personal Narrative of Explorations and Incidents in Texas, New Mexico, California, Sonora, and Chihuahua; connected with the United States and Mexican Boundary Commission, during the years 1850, 1851, 1852, and 1853, by John Russell Bartlett, United States commissioner during the period, Vol. II.

luxuriant crops. At the western end of the valley is a rich tract of grass, where we had our encampment. This is a mile or more from the nearest village of the Coco-Maricopas. On the northern side of the river there is less bottom land, and the irrigation is more difficult. There are a few cultivated spots here; but it is too much exposed to the attacks of their enemies for either tribe to reside upon it.

The villages consist of groups of from 20 to 50 habitations, surrounded by gardens and cultivated fields, intersected in every direction by acequias, which lead the water from the Gila. Their mode of irrigation is the same as that practiced in various parts of Mexico. Their cultivated fields are generally fenced with crooked stakes, wattled with brush, the thorny mesquit predominating; although I noticed large patches of wheat, a long distance from any village, that were not inclosed.

They plow but little, finding their hoes quite sufficient for turning up the light soil. When plowing is resorted to, oxen alone are used. They possess a few carts and wagons, obtained from emigrants, which they use with oxen for agricultural purposes.

I have not cited the agriculture of these tribes as superior to that of all other Indians; although I may be safe in saying that the system is more extensively and methodically practiced than elsewhere. The Yumas and other tribes on the Colorado, irrigate their lands and raise wheat, corn, melons, etc. The Moquis and the Navajos, far to the north, do the same; and the warlike Apaches, who are more nomadic in their habits than any tribe west of the Rocky Mountains, raise corn when driven to extremities. But the Pimos and Coco-Maricopas have made agriculture more of a system. Their lands are better irrigated, their crops are larger, and the flour which they make from their wheat and maize is quite as good as the Mexicans make, except in their gristmills.

Alegro, in recounting the arduous labors of Father Kino, relates other particulars of the Pimos and Coco-Maricopas, and the interviews between them and this zealous missionary. Kino found, in 1698, the most friendly relations existing between them, and noticed the difference in their languages and dress. But their manners and customs were the same; and the worthy Father particularly noticed "their peacefulness and their gentleness * * *." They then irrigated their lands as now, and had large cultivated fields of wheat.

In an anonymous manuscript of a Jesuit, dated 1764 (the Rudo Ensayo, C. H. S.), descriptive of Sonora, the writer speaks of the Pimos who were on the precise spot where we now find them inhabiting both margins of the Gila. The towns of that people, he says, which occupy 10 leagues of the mild vale along it, with some islands, abound in wheat, maize, etc., and yield much cotton.

July 8. At noon, having journeyed about 12 miles through these villages and cultivated fields, we reached a spot near an acequia, where there was grass and a pleasant grove of mesquit trees. Here we pitched our tent, intending to remain a few days.

* * * * * * *

There are not tribes of Indians on the continent of North America more deserving of the attention of the philanthropist than those of which I am speaking. None have ever been found further advanced in the arts and habits of civilized life. None exhibit a more peaceful disposition, or greater simplicity of character; and certainly none excel them in virtue and honesty. They are quite as industrious as their necessities require them to be. Possessing no market for the sale of their produce, they raise but little more than is necessary to supply their wants. To do this with a soil of great fertility and water at their command requires but little labor. Hence, after crops are in, they have nothing to do until the season arrives to gather them. Their granaries are then filled with wheat, corn, beans, pumpkins, squashes, and mesquit beans.

* * * * * * *

The earliest account of this building is that of Mangi, who, in company with Father Kino, visited it in the year 1694, on which he said mass in it (reference to Casa Grande Ruins, C. H. S.), and it was of one government as shown by a main canal, which comes from the river by the plain, running around for the distance of three leagues, and inclosing the inhabitants in its area, being in breadth 10 caras—about 27 feet—and about 4 in depth, through which perhaps was directed one-half the volume of the river, in such a manner that it might serve for a defensive moat, as well as to supply the wards with water and irrigate the plantations in the adjacencies.

The military occupation, together with the rush of the gold seekers to California in the early fifties, marked the coming of the whites in increasing numbers. These people were for the most part travelers or adventurers, but while they thoroughly explored this general territory, not many remained or settled in the country.

The overland stage route from El Paso via Tucson to the Pacific coast passed through the Pima villages on the Gila River Reservation. Both Sacaton and Maricopa wells became important stage stations. The choice of this route was due both to the abundance of agricultural products[1] and to the protection[2] offered by the Pimas.

Official governmental recognition of the Pimas was taken in the late fifties, and of the reports of men sent out to investigate their conditions and their needs, we quote from that of G. Bailey, special agent, Indian Department,[3] written in 1858.

> Their pueblos (Pimas) extend along this stream (the Gila) some 15 miles, and some of them at a distance from the river proper of more than 5 miles, these being supplied with water by acequias. This valley occupied by the Pimas and Maricopas is to a great extent cultivated, and I have never seen richer soil or more beautiful fields. The acequias of crystal water running from pueblo to pueblo all over the valley makes it present an appearance of beauty and civilization that is truly pleasing. The principal products of their labors are corn, wheat, pumpkins, beans, peas, melons, etc. They are a barrier between the Apaches and all western Arizona, and while their present relations continue, travel between Fort Yuma and the Maricopa wells will be as safe as in settlements.

Chapman, in a census for 1858, gives the numbers of Pimas as 4117 and Maricopas 518.

In 1859, an appropriation[4] of $10,000 was made for gifts and an additional $1,000 for a survey of their lands. As a result of this survey, 64,000 acres of the present reservation was set aside by Executive order in 1859. Subsequent additions and some withdrawals have been made from time to time until at present the reservation embraces about 369,000 acres.

The first resident agent[5] on the Gila River Reservation was Ammi M. White, appointed in 1864. White was also a trader and had a store and mill at Casa Blanca. He was the first white man to reside among the Pimas.[6] The first school among the Pimas was opened in 1871 by

---

[1] In a footnote of Russell, 26th Annual Report, Bureau of Ethnology, quoting from J. R. Brown's Adventures in the Apache Country, the following is taken: "In 1858, the first year of the overland mail, the surplus of wheat was 100,000 pounds. Also large crop of beans, pumpkins, melons, etc., all sold to the stage company. In 1860 they sold 400,000 pounds of wheat, all the mail company could purchase. In 1862 they sold to the Government over 100,000 pounds of wheat."

[2] "The Pimas have always been friends of the whites and the enemy of the Apache. They gave succor and assistance to the early settlers and their door was always open to the unfortunate American hard pressed by the savage. They are a peculiar race, and for centuries have lived and labored and passed away in their quiet valley under the shadows of the Sierra de Estrella. Empires have been founded and overturned, wonderful discoveries have been made, the earth has undergone vast changes, but nothing has disturbed the peaceful serenity of the Pima's life. Shut out from the busy world, he is to-day as he was ages ago." (From Patrick Hamilton's The Resources of Arizona printed in 1884, p. 296.)

[3] That part of Bailey's report concerning the Pimas is taken from a report of Lieut. Chapman, S. Ex. Doc. 1, pt. 1, p. 555, 35th Cong., 2nd session.

[4] Act of Congress, Feb. 28, 1859.

[5] Several Indian agents for the whole territory acquired by the Gadsden Purchase had been appointed previous to this time, but they had headquarters in Tucson: John Walker first in 1857; Abraham Lyons in 1862; and Ruggles in 1866.

[6] The first agency buildings were constructed at Sacaton in 1870.

about 10 miles in either direction. The copy of a sketch made by George Pablo,[1] an old Indian resident of the reservation, which is here given is intended to represent the ditches and the irrigated areas as he remembers them, just prior to the coming of the whites. This map appears to agree very well with the records of early explorers and with the statement of other old Indians.

The earliest accounts of the Spaniards, as well as the traditions of the Indians, would point to the conclusion that the Pimas in the early days of the Spanish exploration were distributed over a much larger territory, but that at a later period the Apaches, or perhaps Mexican slave hunters, caused them to confine their activities and their habitations within a comparatively small area. The confined area referred to is represented in the sketch given by Pablo. The location of the old Indian villages, Equitune, Uturitic, San Andres, and Sudacson, mentioned by Padre Garces and named by Kino, is largely a matter of conjecture, but it is thought that at least two of these were located in the area just described.[2]

A complete census of the Pimas was made in 1858 by Lieut. Chapman. This census, covering nine Pima villages and two Maricopa villages, gives a population of 4,117 Pimas and 518 Maricopas. According to the report of the Commissioner of Indian Affairs for January 30, 1914, there were 3,796 Pimas and 300 Maricopas on the reservation.

According to the Pimas, the decrease in their water supply caused the Indians to extend their villages, to leave many of their old fields, and to establish themselves in approximately the same location, where they are to be found at present. The treaty with the Apaches in 1872 also contributed in an important degree to this movement.[3]

EFFECT OF UPPER DIVERSIONS ON WATER SUPPLY OF THE PIMAS.

A review of the statements given by the Indians and printed in volume 1 of the supplemental exhibits accompanying this report is convincing evidence of the disastrous effects of the upper diversions on the water supply of the Pimas. George Pablo (p. 30) compares the condition of the present-day Pimas with that of the Papagoes, and says:

The Gila River is a river which, in the past, supplied us through our various canals with enough water for the irrigation of our lands, but since that water has been taken by the whites and Mexicans above us, I say we are like the Papagoes out on the desert, because the steady flow has gradually ceased.

Juan Manuel (p. 30) says that "white people began to take water from the river about 40 years ago. The first diversion being so small we hardly noticed

---

[1] See statement in vol. 1, p. 29, supplemental exhibits.

[2] In the Rudo Ensayo, written in 1762 (English translation 1894, p. 129), mention is made of two important Pima rancherias on opposite sides of the river, one called Tusonimo and "the other Sudacson, or the Incarnation, where the principal of their chiefs called Tavanimo lived." "Besides these, a third, further down, Santa Theresa (sic), at a copious spring of water. I do not think that Tusonimo can be exactly located now, especially as the different itineraries of this trip give the distance from the last place as either 2 or 4 leagues. But we can not be much out of the way if we set Sudacson on the Gila not far from the place now called Sweetwater, the settlement next below Sacaton." (On the Trail of a Spanish Pioneer, p. 101.)

[3] The treaty which was ratified in 1872 and which was arranged by Gen. Howard resulted in putting the Apaches under military control on the reservation. This treaty was made at the mouth of the San Pedro, and was attenedd by Pimas, Papagoes, Apaches, and by the military authorities. After this treaty, and until 1882, small bands of Apaches from the reservation continued to raid and cause disturbance through this general section of the country. For date of the above treaty, see Report of Commissioner of Indian Affairs, 1872.

it, but they gradually took more out each year till we noticed our loss by not being able to irrigate all our fields. We were forced to vacate them little by little until some 20 years ago, when we were left high and dry."

William Wallace (p. 6) claims "when Florence Canal was construced (1887, C. H. S.) there was no more water left for us in the river to irrigate our fields. We were forced to leave our ditches and fields. Our pride as independent and self-supporting people was forever destroyed."

Miguel (p. 50), of Santan, makes this comment: "We Pimas are poor Pimas now, but in the olden times, while poor in horses and plows, we were rich in harvests."

Juan Lagons (p. 76) was frank enough to state: "I can not refrain from saying that civilization did us more harm than good. We were self-supporting then; had plenty to eat all the year round. When civilization or enlightened people came they robbed us of our water. We were then left without any resources at all."

In the reports of former Indian agents at the reservation, excerpts of which are also printed in the supplemental exhibits, many references are made to the diminishing water supply of the Indians.

In the Annual Report of the Commissioner of Indian Affairs for 1871, J. H. Stout, agent on this reservation, gives a rather interesting side light on the water question. He says in part (p. 59):

People who have lived on the Gila for years tell me there never was before such a thing as a dry bed on this reserve this time of the year. As a matter of course, our Indians are much dissatisfied and blame the settlers who are above us for taking away their water. On Sunday morning last, Chin-Kum, a chief of one of the lower villages, and one of the best chiefs in the reserve, came to me and said that for many years his people "had lived from what they planted," but now they had no water; white men up the river had taken it from them. After telling me of his wrongs he made known the object of his visit, which was to obtain leave to take the warriors of his village, numbering 127, and by force of arms drive the whites from the river.

Kuvit-ke-shin-e-kum, chief of Vavak, called and said he "was going to Salt River with his tribe, as there is no water for his fields, and if the water does not come soon I think they will all leave.

In nearly every report of the various agents the water question is referred to. Probably the first reference to the damages threatening the water supply was given in 1859, in the report of Lieut Mowry, special agent.[1]

From this report the following is quoted:

There are some fine lands on the Gila and any extensive cultivation above the Indian fields will cause trouble about the water for irrigation and inevitably bring about a collision between the settlers and the Indians.

In 1886 Agent Wheeler, of the Gila River Reservation, drew the attention of the Indian Department to the serious effects which would result from the Florence Canal diversion. The action which was taken in this matter and the subsequent efforts to maintain the water rights of the Pima Indians are summarized in the commissioner's annual report of 1904, p. 121. This information can also be found in House Document No. 1506, page 23, Sixty-second Congress, third session.

The San Carlos project, which has been under consideration since 1899, has had for its prime object the provision of an adequate water supply for the Pima Indians. A summary of the many investigations which have been made in connection with this project is given in the report of the Army board of 1914 (H. Doc. No. 791, p. 11). This report represents the most recent investigation of the San Car-

[1] Russel, in 26th Annual Report, Bureau of American Ethnology.

los project and the recommendations contained therein form the basis of the work of the Gila surveys.

HISTORY OF THE GILA RESERVATION CANALS.

The detailed history of the early canals on the reservation must necessarily come from the Indians themselves. With this in mind, many of the older Indians residing in the various districts of the reservation were interviewed.[1]

Whenever possible two or more persons were questioned, independently, in the same subject so as to obtain corroborative evidence.

Indian calendar sticks were also interpreted in order that the different events to which the older Indians referred could be related to our own time or calendar.[2]

FORMERLY USED CANALS OF PREVIOUS CULTIVATION.

The term "previous cultivation" as used in this report, will refer to those tracts of land not being irrigated at the present time, but which show unmistakable evidence of having been irrigated at some past time. This term will likewise include inactive ditches, which were evidently used for irrigation in the past.

Obviously it is impossible to obtain definite or precise information concerning the history of irrigation on the Gila River Reservation during that period of time, which antedates the memory of the oldest inhabitants. Efforts have been made, therefore, to determine the manner and extent of irrigation at a time just prior to the coming of the whites, as well as during the period from that time until the present.

The canals here described are, as a rule, plainly visible on the ground, and are shown on the survey plats of the reservation. The outlines of the previously irrigated areas were traced by the aid of the old borders and ditches. As already stated, these ditches are comparatively modern, most of them having been out of use since the early fifties—that is, subsequent to the advent of the whites, as will be shown later in this report.

The Gila River is particularly a flood or "flash" stream, and as a rule the diversion dams at the heading of the various Indian ditches are washed out during each large flood, consequently the diversion sites or heading are changed often to meet the various new conditions brought about by floods. Frequently old and inactive

---

[1] In the supplemental exhibits accompanying this report will be found statements made by the Indians during the course of these interviews. Three interperters were employed at various times, and although not a few of the men interviewed were able to talk English, a far greater number belonged to an older generation and required the services of an interpreter.

The translations have been made as near verbatim and in keeping with the Indian expressions and idioms as was consistent with at least understandable English.

Louis Nelson, John Enis, and Rudolph Johnson (Pima Indians) were employed as translators, and to these men acknowledgments are due. Especial praise and credit are due Rudolph Johnson for his untiring efforts and keen interest in this work.

[2] These calendar sticks are chronological records kept by a few older men of the tribe. They resemble the ordinary walking cane with numerous markings or characters cut into the wood. Each marking or set of markings represents a yearly period. These indentations served to stimulate the memory of the owner. The Pima year differs from our calendar year, beginning, as it does, at the time of the saguaro harvest. For full description of the calendar sticks see Russell Twenty-sixth Annual Report, Bureau of American Ethnology, p. 36. Interpretations of these calendar sticks are submitted in the supplemental exhibits accompanying this report, vol. 1, p. 91

ditches are found that represent merely the former headings of ditches farther down the valley. Accordingly, in writing a history of the old ditches no account will be taken of these various former headings.

The previously irrigated areas and the canals by which they are supplied will be taken up in the order in which they are found, beginning at the east end of the reservation and proceeding down the river to the west boundary line.

Old Woman's Mouth ditch.—The first ditch[1] at the upper end of the reservation which is now unemployed, but which was formerly in use, is the Old Woman's Mouth, named after its builder.[2]

This ditch was constructed in 1881.[3]

A total of 173 acres was shown to have been irrigated at one time under this ditch. Failure of the water supply was given as the cause of its idleness. Partial disuse of this ditch commenced about 15 years ago, but it has been in use as late as 1904. The flood of 1905 washed out the heading and filled the ditch with silt, resulting in its complete suspension.

Old Woman's Mouth and his coworkers lived in the Blackwater settlement and did their planting and other work from this village. After the failure of their ditch these families still remained in Blackwater district. At least one family still cultivates a few acres under this ditch, but the water is derived from the rains and collected from an adjoining gulch. This ditch, from measurements taken at the time of the survey, had a bottom width of 5 feet, a top width of 8 feet, and a water depth of about 1 foot, the maximum capacity being approximately 20 second-feet. The new Blackwater project already referred to covers practically all of the land previously irrigated by the Old Woman's Mouth ditch.

Cayau ditch.—The Cayau (Woods) ditch was located on the north side of the river opposite the Old Woman's Mouth and had its heading near the section line between secs. 24 and 25, T. 4 S., R. 7 E., G. & S. R. B. & M.

This canal was constructed in 1869[4] by an Indian whose name was Cayau, or Woods. From 1869 until 1880 300 acres were irrigated under this ditch. The scarcity of water in the river and the establishment of the present Santan district, the district where the irrigators formerly under the Cayau ditch now live, are given as the reasons for its inactivity. According to the survey, 235 acres were previously irrigated under the Cayau ditch. This ditch originally had a bottom width of 4 feet, was about 7 feet wide on top, and had a capacity of 15 second-feet.

Within the last five or six years the present North Side Blackwater ditch was extended to the Cayau ditch, and the surplus water of the

---

[1] Another inactive Indian ditch which had a heading somewhat higher up on the river than this Old Woman's Mouth, is designated on the map as the Old Indian (Upper Blackwater) ditch. This ditch was constructed in 1884, but inasmuch as it was never used for irrigation, it has not been treated separately. It appears that this ditch was constructed through land that was afterwards thrown open to the public. The consequent white occupation, in addition to the fact that the ditch was constructed on a very poor grade, probably accounts for its nonuse. The lower end of this ditch was used in connection with the recent Blackwater project, which is discussed elsewhere in this report.

[2] The peculiar name given to this ditch is a nickname applied by the Indians to its original builder or promotor.

[3] See statement, supplemental exhibit, Vol. 1, p. 9.

[4] See statement, vol. 1, p. 9, supplement exhibits accompanying this report.

former was used to irrigate some of the land under the latter. However, very little of the old land has been cultivated as a result of this arrangement, since it appears that the Blackwater ditch is inadequate to supply more than a very small quantity of surplus water. The land under the Cayau ditch, therefore, is now practically idle.

Yaqui Canal.—Next in order from the eastern boundary of the reservation, and diverting from the Little Gila River is the ditch generally known as the Yaqui Canal. While this canal has not yet ceased operations the area irrigated under it at the present time is so limited that it will here be considered under the head of previous irrigation. This canal was constructed in 1891, deriving its name from the Yaqui Indians who worked on the ditch at the time of its construction, and into whose possession it eventually came. This ditch during the dry season derives its water supply from the so-called Blackwater Lake.[1]

This lake is a sort of lagoon or small swamp, and from all accounts the springs by which it is fed yielded much more water in former times than they do at present.

Even the Pimas had their local water trouble, for it appears that the appropriation of the waters of this lake by the Yaqui Canal deprived the previous diverters lower down on the Little Gila of a portion of this flow. The lake, which is situated some three or four hundred feet south of the Little Gila, was connected with that stream by a ditch constructed prior to the Yaqui Canal. The water trouble which ensued as a result of the appropriation of water through the Yaqui Canal was brought to the attention of the agent on the reservation. A decision was rendered in favor of the lower diverters and a new, better, and somewhat larger ditch was built in order that the waters of the lake could more quickly reach the Little Gila. This construction took place in 1902, which date naturally marks the decline of the lands under the Yaqui Canal.

According to the survey, 289 acres over and above the acreage at present under cultivation had previously been cultivated by the use of the Yaqui Canal. It may be stated that this maximum cultivation took place during the period dating from 1890 to 1900. The ditch at present has a top width of 6 feet, bottom width of 3 feet, water depth of 2.5 feet, and a grade of 1 in 1,000. Its capacity is 22 second-feet. When it became necessary to vacate their lands under the Yaqui ditch these Indians took up and cultivated lands under the present Santan Canal. Brief reference will again be made to the Yaqui ditch under the head of "Present irrigation," since it still serves for the irrigation of a limited acreage.

---

[1] Blackwater Lake appears to be simply a natural depression containing several small springs. Several reports are current to the effect that this lake represents an artificial reservoir constructed during some more or less remote period to furnish water to the Little Gila River for irrigation purposes. In this connection it may be stated that while the Little Gila itself is thought to have been built by the Indians or by prehistoric irrigators, yet inquiry among the Indians fails to supply any information supporting the artificial-construction theory regarding the lake. Several of the Indians have pointed out, however, that if this lake had been constructed by any of the early tribes related to them, there would no doubt have remained some tradition in reference to this work. There is a tradition among the Pimas regarding Blackwater Lake, but it is to the effect that it is of fathomless depth, that strange and awesome animals have appeared in it, and that it communicates with the ocean, but no reference is made to its artificial construction. The name Blackwater is derived from this mysterious pool of dark water. For further information, see The Myths and Legends of the Pimas, by J. William Lloyd, p. 241.

Old Santan ditch.—Six miles below the old headworks of the Yaqui Canal, and on the same (south) side of the river, is the diversion site of the Old Santan ditch.[1]

This ditch formerly served to irrigate a strip of land between the Little Gila and the Gila proper, part of which now constitutes the agency farm. A new canal, recently constructed by the Indian irrigation service, and which is described under the head of "Present cultivation," is intended to irrigate practically the same lands as formerly irrigated by this old Santan Canal. George Pablo,[2] who is 63 years old, says that this ditch was built in his childhood, while Miguel[3] says that he helped in its construction, and that it was excavated some years before the battle between the Blackwater Pimas and Santan Pimas.[4]

Mr. Cook, the first missionary among the Pimas, in 1871 established a school near the old Santan village,[5] where the irrigators under this canal used to live; and it is therefore safe to assume that this canal was completed prior to 1870, probably about 1865.

Failure of this canal project took place gradually, beginning in the late seventies or the early eighties, or at the time of the construction of the present Santan Canal on the north side of the river. The date of the latter undertaking was 1879.

The area of land which was observed to have been previously cultivated under this old canal amounts to 1,272 acres, including most of the land under the present agency farm, which embraces an area of 168 acres.[6]

While the line of this old ditch is still plainly visible, it is now so badly filled with silt that, like many others of the older ditches, its original dimensions are difficult to determine. From measurements taken, it would appear that this ditch had a bottom width of 5 feet, top width of 8 feet, water depth of 2 feet, and a grade of 1 in 500. The capacity, therefore, is in excess of 30 second-feet.

Failure of the water supply, as well as the tribal fight already mentioned, are stated to be the reasons for the nonuse of this ditch.

New Mount-Top ditch.—The New Mount Top ditch, called "new" because the Indians who built it originally came from the Old Mount Top settlement near the present village of Sweetwater. This former diversion had its heading at a point in the south side of the Little Gila, just below the Sacaton Agency, in sec. 16, T. 4 S., R. 6 E., G. and S. R. B. and M. This ditch was built in 1868. According to Miguel,[7] of Sacaton, who assisted in its construction, only one crop of grain was harvested before the ditch was abandoned. The builders moved to other locations.

[1] This ditch should not be confused with the modern Santan Canal and district. In former years the present Santan Indians or their predecessors lived on the south side of the river, and their former villages, ditches, etc., were called Santan.

[2] Supplemental exhibits, vol. 1, p. 34.

[3] Supplemental exhibits, vol. 1, p. 50.

[4] This trial fight took place in 1878–79, according to the calendar of Maj. Johnson; also confirmed by Russell, p. 57, 26th American Ethnological Report.

[5] The remains of this old schoolhouse, which was of adobe, are still to be seen about 2 miles west of the present Sacaton Agency, on the road between Sacaton and Casa Blanca. Although the old Santan ditch, and the fields which it served to irrigate, are situated on the opposite side of the Little Gila from the site of their old village, yet it appears that these Indians preferred to cross the Little Gila each day on their way to and from work rather than to pitch their camp on the comparatively low lands near the fields.

[6] The land included in the agency farm was originally irrigated by Antonio Azul, who in later years irrigated the eastern portion of this same area from Cottonwood ditch and the remainder from the old Santan ditch. This land was acquired from Azul for agency purposes in 1892.

[7] See statement, p. 50, vol. 1, supplemental exhibits.

The evidence available on the ground would show that about 182 acres were planted under cultivation. This ditch varied in width from 5 feet near the heading to 3 feet at its lower extremity. Its capacity was at least 10 second-feet. After the failure of this venture the Mount Top villagers appear to have amalgamated with the Sacaton Indians, as they no longer have a separate village.

Old Maricopa ditch.—A few miles further down the Little Gila, in section 7, T. 4 S., R. 6 E., G. & S. R. B. and M., another of these many idle canals had its heading. This, the Old Maricopa ditch, is not to be confused with the Ancient Maricopa ditch, which is also an inactive canal, located near the present Sacaton siding of the Maricopa-Phoenix Railroad. The Old Maricopa ditch was constructed in 1848–49, according to Antonito Azul,[1] who states that this ditch was completed and water turned in at the time that a band of Maricopa Indians went to the Picacho Mountains after mescal, and were ambushed by the Apaches. This incident, according to Maj. Jackson's calendar,[2] took place during the years 1848–49.

The builders of the Old Maricopa ditch were Maricopa Indians, who had withdrawn from the main body of their tribesmen, then cultivating land under the Ancient Maricopa ditch. Upon the failure of the former ditch, these Maricopas reunited with their tribesmen and they or their descendants are now cultivating land near the confluence of the Gila and Salt rivers at the western extremity of the reservation. The date of the inactivity of the Old Maricopa ditch is not definitely known. Apachoes[3] says he thinks the fields were vacated about 50 years ago, but his memory was rather vague on that point. This district, as well as the Ancient Sweetwater district, was undoubtedly under cultivation in 1852, at the time of Bartlett's visit,[4] but was evidently vacated before Rev. Mr. Cook's school was established (1871), since the latter fails to mention this district in his description.[5]

It is believed, therefore, that this ditch became inactive in about the year 1870, which date is in conformity with the information obtained from Apachoes.

This ditch had originally a bottom width of 5 feet, top width of 8 to 10 feet, and capacity of 15 second-feet. The area formerly under cultivation under this ditch, as nearly as could be ascertained from the remaining borders, etc., amounts to 238.5 acres. The Old Maricopa Canal discharges into the Ancient Sweetwater, and it is evident that the lower part of this latter ditch was used as an extension to the former.

A branch ditch taking out of the Old Maricopa Canal a short distance below its heading was added soon after the construction of this canal by a number of Old Mount Top Indians, who desired to cultivate a portion of the alkali lands situated south of the main ditch. Some land was placed under cultivation (6.2 acres), but the soil was so poor that the attempt was soon given up.

Ancient Stotonic.—This ditch, called "Ancient" to distinguish it from the present Stotonic ditch, which heads lower down the Gila River, had its point of diversion about 2 miles below the Old Mari-

---

[1] See statement, p. 17, vol. 1, supplemental exhibit.
[2] See calendar, supplemental exhibit, vol. 1, p. 108.
[3] See statement, vol. 1, p. 1, supplemental exhibits.
[4] See p. 25 of this appendix covering the early history of the Gila River Reservation.
[5] See letter of Dr. Cook, in supplemental exhibits, vol. 1, p. 86.

copa Canal and near the north boundary of sec. 2, T. 4 S., R. 6 E. This inactive canal is one of the very oldest ditches on the reservation, and its heading may be considered practically a former heading of the present Stotonic ditch. Inasmuch as certain lands were covered and irrigated by this old ditch that can not be covered by the present Stotonic, the former will be treated separately.

According to the statements of the oldest living inhabitants, the Ancient Stotonic ditch was in operation as early as they can remember, and so far as the knowledge of the Pimas goes, this ditch, or others in the same vicinity, has been supplying the same body of land continuously since the earliest times. Unquestionably the irrigated lands or rancherias first described by the early Spaniards were located in this vicinity.

An area of 590 acres was found to have been under cultivation under this old canal, exclusive of the land now under cultivation under the present Stotonic. This area was vacated because of the removal of the heading to a point lower down the river and the construction of the present Stotonic Canal.

According to Joseph Head, the change of heading affecting this land took place about 35 years ago, consequently, it may be stated that this land has been unoccupied since about 1880. Several headings have been constructed at various times for this canal, as well as for the present Stotonic, but it is thought that the one covering the greatest area of cultivation is as above stated. This ditch at a point above the uppermost of its old laterals had a bottom width of 6 feet, top width of 10 feet, water depth of 2 feet. With its present grade of about 1 in 1,000, these diversions would give this ditch a carrying capacity of 28 second-feet.

Old Mount Top.—The so-called Mount Top ditch is not a separate ditch, but a branch of the Stotonic. It had no independent heading, but inasmuch as it was built and operated by the Mount Top Indians and also later became useless to them, it will be considered in this report as an independent ditch. This canal took out of the present Stotonic ditch in the SW. ¼ sec. 28, T. 3 S., R. 5 E.

According to the statements of Vanico[1] and Pablo[2] this ditch was built prior to their earliest recollection, and undoubtedly before their births. Irrigation in this district was probably carried on contemporaneously with the former irrigation in the adjacent districts of Stotonic and Casa Blanca. According to Pablo[2] this district was at least partially vacated 45 years ago, or approximately at the time of the construction of the New Mount Top, which is said to have been constructed in 1866.

The area previously cultivated under this ditch, all of which has since been in nonuse, according to the survey, amounted to 718.5 acres.

This ditch has a bottom width of 5 feet, depth of 1½ feet, and is not much wider at the top than at the bottom. Its grade is only 1 in 1,800, giving the ditch a theoretical capacity of about 9 second-feet.

The Mount Top Indians when cultivating these lands were prosperous and occupied a village of no mean size near the conspicuous little butte just south of their fields. This little hill is known to

---

[1] Supplemental exhibits, vol. 1, p. 47.
[2] Supplemental exhibits, vol. 1, p. 80.

the Indians as Rattlesnake Home, because a small cave in its banks was the legendary abode of a monstrous rattlesnake and her numerous young. As we already know, these Mount Top Indians, after having vacated their fields, went to the old Santan district, near the old Cooks School, later joining the present Santan villagers.

Sranuka ditch (Alkali Camp Canal).—The Sranuka ditch was in reality only partially serviceable, since a portion of this old ditch is now known as the Alkali Camp Canal, which will be taken up under the head of "Present irrigation."

This is one of the older ditches, having been in use at the time of the coming of the Whites.[1] Much of this old ditch has been washed out, especially near its original heading which was located nearly opposite the village of Casa Blanca and approximately 2 miles above the present heading of the Alkali Canal. This ditch was one of the longest of the older ditches, extending from the heading just mentioned to a point 1 mile or more beyond the railroad at Sacaton siding, a distance of 8 miles. A large portion of the land previously irrigated under this ditch, as well as a part of the ditch itself, has been washed away by the floods.

Many of the Pimas now living at Gila crossing originally irrigated or farmed in the Sranuka district, but the lands which they irrigated under the Sranuka Canal were gradually vacated, beginning at the time of the first diversion in Gila crossing, i. e., in the late seventies or early eighties. Several new headings have been made for the Sranuka Canal, but the area under irrigation has decreased constantly. In recent years this ditch has been known as Alkali Camp Canal, so named because of the unusually large quantities of alkali to be found in the vicinity of the canal. The extreme western portion of the area irrigated under this old ditch was known by the Indians as the Skunk's district.[2]

Pablo in his sketch showing the distribution of the previously irrigated area is under the impression that the Skunk fields were irrigated by a separate ditch other than the Sranuka. It is believed, however, that Pablo confused the Skunk Ditch with the Santa Cruz, since no evidence of another ditch could be found on the ground.

When the survey was made in the early part of 1914, 736 acres were shown to have been previously irrigated under this ditch. At the extreme lower end of the Sranuka Canal there is a comparatively recent ditch, constructed about 10 years ago to utilize the waste water or the drainage from the Sranuka or present Alkali Camp Canal. Although this new ditch was excavated for a distance of about 2 miles, it was never used, owing to the failure of the water supply. The ditch was built by a few Indians living at Gila Crossing.

Sratuka (Wet Camp) Canal and Snaketown district.—All of the inactive canals thus far described, with the exception of the Cayau, had their headings either in the Little Gila or in the south bank of the Gila River proper. The Sratuka, however, is one other canal which lies on the north side of the main river, its heading being

[1] Supplemental exhibits, vol. 1, p. 75. Also statement of Pablo, p. 30.

[2] This rather peculiar name, Skunk, or Oopia in Pima, comes from a family and their descendants of that name who formerly lived in this section. Whether this was a family name or merely an applied name, my informant did not state. (C. H. S.)

built near the isolated hill known as Double Buttes, or sometimes as Rattlesnake Hill. The former heading of this canal was near the section line between sec. 20–21, T. 3 S., R. 7 E., G. and S. R. B. & M.—that is, about a quarter of a mile above the present Snaketown canal diversion.

The old Sratuka district is identical with the district now known as the Snaketown or Skukaika.

The original Sratuka Indians located their village and also cultivated a small area of land on the south side of the river opposite their canal, which, as already, stated, was situated on the north side. This arrangement, while affording better protection for the Indians, required them to cross the river in order to reach their fields. Although the site of the original village of Sratuka has long since been washed away, there still exists a village of this name on the south side of the river in this same locality, and its farms are now irrigated by the Bapchil Ditch.

The proximity of the former village to the river lowlands accounts for the name Sratuka, which means wet camp. It is stated that many of the fields required only one or two irrigations to mature crops, so close was the water to the surface of the ground.

About the year 1872 many of the Indians living in this district vacated their farms and moved over to the Salt River Valley, where they began the cultivation of lands in the present Salt River Reservation. Their reasons for moving seem to have been several, viz. loss of their lands by floods, scarcity of water, and an invotation by the Mormon settlers to come over and settle near them, and thus afford protection from the Apaches. Some five or six years after this migration some of the Indians remaining at the village of Sratuka crossed the Gila and founded the present village of Snaketown.

Several different headings have from time to time been constructed for this ditch. The original canal, located as it was along the mesa edge, was capable of irrigating an area greater than that covered by the modern Snaketown Canal. The present heading of the Snaketown Canal was constructed subsequent to the disastrous flood of 1905.

The original Sratuka was in existence at the time of the earliest recollection of the present-day Pimas, but, as already indicated, the present-day village of Snaketown, on the north side of the river, is of comparatively recent origin.

The area of land which shows evidence of previous cultivation, and which is not included in the area at present under cultivation, amounted at the time of the survey to 1,273 acres. It is estimated that 500 acres has been washed away by floods since the survey by Meskimons[1] in 1904 shows an area in excess of the above figures by this amount.

The old canal, while badly filled up at present with silt, appears to have had a bottom width of 6 feet, top width of 12 feet, water depth of 2 feet. It has a grade of 1 in 1,200, giving a capacity of at least 30 second-feet.

Bridlestood Canal.—Continuing on down the river, the next no longer used ditch is the Bridlestood,[2] which is located on the same

---

[1] Information concerning this survey is given on p. 97, of this appendix.

[2] The origin of this peculiar name is connected with a certain bush or scrub tree, the branches of which are said to have grown in the shape of a bridle. It seems that this particular tree grew in a prominent place near the principal road or trail leading through this district, and in this way the district became known as "where the bridle stood," or the Bridlestood district.

(north) side of the river. The Bridlestood, like the Snaketown Canal, is a very old district, this canal having been built prior to the remembrance of any of the older Indians. It became idle about the time of the Sranuka, the Skunk, and the old Maricopa—that is, about 25 years ago, or in the late eighties. This old Bridlestood ditch has since been used, in part, by several Indians under the leadership of an Indian known as Paloma, who constructed a ditch to divert the waters of the Gila into this old canal. Some of these old Bridlestood fields were rehabilitated, but were again vacated within a year because of a change in the river channel.

Another attempt to irrigate this territory was later made by a number of these same Indians by means of an extension to the Snaketown Canal. While considerable work seems to have been done of this extension within recent years, no success seems to have resulted from these efforts. A great deal of land, especially at the lower end of the Bridlestood district, has been washed away by the numerous floods of the Gila. The land shown to have been previously irrigated by the Bridlestood ditch amounted to 1,143 acres. This ditch was approximately 4 feet wide at the bottom, 10 feet wide on top, had a maximum water depth of 2 feet and a grade of 1 in 1,000. Its carrying capacity was probably at least 20 second-feet.

Old Santa Cruz Canal.—The remains of the upper portion of the old Santa Cruz Canal are found just below the railroad station at Sacaton siding. Much of this old ditch, as well as the land formerly irrigated by it, has been washed away. This ditch, like many others, was named after the Indians, or rather the village of Indians, by whom it was built. It appears that the Indians who were responsible for its construction afterwards moved to the Santa Cruz River near the lower end of the reservation not far from the Estrella Mountains, and for this reason the ditch, as well as the old idle fields under it, are called by other Indians the Santa Cruz.

The old Santa Cruz Canal, while antedating the coming of the whites, was built within the remembrance of at least some of the older Indians. Pablo[1] mentions it as one of the older ditches, having been in existence longer than he can remember. Ben Thompson,[2] however, states that he thinks it was built when he was a small boy, and that it became inert when he was old enough to fight the Apaches. This would indicate this ditch to be at least 60 years old, the year of its last activity probably being about 1875. Thompson corroborates this by stating that the old Santa Cruz Canal and the old Sranuka ditch became useless about the same time. So much of the area formerly irrigated under this ditch had evidently been washed away by floods that it was found impossible to determine the exact area of previous cultivation. The area remaining undisturbed by the floods and which showed evidence of previous irrigation, amounted to 400 acres. By assuming the probable location of the river bank at former times, it has been estimated that an additional area of 100 acres was at one time irrigated under this ditch.

---

[1] See statement, supplemental exhibits, vol. 1, p. 30.
[2] See statement, supplemental exhibits, vol. 1, p. 27.

The old Santa Cruz ditch was probably 3 feet wide at the bottom, 10 feet wide on top. It had a grade of 1 foot in 1,000, and a probable capacity of 10 second-feet.

Ancient Maricopa Canal.—As in the case of the old Santa Cruz Canal, the heading and a considerable portion of this old ditch have been washed away by the floods. The original intake of the ancient Maricopa Canal was located near the heading of the old Santa Cruz, but on the opposite (north) side of the river. This ditch [1] according to Ben Thompson, was constructed by Maricopa Indians soon after this tribe joined forces with the Pimas. Nearly all of the existing calendars of the older Indians include prominent references to the Maricopas, but their coming to this reservation antedates the earliest of these records. According to Col. Emory [2] these Indians were found by Dr. Anderson at Gila Bend as late as 1828. They were then moving gradually from their old location on the Gulf of California to their present position near the Pimas. It is probable, therefore, that the ancient Maricopa Canal was started about 1830 or 1840. Each Indian who was interviewed upon the subject claimed that the canal was built prior to his knowledge.

As in the Santa Cruz district just across the river, much of the land formerly irrigated by means of the Ancient Maricopa Canal has been washed away. The remaining portion, according to the survey, measured 386 acres, and assuming again the probable former width of the river, it is estimated that at least 750 acres were at one time cultivated under this old ditch. The ditch, as it exists to-day, is 3 feet wide on the bottom, 5 or 6 feet on top, and appears to have had a water depth of 1½ feet. Its grade is 1 in 1,000. With these dimensions it would have a carrying capacity of 10 second-feet.

ACTIVE CANALS OF PRESENT IRRIGATION ON THE GILA RIVER RESERVATION.

North Blackwater (Cholla Mountain) ditch.—This canal, which lies on the north side of the river, has its heading about 3 miles up the river from the east line of the Gila River Reservation, in sec. 12, T. 5 S., R. 8 E. Two other ditches supplying reservation lands have their point of diversion opposite the heading of this ditch, but on the south side of the Gila.

Juan Thomas [3] states that this ditch was in operation when he came to the Blackwater district 38 years ago; that is, prior to 1876. Havilena [4] says this ditch was constructed 49 years ago; that is, in 1865, when he was serving as scout for the United States Government. Samuel Scoffer [5] states that it was constructed at some time prior to his arrival in this district, which was in 1867. It will be reasonable to assume, therefore, that the year 1866 represents very closely the date of its construction.

Juan Thomas also states that at the time of his arrival in the Blackwater district about two-thirds of the land irrigated at the present time was under cultivation. Thomas having arrived there in

---

[1] See statement, supplemental exhibits, vol. 1, p. 27.
[2] See footnote, p. — of this appendix.
[3] See statement, p. 1, vol. 1, supplemental exhibits.
[4] See statement, p. 3, vol. 1, supplemental exhibits.
[5] See statement, p. 9, vol. 1, supplemental exhibits.

1876, it may be safely assumed that with this rate of development the entire district was irrigated by the year 1881.

The North Blackwater ditch has a top width of 11 feet, a bottom width of 5 feet, a water depth of 1½ feet, and a velocity of 15 feet per second; the ditch thus possessing a capacity of 16 second-feet. This canal, at present, is in good condition. At the time of the survey it served to irrigate 941 acres of land, an additional area of 309 acres showing evidences of previous culture. A survey made by Mr. Meskimons in 1904 showed an area of 1,456 acres under cultivation at that time.

Blackwater or Island ditch.—The first ditch constructed for the irrigation of the Blackwater Island district, which lies between the Little Gila and the main channel of the river, was commenced in 1862. Juan Thomas has recorded this date in his calendar,[1] while William Wallace,[2] who claims to have been the chief promoter of the ditch, also gives the year of its construction at 1862. Frank Hayes,[3] states that it was built about 54 years ago and that within four or five years all the land which it could serve to irrigate had been placed under cultivation. In order that this might be possible, the ditch was enlarged from 3 feet to 4 or 5 feet on the bottom.

The present heading of this canal lies in sec. 2, T. 5 S., R. 8 E., about 1 mile upstream from the reservation line. Various other headings, however, have been in use during the past.

Formerly the Island ditch was flumed across the Little Gila to Blackwater Island. Several years prior to 1913 the Little Gila was permitted to choke up, and instead of using the flume, this ditch was then permitted to discharge into the Little Gila, the water being rediverted by means of a dam some distance farther down.

In 1913 the Indian Irrigation Service opened up the Little Gila heading and constructed a new flume to carry this ditch across the Little Gila, as formerly had been done. This work was known as the Little Gila project.

The Island Canal at the present time has a capacity of 35 second-feet. It has a top width of 10 feet, a bottom width of 7 feet, water depth of 2 feet, and has a velocity slightly greater than 3 feet per second. This canal serves to irrigate 1,029 acres, according to the survey of 1914. According to the Meskimons survey in 1904, 1,506 acres were then being irrigated.

Under this canal there are, in addition, 30 acres which have been cultivated at some former date, while 330 acres more are susceptible of irrigation.

Little Gila Canal.—It is generally conceded that the so-called Little Gila River is of artificial construction. Its general location in respect to the topography of the surrounding country, the evident remains of side drainage channels which formerly continued across the present bed of the stream, as well as the directness of the alignment of the channel itself are evidences supporting this belief.

Unquestionably the Little Gila, as originally constructed, was not as large as it is now; its present size and shape is probably due to the action of flood waters which, entering the head of the original canal, not only deepened and widened the channel but also cut a

[1] See statement, p. 1, supplemental exhibits, vol. 1.
[2] See statement, p. 5, supplemental exhibits, vol. 1.
[3] See statement, p. 7, supplemental exhibits, vol. 1.

pathway from the end of the original ditch back to the bed of the main river.

Whether or not the Little Gila Canal was constructed contemporaneously with the other near-by prehistoric canals is, of course, problematical. Needless to state, no knowledge of its artificial construction is possessed by the present day Pimas, and the credit of this enterprise must be given to an unknown race of agricultural people, perhaps ancestors of the Pimas, who had attained a remarkably advanced stage of culture and civilization.

No particular reference to the Little Gila has been found in the narratives of the early Spanish explorers. It is evident that some of the earlier adventuerers into this region were of the opinion that the Little Gila was the main river channel. Russel Bartlett, who was connected with the United States and Mexican boundary survey during the years 1850–1853, and who has been previously quoted,[1] evidently made this mistake, for he states: "We found the river banks about 15 feet high and so abrupt that it was with some difficulty we reached the water." The banks of the Little Gila in many places are 15 feet or more in height, while the banks of the main river are seldom more than 6 or 7 feet high.

During former times no trouble was encountered in keeping the river water diverted into the Little Gila, and the principal ditches serving the land that was irrigated prior to the coming of the whites had their heading in this channel or, in other words, were laterals or subditches of the Little Gila.

With the recent recurring floods, the main river channel has been washed much wider than formerly, and as a result the diversion of the Little Gila has been maintained with some difficulty.

During the disastrous flood of 1905 the old heading was completely washed away and a mile or more of the upper portion of the Little Gila channel was filled with silt, and, as previously stated, this portion of the channel was occupied by the Island ditch.

In February, 1913, it was decided to reopen the Little Gila, and the work in this connection, which was done under the direction of this service, has been known as the Little Gila project.

Little Gila project.—The Little Gila project, which was completed in 1914, had for its primary object the opening up of the Little Gila and the installation of a suitable heading at its point of diversion from the Gila River. This work necessitated the relocation of a portion of Blackwater Island ditch and the excavation and the cleaning out of the channel for a distance of 3,950 feet. The Blackwater Island ditch was reconstructed through a distance of 3,725 feet. A flume was built to carry this ditch across the Little Gila below its heading and a drop was installed to discharge the water into the original Island ditch. Bank protection, both above and below the Little Gila headgate structure, was installed as a part of this project. Two wing dams were built, one above the heading to divert the water against the headgate and one below to protect the downstream bank.

The great flood of December, 1914, did considerable damage to the bank protection and headwork of the Little Gila. The flood

[1] See p. 13 of this appendix.

was of such magnitude that the high water overflowed the river banks in all directions and washed out much of the bank protection, as well as portions of the fill or revetment around the Little Gila structures. Subsequent to the flood a new channel has been cut from the main Gila to the Little Gila and the channel of the Little Gila was again cleaned for a distance of 2,400 feet.

The Indian Island ditch, which closely follows the river bank at the Little Gila heading, was also washed out and 8,200 feet of new ditch was constructed to replace the washed-out portion. The flume carrying the Indian ditch across the Little Gila was also damaged by the flood, and this flume, as well as some other minor structures, were repaired.

The trouble experienced with the Little Gila heading is common with all the ditch headings on the reservation and emphasizes the need of a permanent diversion dam.

The cost of this project during the fiscal year of 1913–14 amounted to $12,984.81, and during the fiscal year 1915 $3,531.27, or, in all $16,516.08.

Blackwater project ditch (B line).—The ditch shown on the map as the Blackwater project ditch (also known as the B line) has its heading 1 mile east of the reservation and was constructed by this service in 1914. This canal was not quite complete at the time of this survey and, of course, no land was yet in cultivation under it. The ditch will serve to irrigate 2,500 acres in the Blackwater district, which includes all of the land in the Old Woman's Mouth district, as well as all land that was intended to be irrigated by the Upper Blackwater ditch, which is described elsewhere in this report as never having been used.

This canal, according to the survey, has a bottom width of 6 feet, top width of 15 feet, water depth of 2 feet, and a grade of 1 in 1,500. Its calculated capacity is 18 second-feet. The total costs for the construction of this ditch up to end of fiscal year 1915 amounted to $7,769.75.

Yaqui Canal.—The history of the so-called Yaqui Canal has already been related under the heading of "Previous cultivation." The area cultivated under this ditch at the present time amounts to only 44 acres. Owing to a continued diminution in the quantity of water available, the lands formerly cultivated under this ditch are gradually reverting to the desert state, and unless a better water supply is soon obtained all remaining cultivation must likewise be suspended.

The land previously cultivated amounts to 290 acres.

Sacaton Flat Canal.—The Sacaton Flat Canal, sometimes called the Upper Stotonic Canal because the ditch was originally built by Indians coming from the Sacaton district, has its heading on the north side of the Little Gila about 1 mile below the Yaqui. According to John Hayes[1] this ditch was built in 1872. Has Makil[2] claims that the canal in question was in operation prior to his residence in that section, stating that he arrived in 1879. Hayes claims also that within five years after work was first begun on the canal all of the land irrigated at the present time had been placed under cultivation. At the time of this survey the area cultivated under this canal was

[1] See statement, p. 7, supplemental exhibits, vol. 1.
[2] See statement, p. 16, supplement exhibits, vol. 1.

899 acres, 384 acres in addition showing evidences of previous cultivation. The survey of Meskimons in 1904 gave 1,105.2 acres as the area then under cultivation.

The Sacaton Flats Canal is 5 feet wide on the bottom and about the same width on top; it has a depth of 2½ feet, a grade of 1 in 800, giving a carrying capacity of 40 second-feet.

Cottonwood ditch.—This ditch, so-called from the numerous large cottonwood trees that line its banks, was constructed in 1872, according to a statement of its builder, Antonito Azul.[1]

Hokee refers us to the ditch captain and promoter, Azul, for the exact date of the construction of this ditch, but states that to the best of his recollection it was constructed 45 years ago. The area cultivated under this ditch at the time of the survey was 819 acres, while 152.9 acres additional were found to have been previously cultivated. The survey of Meskimons in 1904 gives 439 acres as the area then under cultivation. Azul and other farmers cultivating lands under this ditch came from the Sweetwater district, although Hokee Wilson,[2] who also helped to build the ditch, came from the Old Mount Top district.

The Cottonwood ditch is 8 feet wide on the top, 6 feet on the bottom; it had a depth of 1½ feet and a grade of 1 in 1,000, giving a carrying capacity of 20 second-feet.

The Santan Indian Canal.—The Rev. Dr. Cook,[3] in his letter relative to the early irrigation on the reservation, states that "at one large village north of the river and for a distance of near 10 miles there were fine ancient fields without a ditch and near the head of it there was fine strata of rock and river bed, "and while Dr. Cook mentioned further on that he assisted the Indians to overcome the difficulty of getting a ditch started, he fails to mention any dates.

John Manuel,[4] however, says that Dr. Cook made a survey of the above ditch in 1887 and that he "rod for him."

He states that construction began immediately after this survey, but that this ditch was not completed until 1883.

Cos Chin,[5] an Indian 90 years of age, claims that he moved from the Island or "old" Santan district to the "modern" Santan district in 1880 or 1881. It appears from the calendar of Maj. Jackson[6] that attempts to build a canal in this district were made as early as 1869, but it is quite probable that not much work was done until after the survey of Dr. Cook in 1877.

At the time of the survey of 1914 there were cultivated under this ditch 3,319.3 acres, an additional 201 acres showing evidences of

[1] See statement, p. 17, supplemental exhibits, vol. 1.
[2] See statement, p. 41, supplemental exhibits, vol. 1.
[3] See p. 86, supplemental exhibits, vol. 1.
[4] See statement, p. 20, supplemental exhibits, vol. 1.
[5] See statement, p. 61, supplemental exhibits, vol. 1.
[6] See p. 108, supplemental exhibits, vol. 1.

previous cultivation. According to Tor White,[1] the original ditch had a bottom width of 5 feet near its lower extremity and 9 feet near its heading. At present the Old Santan ditch is 10 feet wide on the bottom, 16 feet on top; it has a water depth of about 3 feet and a grade of 1 in 1,500, its capacity, therefore, being at least 75 second-feet.

Lower Santan Canal.—John Manuel[1] claims that there was constructed in 1879 a canal known as the Lower Santan Canal, which a few years later was combined with the Santan Indian Canal.

According to Manuel, this lower canal later was almost entirely washed away. Very few sections of the original ditch remain, but those which were found showed the ditch to have had a cross section about 6 feet wide at the bottom, 11 feet on top, with a water depth of 2 feet. Its capacity was about 15 second-feet.

As already stated, this ditch not long after its construction was used simply as an extension to the Santan Indian Canal. The land lying under the Lower Santan Canal is considered a part of the main Santan district since those two canals were constructed at about the same time and would carry with them priorities which are approximately equal.

The Santan Flood Canal (Sacaton Project).—In December, 1904, the board of engineers of the Reclamation Service submitted a report to the Secretary of the Interior on the question of furnishing water to the Gila River Indian Reservation. In January, 1906, the Secretary of the Interior issued special instructions that surveys be made and plans prepared for the construction of an irrigation system. The investigation was accordingly made under the direction of the chief engineer of the Indian irrigation service, with the result that an irrigation system consisting of a flood water canal supplemented by pumping plants was decided upon. The Reclamation Service, under the direction of the Indian Office, was detailed to carry out these plans. Reimbursable appropriations for the construction of this project were made as follows:

Mar. 3, 1905	$50,000
June 21, 1906	250,000
Apr. 4, 1910	75,000
Mar. 3, 1911	125,000
Total	500,000

Of this amount there remained on hand March 31, 1912, a balance of $32,648.21.[3]

In addition to the above amount, there has been expended by this service for the construction of the distribution system and other necessary work, some $39,837.70.

This project has for its object the irrigation of about 10,000 acres of land on the north side of the river embracing all the territory within the Santan District, including the land covered by the Santan Indian Canal. The plans for the distribution of water in this district, as they were finally evolved and carried out, may be described as follows: The Santan Indian Canal was already located on a low ridge whose general direction parallels the river. Situated on either side of this ditch are the lands of the Indians,

[1] See statement, p. 68, supplemental exhibits, vol. 1.
[2] See statement, p. 20, supplemental exhibits, vol. 1.
[3] H. Rept. No. 1506, p. 569, 62d Cong., 3d sess.

where these people live and are using water for irrigation.. The wells were drilled along a line located from one-half to 1 mile north of the Santan Indian Canal, while a short distance farther north was constructed the large Santan Flood Canal.

Connecting the different wells is a ditch which is joined at its upper end to the flood canal.

A large lateral which takes out of the flood canal and enters the Santan Indian Canal above the uppermost of its laterals, serves to conduct the flood water into the Indian Canal. At frequent intervals along the course of the flood canal, feeder and drain ditches have also been constructed.

The Santan Flood Canal has dimensions as follows: Bottom width, 26 feet; side slopes, 1 to 1; water depth, 4 feet. It has a grade of 0.0003 and its capacity is 300 second-feet.

The lateral already referred to, connecting the flood canal with the Santan Indian Canal, has a bottom width of 10 feet; side slopes, 1 to 1; depth, 3½ feet; and a grade of 0.005. Its capacity is 110 second-feet.

The well ditch (also referred to above) has a bottom width of 6 feet; side slopes, 1½ to 1; grade, between 0.003 and 0.0025. Its capacity is approximately 30 second-feet.

Work was begun on this project on April 20, 1908, with the drilling of the first well. The drilling of the ninth and last well was completed on January 15, 1909. Survey work and the preliminary location of the flood canal was started in May, 1909, and actual construction was commenced in October of the same year.

Opposition to this project[1] soon arose among the Indians, with the result that the United States Reclamation Service suspended operations after the main flood canal had been completed but before work had proceeded very far on the distribution system. Work on this project was resumed by the Indian irrigation service in 1913 shortly after the suspension of work by the Reclamation Service. Since that time, the Indian lands under the canal were surveyed and allotted, the distribution and drainage systems have been completed, and another well had been drilled.

Owing both to the continued opposition of the Indians and to the lack of a diversion dam at the head of the Santan Flood Canal, this canal has been used only in connection with the Santan Indian Canal, although it was always intended that the flood canal should some day entirely supplant the Indian Canal.

The lack of a suitable diversion works at its head has greatly limited the usefulness of the flood canal, since the Indians find it much easier to divert the flow of the Gila directly into the Santan Indian Canal.

At the time of this survey there was under cultivation under this canal a total area of 3,319.3 acres, which is identical with the area cultivated under the Santan Indian ditch. The area cultivated under the Santan Flood Canal was no greater at the time of the survey than that formerly cultivated under the Indian ditch, but much land was being cleared and other efforts were being made at that time to increase this area. It is proposed by the Indian Service to irrigate at least 10,000 acres under this project.

---

[1] Hearing before the Committee on Indian Affairs, House resolutions 330, No. 1, December 21, 1911; No. 2, January 5, 1912.

Agency project at Sacaton.—This project has for its purpose the irrigation of lands on the so-called island, that strip of land lying between the Little Gila and the Gila River just north of the Sacaton Agency. The necessary surveys were commenced in November, 1913, actual construction work started in March, 1914, and the project was completed in June of that year.

This irrigation system consists of one main canal and a number of laterals. Its water supply is obtained by diversion from the Little Gila at the north and south midsection line of section 23, T. 4 S., R. 6 E. The main canal has a bottom width of 6 feet, side slopes, 1½ to 1, water depth 2 feet, maximum grade of 1 in 1,000, and a carrying capacity of 30 second-feet.

The territory to which this ditch now furnishes water embraces the district formerly known as the Old Santan district, as well as a considerable area formerly belonging to the Cottonwood Canal district. This project, including these two areas, mentioned above, was built with the intention to irrigate 2,000 acres. At the time of the survey, some land was already being cleared in anticipation of the completion of the ditch. During the summer of 1914, and after survey had been made, about 30 acres were put under irrigation in addition to the land which was being irrigated by the Cottonwood ditch. Disbursements made for the construction of this project to the end of the fiscal year 1915, have amounted to $26,754.28.

Hendricks ditch.—This canal, which takes out of the Little Gila about 2 miles above Sacaton[1] was constructed by its present owner, Mr. Hendricks, in 1904. The Hendricks ditch served to irrigate 76 acres of land at the time of this survey.

An old ditch known as the Louis Morago, which has its heading about 300 feet east of the present heading of Hendricks ditch, formerly irrigated about 40 acres of the land now irrigated by means of the latter. This ditch was constructed by the Sacaton agency in 1882, but after about two years of use it was found unserviceable.

In connection with this old Morago ditch, another ditch heading in the Big Gila extended across the Cottonwood lands, and, discharging into the Little Gila, supplied water to the Morago ditch. This connecting ditch has been largely effaced by the continued plowing of fields and the excavation of new ditches since the time of its inactivity. Traces of this old ditch, however, are still visible, the approximate location being shown on the survey map of the reservation. Owing to the limited acreage served by this ditch, as well as its short life, it has not been treated under a separate heading.

Casa Blanca Canal project.—This project is situated on the south side of the Little Gila, west of the Sacaton Agency. By means of this canal it is proposed to irrigate some 35,000 acres of land, including the areas of Casa Blanca and Sweetwater, which are irrigated at the present time, and the previously irrigated district of the

[1] Sacaton was merely a stage station in the early sixties, and did not become an Indian village until less than 30 years ago. Previous to this time these Indians were living in the Cottonwood district just adjacent. Sacaton takes its name from a long-bladed grass, a sort of hay, called sacaton grass, which formerly grew in abundance in this vicinity. This word is evidently of Spanish origin, the Pima name for this village being Ku'-u Key (high house), referring to the relatively large houses built by the whites for the agency.

Old Maricopa, Ancient Sweetwater, Mount Top, and the Sranuka. Work was begun on this project in May, 1914, and by the end of that fiscal year the canal had been excavated throughout a length of 18,100 feet. During the fiscal year 1915, 22,100 feet of laterals were constructed for the distribution system and several concrete structures were built. The total expenditures on this project to the end of the fiscal year 1915 were $25,300.34.

This canal has a bottom width of 14 feet; side slopes 1½ to 1, depth, 6 feet; grade, 0.0006; velocity, 3.25 feet per second. Its capacity is consequently 350 second-feet.

Alkali Canal.—Alkali Canal is a name recently applied to a portion of the old Sranuka ditch, which still remains in use. The latter has already been referred to under the head of "Previous Irrigation" as a partially inactive ditch. The so-called Alkali village of to-day is situated approximately 2 miles west of the site of the former Sranuka village, which, for the purpose of protection, had been established close to the town of Casa Blanca.

After peace had been made with the Apaches, Sranuka village was vacated. Many of the Indians found new habitations elsewhere, but a few remained to build the present Alkali village. At the present time this canal is irrigating only 198 acres of land in what was formerly the upper portion of the old Sranuka district. Great quantities of alkali are found in this portion of the old district, giving rise to the more recent name of the canal and of the camp as well. The presence of these injurious salts has greatly limited the extent of cultivation in this district.

Stotonic (or Sweetwater ditch).—The Stotonic ditch (often erroneously called the Casa Blanca)[1] has its present heading near the center of sec. 35, T. 3 S., R. 5 E., at the point where the Little Gila discharges into the main channel of the Gila River. As already pointed out under the title of Ancient Sweetwater (see Previous Irrigation), the present Stotonic ditch is identical with the Ancient Stotonic except that its heading has been moved from a point on the Little Gila to a new location below the junction of this stream with the Big Gila. The motive for this change was undoubtedly a desire on the part of the Indians to take advantage of the flow in both of these streams. This ditch should have a priority identical with the Ancient Stotonic, since all the lands now cultivated under this ditch were cultivated under the ancient ditch.

At the time of this survey 1,559.3 acres were being cultivated under this ditch, and an additional 810 acres had been previously irrigated. This area of previous cultivation does not include that already noted under head of Mount Top ditch or Ancient Sweetwater. A considerable portion of the land formerly irrigated under this ditch has been washed away. It is recorded that the flood of 1869–70 destroyed a flour mill which was built in this section by Ammie White who was the first white person to live among the Pimas, and who later was appointed resident agent. Mr. White resided at the

[1] The name Stotonic, meaning many ants, has been variously applied by the whites to several different villages and canals in this general district. The village called Sweetwater by the whites is the Stotonic village of the Indians, while Casa Blanca village is known to the Indians as Wakey. The Sweetwater Canal, also called the Casa Blanca Canal, is known to the Indians as the Stotonic. The Bapchil Canal in this same district is sometimes also erroneously called the Casa Blanca.

old Casa Blanca or Wakey village, but his flour mill was down near the river bottom.

At the time of this survey the Stotonic ditch had a bottom width of 4 feet, top width of 10 feet, water depth of 2½ feet and a grade of 0.0006, with a capacity of 29 second-feet.

Bapchil (Ooist) Canal.—The Bapchil Canal[1] the heading of which lies a little more than a mile below the Stotonic, possesses a history similar to that of the latter canal, both of these being ancient Pima ditches. This Bapchil ditch, called also Ooist by Pablo[2] and other Indians, serves to irrigate the land below the Stotonic in the same general district. The village and district known as Wet Camp, or in the Indian, Sra-tuka, "full of moisture," is situated under this Bapchil ditch.

At the time of the survey this ditch served to irrigate 1,937 acres of land, an additional 936 acres having been previously irrigated. The canal above its uppermost laterals was being cleaned out at the time of this survey, consequently it was found to be much larger than appears necessary from the area of land which it covers. In that portion of the ditch which had been cleaned a cross-section 14 feet on the bottom, 22 feet on top with a water depth of 2½ feet was measured. With these excessive dimensions, the canal would have a very large capacity. At a point lower down, however, after several lateral diversions had been made, this ditch was found to have a cross-section of 7 feet on top, 3 feet on the bottom, 1½ feet depth, with a grade of 1 in 1,000. This would give a capacity of 10 second-feet.

It is estimated that at least 700 acres of land which were formerly irrigated by this ditch have been washed away by the floods. The previous survey by Meskimons in 1904 shows the irrigated lands to have extended a half mile or more beyond the present river bank.

Snaketown Canal.—On the south side of the river opposite the Bapchil is the present point of diversion of the Snaketown Canal, called in Pima, Skakaik ("many snakes"). Like the Stotonic fields across the river, this district is one of the ancient rancherias of the Pimas, and the history of the early irrigation in this region has already been given under the title of "Previous cultivation." At the time of this survey the area cultivated under this ditch was 354 acres. The area of previous cultivation has already been discussed under that heading. The Meskimons survey of 1904 showed an area of 3,499.1 acres, representing past and present cultivation in this district.

MASS-ACUMULT.

After passing the Alkali Canal no further diversions from the Gila are found until just below the region known as Mass-Acumult. This name, Mass-Acumult, translated means "clear river." This district is a portion of the broad river bottom in which the clear underflow[3] appears in springs, forming numerous little lakes or sloughs dividing the low bottom lands into small tracts or islands. In former years, and even now at favorable times, these lowlands

[1] Bapchil, meaning hook nose in Pima, is a sort of nickname given to the Indians of this locality because they were supposed to possess this facial peculiarity.

[2] See statement of Pablo, vol. 1, p. 80, supplemental exhibits.

[3] For a description of the underground waters of this district, see The Underground Waters of the Gila River Valley, Arizona, Water Supply Paper No. 104, p. 24.

were sometimes cultivated, but there was no artificial irrigation, nor was the land even plowed. The Indians merely planted the seed, relying upon the natural moisture of the ground to mature their crops. Such crops as corn and watermelons, and even a little cotton, were grown. This method of cultivation never became very extensive in this district, not only owing to the limited area suitable for cultivation, but also because of the constant damage of floods. This particular area is situated in a very hazardous position with respect to the river, since every large flood completely changes the topography of this so-called Mass-Acumult district. During the recent flood of 1914 the topography of the bottom lands was completely altered. The river bed was shifted a considerable distance, lakes and ponds were filled up, while the near-by ditches were greatly damaged.

At the time of this survey no land was being cultivated in this district. The survey of Mr. Meskimons, however, gave an area of 168.7 acres as being under cultivation in 1904.

Just below the Mass-Acumult district, and supplied largely by the waters collected in these ponds or clear lakes, is the first diversion of the Gila Crossing district.[1]

At many points between the Mass-Acumult locality and the west line of the Gila River Reservation, and in the districts beyond, more or less water rises to the surface of the river bed. As this water rises it is collected and diverted by several canals, furnishing the principal water supply for the irrigation of the Gila Crossing district, and other districts beyond the reservation.

IRRIGATION AT GILA CROSSING.

The Gila Crossing district is comparatively recent, the first ditch having been constructed in 1873. This district apparently owes its origin to the shortage of water on the Gila farther up on the reservation, the Indians who now far mhere or their antecedents formerly having lived and cultivated fields in the old Sranuka, Bridlestood, Skunk, and other districts.

That the return flow from the Mass-Acumult or from other sources along the river was not used by the Indians in former times is due to the disfavor with which this water was always regarded by the Indians for irrigating purposes. They early realized that the water contained elements deleterious[2] to their plants and they plainly preferred the surface flow. They never used this alkaline water until compelled to do so by the failure of the flood water supply.[3]

Although the Indians still make use of the flood waters at times for irrigation, it is used more especially for neutralizing and fertilizing purposes, irrigation during the time of maximum drought depending entirely upon these seepage or return flows. The floods which are so frequent on the Gila invariably destroy the low dams built by the Indians, necessitating considerable work of maintenance in connection with these canals. This difficulty is increased by the fact that after a heavy flood the return flow usually reappears in entirely new locations.

---

[1] The Gila Crossing district is known to the Pimas as Kawertk-Weercho ("under the hills").
[2] See Analysis, p. 25, Water Supply and Irrigation Paper No. 104.
[3] See statement, supplemental exhibits, vol. 1, pp. 75, 76–78.

According to Mr. Lee, of the Geological Survey, the return or seepage flow in the Gila Crossing district on June 1, 1903, amounted to 2,050 inches.[1]

The development of the underground water in this district, as well as at other points on the reservation, has been undertaken at different times by the Indian Department with a view of increasing the water supply. Owing, however, to the frequent floods to which the river is subject, and its constantly changing condition, these attempts have met only with doubtful success.

Hollen (Simon Webb) ditch.—This ditch has the most easterly heading—that is, it is highest on the Gila River—of the several ditches used for irrigation at Gila Crossing. Its heading is shown on the map as being very near the township line adjacent to sec. 25, T. 2 S., R. 2 E., G. and S. R. B and M. This ditch was constructed in 1877, according to several persons[2] who were connected with its construction. According to their statements, one year was consumed in its construction, and within four years all of the land now being irrigated under this ditch was in cultivation. The area cultivated, as shown by this survey, amounts to 660 acres, while the survey of Meskimons shows an area of 900.4 acres as having been cultivated in 1904. The ditch which was originally only 3 or 4 feet wide is now 6 feet on the bottom, 8 feet on top, has a grade of 1 in 1,500, and, with a water depth of 1 foot, has a capacity of 8 second-feet. Water Supply Paper No. 104 gives its flow on June 1, 1903, as 200 miner's inches, or about one-half the above capacity.

About 2 miles south of the Hollen Canal, but diverting water from the Santa Cruz River, is a small ditch known as the Breckenridge. This ditch serves to irrigate a small acreage nearly adjacent to the upper end of the area irrigated by the Hollen. This ditch was constructed about 13 years ago—that is, in 1902. It has a bottom width of 2½ feet, top width of 3 feet, water depth of 1 foot, and has a grade of 1 in 2,000. At the time of this survey only 5 acres were in cultivation, while 30.8 acres had been cultivated at some previous period.

Hoover ditch.—The first ditch constructed in Gila Crossing district was the Hoover ditch. According to several sources[3] this ditch was constructed in 1873, a year being consumed in its construction. The area under cultivation in 1914 amounted to 954 acres, according to this survey, while the former survey of Meskimons gave 827.1 acres as having been cultivated in 1904. This canal has across section 8 feet wide on the bottom, 10 feet on top, depth of 1 foot, grade of 1 in 1,400, giving a capacity of 12 second-feet. According to the statement of Head, when originally constructed this ditch was 4 feet wide on the bottom and when filled with water was knee-deep. In June, 1903,[4] this ditch was flowing 300 miner's inches.

John Thomas Canal.—This ditch, like the Hollen, lies on the south side of the river, its heading being located very near to the northern boundary of sec. 22, T. 2 S., R. 2 E., G. and S. R. M. This canal, according to information from several sources, was constructed three or four years subsequent to the Hoover ditch, which fixes the date of construction as 1876 or 1877. According to Joseph Head, this ditch

---

[1] Water Supply Paper No. 104, p. 24.
[2] See statements pp. 78–83, supplemental exhibits, vol. 1.
[3] See statement of Joseph Head, p. 80, supplemental exhibits, vol. 1.
[4] See Water Supply Paper No. 104.

was in course of construction for two years, and after three years all of the bottom land had been placed under cultivation.

A branch ditch, known as the Lancisco was also constructed. In 1905 nearly all the bottom land under the John Thomas Canal was washed away by the exceptionally heavy flood of that year. The major portion of the land remaining after the flood was situated under this branch ditch, and for this reason the canal is sometimes known as the Lancisco.

The amount of land being cultivated under this canal at the time of the survey was 587 acres, while 108 acres showed signs of previous irrigation. The survey of Meskimons in 1904 gave an area of 827 acres as being cultivated at that time. This canal has a bottom width of 6 feet, top width of 8 feet, water depth of 1.4 feet, and a grade of 1 in 100, with a carrying capacity of 15 second feet. Water Supply Paper No. 104, already referred to, gives the actual measurement of its flow for June 1, 1903, as 600 miner's inches, or 12 second-feet.

Joseph Head Canal.—The so-called Joseph Head ditch, which properly should come under the head of previous cultivation, is no longer a separate ditch, it having been consolidated with the John Thomas some 10 years ago. This ditch, according to the statement of its builder, Joseph Head,[1] was constructed in 1886.

Other old residents of Gila Crossing also give this date as the time of its construction. Joseph Head states, furthermore, that the ditch was in use 18 years until the disastrous flood of 1905, which took out the heading and a portion of the ditch, as well as considerable land formerly irrigated under it. It was then arranged to conduct the water into this ditch from the John Thomas Canal and a connecting ditch was constructed for this purpose. This method of obtaining water still remains in force.

The land formerly irrigated by this ditch and which is now cultivated under the John Thomas Canal adjoins the lower end of the John Thomas district. According to this survey, 139 acres were being cultivated under the old Joseph Head ditch, an additional 30.3 acres showing evidences of previous cultivation. The survey of Meskimons, which shows these two ditches to have been separate, gave an area of 786.4 acres as being cultivated under the Joseph Head ditch in 1904, including, however, some land later coming under the John Thomas ditch. So much of the upper end of this ditch had been washed out that no cross section was taken. Water Supply Paper No. 104 shows a discharge of 150 miner's inches on June 1, 1903.

Cooperation Canal.—Proceeding down the river, the next diversion following the Hoover is the Cooperation ditch. This ditch is comparatively recent, having been constructed in 1900 by a number of Indians of the younger generation—men who had been given some educational training either at the reservation school or elsewhere. These Indians have endeavored to farm after the manner of the whites and have met with very encouraging results. They have increased the extent of their fields, have built comfortable farm houses, and in general have become more progressive, as they are proud to describe themselves, than the older Indians. They also have inaugu-

---

[1] See statement, p. 80, sup. exh., vol. 1.

rated a system of cooperation which has given rise to the name of their ditch.

At the time of the survey, this canal was irrigating 594 acres of land, an additional 390 acres showing evidences of previous cultivation. At the time of the Meskimons survey in 1904, 314.7 acres were being cultivated. This ditch has a section 6 feet wide on the bottom, 8 feet wide on top, 1 foot deep. Its grade is 1 in 100, giving a carrying capacity of 10 second-feet. Water Supply Paper No. 104, already referred to, gives a flow on June 1, 1903, of 150 miner's inches for this ditch.

Oscar Walker Canal.—This ditch constitutes the lowest diversion from the Gila River on the reservation. It is of small proportions and irrigates a very limited area. This ditch is of comparatively recent date, having been constructed in 1903, and has been in continual operation since that year. At the time of the survey this ditch served to irrigate 13.1 acres, while 45.4 acres additional had been irrigated at some previous time. In 1904, at the time of the Meskimons survey, 28.5 acres are shown to have been irrigated. The ditch is 3 feet wide on the bottom, 5 feet wide on top, has a depth of 1 foot, grade of 1 in 1,000, and a capacity of 4 second-feet. Water Supply Paper No. 104, already referred to, shows a flow of 50 miner's inches.

Irrigation in Maricopa District.

Maricopa Canal.—A short distance northwest of the Gila Crossing district and situated between the Salt and Gila Rivers just above their confluence is found the present Maricopa district. The lands irrigated in this district are served by a ditch diverting water from the Salt River, and although the diversions from the Salt River are not within the scope of this investigation, the survey was extended so as to include this district.

Irrigation in the Maricopa district is relevant to a study of irrigation along the Gila because of the fact that the Indians of the former district formerly cultivated tracts along the Gila, but were later forced to vacate these because of the scarcity of water. It may be assumed, therefore, that this irrigation by means of water from the Salt River represents in a manner the irrigation formerly practiced by these Indians along the Gila.

This Maricopa district is served by one main canal heading several miles northeast of the reservation boundary. At the time of the survey (June, 1914), 1,271 acres were being irrigated in this district, an additional 219 acres showing evidences of previous cultivation.

The water supply is derived largely from the return flow of the Salt River. This flow subsequent to the recent increased use of water for irrigation in the Salt River Valley has doubled in amount, and has now become sufficient to supply not only this canal but to furnish water to several other irrigation canals farther down.

At the point where the Maricopa Canal enters the reservation it has a top width of 8 feet, bottom width of 7 feet; it is 2½ feet deep and has a grade of 1 in 2,000.

In 1903 the Government instituted suit in the United States district court to determine the relative water rights of several canals using water near the lower end of the Salt River. In the evidence submitted during the action it was shown that prior to 1894 the Indians had been irrigating 580 acres; that in 1901, 1,180 acres were under cultivation, and the court decreed that the Indians' lands were entitled to water from the Salt River in accordance with these findings.

A decree in the case above referred to was handed down by Judge Kent in Phoenix, Ariz., on June 11, 1903. A copy of this decree, as well as a supplemental decree of later date, is to be found in volume 4 of the supplemental exhibits accompanying this report.

Historical Analysis of Irrigation on the Gila River Reservation.

The analysis chart shown in the body of this report has been compiled from all the evidence and data gathered during the progress of this investigation and survey. The areas as determined by a survey of the reservation, made in 1904 by Mr. J. R. Meskimons, then superintendent of irrigation of the Indian Service, have been included with other data and are shown on the chart.

The survey of Meskimons was not made in sufficient detail to permit the segregation of the areas in actual cultivation from those previously cultivated. The outlines of the tracts shown on the Meskimons map included, in some instances, both cultivated and previously cultivated areas. However, in the report accompanying his map Mr. Meskimons gave an estimate of the irrigated area based on the results of his survey. A copy of this report is to be found on page 149, volume 1, of supplemental exhibits.

The areas as compiled in the chart shown in the body of the report represents proportional acreage areas covering a period of several years and do not take into consideration single years of exceptional droughts, for which no reliable information could be obtained. The compilations were made after a careful consideration of the life of the several ditches and from evidence obtained from the Indians and from other sources. These estimates, of course, were governed largely by the results of the survey made in connection with this investigation and the Meskimons survey.

It will be seen from the chart that the Indians during former years had a larger area under cultivation than they have at present, and that the irrigated tracts are scattered over a much more extended area of the reservation than they were at the time of the coming of the whites.

The principal factors which led the Indians to locate in the many districts in which they are now farming are the depletion of their low-water surface supply, necessitating the use of the meager seepage flow, peace with the Apaches, and to take advantage of the short period during which flood water was available in order to produce one crop.

The total agricultural yield realized by the Indians has become greatly reduced in recent years, and this one-time proud and powerful race has been forced since the advent of the whites to depend at least partly upon the bounties of the Government.

Florence-Casa Grande District No. 3.

The next oldest irrigated district along the Gila is in the Florence-Casa Grande Valley.

Irrigation in this district started at the time of the coming of the first white settlers to this general territory.

The agricultural development has progressed with varying degrees of success, and a number of different canals have been constructed from time to time.

Several years after the first settlers arrived in this district this territory experienced a mining boom and this mining excitement naturally gave an impetus to other lines of industries. The need for a large and adequate irrigation system for this valley was keenly felt, and efforts were made to induce capital to invest in a large irrigation enterprise. These efforts were finally successful, and in 1887 the Florence Canal project was undertaken. This project marked the most important agricultural development in this section. The many and varied fortunes of this enterprise have already been mentioned in the body of the report, and a more detailed account will be given in this appendix.

As in other districts along the Gila River, a number of canals formerly in use in this district have since become inactive. Some of the formerly used canals of this valley were absorbed by the Florence Canal, while others fell into disuse principally as the result of the failure of the water supply. The great damage occasioned by the frequent floods has also contributed largely to the present state of disuse of these canals.

The previously used ditches of this district will be first considered and in the order of their diversions, beginning at the upper end of the valley and proceeding downstream.

PREVIOUSLY USED CANALS.

Moore ditch (north side of river).—The uppermost of the abandoned ditches in this district is known as the Moore, or Moore and Arthur, ditch. This ditch was constructed in 1888 by Mr. Moore and first used during that year.

The Moore ditch was about 5 miles long heading just below the Double Buttes, and, according to this survey, had been used to supply water to 332.9 acres of land.

In 1903 this ditch was sold to a mining company which intended to use the waters thus acquired for milling purposes. The lands which had been irrigated by this canal were neglected from that time on, and the ditch was abandoned about the year 1905.

A small tract situated at the lower end of this old canal was later irrigated by means of a ditch known as the Ah Lee.

Brash ditch (south side river).—The Brash ditch, which was constructed by a man of that name in 1876–77, formerly served to irrigate land in the extreme upper end of the Florence Valley in what is sometimes called Round Valley.

Mr. Brash claims that the ditch was 5 miles long, that it was 4½ feet wide on the botom, 8 feet wide on top, and 20 inches in depth, and that it was constructed at a cost of $20,000. The first use of water from the Brash ditch took place in 1877, approximately 200 acres of land having been placed under cultivation as early as 1878. The canal was in continuous use until 1891, when, according to Brash, the Florence Canal Co. claimed and diverted the water, and he was forced to abandon the land. According to the survey, 310.4 acres of land are shown to have been previously irrigated under this old canal.

Montezuma (south side).—The Montezuma Ditch & Canal Co. was incorporated December 24, 1875, by Warren Vernoy, George N. Finch, Harvey Robbins, Andreas A. Eschallier, and Granville Wheat. Construction started in 1876, and the ditch was finished in 1877.

The heading of this canal was on the south side of the river in the SE. ¼ of sec. 12, T. 4 S., R. 10 E., just north of the old White house in Round Valley. This ditch followed the river bank to a point where the heading of the O. T. Canal was subsequently constructed, but the river erosion eventually carried away this portion of the ditch. When the O. T. Canal (see p. — of this appendix) was built, a portion of the Montezuma beyond this point was utilized.

The Montezuma Canal was one of the most important of the early ditches in the Florence district. In 1888 this ditch had a capacity of 15 second-feet of water, and according to the annual report of the board of supervisors for 1889 it served to irrigate approximately 1,000 acres of land.

Shortly after the construction of the Florence Canal the water users under the Montezuma began to transfer stock in the latter canal in consideration of water rights in the Florence Canal. The last recorded transfer of this nature bears a date of 1895. From the evidence gathered the Montezuma Canal was in use as late as 1900.

From the survey and from other information collected it is estimated that the Montezuma was used to irrigate approximately 775 acres just prior to its abandonment and absorption by the Florence Canal.

Holland ditch (south side).—In 1868 Pat Holland constructed the ditch which bears his name, but which is sometimes also known as the Holland & Gay. The line of this old ditch passes through the town of Florence, and in places the old banks are still plainly visible.

Primarily this ditch was constructed for the irrigation of the Holland ranch, but later other landowners became interested. In the report of the board of supervisors for 1889 it is stated that 1,000 acres of land were under cultivation from this ditch, the length of which is given as 7 miles. Other sources give 1,200 acres as the maximum acreage under this ditch.

The results of the survey and investigation give 950 acres as the area previously irrigated by this canal.

According to the records on file in the office of the county recorder of Pinal County, the Florence Canal Co. agreed to furnish water for 740 acres situated under the Holland in consideration for the complete transfer of the latter ditch. This instrument was dated February 10, 1894. It has been concluded, from the evidence collected, that the Holland ditch was not used after 1891.

Alamo Amarillo (south side) ditch.—This ditch was constructed about 1868 for the express purpose of irrigating the town property of Florence and land lying immediately adjacent thereto. Water from this ditch was also used for power purposes in the old flour mill situated between Florence and Adamsville. The remains of this old flour mill are still to be seen close to the county road a short distance southwest of Florence.

In 1871 the Alamo Amarillo was extended to the town of Florence and was used extensively for the irrigation of town gardens and lawns as well as the many trees which lined both sides of the streets. The Alamo Amarillo was owned by a corporation of that name, but in 1890 the control of its stock passed into the hands of the Florence Canal Co., though it appears that even prior to that time the Florence Canal Co. had acquired some interests in this ditch. The Alamo Amarillo ditch continued in use until 1905.

It is estimated that 440 acres were cultivated by this ditch prior to its consolidation with the Florence Canal.

Sharpe (north side) ditch.—This ditch was probably constructed about 1877 or 1878 by Sharpe, who owned land on the north side of the Gila opposite the town of Florence.

Its heading was near the east line of sec. 20, T. 4 S., R. 10 E., and from here the ditch extended across the lowlands and around a rocky point which projects out to the river bank. A large portion of this ditch has been completely obliterated, but the location has been pointed out and established by a number of the older residents of that section. Because of the excessive cost of maintenance around the rocky point, mentioned above, this ditch fell into disuse and the irrigation of the lands was discontinued.

The first serious damage to the Sharpe ditch occurred in 1891, but this break in the ditch was repaired. In 1894 the Sharpe ditch was used to carry water to the Stiles ditch, which was located just below the Sharpe. The flood of 1896 destroyed so much of the ditch that it was completely abandoned.

According to the survey, only 14.7 acres show evidence of previous culture. Some land under this ditch has been washed away, but it is possible that some of the previously irrigated land which has never been subject to damage by floods no longer shows visible evidence of former cultivation.

According to data which have been gathered, approximately 160 acres were formerly cultivated under this ditch.

Stiles and Mason and Sylvester-Andrade (north side) ditches.—These two ditches are taken up under a single caption, since they formerly served to irrigate identical lands and because the upper portion of the old Sylvester-Andrade ditch was practically the original heading of the Stiles and Mason ditch.

The Sylvester-Andrade ditch was constructed in 1868–69 and the Stiles and Mason in 1872. The Stiles and Mason headed higher on the river than the Sylvester-Andrade and irrigated some land above the latter ditches. Several years (exact date not known) after the construction of the Stiles and Mason a heavy flood washed out much of the upper end of the Sylvester-Andrade. The Stiles and Mason was then extended to join the older ditch, the land under the latter being irrigated after that time by the Stiles and Mason.

After the first diversion made by the Florence Canal the water supply failed and the Stiles and Mason ditch, as well as the lands irrigated under it, were abandoned.

According to this survey, 106.4 acres are shown to have been previously irrigated under this old ditch. Much of the land formerly irrigated has been destroyed by floods, but according to data available 675 acres were at one time irrigated under this ditch and the Sylvester-Andrade.

White ditch (south side).—As previously mentioned, the first irrigation in the Florence district took place under the White ditch, which was constructed in the vicinity of Adamsville in 1864. Some land was already irrigated under this ditch during that year.

The White ditch was in use until 1891, at which time a large portion was washed out by floods, and it was never rehabilitated as a separate ditch, although portions of this ditch have been used as parts of later ditches.

In the case elsewhere referred to of P. R. Brady et al. *v.* The Florence Canal Co., evidence was submitted to the effect that in 1874 560 acres were being served by this ditch. According to this survey, 384.5 acres are being cultivated at the present time in the territory situated under the White ditch, and no other area in addition to the above was found to have been previously irrigated.

The area originally served by the White ditch is now irrigated by means of the Adamsville Canal.

Walker ditch.—John D. Walker was one of the earliest white settlers in this part of the country. Walker established a trading post on the Gila River Reservation and lived with the Indians as a squaw man. He was at one time a sergeant of the Pima Scouts, after which, in 1868, he took up land near the eastern end of the reservation in the vicinity of Adamsville and constructed the Walker ditch.

No land was placed under cultivation until two years after the construction of the ditch, and it appears from evidence submitted in the case of Brady et al. *v.* The Florence Canal Co. that between two and three hundred acres were at one time cultivated under the Walker ditch.

Most of the land originally irrigated by this ditch is now served by the Padilla ditch, although it is not at all unlikely that some land under the present Price and Powell ditch was also formerly irrigated by the old Walker.

In 1886–87 irrigation under this ditch ceased and the ditch was abandoned. A portion of the old Walker ditch now forms a part of the present Price and Powell ditch.

After due consideration of all available data it is believed that approximately 320 acres of land was irrigated by the old Walker ditch, and in the irrigation analysis of this district this entire area has been credited to the Padilla ditch.

CANALS IN OPERATION IN THE FLORENCE-CASA GRANDE DISTRICT.

Florence Canal.—The Florence Canal & Land Co., the first company which undertook to finance the construction of the Florence Canal, obtained its water right as the result of a filing made on October 13, 1885, by W. S. Foreman, who claimed to appropriate 100,000 miner's inches of water from the Gila River. This filing or water right was granted to J. M. Hurley on March 8, 1886, and Hurley in turn granted all right, title, and interest to the Florence Canal & Land Co. This company was organized in March, 1886, and as Mr. Hurley was one of the incorporators, it is presumed that the corporation was created for the express purpose, among other things, of acquiring his water-right privileges.

The capital stock of the Florence Canal & Land Co. was fixed at $1,000,000, the shares having a par value of $10. It appears that in July, 1886, this corporation filed amended articles of association, changing its name to that of the Florence Canal & Water Co., and also reducing its capital stock to $200,000. This capitalization was represented by 20,000 shares having a par value of $10. In 1886–87 this company constructed approximately 10 miles of canal, beginning at the point of diversion, and this ditch, as originally constructed, was 25 feet wide on the bottom, 30 feet wide on top, having a water depth of 4 feet, and capacity of 125 second-feet. The total length of this canal as finally constructed was approximately 50 miles. About 16 miles of this distance was completed in 1887, while the remaining portion of the ditch, together with the Picacho Reservoir, was not constructed until 1889.

The Florence Canal & Water Co. spent $60,000 in the consturction of the first 10 miles of the ditch, and in so doing exhausted its means for continuing the work which it had undertaken and without receiving any commensurate benefits.

On November 12, 1887, the Florence Canal & Water Co. conveyed all of the said canal with appurtenances to the Florence Canal Co.

The Florence Canal Co. was organized September 1, 1887, its capital stock being $500,000, consisting of 10,000 shares having a par value of $50. The canal system was not managed in a mutual manner, but a common carrier; the Florence Co. sold water to landowners and entrymen and many entries were proved up under the rights thus acquired. These rights were sold at prices from $3 to $15 per acre, each acre being covered by one share of stock and each share representing enough water to irrigate 1 acre.

The contract by which this water was conveyed called for an annual maintenance charge of $1.50 per acre. During the construction of the Florence Canal and for a few years afterwards people rushed into this district and 52,160 acres of land under this canal were filed on, 30,000 acres of which were desert entries. Owing to the failure of the water supply, resulting chiefly from the silting of the canal, title was not perfected to a large portion of this land until many years later. These later titles were acquired principally by homestead and desert entries, reclamation having been effected by pumping.

There appear to be no records in the recorder's office of Pinal County in the nature of contracts or agreements whereby the Florence Canal Co. took over the Montezuma, the Alamo, Amarillo, the Holland, and certain interests in the Brady-Chase Canals, excepting the records of water rights grants of the Florence Canal Co., wherein the said Florence Canal Co. agrees to furnish water to the owners or shareholders of these small canals in consideration of the interests or stock held by these several parties and which were assigned by them to the Florence Canal Co.

Of these transactions some are dated as early as 1888, others as late as 1895. One instrument by which the Florence Canal Co. agreed to furnish water for 740 acres in consideration of the transfer of stock in the Montezuma was dated 1891. In another agreement, dated March 19, 1888, "the Florence Canal Co. further stipulates to furnish the second party from the Alamo Amarillo ditch water for the irrigation of certain lands, when it can be done, instead of the Florence Canal, and at the same price per acre. All rights for prior use of water reserved by second party as though he had retained the said stock in the Alamo Amarillo Ditch Co." While the records show that the Florence Canal Co. obtained an interest in the Brady-Chase ditch, it never gained control of the latter.

The Florence Canal Co. at a time just subsequent to its acquirement of the Florence Canal and franchise executed a mortgage lien on its canal and property, dated August 1, 1889, to the Farmers Loan & Trust Co., a corporation organized under the laws of the State of New York, to secure a bond issue in the sum of $300,000 with which to carry on the construction work. Of this amount, $125,000 was expended in the construction of the Piacacho Reservoir, while the balance was spent on the canal which was completed throughout the entire length originally proposed.

Foreclosure proceedings were instituted on the bond issue above mentioned, and a decree was rendered August 1, 1893, directing the sale of the canal and property to satisfy the plaintiffs in the sum of $379,746.64, being principal and interest secured by the mortgage aforesaid. Title to the property was perfected to the Casa Grande Valley Canal Co., December 19, 1894. The above-named corporation was organized April 16, 1894, by Oren B. Taft, Oren E. Taft, and Charles Hood.

When the Casa Grande Valley Canal Co. came into possession of the property it was by virtue of being the owners of the $300,000 of bonds issued by the Florence Canal Co., the new company being organized solely for the purpose of acquiring the property which these stockholders found themselves obliged to take under the foreclosure proceedings just mentioned.

Upon acquiring this property the stockholders, who were also the bondholders in pro rata shares, assessed themselves voluntarily $40,000 in cash, of which $8,000 was used in the expense of foreclosure and the remainder in the construction of about a mile and a half of new canal to replace a section of the original canal lying just below the point of diversion, this section having proved to be exceedingly faulty, rendering the canal almost useless at time of high water. That that expenditure of the last-mentioned sum ($32,000) was amply justified has been proven by five years of use of the canal since that time, the former difficulty having been entirely overcome. The canal was never cleaned of silt until the year 1900, and was not at that time carrying its full capacity.

On July 1, 1894, the Casa Grande Valley Canal Co. executed a mortgage lien on the canal and all property appurtenant thereto to the Mercantile Trust Co., of New York, to secure a bond issue in the sum of $600,000.

Of the $600,000 of bonds secured by this mortgage only $360,000 have been issued, $240,000 being left with the trustee for future issuance if necessary. The outstanding $360,000 of bonds represent to the stockholders an actual cash outlay of approximately $250,000. This latter sum includes $210,000, which was the amount paid for the $300,000 of Florence Canal Co. bonds at about 70 cents on the dollar, together with the $40,000 which was the amount of the assessment levied by the new stockholders to defray expenses of foreclosure and to reconstruct the upper portion of the canal.

The bondholders of the last company (Casa Grande Valley Canal Co.), were also prorata holders of its outstanding stock, amounting to $292,500, the balance of the stock, amounting to $707,500, never having been issued, remained in the hands of the company.

Owing to the excessive cost of maintenance resulting from the silt-laden waters and the insufficient gradient of the canal, this company was unable properly to maintain its ditch and was compelled to submit to a forced sale of its property for taxes.

This sale took place April 6, 1900, and on March 1, 1901, title was perfected in William English by A. F. Booker, treasurer and ex officio tax collector of Pinal County, Ariz. On May 15, 1901, grantee last mentioned quit claimed all right, title, and interest to Frances E. Taft, wife of Oren B. Taft, who in turn, together with her husband, on March 22, 1904, quit claimed all right, title, and interest in said canal to John W. Sharpe. When Mr. Sharpe became the owner of the canal and property he acquired the appropriations made by the Florence Canal Co. on April 4, 1888, amounting to 40,000 miner's inches in addition to the original rights of S. W. Foreman, who had appropriated 100,000 miner's inches. Subsequent to this time Sharpe acquired the right of Charles D. Reppy, who had appropriated 5,000 miner's inches, making in all a total of 145,000 miner's inches of water now vested in Sharpe.

On August 26, 1905, the Pinal Water Co. was organized for the purpose of taking over the interest of John W. Sharpe, who, as shown, acquired the rights and title to the Casa Grande Valley Canal Co.

The Pinal Water Co. was originally capitalized at $250,000, later increasing its capital to $1,000,000 by amended articles. On February 12, 1907, Mr. Sharpe transferred by quit-claim deed to the Pinal Water Co., the 5,000 miner's inches of water acquired from Charles D. Reppy, heretofore mentioned.

On and after March 23, 1907, certain complaints were filed against the Pinal Water Co., to which the Florence Canal Co., the Casa Grande Valley Canal Co., and John W. Sharpe were made party defendants, in which the plaintiffs in various cases asked for appointment of a receiver, some of which were denied by the court, while in the case of William J. Schulze against the same parties defendant, filed November 15, 1907, Albert C. Sieboth, Esq., was appointed receiver on amended motion December 15, 1907. Mr. Sieboth administered the affairs of the concern until the last few years, during which time various attachments were levied against the canal to satisfy labor claims, materials purchased, etc., and judgments rendered. Other difficulties existed between those owning water rights under the old Florence Canal, whereupon Mr. Sieboth was relieved, on motion, and R. L. Chamlee was appointed receiver of the Casa Grande Valley Canal Co. and the Pinal Water Co.

The receivers permitted the canal to continue in use with the result that more silt was deposited, the capacity of the canal thereby reduced, and much of the land allowed to return to its virgin state.

On March 13, 1909, John W. Sharpe et al. conveyed by means of a quitclaim deed to Charles R. Sligh (spelled Schley in records) the Florence Canal and the Picacho Reservoir.

The Florence Canal was again sold for taxes and pursuant to a judgment rendered on March 25, 1913, against the Casa Grande Canal Co., Pinal Water Co., Pinal Mutual Irrigation Co., John W. Sharpe and Charles R. Sligh, and according to the sheriff's certificate of sale dated May 23, 1913, title to the Florence Canal passed to one H. M. Fennemore. This last title was perfected by sheriff's deed dated May 28, 1914, and shortly thereafter July 29, 1914, Mr. Fennemore conveyed by quitclaim deed all his rights and interest in the Florence Canal to the San Carlos Canal and Irrigation Co., a corporation. This company having the present tax title is now operating the canal, the last receiver, G. W. Smith by name, having been dismissed by an order of the court, dated October 23, 1914.

The Pinal Mutual Irrigation Co., mentioned as one of the defendants in the action, was incorporated in March, 1911, for the purpose of taking over on a cooperative plan, the old Florence canal system. The incorporators of this company are a portion of the original contract holders and owners of land under the old canal who desired to acquire possession of the canal, or otherwise to be in a position to operate the canal on a mutual basis.

It appears also that the Pinal Mutual Irrigating Co. had an option on all rights or interests of Charles R. Sligh, and that this option was obtained prior to the last tax sale referred to above.

Mr. Thomas Weeden, present Register of the Land Office at Phoenix, in the Arizona Blade-Times, November 1, 1913, has written as follows:

> The Pinal Mutual Irrigation Co. also has an option on all the Charles R. Sligh and the Clark estate rights and interest in and to the Casa Grande Valley Canal Co., said interests representing 80 per cent of the stock and bonds of the said Casa Grande Valley Canal Co. Before the Casa Grande Canal Co. went into the hands of the present receiver, John W. Sharpe had purchased a majority of the stock and bonds of the company and he subsequently sold these stocks and bonds to Sligh and Clark and they increased their holdings to 80 per cent of said bonds and stocks. Under this option, above referred to, Charles R. Sligh and the administrator of the Clark estate became stockholders in the Pinal Mutual Irrigation Co. upon the same terms and conditions as do all other stockholders of the company. That is, they take one share of stock for each acre of land they sign up under the system.

By virtue of a quitclaim granted by E. W. Coker and others and dated April 12, 1911, the Pinal Mutual Irrigation Co. came into possession of a certain water-right appropriation, dam site, and canal location, made on March 22, 1911.

This company spent considerable money in surveys, reports, and some heavy "rock cut" construction work on the canal of their proposed project, which had for its object the building of a new canal closely paralleling the Florence Canal and a permanent diversion in the Gila River. An able report on this project was made by the late Mr. J. D. Schuyler in 1911.

Referring again to the Florence Canal, shortly after this sheriff's sale, several of the landowners under this canal who held contracts from the original company petitioned the supreme court to allow the receiver to issue receiver's certificates, these certificates to represent a first lien on the canal and reservoir. This petition was granted and the certificates were issued to the amount of $5 per acre to the landowners under the canal who would spend that amount per acre toward the rehabilitation of the canal. Under this order, a number of landowners got together and cleaned out approximately 15 miles of the old canal, expending about $8,000 in this work and bringing possibly 2,000 acres of land back under cultivation. After this expenditure, the landowners brought suit to foreclose on the lien. The defendants to this action were the Casa Grande Valley Co., Pinal Water Co., H. M. Fennemore, Chas. R. Sligh, and any and all persons claiming any right or title to the canal. It appears, however, that no further action in this suit has been taken, but other landowners, realizing the benefit derived by their neighbors, decided to continue the work of maintenance in order to make the canal more serviceable. These people claimed to be carrying on this work under the statutes of the State of Arizona, which provide that when the proprietors of a ditch fail to supply water for irrigation the landowners may take possession of the canal and do the necessary work, assessing themselves therefor, and that the work thus performed will stand as a lien against the ditch and may be collected as any other lien, through foreclosure proceedings.

Maintenance work of this nature was going on at the time of this investigation, although, as a matter of information, it appears that Mr. Fennemore served notice on the laborers to desist in the work of widening the canal, but that this notice was not heeded by the landowners.

The Florence Canal at the time of this survey was being used to irrigate 3,531.5 acres, and the survey also showed that there are 10,998 acres of previously irrigated land under the canal, while the maximum area irrigated at one time as found in the analysis of irrigation in this district was approximately 7,000 acres.

Ah Lee ditch (*north side*)—The Ah Lee ditch was constructed in 1912 and for the past two or three years has been operated by a Chinese gardener, after whom the ditch takes its name.

The Ah Lee ditch is only about 1 mile long, has a bottom width of 2.5 feet, top width of 5 feet, and water depth of 0.8 foot. The land cultivated by Ah Lee was undoubtedly formerly irrigated by the Moore and Arthur at a time when this latter ditch was in operation.

At the time of this survey no land was actually being irrigated, as the ditch heading had been washed out and a pumping plant was being installed.

While the Ah Lee ditch will be used in connection with the pumping plant it is not likely that a diversion from the river will be again attempted.

This survey showed that the garden tract under this ditch contained 10.3 acres.

McLellan (*north side*).—The original appropriation for this ditch called for sufficient water to irigate 480 acres of land, or three quarter-sections, and in the adjudication suit of 1896 (Brady et al. *v.* Florence Canal) Mr. McLellan claimed there were about 400 acres actually irrigated from this ditch.

This canal was constructed by Canterio Yescas in 1871 and so far as known it has been in continuous use since that year. In 1881 this ditch carried sufficient water to irrigate 400 acres of land.

At the time of the construction of the Florence Canal, McLellan claimed to have had in cultivation under this ditch 400 acres, about 100 acres of which was in alfalfa and 30 acres in orchards, one-half acre in vineyard, and balance of land in grain. Yescas had in addition two acres of alfalfa and a few peach trees. Shortage of water which resulted from the Florence Canal diversion made it necessary for these ranchers to confine their crops to grain alone, and it is claimed that yield of grain decreased to about one-half what it had formerly been.

The irrigated lands lay on what are known as the upper and lower benches, but subsequent to the flood of 1891 the land on the lower bench was no longer irrigated. This lowland was at one time called Parson's Valley.

In 1891 a portion of this ditch washed out, but it was immediately rebuilt on the former alignment. The first irrigation from this ditch took place in 1872. In the report of the board of supervisors of Pinal County, dated 1889, it is stated that the McLellan ditch was three miles long and irrigated some 300 acres.

J. J. Fraser and W. G. Knight, present owners of the McLellan Canal, claim that some 40 acres were irrigated in 1871, and in 1872 there were 280 additional acres put under irrigation, making a total of 320 acres which has been irrigated to the present time. This land lies in secs. 16 and 17, T. 4 S., R. 10 E.

At the time of the survey in 1914 the area under cultivation was found to be 1,901 acres and in addition 12.2 acres showed evidence of former cultivation. An additional 29.2 acres were found to be under fence, but showed no evidence of previous culture.

Old Timers Canal (south side).—Because of the failure of the Florence Canal to furnish water to many of the landowners in the vicinity of Florence, some of these landowners organized the Farmers Ditch Co., a mutual concern incorporated with a capital stock of $50,000 consisting of 5,000 shares. In 1909 this company commenced the construction of a ditch known as the Old Timers Canal which was completed during the following year. This ditch takes out of the river at a point somewhat lower than the Florence Canal, but it runs nearly parallel to the latter and covers much of the territory south of the river which was under irrigation prior to the construction of the Florence Canal. On May 10, 1911, the Farmers Ditch Co. deeded to the Old Timers Canal Co. all of their rights and interests in the Farmers Ditch of which the latter company is the present owner. The Old Timers Canal Co. is capitalized for $44,000 represented by 2,200 shares. Up to the present time 1,968 shares have been issued and are held by 233 different land owners under the canal.

Next to the Florence Canal the Old Timers ditch irrigates the greatest area in the Florence district. It is a well constructed ditch, has a permanent headgate and is well maintained.

This survey showed that during 1914, 1,938.8 acres were under cultivation under this ditch and an additional area of 180.9 acres exhibiting evidences of previous culture.

The Old Timers Canal now serves to irrigate lands that were originally irrigated by the older canals. When this irrigation is credited to the Old Timers Canal as has been done in the irrigation analysis, which is included in this report, this canal possesses a very early priority.

Chino or Brady and Chase ditch (south side).—The ditch now known as the Chino was originally known as the Chase, then as the Brady and Chase, later as the Ruggles, and still later as the Kellner. Its present name has been given it for the reason that several Chinamen have recently been farming under it.

This ditch was constructed in 1867 or 1868, and at the time of the construction of the Florence Canal in 1887 it served to irrigate approximately 200 acres.

In 1873 this ditch was extended and the water used to operate a flour mill from that time until the water shortage which followed construction of the Florence Canal.

It appears as a matter of record that the Florence Canal Co. endeavored to gain a controlling interest in this ditch, but while a small interest was obtained the controlling interests remained intact, and this ditch has always been operated independently of the Florence Canal Co.

The area being cultivated by the Chino ditch at the time of this survey in 1914 was 172 acres, with an additional area of 32.4 acres shown to have been previously cultivated.

Pierson-Nicholas (north side).—This ditch, originally called the Spinas or Swiss ditch, was constructed in 1872 and was first used for irrigation during that year.

According to Mr. Spinas, by whom it was originally constructed, this ditch served to irrigate 320 acres in 1873, and 650 acres in 1877. This survey showed that 950.7 acres were under cultivation in 1914. There is an additional area of 338.8 acres which is fenced and which is claimed by the owner to have been irrigated on several occasions. It appears, however, that this irrigation consisted simply of flooding the land for pasture purposes and that no crops were ever produced.

This ditch was later called the Stewart after the name of the owner to whom it was sold by Spinas. Stewart in turn sold this ditch to its present owner.

The three Pierson brothers in 1891 built a ditch known as the Pierson ditch to irrigate their land which adjoined the Spinas holdings. Their ditch was located near the Spinas ditch. The heavy flood of 1905 washed out the heading of the Pierson ditch as well as a portion of the Spinas, and it was decided to combine the two ditches, using portions of each. This combined ditch has since been called the Pierson-Nicholas.

Price and Powell.—In 1909 Messrs. Price and Powell, of Florence, constructed a ditch which they originally called the Montezuma, but which was later known as the Price and Powell.

In the construction of the Price and Powell ditch a considerable portion of the old Walker, previously referred to, was utilized.

It is quite probable that some of the lands previously irrigated by the old Walker ditch are situated under the Price and Powell, but no definite data could be obtained in this relation. Inasmuch as the owners under the Padilla ditch (hereinafter discussed), claim to have as great an area under cultivation as was known to have been by the Walker ditch, no land under the Price and Powell has been credited as having been irrigated by the Walker ditch.

Owing to the long period (22 years) which elapsed from the time the Walker ditch went out of service until these later ditches were placed in operation, during which period land remained idle, the fact of the early irrigation of these lands appears of little importance. At the time of this investigation 317.4 acres were being irrigated under the Price and Powell ditch.

Adamsville Canal (south side).—This ditch, also known as the Sanford, is believed to have been built in 1866. It was designed to carry not less than 800 miner's inches of water, and its original heading was about three-fourths of a mile below the town of Florence on the south side of the river, approximately at the point where its present heading is located.

The board of supervisors of Pinal County, in their report of 1889, claim that this ditch at that time was 4 miles long and served to irrigate 1,000 acres of land.

The land formerly irrigated by the White ditch was irrigated from the Adamsville ditch after the floods of 1891, which destroyed a large part of the White. The Adamsville and the White ditches were located so as to cover about the same territory, and it is difficult to segregate definitely respective areas served by these two ditches.

At the present time the land around Adamsville owned by W. J. Clemens is irrigated almost entirely from this ditch.

At the time when this survey was in progress several large wells were being drilled on this land, and it is the intention of Mr. Clemens and others to irrigate this land by pumping, and to abandon the use of river water.

At the time of this survey in 1914, 384.5 acres were being cultivated under this ditch and no further land was found to show evidences of previous culture.

Padilla ditch.—What is now known as the Steinfeld Ranch was originally placed under cultivation at about the same time as was the J. D. Walker Ranch.[1] Juan Largo, who first owned and cultivated the Steinfeld land, was an intimate friend of Mr. Walker. They cleared and irrigated these two ranches from the same ditch. The Largo land, like Walker's, was abandoned about the time of the construction of the Florence Canal and remained idle until about four years ago (in 1910). During that year Padilla leased the Steinfeld land and constructed the ditch known as the Padilla ditch.

This survey showed 78.4 acres under cultivation in 1914, and 219.2 acres to have been previously cultivated. The present owner is Albert Steinfeld, of Tucson, Ariz.

The two Padilla brothers cultivated this land for about two years, then turned it back to Steinfeld, since which time it has been leased to various parties.

At the present time it is used exclusively by Indians belonging to the reservation, who besides irrigating the Steinfeld land are irrigating 44 acres situated within the confines of the reservation by means of this ditch.

The Padilla Canal is the last or lowest diversion of the Florence Casa Grande district, the next ditch below this one being located in the Gila River Reservation.

A PROPOSED IRRIGATION PROJECT IN THE FLORENCE-CASA GRANDE VALLEY.

A large project, proposing the diversion of a portion of the flow of the Gila River and the irrigation of a large tract of land in the Florence-Casa Grande Valley, was in course of construction at the time of this investigation.

The main canal of this project is located just above the old Florence Canal and nearly all of the land proposed to be irrigated is the same land as was originally or formerly proposed to be irrigated by the Florence Canal. The construction of this project is being undertaken by the Casa Grande Water Users' Association.

[1] See Walker ditch, supra.

The Casa Grande Water Users' Association came into existence on the 8th day of April, 1911, and claimed as its object the irrigation and development of the Florence-Casa Grande Valley, as well as the protection and benefit of the stockholders. No investigation of the affairs of this company was made by members of this Service, but the following general description of the company is taken from a report submitted on October 30, 1913, by H. G. Wells, a Carey Act inspector of the General Land Office. A full copy of this report is to be found in volume 2 of the Supplemental Exhibits.

The association is capitalized for $5,000,000, divided into 100,000 shares of the par value of $50 each, said shares being assessable. At the time I made examination of the association's books, it had, by contract, disposed of 51,399 shares, but, as I understand it, issued none. In other words, that much has been subscribed for. There had been paid in on such stock so subscribed for $69,532.60, or about $1.35 per share.

Its resources consist of certain water filings on the Gila River and on the San Carlos reservoir site, rights of way and real estate for which $3,350 have been paid, and a grading outfit which has cost approximately $10,000, together with several miles of constructed ditch which will be considered later. So far as I could find, it has no liabilities.

The officers and directors of this company are in no way interested in the promotion or financing of any other system, excepting that some of the officers may be interested in so far as getting water is concerned from what is known as the Old Florence Canal, which will be treated of later in this report. Mr. White is treasurer of a company known as the O. T. Canal Co., which takes water from the Gila River and irrigates 2,200 acres in the immediate vicinity of Florence, which lands are really a part of the lands which were formerly irrigated by the Old Florence Canal. Mr. White, or none of the others, is interested in such a way that they might be called promoters or financiers in connection with any other company.

The titles of this association to whatever water right it has, came to it through original filings made by it, which are evidenced by the certified copies of the files as they appear of record in the office of the county clerk of Pinal County, the first being "notice of appropriation of water and claim of site for dam and reservoir on the Gila River." This is what is known as San Carlos reservoir site. It was filed on by this association on the 3d day of June, 1911, by the Casa Grande Valley Water Users' Association, T. M. Meehan, vice president. This same paper, I think, was offered in the right-of-way matter, wherein this association filed certain papers with the department, in connection with the Casa Grande Valley Water Users' Association intervention in the matter of conflicting applications of J. M. Jamison, for right of way to construct a dam at San Carlos, Ariz., for the purpose of irrigation, and of the Arizona Eastern Railroad Co. to construct a railroad on a low grade through said reservoir site, involving the utilization of Box Canyon on the Gila River.

On February 17, 1912, the department rendered a decision in the above entitled case, in which it stated:

"Accordingly, in view of the foregoing, the application for right of way, filed by the Arizona Eastern Railroad Co. August 3, 1909, is hereby rejected, because of its interference with the San Carlos reservoir site, but this rejection will not preclude the railroad company from presenting another application for right of way for its road along the Gila, at such an elevation as will avoid interference with the reservoir site.

"Upon the present record, therefore, the several applications for rights of way for the reservoir site are accordingly hereby rejected without prejudice to the rights of said applicants, or any one of them, to hereafter submit a new application, supported by such showing as shall reasonably demonstrate the feasibility of the scheme and the capability of the applicants to carry the project to a successful conclusion."

This filing claimed also by appropriation, and attempting to appropriate, for domestic use, for irrigation and power purposes, and for any other beneficial use and purpose, all of the subterranean, surface, normal flow, and storm waters of the Gila River and its tributaries, which may be above the point of diversion, which can be developed, stored, or impounded by means of a storage dam to be constructed across the channel of the canyon of said Gila River at a point about 6 miles west of San Carlos post office, at what is known as Box Canyon. Also, it is the intention to use the channel of said river below the dam to carry the water appropriated and to be stored from time to time in said reservoir, to a suitable point above the town of Florence, in the county of Pinal where said water will be diverted from said channel by means of a canal, said canal being called the Casa Grande Valley Water Users' Association Canal, under construction. It is proposed by this canal to divert the water into a reservoir called the Picacho Reservoir, and from there to carry the water westerly through the Casa Grande Valley Water Users' Association's proposed canal.

On the 28th day of March, 1912, Frederick G. White, acting as the agent of the Casa Grande Valley Water Users' Association, posted a notice on the Gila River, about the center of section 8, T. 4 S., R. 11 E., claiming same to be a notice of appropriation. In this notice, the Casa Grande Valley Water Users' Association cites that it has appropriated, and does thereby appropriate, for irrigation, mechanical, domestic, stock, and any and all beneficial purposes, to be used by its stockholders upon and in connection with irrigable land owned, and to be owned, by them, and for the generating of water power for the generation of electricity, and unappropriated, surplus and flood waters of the Gila River in the county of Pinal, State of Arizona, in and of the amount of 1,500 second-feet, equivalent to 60,000 miner's inches, to be diverted at the point where the notice was posted, said place being on the south bank of said river, in said county and State, and more particularly described as being a point located north 50° 19′ east, 14 feet from the United States Geological Survey bench mark "1574," said point being the south abutment of a proposed dam. It is stated that it is the intention of the appropriator to build and mainain a dam and other necessary and proper diversion works, at the said point, and to construct, maintain, and operate an irrigating canal, beginning at said point and extending in a southwesterly and southerly direction, following a practicable and suitable grade line, to a point southerly and southwesterly from Casa Grande Station on the Southern Pacific Railroad, and located in the southwest corner of section 10, T. 7 S., R. 5 E., of the Gila and Salt River base and meridian, and that said dam, canal, and other diversion works, will be of ample capacity to divert and carry 1,500 second-feet of water as appropriated.

This is the same canal as heretofore referred to, as being the Casa Grande Valley Water Users' Association Canal, under construction, and the Casa Grande Valley Water Users' Association's proposed canal.

Frederick G. White, acting as agent for the Casa Grande Valley Water Users' Association, filed another notice on the 28th day of March, 1912, at a point north 67° west, 269 feet from United States Geological Survey mark "1574." In this notice, the Casa Grande Valley Water Users' Association claims to appropriate for irrigation, mechanical, domestic, stock, and any and all other beneficial purposes, for use by stockholders upon and in connection with irrigable land owned and to be owned by them, and for the generating of water power for the generating of electricity, 1,500 second-feet, equivalent to 60,000 inches, to be diverted at the point where said notice is posted, and with the exception of the point of location of the point of diversion, the language of this certificate, and the other one filed on the same day, which has just been referred to, are identical, and in fact the filings are identical, with the exception that in one case the point of diversion is moved up the river a short distance from where it is in the other. They have a separate canal for about a half mile, when the canal becomes the same. In other words, if one is constructed, the other will not be constructed. The object of the filing of the one which is up the river the farthest, is to avoid interference with the prior claim of J. M. Jamison and his successors to the point of diversion first filed on, or filed nearest to Geological Survey monument "1574."

These are all the filings that this association has made upon the waters of the Gila River, and cover the question as to the title which this association may have to its water rights.

But one class of stock has been contracted for. As I understand it, no stock has been issued and none will be issued until it is paid for in full. At the time the prospective water user arranges for stock he signs a contract agreeing to pay $50 for sufficient water to irrigate each acre of land which he proposes to reclaim. This contract makes the water appurtenant to the land and not to be separated from the land except on consent of the association.

There have been contracts signed for stock amounting to 51,399 shares, out of a total of 100,000 shares for which the association is incorporated, being a little more than half.

Each share of stock carries with it a proportionate part of the amount of water which may be available any one year. This is fully covered in section 8 of the by-laws, as follows:

"The amount of water to be delivered to such owner during any irrigation season shall, subject to the restrictions and limitations prescribed in these by-laws and in the form of stock subscription and contract set out in section 4 of this article, be such proportionate part of all water available for distribution by the association during a given irrigating season, as the number of shares owned by such owner shall bear to the whole number of valid and subsisting shares then outstanding, such water to be delivered for the irrigation of lands at such time during the irrigating season in each year as may be needed for the proper irrigation and cultivation thereof. But nothing in these by-laws or in the form of stock subscription and contracts shall be taken or construed as interfering or intended to interfere with any vested right of prior appropriation of water for the irrigation of the lands of any subscriber for or owner of, shares in this association and in times of scarcity of water the association, in the distribution of the water, other than water developed or stored by it or by means of works under its control, management and direction, shall recognize and give preference, in distribution of water to the land of shareholders priorities thereof, to the amount of water actually and necessarily required for the successful irrigation and cultivation of such lands."

The project had no irrigating capacity at date of examination. About 6 miles of the ditch had been partially built, which will be noted later on.

The project is not delivering the water sold.

The irrigation capacity of the project, as planned, is about 70,000 acres, as I am informed by the secretary of the association. The lands which it is proposed to irrigate are the following:

	Acres.
Unpatented desert-land entries	33,770.28
Homestead entries	4,621.01
Patented lands	9,172.97

There are also lands above and beyond the ditch, for which I did not take the data from the land office records, to see whether they were homestead, desert, or patented lands, to the extent of 5,375 acres, for which contracts for stock are held. This would make a grand total in connection with the project for which contracts for stock are held of 52,939.26 acres.

In addition, there is, under the ditches of this project, 6,720 acres of desert lands which have stock in what is known as the Pinal Mutual Irrigation Co. and no stock in this association; 8,040 acres of patented lands which have stock in the Pinal Mutual; and 20,480 acres of desert entries which have stock in neither of these companies, and, as far as I know, have no feasible way of being reclaimed.

There are also 7,360 acres of homestead entries which have stock in neither of these companies, making a total of 43,600 acres which are under the ditches of this association and could be watered from them were there any water, but which have no interest whatever in the association.

The project is not completed, but as proposed will consist of a ditch which is to be 40 feet wide on the bottom and 6 feet water depth. Side slopes 1¼ to 1, grade 2 feet per mile, giving the ditches a capacity of 957 second-feet. Such a ditch is feasible in the country in which this is being built, there being only one point that is difficult, and that being about a quarter of a mile below the headgate, where it goes across a rocky dike. Aside from this it is practically all plow material.

The per cent of the project completed, based on the area to be irrigated, would be nothing, as while there is, perhaps, about 6 miles of ditch constructed over a length of about 9 miles; it is constructed in a section here and another one there. The 6 miles which is built is not continuous, and the first work is about a quarter of a mile from the point of diversion.

The proportion of the plans completed, based on the cost of construction, was given me by the secretary as being about 15 per cent. However, I can not agree with him there, for the reason that there are about 55 miles to construct. One-half of this amount is of full size, and requires about 36,000 cubic yards to the mile. Of this 27 miles, there is not over 6 miles completed, which is about 22 per cent. Of the other 27 miles, the average capacity would be about one-half of that amount, and nothing has been done on that. I do not consider that there is over 10 per cent of the ditch completed, based on cost of construction. To construct the ditch with proper diversion works would cost at least $300,000. No land is actually under irrigation.

CONCLUSIONS.

I do not consider that the Casa Grande Valley Water Users' Association has any right, or filing, or interest in any filing on the San Carlos Reservoir.

I do not consider that there is any water from the direct flow to amount to anything that could be used to the benefit of his land after the prior rights are taken care of.

RECOMMENDATIONS.

That the question of the association having any storage rights in the San Carlos Reservoir be not considered.

That evidence of water from a constant flow right through the proposed canal of the association be not accepted, either as evidence of annual expenditure or as evidence of water for final proof, and that no extensions of time be granted on any desert land entries holding stock in this association, unless the claimants can show that they have some other means of watering their desert entries aside from stock in this association.

Construction work of the Casa Grande Canal was started in April, 1912, and at the time of this survey, May, 1914, about 9 miles had been completed and the work had been opened up for a distance of 12 miles. Shortly after this later date the large scale upon which the work was being carried on was greatly reduced, and it is believed that on July 1, 1915, no more than the full 12 miles of canal had been finished, or about 15 per cent of the project had been completed, based on the cost of construction.

As a result of the report above quoted the Commissioner of the General Land Office served notice under date of February 28, 1914, on the several desert-land owners who desired to prove up under the canal of the Casa Grande Valley Water Users' Association that their entries were held for rejection and 30 days was given in which the claimant was allowed to make an affirmative showing. A hearing in the above matter was held on March 13, before the local land office and attention was directed to the case of George Lobb, plaintiff, *v.* Peter Avenente, et al., defendants, which has heretofore been mentioned, and which was then pending in the superior court of Pinal County, and the ruling of the commissioner which followed this hearing is in part as follows:

A copy of the summons and complaint in this suit was filed in this office and from these papers it is ascertained that the plaintiff prays the court to adjudge the relative rights of the parties to the action to the appropriation of water from the Gila River for the irrigation of their lands. The association is made a party to the said suit, and the attorneys at the time of the hearing assured me that it was the intention and desire to proceed with due diligence to the hearing of the matter, and they requested that the action of this office be deferred pending the final adjudication of the questions involved.

In the office letters dated February 28, 1914, each claimant was to be allotted 30 days from receipt of notice to submit new annual proofs, or to make an affirmative showing refuting the conclusions of the inspector.

In view of the pending suit above mentioned, you will notify each claimant, as indicated, that he will be allowed 30 days from receipt of notice to file a brief application requesting that action on his entry be suspended pending the adjudication of the suit referred to, and that he be not required to make the showing called for on February 28, 1914.

Accordingly action has been suspended on these entries under the Casa Grande Water Users' Association Canal, pending the outcome of the case referred to.

No decision has as yet been rendered in the above action. Shortly after the beginning of the case, however, the Pinal Mutual Irrigation Co., a corporation and one of the defendants in this action, filed a demurrer to the answers and cross bill of the Casa Grande Valley Water Users' Association, and the points at issue were submitted on briefs and the demurrer was overruled by the court.

As a matter of information and common report, the Casa Grande Water Users' Association have taken an option on all of the land either owned or controlled by Charles R. Sligh, and with this agreement (commonly called the Sligh deal) it is understood that whatever interests Sligh may have in the Florence Canal is to be conveyed along with the land.

It is understood that the price to be paid by the Casa Grande Water Users' Association was $125,000, with a first payment of $25,000. The time in which this first payment was to be made having expired, the company has been granted an extension of time. At the time this report was written—July, 1915—this initial payment had not been made.

COMMENT ON ANALYSIS OF IRRIGATION IN THE FLORENCE-CASA GRANDE DISTRICT.

The data and information from which the analysis of irrigation in this district was compiled has been obtained from a number of different sources.

The proof of appropriation blanks elsewhere referred to were distributed to the different landowners using water now or who had been in past times. Much information was secured in this way. Many of former water users, or perhaps better, entrymen, under the Old Florence Canal have long since left this part of the country, and while an effort was made to get information through the mails from those whose addresses were obtainable, yet not very satisfactory results were obtained. It is also true that a number of those reached by correspondence, as well as others who were personally interviewed, refused to fill out the blank or give any information concerning the irrigation of their land.

Much data referring directly or indirectly to irrigation was collected from the records in the county recorder's office of Pinal County. Abstracts were made and used in the analysis of all water appropriation filings, water-right deeds, transfers of stock and articles of incorporation recorded in this county.

Through the courtesy of Mr. Alfred C. Sieboth, receiver of the Florence Canal, access was had to the books kept by Mr. Sieboth covering the delivery of water from the Florence Canal to the various tracts receiving water during the period of his receivership, from January 1, 1908, to June, 1911. Mr. Dugal Stewart was also kind enough to grant access to the receiver's books covering the deliveries of the Florence Canal from November, 1912, to April, 1914.

Efforts were made toward obtaining access to the books of the Florence Canal Co.; however, no success was attained. Their books have been taken from this part of the country and it is believed that they are now in Chicago.

From the evidence and decree submitted (May, 1897) in the District Court of Pinal County, and in the case of Peter R. Brady et al. *v.* Florence Canal Co. et al., elsewhere referred to and copies of which are to be found in the supplemental exhibits of this report, considerable data was obtained. A much later water-right lawsuit, and which is still pending in case No. 2329, entitled "George Lobb, *v.* Peter Avenete et al.," before the Superior Court, Pinal County, Ariz. The complaint in the above case was opened June 10, 1914, before Judge Lockwood. Evidence was heard by J. W. Walker, appointed referee by the court. A copy of the complaint with names of defendants in this case is to be found in volume 2, of the supplemental exhibits.

At the time of the writing of this report, all of the evidence in the latter case has not been heard; however, abstracts of the evidence, so far submitted, were obtained and used in the analysis.

Much consideration was given to a survey of the irrigated lands made by Mr. Albert T. Colton in 1896, and reported by Mr. Arthur P. Davis in the United States Geological Survey (Water Supply Paper No. 2). A map was prepared by Mr. Colton, together with other data referring to irrigation in this district, accompanied the report submitted by Mr. Davis. Mr. Colton, who is one of the pioneer surveyors of this section of the country, and who is now the water commissioner of the Safford Solomonville Valley, advises that the map referred to was compiled from actual surveys made by himself at that time.

Besides the information supplied by the present water users through the proofs of appropriation, a certain amount of more or less general history of irrigation in the district was obtained from interviews with the older residents, or "old-timers" of the district.

The great difficulty encountered in computing a detailed analysis of irrigation in this district, or in the other districts investigated, was the scarcity of specific or detailed information concerning the history of irrigation. The records in the recorders office, as well as much of the evidence submitted in the water litigation, were alike in the very general nature of the information supplied. The data by which the detailed anaylsis wes made came largely from the present landowners who had remained in the district since its early days. This information, as a rule, favored the interests of the persons giving the information, yet sufficienrt data has been obtained so that any gross exaggerations could be known and modified.

No specific information was obtainable as to the exact dates of irrigation of certain of the previously irrigated areas in the territory along the Florence Canal between the towns of Florence and Casa Grande, and certain assumptions had to be made so as to include these areas in the analysis. Whenever assumptions as to dates were made they were governed by all available information, and as a rule, when assumed dates were used the possible error was confined within narrow limits by other known data.

Observation of the land itself, as well as evidence from other sources, would indicate that a large portion of the previously irrigated lands under the Florence Canal were reclaimed and irrigated sufficiently for patent purposes only, and never produced beneficial crops. Other tracts were irrigated more or less indifferently for a few years and then abandoned. Certain landowners under the Florence Canal claim that their lands have been irrigated when there was absolutely no evidence on the ground or obtainable elsewhere to support such contentions. Certain other owners made claims of previous cultivation by water from the Florence Canal when it was plainly evident that their lands had been reclaimed by pumps or water from other sources. Whenever any doubt existed as to the nature of the irrigation of the land or as to the duration of the irrigation, the land in question was given the benefit of the doubt, and all lands having any evidence of previous irrigation by waters from the Gila River, either as a result of the survey or otherwise, are included in the analysis regardless of how brief was their irrigation or how beneficial was the use of the water.

Inasmuch as the history of irrigation in any district must come largely from the memory of interested parties, as well as from other sources that are more or less in dispute, an anlysis embracing such a history may be in error to a certain extent. In the present investigation so much data has been collected from a number of different sources that it is believed that the analysis submitted in the body of the report is fairly accurate and in conformity with the facts.

Solomonville-Safford Valley District No. 2.

HISTORY OF CANALS.

A brief history of the different canals of the Solomonville-Safford district is here given. Information in this connection has been obtained from a review of the evidence submitted in the case of Smithville Canal Co. *v.* Oregon Irrigation & Canal Co., referred to in the body of the report, and from the data supplied by the present owners through the proof of appropriation blanks distributed during the progress of the survey in this valley.

These canals will be taken up in the order in which they are situated, starting at the upper end of the valley and proceeding down the Gila.

Brown Canal.—The first ditch diverting water from the Gila River in the Solomonville-Safford Valley is the Brown Canal on the north side of the river some 8 or 9 miles above Solomonville. This ditch was constructed in 1896 and in 1904, according to the decree, and was used to irrigate 100 acres on the Brown ranch. In 1905 the Sanchez and the Mejia Canals were consolidated with the Brown.

These two canals, the Sanchez and the Mejia, were located somewhat lower down the river and are much older than the Brown.

The Mejia was one of the early canals, having been constructed in 1877. It was only 3 feet wide until 1883, when it was enlarged to a width of 6 or 7 feet.

The Sanchez ditch was constructed later in 1891, but some of the land under this ditch had been previously (as early as 1883) irrigated by an older ditch known as the old Brown ditch, which was supplanted by the Sanchez in 1891.

The Brown Canal, at the time of this survey, served to irrigate 559.5 acres of land, while 103 acres additional were found to have been cultivated at some previous time. The decree shows 820 acres to have been the combined acreage irrigated under the three canals at the time of the adjudication in 1904.

The present owners, according to the proofs of appropriation which they have furnished, believe they now have a combined area of 1,101 acres under cultivation and that in 1904 they had 779 acres under cultivation. The difference, amounting to 158 acres between the area shown to have been cultivated by this survey and the area given in the decree, is accounted for in part by an overestimation at the time of the decree. It is not believed that the floods which have occurred subsequent to that time have washed away areas of land sufficient to account for this difference.

The Brown Canal Co. has been incorporated with 150 shares, having a par value of $10 per share. Only 94 shares have been issued, these being held by 28 individuals.

Fournese Canal.—The next canal in order down the valley lies on the opposite or east side of the river, and is known as the Fournese.

The Fournese Canal constitutes the original heading and the upper portion of the old San Jose Canal. In 1891 a new heading was constructed for the San Jose Canal a short distance lower down the river and the alignment of the San Jose was shifted in order to embrace a greater area of land. The remaining portion of the old San Jose ditch was later rehabilitated and called the Fournese Canal.

The waters of the Fournese Canal served to irrigate, at the time of this survey, 230.5 acres, an additional 11 acres showing evidence of previous cultivation.

Included in the above areas are 66 acres which are situated under the San Jose Canal, the water of this canal being conveyed over the Fournese Canal by means of flumes. The decree shows the Fournese Canal to have irrigated a constant area of 260 acres from the date of its initial use until at the time of the decree. The area under cultivation at the present time, according to the claims of the owners, amounts to 200 acres. Very little difference was found to exist between the decreed amount and the results of the survey.

The Fournese Canal is incorporated, the capital stock, amounting to $3,375, consists of 45 shares, having a par value of $75. These 45 shares are held by 12 landowners.

San Jose Canal.—The San Jose Canal, which has its heading in the Gila, one-half mile below the Fournese, is the third largest canal in the valley. It is also one of the oldest canals in the valley, its construction having been started during the latter part of 1873. In 1874 it had been built as far west as Solomonville.

In 1891 a new heading was provided for this canal, its alignment was changed, and it was enlarged and otherwise improved. The former heading, as previously stated, now constitutes the heading of the Fournese Canal.

In this same year a company was formed for the purpose of constructing an extension to this canal, beginning at the San Simon Wash, at Solomonville, and continuing us far west as the town of Safford. This portion of the ditch is called the San Jose extension.

At the time of this survey the San Jose Canal was irrigating 3,595.7 acres, an additional acreage of 62.5 acres being shown to have been previously irrigated. According to the adjudication decree, the area under cultivation, in 1914, at the time of the suit, was 3,000 acres. The excess area, shown by the survey, amounting to approximately 600 acres, has evidently been placed under cultivation since 1904.

The San Jose Canal Co. and the San Jose extension are both incorporated companies. The former company is capitalized at $20,000, its stock consisting of 200 shares, of par value $100, and owned by 38 individuals. The San Jose Extension Co. is capitalized at $2,500, its stock consisting of 50 shares, par value $50, being divided among 43 stockholders.

Michelena Canal.—The Michelena Canal is located on the north side of the river about 4 miles above Solomonville. Construction work on this ditch was begun in November, 1873, its width near the heading was made 6 feet and it has usually served to carry one irrigating head.

The first cultivation under this ditch took place in 1874, when about 40 acres were put under irrigation. The results of this survey gave 382.5 acres of present cultivation under this canal and 5.7 acres of previous cultivation. The decree gave 450 acres as the area under cultivation in 1904. While loss by floods may account for some of this difference, it is thought that the acreage given in the decree was slightly overestimated. The present owners are of the opinion that they have 510 acres under cultivation.

The Michelena is a private ditch, not incorporated, and is owned exclusively by two different owners of land under the canal.

Montezuma Canal.—The oldest canal in the valley and second in point of size is known as the Montezuma. This canal was constructed in 1873 to replace a small ditch that had been built during the previous year and which had been used to irrigate a small amount of land prior to the construction of the larger ditch. In 1874 the Montezuma Canal had been excavated as far west as the Sand Wash, its total length then being 5½ miles. As early as 1877, 1,000 acres were being cultivated under this canal.

The Layton town extension of the Montezuma Canal, beginning at the Sand Wash, had its beginning in a small ditch constructed in 1882. Virtually, however, the Layton Town Canal was not constructed until 1891, when this small ditch was greatly enlarged and improved.

The Montezuma Canal was further extended in 1892 and still further a few years later, the latter extension being known as the Thatcher extension.

At its lower terminus the Montezuma wastes into the Union Canal.

The total area of land shown to be in cultivation under this canal at the time of this survey was 4,837.8 acres, while an additional 107 acres presents evidence of former cultivation. The total cultivation, past and present, aggregates 4,944.8 acres. Of this area, 3,150.7 acres lie under the Montezuma proper, 722 under the Layton Town extension, the remainder coming under the later extension. The adjudication decree gave 3,750 acres as the area under cultivation in 1904 under the Montezuma, while the present owners claim to have under cultivation a total of 5,780 acres. Since the date of the decree the cultivated area has been gradually increased, and it is believed that the area according to the decree is a close estimate of the cultivation at that time.

The Montezuma Canal proper and the Layton Town extension are separate incorporations. The users of water under the Thatcher extension own or control stock in the Layton Town extension.

The Montezuma Canal has 191 stockholders. Its capitalization, amounting to $10,000, is represented by 400 shares having a par value of $25 per share. The Layton Town Canal is capitalized for $10,000, represented by 2,000 shares having a par value of $5 each. The Layton Town Canal has 142 stockholders.

Union Canal.—The Union Canal is the largest canal in the Solomonville-Safford Valley. The area irrigated under this canal embraces lands that formerly were irrigated by several other canals, one of which, the Central Canal, was at one time one of the principal canals of this district, serving to irrigate nearly as great an area of land as did the Union.

The old Central Canal, constructed in January, 1873, was originally about 4 miles long and its heading was located just north and a short distance east of Safford. An extension known as the Smithville extension was constructed in 1883. The capacity of the Central Canal just previous to the flood of 1905 was 43.3 cubic feet. The consolidation with the Union was made after this large flood and subsequent to the adjudication decree.

The Union Canal is in reality an extension of what originally was called the Old Mill ditch. The construction of this latter ditch was begun in 1875 and in 1879 it was used almost exclusively to furnish power to the flour mill just east of Safford. A small amount of water was used to irrigate the Old Mill ranch while the balance was allowed to return to the river. Later, in 1882 or 1883, a lateral known as the Anderson ditch was extended from the wasteway below the mill. This lateral served to irrigate considerable land around Safford, especially west of that town.

The main extension of the Mill ditch was constructed in 1886, starting at the point where the Mill ditch turned north to the millrace. After the completion of this extension the Mill ditch became known as the Union Canal.

The Union also absorbed a ditch known as the Darby, which originally had paralleled the Old Mill ditch (Union Canal) and served to irrigate land between the Mill ditch heading and the mill itself. This consolidation took place in 1890. Some land which originally had been irrigated by the Montezuma and the Darby Canal is now irrigated by the Union and was accordingly credited to the Union in the decree.

At the time of this survey the total area being irrigated by the Union Canal was 5,865.9 acres, with an additional 340 acres shown to have been previously irrigated. The combined acreage under the Union and the Central Canals, as given in the decree of 1904, was 5,575, a difference of 291 acres, which evidently is the area placed under cultivation subsequent to the date of decree. The total area under cultivation as given by the present landowners amounts to 8,163 acres, a striking example of the overestimation usually made by farmers.

Both the Union Canal and the Union Extension, are incorporated companies. The capitalization of the former is $25,000, which is represented by 1,000 shares, having a par value of $25 per share. The Union Extension is capitalized at $2,000, this amount being represented by 80 shares of par value $25 per share.

Gonzales and Lee ditches.—The Gonzales Canal, which now serves to irrigate the land formerly irrigated by the Lee, was not taken into consideration in the adjudication decree, because the parties in interest failed to answer their summons as defendants and consequently in the distribution of water as provided in the decree this canal was ignored.

It appears that the Gonzales Canal was constructed in 1896, but after several years of use for irrigation its heading was destroyed by a flood. A pumping plant was then installed to lift water directly from the river and the land was irrigated in this manner until 1905. The great flood of that year washed away the pumping plant as well as a large portion of the irrigated land.

In 1911-12 a portion of this land was again irrigated by pumping and some 25 acres were placed under cultivation. At the time of this survey 38.7 acres were being cultivated under this canal by the use of pumped water.

The Lee ditch, which is situated a short distance below the Gonzales, was constructed about the year 1898 and it has been estimated that 140 acres were irrigated under this old ditch. The flood of 1905 destroyed the greater portion of the irrigated land and also much of this old ditch. The remaining area is now covered by the Gonzales ditch.

The canal is not incorporated, never has been, and is held by the owners of the land which it serves to irrigate.

Sunflower Canal.—The Sunflower Canal, while it was used as an independent canal, had its heading about 1½ miles east of Safford on the south side of the river. At the time of this survey and during all of the irrigation season of 1914, the Sunflower Canal had no separate heading, but was simply used as a lateral or as part of the distribution system of the Union Canal.

The Sunflower Canal is one of the earliest canals of this district. It was constructed during the latter part of 1873, and the first irrigation by its use took place the following year. Originally the ditch was of small cross-section, but it was gradually enlarged as the acreage under cultivation increased.

The Chericahua Cattle Co. were for a long time identified as owners of this canal and it is now often referred to as the Chericahua ditch. In 1891, however, this canal was incorporated and the 600 shares of its capital stock are divided among 7 owners.

According to this survey the lands irrigated by means of this canal amounted to 241.2 acres actually under cultivation with an additional 15.1 acres of previous culture. The decree of 1904 gives 400 acres as the area under cultivation at that time. The present landowners, according to their proofs of appropriation, believe they have a total of 425 acres under cultivation at the present time. Since nearly all the land under this canal is situated close to the bank of the river, it is safe to assume that at least part of the land claimed to have been cultivated in 1904 has since been destroyed by the floods. From the evidence given in the proofs of appropriation, 60 acres are known to have been lost by floods and this number has been added to the acreage at present under cultivation to obtain the corresponding area for 1904.

The Sunflower Canal is capitalized for $10,000, which is represented by 1,000 shares having a par value of $10. Seven stockholders are the owners of this canal.

Graham Canal.—The Graham Canal, which heads in the Gila River a mile east of Safford, but on the opposite side of the river, was constructed in 1878, at first diversion of water having taken place in 1879. When first constructed, this canal was 4 or 5 feet wide on the bottom, but since that time it has been increased to its present width of 6 feet. A gradual increase in the area of land cultivated under this ditch has taken place since its construction, and in 1904, according to the decree, the area irrigated amounted to 962 acres.

According to this survey 999.9 acres were being actually cultivated in 1914, while an additional 166.8 acres showed evidences of previous cultivation. The discrepancy in this case is very slight. This fact, however, should not be assumed to indicate that no new lands were placed under cultivation subsequent to the date of the decree, since it appear in this district, as is the case elsewhere in this valley, that as old lands are abandoned, new tracts are placed under cultivation, with the result that the irrigated area under the several ditches remain much the same.

The Graham Canal is incorporated. The capital stock, amounting to $3,000, is represented by 300 shares having a par value of $10,000. These shares are held by 29 stockholders.

Oregon Canal.—The Oregon Canal, like the Graham, heads on the north side of the river several miles below the Graham. This canal was constructed in 1874, and, according to the decree, it served to irrigate 30 acres of land in 1875. During the following year, this ditch was enlarged, and from that time on the land lying under it was gradually developed. The decree of 1904 gives 1,100 acres as the amount of land then irrigated. The results of this survey show that during 1914, 1,469 acres were actually under cultivation, while 185 acres in addition were shown to have been irrigated at some previous time. According to their proofs of appropriation, the present owners consider that they have 1,315 acres under cultivation. It is believed that the increased irrigated area shown has been put under cultivation since the date of the decree.

The Oregon Canal Co. is incorporated, it is capitalized for $2,500, this stock being represented by 500 shares having a par value of $10. The stock is divided among 50 stockholders.

Smithville Canal.—The Smithville Canal, which has its heading just north of the town of Thatcher and on the south side of the river, was constructed by W. A. Gillespie during the latter part of 1879. By March of the following year this canal had been excavated for a distance of 4¼ miles. Shortly after this portion had been completed, the Smithville Canal was taken over by the incoming Mormon settlers, and in 1880, they had already placed 300 acres of land under irrigation. This cultivation took place in the vicinity of the old town of Smithville, which is known as Pima. The Smithville Canal was strengthened and enlarged in 1881. This ditch is incorporated.

That part of the canal west of the syphon under the Cottonwood Wash is owned by the Smithville Extension Canal Co., which was incorporated in 1909. Some of the land which was covered by this extension had been previously irrigated by the Union Canal and by smaller ditches from the Smithville proper. Considerable land under the Smithville Extension remains to be reclaimed.

The entire area actually under cultivation under the Smithville Canal at the time of this survey amounted to 2,049.3 acres, while an additional area of 374.5 acres was previously irrigated. Of this total about 350 acres were located under the Smithville Extension. The adjudication decree of 1904 credited Smithville Canal Co. with 1760 acres. The land under cultivation since that year has been confined largely to the Smithville Extension district.

The Smithville Canal Co. is capitalized for $5,300, which is represented by 1,060 shares, par value $5. This stock is in the hands of 77 stockholders.

The Smithville Extension is capitalized for $60,000, the stock consisting of 6,000 shares, par value $10, being in the hands of 45 stockholders (July, 1914).

The lack of an adequate water supply at the head of the Smithville Canal during the dry seasons beginning about 1900 gave rise to litigation which terminated into the adjudication decree of the water rights of this valley.

Bryce Canal.—The Bryce Canal, which is situated on the north side of the river, about 2 miles west of the Oregon Canal and serves to irrigate a little land formerly irrigated under the latter canal. The construction of the Bryce Canal was begun in 1882 and it was completed in 1883. This canal is 7½ miles long and covers considerable land that is so situated as to be in imminent danger of erosion by floods.

At the time of this survey in February, 1915, the Bryce Canal was irrigating 593.7 acres, while 19.5 acres in addition had been previously irrigated. The decree credits this canal with 515 acres of irrigated land in 1904. The Bryce Canal has been incorporated, capitalization of 50 shares and has 26 stockholders; capital stock $2,500, value of each share $50.

Dodge Canal.—The Dodge Canal, which heads about a mile east of Pima, was constructed in 1881. The initial length of this canal was about 3 miles, but it was extended first in 1885, and in 1894 it was again extended by the construction of a syphon crossing the Bear Spring Wash at Matthewsville. For a period of about one year this latter extension served to irrigate some 90 acres of land when the syphon was destroyed by floods. About 30 acres of this previously cultivated land is now irrigated by means of the Smithville Extension Canal.

The Dodge Canal suffered severely as the result of the floods of 1914 and 1915. During the time that the survey was in progress, a portion of the canal near the heading, as well as considerable land under the canal, was destroyed by floods in the river. The survey of the remaining land showed 363.4 acres to be under cultivation, and in addition 21.6 acres previously cultivated.

According to the decree this canal was irrigating 450 acres in 1904. It is believed that the latter number closely represents the area under cultivation at the time of the decree and that this area has decreased in amount because of the loss by floods since that time. Considering the location of the Dodge Canal, situated as it is, between the Nevada and the Smithville Canals, it is believed that all the land which it is possible to irrigate under this canal was cultivated at the time of the adjudication suit.

As late as April, 1915, a new heading had not been constructed for this canal, and it was understood that negotiations were under way whereby the irrigators under the Dodge would be supplied with water by the Smithville Canal.

The latter canal is located in such a manner as to cover all the land under the Dodge, and the elimination of the latter canal appears to be logical.

The Dodge Canal is incorporated, and at the time of this investigation 27 landowners were interested in the company.

Nevada Canal.—The construction of this canal was begun in 1877 by two Nevada boys. In 1879 this ditch had a length of 4 miles, but later, in 1885, it was extended. That part of this canal west of the so-called Bear Spring Wash, has been incorporated under the name of Nevada Extension Canal, while the remaining portion from the Bear Spring Wash to the intake has been incorporated as the Nevada Canal. The latter was incorporated in 1884, while the Extension was incorporated in 1911.

At the time of this survey the entire area being cultivated under the Nevada Canal was 1,222.6 acres, only 74 acres in addition showing evidence of former irrigation. The decree gives 800 acres as the area cultivated in 1904, while the present landowners claim 1,200 acres as the area which they believe to be in cultivation.

Considerable land under the Nevada Extension is rapidly being placed under cultivation, and more will be said of this extension under the title of "Future Uses of Gila River Water Above the San Carlos Reservoir."

The Nevada Canal Co. was capitalized for $1,200; it stock consists of 120 shares having a par value of $10. The Nevada Extension Co. has a capital of $6,000, represented by 600 shares which are now owned by 27 shareholders.

These canals, like others in the valley, are common carriers, and while the stockholders of the company, as a rule, are landowners under the canal, the stockholders need not necessarily be landowners, and vice versa.

Curtis Canal.—The Curtis Canal is situated on the north side of the river about 1 mile northwest of Pima. Construction work on this canal started in February, 1881; its width at the upper end was 12 feet, while at the lower end it was 6 feet. Thirty acres were irrigated in 1881, but the canal was enlarged from time to time, as the increased cultivation demanded.

The Kempton Canal, which was eventually absorbed by the Curtis, had its heading lower down but on the same side of the river. This canal was constructed in 1882, and during that year 30 acres were placed under cultivation. The Kempton was incorporated in 1884, and at the time of the decree it was estimated that 850 acres were under cultivation under this ditch, but it also appears that a portion of this area was then being irrigated by the Curtis.

The Curtis Canal was first incorporated in 1885. The present articles of incorporation were filed in 1911. The capital stock of $10,000 is divided into 1,000 shares. At the present time this stock is owned by 59 stockholders.

At the time of this survey (March, 1915) 1,637 acres were in actual cultivation, an additional 75 acres having been previously irrigated. The decree for the two canals gives 1,650 acres as the area under cultivation in 1904. The total area given by the present landowners as being under cultivation in 1914 was 1,874.

While some land has been washed out under this canal, it is believed that as this land was lost, new land has been placed under cultivation so that the total irrigated area has remained about the same.

Fort Thomas Consolidated.—The land cultivated in the vicinity of Fort Thomas has been irrigated by a number of different canals, having their headings a mile or more apart along the south bank of the river. After the flood of 1905 these canals were combined under the name of the Fort Thomas Consolidated. A large new heading was constructed and the area formerly irrigated by the five canals is now served by one.

The earliest of these original ditches appears to be the Thompson, known also as the Clanton, also Peter Moore. The heading for this ditch was 1 mile east of Fort Thomas. Approximately 40 acres were in cultivation under this ditch in 1876.

Another of the five ditches which went to make up the Fort Thomas was first known as the McMurren, later as the Zeckendorf. Although constructed a year or so earlier than the Thompson no irrigation took place under this ditch until 1877. The Collins was situated a little higher than the Thompson and was capable of irrigating the land coming under the latter.

Taking out still higher up on the Gila, and next in order of priority, was the old Reid ditch. This ditch was constructed in 1884, but was not placed in service until 1886, although a few acres lying under this ditch had, as early as 1884, been irrigated by the Collins or Zeckendorf ditch.

The Clavenger ditch, also called Maxey, was constructed in 1883, and served to irrigate lands lying under the Collins. The Collins or Zeckendorf acquired all rights in the Clavenger and the area irrigated by the Clavenger was credited to the Collins.

The Fort Thomas ditch, another of the five, was constructed in 1894, and, according to the decree, 25 acres were already being irrigated in 1895. In 1900 this canal was extended from Fort Thomas to Geronimo, and then served to irrigate all the land previously irrigated by the Military Canal. This latter ditch was constructed in 1896, and during that year 250 acres were put under cultivation.

According to the decree the combined area irrigated under these ditches (Reid, Fort Thomas, and Thompson, Military), in 1904, was 2,140 acres. The survey of 1914 shows 2,441 acres actually under cultivation, and an additional area of 530.2 acres which had been irrigated at some previous time. This comparatively large area of previous cultivation for the most part represents lands that had been cultivated for a brief period and then held without further cultivation pending an expected increase in real estate values. The area shown by this survey represents a gradual increase over the amount cultivated at the time of the decree.

The Fort Thomas Consolidated Canal Co., is capitalized for $10,000, represented by 1,000 shares, par value $10. At the time of this survey this stock was owned by 58 stockholders.

Colvin-Jones.—The Colvin-Jones or the Saline ditch was constructed by the Saline Bros. in 1895, and about 30 acres were placed under cultivation during that year. According to the information available, the heading of the Saline ditch was destroyed in 1905, and very little irrigation took place from that time until 1910, when the Colvin-Jones interests took over this old ditch and increased the cultivated area to the present 93.3 acres, shown by this survey.

The Colvin-Jones Co. is incorporated under the laws of Arizona, capital stock $2,000, divided into 200 shares, par value $10 each. This stock is held by five landowners.

Black & Rose Pumping Plant.—This small pumping plant, lifting water direct from the river, was installed and placed in operation in 1914, and serves to irrigate 11.5 acres. This land was first put under irrigation under the Porter Canal in 1898, when 40 acres were irrigated. In 1905 the canal for some distance downstream from the heading was completely destroyed, making it impossible to use the canal as a gravity ditch. It therefore became necessary to resort to pumping as a means of conveying the water from the river to land to be irrigated.

This canal is not incorporated but is owned by the two parties after whom it is named. The area irrigated by this pumping plant is the final land at present cultivated in the Safford-Solomonville Valley before reaching the San Carlos Indian Reservation.

Old Alexander Canal.—Near the town of Geronimo, which lies just east of the San Carlos Reservation, is a small tract of land which has been previously irrigated. This land was irrigated during only one year (1907) by a Mr. A. C. Alexander, who had charge of the commissary for the railroad construction camp located at this place. With the completion of the railroad construction, the ditch and the cultivated land were abandoned.

IRRIGATION ANALYSIS.

A tabular analysis of the irrigated areas in the Solomonville-Safford District was submitted in the body of the report. The data included therein were collected from several sources as follows:

The areas under cultivation during the years prior to 1904 were obtained for the most part from the findings in the case of Smithville Canal Co. et al. *v.* Oregon Canal Co. et al.

Proof of appropriation blanks were furnished to all the present landowners, but in nearly every case it was found that the areas given in these blanks as irrigated in 1904 were greater than those shown in the findings of the court in the adjudication suit.

A copy of the transcript of evidence in this suit was obtained and is included in the volume of exhibits submitted with this report. The review of this transcript consisting of 892 pages of single-spaced matter was referred to in the body of this report.

Many of the pioneer farmers of this district have died or have moved elsewhere, while the majority of the present landowners know very little regarding the past irrigation of their lands or they were inclined to give exaggerated figures.

The areas cultivated during the years subsequent to the decree have been taken from the proofs of appropriation furnished by the present owners, and adjusted in accordance with the results of the survey

SAN CARLOS INDIAN RESERVATION.

The San Carlos addition to the White Mountain Indian Reservation was established by Executive Order of December 14, 1872.

The White Mountain Reservation was set apart by the War Department in 1871, and selected by the Commissioner of Indian Affairs as one of the Indian reservations upon which the Apache Indians of Arizona might be collected, fed, clothed, and otherwise provided for and protected. (See Executive orders relating to Indian reserves, Annual Report Com. of Ind. Affairs, 1882, p. 246.)

The original San Carlos Reservation extended 15 miles south of the Gila River, and ran parallel to it as far east as the New Mexico line. By Executive order of August 5, 1873, all that portion lying east of and above the site of old Camp Goodwin was restored to the public domain. (In same report as above, p. 250.)

References to the more or less limited early agricultural activities of the Apaches[1] have been made by a number of writers.

Capt. J. G. Bourke, On the Border with Crook, page 42, mentions having camped in and destroyed the small corn fields of the Apaches on Pinto Creek. Geronimo in Geronimo's story of his life, Burrett, page 17, said:

> In that country which lies around the headwaters of the Gila I was reared. This range was our fatherland; among these mountains our wigwams were hidden; the scattered valleys contained our fields; the boundless prairies stretching away on every hand were our pastures; the rocky caverns were our burying places.

Bandolier, who was quoted in the body of this report, has given further descriptions of the Apaches. His writings on this subject appears in Archaeological Institute, volume 3, page 182.

Col. Emory, who was also mentioned in the body of this report as having passed down the Gila in 1846, gives an account of this trip in his "Notes of a military reconnoissance." (Ex. Doc. No. 7, 30th Cong., 1st sess., p. 97.)

In the annual reports of the early Indian agents, excerpts from which are published in volume 1 of the supplemental exhibits accompanying this report, much information is to be had concerning the early irrigation on this reservation.

PREVIOUS IRRIGATION.

As already stated, the irrigable lands of the San Carlos Reservation are made up of small parcels more or less detached, one from another. Frequent attempts, which in some cases have proved successful, have been made to irrigate these parcels of land. Numerous ditches have been constructed from time to time, some of which were never used; others for one irrigation only, while still others remained in service for a time, but eventually nearly all fell finally into disuse.

---

[1] The name Apache is a corruption of the Yuma Indian word, Apa-ahwa-etch, apa meaning man, ahwa hostile, etch being the plural; hence, war or hostile men.

Only the general history of the many formerly used ditches on this reservation will be given in this report. Information concerning previous irrigation has been gathered largely from the reports of former Indian agents of the reservation.

In their various reports these agents have sometimes described the irrigation which took place on this reservation, but they have not distinguished between the various ditches, nor are the present Indian inhabitants able to supply this information. The Indians worked on the ditches ordinarily only when they were paid to do so, and expected the Government to keep the ditches in repair or to build new ones.

Many of these old ditches have been completely washed away, while a large portion of the land under those still remaining has long since become part of the river bottom, and the boundaries of the original cultivation are, of course, impossible of exact determination at the present time.

Many of these various ditches represent merely changed diversions and places of appropriation of preceding ditches. Frequently these changes were necessitated because the land formerly irrigated was washed away or the ditch headings destroyed. Better location for return or seepage flows, concern and disturbances by hostile Indians, and appropriations by the whites higher up on the streams are some of the factors which governed the selection of the irrigated tracts.

From the annual reports of the agents stationed on the reservation, and from information furnished by the older whites[1]—inhabitants who are familiar with early conditions—a brief description of irrigation on the reservation along the Gila and its tributary, the San Carlos, is here given.

Camp Goodwin ditch.—According to Mr. McMurren, the first ditch serving to irrigate land within the present confines of the reservation and along the Gila River was constructed by the militia of old Camp Goodwin. This ditch, which apparently had a short life, was used to irrigate a considerable area of land in the vicinity of the old town of Geronimo at the eastern extremity of the reservation. Nothing further is definitely known of this ditch and practically all of the land formerly irrigated under it with the exception of a small area in the vicinity of the present Bylas farm has been washed away by floods.

Reservation farm ditch (Tonto ditch).—This ditch was built by Maj. Brown, who was stationed at San Carlos during 1873. According to his report about 100 acres of wheat were cultivated during that year. This ditch headed near the junction of the San Carlos and the Gila, and it seems that water was used from either stream, the irrigated land being situated just below the agency grounds on the north side of the river.

The Tonto ditch, which evidently was an enlargement of the above ditch and which had its point of diversion somewhat higher on the Gila, was built, according to Mr. McMurren, in 1878. This ditch

[1] Acknowledgments are due Mr. Lawshe, who lent assistance to the work and who furnished the letters of the army officers, to be found in vol. 1, of exhibits, accompanying this report; also to J. H. Hinton of Fort Thomas; R. S. Knowles, of Geronimo; W. E. Tiffany, H. E. Young, and P. McMurren, of the reservation. Mr. McMurren, who is at present the principal farmer on the reservation, and who in the early days was a scout in the militia, has given valuable and reliable data concerning the past irrigation.

had two headings, one on the San Carlos, the other being located some distance above, on the Gila. From the latter heading the ditch was flumed across the San Carlos.

As might be expected, the flume carrying this ditch across the San Carlos was several times washed out, and in 1881 the agent reported "that many things would have to be taken into consideration before the expensive reconstruction is undertaken." Some time later, however, a new heading was put in, and more or less irrigation took place under this ditch until the disastrous flood of 1905, which destroyed so much of the ditch, as well as the land served by it, that no further irrigation was attempted.

Of the land remaining undisturbed by the river 25 acres are at present in grain, this area being irrigated from the agency ditch which heads in the San Carlos River about a mile above the agency.

In addition to the irrigated areas mentioned above there are at present 200 acres still intact under this ditch which show evidences of previous irrigation.

Desalin.—A ditch known as the Desalin, built by an Indian of that name, was constructed in 1875, and is mentioned in the agent's report of that year. At present this ditch is badly washed out, but the remaining portion indicates that it may have been connected with the lower extremity of the Tonto and used as an extension to that ditch.

The land under this ditch showing previous cultivation amounted to 186 acres over and above the amount given for the Tonto. Some of this area, however, may have been irrigated with water from the Tonto.

Old Yuma or Mohave Ditch.—A band each of Yumas, Mohaves, and Tonto Indians were transferred by the militia from Camp Verde to the San Carlos Reservation in 1876. The Tontos established themselves on the north side of the Gila not far from the San Carlos Fort, while the Yumas and Mohaves occupied a camp site on the opposite side of the river. The Yumas started digging their ditch in April, 1875, and planted a small crop for the fall harvest. The agent's report for that year states that this ditch was 5 feet wide on the bottom, 9 feet on top, 7 feet in depth, and that it exended for a distance of 2 miles. In 1881 the highest flood during a period of 17 years preceding that date carried away all of the gardens and crops of these Indians.

The agent reported in 1888 that the Yumas, Mohaves, and the Tontos were very dissatisfied with their location and desired to return to their own country. In 1892 more of their lands were washed away, and they were still desirous of moving. They were also displeased, according to the agent, on account of orders received directing that they should be moved to the eastern part of the reservation, where a tract had been set aside for them in the vicinity of Bylas. It appears, however, that they all did not take advantage of this opportunity. Mr. McMurren states that he helped to extend the ditch in 1894 and that more or less irrigation took place under it until the flood of 1905.

In 1902 the dissatisfied Yumas and Mohaves, following the policy of the agent in charge, were allowed to go off the reservation to work for the white farmers. The agent states in his report of that year that their departure resulted in a decrease of 437 in the census within one year.

Under this Old Yuma or Mohave Canal, and located on the south side of the river, there still remain 171 acres of land showing evidences of previous culture.

Old ditches at Naches.—The old ditch on the north side of the river opposite Naches, called the "Eskiminzim" (or S. H. 1), after its builder, a well-known chief of that name, was constructed about the year 1882. According to Mr. McMurren, although the heading had previously been rebuilt several times, this ditch was inactive after the flood of 1905.

The land shown to have been cultivated by the ditch and still undamaged by the river, amounted to 218 acres at the time of this survey.

The ditch on the south side of the river at Naches was constructed in 1881. Mr. McMurren corroborates this date. It is described in the agent's report of that year as being 5 miles long, having a bottom width of 5 feet, the upper extremity for three-fourths of a mile being 11 feet deep. The ditch, having been built by the agent, was known as the Government ditch. After the flood of 1905 it likewise was unemployed. Ninety-two acres still remain of the area previously irrigated under this ditch.

Old ditches between Naches and Bylas.—Ascending the river from Naches, the remains of old ditches may be seen at several places, notably one at Dewey Flat. East of Dewey Flat on the opposite side of the river is another old ditch with previously irrigated land still in evidence, while opposite the railroad station of Calva were found two inactive canals, which are quite distinct from those of the Bylas districts. The one on the south side, known as the J. C. Band ditch, was in service as late at 1894. The ditch opposite on the north side, known as Old Mohave, has been almost entirely washed away, and none of the remaining land shows evidence of former cultivation, although parts of the ditch are still visible.

The areas showing former cultivation under these old ditches are as follows:

South side Dewey Flat (Mohave)	46
North side Dewey Flat	74
Opposite Calva, south side (C. J. Band)	41
Opposite Calva, north side (Old Mohave), no area remaining.	

Between present Bylas district and Calva on the south side of the river there were, in addition, 168 acres undoubtedly irrigated at one time under the Dewey extension of the Bylas ditch. (See below.)

Owing to the uncertainty existing as to the time when these tracts were under irrigation and to the extent of the area formerly irrigated, these figures are of no especial value and are given merely to show that many attempts have been made in the past to irrigate the lands along this portion of the Gila.

BYLAS DISTRICT.

The only ditches now taking water direct from the Gila River within the San Carlos Reservation are two in the Bylas district, one on the north side of the river, the other on the south, or Bylas, side.

According to the annual report of the San Carlos agent for 1878, a subagencey was established at Bylas that year. This subagency was moved to San Carlos in 1883. The same report states that two ditches were started in that year (1878), but were not finished before the fall crops. No further mention of this district is made in the annual reports for some time. Both Mr. McMurren and Mr. Hinton claim that the north side Bylas ditch was finished in 1881 and the south side ditch in 1882. Both of these ditches have had several different headings.

The south side ditch, called the South Bylas, to distinguish it from the Coyotero (or North Bylas) had its original heading opposite Black Point. This heading was washed out and the next heading was constructed at or near the old town of Geronimo. According to Mr. McMurren, this Geronimo heading was constructed in 1898.

In 1891, the agent remarks that "the Geronimo ditch has been extended to cover 300 acres." A later heading was constructed just above the Black Point, approximately at the same location as the present heading. After the flood of 1905, which very seriously damaged the canals, as well as much of the irrigated land, and until 1912, nor irrigation was again undertaken in the South Bylas district.

The present South Bylas Canal heading, constructed by Mr. McMurren in 1912, has been in operation since that time.

The Coyotero (or North Bylas) ditch was constructed in 1881, but, like the ditch on the south side, its diversion point was changed several times. The flood of 1905 proved disastrous for this canal, and it appears that from that year until 1910 it was not used. During the latter year (1910) a new heading was constructed which has remained in use ever since.

The area which was being cultivated on the south side of the river under the South Bylas ditch at the time of survey amounted to 591.5 acres. Before the survey of this district was completed during December, 1914, a heavy flood reduced this area by 47 acres.

On the north side of the river opposite Bylas, under the Coyotero ditch, there were 409 acres in cultivation at the time of this survey. An area of 174 acres was found to have been previously irrigated, while 17.2 acres of land was washed away during the December flood and subsequent to this survey. Summing up the areas of the Bylas district, as shown by this survey, a total of 1,000.5 acres were found to be under cultivation on both sides of the river.

RÉSUMÉ OF IRRIGATION ON THE SAN CARLOS RESERVATION.

The following table showing the areas irrigated during the different years has been made up principally from the reports and statements of the Indian agents at San Carlos, these being practically the only available source of definite information concerning former irrigation on this reservation. Inasmuch as this early irrigation was carried on under the direct supervision of these agents, and also in view of the fact that irrigation was never widely practiced on the San Carlos Reservation, there is no reason to suppose this information to be greatly in error.

The statistics and excerpts from the reports are given in volume 1, of supplemental exhibits, accompanying this report.

It should be explained that the statistical information concerning the cultivated area which is embodied in the annual reports of the several Commissioners of Indian Affairs for the years 1874 to 1898 covers not only the cultivated areas along the Gila and San Carlos Rivers but also the area cultivated on the Black River of the White Mountain Reservation as well.

In the tabulation which follows these areas have been segregated and are shown under their respective headings.

Year.	Total acres given in statistics	Total irrigation on Gila.	San Carlos.	Black River.	Year.	Total acres given in statistics.	Total irrigation on Gila.	San Carlos.	Black River.
		Acres.	*Acres.*	*Acres.*			*Acres.*	*Acres.*	*Acres.*
1873	100	[1] 100	....	....	1880	125	[1] 70	[1] 30	[1] 25
1874	....	[2] 200	....	140	1881	1,000	[2] 560	[2] 240	[2] 200
1875	320	[1] 200	[1] 30	[1] 90	1882	500	....	....	....
1876	545	[2] 340	[1] 50	[2] 155	1883	1,000	[2] 560	[2] 240	[2] 200
1877	300	200	30	[2] 70	1884	1,000	[2] 560	[2] 240	[2] 200
1878	120	[1] 20	[1] 20	[2] 80	1885	....	....	....	....
1879	100	[1] 45	[1] 30	[1] 25	1886	1,900	[2] 1,050	[2] 450	[2] 400

[1] Given by agent in annual report. [2] Estimated.

1181: Using same proportion of increase.

1886: Using same ratio of increase but assuming a maximum irrigated area of 450 acres on the San Carlos. According to information obtained no more than this acreage was irrigated on San Carlos during the earlier periods.

Year.	Total acres given in statistics	Total irrigation on Gila.	San Carlos.	Black River.	Year.	Total acres given in statistics.	Total irrigation on Gila.	San Carlos.	Black River.
1887	....	([1])	....	....	1894	3,900	[2] 1,725	[2] 450	[2] 1,750
1888	1,060	[2] 460	[2] 400	200	1895	3,000	[2] 1,250	[2] 450	[2] 1,300
1889	2,390	[2] 1,450	450	290	1896	3,000	[2] 1,250	[2] 450	[2] 1,300
1890	4,600	....	....	([3])	1897	3,000	[2] 1,250	[2] 450	[2] 1,300
1891	....	([1])	....	....	1898	2,000	[2] 1,250	[2] 450	[6] 1,218
1892	{ [4] 1,200 / [5] 1,635 }	1,185	450	1,200	1899	2,000	[2] 1,550	[2] 450	[6] 1,240
1893	3,925	[2] 1,725	[2] 450	[2] 1,750	1900	2,500	[2] 2,000	[2] 500	[6] 1,260

In 1886-87 many ditches put in. (See letter of Jesse M. I ce, appendix.) Volume 1, supplemental exhibit

In 1888 agent reports all available lands on San Carlos irrigated.

In 1889, 940 acres of land was put under cultivation. This has all been credited to the Gila River.

In 1893 statistics give an increase of 1,110 acres broken during the year and a half. This has been credited to Gila and White Rivers.

[1] No report.
[2] Estimated.
[3] Not considered reliable.
[4] Area of White Mountain Apaches at White Mountain.
[5] Area of San Carlos Yumas and Aribaipi Apaches at San Carlos.
[6] Statistics.

Year.	Statistics.	Gila.	San Carlos.	White River.	Year.	Statistics.	Gila.	San Carlos.	White River.
	Acres.	*Acres.*	*Acres.*	*Acres.*		*Acres.*	*Acres.*	*Acres.*	*Acres.*
1901	3,000	2,500	500	[1] 1,087	1908	([2])	([2])	([2])	([2])
1902	2,450	2,500	450	[1] 1,087	1909	([2])	([2])	([2])	([2])
1903	([2])	....	....	....	1910	....	400	650	....
1904	1,285	835	450	[1] 1,082	1911	....	570	650	....
1905	([3])	([3])	([3])	([3])	1912	1,100	600	500	[1] 1,400
1906	([4])	([4])	480	....	1913	....	....	700	....
1907	([2])	([2])	([2])	([2])	1914	....	1,000.5	936	

In 1902 decreased amount due to drought according to agent.

In 1905 agents speak of the large flood, also cultivation without irrigation.

In 1906 from data furnished by Mr. McMurren.

[1] Statistics. [3] No irrigation on account of floods.
[2] No report. [4] No irrigation.

COMMENTS ON SAN CARLOS IRRIGATION.

The foregoing table is believed to be a reasonably accurate analysis of irrigation on this reservation.

While our surveys show that the entire area of land found to have been irrigated at sometime or other is in excess of the amounts tabulated, it is quite evident from the reports of the agents and from information gathered from other sources that various parcels were irrigated at different times, and that the area irrigated during each succeeding year since the initial irrigation is represented very closely in the above table.

Very little satisfactory evidence could be obtained from the Indians themselves in regard to past irrigation on the reservation. All the information which the Indians were able to furnish proved to be very general in its nature and as nothing tangible concerning the early irrigation seemed to be forthcoming from this source it was decided early in the investigation that it would be a waste of time to attempt to obtain information from these Indians.

An analysis of irrigation in five-year periods, similiar to those obtained for the Duncan and Solomonville districts has been given in the body of the report for this reservation.

All the irrigation along the Gila within the San Carlos Reservation has been credited to the two canals of the Bylas district, which are the only canals diverting water from the Gila at the present time. It is considered that these ditches represent merely the diversions which formerly took place lower down on the river and that changes of the points of diversion of the water as well as its use for irrigation on different tracts of land involves no losses of priority.

WINKELMAN SECTION.

The history of irrigation in the Winkelman section has been given in the body of the report. The following tabulation is a concise summary of the irrigation data obtained during the investigation.

Name of ditch.	Year constructed.	Year of last use.	Present irrigation.	Previous irrigation.	Additional irrigable land under ditch.	Irrigation by well water.	By pump from river.	Cultivated but not by irrigation.	Irrigated land not under ditch.
			Acres.	*Acres.*	*Acres.*	*Acres.*	*Acres.*	*Acres.*	*Acres.*
Old Settler	1907	1910							
Winkelman	1885	1910		468	285				
Braceamonte	1880		53	45	50			(1)	(1)
Escalonte (about)	1905		61		35				
Small ditches from Rallings			50						
Branaman ditch	1880		150	35	123	20			
Old Branaman (prior)	1880			10	33		22	44	
Gilson	1910		17	7	80				
Not under a ditch						63			
Irrigable land not under a ditch									350
Pool Canal	1910						12		
Upper Canyon	1912		15						
Glasper Ditch	1880	[2] 1915							
Totals			301	565	606	83	34	44	350
By water pumped			34						
Total from river			335						

[1] Abandoned and reclaimed. [2] All land washed out.

NOTE.—All of the land in the Winkelman section lying on the north side of the river is owned by the Ray Consolidated Copper Co., and has been acquired for the deposition of the concentrator tailings. The tailings have now rendered useless for agriculture all but 50 acres of land which was formerly irrigated, and it is the intention of the company to cover this area as well as all bottom land in this vicinity.

DUNCAN VALLEY—A BRIEF HISTORY OF THE INDIVIDUAL CANALS OF THE DUNCAN VALLEY.

The canals are given in the order they appear, beginning at the upper end of the valley and proceeding downstream.

Sunset Canal.—The first known irrigation in this district took place on land now being served by the Sunset Canal and was carried on by means of a very small ditch constructed in 1876. In 1883, the Telles ditch was constructed and more land put under cultivation, and a few years later the Sunset Canal interests which owned a small canal made an agreement with the Telles interests to use the Telles ditch. It appears, however, that the Telles interests did not keep up the assessment work on their ditch, and because of this failure, they were denied the use of water by the owners of the Sunset Canal, whereas the Telles interests cut the ditch; an arrest followed and the case came up for trial in Silver City and resulted in a decision for the plaintiffs. This is the only suit involving water rights that ever came to trial in the Duncan Valley.

Several small ditches, mostly in New Mexico, like the Miller and Rucker, were constructed in the early eighties, the Hughes ditch constructed somewhat later, and others with names unknown, irrigated small tracts of land along the river, some of which have since been washed away, while those remaining are now covered by the Sunset Canal.

All of the land irrigated by the Sunset Canal is in the State of New Mexico. The landowners under the Sunset, according to their claims of appropriation, estimated that they were cultivating 832 acres of land, whereas the survey shows 694 acres.

The Sunset Canal Co. was incorporated under the laws of New Mexico and has 128 outstanding shares held by six different individuals or interests, the Gila Ranch Co. owning a majority of the stock.

Cosper Martin and Wilson, also called the P. & M.—This ditch represents a consolidation of two ditches, the Cosper Martin and the Wilson. The latter ditch is much the older of the two, having been constructed in 1879. The consolidation was effected in 1909. The old Wilson Canal was one of the early important canals in this district, and as early as 1880 served to irrigate more than 200 acres. This ditch is now serving land formerly irrigated by the Hill ditch which was constructed in 1887, and the Rolston, constructed in 1892, and to a certain extent, the old Willet ditch.

Like the Sunset Canal, this ditch and the land which it serves to irrigate are situated altogether in New Mexico.

The survey shows 483.5 acres to be under cultivation, which is a larger amount than that estimated by the present owners.

The company owning the canal was incorporated under the statutes of New Mexico. Thirty-six shares of stock have been issued, all held by landowners under the canal.

Cosper and Windham.—The Cosper and Windham Canal was constructed in 1886–87, and its location has remained much the same since it was originally constructed.

This ditch, when first constructed, was situated entirely in New Mexico, but it was extended across the State line in 1889 in order to cover the Parks Ranch.

As a result of the survey 641.6 acres were shown to be in cultivation, 541.8 acres in New Mexico, and the remaining 126.7 acres in Arizona.

The Cosper and Windham is owned by a company of 17 landowners. Having holdings under the canal, these landowners own various amounts of the 60 shares issued by the corporation. This company, like the two preceding, was incorporated under the laws of New Mexico.

Model Canal.—A greater part of the land irrigated at the present time by the Model Canal was formerly served by a ditch called the Johnson and Black, and later the Franklin. The Johnson and Black ditch was first constructed about 1882, but it was enlarged a few years later. In 1895 a colony of Mormons settled in this region near the village of Franklin and this ditch was then called the Franklin Canal.

According to Mr. Thomas Nations, who claims to have assisted in its construction, the Model Canal was begun in 1893, and was completed in 1895. With the completion of the Model Canal the Franklin was abandoned and the water rights of the latter were taken over by the Model and stock issued in accordance.

The area cultivated under the Model Canal was 1,819.5 acres at the time of the survey, and of this area 278.9 acres were situated in New Mexico. The sum of the areas given by the different landowners amounts to 2,019 acres.

The Model Canal Co. was incorporated July 5, 1899, capital stock $5,000, divided into 200 shares. By an amendment to the articles of incorporation on September 12, 1908, the capital stock was increased to $10,000, divided into 400 shares. Of these 400 shares, 343 have been issued and are held by 53 landowners under the canal.

The Shriver Canal.—The Shriver Canal is situated altogether in New Mexico, below, and on the same side of the river as the Model Canal. It was constructed in 1887, and about 50 acres were placed under irigation during the first year. In 1890 the acreage under cultivation was equal to that cultivated at the present time. The survey shows an area of 66 acres cultivated in 1914, whereas Mr. Shriver, the sole owner, claims that at one time 100 acres were under cultivation. Evidently some of this land has recently been destroyed by floods.

The Valley or Boone Canal.—This canal was constructed in 1887 by a Mr. Boone, and the ditch as well as the area cultivated under it has been gradually enlarged. Prior to the construction of the Valley Canal, and as early as 1884, there was a ditch known as the Buck Tyson, which served to irrigate a small portion of land that is now irrigated by the Valley Canal. Most of the land formerly irrigated by the Buck Tyson Canal has been washed away, and information concerning the land under it was so meager that it was not considered in the analysis.

Further down the river from the old Tyson ditch was the Watters and Oliver ditch, built in 1888, but which was destroyed by the flood of 1897. Still later, in 1895, was constructed the Angle ditch, which served to irrigate the same land formerly covered by the Buck Tyson ditch. This ditch also was washed out in 1897. It appears that a small Mexican ditch also served to irrigate some land in this section prior to the flood of 1897.

The results of the survey show 1,220.5 acres actually under cultivation and 46.5 acres of previous cultivation. The Valley Canal Co. was incorporated as early as June 29, 1888. Its capital stock is divided into 97 shares, held by 23 landowners under the canal.

The Burtcher (Ward & Courtney) Canal.—This ditch, formerly called the Ward & Courtney Canal, was constructed in the early eighties or late seventies, the exact date not being known. In 1885 about 150 acres were irrigated by this canal. The Ward & Courtney also formerly supplied the water for irrigation and stock purposes in the town of Duncan. About 1887 a disagreement arose between the town people and the Ward & Courtney owners as to the distribution of water. As a result of this controversy the town people constructed a ditch for their own purposes in 1896 (approximately) and this canal was called the Duncan or Town ditch.

This town ditch continued in use until about 1909, when the Duncan Canal Extension was constructed and this latter canal then served the lands in the immediate vicinity of Duncan.

The Burtcher or Ward & Courtney Canal has its capital stock divided into 420 shares and this stock is held by 14 landowners under the canal.

This Burtcher Canal was irrigating 163.5 acres at the time of the survey, although 300 acres was the total area given by the landowners.

The Duncan Extension.—The Duncan Extension, which in reality is an extension of the Burtcher Canal, is treated as a separate ditch inasmuch as this canal has for its principal purpose the collection and diversion of the waste waters of the Model Canal. Although it is connected to the Burtcher, the incorporators of this canal claim it to be their purpose to obtain water for their ditch by first passing it through the Model Canal.

The Duncan Canal Extension serves the land formerly irrigated by the original Duncan Canal, which was constructed in 1886 or 1887, and which superseded the Ward & Courtney (Burtcher) Canal, and in the analysis this early priority has been credited to the Duncan Extension Canal.

The Duncan Canal Extension served to irrigate 67.5 acres at the time of this survey, whereas the owners under the canal were of the opinion they were irrigating 150 acres. This discrepancy may arise from the fact that a portion of the land upon which the town of Duncan is situated was formerly irrigated by this ditch but was not included in the above survey figures.

The Black & McCloskey Canal.—This ditch was constructed in 1897–98 and an appropriation filed February 20, 1901.

Previous to the construction of the Black & McCloskey about two-thirds of the land cultivated at the present time was being irrigated by means of the Duncan Canal, and this priority has been credited to this canal in the analysis.

At the time of this survey (October, 1914), 153 acres were being irrigated from this canal, while the area given by the landowners in the proofs of appropriation was 207 acres.

The stock of the Black & McCloskey Canal Co. is divided into seven shares, which are held by five persons. Articles of incorporation were never filed.

The Colmenero Canal.—The Colmenero Canal was constructed in 1890. During that year 20 acres were put under cultivation and a gradual increase in the irrigated area has taken place since that time.

This ditch was irrigating 390 acres of land at the time of this survey, which amount corresponds closely to the acreage given by the landowners.

The Colmenero Canal Co. was incorporated in March, 1897, with a capital of $2,400, divided into 240 shares of the par value of $10 each. These shares have all been issued and are now owned by 16 individuals holding land under the canal.

The Sexton Canal.—The Sexton Canal, heading just below the town of Sheldon, was constructed in 1901. The ditch is about 2 miles long and irrigates 75.5 acres, an additional 19 acres having been previously irrigated.

The Billingsley ditch.—This is a small ditch constructed and still owned by Mr. Billingsley. It was built in 1907 and originally served to irrigate only 40 acres of land, but was irrigating 82 acres at the time of this survey.

The York Canal.—This canal was originally called the Greaser Flat Canal, later the English & Herrel Canal, and finally the York Canal.

So far as could be learned, this canal, or rather a small ditch irrigating part of the land under the present York Canal, was constructed about the year 1881 by several Mexicans. In 1886, or thereabout, the "C A" Cattle Co. bought out the Mexicans and proceeded to enlarge the canal. Difficulty was encountered because of the solid rock through which part of this ditch had to be carried, and it appears that several attempts at reconstruction of the canal may have been abandoned for a time.

In 1905 Herrel and English took this canal over, rebuilt a portion of it, and also extended it. The permanent heading, consisting of a tunnel cut through the cliff into the York Box Canyon, was constructed in 1909, just after the incorporation of the York Canal Co.

What is really the only permanent diversion dam on the entire Gila is the lower weir constructed across the channel forming the division for this canal.

This canal served to irrigate 265 acres at the time of this survey, and 29 acres was shown to have been previously irrigated. This area corresponds very closely with the estimates furnished by the several landowners under the canal.

The York Canal Co. was incorporated in 1909, with a capitalization of $3,000, divided into 300 shares. These shares are held by five landowners under the canal.

PUMPING PLANTS.

In the narrow section of the valley extending from Sheldon to Guthrie 10 pumping plants have been installed and serve to irrigate small patches of land. These pumps are of the centrifugal type, driven by gasoline engines, and lift the water direct from the river. They are usually located advantageously with respect to the low-water flow.

These plants are operated by individual owners, and most of them are of recent date. In some instances the pumps were installed because of the failure of former gravity irrigating ditches. A brief description of these plants follow:

Just below the Sexton Canal is located a small pumping plant station owned by Phil McNair, who has been irrigating his land since 1913. At the present time he has 11.5 acres under irrigation.

On the west bank of the Gila, at York, Ariz., two pumping plants are situated. One is owned by Edwards and Cauthens, the other by J. F. Goolsby.

The land under the Edwards and Cauthens pumping plant has been irrigated since 1906, but it is claimed by present owners that this land was first irrigated by means of a syphon from the York Canal. The area which is being irrigated by this pumping plant is 18.5 acres. In addition to this amount, 5.5 acres could be irrigated.

Under the Goolsby pumping plant there are 10 acres of irrigated land, 16.5 acres show evidences of previous irrigation and could be irrigated with the expenditure of a little labor in clearing and leveling of the adjoining fields. This land was first irrigated about 10 years ago.

The small pumping plant located on the east bank of York, Ariz., is owned and operated by Earnest Shade, who has been irrigating by this method since 1911. The pumping plant irrigates 6 acres of land in garden truck, but a larger area of land could be placed under irrigation by clearing and extending the present irrigating system.

Down the river 2 or 3 miles, on the same bank, is located another pumping plant, which is owned and operated by J. W. Foote. This pumping plant has been in operation since April, 1914, and has irrigated 7 acres of garden-truck land. An additional area of 5 or 10 acres could be irrigated by this pump.

Just below this pumping station is another plant owned and operated by A. C. and T. A. Angle, of Guthrie, Ariz. This pumping plant has been in use since 1908 and irrigates 15 acres of land.

Across the river from this farm is located J. H. Brown's pumping plant, which has been in use for irrigation since 1913. This land was formerly irrigated by a gravity ditch constructed about the year 1900. Since that time floods have destroyed this canal and heading, and the pumping has been resorted to as a means of supplying the ditch with water from the river. Eleven acres are irrigated by this plant.

Just below Mr. Brown's plant is the pumping plant owned by R. S. Medina, which will be placed in operation during the year 1015. Some 10 acres will be irrigated by this pumping system. This land, according to Mr. Medina, has never before been irrigated.

C. M. Short's pumping plant, which is located at Guthrie, Ariz., was constructed in 1907. Previous to that time a gravity canal was in use here, but in 1907 this was destroyed by floods. This canal had been in use since 1885, and the irrigation of this tract of land dates back to that time. At one time a self-operated water-lifting wheel was installed, but this did not prove to be a successful venture. This pumping plant irrigates 35 acres of garden-truck land.

Between the Guthrie Canyon and the first diversion, which is made for the Solomonville Valley, there are three small pumping plants irrigating small areas near the mouth of the San Francisco River.

The Gila River surveys were not extended to include this small acreage, but the information which has been gathered concerning this cultivation was to the effect that on the east and west sides of the river about 60 acres of land has been irrigated continuously since 1899 by E. Funtes and Telles, two Mexicans, who sell their produce in Morenci and Clifton.

Farther down the river on the north side is located John Velton's farm of 20 acres, which has been under cultivation since 1902.

Another farm, still farther down the river on the south side, consists of 10 acres of cultivated land, which has been irrigated since 1899 by Albert Suvia.

Below the Suvia farm the Gila River flows through a narrow box canyon until it reaches the Solomoville valley.

IRRIGATION ANALYSIS.

The irrigation analysis, under the different dates representing five-year periods, has been based upon actually cultivated areas. The areas under the 1914 column represent the areas actually cultivated at time of and as shown by this survey.

As related in the body of the report the irrigation of many of the tracts in the Duncan Valley has not been carried on continuously under the same ditches, but a great deal of land, especially the irrigated areas in New Mexico, have been served at various times by a number of small ditches. It was found practically impossible, however, to ascertain the detailed history of these numerous small ditches.

After obtaining the general history of irrigation in this valley from all available sources the analysis of priorities was estimated from these general data and from the information furnished by the landowners in the claims of appropriation. In each case the landowner has been requested to give an estimate of the land he had under cultivation during previous times and at the time of the survey, and these estimates were then compared with the results of the survey. Where discrepancies occurred a proportional adjustment of the estimates was made, and the area thus arrived at was credited to the canal now serving the land.

Many of the former landowners have sold out and left the country, and the evidence readily obtainable was not altogether satisfactory. Some errors in the analysis may occur, yet it is believed that for all practical purposes they are substantially correct.

IRRIGATION ON THE TRIBUTARIES OF THE GILA (DISTRICT NO. 6).

A reconnaissance survey was made to ascertain the extent and nature of the irrigation along all of the important tributaries of the Gila with the exception of the Salt River. The irrigation on the extreme upper reaches of the Gila was also covered by a reconnaissance survey.

A summary of the irrigation in the several districts, as well as the general conditions pertaining thereto, is given in the following report.

These tributaries will be taken up separately in the order in which they join the Gila, beginning with the San Pedro, and proceeding upstream.

SAN PEDRO RIVER.

The San Pedro River rises in the Huachuca Mountain range, in northern Sonora, Mexico, and, flowing in a northeasterly direction, crosses the international boundary line into Cochise County, Ariz., at a point one-half mile east of international boundary line, survey monument No. 98. It continues in the same direction for about 6 miles, then takes a course of about north by west, and leaves Cochise County at a point 3 miles south of its northwest corner. It then flows through the northwest corner of Pima County into Pinal County; thence in the same direction, north by west, to its confluence with the Gila River in the center of sec. 23, T. 5 S., R. 15 E., G. & S. R. B. & M.

After crossing the international boundary into the United States the river flows through a narrow valley with hills on either side which confine the irrigable land to narrow strips along the river bottom. In places the hills open out, forming small valleys of excellent farming land. Of these valleys, the St. David and Benson are the largest, and are practically a single valley, being interrupted only by points of the mesa which project out to the river.

Irrigation on the San Pedro River has been practiced since ancient times. When the first Spanish explorers came into this region during the sixteenth century, they found Indians irrigating land along this river. Several of the trails between Mexico and northern Arizona followed the San Pedro along the greater part of its course, and mention is made in the narratives of the early Spanish explorers of the Indian ranchos along this river.

In more recent years Mexicans have immigrated to this valley and have irrigated small patches of land. Some of these parcels have been continuously irrigated to the present time, this being especially true of the lands along the upper part of the river, on the old Spanish grants, and in the lower Benson Valley.

The whites began to irrigate lands along the San Pedro in the early sixties. The number of new ditches and irrigated fields increased rapidly until the occurence of the floods of 1894 and 1895. These floods did great damage, washing out a number of ditch headings and destroying many acres of irrigated and irrigable land. Other destructive floods occurred in 1905 and again in 1914. The flood damages were so great as to make further irrigation impractical at some points along the river, besides rendering it more difficult and expensive in all irrigated districts. In spite of these floods, however, the total irrigated acreage has gradually increased.

From the annual report of the Indian agent of the San Carlos Indian Reservation it has been learned that prior to 1868, about 75 Indians irrigated small tracts along this river and Aravaipa

Creek, a tributary. Many of these Indians either have abandoned their lands or have been forced out by the whites, and those few who remain at the present time are cultivating only a few acres.

IRRIGATION BY DISTRICTS.

Mexican land grants.—There is no irrigation along the San Pedro in the Republic of Mexico. The first irrigated area is on the upper course of this river, situated near the town of Hereford, near the south boundary of the San Rafael Del Valle grant, and is served by the Hereford Canal. On this grant and on the Rancho San Juan de las Boquillas y Nogales, which is also an old Mexican land grant, there are four ditches irrigating land as follows:

	Acres.
Hereford Canal	312
Boquillas (east side) Canal	296
Boquillas (west side) Canal	286
Union or Hill	364
Total	1,258

Of the Union or Hill ditch, a 230/380 part interest is owned by the Boquillas Land & Cattle Co., owners of the grant lands, who irrigate 244 acres of said land. The remaining 120 acres of irrigated land is owned by a number of ranchers living in the upper St. David Valley.

The Boquillas east and west side ditches are provided with a single diversion dam, the ditches taking out on opposite sides of the river.

In the land-grant areas there were about 100 acres irrigated in 1901, when the land was purchased by the present holders. This acreage has been gradually increased since that date.

The oldest ditches in this district are now obliterated and no definite data could be obtained concerning the number, location, and area served. It is evident, however, that they were small, irrigated small areas, and that all land originally served by these ditches which has not been washed away is now irrigated under the present ditch.

St. David district.—Proceeding down the river, the next irrigated area is the St. David district.

On the west side of the river in this district there are no ditches diverting water from the river, but a few small patches of land are irrigated by means of artesian wells.

On the east side of the river are located the Union or Hill ditch, already mentioned, in the Grant land district, which irrigates 120 acres in this district, and the St. David Canal. Besides these two canals, water from numerous artesian wells is used for irrigation.

Prior to 1877 there were only a few scattered settlers in this district, but during that year a Mormon colony came in and the Union or Hill ditch was constructed. The earthquake of 1887 opened a fissure from which water flowed for some time and led to the discovery of artesian water during that year. During this period and until 1902 the area under irrigation increased rapidly. In 1902 the water supply first became noticeably inadequate and trouble began to be experienced with the ditch headings. About this time a single high-line system was advocated, and the St. David Cooperative Commercial and Development Association was organized and began the construction of the high-line ditch, using the heading of the Union or Hill Canal. Considerable work was done on this canal but it never was completed. In 1903 the Boquillas Land & Cattle Co., owners of the grant land on which the heading of this canal was situated, served an injunction on the parties owning the canal. The water rights of this project were adjudicated November 3, 1906, decree being rendered by Fletcher M. Doan, then judge of the superior court of Arizona, in the district court of the second judicial district, county of Cochise, Territory of Arizona, in action No. 3723, Boquillas Land & Cattle Co., plaintiff, *v.* St. David Cooperative Commercial and Development Association (a corporation) et al., defendants.

In this action the court found: That the Boquillas Land & Cattle Co. had acquired an undivided interest in the San Juan De Las Boquillas y Nogales grant, on which land the ditches in the aforesaid action had their diversion. That the defendants have no right, title, or interest in or to that ditch commonly known as the Union or Hill Canal, and were perpetually enjoined from entering upon this land for any purpose whatever, except the defendants J. N. Curtis, Lyman Curtis, Samuel Curtis, and John Summers, were permitted to aid in the construction of a canal for purpose of conveying water for 380 acres of land, the defendants to have 120/380 of the water for use of their own land, amounting to 120 acres, the plaintiff to have water from the same canal for 260 acres.

The St. David Canal, built in 1878, is owned by a mutual company, the shares of which are held by the landowners and the water users under the canal. The water and the maintenance expense are proportioned according to the number of shares owned.

During the time of the construction of a higher ditch by the St. David Cooperative Commercial and Development Association the heading of the St. David Canal was washed out. In anticipation of the new canal this heading was not replaced until two years had elapsed, and the land lay idle during that time. Also, during the three years of the above-mentioned litigation the Union or Hill ditch was not used and the land under it lay idle.

The areas irrigated by means of the St. David Canal and artesian wells in the St. David Valley are as follows:

	Acres.
St. David Canal only	820
St. David Canal and artesian wells	100
Artesian wells only	63
Total	983

Artesian wells in this district vary in depth from 150 to 900 feet and have an average diameter of about 3 inches.

The maximum flow is about 80 gallons per minute. These wells are used for domestic purposes and for irrigation. In a number of cases the artesian water is used in connection with the water from the canal. Attention is invited to a report on the underground water of supply of this valley made by Willis T. Lee in 1903 and published in the second annual report of the Reclamation Service, 1903 and 1904, pages 165 to 170, inclusive.

Benson Valley.—In the Benson district there are no ditches in operation on the west side of the river, but a few patches in the vicinity of Benson are irrigated by the use of artesian water. On the east side of the river all of the cultivated land is irrigated by water from the Benson Canal.

The Benson Canal was built in 1909 and 1910 by the Benson Canal Co. (a corporation). This company is a mutual organization owned and maintained by the land owners and water users under the canal, no water being sold. Each share is assessed for one one-hundredth part of maintenance expenses and entitles the owner to one one-hundredth part of the water carried by the ditch at any stage. At the present time 1,007 acres are irrigated under this canal. There are no other ditches in active operation in the district.

In the upper part of the Benson Valley the irrigated lands were reclaimed since the completion of the Benson Canal, where, as in the lower portion of the valley, in what is known as the "Tres Alamos" district, considerable land was irrigated during previous times.

This previously irrigated land, having an aggregate area of 460 acres, was served by three ditches, as follows:

	Acres.
Old Gujalba Canal	80
Old Dunbar Canal	300
Old Etz Everhardy Canal	80
Total	460

Of the land previously irrigated by the old Dunbar Canal, 20 acres are now being irrigated by direct pumping from the river.

The irrigation in the Tres Alamos district is the oldest on the river. The whites began the practice of irrigation here in 1868. In 1890 the river had cut its channel to such a depth that diversions were impracticable and a gradual abandonment of this land took place. In 1900 all of these older ditches had been abandoned.

Pool district.—The Pool district is a long, narrow valley or series of small valleys situated between the Benson and Reddington districts. Inasmuch as the valley is very irregular in character, the irigated areas are scattered over a long distance. This land was originally served by eight ditches, but owing to various causes only four ditches are now being used.

The following tabulation shows the ditches in operation or abandoned, with the respective cultivated or previously cultivated areas:

	Acres irrigated.	Acres previously irrigated.
Apadoca Canal	80	
Redus McKinney and Cook Canal	45	
Rivero Canal		20
Pool Canal		
East side		180
West side		40
Boetonas Canal		100
Monguia Canal	40	
Sozo Canal	80	
Total	245	340

This district has been under cultivation for many years, having been settled by the early Mexican immigrants. It is still largely owned by Mexicans.

Reddington district.—The Reddington district is owned principally by the Bayles & Berkalew Cattle Co., and is served by five ditches, one of which irrigates a small homestead, while the others serve the land owned by the company. The ditches and areas irrigated in this district are as follows:

	Acres.
Wheaton, Warren, and Ryan ditch	400
Old Los Angeles	700
Bollen	100
Marcum	300
Moran	22
Total	1,422

The first four ditches serve the company ranch.

This district has been under irrigation since the early seventies and the areas cultivated have been gradually increased since that time.

Mammoth district.—Below the Reddington district the next irrigation begins 9 miles above and extends to the town of Mammoth. This district was formerly served by five ditches, but one of these, the Rhodes ditch, recently has been abandoned.

The ditches and areas served are as follows:

	Acres irrigated.	Acres previously irrigated.
Rhodes ditch		30
Action ditch	30	
Action and Cheek ditch	320	
Hawes ditch	65	
Smith ditch	200	
Total	615	30

Some of this land was under cultivation prior to 1890, but the larger portion has been reclaimed more recently.

Aravaipa district.—The Aravaipa district lies between Mammoth and the Aravaipa Creek and is served by the five ditches designated as follows, the respective areas under irrigation also being given:

	Acres irrigated.	Acres previously irrigated.
Cronley Girard ditch No. 1	100	
Cronley Girard ditch No. 2	10	40
Buzan ditch	50	10
Willis	90	
Pusch No. 1	50	
Total	305	50

Practically all of the irrigation in this district took place since 1880. The Wills ditch, however, which was the old Fort Grant ditch, was constructed by the militia prior to 1868. Since 1880 the area under irrigation has gradually been increased, although some of the area previously irrigated has been lost by erosion.

Feldman and Winkelman district.—From the mouth of the Aravaipa to the confluence of the San Pedro with the Gila the irrigated area is practically continuous. It is confined to narrow strips and is divided in about equal proportions on the two sides of the river.

There are 13 ditches in this district irrigating land, as follows:

	Acres irrigated.	Acres previously irrigated.
Cook ditch	250	....
Pusch ditch, No. 2	190	....
Finch ditch, No. 1	3	60
Finch ditch, No. 2	50	15
Indian ditch, No. 1	8	....
Indian ditch, No. 2	12	....
Mallor	132	68
Liningle and Young ditch	25	25
Wilcox ditch	200	40
Old Cunningham or Raey Beans Snyder ditch	....	30
Latin ditch	80	....
Lilley-Bates ditch	62	....
Total	1,015	268

The land in this district has been irrigated intermittently for many years. Apache Indians were irrigating small patches prior to 1868, while a few white settlers began to cultivate small patches soon after that. From 1870 to the present time the irrigated area has steadily increased in spite of the heavy losses caused by floods.

IRRIGATION ON THE TRIBUTARIES OF THE SAN PEDRO.

Babacomari Creek.—The Babacomari Creek flows easterly through the Babacomari grant to its confluence with the San Pedro River at Fairbanks.

There are 76 acres under irrigation on this stream, this entire area being served by one ditch, the Kimball or Babacomari ditch which was constructed prior to 1900 and has been in continuous use since that time.

On page 170 of the Third Annual Report of the Reclamation Service, 1903–04, mention is made of a proposed dam on this stream. However, no further action in this matter has been taken. Recently the Boquillas Land & Cattle Co., a large cattle and landholding company, have purchased all of this land, but they have no intention of promoting this project.

Aravaipa Creek.—The Aravaipa Creek rises in the Galiuro Range and flows in a westerly direction to its confluence with the San Pedro River near the center of sec. 9, T. 7 S., R. 16 E., G. & S. R. B. M.

About 5 miles above the mouth of this creek the stream bed passes through a box canyon for a short distance. Above this canyon the creek basin opens out into a series of small valleys, all of which are now under irrigation. Fifteen small ditches in this section serve to irrigate approximately 170 acres of land.

Below this canyon there is one ditch in operation serving 500 acres.

Beginning in the late sixties and prior to 1887 a considerable area of land, both above and below the Box Canyon on the Aravaipa, was cultivated by the Apache Indians, but its extent can not be definitely determined. With the coming of the whites the Indians were gradually forced from their holdings, until at the present time only one ranch of 8 acres in extent remains in the possession of the Indians.

SUMMARY OF IRRIGATION IN THE SAN PEDRO BASIN.

On the San Pedro River there are 46 ditches serving a total of 6,860 acres of irrigated land.

Following is a tabulation of all of the ditches, showing the acreage previously irrigated, area irrigated at present, irrigable land under ditches, and land under ditches but irrigated entirely or partially by artesian wells:

Distribution areas by ditches on San Pedro River.

Ditches.	Year built.	Year last used.	Acres cultivated.	Acres previously cultivated.	Additional irrigated area.	Irrigated by wells.
Hereford	Prior to 1901		312		160	
Boquillas:						
East side [1]	do		296		200	
West side [1]	do		286		150	
Union	1877		364		220	
St. David	1878		920	223	1,109	163
Benson	1909		1,007		1,215	11
Grijalba	1873	1900		80	240	
Dunbar [2]	1868	1890	20	300	300	
Everhardy	1906	1909		80	300	
Apocado	1879		80		220	
Redus-McKinney	1905		45		60	
Rivero	1880	1903		20		
Pool:						
East side	Prior to 1880	1905		180	300	
West side	1912	1914		40		
Basquiz	1898		35			
Boetonas	1895	1907		100	90	
Monguia	1885		40			
Sozo	1890		80		60	
Wheaton	1890		300		80	
Los Angeles	1878		700		120	
Bollen	In the eighties		100	20		
Marcum	1890		300		110	
Moran	1905		23			
Rhodes	Prior to 1910	1915		30		
Acton	1890		30			
Acton and Clark	1883		320		400	
Hawes	Prior to 1910		65			
Smith	Prior to 1895		200		75	
Cronley 1	Prior to 1903		100			
Cronley 2	1892		10	40	15	
Buzan	1907		50	10		
Wills [3]	In the seventies		95		30	
Pusch	1879		50			
Cook	1877		250		260	
Pusch 2	1894		190		100	
Finch 1 [4]	1890		3	60		
Finch 2	1875		50	15	20	
Indian 1	1890		8			
Indian 2	1883		30		12	
Mallor	1909		3		4	
Livingle and Young	1878		132	68	40	
Wilcox	1880		25	25	80	
Snyder	1900	1912		30		
Raey Bros [5]	1880		200	40		
Latin	1885		80		30	
Lilley-Bates [6]	1890, 1907		62	25	75	
Total			6,860	1,386	6,025	174

[1] Using same diversion.
[2] Irrigated 20 acres by pump.
[3] Old Fort Grant Canal.
[4] 57 acres washed out in 1915.
[5] Old Cunningham ditch.
[6] Bates built in 1890; Lilley built in 1907.

Nature of the Land and Ditch Ownership Along the San Pedro.—Practically all of the bottom land above the St. David Valley, the major portion of which is included in the old Spanish grants, is owned by the Boquillas Land & Cattle Co.

In the St. David and Benson Valleys the irrigated land consists of small ranches originally taken up as homesteads.

In the lower Benson Valley and in the Pool districts the ranches range from 80 to 1,000 acres in area and are owned by companies or by individuals.

The land in the Redington district is practically all owned by one company, the Bayles & Berkalew Cattle Co. A few small homesteads also have been taken up by other parties. Below the Redington district and down to the confluence of the San Pedro and the Gila the ranches vary in size from 40 to 3,000 acres and are owned by the companies or the individuals. The ditches are owned by the companies or the individuals owning the land. In the St. David and Benson districts the canals are owned by mutual corporations. The landowners hold the stock and the water is distributed in proportion to their holdings in the company.

Water Supply.—During the greater part of the year the discharge of the San Pedro River is spasmodic and flashy in character, floods occurring at irregular but frequent intervals. During the months of May, June, and a part of July there is a decided shortage of water for irrigation purposes.

At the time of the immigation of the first whites to this valley and until about 1887 the regimé of the river was entirely different from that which exists at present. The channel was shallow and much smaller than at present, and some water flowed in the upper portion of the valley during the entire year, while near its mouth the stream occasionally disappears entirely during the dry months. Disastrous floods were unknown until comparatively recent years. In the Benson Valley the river channel was very little below the average level of the valley flood, and the frequent freshets during the flood season, especially in the lower portion of the valley, spread over the bottom land giving to swamps covered with profuse vegetation.

It is reported that the severe earthquake of 1887 caused the San Pedro to begin to cut a deeper channel. This erosion has continued to the present time. In 1894-95 there ocurred a heavy flood which greatly eroded both the banks and bed of the river. In the vicinity of Benson the river bed has been cut to a depth of from 35 to 40 feet.

Prior to the incoming of the whites there was an abundance of grass and other vegetation in the watershed and the discharge of the river was much more regular and less flashy in character. Overstocking the cattle ranges and consequent denudation of vegetation has been responsible for the altered nature of the run-off.

A number of discharge measurements have been made on the San Pedro by the Reclamation Service and the Geological Survey at various points and during various periods. The following discharge measurements were taken from a supplemental report of the Benson Canal by Field Examiner R. G. Mead to the Commissioner of the General Land Office:

Mean monthly discharge of San Pedro River, Ariz., at Charleston.

[Drainage area, approximately 1,200 square miles.]

Month.	1904	1905	1906
	Second-feet.	*Second-feet.*	*Second-feet.*
March	20.3	152.0	65.2
April	21.5	60.5	28.9
May	28.7	29.8	18.7
June	12.8	30.6	8.0
July	870.0	47.2	32.7
August	735.0	125.0	147.0

The following discharge measurements of the San Pedro River were obtained near Lewis Springs during the year 1911, and the data published in Water Supply Paper No. 309, page 329:

	Discharge (second-feet).
January 19	23
March 11	15
April 11	18
July 14	100
August 23	70
September 25	25
November 15	12

The following discharge measurements of the San Pedro River at Fairbanks for the year 1912 were obtained from Water Supply Paper No. 329, page 219:

	Discharge (second-feet).
September 28	15
October 10	14
November 28	18
December 10	11

Since 1912 a measurement station has been maintained continually on the river 2 miles above Fairbanks, under the supervision of C. C. Jacob, district engineer United States Geological Survey, with headquarters at Phoenix, Ariz.

During the trip down the San Pedro for this investigation nine current-meter measurements were made at irregular intervals of distance. The results of these measurements are on file with Mr. Jacob at Phoenix and are also included herewith, as follows:

San Pedro River at—	Date (1915).	Second-feet.
5,400 feet below St. David Canal diversion	Apr. 13-15	26.03
Benson, 3 miles below Benson Canal, Benson Canal diverting and turning water back into river through spillway.	Apr. 14	30.25
Benson, 3 miles below Benson Canal diversion, Benson Canal	Apr. 18	3.43
Narrows, 20 miles below Benson	Apr. 20, 5 p. m.	9.28
	Apr. 21, 8 a. m.	7.33
5 miles above Reddington	Apr. 25	26.76
East line of T. 9 S., R. 17 E	Apr. 27	33.37
2 miles above Mammoth	Apr. 28	44.87
3 miles above mouth of Aravaipa Creek	Apr. 30	44.25
On Aravaipa Creek, 3,000 feet above confluence	do	21.00
San Pedro River, 150 feet above confluence with Gila	May 5	92.83

Underground flow of San Pedro River.—The material of the river channel consists principally of loose shifting sand and gravel which has considerable depth to bedrock, thus permitting a large amount of water to flow under the surface. During the summer season, when the basin is apparently dry, there occurs at various points in the river bed notable return or seepage flows. This return water generally rises at points where the bedrock is near the surface. By locating the headwork of a ditch near such a point it sometimes happens that the ditch may receive an ample supply of water for irrigation notwithstanding the fact that a second ditch heading at another point but a short distance up the river may be diverting all of the surface flow at that point. This condition is most noticeable between the St. David and Benson Canals and the Cook and Pusch Canals, in the Winkelman districts.

To illustrate this phenomenon, two examples may be given. At the time of this investigation the St. David Canal was diverting 16 second-feet of water or practically the entire surface flow, only 4 second-feet being permitted to escape past the diversion weir. One mile below the weir a current metter measurement was made, which gave a surface discharge of 26.63 second-feet.

The Pusch No. 2 Canal and the Cook Canal have their headings only 400 feet apart. When the water is low, the first-named canal may divert apparently all of the surface flow, but in the space intervening between the two headings water will rise to the surface to supply the second. This is unusual, however, since during the dry season there are few places along the river where there is sufficient flow to furnish an irrigating head. A majority of the ditches are sometimes without water, and none of them have an adequate supply at all times.

Probable future uses for irrigation.—Increased future irrigation by direct diversion on the San Pedro River seems to be fraught with more or less risk, as the cost of maintaining irrigation systems along this stream is very great. This is due to the high river banks of soft material and to the spasmodic and flashy character of the river flow. The cost of maintenance of the headings and ditches now in use is very great. Two concrete diversion dams, owned by the Boquillas Land & Cattle Co., the only concrete irrigation structures on the river, were destroyed by the floods of the past season. It is stated, however, that these diversion dams are to be immediately replaced.

Of the old ditches not in use at the present time there are only two small ones, the Bortonoa and Rhodes ditches, for which there is an expressed intention of rebuilding new headings. It is intended, however, to use portions of the Old Dunbar, the two Pool ditches, and the Snyder ditch in conjunction with pumping systems which are to lift the water directly from the river. In the Benson district W. R. Rollons is also installing a pumping system, taking water from the river. The aggregate area to be irrigated under these proposed systems is 600 acres.

Messrs. Bayles and Bukalew, landowners in the Reddington district, propose to construct one or two new ditches and to extend the present ditches to cover 1,300 acres in addition to the area irrigated at the present time.

Under all of the ditches along the San Pedro River there are 7,500 acres of irrigable land, 1,200 acres of which has never been cultivated and 1,400 acres of which has previously been cultivated.

From a consideration of the shortage of water for the ditches now in use during the dry season, and the high cost of construction and maintenance of the headings and diversion dams, it is evident that the future irrigation along the San Pedro River must be very limited unless a reservoir to conserve and regulate the flood water be constructed. The St. David and Benson Valleys, together with the surrounding mesa, embrace a large tract of irrigable land, constituting the only area of sufficient extent to justify such a project. For this the Charleston Reservoir has been proposed.

An investigation of the Charleston project has been made by the Reclamation Service, and a copy of the findings is given in the third annual report of the Reclamation Service, 1903 and 1904, pages 157 to 170, inclusive.

The following is an excerpt from the summary of the report of the board of consulting engineers who reviewed the report made by H. R. Evans for the Reclamation Service:

> The limited time during which measurements of the run-off from the storage basin above proposed storage reservoir have been made renders an estimate of the dependable water supply largely an assumption.
>
> The increasing demands in Mexico for water incident to extensions and increasing mining operations should be carefully considered, since one-half or more of the drainage area of the San Pedro project is in Mexico. Also the rights of the Indians lower down on the Gila River should be considered before definitely determining the merits of this project.

The consulting board further advised that investigations be made of the available water supply and the probable future requirements for water in the portion of the drainage area lying in Mexico. No further action has been taken by the Government in this project.

The San Pedro project is proposed to irrigate 20,000 acres, 2,000 of which are now under irrigation. Without this project or one similar not more than 3,000 acres of land in addition to that now irrigated in this district could feasibly be placed under irrigation by direct diversion from the river.

Subsequent to the investigations of the above-mentioned project, the El Paso & Southwestern Railroad, which crosses the reservoir site, has reconstructed its line, replacing the old tracks with thoroughly modern construction. As the construction of this project would entail the removal of this railroad, this item of expense has now become considerably greater than when originally considered.

It is reasonable to expect that the construction of this project rests entirely with the Government. There has been no expression of the intentions of private capital to undertake the project. The cost will be approximately $1,000,000, but the long period which must intervene before returns will be realized on the investment, and the fact that all of the land is either owned in small private holdings or is held by the Government do not make this project alluring to capitalists.

IRRIGABLE BOTTOM LAND BY DISTRICTS NOW UNDER DITCHES.

San Pedro River.—The following table gives the areas of irrigable bottom land along the San Pedro River which are not covered by ditches:

	Acres.
Grant district	1,500
Benson district	3,000
St. David district	2,000
Pool district	4,200
Reddington district	1,500
Mammoth district	1,300
Aravaipa district	1,800
Feldman and Winkelman districts	2,200
Total	17,500

Summary and conclusions.—On the San Pedro River there have been found to be 6,860 acres of cultivated land irrigated by 46 ditches, 6,025 acres irrigable land situated under ditches but never irrigated, 1,400 acres of land previously irrigated but now no longer irrigated, and 17,500 acres of land irrigable from the river which has never been under ditch.

Taking into consideration the fact that the water supply is generally inadequate during the dry season, it is concluded that in the future, the diversions of water on the San Pedro will not become greatly in excess of the diversions now being made. The volume of water which this river contributes to the flow of the Gila may be expected to continue in the same proportion in future years as in the past. It should also be added that the discharge of the San Pedro is insignificant during the dry seasons and that the greatest part of the flow contributed to the Gila by this tributary is discharged during times of floods or when there is sufficient water on both rivers for all requirements.

THE SAN CARLOS RIVER.

The San Carlos River Basin is located in the southeastern part of Gila County, and in the northwestern part of Graham County. For a distance of 25 miles, the boundary line separating these two counties follows the course of the San Carlos River. On the north and east this basin is bounded by the Natanes Plateau and on the north and west by Apache, Pinal, and El Capitan Mountains. The southern limit of this drainage basin is the Gila River.

The San Carlos River Basin consists generally of mountainous country, its valleys are narrow and winding, the streams or creeks flowing in these valleys are generally torrential in character. Among the many creeks or washes which flow into the San Carlos River there are but six creeks that may be regarded as important.

The valley of the San Carlos at its widest parts, where the towns of Rice and San Carlos are located, is not more than 4,000 feet in width; and in many places is but 200 feet in width.

The maximum elevation of the San Carlos at its headwaters is approximately 3,000 feet above sea level. At its confluence with the Gila River the San Carlos has an elevation of 2,410 feet above sea level.

The climate of this valley is more temperate than that found in the southern parts of the State.

The cultivated area along the San Carlos, begins at a point 3 miles northeast of the town of Rice and extends to the Gila River, a distance of 15 miles. Practically all of the irrigable land is farmed by Apache Indians of the San Carlos Reservation.

The soil throughout the valley is silt alluvium and is very fertile. The valley is divided into two districts, the first district comprising that part of the valley from Paridot farm to the upper limits of the irrigable lands, the second district comprising that part of the valley from Paridot to the junction of the San Carlos and the Gila Rivers, and known as the agency district. These two districts are presided over by two Government farmers who superintend the construction of headings, headgates, canals laterals, borders, and general irrigation work on the Indian farms in their respective districts.

The first irrigation along this river took place in 1875, according to the report of the agent in charge, in the vicinity of the town of Rice. The development of the irrigated area as given by the agents in their annual reports and as estimated from other available data it is given in tabulated form on page 236 of this appendix, in connection with the history of irrigation along the Gila and on the San Carlos Reservation.

Many of the original canals have been destroyed by floods, which occur frequently in this region. Traces of some of these old canals may still be observed on the ground, but many have been completely obliterated.

Great difficulty is met in maintaining the headings of the 24 canals along the river which supply water to the irrigated land. The canals are not of large capacity nor do any of them serve to irrigate large tracts of land. The ordinary canal in this valley irrigates on an average 40 acres of land and supports four or five Indian families.

In the following tabulation are shown the names of the canals as found in the different districts, the areas at present cultivated, the area previously cultivated, and the area under the various canals not cultivated but fenced.

There are 24 canals in operation in these two districts. In the Paridot farm district there are 12 canals which serve to irrigate 453.9 acres of land. There are 229 acres of land previously cultivated and also 165.5 acres of land not cultivated but fenced and under canals. In the San Carlos, or "agency," farm district there are 12 canals which serve to irrigate 482.1 acres of cultivated land. An area of 255 acres has been previously cultivated, and there are in addition 196.1 acres of land not culivated but fenced and under canals.

List of canals San Carlos River, San Carlos Indian Reservation.

Canals.	Cultivated land.	Previously cultivated land.	Not cultivated land.
	Acres.	*Acres.*	*Acres.*
Paridot farm district:			
1. C. B. 1	32.4	12.1	0.9
2. C. B. 23	29.0	....	....
3. C. A. 11	24.7	20.8	17.4
4. Talkali	54.5	72.2	69.2
5. S. N. 1	26.0	10.6	4.6
6. S. B. 47	24.7	....	27.1
7. Hoffman	15.0	....	1.8
8. T. B. 4 (old)	....	46.9	....
9. S. B. 13 "Nosie"	67.2	27.4	1.2
10. Antonio	64.2	6.3	20.6
11. Paridot farm	108.5	16.2	15.1
12. Hopkins	7.7	16.5	7.6
	453.9	229.0	165.5
San Carlos district:			
13. S. F. 11	7.6	....	2.8
14. Capt. Jack	20.9	3.0	....
15. S. O	11.0	....	2.8
16. Victor	18.2	50.0	2.3
17. S. J. 53	6.2	27.4	1.5
18. S. H. 7	26.9	2.2	....
19. Tony Lee	27.6	....	4.8
20. Sabe Mucho	74.1	12.2	16.9
21. Big John	52.1	43.0	15.4
22. T. D. 2	26.2	6.4	14.7
23. T. A. 21	5.6	12.2	13.3
24. Agency	205.7	98.7	121.6
	482.1	255.1	196.1
Total	936.0	484.1	361.6

Analysis of irrigation on San Carlos Reservation, Arizona, Paridot and San Carlos districts.

Name of canal.	Date of construction.	Date of abandonment.	Area by United States Irrigation Service Survey, 1914.		
			Acres cultivated.	Acres previously cultivated.	Acres not cultivated (fenced).
Paridot farm district:					
1. C. B. 1	1892	....	32.4	12.1	0.9
2. C. B. 23	(1)	(1)	29.0	....	....
3. C. A. 11	1898	....	24.7	20.8	17.4
4. Talkali	(1)	....	54.5	72.2	69.2
5. S. N. 1	1898	....	26.0	10.6	4.6
6. S. B. 47	1897	....	24.7	....	27.1
7. Hoffman	1885-1890	....	15.0	....	1.8
8. T. B. 4	(1)	(1)	....	46.9	....
9. S. B. 13	1885-1890	....	67.2	27.4	1.2
10. Antonio	1885-1890	....	64.2	6.3	20.6
11. Paridot	1885-1890	....	108.5	16.2	15.1
12. Hopkins	1911	....	7.7	15.5	7.6
San Carlos district:					
13. S. F. 11	1910	....	7.6	....	2.8
14. Capt. Jack	1896	....	20.9	3.0	....
15. S. O	1888	....	11.0	....	2.8
16. Victor	1890	....	18.2	50.0	2.3
17. S. J. 53	1902	....	6.2	27.4	1.5
18. S. H. 7	1904	....	26.9	2.2	....
19. Tony Lee	1908	....	27.6	....	4.8
20. Sabe Mucho	1898	....	74.1	12.2	16.9
21. Big John	1898	....	52.1	43.0	15.4
22. T. D. 2	1900	....	26.2	6.4	14.7
23. T. A. 21	1904	....	5.6	12.2	13.3
24. Agency	1900	....	205.7	98.7	121.6
Total	....	....	936.0	484.1	361.9

[1] Unknown.

Analysis of irrigation on San Carlos Reservation, Arizona, Paridot and San Carlos districts—Continued.

Name of canal.	Priorities in five-year periods as estimated from all available evidence.								
	1875	1880	1885	1890	1895	1900	1905	1910	1915
Paridot farm district:									
1. C. C. 1	......	......	......	......	20	20	15	25	32.4
2. C. B. 23	10	10	30	30	30	30	25	25	29.0
3. C. A. 11	......	......	......	......	......	15	5	20	24.7
4. Talkali	......	10	40	50	55	55	45	45	54.5
5. S. N. 1	......	......	......	......	......	20	10	15	26.0
6. S. B. 47	......	......	......	......	......	20	10	15	24.7
7. Hoffman	......	......	15	15	15	15	10	10	15.0
8. T. B. 4	20	10	45	45	45	30	15	15	......
9. S. B. 13	......	......	40	25	30	30	25	40	67.2
10. Antonio	......	......	......	40	50	50	45	40	64.2
11. Paridot	......	......	45	45	60	60	55	50	108.5
12. Hopkins	......	......	......	......	......	......	......	......	7.7
San Carlos district:									
13. S. F. 11	......	......	......	......	......	......	......	5	7.6
14. Capt. Jack	......	......	......	......	......	15	15	10	20.9
15. S. O	......	......	10	10	10	10	5	5	11.0
16. Victor	......	......	20	20	20	20	5	20	18.2
17. S. J. 53	......	......	......	......	......	......	10	5	6.2
18. S. H. 7	......	......	......	......	......	......	10	15	26.9
19. Tony Lee	......	......	......	......	......	......	......	15	27.6
20. Sabe Mucho	......	......	......	......	......	30	20	40	74.1
21. Big John	......	......	......	......	......	30	20	30	52.1
22. T. D. 2	......	......	......	......	......	10	5	10	26.2
23. T. A. 21	......	......	......	......	5	5	5	5	5.6
24. Agency	......	......	......	......	......	50	100	190	205.7
Total	30	30	215	280	350	515	455	650	937.0
Total given by agents in annual reports	30	30	......	......	450	500	480	......	......

Future uses of water from the San Carlos.—In view of the fact that the flow of the San Carlos River during the dry season is not greatly in excess of the requirements of the present cultivation, no large increase in the irrigated areas can be expected. Owing to the fact that the land now irrigated is situated in a narrow valley and in close proximity to the river, favorable to return flow, it is not thought that the present uses or possible future uses of the river waters should have any appreciable effect upon the water supply for irrigation lower down on the Gila proper.

EAGLE CREEK.

Eagle Creek rises in the Blue Range, in the northeast corner of Graham County, Ariz., flows eastward and crosses into Greenlee County; then turning in a southerly direction, it forms the boundary between these two counties and finally empties into the Gila River, 1 mile east of the point where the Gila River leaves Greenlee and enters Graham County.

Districts.—For convenience we will divide the irrigated area along Eagle Creek into two districts. The upper district, which is about 14 miles in length, and which includes the larger valleys, we will term the Double Circle district. The lower district, which includes the box canyon through which this tributary flows, and in which the irrigated areas are scattered, we will designate the Canyon district.

From the Indian agent's report of the San Carlos Indian Reservation for the year 1878 it is learned that 119 Indians were farming along Eagle Creek at that time. The report did not state the acreage cultivated by Indians or other information concerning their lands.

The Indians apparently abandoned their farms because of the destruction of their ditches and erosion of their lands by the floods. There is evidence along the stream of very early irrigation, which apparently had to be abandoned because of the great damage done to the land by floods. These farms belonged probably to Apaches.

Prior to the arrival of the first white settlers in this region in the eighties a few Mexicans had taken up small farms along the stream. The holdings of the whites and primarily cattle ranches, and crops are raised mainly for domestic consumption, since practically all irrigated areas along this creek are inaccessible by means of wagons, and can be reached only by pack outfits.

Double Circle district.—The Double Circle district, beginning at the Honeymoon Ranger Station and extending downstream about 18 miles, is settled and farmed by cattlemen.

In this district 16 ditches are serving the irrigated land, as follows:

	Acres.
Honeymoon Ranger Station district	20
Garnet district	30
Swafford district	40
Brown district	30
Patty district	7
Miller district	18
Harris district	30
Nicholas district	48
Filleman district	20
Miller district	20
Davis district	10
Shannon district	22
Montgomery district	50
Harrison No. 1 district	40
Harrison No. 2 district	100
Cook district	5
Total	490

Canyon district.—In the Canyon district the irrigated areas are small and served by small ditches about 1 foot deep and 1 foot in width at the top. This land is farmed principally by Mexicans, and is served by eight ditches as follows:

	Acres.
Guadilano ditch	3
Basa ditch	4
Poney ditch	45
Llano ditch	10
Gaino ditch	2
Gomex No. 1 ditch	2
Gomex No. 2 ditch	2
Talamente ditch	5
Total	73

The Mormon Water Co. has a large pumping station at the lower end of the Canyon district and due west of Clifton. They formerly maintained a small dam about 12 feet in height on the creek which submerged the present Talamente Ranch. This dam was washed out in 1903, but it has been superceded by a small diversion dam of rock and brush. This pumping plant delivers 2,000,000 gallons of water every 24 hours, of which from 1,000,000 to 1,500,000 gallons is taken directly from the creek, depending upon the stage. The balance of the water is supplied from wells. The Clifton and Morenci mining camps obtain their water supply from this pumping plant.

Summary of irrigation on Eagle Creek.—The irrigation on the stream is supplied by 24 ditches diverting from the creek, most of which are now serving all of the land irrigable by them. The following is a list of the ditches, areas served, and additional land that can be irrigated from present ditches:

Ditches and areas served, Eagle Creek.

Canals.	Year constructed.	Year of last use.	Acres irrigated.	Acres irrigable.	Remarks.
Honey Moon Ranger Station	[1] 1912		20		
Garret	1910		30		
Swafford	1910		40		
Brown	1910		30		
Patty	1910		7		
Miller	1910		18		
Harris	1910		30		
Nicholas	1910		48		
Filleman	1910		20		
Miller	1910		20		
Davis	1910		10		
Shannon	1890		22	40	Double circle.
Montgomery	1890		50	50	
Harrison No. 1	1903		40	20	
Harrison No. 2	1900		100	17	
Cook	1911		5	6	By pump.
Guadillano	1909		3		
Bass	1910		4		
Posey	1889		45		
Llano	1910		10		
Gaino	1905		2		Canyon district.
Gomes No. 1	1910		2		
Gomes No. 2	1910		2		
Talamente	1903		5		
Total			563	134	

[1] Prior to 1912.

Probable future uses.—Owing to the inaccessible nature of the entire valley and also to the fact that the irrigable area is so confined, it is reasonable to expect that no great increase of the area under irrigation will take place in the future.

It should be emphasized that the Canyon district is from 15 to 50 miles from the railroad and the Double Circle district from 50 to 80 miles, that the ranches are reached only by pack outfits, and that stock raising and not farming is the chief occupation.

THE SAN FRANCISCO RIVER, ARIZ. AND N. MEX.

The San Francisco River is one of the largest and most important of the tributaries of the Gila. Rising in the southeastern part of Apache County, Ariz., it flows into New Mexico, thence southwesterly into Arizona to its confluence with the Gila about 9 miles below the town of Clifton and about 24 miles above the town of Solomonville.

The valleys of Alpine and Luna, on the head of the stream, are open, sloping gradually upward to the surrounding hills. At the lower extremity of Luna Valley the river enters a canyon and throughout the remainder of its course flows through a mountainous country in narrow valleys or deep canyons. The outlines of the bottom lands or valleys are very irregular.

The ditches are supplied with water from the river by direct diversion, except near Clifton, where the water is lifted from the river by means of pumps. The water is conveyed to the fields by main ditches and laterals; for alfalfa and grain it is controlled in the fields by use of borders, while the furrows method is used for other crops.

History of irrigation along the San Francisco.—The practice of irrigation along this stream antedates the coming of Americans by a number of years. When the first American settlers arrived in this country, in the early eighties, a number of Mexican ranches had already been under cultivation for some time. A few of these ranches are still in possession of Mexicans.

Alpine district.—In the Alpine district regular irrigation is not necessary, since the land is subirrigated. During the dry season irrigation is sometimes practiced, but at such times there is seldom sufficient water, although use is made of all the water available from the river. At the present time 980 acres are being cultivated in this district.

Luna district.—The Luna Valley is irrigated from a reservoir on the river, located 10 miles above Luna at the lower extremity of Alpine Valley. The impounding dam by which the reservoir was created is of earth, is 20 feet in height, and the reservoir is of sufficient capacity, supplementing the normal flow of the stream during the summer, to irrigate about 1,000 acres. The river channel is used to conduct the stored water from the reservoir to a point about 2 miles above Luna, where the two main canal diversions take place.

This reservoir project was constructed in 1892 under a 25-year franchise, which will expire in 1917. It is the intention of the company, however, to renew its franchise at the date of expiration. While the project will supply about 1,000 acres, the ditches are inadequate to serve an area larger than that now irrigated. It is also intended to enlarge these ditches.

This reservoir now serves to irrigate 300 acres of land by means of two main ditches. Besides the above area, there are 80 acres situated at various points in the valley, which are irrigated from small side drainage streams. In addition to the above area, it is estimated that 2,200 acres are susceptible of irrigation in the Luna Valley.

Prior to the construction of the reservior, several small ditches were serving the land now under the reservoir project. All of these rights have been taken over by the irrigation company.

Reserve district.—Between the Luna Valley and the Reserve district, no irrigation takes place. The Reserve district begins 7 miles below the Luna Valley and extends to the Apache National Reserve. This district is served by eight ditches, irrigating small patches on either side of the river. The Reserve Valley is narrow, and the irrigated land is cut up into small tracts.

A list of the ditches in this district and the areas which they serve to irrigate are given in the following table:

Canal.	Irrigated.	Irrigable.	Canal.	Irrigated.	Irrigable.
	Acres.	*Acres.*		*Acres.*	*Acres.*
Lewis ditch	10	12	Romero No. 2	13	
Allen or McCarthy	11		Jones	6	
Romero No. 1	10		Manor	8	
Henley	28				
May	20		Total	166	12
Balla	60				

This district was cultivated by Mexicans prior to the coming of Americans, who began to settle here in the early eighties. Some of the old Mexican ditches are still in use to-day.

Frisco or Plaza district.—Proceeding down the stream the next irrigated lands reached are situated in what is known as the Frisco or Plaza district. This includes an old Mexican settlement and embraces all the lands in the Frisco and Plaza Valley, as well as the lands along the river as far down as the Martinez Ranch, 20 miles below Frisco.

At Frisco the valley opens out and is fairly wide, but below Frisco the irrigated lands are confined to small areas on either side of the river.

There are 11 ditches serving lands as follows:

Canal.	Irrigated.	Previously cultivated.	Irrigable.
	Acres.	*Acres.*	*Acres.*
Kiehue ditch	50		
Frisco ditch	92		
Hitower ditch	80		
Plaza, east side	77		
Plaza, west side	87		60
Barrara Jerome	18		10
Cordova		6	
Romero	10		
Jim Kelly	10		
Felica	15		
Martinez		5	
Total	439	11	70

A portion of the area tabulated above was under irrigation a number of years prior to the coming of the early white settlers in 1880. During recent years the erosive action of the floods has destroyed a large acreage of cultivated land bordering on the stream.

Alma district.—The next irrigation below the Frisco is the Alma, which embraces the entire Alma Valley. A major portion of the land in this valley is owned by the well known "W. S." Ranch Co.

At the head of this district the valley is very narrow but it widens out in the vicinity of Alma. At Alma the San Francisco is joined by a tributary called Mineral Creek.

In this district are 6 ditches which serve to irrigate lands as follows:

Canals.	Irrigated.	Previously cultivated.	Irrigable.
	Acres.	*Acres.*	*Acres.*
Wm. Spurgen	2		
S. F. Spurgen	30	10	
"W S" East No. 1	100		
"W S" East No. 2	50		100
"W S" West	100		
Alma Town	43		
Total	325	10	100

Some of this land has been cultivated for many years, and, as in the case of the Frisco district, lands were cultivated here prior to the coming of the whites.

Pleasanton district.—The Pleasanton district includes what is commonly known as the Pleasanton Valley. This valley is the lowest open valley on the stream, is in a high state of cultivation, and presents a very prosperous appearance. Irrigation began in this district prior to 1880 and reached its present stage of development about 1900.

In this valley there are three ditches which divert water from the river, while one other ditch receives its water by pumping from wells. The irrigated areas are as follows:

Canals.	Acres irrigated.
Holt & Goddard	202
Sibe	40
Goddard	75
York's well	12
Total	329

There are in this valley about 300 acres of illigable land not under ditch.

Clifton district.—The Clifton district includes the land extending from Pleasanton Valley as far down the stream as Clifton. The river in this district is confined in a deep, narrow canyon, which widens out slightly in places, forming several restricted valleys. Irrigation is carried on in the most favorable of these valleys.

There are five ditches serving to irrigate areas, as follows:

Canals.	Acres irrigated.
Sliger ditch	55
Keppler	[1] 5
Sweeting	[1] 4
Harper	[1] 20
Potter	[1] 28
Total	112

With the exception of the Sliger ditch, which diverts directly from the river, all of the above ditches are supplied by water pumped directly from the river.

About 2 miles above Clifton the Arizona Copper Co. diverts some of the flow of the river for power purposes, but the entire flow so diverted is later returned to the stream.

No irrigation takes place on the San Francisco below the Clifton district.

Summary of irrigation on the entire San Francisco River.—In the Alpine Valley 980 acres are under cultivation, the land being subirrigated. Below the Alpine Valley and throughout the remaining course of the river the land is irrigated either by ditches diverting directly from the river or by ditches supplied by direct pumping from the river.

There are in all 37 ditches along the stream, which serve to irrigate 1,739 acres. In addition to this area 21 acres have been previously cultivated, while 2,682 acres are irrigable and located either under the present ditches or under their possible extensions.

[1] Diverted by pump.

The following is a tabulation of the ditches and the areas situated under each:

Ditches.	Year constructed.	Year of last use.	Acres cultivated.	Acres previously cultivated.	Irrigable.	Subirrigated.	Remarks.
Alpine district					300	980	
Luna Irrigation Co.			300		2,200		Reservoir sufficient for 1,000 acres additional.
By tributaries Luna Valley.			80				
Lewis	1895		10		12		Expect to build another ditch.
Allen, prior to	1900		11				
Romero No. 1	1900		10				
Nemley	1878		28				
May	1885		20				
Balla	1870		60				
Romero No. 2	1880		13				
Jones	1910		6				
Manor	1910		8				
Kienue	1880		50				
Frisco	1885		92				
Hitower	1900		80				
Plaza E. S	1885		77				
Plaza W. S	1885		87		60		
Barrara	1913		18		10		May build ditch to cover.
Cordova	1900	1909		6			
Romero	1900		10				
Kelly	1900		10				
[illegible]	1880		15				
Martinez	1900	1910		5			Being rebuilt, 7 acres to be covered by ditch.
Spurgen	1885		2				
S. F Spurgen	1885		30	10			
W. S. East S. 1	1885		100				
W. S. East S. 2	1911		50		100		May build 2 ditches to serve irrigable land.
W. S. West S. 3	1885		100				
Alma Town	1880		43				
Holt	1880		202				
Sibe	1880		40				
Goddard	1900		75				
Sligger	1890		55				
Kepper	1900		5				
Sweeting	1900		4				
Harper	1900		20				
Potter	1900		2				
Total			1,739	21	2,682	980	12 by well.

Irrigation on small tributaries:	Acres, approximately.
Center Fire Creek	300
Mineral Creek	200
Glenwood Springs	30
White Water Creek	30
Tularose River	200
Total	780

Ditch ownership.—The Luna Irrigation Co., which operates the Luna Reservoir, is a mutual corporation, owned by the water users under the project, each shareholder being assessed for the expenses and the water apportioned according to the number of shares controlled.

The remainder of the ditches are classed as individual or partnership ditches. Each ditch in the latter class is owned by two or more partners, each sharing the expense of maintenance according to the interest held in the ditch and receiving the water in the same proportion.

Water supply for irrigation on the San Francisco River.—Notwithstanding the high altitude of the greater portion of the drainage area, the run-off of this tributary of the Gila is torrential and flashy in character, and while the flow is continuous, yet it becomes very low during the dry seasons.

Discharge measurements have been made for a number of years at Alma, N. Mex., which is above the confluence of the San Francisco and the Blue Rivers. The results of these measurements are to be found in Water Supply Papers No. 269, page 224, and No. 309, page 234. These measurements show that the flow at Alma varies from a maximum of nearly 1,000 second-feet to a minimum of 6.9 second-feet and that the average monthly flow varies from 100 to 300 second-feet.

Discharge measurements made in 1911 below the confluence of the San Francisco with the Blue, at a point 1½ miles above Clifton and published in Water Supply Paper No. 309, page 235, give a maximum discharge of 1,240 second-feet, a minimum discharge of 56 second-feet, and a mean or average flow of 325 second-feet.

From these measurements it will be seen that there is an adequate water supply for irrigation purposes in the several districts along the San Francisco, as well as in the extreme upper valleys known as the Alpine and the Luna districts. In the Alpine Valley most of the land is subirrigated, while a reservoir in the Luna Valley conserves the irrigation waters in that district.

Probable future uses.—In the following table is given an estimate of the areas subject to cultivation in the different districts along the San Francisco River:

	Acres.
Alpine Valley	300
Luna	2,200
Reserve	80
Frisco or Plaza	170
Alma	150
Pleasanton	300
Total	3,200

As already stated, irrigation in the Alpine district is not necessary. In the Luna Valley, with the reservoir at its present height and capacity, an additional area of 1,000 acres could be served, the only change necessary being the enlargement of the present ditches.

In the Reserve and Frisco Valleys, there seems to be no likelihood of an increase in the area under irrigation. In the Alma and the Pleasanton Valleys, extensions of the present ditches are contemplated and it may be reasonable to expect that the entire cultivatable area in these valleys may be irrigated in the near future. It is believed that if present conditions continue in force, at least 1,500 acres in addition to the land now irrigated can reasonably be expected to be put under cultivation on the San Francisco within a short time.

Irrigation on the tributaries of the San Francisco.—Besides the Blue River, there are several lesser tributaries to the San Francisco and some irrigation takes place along these small streams. On the Center Fire Creek, which joins the San Francisco 6 miles below the town of Luna, an area of about 300 acres is being irrigated at present. Along the Tularosa River, which contributes its flow to the

San Francisco at a point just below Frisco, approximately 200 acres are being cultivated, the exact area not being known. On Mineral Creek, which joins the San Francisco at Alma, about 200 acres are being cultivated at the present time. On Whitewater Creek, which empties into the San Francisco just above Pleasanton Valley, about 30 acres are being cultivated by diversions from the river, and an additional 50 acres are cultivated from Glenwood Spring in the White Water Creek Valley.

IRRIGATION ALONG THE BLUE RIVER.

The Blue River, rising in the southeastern corner of Apache County, Ariz., flows in a southeasterly direction, across the northeast corner of Greenlee County, and one-half mile into New Mexico, crossing the State line 3 miles south of the southern boundary of Apache County; thence taking a course west of south, the river returns into Greenlee County and discharges into the San Francisco River, 20 miles above the town of Clifton, the county seat of Greenlee County.

At the point where the river enters New Mexico, a branch stream, the Dry Blue, enters the Blue River from the northeast. Above this fork, or junction, the main stream is known as the Campbell Blue. The Dry Blue is a small stream heading about 4 miles south of Luna, N. Mex.

The Blue River flows in a narrow canyon throughout its entire length, the surrounding country being very rough and mountainous, with numerous washes entering the river bed.

The few valleys which occur along the course of the river are small and narrow, and the river, in traversing these, leaves many small irrigable tracts on either side of the channel. Just above the forks, on the Campbell Blue, is a small valley about 1½ miles in length and about 1,500 feet in width, which constitutes the largest on the river.

When the American settlers began to arrive in this region, about 1885, they found a few Mexicans farming small areas along the Blue River. Several of these old Mexican farms have since been abandoned.

Evidences of prehistoric irrigations, as well as ruins and caves of ancient cliffdwellers, are found at different places along the Blue River. Some of the ditches now used along the head waters of the Blue River are said to have been originally constructed by the ancient cliffdwellers.

Since 1885 the extent of irrigation along the Blue River has slowly increased, in spite of the fact that considerable land has been lost by flood erosion.

On the Campbell Blue there are two ranches which are irrigated by means of four ditches, while below the forks, or on the Blue River proper, the irrigated areas are situated at irregular intervals. From the forks of the Blue River to the confluence with the San Francisco there are in all 22 ditches, which serve to irrigate a number of small patches of land.

Summary.—On the entire stream system of the Blue River there are 26 ditches, all of which are now in use except one, the Carthy ditch.

The following table shows the date of construction and abandonment of each ditch, the area irrigated at present, the areas previously irrigated, and the irrigable area under the ditches:

Areas under ditch Blue River, Ariz.

Canal.	Year constructed.	Year of last use.	Acres cultivated.	Acres previously cultivated.	Acres irrigable.
Peary, No. 1	1890		10		
Peary, No. 2	1890		11		
Peary, No. 3	1890		4		
McMilligan	1885		20		75
Old Bob Cat, Ranger Station	1895		11		9
Old Saw Mill	1914		5		12
Martin, No. 1	1915		6		5
Martin, No. 2	1890		20	5	
Martin, No. 3	1890		8		10
Blue Ranger	1911		15		5
Station	1910				
Balker & Slaughter, No. 1	1910		1½		1
Balker & Slaughter, No. 2	1910				
Carthy	1910	1911		10	
Snyder	1910		7		
Jones, No. 1	1893		10		
Jones, No. 2	1914		2		
Jones, No. 3	1892		10		3
Castro	1886		7		35
Thomas, No. 1	1914		6		2
Thomas, No. 2	1885		14		6
Hale	1913		2		
Hollis	1887				
McKitrick	1887		6		
McKean	1890		13		5
Bell	1885		10		5
Base Line			16		
Ranger Station (prehistoric)			5		
Total			241	15	174
Land on Campbell Blue			45		75
Land below fork			196	15	99

Ditch ownership.—The ditches are individually owned, none serving more than one ranch.

Water supply.—The flow of the river is flashy and intermittent, dependant upon the rainfall and upon the drainage area. During the winter considerable snow falls upon parts of the basin, which frequently remains until late in the season, and sometimes causing torrential floods after a warm rain. During May, June, and July the water supply is derived from springs or seepage water from the basin, the flow becomes very small and often the stream bed is dry at numerous places along its course during these months. The summer rains usually begin late in July.

During the progress of this investigation two float measurements were taken on the Blue River, with results as follows:

	Second-feet.
July 11, 1915, 500 feet below forks	8.97
July 10, 1915, ½ mile above base line ranger station	46.50

These measurements were taken at points located about 30 miles apart, at a time when the stage of the river was slowly falling. Between these points several streams of various sizes join the river, a few of which were discharging as much as the river itself at the point of the first measurement, or as either of the forks. Inasmuch as the river bed is composed of sand and bowlders the underflow is evidently considerable.

Probable future uses.—As shown in the summary of this report there are 189 acres of irrigable land under ditches which at present is not cultivated. Plans have been formulated, however, to construct five additional ditches to serve 46 acres not under ditch at the present time. This entire area is situated on the Blue, below the forks, a total of 235 acres of irrigable land being considered available future irrigation.

The remaining irrigable areas on the streams are all in small patches, and a number of these are almost too sandy for cultivation.

Owing to the precarious location of the irrigated lands with respect to floods, as well as to the meagerness of the water supply, it is not believed that the irrigated area will greatly increase in amount during future years.

Irrigation on the Headwaters of the Gila River, N. Mex.

HEADQUARTERS ABOVE DUNCAN VALLEY.

In this portion of the report only the headwaters or that portion of the Gila River situated above the so-called Duncan Valley will be considered.

The Gila River rises in southern Socorro County, N. Mex., flows in a southewesterly direction to a point near the Arizona State line, then it takes a northwesterly bearing and flows into Arizona. For a distance of 40 miles before the Gila reaches the valley in which the Gila post office is situated, the river flows through a deep, narrow canyon. On some of the numerous forks which unite to form the upper Gila there are a few small irrigated areas.

From the Gila post office down to the Duncan Valley, a distance of about 40 miles, the country adjacent to the Gila is wholly mountainous in character and the stream flows through a narrow canyon, which frequently widens out, forming small valleys, all of which are well cultivated.

In the Gila Canyon, about 35 miles above the Gila post office, N. Mex., are found ancient cliff dwellings of considerable extent. Doubtless the ancient inhabitants of these dwellings carried on some irrigation along the river.

The territory along the headwaters of the Gila was settled by the American immigrants in the early eighties. For perhaps 10 years prior to this time Mexican ranchers had been carrying on some irrigation in this section, although only a small portion of the land at present under cultivation was originally reclaimed by Mexicans. With the advent of the white settlers, the arable areas were soon placed under irrigation and as early as 1900 all of the lands cultivated at the present time had been reclaimed.

With the exception of a few scattered tracts of irrigated land on the extreme headwaters of the Gila, the first irrigation to be found in proceeding down the river is in the valley in which is situated Gila post office. This district is irrigated by four ditches, the land being owned largely by the L. C. Cattle Co. Irrigation began here about the year 1880.

The cultivated areas under these four ditches are as follows:

Shelby ditch, west side of river	750
Fort West ditch, east side of river	710
Bill Bros. ditch, west side of river	300
Middle ditch, east side of river	220
Total	1,980

Cliff district.—The cliff district is situated just below the Gila district, the two being separated only by a point of high land projecting from the mesa.

Irrigation was first carried on in this district in 1880 and the reclaimed area was gradually increased until 1900, at which time all of the land irrigated at the present time had been placed under cultivation.

In this district there are five ditches now in use and one abandoned ditch, with areas cultivated and previously cultivated as follows:

Canals.	Irrigable.	Previously cultivated.
	Acres.	*Acres.*
Clark ditch No. 1	125	
Clark ditch No. 2 (abandoned)		30
Clark ditch No. 3	45	
Mose ditch	104	
Lyons	70	
McCauley	180	
Total	524	30

The lower end of this district becomes very narrow and the valley is extremely irregular in outline.

Red Rock district.—The Red Rock district is situated in what is known as the Red Rock Valley and includes the Fuller Ranch, 6 miles below the valley proper.

This valley is also irregular in shape, being composed as it were, of a series of smaller valleys. Although practically all of the arable land may be irrigated by means of the ditches as they are now constructed; not all of this land has been brought under cultivation.

There are nine ditches now in use which serve areas as follows:

	Acres.
Woods ditch	387
Knox-Tony	173
Jenigan	55
Martin & Cludt	27
Roy Harper	140
Robinson	60
Jim Harper	70
Maveric flat	125
Fuller	80
Total	1,117

Summary.—On the Gila River above the Duncan Valley, there are at the present time 18 ditches which serve to irrigate 3,621 acres of land. This area does not include the small scattered patches of irrigated land situated near the extreme headwaters of the Gila.

A table showing all the irrigation by ditches on the Upper Gila, above the Duncan Valley, follows:

Canal.	Year constructed.	Year of last use.	Irrigated.	Previously cultivated.	Irrigable.	Remarks.
			Acres.	*Acres.*	*Acres.*	
Shelly Prior	1895		750			West side of river.
Fort West	1885		710			East side of river.
Bell Bros	1890		300			West side of river.
Middle	1895		220			East side of river.
Clark, No. 1	1895		125		*50*	Do.
Clark, No. 2	1890	1907		30		West side of river.
Clark, No. 3	1881		45			Do.
Mose	1881		104		10	East side of river.
Lyons	1890		70		30	West side of river.
McCauley Prior	1890		180			East side of river.
Woods	1885		387		20	North side of river.
Knox-Tony Prior	1895		173		20	South side of river.
Jenigan	1910		55		*15*	North side of river.
Martin & Cludt	1905		27			Do.
Roy Harper	1885		140			South side of river.
Robinson	1890		60		*28*	Do.
Jim Harper	1890		70		*40*	Do.
Maveric Flat	1890		125		*50*	Do.
Fuller	1902		80		5	North side of river.
Total			3,621	30	268	

NOTE.—The figures in italics represent irrigable areas not now under the ditch opposite, but for which there have been expressed intention to raise the ditch grades so that those additional areas may be covered.

Water supply.—All of the ditches in the upper Gila district are owned cooperatively by the landowners under the canal, the maintenance cost and the available water being apportioned in accordance to the interest of each.

The run-off is intermittent and flashy in character, and floods have wrought great damage to ditches and have destroyed a large area of irrigated and irrigable land by excessive erosion.

The rains begin late in the summer and occur at irregular intervals until the late winter or early spring, at which time the rainfall reaches its maximum. It then diminishes until about the 1st of May, the beginning of the dry period.

In order to determine the flow on the upper Gila, meter measurements have been made near Cliff and at Red Rock. The results of these measurements are to be found in Water Supply Paper No. 349, pages 176–177; No. 269, page 221; No. 309, page 229.

From these measurements, it may be seen that the flow above the Red Rock Valley ranges from 850 second-feet to 40 second-feet, that the flow continues throughout the year, and that the water supply for irrigation is more than sufficient for the area irrigated at the present time and for the remaining irrigable lands which have not yet been placed under cultivation.

Probable future uses of waters of the Gila above the Duncan Valley.—Referring to the areas already tabulated, it is seen that 135 acres are susceptible of irrigation under the present ditches. By rebuilding some of these ditches on a higher grade line, which can be done in several instances, an increased area could be brought under cultivation.

Considering the probability of losses by floods and the limited extent of the arable land, it is not believed that the future uses of the Gila waters in this section will be greatly in excess of the present uses.

Investigations have been made and are being carried on to a limited extent at the present time in connection with a proposed reservoir

Water supply for irrigation on the San Francisco River.—Notwithstanding the high altitude of the greater portion of the drainage area, the run-off of this tributary of the Gila is torrential and flashy in character, and while the flow is continuous, yet it becomes very low during the dry seasons.

Discharge measurements have been made for a number of years at Alma, N. Mex., which is above the confluence of the San Francisco and the Blue Rivers. The results of these measurements are to be found in Water Supply Papers No. 269, page 224, and No. 309, page 234. These measurements show that the flow at Alma varies from a maximum of nearly 1,000 second-feet to a minimum of 6.9 second-feet and that the average monthly flow varies from 100 to 300 second-feet.

Discharge measurements made in 1911 below the confluence of the San Francisco with the Blue, at a point 1½ miles above Clifton and published in Water Supply Paper No. 309, page 235, give a maximum discharge of 1,240 second-feet, a minimum discharge of 56 second-feet, and a mean or average flow of 325 second-feet.

From these measurements it will be seen that there is an adequate water supply for irrigation purposes in the several districts along the San Francisco, as well as in the extreme upper valleys known as the Alpine and the Luna districts. In the Alpine Valley most of the land is subirrigated, while a reservoir in the Luna Valley conserves the irrigation waters in that district.

Probable future uses.—In the following table is given an estimate of the areas subject to cultivation in the different districts along the San Francisco River:

	Acres.
Alpine Valley	300
Luna	2,200
Reserve	80
Frisco or Plaza	170
Alma	150
Pleasanton	300
Total	3,200

As already stated, irrigation in the Alpine district is not necessary. In the Luna Valley, with the reservoir at its present height and capacity, an additional area of 1,000 acres could be served, the only change necessary being the enlargement of the present ditches.

In the Reserve and Frisco Valleys, there seems to be no likelihood of an increase in the area under irrigation. In the Alma and the Pleasanton Valleys, extensions of the present ditches are contemplated and it may be reasonable to expect that the entire cultivatable area in these valleys may be irrigated in the near future. It is believed that if present conditions continue in force, at least 1,500 acres in addition to the land now irrigated can reasonably be expected to be put under cultivation on the San Francisco within a short time.

Irrigation on the tributaries of the San Francisco.—Besides the Blue River, there are several lesser tributaries to the San Francisco and some irrigation takes place along these small streams. On the Center Fire Creek, which joins the San Francisco 6 miles below the town of Luna, an area of about 300 acres is being irrigated at present. Along the Tularosa River, which contributes its flow to the

San Francisco at a point just below Frisco, approximately 200 acres are being cultivated, the exact area not being known. On Mineral Creek, which joins the San Francisco at Alma, about 200 acres are being cultivated at the present time. On Whitewater Creek, which empties into the San Francisco just above Pleasanton Valley, about 30 acres are being cultivated by diversions from the river, and an additional 50 acres are cultivated from Glenwood Spring in the White Water Creek Valley.

IRRIGATION ALONG THE BLUE RIVER.

The Blue River, rising in the southeastern corner of Apache County, Ariz., flows in a southeasterly direction, across the northeast corner of Greenlee County, and one-half mile into New Mexico, crossing the State line 3 miles south of the southern boundary of Apache County; thence taking a course west of south, the river returns into Greenlee County and discharges into the San Francisco River, 20 miles above the town of Clifton, the county seat of Greenlee County.

At the point where the river enters New Mexico, a branch stream, the Dry Blue, enters the Blue River from the northeast. Above this fork, or junction, the main stream is known as the Campbell Blue. The Dry Blue is a small stream heading about 4 miles south of Luna, N. Mex.

The Blue River flows in a narrow canyon throughout its entire length, the surrounding country being very rough and mountainous, with numerous washes entering the river bed.

The few valleys which occur along the course of the river are small and narrow, and the river, in traversing these, leaves many small irrigable tracts on either side of the channel. Just above the forks, on the Campbell Blue, is a small valley about 1½ miles in length and about 1,500 feet in width, which constitutes the largest on the river.

When the American settlers began to arrive in this region, about 1885, they found a few Mexicans farming small areas along the Blue River. Several of these old Mexican farms have since been abandoned.

Evidences of prehistoric irrigations, as well as ruins and caves of ancient cliffdwellers, are found at different places along the Blue River. Some of the ditches now used along the head waters of the Blue River are said to have been originally constructed by the ancient cliffdwellers.

Since 1885 the extent of irrigation along the Blue River has slowly increased, in spite of the fact that considerable land has been lost by flood erosion.

On the Campbell Blue there are two ranches which are irrigated by means of four ditches, while below the forks, or on the Blue River proper, the irrigated areas are situated at irregular intervals. From the forks of the Blue River to the confluence with the San Francisco there are in all 22 ditches, which serve to irrigate a number of small patches of land.

Summary.—On the entire stream system of the Blue River there are 26 ditches, all of which are now in use except one, the Carthy ditch.

to a limited extent by the Antelope Valley Canal Co. This diversion is elsewhere referred to under head of present canals.

In the Maricopa County group three canals, the Enterprise, the Arlington, and the Buckeye, are at present in operation. These abandoned irrigation projects were constructed with little regard to the water supply, and that consequently, after brief attempts at cultivation, they were gradually abandoned. A few have from time to time been put in shape and used, only to be soon again abandoned. Others, like the Mohawk or the Palomas, have had comparatively longer periods of usefulness or prosperity. The Mohawk and Palomas districts, situated on opposite sides of the river, enjoyed for a period of four or five years prior to 1890 a rapid agricultural development, and reports[1] give from one to three thousand acres as having been under cultivation.

According to the State governor's report[2] of 1900, the shortage of water, with the usual accompanying litigation, caused many to abandon their homes.

Intermittent irrigation continued, however, until the disastrous flood of 1905, when the canal headings were so badly washed out that these old districts were completely abandoned. In 1914 a little overflow irrigation was going on in the Palomas Valley, while in the Mohawk Valley some 500 acres were being partially or rather unsuccessfully irrigated by means of pumps. The canals below the Palomas and the Mohawk Canals, such as the Redondo, the Araby, etc., evidently went out of commission some time prior to the flood of 1905; that is, before the canals higher up on the Gila or in the Mohawk Valley went out of service. At Sentinel, above the Antelope Valley, are the diversion site and headworks of the South Gila (Sentinel) Canal, now owned by the Southwestern Fruit & Irrigation Co. This canal was constructed in the late eighties and is 22 miles long.[3]

Several unsuccessful attempts have been made to construct a permanent diversion dam at the canal heading, but without success. No land was ever cultivated under this project, and it was only during times of flood that water flowed in the canal. Within the past two years construction work has been carried on to provide the canal with suitable headworks, and it is claimed by the

---

[1] No reliable information concerning the exact amount of cultivation at any one time was readily available. The writer during a hurried trip through this section was advised by some of the old-timers that about 3,000 acres had been under cultivation in this section. As nearly as could be observed during this trip through the Palomas Valley, at least 1,000 acres had been under cultivation at one time or another. Mr. A. P. Davis, in Water Supply Paper No. 2, p. 94 (U. S. G. S.) estimates from the best data then available that in 1897, 1,000 acres were under cultivation along the Gila in Yuma County, which would include both the Mohawk and the Antelope districts. (C. H. S.)

[2] The largest canal taking water from the Gila is the Mohawk which heads above the town of that name. It is 23 miles in length; cost probably $50,000 and covers between 25,000 and 30,000 acres of land. For several years prior to 1899, the canal was out of use and many of the farmers left the valley. In that year it was again put into condition and the water supply having been plentiful, a small acreage was brought under cultivation. (Governor's Report, 1901.)

There are large tracts of good land along the banks of the Gila River, aggregating 30,000 acres or more lying in the Mohawk Valley, but the water supply can not be depended upon and the rainfall is slight. The history of irrigation in the Gila Valley is full of expensive litigation due to the continued contests in the courts over prior water rights. A number of canals on the Gila near the headwaters are being enlarged and new ones taken out from time to time. As a consequence, the periods of scarcity or of no water in the canals below are more and more prolonged each year. (Governor's Report, 1901.)

[3] The proposed dam and a brief description of this project is given in Water Supply Paper No. 2, p. 76.

company that they intend to construct a high dam at this point for storage purposes.

Above the Sentinel or South Gila project and about 20 miles northwest of Gila Bend is the old Dendora Canal project. The canal was excavated in 1882 for a distance of about 7 miles, and a 4-foot rock-fill dam was constructed across the Gila. During the first flood after its construction the dam went out and no land was ever put under cultivation. It was proposed to irrigate about 5,000 acres in the Oatman Flat district by this project. The construction of a storage dam also was contemplated. Efforts to rehabilitate this canal have been made, but without success.

In the vicinity of Gila Bend and in the territory just above are to be found several large abandoned canals and irrigation projects.

The Citrus Canal, which has its heading within the Gila River Reservation, was built in the early eighties. Like many others, it had but a short life. In a report of ex-Superintendent of Irrigation J. W. Martin, of this service, dated August 4, 1909, the following reference is made to this canal: "It has been out of use for some years and the headgates are filled with mud."

The next large abandoned canal above the Citrus is the lower Gila Bend. According to the governor's report this canal was constructed in 1885 and in 1900 had been out of use for several years.

Subsequent to the latter date a new heading was constructed and the canal was successfully operated until 1908, when its heading was again destroyed by flood. Since 1908 this canal has been continuously out of service.

The largest of these ill-advised and now abandoned projects is variously known as the East Riverside, Gila Bend, or Peoria Canal. The main canal for this project had its heading at what is known as Woolseys Butte, the present site of the Enterprise Canal heading. This project was started in 1891, and it is reported that $1,000,000 was spent in its construction. A brief description of this project may be found in Water Supply Paper No. 2, page 47.

After a large portion of the dam was washed out for a second time in 1895 and still further in 1905, no water is known to have flowed through this canal except in times of extremely high flow and no successful irrigation had been carried on under this canal since the flood of 1905.

During the few years that this ditch was in commission it is reported that about 1,000 acres were put under cultivation. On a large portion of this land but one crop (grain) was ever grown, while other smaller patches of land were cultivated for several years. Most of the land formerly irrigated under this ditch has since been washed away.

This company, as well as several others having projects below the Gila River Reservation, have made filings and have expressed their intentions to construct large dams and store the waters of the Gila. Nothing, however, has been done toward the fulfillment of these proposals.

Other canals of lesser proportions than those discussed above have been constructed on the Lower Gila, but all of these ditches, like the larger canals, have been out of commission for at least 10 years.

RÉSUMÉ OF PREVIOUS CULTIVATION AND ABANDONED PROJECTS WEST OF GILA RIVER RESERVATION.

The detailed or complete history of these abandoned canals is not readily available, and, as already pointed out, they were not considered to have sufficient bearing upon this investigation to warrant the expense that would be necessary to obtain this information. Not much has been written regarding these old ditches, and information in their locality is very meager. However, it is generally known that they were for the most part ill-advised and that they were never put to beneficial use. Certain work, such as the occasional cleaning out of a portion of the canal or headworks, has been done on a few of these canals,[1] but this work has been carried on in a desultory manner which has been productive of no beneficial results. Owing to the very limited supply of water available during the dry season, which is discussed elsewhere in this report under the head of "Water supply," it is quite obvious that irrigation in this section, using river flood water alone, is hardly feasible. The shortage of water supply undoubtedly accounts for these many abandonments and the present general disuse of these numerous and expensive canals.

PRESENT IRRIGATION WEST OF THE GILA RIVER RESERVATION.

Buckeye Canal.—At the west line of the Gila River Reservation the Gila is joined by its principal tributary, the Salt. About 3 miles farther west, down the river, the Gila receives the discharge of a smaller tributary, the Agua Fria. The latter stream, especially near its mouth, is dry the greater part of the year. Just below the mouth of the Agua Fria is the rock and brush diversion dam of the Buckeye Canal. This diversion is made from the north bank of the Gila in sec. 34, T. 1 N., R. 1 W., G. and S. R. B. and M.

This canal is 24 miles long, and is intended to irrigate about 20,000 acres of land, all lying on the north side of the river. The appropriation of water for this ditch is based on a filing made in 1885. Construction started during the same year. The first irrigation took place about 1888. Each year thereafter the amount of land irrigated was increased, and at the time of this survey 14,540 acres were under cultivation. In 1903[2] between 10,000 and 12,000 acres were under cultivation. This canal is owned by a mutual company composed of the farmers under the canal. Not all of the water users, however, are stockholders, as some of these farmers buy outright the water needed for their lands. During May, 1914, the stockholders of this canal company authorized a bond issue of $30,000 to be used for the draining, washing, and reclaiming of alkali lands to the extent of 3,500 acres. No reclamation has yet (1914) been undertaken under this bond issue.

Of the total land area under cultivation, about 90 per cent is in alfalfa, the remaining 10 per cent being in grain, sorghum, and pasture. Cattle grazing and feeding is also an important industry in this section. At a point one-half mile below its heading, there is

---

[1] On the Lower Gila, there was, and to a certain extent there still exists a custom or practice among the owners of or interested parties in a canal to do a certain amount of assessment work on their canal each year, and thus hold their "franchise."

[2] Report of the Governor of Arizona to the Secretary of the Interior, 1903, p. 81.

a bridge across the Buckeye Canal. The canal at this point is 15 feet wide on the bottom, 25 feet wide on top, and has a water depth of 3½ feet. On May 29, 1914, this canal was flowing, by actual measurement, 109 second-feet. This measurement was taken during the low-water season and represents, at least during that year, the minimum flow. The maximum capacity of the canal is 200 second-feet.

Arlington Canal.—The next canal diversion[1] down the river from the Buckeye is the Arlington. This canal lies on the north side of the Gila River; that is, on the same side as the Buckeye, but about 13 miles farther down. The Buckeye and the Arlington districts are situated in the same general valley, which is practically a westward extension of the larger Salt River Valley. The Hassayampa River, which joins the Gila about 7½ miles below the Arlington diversion, is generally considered to be the dividing line between these two districts, although the Buckeye is siphoned across the Hassayampa River, and irrigates a small acreage on its western bank.

The Arlington Canal is owned by the Arlington Canal Co., a cooperative organization composed of farmers who own the land under the canal. This canal was built in 1889–90, the notice of water appropriation having been filed in July, 1907. This canal, at the time of the survey, was irrigating about 4,800 acres, and is intended to irrigate several hundred acres more lying under the canal. A permanent low-water concrete diversion dam was constructed in 1913–14, and considerable work was done on this project. The irrigated land is pract ca l all planted to alfalfa, and cattle feeding is an important industry. l y

The main canal is about 15 miles long, and at a point above the uppermost of its laterals had, at the time of this survey, a bottom width of 10 feet, top width 17 feet, and water depth 3 feet. By actual meter measurement, made on June 1, 1914, a flow of 53 second-feet was recorded. This quantity, according to several farmers in the district, represented practically the minimum flow during the year. The canal when full would have a maximum capacity of about 75 second-feet. The siphon built to carry this canal under the Hassayampa River is 300 feet long, having a rectangular section of 4 by 6 inches in the clear.

Joshlin ditch.—This ditch is on the opposite or south side of the river from the Buckeye district and has its heading at a distance of one-half mile below the point of diversion of the Arlington Canal. The ditch is owned by Mr. Joshlin and was constructed in 1911. At the time of this survey the land cultivated under this ditch approximated 225 acres. This ditch is of small section; bottom width 2 or 3 feet, top width 5 feet, water depth 1 foot. By actual meter measurement made on June 1, 1914, a flow of only 1.4 second-feet was recorded. Owing to the nearness of this diversion to the intake of the Arlington Canal, very little water is available during

[1] About 3 miles below the Buckeye Canal, but above the Arlington, is found a small pumping plant known as the Corbett. This plant pumps directly from the river, and at the time of this survey was irrigating about 120 acres, the water being conducted through a small ditch. The plant consists of a gas engine and a 14-inch centrifugal pump, which has been in operation for about five years.

the dry season. It appears that no efforts will be made to further increase the area of cultivation under this ditch.

James Bent Canal.—The water from the James Bent Canal is diverted from the east bank of the Gila River at a point 13 miles below the Arlington heading. It serves to irrigate about 300 acres near Gila Bend, the first appropriation having been made in 1910. At the time of the survey this ditch was found in a bad state of repair, while the land covered by it appeared to be reverting rapidly to a state of disuse or abandonment.

The cross section of the ditch in its present condition has a bottom width of 4 feet, top width of 6 feet, and a possible water depth of 2 feet. On June 1, 1914, the canal was flowing 4½ second-feet, according to actual meter measurements. Originally, the capacity of the ditch was probably 10 or perhaps 15 second-feet, although its grade and the consequent velocity are very small. The water supply for this canal appears to be inadequate, particularly since the proprietors of the Enterprise Canal, who divert water 2 miles below, claim prior right. Friction has already developed and legal procedure has been threatened.

Enterprise Canal.—A low mountain ridge entering the valley on the north side of the river terminates the Arlington and Buckeye region. This ridge ends abruptly, terminating at the river's edge in a steep bluff which has been called Woolseys Butte. The close proximity of the Estrella Mountains on the south side of the river to Woolseys Butte, forms a relatively narrow chanel through which flows the river. This short narrow canyon makes a very favorable diversion site, and at present is used for that purpose by the Enterprise Canal Co. Formerly it was used as the dam site for the Upper Gila Bend project elsewhere referred to under the head of "Previous irrigation." The diversion for the Enterprise Canal is located in section 28, T. 2 S., R. 5 W., G. and S. R., B. and M. The greater portion of this canal was constructed during the year 1885, the original heading having been 1½ miles below the present site. The present diversion works were constructed in 1901–2.

The Enterprise Canal is owned by a corporation known as the Enterprise Canal Co. The stockholders are the owners of the land irrigated, and for the most part are engaged in cattle-raising. At the time of this survey about 700 acres were being irrigated by this canal, while 2,000 acres in addition are susceptible of irrigation. During the years of heavy flow in the river, new land other than the above is cultivated. Nearly all of the land is planted to alfalfa, but some sorghum and grain are also grown.

To the favorable location of the dam apparently is due the excellent supply of return water which is provided. Meter measurement of the flow in this canal, made on May 30, 1914, showed that a diversion of 25 second-feet was taking place. This quantity was somewhat in excess of the minimum flow, according to Mr. Montgomery, president of the Enterprise Canal Co., who stated that during the dry season probably not more than 15 second-feet could be depended upon. This canal has a bottom width of 4 feet, top width of 10½ feet and a water depth of 2.5 feet.

Papago (Farmers' Ditch or Anderson Canal).—Below the Enterprise diversion, no canals are at present taking water from the Gila within a distance of 19 miles, or until the Papago Canal on the Gila Bend Indian Reservation[1] is reached.

The Papago Canal was constructed in 1891 by L. S. Anderson. For several years prior to that date the land under this canal was irrigated from the lower Gila Bend (Riverside) Canal. As already stated, this latter canal was constructed in 1885 and was abandoned some time prior to 1900.

A five-sixths interest in the Papago Canal was held by Mr. Anderson. The Gila Bend Indians hold the remaining one-sixth interest and they have irrigated about 82 acres by means of the water thus obtained.

The Papago Canal is 8 feet wide on the bottom, 15 feet wide on top, has a water depth of about 2 feet, and a maximum capacity of about 30 second-feet. No meter measurements were made at the time of this survey owing to the small quantity of water then flowing into the canal.

Several investigations and surveys have been made by the Indian Department with a view of providing additional water for this reservation, but as yet no money has been appropriated for the work. The Gila Land & Cattle Co., which owns and cultivates land to the west of the Gila River Reservation, has acquired Mr. Anderson's five-sixth interest in the canal, and was irrigating at the time of this survey 730 acres.

Antelope Valley Canal.—At the present time between the Anderson heading at Gila Bend and the mouth of the Gila at Yuma the Antelope Valley Canal is the only diversion of importance.[2]

The present Antelope Valley Canal has its heading in the SW. ¼ sec. 21, T. 8 S., R. 17 W., G. and S. R. B. and M. This was also the point of diversion of the Old Antelope Canal, which was mentioned in the report of citizens' executive committee of Yuma County for 1889 (previously mentioned in this report), and it therefore appears that the present Antelope Valley Canal project is a rehabilitation of the Old Antelope Canal. The present Antelope Valley Canal Co. bases its water rights upon a filing made May 1, 1908, on 5,000 inches of water. Filings for a right of way and reservoir site were made and approved at the Phoenix land office on April 15, 1909. The Antelope Valley Canal Co. has applied to the United States land office asking that stock in this company be accepted as final proof in desert entries under the canal.

A report favorable to the project was submitted in 1914 by R. G. Mead, field engineer of the land office, and a further supplemental report, also favorable, was submitted in April of this year (1915). From a copy of these two reports kindly furnished by Mr. Mead, the following information has been obtained:

The project is intended to irrigate 10,000 acres during five months of the year. Delivery of water began in 1909. The acreage ready to receive water on

---

[1] The Gila Bend Reservation, comprising all of T. 5 S., R. 5 W. excepting section 18, was withdrawn from public entry and set aside as an Indian reservation by an Executive order of Dec. 12, 1882. On June 19, 1909, section 16 and sections 19 to 30, inclusive, were restored to the public domain. This reservation, which is about 3 miles from the station of Gila, on the Southern Pacific Railroad, is used by Papago Indians, where about 500 of them make their winter headquarters. During the heat of the summer, but few Indians remain at the reservation.

[2] In addition to the Antelope Canal, there is at least one of the older or abandoned canals which takes water from the river during extreme high water and is supplemented by pumps during the remainder of the irrigating season.

November 1, 1914, was 977, and since that date 125 acres additional have been put under cultivation.

The company is a mutual organization composed of landowners under the canal. Until two years ago, when a good heading was put in, the Antelope Canal was supplied with water by means of a pump, the water being drawn directly from the river. This pumping plant is no longer in use. A number of the farmers under this canal are installing auxiliary pumping plants to supplement the floodwater supply.

In the report of the Director of the Geological Survey to the Commissioner of the General Land Office, under date of April 27, 1915, and referring to the probable water supply of the Antelope Valley Canal Co., the comment is made that during the winters of 1903–4 and 1904–5 agricultural operations would have failed, and the fact that "the company is delivering so small a proportion of the water which by sale of stock it is bound to deliver to 8,040 acres may or may not be significant of an inadequate water supply, but it raises a question concerning the system which should be explained." Mr. Mead, however, takes the position that the water supply is adequate for the project, and accordingly has made a favorable report. At the time of the writing of this report no decision had been rendered by the Commissioner of the Land Office in regard to the application of this company.

WATER SUPPLY FOR IRRIGATION WEST OF THE GILA RIVER RESERVATION.

With the exception of the gauge recently established near Florence in connection with this investigation, the first gauging station on the Gila above the diversion west of the Gila River Reservation is located at Kelvin, a distance of 90 miles upstream from the west line of that reservation. Between this station and the Buckeye district many diversions take water from the Gila and at least two tributaries contribute to its flow. The records of this station are therefore of no great value, especially during periods of low water, in determining the available supply below the reservation.

On the river just opposite the railroad station of Sentinel a gauging station has been in operation for the past two years. This station is situated approximately in the center of the district under consideration, being just above the Palomas and Mohawk Valleys, and just below the Gila Bend territory.

For four years a gauging station was maintained on the Gila at Gila City, 14 miles above Yuma, and inasmuch as this station is situated at what might be called the end of the district under consideration some idea of the river flow in this district may be had from these observations. They are given below.

At Yuma the Reclamation Service has made observations of the flow of the Gila since 1903. In the following tabulation the flow for the years 1907 to 1912, inclusive, have been taken from the records furnished by that service:

GILA CITY.

	1903	1904	1905	1906
	Acre-feet.	*Acre-feet.*	*Acre-feet.*	*Acre-feet.*
January			189,200	136,000
February			680,300	168,000
March			1,020,000	576,000
April	30,228		768,200	422,000
May	799		299,700	122,000
June			43,140	4,580
July		5,792	4,341	
August	9,200	130,600		25,100
September	7,319	41,700	2,957	4,280
October	13,650	32,800	11,010	
November		6,486	271,200	
December			375,100	332,000
Total[1]	61,196	226,400	3,665,200	1,790,000

[1] Data from Water Supply Paper No. 100; 1904 data from Water Supply Paper No. 133; 1905 data from Water Supply Paper No. 175 at Gila City; 1906 data from Water Supply Paper No. 211 at Gila City.

YUMA.

	1907	1908	1909	1910	1911	1912
	Acre-feet.	*Acre-feet.*	*Acre-feet.*	*Acre-feet.*	*Acre-feet.*	*Acre-feet.*
January	63,500		71,900	213,000	60,000	
February	59,400	391,500	175,100	9,200	40,000	
March	289,000	162,600	147,400	500	84,000	121,000
April	71,500		96,000	1,500		70,000
May			14,200			600
June						
July			21,000		34,700	12,500
August		94,700	54,500			39,700
September	400	44,200	81,000			
October	93,200				30,200	1,400
November	58,000				17,300	
December	13,600	404,000				
Total[1]	648,600	1,097,000	661,200	224,200	266,200	245,200

[1] 1907-1912, U. S. Reclamation Service, Yuma.

SENTINEL.

	1913	1914		1913	1914
	Acre-feet.	*Acre-feet.*		*Acre-feet.*	*Acre-feet.*
January		39,600	August	2,350	42,700
February		146,000	September		29,900
March		22,800	October		(1)
April		2,810	November	5,000	(1)
May		30	December	170,000	(1)
June					
July	120	12,700	Total[2]	24,470	296,540

[1] Not available.
[2] Water measurement data at Sentinel, 1913–1914, supplied by Mr. C. Jacob, district engineer, U. S. G. S., Phoenix, Ariz.

It will be seen from the above table that the annual run-off at this station ranges from as little as 24,470 acre-feet in 1913 to as much as 3,665,200 acre-feet in 1905. It is also apparent that the river is frequently dry during the time of maximum irrigation draft and that the dry season is often of considerable duration. It is, therefore, very questionable whether flood-water irrigation can be successfully practiced on the Lower Gila.

Attention is directed to the fact that the few measurements available include the two highest flood years of recent times, namely, the years 1905 and 1914. Considering only these measurements, a high average annual run-off would be found, and any conclusions based on these data might therefore be misleading.

Comparisons of the run-off of the Gila River observed at Yuma and at Sentinel with the run-off measured farther up the stream at Kelvin and at San Carlos, and with measurements made for the same period on the Salt River, indicate that during a period covering seven years prior to 1905 this portion of the valley experienced a very serious drought.

SEEPAGE OR RETURN FLOW.

The success of irrigation immediately below the Gila River reservation and as far down the river as Gila Bend has been due to the return or seepage flow at the various points in the river bottom. This return flow is used almost entirely by the most successful of these canals, especially during the dry years and the dry season. No measurements of the flow in these different districts covering a considerable period of time have been made, so that the amount of this return flow is not definiately known. Measurements made about June 1, 1914, on the canals above Gila Bend, and which have already been referred to, record a combined flow of 193 second-feet at the time they were made. From conversation with the farmers living in this district it was ascertained that the above measurements were made at a time of low water supply, so that the amounts here given represent the minimum flow during the year.

In considering the return flow on the Lower Gila, it is important to examine the effects of the extensive irrigation which has taken place in the Salt River Valley under the Roosevelt project. Mr. H. L. Hancock, water commissioner of the Buckeye district, states that the return flow at the head of the Buckeye Canal has increased at least 100 per cent since the Roosevelt project has been in operation. An increased return flow has also been observed at the headings of other canals as far west as Gila Bend. Inasmuch as practically the entire return flow is diverted from the river at each of the various canal intakes, it can not be expected that the return flow coming to the lower canals would be in proportion to that received by those above. Very little, if any, return surface flow is available from the river below Gila Bend.

SUMMARY AND CONCLUSIONS RELATIVE TO PRESENT AND FUTURE USES OF WATER ALONG THE GILA WEST OF THE GILA RIVER RESERVATION.

1. The total area of land at present (1914) under cultivation west of the Gila River Reservation and irrigated by means of the eight ditches taking water from the Gila River amounts to 24,095 acres. Of this area, all but 1,100 acres is situated within the Gila Bend, the Enterprise, and the Buckeye districts.

2. That nearly all of the land at present under cultivation in this section has been reclaimed within comparatively recent times (since 1880) while the older or first-irrigated districts are no longer cultivated, owing, apparently, to failure of the water supply.

3. That by far the greater portion of the area at present under cultivation below the Gila River Reservation is dependent upon return water flow for its successful irrigation, and that the fluctua-

tions in the flow of the Gila River are so great and the water supply is so meager during the dry months as to preclude the possibility of successful irrigation using flood water alone.

4. That the increased irrigation on the Gila River Reservation and at Florence, in the event of a storage dam at San Carlos, would increase the return flow west of the reservation, and that this section would consequently benefit thereby.

5. That the regulation and control of the flood waters of the Gila by a reservoir at San Carlos would not meet with the disapproval of the majority of the present water users west of the Gila River Reservation.[1]

6. Past experiences have proven that irrigation projects in this portion of the Gila Basin depending upon the normal or flood-water flow are at best very uncertain ventures, and it is not expected, nor is it at all likely, that further diversions will be attempted.

7. It is also fairly certain that no storage project involving a high storage dam to provide water for the irrigation of lands west of the Gila River Reservation will be constructed by private or corporate enterprises for these principal reasons:

(*a*) The available water supply is insufficient, especially in view of the unquestionable superior rights of other water users higher up on the Gila and its tributaries.

(*b*) That the capital necessary for the construction of a large storage reservoir project such as would be required for this development would not be forthcoming from private sources, especially in view of the long time which must elapse before returns would be realized.

(*c*) Doubtful existence of a suitable reservoir and dam site on the lower Gila.

8. That below their confluence the waters of the Salt River hold the same relation to the total available water supply as do the waters of the Upper Gila itself. In the suit which adjudicated the water rights on the Salt River, resulting in the Kent decree, the users of water below the confluence were not made parties to this suit. In the adjudication suit known as the Nels Benson *v.* John Allison et al., which is still pending and which has for its object the adjudication of the relative rights of the Buckeye Canal, none of the parties diverting water from the Gila River on or above the Gila River Reservation or below the Buckeye Canal were made parties to this action, and their rights, of course, were not affected.

9. Accordingly, in view of the facts set forth above, the conclusion is drawn that the present irrigation west of the Gila River Reservation on the Gila would not suffer in the event of the San Carlos project, nor is it considered that the water rights, if any exist, west of the reservation, need be taken into consideration in the determination of the amount of water legally available for the San Carlos project.

---

[1] In interviews with Mr. Brown, president, Mr. Nels Benson, director of the Buckeye Canal Co., and Mr. Montgomery, president of the Enterprise Canal and a director in the Arlington Canal, these gentlemen informed the writer that the flood waters of the Gila usually did more damage than good and that although their lands required some flood waters for fertilizing and leveling purposes, they considered that if the San Carlos Reservoir were constructed they would still receive sufficient flood water from the various tributaries, such as the San Pedro, the Santa Cruz, the Verde, and from the several other lesser tributaries to supply their needs. (C. H. S.)

APPENDIXES TO

San Carlos Water Supply and Cost Report

APPENDIXES B AND C

Appendix B—HYDROGRAPHY, GILA BASIN, by H. K. PALMER, Assistant Engineer, U. S. Indian Irrigation Service.

REPORT ON THE HYDROGRAPHIC INVESTIGATION OF THE GILA RIVER, by C. C. JACOB, District Engineer, Water Resources Branch, U. S. G. S.

Appendix C—MAXIMUM AND MINIMUM COST OF THE SAN CARLOS PROJECT, by H. V. CLOTTS, Assistant Engineer, U. S. Indian Irrigation Service.

HYDROGRAPHY, GILA BASIN, ARIZONA.

The watershed of the Gila River has been described in detail in this report, so its essential features only need be mentioned here.

The Gila River and one of its principal tributaries, the San Francisco, rise in the mountains of western New Mexico and eastern Arizona. Some water is also received from the San Carlos River, at the western end of the Solomonvile-Safford Valley, and from the San Pedro a few miles above the mining town of Kelvin, not far above the mouth of the canyon where the Gila emerges onto the desert plain of southwestern Arizona. The watershed of the Gila includes the following areas above the San Carlos Dam site:

	Square miles.
In Arizona	7,378
In New Mexico	6,077
Total	13,455

As shown on the accompanying key map No. 1, the river traverses the Duncan, Solomonville-Safford, and Winkelman valleys above the mouth of the canyon mentioned above. In all of these valleys more or less water is diverted from the river for irrigation, a portion of which in each case returns underground. After leaving the mountains, 16 miles above Florence, the low-water flow of the river seeps away in the sand so rapidly and the Florence diversions are so great that it is only during times of moderately high water that enough reaches the Indians lands around Sacaton to permit irrigation.

Except where it is confined in box canyons the river course occupies a wide sandy bed, the water saturating the sand on both sides of the stream to within a few inches of the surface. On account of the hot, dry climate a great loss is occasioned by the excessive evaporation which is a factor of vital importance especially during times of low water flow. Acting as it does over a wide sandy area whose width is not dependent upon the stage of the river, the evaporation from the ground surface depends only on climatic conditions and not on the amount of the surface flow. The evaporation from the water surface alone depends on the stage of the river. This large evaporation loss tends to amplify the fluctuations of the run-off in the lower sections.

The upper Gila and San Francisco Rivers rise in forested areas and are typical mountain streams, subject to great floods resulting from the rains which occur during the winter and summer seasons. The lower sections of the Gila and its tributaries receive water also from barren lands where the run-off is large and this results in short floods of varying magnitude following every rain storm. At the dam site, in cases of drought, the river sometimes becomes entirely dry but at its highest flood it has been known to discharge more than 100,000 second feet.

It is believed that in former times, water flowed past the Indian land at Sacatan at all stages of the river, but during recent years, that is, since irrigation has been carried on extensively in the upper valleys and at Florence the flow during the low water season it has entirely disappeared before reaching Sacatan. The depletion of the water supply began to be felt 20 years ago and several reports on this subject have been written between 1899 and 1914. The last of these reports, that of the Army Board, summarizes the findings of all previous investigations. In each of these reports, the need of storing the flood water is brought out and the more recent reports agree upon the site for the dam below the town of San Carlos, at the head of the box canyon, which the river enters at that point.

As a result of the torrential character of the river, the hydrographic conditions are naturally divided in two well defined groups, low water and flood water. All previous reports have laid the greatest stress on the flood conditions, merely summarizing the low water conditions to show the necessity for building the dam. In this report these two groups will be considered separately and each will be fully discussed.

Flood Conditions.

The torrential character of the run-off makes it impossible to use a large portion of the flow of the Gila for irrigation unless storage facilities are provided. At the same time, the annual run-off varies so greatly (from a minimum of 99,900 acre-feet in 1902 to a maximum of 1,011,000 in 1905), that sufficient storage must be provided to carry over the supply for several years.

The run-off at the dam site, below the town of San Carlos, is shown by the table at the end of this appendix. The measurements of the run-off at this point have not been continuous, so it has been necessary to supply the missing observations by the use of measurements made at other points modified by a proper factor. Up to and including 1912, the run-off has been computed by the Army board. For 1913 and the first 4 months of 1914 similar computations have been made by the Geological Survey, and since the latter date the figures are based on measurements made at the dam site. This run-off has been plotted and is shown on Plate No. 65.

This diagram shows that a few wet years are generally followed by a succession of dry years, and a comparison of wet and dry periods seems to indicate the existence of a cycle of about 9 years. The table shows that during the period from 1895 to 1903, inclusive, the average annual run-off amounted to 282,000 acre-feet, while during the period from 1904 to 1912, inclusive, it amounted to 413,000 acre-feet. The average annual run-off based on 21 years, 1890, and 1895 to 1914, inclusive, for which records are available, is 359,878 acre-feet. This is higher than the average of the two periods because the very wet year 1914 contributed 742,350 acre-feet amounting to 212 per cent of the average. The run-off during 1913 amounted to 230,330 acre-feet or 64 per cent of the average. With such uncertainty in the periodic run-off, it is obviously difficult to estimate how much water it is economically possible to utilize by means of a stroage reservoir. By combining the two 9-year cycles of which we have records, superimposing the years which have corresponding positions in their respective cycles, viz: 1895 and 1904, 1896 and 1905, etc., a mean cycle has been obtained which, it is believed, represents more nearly the normal cycle of the Gila River. The annual run-off as given by this mean cycle is 349,960 acre-feet.

RESERVOIR, SIZE, AND BEHAVIOR.

During the 21 years for which we have records the run-off for 9 years was above the normal, while for 12 years the run-off fell below the normal. In this ratio, out of 9 years there would probably be 4 wet years and 5 dry years. A reservoir having a capacity equal to 2 years' normal run-off would be theoretically sufficient to furnish a continuous draft equal to the normal flow if the mean average run-off during the 5 dry years did not fall below 71 per cent of the normal. In the same way, a reservoir holding three times the normal run-off would require an average run-off during the following 5 dry years of not less than 62½ per cent of the normal. Since the added benefit of a still larger reservoir could be realized only at an unproportionally greater cost, and since it would be open to the further objection of the greatly increased probability of not being filled during the wet period, the economic size of the reservoir is found to be one having a capacity between two and three times the normal annual run-off.

The physical conditions at the dam site are such that most any height of dam is permissible. A careful study of the behavior of the stream indicates that a dam 180 feet high to the crest of the spillway, impounding 714,450 acre-feet would be the most suitable. The capacity of this reservoir at various depths is shown in the following table:

Capacity of reservoir.

Contour.	Area.	Capacity.	Contour.	Area.	Capacity.
	Acre.	*Acre-feet.*		*Acre.*	*Acre-feet.*
10 feet	17	85	120 feet	5,191	183,605
20 feet	41	375	130 feet	6,230	240,710
30 feet	84	1,000	140 feet	7,380	308,760
40 feet	210	2,470	150 feet	8,698	389,150
50 feet	488	5,960	160 feet	10,148	483,380
60 feet	934	13,070	170 feet	11,433	591,285
70 feet	1,549	25,485	180 feet	13,200	714,450
80 feet	2,195	44,205	190 feet	14,872	854,810
90 feet	2,624	68,300	200 feet	16,153	1,009,935
100 feet	3,475	98,795	210 feet	17,131	1,176,355
110 feet	4,148	136,910	220 feet	18,109	1,352,555

According to this table, the use of 10-foot spillway gates would increase the capacity of the reservoir to 854,810-acre feet. The behavior of this reservoir, with and without spillway gates is shown by plates Nos. 65 and 66.

Diagram No. 66 shows the mass curve of the actual run-off of the Gila River. This diagram indicates, at any selected time, the total value of water that has passed the dam site since the beginning of the period in question. In the preparation of this curve, the year 1890 was substituted for the year 1894, since measurements were on record for 1890 and not for 1894. Plotted on the same diagram are several draft curves which show the total volume of water drawn from the reservoir under various assumptions. The vertical distance between the run-off and draft curves indicates the amount of water stored in the reservoir at any particular moment.

Because of the variable demands of water during different months of the year the draft curve should not be straight, but it was found on trial that the variations from a straight line were too small to effect the final result. The slope of the draft lines is increased to take into account the loss by evaporation, which depends on the area of the water surface, and consequently on the amount of water in the reservoir. The annual loss in acre-feet based on an assumed exaporation of 60 inches per year is shown in the following table:

Annual Evaporation from reservoir.

Volume of water in reservoir.	Annual evaporation.	Volume of water in reservoir.	Annual evaporation.
	Acre-feet.		*Acre-feet.*
100,000	17,500	500,000	51,000
200,000	27,500	600,000	58,000
300,000	36,000	700,000	65,000
400,000	44,000	800,000	71,300

In calculating the evaporation, the average contents of the reservoir for the year in question was taken as a basis to avoid the irregularities in evaporation during various months of the year.

It is obvious that as soon as the reservoir is completely filled which condition is indicated when the vertical ordinates between the run-off and draft curves becomes equal to the ordinate representing the capacity of the reservoir, the overflow from the spillway will be added to the discharge through the gates and the draft curve will parallel the mass curve until the draft begins to exceed the run-off. To determine the minimum storage required for any given draft, the draft line may be drawn backward from a given point on the run-off curve beyond which it is permissible for the reservoir to be empty, to a point where its ordinate distance from the run-off curve is a maximum. This maximum ordinate will represent the minimum capacity which must be provided for during the cycle assumed. With this amount of storage, the assumed draft can be maintained throughout the required period.

The mass curve of the actual run-off indicates that between 1894 and 1904, 225,000 acre-feet per year was very slightly in excess of the draft which could have been maintained throughout that period. With a draft of 300,000 acre-feet per year, the reservoir would not have filled to the spillway level and the reservoir would have become dry in 1902. Since 1905, the run-off has been so great that the reservoir would have been adequate to supply continuously more than 300,000 acre-feet per year. The minimum reservoir capacity required to supply 300,000 acre-feet per year during this period was 380,000 acre-feet.

The er from 1895 to 1904 was one of exceptional dryness in the Gila Basin corresponded with the dryest period known in the history of Southern California, where rainfall records are much more complete. The period following has been one of much greater rainfall and run-off than the average. It is probably safe to consider these two as extreme examples. The behavior of the reservoir during a normal cycle is shown on the mass curve diagram plate No. 65. This curve shows that the reservoir should be able to supply 300,000 acre-feet per year without the use of spillway gates, and that the reservoir would become practically empty at the end of this cycle.

According to this mean cycle, the minimum reservoir capacity required to supply a uniform draft amounting to 225,000 acre-feet per year would be 230,000 acre-feet; to supply 250,000 acre-feet per year, 370,000 acre-feet; and to supply 300,000 acre-feet per year, 714,450 acre-feet.

The effect of combining several actual cycles into a mean cycle as was done above is to smooth out the irregularities in the individual curves. These irregularities are due to the fluctuations of the flow which in most western streams vary within wide limits. In a case like that of the San Carlos Project the smoothness of this curve is an important factor in determining the required storage. The effect of this smoothing of the mass curve is shown by comparing the different capacities required to furnish a given annual draft. During the first dry period (1895–1904) the storage required to furnish 300,000 acre-feet annually was 1,255,000 acre-feet; during the second wet period (1904–1913) only 400,000 would have been required. The average of these capacities is 827,000 acre-feet, yet when the curve is smooth out by averaging correspond years, the required capacity is only 714,000 acre-feet. There is a range here of 855,000 acre-feet in the capacity according to the various methods of computation. Assuming this to be the extreme range, then the required capacity according to the normal cycle is 314,000 acre-feet greater than the minimum and 541,000 acre-feet less than the maximum.

In other words the chances are 3 in favor to 5 against any 9-year period being sufficiently regular to supply 300,000 acre-feet per year. For quantity alone, the chances that the supply will be sufficient are $\sqrt{\frac{1}{2}} \times \frac{3}{5} = 43$ per cent in favor, to 57 per cent against. These figures are merely rough approximations and are given merely to show that the use of the mean curve gives results which appear more favorable than they really are. To supply 300,000 acre-feet, spillway gates should be provided as they would lessen the possibility of crop failures during unusually dry years.

SIZE OF SPILLWAY REQUIRED.

From an estimated hydrograph of the great flood of December, 1914, submitted by Mr. Jacob, of the Geological Survey, it is seen that a maximum discharge of 41,000 second-feet was estimated and within five days there were four distinct flood crests, three of which reached a maximum of about 20,000 second-feet. High-water marks in the channel as well as other known data would indicate that previous floods at this point have reached a maximum of nearly twice the amounts given above, and it should be stated that the hydrograph mentioned was prepared by Mr. Jacob from high-water marks observed after the regular gauging station had been destroyed by the flood, and no great accuracy is claimed by Mr. Jacob for this datum. In order to design the spillway to meet maximum conditions, a flood has been assumed in which the flow at all times is just double the flows shown on the hydrograph mentioned above. This modified run-off has been plotted on diagram No. 65 to a scale of 1 inch vertical to 10,000 second-feet and 1 inch horizontal to 24 hours. One square inch is therefore equal to 20,000 acre-feet (approximately). The area of the water surface at the 180-foot contour (spillway level) is 13,200 acres. At elevations above the spillway crest, this area increases fairly uniformly at a rate of 159 acres per foot of rise. Variations from this uniform rate of increase are too small to be considered in this investigation.

The formula used for the discharge of the spillway is $Q=3.1\ h^{3/2}$ per foot of length of spillway, Q being expressed in second-feet and h in feet. In the diagram No. 65 the area between the run-off curve and the horizontal axis represents the amount of water which has entered the reservoir. In the same manner the area between a curve showing the discharge over the spillway and the horizontal axis represents the amount of water that has flowed out, while the difference between the two areas represents the amount of water in the reservoir above the spillway level. From this the height of the water surface above the spillway level may be determined and the corresponding amount of water flowing over the spillway, which must check the final ordinate of the spillway curve. The reduction from the planimeter reading in square inches to second-feet per foot of spillway is made directly by means of the curve, which is plotted directly above the run-off diagram. In plotting the discharge curve the discharge of the spillway is assumed for a short period (one-half day for instance), and the area for that time between the run-off and discharge curve is determined by means of the planimeter. With the assumed length of spillway and the planimeter reading, the discharge at the end of the short period is computed. If this differs materially from the assumed discharge, it is again necessary to measure the new area and find a new value for the discharge, the approximations being continued until the resulting discharge equals the discharge assumed. In general, one or two approximations are sufficient. When the discharge curve is found for one short period it is continued to the next in the same manner, and so on as far as desired. So long as the flow into the reservoir exceeds the discharge over the spillway, the water level continues to rise while the discharge over the spillway rapidly increases. In a similar manner, when the inflow is less than the outflow, the spillway discharge decreases. Therefore the maximum height of the spillway curve will be at the point of intersection of the two curves.

In this way the maximum discharge of a 300-foot spillway with water at the crest of the spillway at the beginning of the modified flood assumed is 36,200 second-feet, corresponding to a depth of 11.5 feet over the spillway.

To consider the effect of spillway gates with the gates ready to open when the flood begins, the spillway curve must start at a discharge corresponding to the depth of water when they open. In this case the area between the two curves will give the amount of water in the reservoir above the top of the gates; then to ascertain the volume of water above the crest of the spillway we must add the planimeter reading corresponding to the initial height. For $h=10$ feet (10-foot gates) $R=7$ square inches. Curve No. 2 gives the discharge over a 300-foot spillway with 10-foot gates and shows the maximum flood to be 45,300 second-feet, corresponding to a depth of 13.4 feet of water over the spillway crest. The effect of the gates therefore is to increase the high-water level 2 feet.

In the same manner, it is ascertained that a 240-foot spillway with 10-foot gates will pass a maximum stream of 41,000 second-feet with a depth of 14.5 feet over the spillway crest.

To make reasonably certain that the spillway would pass the maximum flood likely to occur, the duration of the flood will now be assumed to be twice that of the flood of December, 1914, and the intensity of the flood will also be doubled as was done in the preceding cases. In this case 1 square inch would represent 40,000 acre-feet. A flood of this duration as shown by curve No. 4 would yield a maximum discharge over the spillway of 51,500 second-feet giving a maximum depth of 17 feet over the spillway. The assumptions in this case include 10-foot gates as before.

If spillway gates are installed the intermediate piers will take up sufficient space to reduce the clear width of spillway from 300 feet to 240 feet. Therefore, from a structural point of view we should compare the 300-foot spillway without gates with the 240-foot spillway with gates, in which case the effect of the gates is to raise the extreme high-water level 3 feet.

SILT ACCUMULATION.

All previous investigations have taken cognizance of the large deposits of silt which would accumulate in the reservoir and have given this problem considerable study.

After careful consideration of all available data, the Army board adopted the value of 1.3 per cent as representing the average ratio between the volume of the silt and run-off; and they assumed further that about one-sixth of the silt would remain in suspension or would be sluiced out through the dam, leaving an accumulation of 1.1 per cent in the reservoir. The average annual run-off as shown above is 359,880 acre-feet, making the annual accumulation of silt about 3,959 acre-feet. If desilting is not resorted to, it is evident that the value of the reservoir will remain unimpaired for a certain length of time, depending on the surplus capacity which can be filled with silt. Based on the mean 9-year cycle, an annual draft of 300,000 acre-feet will leave no margin for silt unless spillway gates are installed. The use of these gates (10 feet in height) would increase the capacity from 714,450 acre-feet to 854,810, giving a surplus capacity of 140,360 acre-feet, which is equivalent to the silt accumulation of 37 years. The length of time which would elapse before the accumulation of silt would begin to cut down the required capacity of the reservoir is shown by the following table:

Annual draft.	Required capacity.	Surplus capacity available for silt.	Number of years elapsing until entire surplus capacity is occupied by silt.	
			Without gates.	With gates.
Acre-feet.	*Acre-feet.*	*Acre-feet.*		
300,000	714,450	....	....	37
250,000	370,000	344,450	91	128
225,000	230,000	484,400	127	164

Attention is called to the fact that the above table is based on the mean cycle and that the time elapsing under actual conditions might depart considerably from these figures. After the entire surplus capacity is filled with silt, the probability that the reservoir will still meet the requirements is the same as found before or 4 for to 6 against. To ascertain the number of years when the deposition of silt will begin to cut down the required storage capacity in the dryest periods, it is necessary to refer to the dry cycle rather than to the mean cycle.

In this case an annual draft of 225,000-acre feet is a little too great to be maintained by the storage capacity available even assuming that no silt deposit be permitted to accumulate. By the use of spillway gates, however, it would require 36 years before the silt would affect the necessary storage capacity if the dry cycle is assumed, against 164 years assuming the normal cycle. This, however, is an extreme case as it is not likely that there will be another drought for manydyears as intense as the one shown during the first period on recor .

WATER SUPPLY BELOW SAN CARLOS DAM.

The Army Board found evidence of some inflow along the river below the dam site in addition to the run-off of the San Pedro River. Lippincott [1] found the annual run-off at the Buttes to be 10 per cent greater than at San Carlos. A few of the observations made during this investigation showed that the flow at the Buttes, especially during low stages of the river, to be 20 per cent in excess of the flow at San Carlos. Because of the fact that practically the entire run-off from the San Pedro and other sources is discharged during the rainy months the Army Board disregarded it except to say that the flow from the dam could be regulated to give a constant flow below the mouth of the San Pedro.

The data available at the present time are not sufficiently complete to warrant our depending on receiving from the San Pedro and other sources a flow more than that required to make up for the evaporation below the dam site, which would probably amount to about 5,000 acre-feet per year. However, this flow would serve a further purpose of partially supplying the underground water beds which would be depleted by diverting the flow of the Gila through canals. On a basis of 100 second-feet seepage, as explained below

[1] Water Supply Paper No. 33.

under the head of Low-water conditions, these sands would absorb 73,000 acre-feet per year.

Assuming the mean flow of the San Pedro to be about one-tenth that of the Gila, its total annual flow would be approximately 35,000 acre-feet. Subtracting 5,000 acre-feet for evaporation would leave 30,000 acre-feet available for storage in the underground channels or 41 per cent of the volume required to produce saturation. Any water flowing over the spillway of the dam would still further increase this percentage but at best the water plane would be lowered by the construction of the dam thus increasing the lift of such pumping plants as would be operated after the completion of the project.

Willis T. Lee[1] makes an estimate of the minimum amount of the underground water passing through the Florence Valley of 35,830 acre-feet per annum. This based on a depth of water bearing gravel of 136 feet, a width of 4 miles and porosity of 40 per cent. This gives a velocity of 1,360 feet per year which may be easily increased to 2 miles owing to the uncertainty of conditions. The depth of the gravels is undoubtedly greater than 136 feet, and their width more than 4 miles. He therefore considers it probable that the underground flow amounts to more than 100,000 acre-feet per year and less than 600,000 acre-feet. A part of this flow is derived from the drainage areas north and south of the river, but a far greater portion is supplied by the Gila itself.

At the present time the underground flow is brought to the surface at the comparatively narrow portion of the valley near Gila Crossing, but it is impossible to predict whether the dam at San Carlos and the canal to the Indian lands will divert sufficient water to dry these surface flows. The contraction of the strata as the river approaches narrow portions of the valley tends to hold the water plane at or near the surface and the effect of the diminution of the water supply will be to decrease the slope of this plane. This will decrease the area within which the ground water lies within 8 feet of the surface, thereby diminishing the evaporation. At the same time the irrigation of a greater area which would be brought about by the project would increase the return flow. Since the effect of the dam will be to hold the flood waters back and to deliver from one-quarter to one-third of the run-off through the ground as return flow, it is likely that the return flow during low water season will be increased rather than diminished.

Low Water Conditions.

In case no large storage reservoir is constructed on the Gila River the low water conditions are most important to the irrigation of the lower valleys. At times of flood there is a large surplus flow in excess of all ordinary demands for irrigation and this surplus is still further increased by the fact that floods follow closely each rainfall and therefore the maximum run-off is available at times when the irrigation demand is a minimum. In order to arrive at the normal loss of water which results from seepage and evaporation between Kelvin and Sacaton, use has been made of the following table and a diagram No. 73 showing the typical fluctuation of the river during a moderately high stage. A low stage was not

[1] Underground Water of Gila Valley, Arizona, Water Supply and Irrigation Paper No. 104, 1904, p. 60.

selected in the determination of these losses since it would show no flow at all at Sacaton and leave the normal loss between Kelvin and Sacaton problematical. The exact fluctuations through the Duncan and Solomonville-Safford Valleys have been estimated since no measurements have ever been made of the river flow except at the ends of these valleys. The total diversions in the Solomonville canals exceed the discharge of the river at the head of the Solomonville Valley, the return water and inflow supplying nearly all of the water at the dam site. as will be explained later.

Flow of Gila River at various points.

	Miles.	Nov. 1, 1914.	June 16, 1915.
Duncan		280	240
Duncan canals		− 25	−115
Guthrie	25	240	145
San Francisco	31	115	190
Solomonville	43	320	335
Solomonville canals		−355	−395
San Carlos Creek	113	30	5
San Carlos Dam site	118	415	205
Kelvin	153	560	260
Florence canals		− 10	− 75
Sacaton	183	415	65

NOTE.—Minus signs denote totals diverted.

In considering the low-water conditions, the most important point along the Gila River is near Sacaton, or at the east boundary line of the Gila River Indian Reservation. It will be much easier to consider the hydrographic conditions near Sacaton, first, where they are simple, and, later, those of the Solomonville-Safford Valley. In the Duncan Valley the conditions become so complex as to make it best, with the data now available, not to attempt to trace to a mathematical conclusion the influence its use there would have upon the flow at Sacaton, but its influence will be of the same character as a of the Solomonville-Safford Valley, though much less noticeablth t

The data, on which this study is based, comprises a series of measurements with automatic gauges at several points between Duncan and Sacaton, during a period from May, 1914, to June, 1915, inclusive. A detailed description of this series of measurements is given in the report of Mr. C. C. Jacob, which is included in this appendix, and need not be repeated here. Unfortunately, it rained nearly every month during which the investigation was carried on, thus causing abnormal fluctuations in the river. It has been almost impossible, therefore, to obtain reliable results by the use of these data, and, consequently, much more dependence has been placed on pure theory than would otherwise be desired.

FLORENCE DISTRICT.

The conditions in the Florence Valley, and in the region farther west, are very simple. The river emerges from the mountain 16 miles east of Florence, at a point about 4 miles above the Florence Canal heading. From this point to Yuma the valley of the Gila consists of an alluvial fill of considerable width, except where narrows existed in the earlier valley, which is now deeply buried by the deposits of silt and sand. The absorptive capacity of this alluvium is very great, and begins noticeably to affect the flow of the river immediately after it passes The Buttes, 4 miles above the Florence Canal heading. So long as the sands remain saturated, the water continues to flow at Sacaton, but, when the run-off below the Florence Canal becomes less than the quantity absorbed by the sands, the flow ceases, and the water-plane begins to fall below the river bed. The flow does not reappear until the sands have been resaturated by the next succeeding flood.

In order to determine the amount of the seepage losses between Kelvin and Sacaton, a diagram (No. 73) was prepared, in which the flows at Kelvin, less the diversions at Florence, were plotted as absiscas, and the flows at Sacaton, on the same dates, as ordinates. Attention is also directed to the tables showing losses and inflows which are given at the end of this report. Inasmuch as a zero measurement at Sacaton would not indicate at what particular point between Florence and Sacaton the river flow disappears entirely, such measurements would be of no value. The records used in the preparation of this diagram were, therefore, confined to those dates on which actual flows were recorded at the Sacaton gauge. The dates chosen were those closely following storms, in order to make certain that the sands were still saturated. The results of this plotting indicate that a seepage loss of 110 second-feet takes place during the lower stages of the river, with an additional transmission loss of 10 per cent of the remaining flow. Because of the simplicity of the conditions this result may be considered fairly reliable, and shows the need for a canal from the mouth of the canyon to Sacaton, whether a storage dam be built or not. On account of the great extent of the valley fill, the return flow from irrigation will not be so apparent as in the upper valleys.

WINKELMAN DISTRICT.

This valley lies between Kelvin and the mouth of the San Pedro River. It is a small valley, with very sandy soil, where only a small quantity of water is diverted, which in no case is carried far from the river, so a large proportion returns to the river channel. The net loss is so small in this district that it will not be considered.

SOLOMONVILLE-SAFFORD VALLEY.

Except during the fairly high stages of the river the total quantity of water diverted for the several canals of the Solomonville-Safford Valley exceeds the flow of the river at the head of the valley. This apparently paradoxical condition is the result of a relatively large return flow of water from the irrigation ditches and the other underground flow from the watershed adjacent to the valley. The inflow from two sources can be segregated only by making an accurate series of measurements extending over a long period which should include typical wet and dry years. Until such series of observations is available the only possible method of arriving at a value for the return flow from irrigation is by basing it on purely theoretical assumptions. The amount of this return flow is of great importance in determining the effect which irrigation near Solomonville has on the discharge of the river at Sacaton.

A series of measurements along the river between Solomonville and the dam site has been made by Mr. Jacob for the purpose of determining the amount of the inflow, but no effort has been made by him to segregate this flow into its component parts. The results of these measurements is shown on plate No. 71, which accompanied his report. According to this set of measurements, the entire discharge of 96 second-feet recorded at the head of the Solomonville Valley was diverted within the first 15 miles. Six canals diverted the return water below this point, each canal diverting at its heading all the water flowing in the river. Between the lowest canal heading and the dam site the inflow amounted to 28 second-feet. The total inflow observed between the head of the valley and the dam site was 92 second-feet.

This 92 second-feet represents the volume of the inflow appearing in the bed of the stream less the evaporation from the water surface. Except on the high knolls, the sands on both sides of the river are saturated almost to the surface, and it is therefore necessary to consider the evaporation from these sand beds.

Bowie[1] gives a table of the amount of evaporation from irrigated land when covered with various depths of dry mulch. The 4-inch thickness of mulch seems best to fit the case. On this basis the evaporation amounts to 0.13 inch for the first three days and 0.03 inch during the next four days. By plotting these results, it is found that the initial rate of evaporation is 0.58-inch per week. This would be the condition when the saturation of the lower layers is maintained by underflow. In the same experiment Bowie found the evaporation from a water surface to be 1.94 inches per week, making the soil evaporation 30 per cent of the evaporation from a water surface. The following table, taken from Appendix E of the report of the Army board, gives the monthly gross evaporation based on an annual evaporation of 73 inches, and monthly percentage of the total for the year. These figures are based on the Tucson records and the supposed soil evaporation:

Evaporation table.

Month	Per cent of annual.	Gross monthly evaporation—	
		From water surface.	From soil.
January	3.4	2.48	0.75
February	4.3	3.14	.94
March	6.9	5.04	1.51
April	9 4	6.86	2.06
May	11.9	8.69	2.60
June	13.8	10.08	3.02
July	12.7	9.27	2.78
August	10.7	7.81	2.34
September	9.8	7.15	2.14
October	8.1	5.91	1.78
November	5.0	3.65	1.10
December	4.0	2.92	.88
Total	100.0	73.00	21.90

[1] "P[illegible]ation," p. 31.

The bed of the Gila River is not level transversely but contains many mounds or ridges covered with vegetation. In this discussion it is assumed that the areas covered with vegetation transpire as much water as is evaporated from the surface of the bare sand. The area of the river bed in the Solomonville-Safford Valley above the Consolidated Canal heading is 5,730 acres. According to the above table, the evaporation from this area during the month of June, when it reaches its maximum, would amount to 1,433 acre-feet, which is equivalent to a continuous flow of 24 second-feet. Between the Consolidated Canal and the dam site the area of the river bed is 10,325 acres, from which the June evaporation would amount to 2,581 acre-feet, equivalent to a continuous flow of 43 second-feet. The total evaporation from the river bed in the Solomonville-Safford Valley is therefore equivalent to 67 second-feet. Adding this to the 92 second-feet actually measured gives the total inflow of 159 second-feet.

A further study of inflow was made by comparing the various measured flows along the river for every fifth day between May, 1914, and June, 1915, except during the period of very high water between December 15 and April 15, when the river reached such a high stage that measurements were not accurate enough to give reliable data. The inflow is taken as the difference between the net loss and the gross loss.

The net loss is the loss of water shown by measurements at the gauging stations, being the sum of the discharge of the Gila River at Solomonville (S) and that of the San Carlos River (B), (or the surface flow coming into the valley), less the flow at the dam site (D), (the surface flow leaving the valley). The gross loss consists of the sum of the diversion for all the canals (C) and the evaporation (E). Expressed as an equation—

$$X=(C+E)-(S+B-D)$$

The value of E (evaporation) was changed from month to month to agree with the values found by the Army board, and was omitted on all dates when more than one-tenth of an inch of rainfall was observed. These results have been plotted on diagram No. 67, which shows also the total diversion for the canals of the Solomonville-Safford Valley and the total surface flow at Solomonville. The curve of inflow is fairly regular, except at times of great fluctuation in the flow of the river. It is to be observed that at times of an increasing run-off the inflow decreases and sometimes even becomes negative, indicating that storage of water is taking place. This is explained by the fact that at such times the stream occupies a wider channel, thus tending to saturate the top layers of the sand bed. When the surface flow decreased the inflow would apparently increase above the normal since the saturated sands would tend to give up their storage. It will be noticed that, omitting the times of fluctuation in the river flow, the inflow follows fairly closely to the diversion of the canals in the Solomonville-Safford Valley, indicating that the inflow depends very largely upon the amount of water used for irrigation. According to this diagram, the inflow during low stages of the river is about 180 second-feet and during high water stages between 300 and 400 second-feet. Unfortunately, we have no record of the quantity of water wasted from the canals back into the river during high water, so this appears here as a part of the inflow.

Occasionally there is no flow whatever at the dam site, despite the fact that a certain amount of inflow is received by the river below the irrigated section of the Solomonville-Safford Valley. To explain this phenomenon, a case will be considered when the flow at Solomonville is so small that no water is wasted to return to the river underground below the lowest ditch heading. Theoretical consideration, to be shown later, indicates that the low-water inflow averages 230 second-feet, during the irrigation season, leaving an amount which varies probably from 10 to 150 second-feet to flow in from the adjacent watershed. Forty-five of the 75 miles between Solomonville and the dam site lie below the lowest diversion, leaving 60 per cent of the low-water inflow to return to the surface below this point. The evaporation from this point to the dam site amounts to 43 second-feet, which, during dry seasons, may frequently exceed the inflow.

In order to get some idea of the net amount of water consumed on the lands irrigated at the present time, an effort was made to determine the probable amount of the evaporation loss and transpiration over the irrigated land. The basis for determining the transpiration including the ground evaporation around the plants was certain experimental data bearing upon the amount of water required to produce a pound of various dry crops.[1] In making this estimate, it was assumed that half the acreage was devoted to alfalfa, one-fourth to barley and corn in successive crops, and one-fourth to wheat and cotton. Assuming all these crops to be planted on an average acre, we have the following estimate of water required:

Crop yield.	Pounds of water per pound of crop.	Per cent of acreage.	Pounds of water.
Barley, 2,100 pounds	350	25	184,000
Wheat, 2,000 pounds	496	25	248,000
Cotton, 700 pounds	657	25	115,000
Corn, 2,000 pounds	342	25	175,000
Alfalfa, 12,000 pounds	834	50	5,000,000
Total			[1]5,722,000

[1] 5,722,000 pounds of water = 2.1 acre-feet.

To allow for the evaporation of canals it was assumed that water would seep downward and outward from the sides of the canal, forming a wet prism with side slopes of 1:1. Considering this to be the case, and assuming the depth from which soil evaporation will take place as 8 feet,[2] the evaporation from the surface can be taken at the rate of 4 feet per year, decreasing to zero at a depth of 8 feet,

[1] "Relative Water Requirements of Plants," by Briggs and Shantz, Journal of Agricultural Research, No. 1, vol. III.
[2] Lee, Water Supply Paper, No. 294, p. 58.

and the average evaporation from the soil adjacent to the canals is therefore taken as 2 feet per year over a width of 16 feet. The average width of water surface is taken as 7 feet for main canals and 3 feet for laterals. The average annual rainfall, which amounts to 13 inches, reduces the evaporation from the soil by about 25 per cent and adds to the flow of the canal a volume of water equivalent to a depth of 1.1 feet falling on an area one foot wider than the water surface. Assuming main canals to be in operation eight-tenths of the year and the laterals four-tenths, we obtain 5.5 acre-feet and 1.82 acre-feet, respectively, as the net annual evaporation from main canal and laterals per mile.

It is assumed that any additional seepage water will penetrate to a greater depth than 8 feet, and will be unaffected by evaporation, and, joining the underground stream, will return to the river. Taking these values as a basis, the net loss in the Solomonville-Safford Valley would be 57,553 acre-feet per year, derived as follows:

	Acre-feet.
Evaporation from 170 miles main canal, at 5.5 acre-feet per mile	933
Evaporation from 342 miles laterals, at 1.8 acre-feet per mile	620
Transpiration from 26,633 acres cultivated, at 2.1 acre-feet per acre	56,000
Total	57,553

The discharge measurements made during 1914–15 show that the total annual diversions by all canals in the Solomonville-Safford Valley amounted to 189,285 acre-feet. Considering that this total diversion is diminished by 57,533 acre-feet through transpiration by plants and evaporation in the canals, the return flow should amount to 131,752 acre-feet, which flowing within the period of 0.8 of a year is equivalent to 230 second-feet. Owing to the excessive diversions and the wasteful methods of irrigation which greatly increase the loss by evaporation, the actual amount of the return water flow would probably be much less than the value derived above.

Between the dam site and Kelvin, a distance of 35 miles, an evaporation loss of about 6 second-feet takes place in June, assuming 100 feet to be the average width of the water surface and 10 inches to be the evaporation during that month. During other months the evaporation loss would be correspondingly less. The San Pedro River adds to the flow of the Gila in this section. No direct measurements have been made of the flow of the San Pedro near the confluence of the two streams, but, as previously stated, recent investigations indicate that the low water of the San Pedro at this point may be about one-fifth that of the Gila at the dam site. The first investigation made by Lippincott in 1899[1] indicates that the total run-off of the San Pedro was one-tenth of the Gila. This probably very closely represents the relative flow at high water.

Summary of Flow Losses and Gains Along the Gila.

The following summary gives an estimate of the losses and gains taking place between Solomonville and Sacaton.

[1] U. S. Geological Survey, Water Supply Paper No. 33.

149700—19—vol 2——16

LOSSES.

1. Diversion at Solomonville, taking the entire flow of the stream, up to about 225 second-feet.
2. Evaporation from river bed between Solomonville and Kelvin, amounting to about 73 second-feet in June. This would increase somewhat for higher stages of the river.
3. Diversions in the canals of the Florence district, the quantity depending on the amount of water in the river, but averaging about 50 second-feet.
4. Seepage in the sand between Kelvin and Sacaton, amounting to 110 second-feet; more following a protracted drought.

GAINS.

1. Underground flow from adjacent watershed and return flow from canals in Solomonville valley, amounting to from 180 to 300 second-feet. Decreasing the irrigation decreases the return flow in the approximate ratio of 0.7 acre-feet of return flow for each acre-foot of diversion.
2. Flow of San Carlos River negligible during low water.
3. Flow of San Pedro River varying from one-fifth the flow of the Gila at the dam site during low water to one-tenth of the flow during high water.

In tabular form this is as follows:

	Gain.	Loss.
	Second-feet.	*Second-feet.*
River discharge at Solomonville	243	
Evaporation, Solomonville to Kelvin		73
Solomonville Canals		225
Florence Canals		50
Solomonville underground and return	180	
San Pedro River	35	
Seepage between Kelvin and Sacaton		110
Available for Indian uses at Sacaton		
Total	458	458

The above table shows the conditions as they exist to-day according to the most reasonable theory. Adopting the same basis for calculations as to effects under the assumption that no water be diverted at Solomonville and at Florence, we get the following results:

	Gains.	Loss.
	Second-feet.	*Second-feet.*
River discharge at Solomonville	243	
Evaporation, Solomonville to Kelvin		73
Inflow, Solomonville Valley	110	
San Pedro River	35	
Seepage in sand above Sacaton		110
Transmission loss between Kelvin and Sacaton		10
Available at Sacaton		95
Total	288	288

A comparison of these two tables shows that the effect of diverting 225 second-feet in the Solomonville Valley and 50 second-feet at Florence is sufficient to diminish the flow at Sacaton by 95 second-feet. The 50 second-feet diverted at Florence would be equivalent to 45 second-feet at Sacaton after deducting the transmission loss of 10 per cent; therefore the diversion of 225 second-feet at Solomonville represents 50 second-feet at Sacaton, or, in other words, the transmission loss is 78 per cent. This loss is much greater in proportion to the distance than the 10 per cent loss from Kelvin to Sacaton. The transmission loss can not be stated as a constant proportion of the run-off for all stages of the river, since a large portion of it is a constant independent of the flow. At low stages it is greater than 80 per cent, and at high stages it is less. For the average stage, however, 60 per cent may be taken as the most probable value until a better value can be obtained by a series of careful measurements extending over several years.

It is a notable fact that at certain times the quantity of water flowing past the dam site at San Carlos exceeds the flow at Solomonville, although at the same time diversions may be taking place in the Solomonville-Safford Valley, and this has been taken by some as proof that irrigation in the Solomonville Valley produces no diminution in the natural flow of the river below the valley. If the theory set forth above is correct, then at any time when the quantity of water actually used for irrigation added to the amount of evaporation between Solomonville and the dam site is less than the inflow on this district there will be an actual increase in the flow of the river between these two gauging stations. References to the diagram of the inflow shows that this condition generally occurs each year about the end of the irrigation season, in October and November, when the amount of water used for irrigation is rapidly falling off and much water in the canals is wasted back into the river, and yet when the return water from irrigation earlier in the season is still flowing into the river from lands situated some distance from the stream.

Table showing losses between Kelvin and Sacaton.

Date.	Kelvin.	Florence canal.	Kelvin, less Florence canal.	Sacaton.	Loss.
1914.					
Oct. 21	525	40	485	340	145
Oct. 26	510	30	480	350	130
Nov. 1	560	10	550	415	135
Nov. 5	580	5	575	560	115
Nov. 26	615	20	595	390	205
Dec. 1	470	....	470	300	170
Dec. 11	585	60	525	290	235
Dec. 16	450	50	400	260	140
1915.					
June 1	515	60	455	310	145
June 6	425	85	340	125	215
June 11	336	115	220	90	130
June 16	260	75	185	65	120
June 21	215	75	140	15	125
June 26	165	70	95	5	90

Table showing diversion and inflow in Solomonville-Safford Valley.

Canal.	Mile.	Diversion.	Inflow.
Brown	0.8	4.0	....
San Jose	2.4	26.0	....
Michelena	4.0	1.2	....
Montezuma	7.0	22.0	....
Union	8.4	34.8	....
Do	12.0	....	11.5
Graham	12.8	15.0	....
Do	14.2	....	6.0
Oregon	14.4	17.0	6.5
Smithville	15.8	12.0	12.0
Bryce	18.3	10.0	10.0
Dodge	20.3	3.0	3.0
Nevada	22.6	2.0	2.0
Curtis	24.8	11.0	11.0
Consolidated	28.4	2.0	2.0
Dam site	46.0	....	28.0
	....	160.0	92.0

Run-off of Gila River at dam site (San Carlos).

[Acre-feet.]

Year.	January.	February.	March.	April.	May.	June.	July.	August.	September.	October.	November.	December.	Total.
1890[1]	37,631	28,890	21,416	12,745	4,815	1,500	7,196	173,600	6,854	8,690	11,353	15,218	329,908
1895	(56,000)	(14,000)	(5,000)	(0)	17,000	5,000	(25,000)	86,602	43,485	87,269	59,070	41,559	438,985
1896	21,914	10,824	13,392	9,640	1,771	268	79,744	44,825	52,483	229,381	55,535	34,808	554,585
1897	71,167	44,135	38,849	37,166	12,396	2,785	31,267	44,216	126,976	(51,000)	(0)	(5,000)	464,957
1898	35,417	24,242	26,175	29,294	16,159	13,496	111,895	29,716	14,459	4,372	5,409	16,878	327,512
1899	17,597	11,946	7,194	3,320	996	276	73,800	25,100	24,800	(15,000)	(10,000)	(5,000)	194,529
1900	5,000	10,000	50,000	306	150	33	16	12,200	55,800	3,690	10,500	6,270	153,965
1901	8,670	61,600	26,200	3,530	338	156	23,200	29,600	12,600	4,150	13,300	6,760	190,104
1902	6,119	3,078	625				1,309	48,698	5,821			34,286	99,936
1903	10,400	2,960	2,200	3,010	136	6,370	3,280	59,200	13,300	6,520	3,300	2,180	112,856
1904	1,949	1,875	676	315	535		3,793	58,540	13,800	50,730	6,664	18,820	162,697
1905	56,808	142,644	263,112	237,396	55,519	15,200	6,120	27,100	32,400	9,160	112,020	53,603	1,011,082
1906	20,916	53,040	116,640	58,800	20,652	5,227	8,820	38,484	10,308	7,015	8,664	78,120	426,686
1907	200,640	105,360	68,520	44,400	21,456	13,236	15,564	52,560	50,928	19,956	26,232	17,052	635,904
1908	(30,000)	(72,000)	(42,000)	(38,000)	(9,000)	(0)	(33,000)	(50,000)	(12,000)	(5,000)	(11,000)	(36,000)	(338,000)
1909	11,436	17,760	80,040	47,520	17,616	3,937	13,440	29,736	23,244	7,662	7,877	13,116	273,384
1910	27,456	12,683	11,165	8,899	3,784	2,904	2,783	5,764	5,346	7,788	11,440	9,944	109,956
1911	27,665	19,239	114,290	19,525	744	3,067	57,310	16,115	29,590	54,340	17,985	15,985	375,767
1912	11,825	7,733	123,530	43,780	21,329	19,855	64,240	22,660	21,021	18,612	14,845	14,542	383,972
1913	9,920	14,730	37,510	28,820	14,900	7,340	8,300	12,400	19,350	25,000	29,260	22,800	230,330
1914	18,440	19,360	26,600	13,170	510	4,320	59,500	66,300	36,100	72,100	46,500	379,450	742,350
1915	148,850	219,600	219,800	230,500	69,500	69,500							
Total	686,970	678,099	1,075,134	639,636	219,806	102,972	634,077	934,416	610,665	687,435	460,954	827,301	7,557,465
Mean	32,713	32,290	51,197	30,459	10,467	4,903	30,194	44,496	29,079	32,735	21,950	39,395	359,878

[1] Seasonal year, Sept. 1, 1889–Aug. 31, 1890.

Figures in parentheses are estimated

Table showing sources of Gila run-off data for San Carlos dam site.

Year.	Whence obtained.	Source of information.
1890	Buttes minus 10 per cent [1]	W. S. P. No. 33, p. 30.
1895	Buttes minus 10 per cent, Aug. 1 to Dec. 31	Do.
1896	Buttes minus 10 per cent	Do.
1897	Buttes minus 10 per cent, Jan. 1 to Oct. 3	Do.
1898	Buttes minus 10 per cent	Do.
1899	Buttes minus 10 per cent, Jan. 1 to July 10, and San Carlos, July 10 to Sept. 1.	Do.
1900	San Carlos, Apr. 3 to Dec. 31	Blue-print record.
1901	San Carlos	Do.
1902	....do	W. S. P. No. 85, p.—, rejecting blue-print record.
1903	....do	Blue-print record.
1904	....do	Do.
1905	San Carlos and Cliff, and Alma plus 20 per cent	W. S. P. No. 175, pp. 162, 170.
1906	Cliff and Cliff and Alma plus 20 per cent	W. S. P. No. 211, pp. 123, 128.
1907	....do	W. S. P. No. 249, pp. 176, 178, 179, 180.
1908	Supplied from rainfall and mean of same months in other years.	
1909	Redrock and Alma plus 20 per cent	W. S. P. No. 269, pp. 221, 224.
1910	Redrock and Clifton plus 10 per cent (Clifton deduced from Alma).	W. S. P. No. 289, pp. 202, 207, 208, and blue-print record.
1911	Guthrie and Clifton plus 10 per cent	Blue-print record.
1912	....do	Do.
1913	....do	Do.
1914	January–April, Guthrie and Clifton plus 10 per cent	Do.
1914	May–December, measurements San Carlos	Do.
1915	January–June, measurements San Carlos	Do.
1915 [2]		

[1] Kelvin in 1911=426,220; in 1912=450,691.

[2] Not included in totals.

Water received from underground resources, Solomonville Valley.

Date.	Solomonville Canal (C).	Evaporation (E).	Flow at Solomonville (S).	Flow at San Carlos (B).	Flow at dam (D).	S+B−D.	C+E.	X.
1914.								
May 5	255	55	135	....	22	113	310	197
May 10	230	55	125	....	10	115	285	170
May 15	212	55	100	....	5	95	267	172
May 20	196	55	90	....	5	85	251	166
May 25	183	55	80	....	5	75	238	163
May 30	190	....	80	....	5	75	190	125
June 5	320	63	195	....	10	185	383	198
June 10	216	63	105	....	6	95	279	184
June 15	190	60	73	....	5	68	250	182
June 20	385	63	230	10	100	140	445	305
June 25	280	63	180	....	240	− 60	343	403
June 30	180	63	245	....	70	175	243	68
July 5	325	58	980	....	410	570	383	− 187
July 10	360	58	820	....	700	120	418	298
July 15	390	58	775	....	430	345	448	103
July 20	415	....	1,625	....	740	885	515	− 470
July 25	420	58	2,400	....	1,400	1,000	478	− 522
July 31	330	....	2,560	60	1,915	705	330	− 375
Aug. 5	330	....	969	10	900	70	330	260
Aug. 10	300	50	1,075	15	1,150	− 60	350	290
Aug. 15	300	50	1,525	15	600	− 60	350	290
Aug. 20	360	50	1,000	15	775	240	410	170
Aug. 25	355	50	1,800	115	1,115	700	405	− 295
Aug. 31	350	50	2,125	90	1,800	415	400	− 15
Sept. 5	340	45	1,090	40	1,490	− 360	385	745
Sept. 10	335	....	660	25	725	− 40	335	375
Sept. 15	325	45	540	55	565	30	370	340
Sept. 20	390	....	435	35	400	70	390	320
Sept. 25	420	45	375	20	280	115	465	350
Sept. 30	335	45	220	10	220	10	380	370
Oct. 5	15	....	4,750	75	1,960	2,860	15	−2,845
Oct. 10	75	40	2,250	35	2,870	− 585	110	695
Oct. 15	160	35	610	20	960	− 330	195	525
Oct. 20	300	....	375	10	900	− 515	300	815
Oct. 25	375	....	435	90	550	− 25	375	400
Oct. 31	350	....	320	35	415	− 60	350	410
Nov. 5	380	20	305	25	380	− 50	400	450
Nov. 10	460	....	290	60	280	70	460	530
Nov. 15	400	20	2,360	150	2,000	510	420	− 90

Water received from underground resources, Solomonville Valley—Continued.

Date.	Solomonville Canal (C).	Evaporation (E).	Flow at Solomonville (S).	Flow at San Carlos (B).	Flow at dam (D).	S+B−D.	C+E.	X.
1914.								
Nov. 20	250	20	775	40	925	− 110	270	380
Nov. 25	340	20	510	40	585	− 35	360	395
Nov. 30	430	....	410	50	490	− 30	430	460
Dec. 5	390	....	435	60	525	− 30	390	420
Dec. 10	385	20	370	65	500	− 65	405	470
Dec. 15	385	....	330	70	490	− 90	385	475
Dec. 20	....	....	....	....	....	....	....	....
Dec. 25	....	....	....	....	....	....	....	....
Dec. 30	....	....	....	....	....	....	....	....
1915.								
Apr. 15	515	40	4,060	40	3,440	660	555	− 105
Apr. 20	415	40	2,885	10	2,800	95	455	360
Apr. 25	350	40	2,515	20	2,300	235	390	155
Apr. 30	290	40	2,250	40	2,025	265	330	65
May 5	375	55	1,675	130	2,065	− 260	430	690
May 10	275	55	1,100	65	1,500	− 335	330	665
May 15	320	55	1,125	15	1,140	....	375	375
May 20	400	55	1,115	10	1,130	− 5	455	460
May 25	400	55	825	5	620	210	455	245
May 30	510	35	650	5	465	180	565	385
June 5	505	....	500	10	315	175	505	330
June 10	520	65	435	5	265	165	585	420
June 15	400	65	355	5	205	145	465	320
June 20	360	65	280	....	175	105	425	320
June 25	300	65	190	....	115	75	365	290
June 30	240	65	130	....	60	70	305	235

REPORT ON HYDROGRAPHIC INVESTIGATION OF GILA RIVER BASIN IN COOPERATION WITH THE UNITED STATES INDIAN SERVICE, 1914–15.

[By C. O. Jacob, district engineer.]

This investigation is confined to that part of the Gila Basin above the eastern boundary of the Gila River Indian Reservation. This stream drains an area of varied topography and physiography, and general statements applying to the basin as a unit are impossible. It is really a complete river system made up of a number of minor basins whose individual characteristics have very little in common.

The upper San Francisco and the Gila above the Red Rock Valley are typical mountain streams, although they, in common with all streams of the Southwest are subject to sudden and more or less violent floods resulting from heavy rainfall concentrated over small areas. They both maintain fairly steady flows throughout the spring months, subject to the sudden fluctuations in stage just mentioned. If we accept the theory of " forest storage " of rainfall the explanation of both these conditions follows readily, since both drainage areas are made up of heavily forested areas and also barren areas of igneous rock with steep slopes.

The San Francisco and upper Gila occupy canyons eroded through Tertiary gravels, conglomerates, and lavas, and frequently through the older formations. These canyons vary considerably in width, and in a few places small valleys have been formed where the land is cultivated. The largest of these cultivated areas is the Duncan Valley, which lies both in Arizona and New Mexico. Below the junction of the two streams the river occupies a box canyon about

20 miles in length, changes direction to the northwest, and traverses the long, narrow central Gila Valley to its junction with San Carlos Cr ek. This latter stream drains an area of steep slopes and plateaus built up principally of recent lava flows, and generally barren. Its normal flow, therefore, is very small, and it also is subject to sudden floods. The central Gila Valley is confined on the southwest by a mountain range drained by numerous short canyons and washes whose slopes decrease rapidly as they pass through the foothills to the valley.

There are a few small streams more or less permanent in character in the upper reaches of some of the larger canyons, but this water is lost in the débris of the foothills and upper mesas. Below San Carlos the Gila River occupies another box canyon until it passes the buttes above Florence, where it enters the lower Gila Valley. This valley has been formed by a process of aggradation in which the original topography has become obliterated, and only the higher ridges and peaks of what were once mountain ranges are visible above the deposits of débris constituting the present valley fill.

The San Pedro River, the most important tributary from the south, joins the main stream in the canyon about 25 miles below San Carlos. While its normal discharge at its mouth is very small, this stream is subject to unusually heavy floods, particularly in the winter, when the broad desert areas which it drains have become saturated by prolonged rainfall, so that a high percentage of the subsequent precipitation is carred off by the stream. The effect of this stream on the flow of the Gila River during the floods of December, January, and February, 1915, is particularly noticeable. In addition to the streams mentioned above, there are many other minor stream courses normally dry, which contribute to the flow of the main stream frequently throughout the year in a complex manner depending on the distribution and intensity of the local rainfall.

We can expect, therefore, to find the flow of the Gila River erratic, particularly during times of considerable rainfall. Parts of the three principal Gila valleys, as well as several smaller areas, are being irrigated from the Gila River. The water is diverted directly from the stream by brush dams, each canal having its own heading. The distribution of the water to the various canals is handled independently in each valley, and in general it can be stated that the canals of each valley, considered as a unit, take all the water from the river they can get.

The effect of this diversion on the stream flow during periods of high water is not apparent, due principally to the fact that in flow from washes and dry canyons and seepage and evaporation losses from flooded river bottoms can not be estimated. During periods of low water, however, the effect of the diversion becomes very apparent; painfully so to parties in the lower valleys. For example, we have for the dry months of May and June for the past four years the following mean daily discharges in second-feet:

Year.	Gila-Kelvin.	Gila-Solomonville.	Loss.
1912.			
May	55.7	315.1	259.4
June	9.6	304.1	294.5
1913.			
May	67.9	220.4	152.5
June	15.8	112.1	96.3
1914.			
May	7.1	99.9	92.8
June	61.5	141.6	80.1
1915.			
May	1,173	1,067	[1] 106
June	257	300	43

[1] Gain.

This table shows that for the dry spring period when growing crops must require irrigation, there was absolutely no water in the river at Sacaton; in fact the Florence canals had only a partial supply. The year 1915 was the most favorable of any for which there is a record, and the dry spring season was very short, coming in June and the first half of July.

NATURE AND SCOPE OF THE INVESTIGATION.

The purpose of this investigation was to determine the quantity of water flowing in the river at several definite points during the period covered by the study as well as the quantities diverted by the various canals in the three valleys. In particular it was desired to determine the effect of all upper diversions on the stream flow at the Gila Reservation line.

During the spring and summer of 1914, automatic recording gauges were installed at the following points, which are referred to as "river stations" in this report: (1) Gila River above Duncan; (2) Gila River at Guthrie; (3) San Francisco at Clifton; (4) Gila River above Solomonville; (5) San Carlos Creek at San Carlos; (6) Gila River below San Carlos; (7) Gila River at Kelvin; (8) Gila River above Sacaton; and staff gauges were placed on the following canals:

Duncan Valley.—Casper and Windham, Model, Duncan, Sunset, York, Casper and Martin, Valley, Black and McCloskey, Colmenero.

Solomonville Valley.—Brown, Montezuma, Michelena, Dodge, Curtis, Fournese, Sunflower, Bryce, Nevada, Graham, San Jose, Union, Smithville, Consolidated, Oregon.

Florence Valley.—Florence, Price and Powell, North Side Blackwater, O. T., Pierson and Nicholas.

At all the river stations except the Gila at San Carlos the stream bed consists of sand and gravel and the sections were subject to frequent shifts, particularly during flood stages. This made it impossible to secure permanent ratings of the stations and frequent discharge measurements were required. The probable error of the station estimates is consequently greater than had been expected. The high-stage estimates are especially liable to be in error, and for the larger floods of December and January the estimates can only be considered as approximate.

The canal sections were much more permanent, but the gauge heights were affected frequently by back water from "checks" below the station.

A number of breaks for short periods occurred in the automatic gauge records, and for these periods the gauge heights were interpolated by comparison with the other stations. These breaks were due to (1) a defect in the mechanism of the gauges, resulting in their being occasionally put out of commission by floods, (2) silt filling in the float chamber during a receding flood and (3) malicious persons interfering with the gauge. The latter was not of frequent occurrence. An attempt was made to maintain an automatic gauge near the eastern boundary of the Gila Reservation, in spite of the unfavorable conditions. A complete equipment was installed, but during the high stages of September the river channel shifted several hundred yards from the gauge, destroying the south cable anchorage. The channel was so altered that it was necessary to discontinue the station, and wading discharge measurements were made thereafter whenever the stage of the river would permit.

The exceptional flood of December, 1914, probably exceeding any thus far recorded on the Gila River, carried away the gauge at the San Carlos dam site and damaged the installation at Kelvin so that it had to be abandoned temporarily and staff gauge observations substituted. Other stations were slightly damaged, but the records were continued. This flood also destroyed all the canal headings in the basin, and many other structures, as well as much arable land. The canals were put in commission again in March and April.

The canal stations were located above all diversions therefrom, and in a few instances above sluiceways through which water was occasionally wasted back into the river or into other canals. The canal staff gauges were read daily, or twice each day for some stations, by local parties employed as observers. The work was begun first in April, 1914, on the Solomonville canals; gauges were installed on the Duncan and Florence canals in September.

An examination will show that the period May, 1914, to June, 1915, was a very unfavorable one for such an investigation. Obviously we are concerned only incidentally with flood discharges in this study. When there is a flow of several hundred or thousand second-feet past the reservation it is of small consequence whether the flow at Solomonville is slightly greater, from the standpoint of the irrigation problem. The dry periods are the critical periods of our investigations, and unfortunately the months of low discharge were not numerous during the period studied; in fact, the only months that can be profitably studied are May and June, 1914, and May and June, 1915, and the first half of July, 1915.

In applying the results of this investigation the following considerations should be borne in mind.

(1) The flood estimates for the river stations are approximate only.

(2) Estimates for individual canals are not in all cases reliable, due to disturbing back-water conditions, etc. The totals for the various canals in each valley should be fairly accurate, but the fact that water is frequently wasted from one canal to another should be kept in mind. It is not probable that all of the water measured was actually applied to the land. It was not practicable during this

investigation to determine this waste water and it is therefore ignored in this study.

(3) Many sources of inflow between gauging stations could not be determined. Under this class are included washes and canyons normally dry, springs having their source in the mountain ranges parallel to the valley, and large areas of flat land which, becoming saturated by prolonged rainfall, contributed to the run-off.

TABULATION OF DATA.

(a) *Discharge measurements.*—Current meter measurements were made at the river and canal stations throughout the period of the investigation. In all 232 discharge measurements were made at the river stations, distributed as follows:

Gila near Duncan	20
Gila at Guthrie	26
San Francisco at Clifton	24
Gila near Solomonville	48
San Carlos at San Carlos	19
Gila near San Carlos	23
Gila at Kelvin	41
Gila near Sacaton	31
Total	232

A total of 386 canal discharge measurements were made, as follows: Solomonville Valley 259, Duncan Valley 59, Florence 68.

(b) *Daily discharge.*—The mean daily discharge at each river and canal station was computed from the daily gauge height records and the rating curves determined from the discharge measurements.

These estimated discharges at the river stations are considered fairly accurate for low and medium stages as mentioned above, but in most cases the maximum floods greatly exceeded the limits of the station rating; this fact, taken in connection with the shifting stream bed, renders accurate flood estimates impossible from the data secured. It is considered, however, that they are sufficiently near the truth for studies of storage possibilities, since the season run-off greatly exceeded the maximum possible storage on the stream.

Maximum discharges in second-feet (mean for one day) were determined for the following stations:

Gila at Guthrie, 14,300, December.

San Francisco near Clifton, 14,600, December.

Gila near Solomonville, 31,000, December.

Gila at Kelvin, 90,000, December.

Gila near San Carlos, 32,800, December (estimated from high-water mark).

The sum of the Guthrie and Clifton discharges checks fairly well with that for Solomonville, but the San Carlos maximum is evidently too low. It is possible that the true high-water mark was not determined.

The daily discharges for individual canals are liable to be in error, owing to backwater effects at the gage, produced by dams and checks in the canal below the station. The totals for all the canals in each valley however are considered fairly accurate.

A study of the accompanying hydrograph shows several interesting conditions. The discharge in second-feet, average over five-day periods, are plotted as ordinates, with the time as absissas for each river station and for the sum of the corresponding discharge for all the canals in each valley. Daily rainfall in hundredths inches is plotted for the three rainfall stations—Clifton, Thatcher, and Dudleyville. These are designated by circles. The remarkable fact is noted in this connection, that rainstorms occurred in this basin every month during the investigation, and every month had its resulting flood crest. Only a few periods of reasonably steady flow occurred, and these were selected for more intensive study and the plotting of mass curves for the various stations. They are as follows:

1914: May 1 to June 21, (1); September 6 to September 30, (2); October 16 to December 16, (3).

1915: January 1 to January 26; March 1 to March 21; May 16 to June 30.

The last period could have been extended to July 16 before the occurrence of the July floods, but some of the data for July were not available when this report was prepared.

First period.—At the beginning of this period, there was approximately 60 second-feet passing the Duncan Station, and this flow continued constant throughout the first half of May. There is no record of the Duncan canals for this period, but from later records it is probable that all this flow was taken out in the Duncan Valley. At Guthrie 35 second-feet was flowing in the river the first of the month, which had decreased to 22 second-feet by the 11th and remained at that stage until the 25th. It is probable that this water was all return flow from the irrigated lands and from seepage from rainfall the preceding two months. The flow at Guthrie added to that of the San Francisco River approximately 45 second-feet and the smaller inflow from Bonito and Eagle Creeks resulted in a mean discharge of 135 second-feet for the first 5-day period at the Solomonville Station. The four upper canals—Brown, San Jose, Montezuma, and Union—diverted 132 second-feet, practically all of the flow in the river, during the same period. The following is a tabulation of the water in the river at Solomonville Station during May and June, and the water diverted by these four "major" canals.

Period	1-5	6-10	11-15	16-20	21-25	25-31
MAY, 1914.						
Brown	10	9	8	7	2	2
San Jose	34	33	32	31	31	31
Montezuma	33	32	31	32	32	31
Union	35	46	34	22	16	23
Total for canals	132	120	105	92	81	87
Gila near Solomonville	135	123	100	90	78	78
Difference	3	3	5	2	3	9
JUNE, 1414.						
Total for canals	171	104	89	172	131	83
Solomonville	199	101	74	230	179	67
	18	−3	−15	58	48	−16
JUNE, 1915.						
Canals	322	353	241	213	190	155
Solomonville	493	424	336	261	174	144
Difference	171	81	95	48	16	41

The 11 other minor canals down this valley were using about 120 second-feet of water the first five-day period, which had decreased to about 100 second-feet at the end of the month. Practically all of this water was return flow from the upper irrigated area and spring water proper, having its source in the mountain ranges parallel to the valley. It was not possible to distinguish between these two sources of inflow. From the hydrograph and mass curves, therefore the canals are apparently using about twice as much water as is flowing in the river at the upper end of the valley, during these periods of minimum flow. Attention is directed in passing to the effect of the diversion in the Duncan Valley on the small rise in the river at the Duncan station. Very little of this water reached the Guthrie station, and the sharp rise occuring at Solomonville scarcely affected the San Carlos station.

Of the 135 second-feet flowing in the river at Solomonville the first of the month only 22 second-feet reach San Carlos, and this flow gradually decreased to 5 second-feet at the end of May. The flow at Kelvin was 16 second-feet at the beginning of May and 2 second-feet at the end. All of this flow was diverted by the Florence Canal, and the river at the Agency line was dry during May and practically all of June. The rainstorms occurring in the Valley during the middle of June destroyed the hydrographic relation obtaining throughout May, still the effect of the diversions is clear throughout the month.

Second period.—The floods of the latter part of August affected conditions throughout the month of September. The storage effect of the sands of the river bed is particularly noticeable. For instance, a considerable loss is noted from Solomonville to San Carlos the last two periods of August, but after the crest of the flood had passed, the flow at San Carlos exceeded that at Solomonville up until the middle of September, when the loss through diversion began to exceed the return flow from the saturated sands. This effect can be detected after practically every flood throughout the year. The effect of the diversion on the river discharge is therefore only apparent during the last few days of September, and is greatly reduced by the inflow produced by previous floods and by the local rainfall during the middle of the month.

Third period (October–December).—Here the effects of the high water the first part of October and the frequent rainstorms occurring throughout the period almost completely mask the effects of the diversion. The storage effect of the irrigated area and river sands is very apparent.

This period ends abruptly on December 17, the beginning of the largest flood of the year, and very probably the largest of which there is any record. The flood originated in the upper San Francisco and Gila drainages, and rapidly reached a maximum at San Carlos, and added to the extreme stage of the San Pedro produced and maintained a stage at Kelvin above any previous high-water marks. The stream fell rapidly during January, but another flood occurred on January 30 and 31 bringing the stream to nearly the same maximum as was reached in December.

Some very interesting hydrographs were obtained from the automatic gage records of these floods at the various stations.

A few of the canal headings in the Solomonville district were rebuilt in March, and by April most of the canals were taking water. The river fell rapidly after the April flood, the discharge falling off at the three lower stations from approximately 5,000 second-feet on April 12 to approximately 2,200 second-feet on April 30.

Fourth period (January 1 to 25).—All canals were out of commission during this period and the stream flow increases downstream, as follows:

	Run-off in second-feet, days Jan. 1-25, 1915.	Increment.	Source of increment.
Duncan	10,200	1,100	Side washes and seepage from irrigated lands.
Guthrie	11,300	8,000	San Francisco River.
Guthrie and Clifton	19,300	5,400	Eagle, Bonito, and minor creeks.
Solomonville	24,700		
Gila, near San Carlos (less San Carlos Creek).	26,000	1,300	Side washes and seepage from irrigated lands.
Kelvin	60,500	24,500	San Pedro River, Mineral Creek and minor creeks

The mean discharge at Kelvin for the five-day period ending December 25 was approximately 1,000 second-feet; at San Carlos, 700 second-feet; at Solomonville, 615 second-feet; at Guthrie, 130 second-feet; and at Duncan, 95 second-feet.

Fifth period (March 1-20).—The heavy local rainfall during the first half of March complicated the discharge relations in the basin. Practically no water was taken out by the canals, and the mass curves for Duncan and Guthrie, Solomonville, San Carlos, and Kelvin run closely parellel.

Sixth period (May 16-June 30).—Throughout this period the stream fell rapidly, and practically all canals were taking water. Total run-off in acre-feet for the period was as follows:

May 16–June 30.

Station.	Total run-off, second-feet, days.	Apparent gain or loss.	Net gain or loss.	Remarks.
Duncan	15,950	5,305	545	Return flow.
Duncan canals	5,850			
Guthrie	10,645			
Guthrie and Clifton	22,620	[1] 70	[1] 70	
Solomonville	22,550	[1] 5,400	13,400	Do.
Solomonville canals	18,800			
San Carlos	17,150	[2] 2,600		San Pedro, etc.
Kelvin	19,750			
Florence canals	3,100	5,990	2,890	Net seepage loss, Kelvin to Sacaton.
Sacaton	13,760			

[1] Loss. [2] Gain.

During this period the effect of the various diversions is very plain, though there is at least one discrepancy in the results. It is difficult to see why there should be such a heavy seepage loss as is shown between Kelvin and Sacaton. However, this particular month's record is supported by 8 discharge measurements made at Kelvin on May 14, 27, 28, June 15, and July 2, and 10 discharge measurements made at the reservation line May 29 to June 25. For example, the measured discharge at Kelvin on June 15 was 231 second-feet and on June 16 at the reservation line there was a flow of only 30 second-feet. At this time the Florence canals were diverting approximately 77 second-feet. The difference, or 118 second-feet, is the measured seepage loss from Kelvin to Sacaton on that date. Earlier in the period the loss is shown to be still greater. The valley fill below Florence is very deep and doubtless has great storage capacity, still, in view of the preceding high-water conditions in this basin, it is hard to account for such a heavy loss in so short a distance. Further investigations will be undertaken to confirm this as soon as the river is flowing again at the reservation line.

The accompanying mass curves for the six periods just described give the total run-off in second-feet days (one second-foot day equals approximately 2 acre-feet) for the different river stations and canals for the periods.

SEEPAGE INVESTIGATION.

By July 1, 1915, the flow of the river had become practically constant at Solomonville, and a series of measurements was begun, commencing above the Solomonville Gaging Station and extending downstream to determine the actual extent and distribution of the return flow from the irrigated lands. Approximately 96 second-feet was flowing past the Solomonville station during the period July 10–16. Discharge measurements were made above and below the various canal headings, the Oregon canal being reached on July 17, when a sudden rise in the stream temporarily ended the investigation. From gage-height observations on the other canals during the same period it was possible to fill out the missing data. Discharge measurements were made early in July on the Florence canals and finally all the data available were plotted on the accompanying sheet. Practically all of the water flowing at the Solomonville gaging station was diverted by the first four canals, the others using the return flow. From the last (consolidated) canal heading to the gaging station at San Carlos the return flow was 28 second-feet. San Carlos Creek was dry during this time. This flow increased to 69 second-feet at Kelvin. Of this the Florence canals diverted 53 second-feet, there being a seepage loss of 16 second-feet between Kelvin and Florence. No water was flowing at the reservation line.

It is not possible to show from these or the other available data just what percentage of the 90 second-feet flowing at Solomonville would have reached Sacaton had there been no diversion above. The facts derived from the partial seepage investigation may be summarized as follows:

1. The first four Solomonville canals divert all the water passing the Solomonville gauging station during very low stages.
2. The other canals down the valley divert the return flow and spring water, the total quantity nearly equaling the quantity diverted by the larger canals.
3. There was an inflow from seepage and springs below the irrigated area and above San Carlos Dam site of 28 second-feet.

4. The inflow between San Carlos and Kelvin was approximately 40 second-feet.
5. Fifty-three second-feet was used by the Florence canals.
6. Sixteen second-feet was lost by seepage somewhere between Kelvin and Florence.
7. No water reached the Indian lands at Sacaton.

CONCLUSIONS.

The period covered by this study was very unfavorable on account of the unusual weather conditions prevailing. Only very short periods of water deficiency occurred, and these were greatly affected by preceding floods or by local rainfall during the period. The following facts were determined:

1. The daily discharge of the river at seven different points in the basin.
2. The approximate quantities of water used by the various canals in the basin and their distribution throughout the year.
3. The approximate effect on the river discharge of the diversions in the basin for irrigation during periods of low discharge.

The effect of the canal diversions on the stream flow could not be determined for flood periods, nor the absolute quantitative effect of the various diversions on the low-stage flow. It is shown, however, in the preceding discussion that such an effect exists and that the canals in the three Gila valleys divert all of the river flow in addition to the seepage and spring flow when the stream falls below 150 to 200 second-feet at Solomonville.

The field data were collected by J. B. Spiegel, E. S. Borgquist, and M. D. Anderson, under the direction of C. C. Jacob, district engineer.

C. C. Jacob,
District Engineer, United States Geological Survey, Water Resources Branch.

Phoenix, Ariz., *September 18, 1915.*

MAXIMUM AND MINIMUM COSTS

The item in the Indian appropriation act, which act has been already referred to, providing for an investigation to determine the water supply legally available for the San Carlos project, also calls for a report on the "Maximum and minimum cost of the San Carlos irrigation project, including dam and necessary canals, ditches, and laterals."

It is assumed that by "maximum cost" is meant that cost per acre which is found by using the most conservative assumptions as to the available annual draft and as to the duty of water. By "minimum cost" is meant that cost per acre which is found by using a draft which can be maintained at all times except possibly for a short period which may recur only at intervals of a long period of years, and by using a duty of water which it is believed will develop the full possibilities of the project.

LANDS TO BE TAKEN INTO THE PROJECT.

It is shown by the surveys made in connection with this investigation that the Pima Indians on the Gila River Reservation, have 14,356 acres of land under irrigation from the Gila River, and an additional 11,315 acres show previous cultivation to have taken place some time or other. In the Florence-Casa Grande district, 7,563.4 acres are under irrigation, and 12,217 acres in addition were found to have been irrigated less recently.

Contending, as did the Army board, that the Indians should at least have sufficient water to supply 10 acres per capita present population, the total Indian lands to be supplied with water would amount to 40,000 acres. Of this area 5,000 acres are already supplied by pumps, as in the Santan district, so that the total area of Indian lands to be supplied by the San Carlos project would amount to 35,000 acres.

As stated heretofore, it is believed that a total annual supply of 300,000 acre-feet may be safely assumed and that the San Pedro and other tributaries of the Gila contribute to the flow an amount at least equal to that lost by seepage and evaporation between the impounding dam and the diversion weir. Assuming concrete lined canals, and 20 per cent loss by evaporation and seepage between the diversion dam and the land, we would have 240,000 acre-feet available for irrigation. This amount of water would supply, assuming a water duty of 3 acre-feet per acre, 80,000 acres of land. Allowing 35,000 acres for the Indians, the balance of 45,000 acres would be the area of private land to come under the proposed project.

With unlined canals, it would be necessary to figure the seepage and evaporation losses at 30 per cent of the volume of water at the head of the system. Using this percentage, we would have available 210,000 acre-feet of water, or enough to supply 70,000 acres of land at the assumed duty of 3 acre-feet per acre. A project of 70,000 acres should be divided equally between the whites and the Indians.

WASTE LAND.

As to the area of waste lands, such as canals, pastures, fallow lands, etc., that is included with the area to come under a project, and to which no water is actually applied, it is here assumed that this additional area is taken into account in the unit area of the water duty, or in other words, the assumed three acre-feet of water will be actually applied to an acre of land, less the usual small percentage of that area allowable for pasturage, or waste lands.

PRIVATE LANDS.

The private lands to be taken into the project are considered to be located in the same area as set forth in the Army board report. Nearness of this land to the water supply has governed this selection.

Maps showing the tentative location of the distribution system have been prepared and are to be found in volume of maps, Nos. 54 and 55 of this report.

For the territory immediately surrounding Florence it is proposed that the present O. T. Canal be enlarged and extended and used as a part of the distribution system; all other ditches to be new.

At the present time there are approximately 1,200 acres of land irrigated on the north side of the river in the Florence-Casa Grande district. It is proposed to build a distribution system for the area on the south side only, but to allow sufficient water to flow past the diversion dam to irrigate this area of 1,200 acres. Owing to the fact that the ditches which serve to irrigate this area on the north side of the river divert their water from the river at no great distance below the site of the proposed dam, it is not believed that evaporation or seepage losses will be excessive. To construct a new ditch from the proposed diversion dam for the irrigation of this small area on the north side of the river would be inadvisable, owing to the excessive cost.

It is assumed, therefore, that if an 80,000-acre project is determined upon, the Florence-Casa Grande district will receive water for 45,000 acres, 43,800 acres of which are located on the south side of the river and 1,200 acres are situated on the north side.

INDIAN LANDS.

Upon entering the reservation the main canal is to continue along the ridge until it reaches the vicinity of Blackwater, where it will empty into the Little Gila. The Little Gila will be used to conduct the water for a distance of 4½ miles, at the end of which distance part of the water is to be diverted diagonally across the island to the Gila River and to empty into the river just above the Santan, or flood-water diversion dam. From the Santan diversion dam it is proposed to construct a canal back to the Little Gila. The purpose of this latter canal is to provide surplus flood water for the Casa Blanca and agency districts when it may not be necessary to draw into the Little Gila just above the head gates of the canal serving the agency project.

The diversion for the Casa Blanca project is situated about 8 miles below the agency project diversion. The Little Gila accordingly would be used as a conduit for a distance of 12 miles.

It is not proposed to use the stored waters west of the Casa Blanca district, since the area to be served in this district, together with the areas to be served in the districts east of this will make up the acreage allotted to the Indians. The acreages to be served with water from theproposed San Carlos project for the different districts are as follows:

	Acres.
Blackwater	3,000
Sacaton Flats and Agency districts	4,000
Santan district	5,000
Casa Blanca district	23,000
Total	35,000

Of the 3,000 acres comprising the Blackwater district about 2,000 acres are on the south side of the river adjacent to the proposed Pima Canal, and in reality merely form an extension of the Florence district. At the extreme eastern end of the reservation one of the laterals from the Pima Canal would be carried across the Little Gila on a flume and irrigate approximately 1,000 acres on the "island," or that strip of territory between the Little Gila and the main channel of the Gila River.

For the Sacaton Flat district, it is assumed that the ditch serving this district will head at the same point as does the large canal which serves to conduct the water for the Santan district from the Little Gila across to the Gila River. The Sacaton Flat district is contiguous to and situated just above the so-called agency district.

PORTIONS OF RESERVATION SYSTEM NOW CONSTRUCTED.

The diversion dam and headgates, as well as the distribution system for the agency district have already been constructed and only the actual cost of construction of this project is considered as a charge against the San Carlos project. While it is true that the structures on the agency system, as now constructed, are of the wooden variety, yet they are built in a very substantial manner and undoubtedly will be used for many years to come, so that it would hardly be considered fair to tax the San Carlos project with the replacement of these wooden structures with concrete construction.

The actual cost of the agency system was $18,747, which amount is assumed to be chargeable against the San Carlos project.

As discussed elsewhere, only 5,000 acres of the Sacaton district are to be taken into the San Carlos project.

Considering the distribution of the expenditures already made on this system as submitted by the Reclamation Service, together with the analysis of the cost of the work so far done by the Indian Service a figure of $88.633 has been arrived at, which represents an equitable portion of the total cost chargeable to the San Carlos project for the irrigation of 5,000 acres in the Santan district, or the Sacaton project.

Work on the Casa Blanca system started during the fiscal year 1914, and at the end of the fiscal year 1915, $23,900 had been spent in actual construction. This entire amount is considered as being chargeable to San Carlos project.

Duty of Water.

All things considered it is concluded that the duty of water assumed at 2 acres per acre-foot on the land, as proposed by the Army board, is too high.

It is conceded that 2 acre-feet of water is sufficient for the successful maturing of one crop, or for the irrigation of orchards, yet a one-crop project is manifestly not advisable and the climate is not suitable for extensive fruit growing.

The San Carlos project is primarily an Indian relief project and the Indians should therefore be given first consideration. An extremely high duty of water involves a very intelligent and economical use of every drop of water, and it is not to be expected that the Indians will be able to make a success of the project under such conditions.

The Army board points out that:

> It is true that in the beginning a farmer raising crops of the latter kind (alfalfa and most fruits) would not be able to cultivate his entire acreage.

This appears to be simply a statement to the effect that some land is to be taken into the project that will be of little value toward the payment of the cost of that project and that the 2 acre-feet duty of water in reality is too high or that the project is too large.

In paragraph 142 of their report the Army board states:

> It should not be overlooked, however, that in average and wet years the quantity of stored water available under the project will exceed 2 acre-feet per year, and that rainfall in the Florence-Casa Grande district averages 10 inches annually.

This statement conveys an impression not intended by the Army board. It was afterwards learned and it is also apparent that the clause, "the quantity of stored water available," etc., should have been written so as to read, "the quantity of overflow and other water available would exceed 2 acre-feet," etc. Had the stored water in excess of 2 acre-feet been used in average and wet years, of course, no safeguard could be guaranteed against a critically dry period. However, it may be pointed out that when the excess over 2 acre-feet was most needed it probably would not be available.

Data on the duty of water are of little value, unless accompanied by corresponding rainfall, length of irrigation season, character of soil, etc. While it is true that crops are raised in California and elsewhere on a comparatively high duty of water and, in fact, certain crops (principally beans) are raised along the coast of California without any [illegible] at all, yet when rainfall and other factors are taken into consideration the duty is not as high as would first appear.

Considerable information is now available covering the duty of water at different places and under various conditions, and it appears from a careful consideration of all these data, that the duty of water ranges within rather wide limits under the various conditions, and it is extremely difficult to reduce this relation to a common standard. The only safe criterion for making comparisons seems to be that all conditions must be practically the same.

From the center of the area to be irrigated by the proposed San Carlos project to the center of the area now being served under the Roosevelt project, is a distance of 40 miles, the lower end of the Santan district or the reservation which would come under the San Carlos project, is not quite 15 miles from the Pempe Canal of the Roosevelt system. The soil conditions on the two projects are much the same, and needless to say, so are the climatic conditions. There should be no valid reason therefore why the actual duty of water as found on the Salt River project should not apply to the near-by proposed project of San Carlos. Obviously it would be inconsistent for the Government to expect the Indians and the settlers under the San Carlos project to attain a materially higher duty of water than has resulted under the Roosevelt system.

The following figures procured through the courtesy of Mr. C. H. Fitch, project manager, Salt River project, gives the duty of water by years for the past six years on the Salt River project. The figures are acre-feet per acre actually delivered to the land.

Year	Acre-feet
1909	4.20
1910	3.60
1911	3.53
1912	3.94
1913	3.58
1914	2.62
Average	3.58

On the Yuma project, which is situated at a distance of 180 miles west of the lands to be irrigated under the San Carlos project, the average duty of water for the four years prior to 1913 was 5.1, and the average rainfall was 5 inches less at Yuma than at Florence.

On the Carlsbad project in New Mexico, some 420 miles to the east, the average duty of water during the same four-year period was 2.5 acre-feet, the average rainfall being 15 inches and the length of the irrigation season in this district 260 days, whereas under the Yuma and Salt River projects, perennial irrigation is practiced.

In Idaho, the State board of land commissioners entered into a cooperative agreement with the irrigation investigators of the office of Experiment Station, United States Department of Agriculture, for the purpose of determining the economic duty of water in Idaho. This investigation started in 1909 and was carried through 1913, at a cost of a little over $55,000. Some of the conclusions as the result of this investigation taken from the eighth biennial report of the State engineer of Idaho, and prepared by Mr. Don H. Bark, of the agricultural department, follows:

The duty for projects planted to diversified crops on the average clay loam soils of south Idaho should be sufficient so that 2 acre-feet per acre can be retained on each irrigated acre.

A sufficient quantity should be delivered to each individual over and above the 2 acre-feet so that he may, if unavoidable, waste not to exceed 12.5 per cent of the water delivered to him.

The rainfall in southern Idaho averages about 13 inches per annum and the irrigation season has a duration of several months.

Irrigation investigations conducted in California under cooperative agreement between the Office of Experiment Station, United States Department of Agriculture and the California State Department of Engineering during 1913 and 1914 resulted in a number of water duty determinations. These investigations were directed to studies of the duty of water for alfalfa, on a large number of farms in Sacramento Valley, where climatic and other conditions are somewhat similar to those obtaining in the Arizona territory. The results of these experiments were published in Bulletin No. 1, of the California State Department of Engineering.

From this bulletin it is seen that at Gridley, during the season from November 1, 1912, to October, 31, 1913, the rainfall was 1.16 feet, and the average amount of water applied to the land on 14 farms was 3.31 feet in depth. At Los Molinos during 1913 the rainfall was the same as at Gridley, the average duty of water on 9 farms was 5.57 acre-feet.

On 11 farms at Los Molinos during 1914 the amount of water applied to the land amounted to 4.74 acre-feet and the rainfall was 2.74 feet. On 5 farms at Orland during 1913 the amount of water applied to the land was 3.78 with 0.82 foot rainfall. At this same place the rainfall was 2.39 feet during 1914, and the average amount of water applied to the land was 4.83 acre-feet. At Woodland during 1913 the average amount of water applied to the land on 12 farms was 2.94 acre-feet and the rainfall was 0.61 foot. During 1914 the rainfall at Woodland was 2.45 feet, and the average amount of water applied to the land was 1.8 acre-feet. At Dixon during 1913 the rainfall was 0.61 foot, and the average amount of water applied to the land on 7 farms was 2.92 acre-feet. At Willows during 1914 the rainfall was 2.39 feet, and the depth of water applied to the land on 6 farms was 1.71 acre-feet.

In nearly all of the above investigations five different cuttings were made and the yields carefully determined, and it is seen from the tables covering the results of the above investigation that where the amount of water applied to the land is relatively low, as at Willows, there is a marked dropping off in the yield.

From a diagram published in this same bulletin and showing the results of water duty investigation covering a period of five years conducted at the California State experiment farm at Davis, it is shown that the yield of alfalfa per acre irrigated increases with the amount of water applied to the land until a total depth of 36 inches is reached; the yield with 49 inches applied to the land is about the same as when only 36 inches were applied and the yield began to decrease after the 48-inch depth was reached, and the yield for 60 inches was practically the same as for 30 inches. The yield difference between the 2 acre-feet and the 3 acre-feet was a little over 1½ tons in favor of the 3 acre-feet duty.

This bulletin also publishes some results from duty of water investigations conducted in the Imperial Valley. Inasmuch as the irrigation conditions in the Imperial Valley are very similar to those obtaining in the territory to come under the San Carlos project, the following is quoted from page 32 of this bulletin:

INVESTIGATIONS OF DUTY OF WATER IN IMPERIAL VALLEY.

Experiments were begun early in 1914, in cooperation with the University of California, to measure the duty of water in Imperial Valley and to determine what becomes of the water applied in irrigation.

It is generally realized that a knowledge of the duty of water in Imperial Valley is of much value not only to that section but to others in California and throughout the Southwest. Land holdings there are large and water is comparatively cheap, consequently much of the irrigation in the past has been carelessly done. This section has some peculiar conditions not generally found in the irrigated districts throughout the West. The soils are tight and they take water slowly. The irrigation season extends throughout the year. The summers are very hot, the atmosphere is dry, and evaporation is excessive.

In 1906 the average use of water on 120,000 acres of land under Imperial Water Companies Nos. 1, 4, 5, and 7 was 2.04 acre-feet per acre. At that time a large portion of the land was growing barley as a temporary crop. Much of the barley has now given place to alfalfa, cotton, and cantaloupes. Many of the barley growers use only 1 acre-foot per acre, as shown by the water company charges. Alfalfa requires more water than any other crop, and the company records indicate that from 3 to 4 acre-feet is used for its production. The change from grain to alfalfa has brought an increased use of water, and the average duty in 1913 was approximately 2.25 acre-feet per acre. It has also brought about a different distribution of the water throughout the year. During the early period the maximum use was in March, when alfalfa, barley, melons, and almost every crop grown, except corn, was given water. The maximum use in 1913 was in July, when Alfalfa must be given a plentiful supply.

Mr. R. S. Carberry, superintendent of Imperial Water Co. No. 1, states in his annual report for 1912 that 17 typical farms in the No. 1 territory were selected from which to determine the duty of water for the leading crops, as shown by the companies' water deliveries. The averages in acre-feet of water supplied per acre were: Alfalfa, 4.19; corn, 2.18; cantaloupes, 1.621, and barley, 1. Imperial Water Co. No. 7 determined the average amount used for alfalfa in its district during 1913 from the water charges to be from 3.5 to 4 acre-feet per acre.

Reference has been made to a large number of water-duty determinations, the results of which are found in a recent publication entitled "Irrigation Practice and Engineering," by Etcheverry, volume 1, pages 68 to 92.

GROSS DUTY OF WATER ALONG GILA RIVER.

The gross duty of water, as shown by the amounts actually diverted in a number of canals along the Gila River, is shown in the following tabulation:

The quantities given represent the actual flow in the canals near the points of their respective diversions, and do not represent the amount of water actually applied to the land since a part of the flow is lost by evaporation and seepage. It is also probable that in some instances a small portion is returned directly to the river and rediverted.

Measurements of the flow in most of the canals of the Solomonville-Safford Valley extending over the period of one year, were made at intervals sufficiently frequent so that a reliable record of the amount of water actually diverted has been obtained.

The only suitable measurements of the flow in the canals of the Florence and Duncan districts extend over a period of only nine months and it was necessary to estimate the flow for the balance of the year. The same is true of the duty of water determinations. In making this estimate, the mean monthly flow was used for the month during which no records were available.

Owing to the adverse river conditions at the time when the measurements were made, many of the canals in the Duncan and Florence-Casa Grande districts were not in service, and only such canals as were kept in fairly continuous use have been selected in making these tabulations.

It should be stated in this connection that as a rule the canals are made to divert all the water they can carry regardless of the requirements of the land under them and consequently these determinations are of no especial value as regards actual crop requirements. Attention is also directed to the excessive use of water in the district where water is plentiful, as in the Solomonville-Safford Valley, in comparison with the more economical duty in the districts where water is scarce, as in the Florence Valley.

Canals in Duncan district.	Diverted and measured for 9 months, October, 1914, to June 30, 1915.	Total estimated for 12 months.	Cultivated	Duty of water.
	Acre-feet.	*Acre-feet.*	*Acres.*	*Acre-feet.*
Sunset	6,426	8,470	694.0	12.1
Model	5,546	7,270	1,819.5	4.0
Valley	4,678	6,240	1,220.5	5.0
Total or mean	16,650	21,980	3,734.0	5.9

Canals in Solomonville-Safford district.	Actually measured, Apr. 1, 1914, to April, 1915.	Total estimated for 12 months.	Cultivated.	Duty of water.
	Acre-feet.	*Acre-feet.*	*Acres.*	*Acre-feet.*
Brown	3,916	....	559.5	7.0
Fournese	4,056	....	230.5	17.6
San Jose	25,986	....	3,595.7	7.0
Michelena	2,256	....	382.5	5.9
Montezuma	37,734	....	4,837.8	7.8
Union	37,541	....	5,865.9	6.4
Graham	10,698	....	999.9	10.7
Oregon	10,431	....	1,469.2	7.1
Smithville	14,754	....	2,049.3	7.2
Bryce	4,808	....	593.7	8.1
Nevada	6,479	....	1,222.6	5.3
Curtis	13,262	....	1,637.3	8.1
Consolidated	14,027	....	2,441.0	5.7
Total or mean	185,938	....	25,885.0	7.1

Canals in Florence district.	Actually measured, 9 months, October, 1914, to June 30, 1915.	Total estimated for year.	Cultivated.	Duty of water.
	Acre-feet.	*Acre-feet.*	*Acres.*	*Acre-feet.*
Florence	11,394	15,192	3,531.5	4.3
Pierson-Nicholas	2,996	3,992	950.7	4.2
Total or mean	14,390	19,184	4,482.2	4.2
Total or mean for 3 districts	216,978	227,102	34,101.2	6.6

Mr. Schuyler, in his report of December 5, 1911, for the Pinal Mutual Irrigation Co., of Florence, states that—

The duty of water in that (Florence) section should be as high as 1 acre irrigated for each 5 acre-feet diverted from the river.

Mr. Sieboth, who was chief engineer of the Pinal Mutual Irrigation Co. at the time of Mr. Schuyler's report, and who is well and favorably known throughout this section, claims that a grain crop can be matured in the Florence district on a water duty basis of 1.6 acre-feet applied to the land.

Mr. Quinton, in a report on the Florence Canal dated September, 1909, said:

Experiments with irrigation in this locality have shown that three irrigations for grain and three irrigations each of 6 inches in depth for corn, milo maize, or sorghum, are sufficient with the rainfall, some of which comes in heavy showers during the growing season, to insure abundant crops. Suppose that the irrigation season is eight months, and six irrigations each 6 inches in depth are made on the land. The depth of water delivered to the land in one season is therefore 3 feet.

CONCLUSION.

After careful consideration, it is believed that the project should be based upon the plan of conserving, as far as practicable, all of the available water supply of the Gila River and the utilization of this supply on the lands in sufficient quantity to insure the success of perennial crops.

In view of the foregoing data, special attention being drawn to practices and results as worked out in the nearby Salt River project and the high cost of water delivered under any project using the San Carlos dam and reservoir site, it is not believed that the Government would be justified in adopting a 2 acre-foot duty of water for this project, and it is further believed that a higher duty than 2 acre-feet per acre may not be assumed with safety. Accordingly, the 3 acre-feet per acre will be assumed in all calculations involving the duty of water in the estimate of the minimum cost of the San Carlos project.

IRRIGATION PLAN.

The proposed irrigation plan of the San Carlos project as adopted in these estimates is the same as that proposed by the Army board. It provides for an impounding dam on the Gila River in the San Carlos Box Canyon and for the diversion of the river water above Florence by means of a low weir into a main canal on the south side of the river. The main canal extends along the south side of the Florence Valley for a distance of 15 miles when it is divided into two branches; the Pima branch turns west and enters the Gila River Indian Reservation after traversing a distance of 10 miles; the other branch, called the Picacho, continues south and forms a part of the Florence-Casa Grande distribution system.

The Picacho branch will extend as far as the Picacho Reservoir, which, if need be, could be used as an auxiliary reservoir.

RESERVOIR.

In the extreme lower end of the Solomonville-Safford Valley and within the area which would be submerged by the proposed reservoir lies the San Carlos Indian Agency, including the towns of San Carlos, the Indian lands, roads, and houses, and a portion of the Arizona & Eastern Railroad, with its bridges across the Gila and San Carlos Rivers.

In plotting the behavior diagrams the impounding areas of the reservoir for the different heights of dam have been ascertained from the survey made of this site by this service in the course of the Gila River surveys. The survey from which the Army board derived their estimates was based on survey made in 1899 by the United States Geological Survey. No material discrepancy exists between the rseults of these two surveys. At the 180-foot contour, the 1914 survey gave 4,826 acre-feet more capacity for the reservoir than did the Geological Survey of 1899. The capacity at other levels were in proportion.

FLOWAGE DAMAGE.

The flow damage that would result from a dam 180 feet high to spillway without spillway gates has been taken as computed by the Army board.

The increased acreage submerged as the result of adding the proposed 10-foot shutter gates in the spillway does not materially increase the flow damages.

The plane-table survey made in connection with this investigation in this portion of the San Carlos Reservation shows that in the submerged area there were irrigated at the time of this survey (January, 1915) 442.6 acres under actual cultivation. In addition to this 252 acres have been previously cultivated and 201.5 acres of land fenced.

In addition to the above acreage there were found to be 1,270 acres susceptible of cultivation. The actual survey, therefore, shows a smaller area irrigated than that given in the original estimate of the Indian Service and a larger area susceptible of irrigation, the net result being approximately the same. A larger area also should be included under the head of grazing land.

The modifications by the Army board of the estimate covering the flow damages to the San Carlos Agency submitted by this service seems fair, and it is believed that $200,000 is an equitable appraisement of these damages.

The cost of moving the railway line of the Arizona & Eastern Railroad Co., to avoid the water line of the reservoir is taken from the brief submitted by the railroad company, and which sum was also adopted by the Army board.

It is not believed that the project should be expected to pay the San Carlos Indians anything for the dam site itself.

EVAPORATION FROM RESERVOIR.

No data was obtained in this investigation bearing on the amount of evaporation from the reservoir and the results as arrived at by the Army board are adopted.

SILT AND THE METHOD OF DESILTING.

An especially commendable portion of the Army board's report was their investigation to determine the quantity of silt carried by the waters of the Gila River. Until more is known of reservoir projects on silt-laden streams, there will always be some doubt as to the volume which silt may be expected to occupy in the reservoir. The question as to the percentage of voids in the silt when the reservoir is full of water is an open one. The Army board has given every phase of this question due consideration and it is believed that with the data so far available, their results can not be questioned.

The silt, as well as the desilting problem, have received much consideration, but it must be admitted that no satisfactory solution has been found. The Army board's system of desilting by dredges appears to be the only known feasible solution.

The silt problem is of prime importance in connection with the San Carlos project since it constitutes the main drawback to any project having to do with the storage of silt-laden water.

The Army board estimated that the cost of desilting would not exceed about 5 cents per cubic yard. This may be a reasonable cost, yet the lack of precedents covering actual operations under similar conditions renders this matter open to question. In fact the general question as to the economic advisability of storage projects on rivers carrying large quantities of silt may only be decided favorably by the invention of more suitable methods of desilting.

DAM SITE AND IMPOUNDING DAM.

In making the estimates for this report, the same dam site (i. e., the upper dam site) as selected by the Army board was adopted.

This site is located at the upper extremity of the Box Canyon of the Gila River, which extends from the mouth of the San Pedro to a point about 7 miles below San Carlos. Above the dam site lies the Solomonville Valley, which extends upstream a distance of 70 miles.

PROPERTIES AND DATA PERTAINING TO THE DAM AND RESERVOIR.

Assuming a dam 180 feet high to spillway level and 200 feet to crest, the following properties and data have been deduced and used in the design:

Elevation of stream bed	feet	2,308
Elevation of spillway	do	2,488
Elevation of crest or roadway	do	2,508
Area of reservoir at elevation 2,488	acres	13,200
Area of reservoir at elevation 2,498	do	14,870
Capacity of reservoir at elevation 2,488	acre-feet	714,450
Capacity of reservoir at elevation 2,498	do	854,800
Length of reservoir at elevation 2,488	miles	16
Maximum depth of rock surface below stream bed (p. 78 Army board report)	feet	23
Probable depth of excavation into solid rock, assumed	do	10
Maximum height of dam at lowest excavation	do	233
Length of dam on crest	do	542

Assumed weight of Cyclopean masonry, 150 pounds per cubic foot.
Assumed uplift, full water pressure at heel varying uniformly to zero at toe.
Water pressure, due to full height of dam, at 62.5 pounds per cubic foot.
Wind pressure, 50 pounds per square foot of vertical projection.
Maximum safe-bearing power of rock, 16 tons per square foot.

Area of Gila Basin above San Carlos, $13,455 square miles. (See p. 22, Water Supply Paper, No. 33.)

Mean annual rainfall on the watershed above dam site, incomplete records, 1867–1899, 12.87 inches (p. 18, Water Supply Paper, No. 33); maximum flood flow 1905 at San Carlos, 150,000 second-feet (p. 24, Army board report).

Average run-off, incomplete records, 1890–1912, based on a proportion of 90 per cent of the run-off at the Buttes, 346,568 acre-feet (see p. 28 Army board report); average to 1915, 359,880; maximum run-off, 1905, 1,011,082 acre-feet (p. 28 Army board report); minimum run-off, 1902, 99,936 acre-feet (p. 28 Army board report).

For rainfall and run-off records in full, see "Hydrograph" in this appendix.

PHYSICAL FEATURES OF DAM SITE.

Map No. 56 gives the locations of what are known as the upper and lower dam sites showing the positions of all lines of test holes drilled by the United States Geological Survey, United States Reclamation Service, and by the Army board during the years 1899, 1903, and 1913. Owing to the greater depth to bed rock, 74 feet, and to the pronounced fault at the lower site, the final selection of the Army board in favor of the upper site is thought to have been well chosen.

At the upper site, as well as at the lower one, the strata dip down stream, and while the straight gravity type dam has been decided upon, the location of the dam between lines G and J (diamond drill lines shown on map No. 56), placing it between converging canyon walls, will insure against sliding.

The rock at this site is principally quartzite and quartzitic sandstone. The bed rock is in sight and appears sound. The proposed dam is of the spillway type and the material excavated for the spillway would be of a quality fit for use in the construction of the dam. Any additional material needed could be secured at reasonable cost by extending the quarry on the spillway level.

ACCESSIBILITY.

The dam site is at present inaccessible to wagons and it will be necessary to build a road from the dam site to the Arizona & Eastern R. R. at a point near Rice, a distance of about 10 miles. This will require very heavy construction.

DESIGN OF DAM.

The type decided upon is the straight plan gravity type with spillways, calculated to resist water pressure to the full height of 200 feet, with uplift due to a full head of water at the heel and varying uniformly to zero at the toe.

Wind pressure is taken at 50 pounds per square foot of vertical projection. A width of 16 feet on the crest was assumed for roadway purposes. Cyclopean masonry construction with 30 per cent large stone was decided as the best as well as the most economical construction, giving a weight of 150 pounds per cubic foot.

Trial profiles were assumed for the cross section of the dam and analyzed graphically to determine the proper dimensions for various heights. The final profile is shown on plan 58. The back face is vertical for the first 40 feet, thence on a batter of 1:10. The front face is vertical for 5 feet, thence on a curve of 45-foot radius, thence on a tangent with a slope of 147 to 190. The section is so designed that the resultant lines of pressure, with the dam either full, including uplift, or empty, with wind blowing upstream, will fall within the middle third at any and all sections. The final profile was then checked mathematically at all critical points. The maximum pressure upon the foundation is found to be 15.5 tons per square foot at the heel, with the reservoir empty and the wind blowing upstream. The pressure at the toe is a maximum of 13.15 tons per square foot, with the reservoir full and with the uplift. The minimum angle of friction is 52°, 16¾′ when reservoir is full, including uplift.

A cut-off wall is shown with the depth equal to one-twelfth the height of the dam and the width equal to one-fifteenth the width of the dam at the base. It is expected, however, that the width and depth be varied to suit the character of the rock. The cut-off wall should be near the upstream edge of the dam.

It is assumed that the necessary depth of excavation for the foundation of the dam will be 10 feet (or less) into the solid rock, and with the cut-off wall it is not proposed to drill holes in the bottom of the trench for the purpose of forcing grout into the crevices of the underlying rock unless the nature of the material seems upon excavation to be more seamy than is indicated on the surface.

A drainage tunnel is provided in the dam with vertical 6-inch pipes spaced 10 feet apart, extending from the tunnel to the bottom of the cut-off wall on the downstream side. This tunnel is provided with a 24-inch cast-iron pipe outlet through the dam to carry off any water which may seep through under the cut-off wall, thereby relieving hydrostatic pressure.

This tunnel is connected with the inclined inspection gallery which connects the valve chambers for the 60-inch balanced valves.

The entrance to the inclined gallery is near the top of the dam, and will be reached from the crest by descending a short stairway secured to the downstream face of the dam.

Three 60-inch balanced valves are spaced 70, 125, 180 feet, respectively, from the top of the dam to control the discharge which will be through cast-iron pipes directly through the dam.

A substantial as well as ornamental type of railing is to be placed on each side of the roadway crest.

It is believed that the diversion of flood waters during construction can be successfully accomplished by building in steps on alternate sides of the foundation until a height is reached where storage will begin.

The location of the dam permits the construction of a spillway at each end, the excavation for which will furnish a quality of rock suitable for use in the construction of the dam. The diagram on sheet No. 65 was constructed from an estimated hydrograph of the December, 1914, flood at San Carlos by doubling the flow.

It is shown that the maximum depth over the spillway for a width of 300 feet is 11.5 feet, which is not deemed excessive, hence two 150-foot spillways are provided.

If sufficient good rock is not obtained from the construction of the spillways, it would be only necessary to extend the excavation further into the hill to supply this deficiency.

In order to provide a roadway across the dam and spillways two 150-foot bridge spans will be required, for which it is proposed to use steel structures, or if automatic gates be put in requiring piers, short-span concrete structures could be used to advantage.

The dam is to be constructed of cyclopean masonry, and it is assumed that it will be most economical both at the quarry and in the masonry to use about 30 per cent plums. Each cubic yard of the dam will then require 0.3 cubic yard plums, 0.91 barrel cement, 0.32 cubic yard sand, 0.64 cubic yard crushed rock based upon a concrete mixture of 1:2½:5, 45 per cent voids in the crushed rock, and cement at 3.8 cubic feet per barrel.

Estimate of Quantities.

Excavation:		
Total area of base ... square feet		77,400
Excavation into rock ... feet		10
Dam foundation:		
Rock below low water ... cubic yards	17,560	
Rock below low water (cut-off) ... do	2,000	
Rock above low water ... do	9,110	
		28,670
Spillways:		
Rock above low water, west	125,000	
Rock above low water, east	72,000	
		197,000
Total rock excavation		225,670
Dam foundation. Sand gravel below low water		23,770
Total excavation		249,440
Concrete:		
Dam below low water		17,560
Cut-off wall below low water		2,000
Dam above low water		265,910
Spillway crest and right wall		640
Bridge abutments		120
Total		286,230
Concrete material (cubic yards) required:		
Cement, 0.91×286,230=260,470 barrels.		
Plums, 30 per cent of 286,230		85,870
Crushed rock 0.64×286,230=183,200 cubic yards; 45 per cent voids		100,800
Sand, 0.32×286,230=91,600 cubic yards; 35 per cent voids		59,500
Total amount of rock in place required		246,170

NOTE.—The amount of rock required for concrete just about equals the total amount of excavation. It is likely, however, that not all of the rock excavated will be available for concrete, and making allowance for a wastage of 20 per cent there will be required 246,170=199,550=46,620 cubic yards of additional rock which can easily be obtained by quarrying on the spillway level.

Miscellaneous material.

60-inch balanced valves	3
60-inch cast-iron pipes ... feet	315
24-inch cast-iron pipes ... do	140
6-inch drill hole ... do	500
6-inch inside diameter casing ... do	500
Iron stairway, 4 feet wide 24 feet deep.	

Estimate of unit cost.

[Adapted from the Elephant Butte Dam.]

Unit cost per cubic yard concrete, 70 per cent 1:2½:5 with 30 per cent plums:	
Cement, 0.91 barrel, at $3.48	$3.17
Hauling crushed rock, 0.64 cubic yard, at 28 cents	.179
Crushing, 0.64 cubic yard, at 25 cents	.16
Hauling sand, 0.32 cubic yard, at 28 cents	.09
Crushing, 0.32 cubic yard, at 59 cents	.165
Hauling plums, cableway, 0.30 cubic yard, at 29.8 cents	.089
Placing plums, derrick, 0.30 cubic yard, at 12 cents	.035
Placing concrete, derrick, 0.70 cubic yard, at 12 cents	.084
Hauling concrete, cableway, 0.70 cubic yard, at 19.8 cents	.139
Mixing concrete, 0.70 cubic yard, at 23.2 cents	.162
Placing concrete in forms, 0.70 cubic yard, at 16.1 cents	.113
Water, 0.70 cubic yard, at 2 cents	.014
Forms, 1 cubic yard, at 12.6 cents	.126
Pump and light, 1 cubic yard, at 3.6 cents	.036
Miscellaneous repairs and depreciation, 1 cubic yard, at 2.4 cents	.024
Total, per cubic yard	4.586

Miscellaneous items of unit cost, adapted from costs of various projects.

Foundation excavation:		
Rock	per cubic yard	$1.55
Sand and gravel	do	1.00
Spillway and quarry excavation:		
Crusher rock	do	1.57
Plums	do	1.28
Waste	do	1.62
Hauling crushed rock from quarry to crusher	do	.28
Crushing rock	do	.25
Crushing sand	do	.59
Hauling plums by cableway	do	.30
Drilling 6-inch holes for drainage tunnel	per foot	2.00
Cement, $1.40 at Los Angeles, plus freight at $8.50, less 20 per cent, plus 7 cents for handling and 20 cents per ton-mile wagon haul equals $1.40 plus $1.63 plus 7 cents plus 38 cents	per barrel	3.48
60-inch balanced valve installed	each	10,000.00
60-inch cast-iron pipe, at 600 pounds per foot	per foot	24.00
24-inch cast-iron pipe, at 150 pounds per foot	do	6.00
Bridge steel, at 4 cents per pound plus 1 cent for erection, per pound		.05

Estimated cost of the San Carlos Dam.

Excavation:	
Solid rock below low water—	
Dam foundation, 17,560 cubic yards, at $2.75	$48,290
Cut-off wall, 2,000 cubic yards, at $2.75	5,500
Above low water—	
Dam foundation, 9,110 cubic yards, at $1.40	12,754
West spillway, 125,000 cubic yards, at $1.40	175,000
East spillway, 72,000 cubic yards, at $1.40	100,800
Extra for aggregate, 46,620 cubic yards, at $1.40	65,268
Sand and gravel below low water, dam foundation, 23,770 cubic yards, at $1	23,770
Total excavation all classes, 296,060 cubic yards, at $1.457	431,380
Concrete, all classes, 286,230 cubic yards, at $4.60	1,316,660

Appurtenances:	
3 balanced valves, 60-inch, at $10,000	$30,000
Discharge pipe, cast-iron, 60-inch, 315 feet, at 30 cents	9,450
Drain pipe, cast-iron, 24-inch, 140 feet, at 8 cents	1,120
Drain pipe casing, 6-inch, 500 feet, at 60 cents	300
Railing and pilasters, 1,084 feet, at 10 cents	10,840
Lighting fixtures	1,800
Total	53,510
Bridges over spillways, two 150-foot steel spans:	
Steel, 600,000 pounds, at $0.0375	22,500
Erection, at $0.0075	4,500
Railroad freight, 300 tons, at $6.50	1,950
Team freight, 3,000 ton-miles, at $0.20	600
Floor system material, 3,000 feet, b. m., at $16	480
Labor, 3,000 feet, b. m., at $4	120
Railroad freight, 50 tons, at $10	500
Team freight, 500 ton-miles, at $0.02	100
Total	30,750
Extra for 10-foot shutter gates and concrete bridges	35,000
Preliminary construction costs:	
River diversion	50,000
Road from near Rice	50,000
Telephone from Rice	5,100
Total	105,100
Camp expense:	
Camp construction, 20 buildings, at $500	10,000
Camp maintenance, 3 years, at $2,000	6,000
Water-supply system	10,000
Sanitation	10,000
Total	36,000
Plant not including buildings:	
Equipment depreciation on $180,000 for 3 years, at 10 per cent	54,000
Railroad freight to Rice and return, say, from Los Angeles, 1,000 tons each way, 2,000 tons at $8	16,000
Team freight both ways on 1,000 tons 2,000 ton-miles, at 25 cents	5,000
Total	75,000
Interests, taxes, etc.:	
Interest on capital, $400,000, 3 years, at 8 per cent	96,000
Taxes on property, one-half of $125,000 for 3 years at $1.60	3,000
Bonds for performance of contract, $3,000,000, at 1 per cent	30,000
Labor insurance on pay roll of $1,100,000 at 2 per cent	22,000
Total	151,000
Superintendence, engineering, etc.:	
Superintendence	20,000
Engineering	30,000
Inspection	40,000
Cement testing	2,000
Total	92,000
Washington office and overhead charges	200,000

Property damage:	
Reservation lands	$91,865
Government buildings	84,013
Indian buildings	1,900
Arizona & Eastern R. R.	680,192
Total	857,970

Summary of costs of San Carlos Dam.

Excavation	$431,380
Concrete	1,316,660
Appurtenances	53,510
Bridges over spillway	80,750
Extra for shutter gates and concrete bridges	35,000
Preliminary construction costs	105,100
Camp expense	36,000
Plant expense	75,000
Interest, bonds, taxes, and insurance	151,000
Superintendence, engineering, and inspection	92,000
Overhead charges	200,000
Property damages	857,970
Total	3,384,370

FLORENCE DIVERSION DAM.

LOCATION.

The site known as the Slight heading at the rocky point near the present heading of the Florence Canal has been tentatively chosen as the most practicable location for the diversion dam. At this site both abutments would be in solid rock and the channel is comparatively narrow. The main canal from such a diversion would follow an alignment almost identical with that of the old Florence Canal and would avoid a portion of the costly rock cut that would be a necessary part of the canal were a considerably higher heading selected.

The diversion dam as now proposed would be too low to divert water into the Casa Grande Valley Water Users' Association canal, as the proposed heading of this later canal is situated about one-half mile upstream from the site herein selected.

It should be pointed out, however, that if it were decided to build an unlined canal and the Casa Grande Valley Water Users' canal could be purchased on the basis of its value to the project, the diversion dam could be raised the additional 3 feet necessary to conform to the grade of the canal at an additional cost of $30,610, and the increased cost of the distribution system in the event of the use of the Casa Grande Water Users' Association canal would amount to $6,200.

Following engineering practice a dam of the East Indian weir type has been selected. A brief description of this dam, together with the cost analysis, follows:

DESCRIPTION OF DIVERSION DAM, AND DATA USED IN THE DESIGN.

The site selected is about 12 miles above Florence, where the Gila River flows between rock walls about 400 feet apart. While the rock banks afford substantial foundation for the end structures, bedrock drops to a great depth in the middle of the channel, so that it becomes imperative to use the Indian weir or floating type of dam. In this type, destructive percolation under the dam due to the head of water back of the dam is overcome by constructing impervious concrete aprons and driving sheet piling, thus controlling the path and the velocity of percolation under the dam.

At this site it is found that a weir crest 8 feet above the stream bed will be sufficient to divert the water into a canal, the bottom of which is to be about the same elevation as the present Florence Canal.

The following data are used in the design of the dam:

	Feet.
Elevation of present bed of Gila River	1,553.0
Elevation of present intake, Florence Canal	1,554.2
Elevation of high-water line, 1914 flood	1,562.7

Width of stream bed, 355 feet; width of stream surface at high-water line, 395 feet.

Approximate slope at river at this point, 13.37 feet per mile.

Probable depth of flood flow, 13 feet, allowing for scour.

Calculated flow, 1914 flood, S=13.37 feet per mile=0.00253; d=13 feet; bottom width, 355 feet; top-flood width, 395 feet; A=4,875, P=382, R=12.76.

If n=0.018, C=118.0, V=21.2, Q=103,300 second-feet.

If n=0.020, C=107.7, V=19.32, Q=94,200 second-feet.

If n=0.025, C=88.7, V=15.93, Q=77,700 second-feet.

A maximum flood of 150,000 second-feet will be used, however, to agree with the assumption at San Carlos, which for a crest length of 440 feet gives a unit discharge of 341 second-feet per foot of weir.

If b=440, d=16, A=7,040, p=472, r=14.9, S=0.00253. V=21.2, n=0.020. Q will be about 150,000 second-feet and the river flow 16 feet deep.

DESIGN OF DIVERSION DAM.

W. G. Bligh, in his Practical Design of Irrigation Works, gives the following formulas for the design of this type of dam:

NOTATION.

C= a coefficient of percolation derived from observation of many structures of this type in Europe. For the Gila River sand it is taken at 15.

q= number second-feet of maximum flood passing over dam, 150.000÷440=341 second-feet per foot.

p= specific gravity of masonry 2.4

p–1= specific gravity of masonry when submerged 1.4

H= maximum head of water on any point **X**. This occurs when the water is level with crest.

A_1= The distance of percolation of the point X from the upstream end of the impervious apron.

$2b$= total distance of percolation required and is equal to CH.

L= total breadth of impermeable apron and talus downstream from back face of dam and equals

$$10\,C\sqrt{\frac{H}{10}}\times\sqrt{q/75}$$

W= breadth of impermeable apron downstream equals

$$4\,C\sqrt{H/13}$$

The cut-off walls or sheet piling and curtain walls are considered by Bligh as furnishing twice their depth of percolation distance.

$t=\frac{4\,(H-h)}{3\,(p-1)}$, where $h=\frac{A_1}{C}$, t=thickness of downstream end of apron at any point distant A, from the upstream end of the impervious apron.

X= breadth of base of weir proper$=\frac{H+d}{\sqrt{p}}$ where d=depth of water over crest=16 feet.

Substituting known quantities in the equations,
$2b = CH = 15 \times = 120$ total distance of percolation required.

$$L = 10\ C\sqrt{\frac{H}{10}} \times \sqrt{q/75} = 10 \times 15\sqrt{8/10} \times \sqrt{\frac{341}{75}} = 286$$ the total length of permmeable apron and talus downstream.

$$W = 4\ C\sqrt{\frac{H}{13}} - 4 \times 15\sqrt{8/13} - 47.1$$ breadth of impermeable apron downstream.

Cut-off wall, 12-foot sheet piling projecting 11 feet below the 5-foot concrete base gives 22 feet, and two 6-foot curtain walls give 23.5 feet, a total of 45.5 feet of percolation. The breadth of upstream apron required is $120 - (47.1 + 45.5) = 27.4$.

The breadth of talus required is $286 - 47.1 = 238.9$.

$$X = \frac{H + d}{\sqrt{p}} = \frac{8 + 16}{\sqrt{2.4}} = 15.47 = \text{breadth of base of weir.}$$

$$h = \frac{A^1}{C} = \frac{6 + 3.5 + 2.5 + 27.4 + 15.5}{15} = \frac{54.9}{15} = 3.66$$

$$t = \frac{4(H\ \ h)}{3(p - 1)} = \frac{4(8 - 3.66)}{3 \times 1.4} = 4.14 = \text{thickness of base of weir.}$$

After due consideration the following dimensions, shown on plan No. 59, were adopted and estimates made thereon. The length of upstream apron 20 feet, downstream apron 50 feet, including base of weir which is 15 feet, breadth of talus 230 feet, sheet piling 12 feet, 11 feet below concrete, thickness of base at toe of weir 5 feet, thickness of upstream apron 1.5 feet, downstream apron 5 to 2½ feet, talus 4 to 2½ feet, curtain walls 6 by 2½ feet, width of weir on top 6 feet with Ogee rollerway.

The weir and impervious aprons are to be of 1 : 2½ : 5 rubble concrete with 40 per cent plums. The end structures of straight 1 : 2½ : 5 concrete reinforced only in exceptional cases, and the talus of 75 per cent of large rock carefully placed and grouted with 1 : 2½ : 5 concrete, small size rock to be used, the surface to be left rough.

On account of the great amount of silt carried by the Gila River especial attention was paid to the design of intake and sluice gates. By reference to plan No. 59 it will be seen that the intake or regulator gates are set perpendicular to the axis of the weir or parallel to the direction of flow and flush with the face of outside training wall. In addition, the 16 regulator gates close upon a sill 4 feet above the bottom of the sluiceway. There are four separate sluiceway channels, with a total sluice gate opening of 20 feet, the channels being separated by concrete walls 4 feet high to facilitate sluicing when the water is low. On the river side of the sluiceway is a training wall with its crest 1 foot below the crest of the weir.

It is proposed to operate the sluice gates by a special type of hydraulic jack outlined on plan No. 60, which will not obstruct the flow of water over the gates, thus leaving a deposit of sand in front of the intake. The intake gates are also operated by hydraulic jacks of the regular pattern.

The principal diversion is on the south side, and the heading has been designed for 1,000 second-feet capacity.

The plan shows a large canal or sand trap of 40-foot base for a length of 2,000 feet, at the lower end of which are six 5-foot gates opening into a 40-foot channel to the river for flushing purposes. The grade and size of this canal are such that under a normal flow of 1,000 second-feet the velocity would be 2 feet per second (the velocity in the canal for 16 miles below to be 7½ feet per second) and the scouring velocity of the sand trap 6.8 feet per second.

At the entrance to the canal six emergency gates are so placed that they could be quickly closed in case of a sudden rise in the river and a failure of the regulator gates to operate, and the sand trap or upper part of the canal is provided with a 300-foot spillway to care for floods.

The plan also shows a diversion on the north side of the river. This north-side turnout is to be used for the purpose of diverting sufficient water for the irrigation of about 1,200 acres of land situated on the north side of the river and about 12 miles below the dam.

Summary of quantities.

EXCAVATION.

	Below low water.		Above low water.	
	Solid rock.	Sand, silt.	Solid rock.	Loose rock, sand.
	Cubic yards.	*Cubic yards.*	*Cubic yards.*	*Cubic yards*
North side head works	20		750	250
South side head works	370		11,020	3,600
Main dam		4,700		
North Canal sand traps			2,120	3,180
South Canal sand traps			30,000	10,000
Total	390	4,700	43,890	17,030
Total excavation				60,920

CONCRETE.

	Below low water.	Above low water.
	Cubic yards.	*Cubic yards.*
North end works		1,020
South end works		2,057
Main dam and 2 aprons	3,578	1,960
North side canal works		53
South side canal works		510
Total	3,578	5,600

Total concrete, 9,178 cubic yards.

Talus grouted, 1,227 cubic yards.

Paving and riprap, probably none.

Sheet piling, 340 feet of 6 by 12 inch by 12-foot tongued and grooved, 25,000 feet b. m., 4,100 linear feet.

Hydraulic gates, five 2½ by 5 cast iron, sixteen 4 by 5 cast iron, one 3 by 5 cast iron.

Screw gates, six 4 by 5 cast iron, seven 2 by 5 cast iron, one 3 by 5 cast iron.

Emergency gates, six 7 by 5.5 wood, one 4 by 5.5 wood.

Total weight of gates, 20,100 pounds.

SANTAN DIVERSION DAM.

[Taken from report of C. R. Olberg, Nov. 25, 1914.]

LOCATION.

This dam is located about 2 miles east of Sacaton, immediately below the heading of the flood canal which was constructed by the Reclamation Service on the north bank of the Gila River.

PHYSICAL CONDITIONS OF THE SITE.

At this point the flood channel was 1,700 feet in width at the time the above report was made, but the south bank has since washed out, leaving the channel about 2,200 feet wide.

On the north side the bank is a high rocky butte, while the bank on the south side is about 8 or 10 feet in height.

The channel is narrower here than at other points in this vicinity and the rocky point would furnish all the rock needed for the construction of the dam.

Map No. 62 shows the topography of the site and the location of the proposed dam and headworks. Map No. 64 shows a cross section of the river channel on the center line of the dam.

DATA PERTAINING TO THE DAM SITE.

	Feet.
Elevation of bed of Gila River	1,286
Elevation of deck present United States Reclamation Service headgate	1,296
Elevation of floor present United States Reclamation Service headgate	1,284.6
Elevation top of riprap at United States Reclamation Service headgate	1,305
Elevation top of south bank	1,294
Approximate slope of river bed 1.9 feet in 1,100=0.00173 width of old channel	1,700
Depth of flood water taken from high-water marks found by survey	7.1

Assuming $n=0.02$, $c=101$, $V=11.15$, $Q=134,580$ second-feet. However, 150,000 second-feet was used in the design. This gives a height of 7.8 feet over the crest.

TYPE OF DAM.

The deep sandy foundation requires a floating or Indian weir type of dam and the section shown on plan No. 63 was designed accordingly.

A dam 3 feet high is found to be sufficient to divert water to the existing Santan flood canal and to the proposed canal from the south end of the dam to the Little Gila.

DESIGN.

The formulæ of W. G. Bligh in his Practical Design of Irrigation Works were used in the design of this dam and are the same as were used in the design of the Florence diversion dam already described in this report, hence will not be repeated here.

The dimensions arrived at by the use of the formulæ and somewhat modified by practical consideration are as follows:

Length of upstream apron, 25 feet; length of downstream apron, 35 feet, including base of weir, which is 3.5 feet; breadth of talus, 55 feet; sheet piling, 15 feet below concrete; thickness of base at toe of weir, 2 feet; thickness of upstream apron, 1 foot reinforced concrete and 1 foot clay puddle; thickness of downstream apron, 2 feet to 1 foot 6 inches reinforced concrete; talus, 3 feet to 1 foot 6 inches; curtain walls, 3 feet by 1 foot 6 inches; width of weir on top, 1 foot 6 inches.

The weir and impervious aprons are to be of 1:2:4 reinforced concrete and the headworks also of reinforced concrete.

Unit costs.

Cement at Colton	$1.40
Railroad freight to Casa Grande	1.00
Team freight	.60
Total (per barrel)	3.00
Lumber at San Pedro	14.00
Railroad freight	11.50
Team freight	4.50
Total (per M)	30.00
Reinforcing steel at San Pedro	.0175
Railroad freight	.0083
Team freight and handling	.0042
Total (per pound)	.03
Sand (per cubic yard	1.00
Stone (per cubic yard)	1.00
Concrete, 1:2:4 (per cubic yard):	
Cement	4.38
Sand	.41
Stone	1.23
Mixing and placing	1.50
Total	7.50
Form work (per cubic yard)	1.40
Sheet piling (per linear foot)	4.85

ESTIMATE OF BANK PROTECTION AT SOUTH END OF SANTAN DAM, AT POINT OF RECENT EROSION.

The length of dam will be 1,850 feet, or 150 feet longer than estimated in 1914.

The bank protection downstream will consist of 100 feet of 12 by 12 inches by 24 feet reinforced concrete sheet piling extending 8 feet above the present bed of the river and backed by an earth fill 10 feet wide on top with 1½ to 1 slope. Beyond this extends 500 feet of rock filled timber cribs 8 feet high by 6 feet wide of 8 by 8 timbers, resting on the sand at the low-water level and protected from under cutting by 6 by 12 inches by 16 feet wood sheet piling.

Above the dam the protection will consist of 200 feet of concrete sheet piling 20 feet long, extending 11 feet above the stream bed or 8 feet above the crest of the dam, also backed by an earth fill 8 feet high. Beyond this will be 1,200 feet of rock-fill crib 11 feet high by

8 feet wide, and beyond this 1,200 feet of 30-foot wood piling 8 feet on centers with 11 feet above present bed of stream, faced with 44 strands of barbed wire 3 inches apart.

The concrete piling, reinforced with four ⅝-inch twist-steel rods, will cost as follows:

6,400 cubic feet concrete, at $0.25	$1,600
34,000 pounds steel ($2.60 plus $0.83 plus $0.25), at $0.0368	1,250
Forms (pipe wire, labor on steel, 6,400 feet), at $0.30	1,920
Driving, 6,400 feet, at $0.45	2,880
Total, 6,400 linear feet, at $1.20	7,650
Back fill, 1,460 cubic yards, at $0.25	365
Timber crib:	
Timber, 222,000 feet board measure, at $16 cost, plus $10.50 railroad, plus $7.50 team, plus $6 labor, at $40	8,880
Sheet piling, 92,000 feet board measure, at $16 cost, plus $10.50 railroad, plus $7.50 team, plus $20 driving, at $54	5,000
Rock fill, 3,025 cubic yards, at $2	6,050
Bolts and washers, 5,040 pounds, at $0.03, plus $0.01, plus $0.0025, at $0.0425	215
Pile and wire extension:	
4,500 linear feet 16 by 8 inch by 30 foot piles, at $0.16 cost, plus $0.13 railroad, plus $0.08 team, plus $0.20 driving, at $0.57	2,565
52,800 feet (10 miles), 3,600 pounds, barbed wire, at $0.032 cost, plus $0.01 railroad, plus $0.0025 team, plus $0.02 labor, at $0.0645	232
52,800 staples, 725 pounds, at $0.032 cost, plus $0.01 railroad, plus $0.0025 team, at $0.0445	42
Total cost	30,990
Engineering and contingencies	3,010
	34,000

Santan diversion dam (without bridge).

[Taken from report of C. R. Olberg, Nov. 25, 1914.]

Excavation	$5,730
Concrete (2,860 cubic yards, at $7.50)	21,450
Rear and fore aprons	30,000
Talus	17,610
Cut-off walls	10,000
Puddle	1,570
Sluice and head gates	6,000
Head works	1,250
Form work and lumber	4,000
Reinforcing steel	742
Plant, equipment, and installation	6,000
Camp	1,000
Office and overhead	7,920
Engineering and contingencies, 10 per cent	11,327
Estimated additional cost for increased length due to erosion by flood since estimate was made	15,000
Bank protection on south side	34,000
Total	173,599

DISTRIBUTION SYSTEM FOR IRRIGATION OF 80,000 ACRES.

DESCRIPTION AND OUTLINE.

In this estimate the main canal, the Pima, and the Picacho branches are considered to be lined with concrete. The remaining canals and sublaterals are unlined. Structures are considered to be constructed of reinforced concrete.

The main canal, starting from the Florence diversion dam, has been assumed to have a bottom width of 22 feet, side slope ½:1, depth 6 feet, and capacity of 1,000 second-feet. The Picacho branch has an assumed width of 6 feet on the bottom, 1:1 side slope, 5 feet depth, and 350 second-feet capacity. The Pima branch was given an average section of 5 feet bottom width, 1:1 side slope, 5 feet depth, capacity 500 second-feet.

The large capacity of the Pima branch results from the steep grade which could be given to this canal.

The large main distribution canals on the reservation have for the most part already been constructed, and only the actual cost of construction chargeable to the San Carlos project has been included in the estimate.

The distribution system as proposed and as assumed in this estimate is designed so that water will be delivered to each 160-acre tract at its highest point. It is considered that the farmer will build at his own expense any further or subsidiary ditches.

The laterals and sublaterals are assumed to be provided with suitable concrete turnout structures and wooden bridges. The bottom width of the laterals vary from 8 to 3 feet. The concrete lining for the main canal is figured as having a 4-inch thickness on sides and bottom. The lining for the Pima and Picacho branches is assumed to be 3 inches thick.

The estimate for the diversion dam on the reservation has been taken from a previous report by Mr. Olberg, submitted November 25, 1914. The instructions calling for this report called for an estimate of a combined bridge and weir across the Gila River on the Gila River Reservation. Estimates were submitted for the diversion weir without the superimposed bridge as well as the estimate for the combined structure. Should the Government decide to build this diversion dam it would be wise to include the bridge feature, since a bridge across the Gila is much needed by the Indians on the reservation, as well as by other persons. However, it is not considered in this estimate that the additional cost of a bridge structure is a proper charge against the San Carlos project. Subsequent to the date of submitting the above report several heavy floods have widened the river channel at the proposed diversion dam site, consequently the length of the dam must be increased to meet this new condition, and in the estimate given as already shown this necessary increased length has been taken into account.

In the calculations for the cost of excavation, the following unit costs were used. These unit costs include clearing and grubbing the right of way. Rock excavation, first class $1 per yard, loose rock and gravel, second class 50 cents per yard; earth excavation 20 cents per yard.

The unit cost of concrete lining was assumed at $12.50 per cubic yard in place, including necessary excavation and back fill. Reinforced concrete for structures was assumed to cost $24 per cubic yard in place.

The cost data for the distribution system was obtained by first laying out on the maps made in the course of this investigation as already related, a tentative distribution system, and the necessary lengths of canals, number of structures, etc., were determined in this manner. While it is possible that in the event of the construction of the San Carlos project the location of the distribution system will depend upon an adjudication or upon other contingences, yet it is believed that the possible changes in the distribution system would not materially affect these costs.

In the following estimate of distribution costs the main canal, the Pima and Picacho branches are assumed to be lined with concrete. With the canals thus protected it was considered that the seepage and evaporation losses would amount to 20 per cent of the available supply at the intake, while if the main canals were left unlined the losses would amount to 30 per cent.

In the final summary of costs this alternative is shown:

Detailed cost of the project distribution system.

Item	Cost	Total
Main Canal (concrete lined); length, 78,000 feet; b = 22 feet; d = 6 feet; side slopes, ½:1; capacity, 1,000 second-feet; lining, 4 inches thick:		
Excavation for canal and drains, etc	$204,000	
Lining	390,000	
Structures	12,000	
Bridges and culverts	8,000	
Engineering and contingencies (10 per cent)	61,400	
		$675,400
Picacho Branch Canal (lined); length, 39,000 feet; b = 6; d = 5; side slopes, 1:1; capacity, 350 second-feet; lining, 3 inches thick:		
Excavation	14,400	
Lining	117,000	
Structures	9,000	
Bridges and culverts	5,000	
Engineering and contingencies (10 per cent)	14,540	
		159,940
Pima Branch Canal (lined); length, 72,000 feet; b = 5; d = 5; side slopes, 1:1; capacity, 500 second-feet; lining, 3 inches thick:		
Excavation	26,620	
Lining	198,000	
Structures	28,500	
Bridges and culverts	15,000	
Engineering and contingencies (10 per cent)	26,812	
		294,932
Distributors and laterals of the Florence-Casa Grande district:		
O. T. Canal (unlined), 58,000 feet—		
Excavation, extension, cleaning, widening	9,200	
Excavation of laterals	5,600	
Structures, concrete	16,200	
Bridges, culverts, etc	5,000	
Engineering and contingencies (10 per cent)	3,600	
		39,600
Main laterals, total length, 182,000 feet; b = 8 feet; d = 3; side slopes, 1½:1:		
Excavation	76,000	
Structures	56,700	
Bridges and culverts	10,000	
Engineering and contingencies (10 per cent)	14,270	
		156,070
Sublaterals, total length 355,400 feet, or 67 miles:		
Excavation	36,800	
Structures	43,500	
Bridges and culverts	5,000	
Engineering and contingencies (10 per cent)	8,542	
		93,962
Total cost, Florence-Casa Grande distribution system		290,532

Item	Cost	Total
Distributors and laterals of the reservation:		
Blackwater district—		
Excavation, main laterals	$11,800	
Structures, main laterals	10,200	
Excavation, sublaterals	2,400	
Structures, sublaterals	2,100	
Bridges, culverts, etc	2,500	
Engineering and contingencies, 10 per cent	2,900	
		$31,900
Sacaton Flat district—		
Enlarging and cleaning present canal	8,800	
Excavation, sublaterals	2,280	
Bridges, culverts, etc	3,000	
Structures	1,500	
Engineering and contingencies, 10 per cent	1,558	
		17,138
Agency district, actual cost chargeable against San Carlos project—		
Excavation	4,918	
Structures	10,829	
Bridges, culverts, etc	800	
Engineering superintendence	2,200	
		18,747
Casa Blanca district actual costs chargeable against San Carlos project: Excavation (principally) to date		23,900
Main canal—		
Excavation unfinished	17,400	
Structures including turnout	9,000	
Bridges and culverts	1,000	
Engineering and contingencies, 10 per cent	3,000	
		54,300
Main laterals—		
Excavation unfinished laterals	53,520	
Structures	21,970	
Bridges, spillways	9,630	
Engineering and contingencies, 10 per cent	8,512	
		93,632
Sublaterals—		
Excavation	24,100	
Structures	19,400	
Bridges, spillways, culverts	4,900	
Engineering and contingencies, 10 per cent	4,840	
		53,240
Connection canal, Little Gila to Gila River—		
Excavation	3,720	
Structures	5,500	
Bridges	750	
Engineering and contingencies, 10 per cent	997	
		10,967
Connection canal, Gila River to Little Gila—		
Excavation	6,310	
Bridges and flume	600	
Engineering and contingencies, 10 per cent	691	
		7,601
Santan flood canal and distribution system cost to date chargeable to the San Carlos project—		
Excavation	48,242	
Structures	34,095	
Bridges, etc	2,646	
Engineering and etc	3,650	
		88,633
Total cost reservation distribution system		376,158

ADDITIONAL COST TO PROJECT (PURCHASE OF WATER RIGHTS).

In the construction of the San Carlos project the water rights effected would either have to be bought outright or a portion of the stored water would have to be distributed to satisfy them. This subject has been fully discussed in the body of the report and it is needless to make repetition here.

Without an adjudication it is extremely difficult to place a figure on the value of water rights in the territory affected by the San Carlos project. It is considered, however, that the only tangible basis upon which to estimate the value of these rights is to use only the class A lands, or those which are under irrigation at present and which have been continuously irrigated for some time. Under the irrigation conditions now obtaining it may be assumed that a water right in this territory entitles the owners to sufficient water for the irrigation of at least one grain crop. Taking this into consideration, together with the value of the reclaimedd land and the distribution system, it is assumed; for the purpose of this report, that a water right in this district is worth $50 per acre.

On the reservation there were under irrigation by the use of the water of the Gila River at the time of this survey (1914) 14,356 acres. In the Florence-Casa Grande district there were under irrigation at the same time 7,563.4 acres, making a total of 21,919 acres that may be said to have rights under the Florence diversion.

Figuring that these rights are worth $50 per acre to the project, the value settled on above, then the additional cost of the San Carlos project for water rights would be $1,095,950.

In this cost, as is thus previously deduced, it has been considered that the pro rata costs should be equally divided between the Indian land and the private land, and that the cost of the irrigation of any one acre should be pro rated from the total cost of irrigation of the entire acreage coming under the project.

PERCENTAGE OF CONVEYED WATER LOST IN CANALS.

Numerous investigations have been made of canal losses by seepage and evaporation, and a review of the results of these investigations would point to the effect that the quantities of water lost from different canals, and even from different sections of the same canals, are so variable that no general rule can be adduced.

These investigations prove, however, that seepage losses from unlined canals are excessive and the need or value of cement lining is strongly brought out.

On the Salt River project, where soil and climatic conditions are similar to those obtaining in the Florence district, the evaporation and seepage losses are very high. According to Mr. C. H. Fitch, manager Salt River project, from 33 to 45 per cent of the water diverted at the Granite Reef diversion dam is lost by seepage and evaporation.

Canals carrying silt-laden waters have a considerable less loss from seepage than other canals which carry only clear water, and it is also noticeable that these losses grow less as the canal is used, and, in a few instances, it has been observed that the continued deposition of silt has made an absolutely impervious canal lining.

Mr. A. P. Davis, in Water Supply Paper, No. 73, estimates the amount of silt deposited in the Salt River Reservoir to be approximately 1,000 acre-feet per year, which amount by comparison would show that the Gila River carries four times as much silt as does the Salt River. It therefore seems reasonable to assume that seepage losses in unlined canals of the proposed San Sarlos project would not be as heavy as occurs along the Salt River, and taking this fact and all other things into consideration it is concluded that 30 per cent loss for unlined canals between the diversion dam and the land is a fair estimate and this assumption has been used in this report.

For lined canals the Army board assumed a loss of 20 per cent between the diverting dam and the land. A study of the available data covering losses in lined canals would seem to indicate that this percentage is a very liberal estimate, and it is believed that these losses would be somewhat less than 20 per cent in the lined canals. Inasmuch as the short laterals of the distribution system are not to be lined some heavier losses may occur there, so this would probably compensate for the smaller losses in the main canals. At any rate it is believed that the 20 per cent seepage and evaporation loss as adopted by the Army board is a safe estimate and has been accepted for purpose of calculation in this report.

Total Cost of Project.

In the estimate of the minimum cost concrete lining was figured for the main canals above the reservation, but not for the ditches of the distribution system. It appears useless to speculate upon the cost of lined canals and ditches for the distribution system on the reservation. Practically all of the main canals for the distribution system on the reservation have already been constructed, while the distribution system itself for 12,000 acres of land of the 35,000 to come under the project also has been constructed and in operation. Twelve miles of the Little Gila River is to be utilized as a part of the reservation distribution system. To backfill these present canals to make suitable cross sections for them and then line with concrete and to change the structures to meet these new requirements would cost more than the resultant gain.

In the Florence-Casa Grande section of the area coming under the project, the ditches and canals would have to be excavated and concrete lining may be advisable. In the minimum cost, concrete lined distribution systems were not considered for either the Florence or the reservation distribution system, as it hardly seemed fair to tax the Indians with the increased Florence cost when it was impractical for them to have the lined system. Another angle to this is that the distribution system on the reservation costs more than the Florence distribution system, so that lined canals in the Florence district would offset the overcost of the reservation.

SUMMARY OF COSTS OF THE SAN CARLOS PROJECT.

The following summaries of costs under the various interpretations of the meaning of maximum and minimum costs show the total costs as well as the costs per acre, the amount of the equal annual payments without interest and with 3 per cent compound interest.

MAXIMUM COST OF SAN CARLOS PROJECT.

Assumed draft, 300,000 acre-feet; duty, 3 acre-feet; canal losses, 20 per cent; Indian land, 35,000 acres; private land, 45,000 acres:

Impounding dam, including flow damages	$3,384,370.00
Florence diversion dam	142,622.00
Santan diversion dam	173,599.00
Main canal (lined)	675,400.00
Picacho branch (lined)	159,940.00
Pima branch (lined)	294,932.00
Florence-Casa Grande distribution (unlined)	290,532.00
Reservation distribution (unlined)	376,158.00
Total	5,497,533.00
Cost per acre	68.72
Assuming this amount to be paid in 20 equal payments, without interest, each payment will be	3.44
With interest at 3 per cent, compounded annually, each payment will be	4.62
Including the cost of water rights at $50 per acre for the 21,919 acres, the total cost will be	6,593,503.00
Cost per acre	82.42
Each of 20 equal annual payments, without interest	4.12
Each of 20 equal annual payments, with 3 per cent compound interest	5.53

MINIMUM COST OF SAN CARLOS PROJECT.

Assumed draft, 250,000 acre-feet; duty, 4 acre-feet; canal losses, 20 per cent; Indian lands, 35,000 acres; private land, 15,000 acres:

Impounding dam, including flow damages	$3,384,370.00
Florence diversion dam	128,360.00
Santan diversion dam	173,599.00
Main canal (lined)	606,170.00
Pima	334,680.00
Florence-Casa Grande distribution (unlined)	84,240.00
Reservation	376,158.00
Total cost	5,087,577.00
Cost per acre	101.75
Assuming this amount to be paid in 20 equal payments, without interest, each payment will be	5.09
With interest at 3 per cent, compounded annually, each annual payment will be	6.83
Including the cost of water rights at $50 per acre for 21,919 acres, the total cost will be	6,183,527.00
Cost per acre	123.67
Each of 20 equal payments, without interest	6.18
Each of 20 equal annual payments, with 3 per cent compound interest	8.29

Table of first costs and annual charges (including water rights).

	Without interest.		3 per cent compound interest.	
	Maximum.	Minimum.	Maximum.	Minimum.
Total cost	$6,183,527	$6,593,503	$6,183,527	$6,593,503
Cost per acre	123.67	82.42	123.67	82.42
Annual payment	6.18	4.12	8.29	5.53
Operation and maintenance	1.50	1.50	1.50	1.50
Total	7.68	5.62	9.79	7.03
Desilting	6.39	4.00	6.39	4.00
Operation and maintenance	1.50	1.50	1.50	1.50
Total	7.89	5.50	7.89	5.50
Annual payment	6.18	4.12	8.29	5.53
Operation and maintenance	1.50	1.50	1.50	1.50
Desilting	6.39	4.00	6.39	4.00
Total	14.07	9.62	16.18	11.03

Cost of San Carlos Project Under Alternative Assumptions.

FIRST ALTERNATIVE.

Draft, 300,000 acre-feet; duty, 3 acre-feet; canal losses, 30 per cent; Indian land, 35,000 acres; private land, 35,000 acres. This is the same as in the minimum cost, except that the main canals are unlined.

Total cost	$5,016,259.00
Cost per acre	71.66
Each of 20 equal annual payments, without interest	3.58
Each of 20 equal annual payments, with 3 per cent compound interest	4.82
Total cost, including water rights	6,078,209.00
Cost per acre	87.32
Each of 20 equal annual payments, without interest	4.37
Each of 20 equal annual payments, with 3 per cent compound interest	5.86

SECOND ALTERNATIVE.

Draft, 250,000 acre-feet; duty, 3 acre-feet; canal losses, 20 per cent; Indian land, 35,000 acres; private land, 31,667 acres. This is the same as in the maximum cost, except that the duty is 3 acre-feet, instead of 4 acre-feet, and the cost of the distribution canals reduced on account of smaller draft.

Total cost	$5,058,105.00
Cost per acre	75.87
Each of 20 equal annual payments, without interest	3.79
Each of 20 equal annual payments, with 3 per cent compound interest	5.08
Total cost, including water rights	6,154,055.00
Cost per acre	92.31
Each of 20 equal annual payments, without interest	4.62
Each of 20 equal annual payments, with 3 per cent compound interest	6.18

In comparing the cost per acre under alternatives (1) with unlined canals, and the cost per acre under the minimum cost with lined canals it is seen that the concrete lined canals would effect a considerable saving owing to the fact that a greater acreage could be irrigated with lined canals.

While it is difficult to foretell what the evaporation and seepage losses will be, yet since no greater difference in cost is shown and considering the advantages of lined canals especially with respect to maintenance, it is believed that concrete lining should be used.

Operation and Maintenance.

The cost of operation and maintenance placed at $1.50 per acre per year by the Army board appears to be a satisfactory and liberal estimate. A review of the operation costs on the United States reclamation projects, as submitted in the annual reports of the Reclamation Service, shows that with a few exceptions the projects at present delivering water to the land are operated at a cost slightly less than the above assumed for the San Carlos.

The plan of having the payments for the project extend over a period of 20 years is considered an advisable one. This scheme, as pointed out by the Army board, would not burden the farmers too heavily during the initial stages of development under the project.

As previously mentioned, there arises considerable doubt as to the possibility, under present conditions, of performing desilting operations at a cost of 5 cents per cubic yard. It is recognized, however, that by the time desilting is necessary it is quite probable that new methods will have been evolved or present ones perfected so that desilting can be performed at a cost within the estimate of the Army board.

Alternative Projects.

The foregoing costs are based upon the assumption that the San Carlos Storage Reservoir would be included in the project. If, however, the San Carlos Reservoir is not constructed in the immediate future, other means should be found to supply water for the lands belonging to the Pima Indians on the Gila River Indian Reservation.

The irrigation of the Florence-Caca Grande section and the Gila River Reservation can be accomplished without the San Carlos Reservoir by the construction of the two diversion dams at Florence and Santan. The project would, however, be based upon a supply of water for one crop per year instead of a full supply basis.

The actual amount of water available during the eight months between October and May, based upon the mean low-water flow and a maximum diversion of 1,000 second-feet, is 193,400 acre-feet.

With unlined canals the percentage of loss in the distribution system would be the same as that assumed in the previous calculation, that is 30 per cent, leaving 135,380 acre-feet to apply upon the land.

It has been demonstrated that to successfully produce one crop of grain in the vicinity of Florence and the Gila River Indian Reservation a duty of 1.5 acre-feet is required. On this basis a total of 90,000 acres of land could be irrigated.

With a view, however, to the eventual construction of the San Carlos Dam and the adoption of an 80,000-acre project with perennial irrigation, it is deemed wise to limit the area to that amount.

Under this plan it will be necessary to adjudicate the water rights appurtenant to the land now under irrigation in the vicinity of Florence and on the Gila Indian Reservation.

The construction of the diversion dam and the distribution systems under this plan would not differ materially from that under the plan including the storage reservoir, as the canals were originally designed to carry the flood waters entering the Gila below the San Carlos Dam.

The following costs have been determined to apply to the construction of the flood water diversion project under these assumptions:

Assumed draft, 193,400 acre-feet; duty, 1.5 acre-feet; canal losses, 30 per cent for unlined canals; Indian lands to be irrigated, 35,000 acres; private land, 45,000 acres:

Florence diversion dam	$142,622.00
Santan diverison dam	173,599.00
Main canal, unlined	461,692.00
Picacho branch	56,056.00
Pima branch	131,230.00
Florence-Casa Grande distribution, unlined	290,532.00
Reservation distribution, unlined	376,158.00
Total cost	1,631,889.00
Cost per acre	20.40

It would probably be advisable to have cement-lined canals to connect with the reservation distribution system, and in this case the cost items would be as follows:

Florence diversion dam	$142,622.00
Santan diversion dam	173,599.00
Main canal, lined	675,400.00
Pima branch, lined	294,932.00
Picacho branch, unlined	56,056.00
Florence-Casa Grande distribution system	290,532.00
Reservation distribution system	376,158.00
Total cost	2,009,299.00
Cost per acre, for 80,000 acres	25.11

PROJECT WITH DIVERSION DAMS AND MAIN CANAL.

The cost of the diversion dam and main canals alone is estimated to be as follows:

Florence diversion dam	$142,622.00
Santan diversion dam	173,599.00
Main canal, lined	675,400.00
Pima branch, lined	294,932.00
Picacho branch, unlined	56,056.00
Connecting canal, Pima to Gila River	10,967.00
Connecting canal, Gila to Little Gila	7,601.00
Total	1,361,177.00
Cost per acre, for 80,000 acres	17.01
If confined to the 21,919 acres now irrigated, the cost per acre would be	62.10

RESERVATION PROJECT.

A one-crop project for the reservation alone would have cost items as follows:

Santan diversion dam	$173, 599. 00
Reservation distribution system	365, 191. 00
Total cost	538, 790. 00
Cost per acre, for 35,000 acres	15, 39

With only a diversion dam at Santan, the connecting canal from the Little Gila to the main Gila would not be necessary. No lands could be irrigated in the vicinity of Blackwater; however, the Casa Blanca Canal system could be extended to serve an additional 3,000 acres to make up for the area which under the regular San Carlos project was to be irrigated near Blackwater. It is considered that the costs incident to this change would remain the same.

Of the above total cost, $131,280 has already been expended, and therefore, in order to complete the system, a further expenditure of $407,510 must be made.

APPENDIXES B AND C

APPENDIX B—GRATUITIES CONVERTED INTO REIMBURSABLES BY THE ACT OF AUGUST 1, 1914

APPENDIX C—COMPILATION OF LAWS RELATING TO INDIAN IRRIGATION PROJECTS

APPENDIX B.

GRATUITIES CONVERTED INTO REIMBURSABLES BY THE ACT OF AUGUST 1, 1914.

Mr. MERITT. The following are the costs for the various Indian projects, expended from the appropriation, "Irrigation, Indian reservations," from 1884 to June 30, 1914, same having been made reimbursable by the act of August 1, 1914.

The amounts shown under "Billings office," "Southern California and general," and "Headquarters, Albuquerque" and "Miscellaneous investigations" have either been pro rated to the projects since July 1, 1914, or are being allocated as fast as the expenditures can be analyzed and audited by the field cost accountant.

Costs for the various Indian projects.

DISTRICT NO. 1.	
Ahtanum, Wash	$48,341.19
Colville, Wash	2,567.84
Fort Bidwell, Calif	68.48
Hoopa Valley, Calif	953.23
Klamath, Oreg	29,952.90
Muckleshoot, Wash	1,208.49
Round Valley, Calif	2,554.20
Satus, Wash	1,654.19
Simcoe-Toppenish, Wash	632.37
Spokane, Wash	102.08
Umatilla, Oreg	1,182.40
Warm Springs, Oreg	6,259.37
Yakima, Wash	110,606.63
Quinaielt, Wash	266.95
DISTRICT NO. 2.	
Carson allotments, Nev	77,650.00
Carson School, Nev	1,827.01
Coeur d'Alene, Idaho	247.05
Fort Hall, Idaho	19,453.24
Lapwai, Idaho	3,306.74
Lemhi, Idaho	2,152.31
Lovelocks, Nev	116.92
McDermitt, Nev	5,629.98
Moapa, Nev	10,229.67
Pyramid Lake, Nev	39,445.10
Shivwits, Utah	1,444.28
Uintah, Utah	124,754.59
Walker River, Nev	111,954.75
Western Shoshone, Nev	39,508.28
DISTRICT NO. 3.	
Billings Office, Mont	$3,498.03
Crow, Mont	143,050.59
Flathead, Mont	17,314.58
Fort Belknap, Mont	9,052.61
Fort Peck, Mont	10,992.66
Fort Shaw, Mont	1,382.41
Pine Ridge, S. Dak	8,037.73
Rosebud, S. Dak	749.67
Tongue River, Mont	73,109.62
Wind River, Wyo	75,572.23
DISTRICT NO. 4.	
Agua Caliente, Calif	2,752.84
Ak Chin, Calif	18.44
Augustine, Calif	25.58
Bishop, Calif	157.15
Cabezon, Calif	370.44
Cahuilla, Calif	6,011.51
Campo, Calif	4,154.15
Camp McDowell, Ariz	27,609.99
Capitan Grande, Calif	2,261.72
Coachella Valley, Calif	360.81
Colorado River, Ariz	16,527.70
Cosmit, Calif	31.17
Fort Apache, Ariz	14,358.96
Fort Mojave, Ariz	14,364.97
Friant, Calif	185.52
Garden of Eden, Calif	870.06
Gila Bend, Ariz	1,830.15
Inaja, Calif	35.93

DISTRICT NO. 4—continued.

Inyo & Mono, Calif	$226.67
La Jolla, Calif	5,725.41
Los Conejos, Calif	66.37
Los Coyotes, Calif	69.14
Martinez, Calif	26,047.80
Mesa Grande, Calif	3,350.06
Mission, Calif	1,924.71
Mission Creek, Calif	320.20
Morongo, Calif	40,468.45
Owens Valley, Calif	4,303.91
Pala, Calif	70,797.98
Palm Springs, Calif	2,375.57
Papago (nomadic) surveys, Ariz	1,006.12
Papago Indian villages, Ariz	1,045.63
Papago, San Xavier, Ariz	20,167.43
Pechanga, Calif	284.00
Perris, Calif	3,179.74
Pima General, Ariz	41,275.58
Agency	25,626.18
Blackwater	6,105.50
Casa Blanca	10,955.69
Little Gila	13,581.24
Gila River investigation	1,480.05
Gila River surveys	18,215.43
Sacaton	5,408.57
Rice School, Ariz	71.83
Rincon, Calif	41,366.52
Salt River, Ariz	5,955.75
San Carlos, Ariz	53,449.85
San Manuel, Calif	154.56
San Pascual, Calif	2,249.47
Santa Rosa, Calif	1,479.43
Santa Ynez, Calif	3,118.52
Santa Ysabel, Calif	299.37
Soboba, Calif	22,443.43
Sherman Institute, Calif	1,437.27
Sycuan, Calif	2,443.42
Torres, Calif	4,722.50
Torres and Cabezon, Calif	11,620.53
Tule River, Calif	7,802.28
Tuolumne, Calif	5,211.78
Volcan, Calif	6,403.20
Yuma, Calif	2,746.18
Southern California and general	8,318.96

DISTRICT NO. 5.

Albuquerque School, New Mexico	34.80
Black Creek, Ariz	239.81

DISTRICT NO. 5—continued.

Black Falls, Ariz	$521.55
Blue Canyon, Ariz	311.66
Crown Point, N. Mex	18.55
Crystal, Ariz	85.76
Fort Lewis, Ariz	480.69
Hogback, N. Mex	204,050.86
Leupp, Ariz	1,509.65
Mescalero, N. Mex	7,979.58
Pueblo Bonito, N. Mex	341.21
Navajo and Moqui, Ariz	97,637.89
Red Lake, Ariz	1,005.06
Seven Lakes, N. Mex	1,448.81
Tohatchi, Ariz	44.69
Tuba, Ariz	30,527.85
Wheatfields, Ariz	3,181.05
Acoma, N. Mex	919.48
Cochiti, N. Mex	18,451.40
Keams Canyon, Ariz	1,023.00
Isleta, N. Mex	3,925.42
Laguna, N. Mex	9,043.34
Laguna and Mesita, N. Mex	8,790.65
Laguna and Paguate, N. Mex	45.37
Jemez, N. Mex	1,723.88
Pueblos, miscellaneous, N. Mex	798.40
Nambe, N. Mex	27.47
Santa Ana, N. Mex	441.24
Santa Clara, N. Mex	3,226.65
Sandia, N. Mex	1,378.33
Santo Domingo, N. Mex	424.52
San Felipe, N. Mex	3,816.32
San Ildefonso, N. Mex	20,763.70
Santa Fe, N. Mex	3,422.74
Taos, N. Mex	3,795.44
Tesuque, N. Mex	502.43
Zia, N. Mex	149.42
Diminished Southern Ute, Colo	4,370.31
Havasupai, Ariz	1,614.05
Jicarilla Apache, N. Mex	3,653.34
Southern Ute, Colo	162,060.49
Zuni, N. Mex	539,755.46
Headquarters Albuquerque, N. Mex	9,876.80
Western Navajo, Ariz	12,197.05
Ponca, Okla	297.78
Miscellaneous investigations, including chief engineer's office expenses from the year 1884 to June 30, 1914	87,613.93
Total	2,817,582.11

APPENDIX C.

Mr. MERITT. Mr. Chairman, in compliance with the request of the committee, the following is a compilation of the various laws relating to the Indian irrigation projects on Indian reservations:

ARIZONA.

COLORADO RIVER.

Act March 2, 1867 (14 Stat., 514): For expense of collecting and locating the Colorado River Indians in Arizona, on a reservation set apart for them by section first, act of March third, eighteen hundred and sixty-five, including the expense of constructing a canal for irrigating said reservation, fifty thousand dollars.

Act July 27, 1868 (15 Stat. 222): For completing the construction of irrigating canal on the Colorado Reservation in Arizona, fifty thousand dollars.

Act May 29, 1872 (17 Stat., 188): Collecting and locating the Colorado River Indians in Arizona.

For completing the construction of the irrigating canal on the Colorado Reservation in Arizona, twenty thousand dollars.

Act April 21, 1904 (33 Stat., 224): SEC. 25. That in carrying out any irrigation enterprise which may be undertaken under the provisions of the reclamation act of June seventeenth, nineteen hundred and two, and which may make possible and provide for, in connection with the reclamation of other lands, the reclamation of all or any portion of the irrigable lands on the Yuma and Colorado River Indian reservations in California and Arizona, the Secretary of the Interior is hereby authorized to divert the waters of the Colorado River and to reclaim, utilize, and dispose of any lands in said reservations which may be irrigable by such works in like manner as though the same were a part of the public domain: *Provided*, That there shall be reserved for and allotted to each of the Indians belonging on the said reservations five acres of the irrigable lands. The remainder of the lands irrigable in said reservations shall be disposed of to settlers under the provisions of the reclamation act: *Provided further*, That there shall be added to the charges required to be paid under said act by settlers upon the unallotted Indian lands such sum per acre as in the opinion of the Secretary of the Inierior shall fairly represent the value of the unallotted lands in said reservations before reclamation; said sum to be paid in annual installments in the same manner as the charges under the reclamation act. Such additional sum per acre, when paid, shall be used to pay into the reclamation fund the charges for the reclamation of the said allotted lands, and the remainder thereof shall be placed to the credit of said Indians and shall be expended from time to time, under the direction of the Secretary of the Interior, for their benefit.

Act March 16, 1908 (35 Stat., 43): *Be it enacted by the Senate and House of Representatives of the United States of America in Congress assembled*, That, subject to the approval of the Secretary of the Interior, additional lands not exceeding forty acres in area, adjacent to its approved right of way in the Colorado River Indian Reservation, in the Territory of Arizona, be, and the same are hereby, granted for additional station grounds and terminal facilities to the Arizona and California Railway Company, a corporation organized under the laws of said Territory, subject to the payment by said company of full compensation therefor in the manner provided in section three of the act approved March second, eighteen hundred and ninety-nine, entitled "An act to provide for the acquiring of rights of way by railroad companies through Indian reservations, Indian lands, Indian allotments, and for other purposes": *Provided*, That such additional lands are granted subject to the right of the United States to cross the same and the works constructed thereon, with canals or water conduits of any kind or with roadways, or transmission lines for telephone, telegraph, or electric power, which may in the future be built by the United States across such lands; and the said company shall build and maintain at its own expense all structures that may be required at crossings, and in accepting this grant shall release the United States from all damages which may result from the construction and use of such crossings, canals, conduits, and lines.

Act April 4, 1910 (36 Stat., 273): For the construction of a pumping plant to be used for irrigation purposes on the Colorado River Reservation, together with the necessary canals and laterals, for the utilization of water in connection therewith, for the purpose of securing an appropriation of water for the irrigation of approximately one hundred and fifty thousand acres of land, fifty thousand dollars, to be reimbursed from the sale of the surplus lands of the reservation.

Act February 15, 1911 (36 Stat., 909): *Be it enacted by the Senate and House of Representatives of the United States of America in Congress assembled*, That the Chucawalla Development Company, a corporation organized under the laws of the State of California, its successors and assigns, be, and they are hereby authorized to construct, maintain, and operate a dam across the Colorado River at the mouth of Pyramid Canyon, known as "Bulls Head damsite," about twenty-two miles north of Fort Mohave, Mohave County, Arizona, and a portion of said site being located in Lincoln County, Nevada; also a diversion intake dam, ten feet high, to be located at or near Black Point, about twenty miles north and upstream from the town of Ehrenburg, Yuma County, Arizona, and about twenty miles north and above the town of Blythe, Riverside County, California, in accordance with the provisions of the act approved June twenty-third, nineteen hundred and ten, entitled "An act to amend an act entitled 'An act to regulate the construction of dams across navigable waters,' approved June twenty-first, nineteen hundred and six": *Provided*, That the actual construction of said dams shall be begun within two years and completed within five years from the date of the passage of this act: *And provided further*, That the actual construction of said dams shall not be commenced until the plans and specifications therefor shall have been presented to and approved by the Secretary of the Interior in addition to the requirements of the act approved June twenty-third, nineteen hundred and ten, entitled, "An act to amend an act entitled 'An act to regulate the construction of dams across navigable waters,' approved June twenty-first, nineteen hundred and six," and in approving the plans and specifications, the Secretary of the Interior may impose such conditions as to him shall seem proper for the protection of the public interests of Indians and of the United States.

SEC. 2. That the right to amend, alter, or repeal this act is hereby expressly reserved.

Act March 3, 1911 (36 Stat., 1063): The first proviso in section twenty-five of the Indian appropriation act, approved April twenty-first, nineteen hundred and four (33 Stat. L. 224), is hereby amended so that the first sentence in said proviso shall read as follows: "*Provided*, That there shall be reserved for and allotted to each of the Indians belonging on the said reservation ten acres of the irrigable lands;" and there is hereby appropriated the sum of eighteen thousand dollars, or so much thereof as may be necessary, to defray the cost of the irrigation of the increased allotments, for the fiscal year nineteen hundred and twelve: *Provided*, That the entire cost of irrigation of the allotted lands shall be reimbursed to the United States from any funds received from the sale of the surplus lands of the reservations or from any other funds that may become available for such purpose: *Provided further*, That in the event any allottee shall receive a patent in fee to an allotment of land irrigated under this project, before the United States shall have been wholly reimbursed as herein provided, then the proportionate cost of the project to be apportioned equitably by the Secretary of the Interior, shall become a first lien on such allotment, and the fact of such lien shall be recited on the face of each patent in fee issued and the amount of the lien set forth thereon, which said lien, however, shall not be enforced so long as the original allottee, or his heirs, shall actually occupy the allotment as a homestead, and the receipt of the Secretary of the Interior or of the officer, agent, or employee duly authorized by him for that purpose, for the payment of the amount assessed against any allotment as herein provided shall, when duly recorded by the recorder of deeds in the county wherein the land is located, operate as a satisfaction of such lien.

Act March 3, 1911 (36 Stat., 1081): *Be it enacted by the Senate and House of Representatives of the United States of America in Congress assembled*, That the Greeley-Arizona Irrigation Company, a corporation organized under the laws of Arizona, is hereby authorized to construct, maintain, and operate a diversion dam in and across the Colorado River at a place known as Head Gate Rock, near Parker, Yuma County, in the Territory of Arizona, in accordance with the provisions of the act approved June twenty-third,

nineteen hundred and ten, entitled "An act to amend an act entitled 'An act to regulate the construction of dams across navigable waters,' approved June twenty-first, nineteen hundred and six": *Provided*, That the actual construction of said dam shall be begun within two years and completed within four years from the date of the passage of this act: *And provided further*, That the actual construction of said dam shall not be commenced until the plans and specifications therefor shall have been presented to and approved by the Secretary of the Interior in addition to the requirements of the act approved June twenty-third, nineteen hundred and ten, entitled "An act to amend an act entitled 'An act to regulate the construction of dams across navigable waters,' approved June twenty-first, nineteen hundred and six," and, in approving the plans and specifications, the Secretary of the Interior may impose such conditions as to him shall seem proper for the protection of the public interests of Indians and the United States.

SEC. 2. That the right to alter, amend, or repeal this Act is hereby expressly reserved.

Act August 24, 1912 (37 Stat., 523): For continuing the construction of necessary channels and laterals for the utilization of water in connection with the pumping plant for irrigation purposes on the Colorado River Indian Reservation, Arizona, as provided in the act of April fourth, nineteen hundred and ten (Thirty-sixth Statutes at Large, page two hundred and seventy-three), for the purpose of securing an appropriation of water for the irrigation of approximately one hundred and fifty thousand acres of land and for maintaining and operating the pumping plant, thirty-five thousand dollars, reimbursable as provided in said act. (Act of April fourth, nineteen hundred and ten, volume thirty-six, page two hundred and seventy-three, section three.)

Act June 30, 1913 (38 Stat., 85): For completion of the construction of necessary channels and laterals for the utilization of water in connection with the pumping plant for irrigation purposes on the Colorado River Indian Reservation, Arizona, as provided in the act of April fourth, nineteen hundred and ten (36 Stat. L., 273), for the purpose of securing an appropriation of water for the irrigation of approximately one hundred and fifty thousand acres of land and for maintaining and operating the pumping plant, $25,000, reimbursable as provided in said act, and to remain available until expended.

Act August 1, 1914 (38 Stat., 587): For the construction and repair of necessary channels and laterals for the utilization of water in connection with the pumping plant for irrigation purposes on the Colorado River Indian Reservation, Arizona, as provided in the act of April fourth, nineteen hundred and ten (36 Stat. L., 273), for the purpose of securing an appropriation of water for the irrigation of approximately one hundred and fifty thousand acres of land and for maintaining and operating the pumping plant, $15,000, reimbursable as provided in said act, and to remain available until expended.

Joint resolution March 4, 1915 (38 Stat., 1228). Reenacted the last foregoing item for the fiscal year 1916.

Act May 18, 1916 (39 Stat., 129): For the construction and repair of necessary channels and laterals for the utilization of water in connection with the pumping plant for irrigation purposes on the Colorado River Indian Reservation, Arizona, as provided in the act of April fourth, nineteen hundred and ten (Thirty-sixth Statutes at Large, page two hundred and seventy-three), for the purpose of securing an appropriation of water for the irrigation of approximately one hundred and fifty thousand acres of land and for maintaining and operating the pumping plant, $15,000, reimbursable as provided in said act, and to remain available until expended.

Act March 2, 1917 (39 Stat., 974): For the construction and repair of necessary channels and laterals for the utilization of water in connection with the pumping plant for irrigation purposes on the Colorado River Indian Reservation, Arizona, as provided in the act of April fourth, nineteen hundred and ten (Thirty-sixth Statutes at Large, page two hundred and seventy-three), for the purpose of securing an appropriation of water for the irrigation of approximately one hundred and fifty thousand acres of land and for maintaining and operating the pumping plant, canals, and structures, $15,000, reimbursable as provided in said act, and to remain available until expended.

Act May 25, 1918 (40 Stat., 568): For continuing the construction of the pumping plant for irrigation purposes on the Colorado River Indian Reservation, Arizona, by the installation of additional pumping machinery, and for continuing the construction of the necessary canals and laterals for the utilization of water in connection therewith, as provided in the act of April fourth, nineteen hundred and ten (Thirty-sixth Statutes at Large, page two hundred and seventy-three), and for maintaining and operating the pumping plant, canals, and structures, $20,000, reimbursable as provided in said act; and for continuing the purpose of securing an appropriation of water for the irrigation of approximately one hundred and fifty thousand acres of land on said reservation by the conduct of surveys and the preparation of plans and estimates for a complete irrigation system to supply water to said land, $50,000, reimbursable from funds in the Treasury of the United States to the credit of the Indians of said reservation arising from the proceeds from the sale of town lots authorized by the act of April thirteenth, nineteen hundred and eight (Thirty-fifth Statutes at Large, page 77); in all, $70,000.

Act June 30, 1919 (41 Stat., 10): For continuing the construction of the pumping plant for irrigation purposes on the Colorado River Indian Reservation, Arizona, by the installation of a settling basin, $11,000, and for continuing the construction of the necessary canals and laterals for the utilization of water in connection with said pumping plant, as provided in the act of April 4, 1910 (Thirty-sixth Statutes at Large, page 273), $82,000, and for maintaining and operating the pumping plant, canals, and structures, $41,000, reimbusable as provided in said act; and for continuing the purpose of securing an appropriation of water for the irrigation of approximately one hundred and fifty thousand acres of land on said reservation by the conduct of surveys, and the preparation of plans, and estimates for a complete irrigation system to supply water to said land, $54,000, reimbursable from funds in the Treasury of the United

States to the credit of the Indians of said reservation arising from the proceeds from the sale of town lots authorized by the act of April 13, 1908 (Thirty-fifth Statutes at Large, page 77); in all, $188,000.

FORT APACHE.

Act June 30, 1919 (41 Stat., 11): The Secretary of the Interior is hereby authorized to withdraw from the Treasury of the United States the sum of $17,600 of any tribal funds on deposit to the credit of the Indians of the Fort Apache Reservation in Arizona, and to expend the same, in connection with an equal sum of the funds appropriated in this act for Indian school and agency buildings, for reconstructing, repairing, and improving the power plant and irrigation system on the Fort Apache Indian Reservation, Arizona: *Provided*, That the tribal funds so expended shall be reimbursed to the tribe by the Indians benefited under such rules and regulations as may be prescribed by the Secretary of the Interior: *And provided further*, That the sum of $17,600 of the amount appropriated in this act for Indian school and agency buildings is hereby set apart and reserved for this purpose.

FORT MOJAVE.

Act July 13, 1892 (27 Stat., 142): For support of Indian pupils * * * ; necessary repairs, buildings, fencing, and irrigation at Indian industrial school at Fort Mojave, Arizona, and for pay of superintendent of said school, at one thousand five hundred dollars per annum, thirty-two thousand five hundred dollars: *Provided*, That not more than ten thousand dollars of this amount shall be used for the erection and repairs of buildings.

Act April 21, 1904 (33 Stat., 212): * * * at the Indian School, Fort Mojave, Arizona, * * * one eighty-horsepower boiler for irrigation, one thousand six hundred dollars; * * *

Act March 3, 1905 (33 Stat., 1074): * * * at the Indian School, Fort Mojave, Arizona, * * * for power house and steam pumps, six thousand dollars; * * *

Act August 24, 1912 (37 Stat., 523): For constructing dike to protect allotments on the Fort Mojave Indian Reservation, twenty-five thousand dollars.

Act August 1, 1914 (38 Stat., 588): For maintaining, strengthening, and raising the dike constructed to protect the irrigable lands on the Fort Mojave Reservation, Arizona, from damage by floods, $5,000, reimbursable out of any funds of said Indians now or hereafter available.

Joint resolution March 4, 1915 (38 Stat., 1228) reenacted the item of August 1, 1914, for the fiscal year 1916.

Appropriations recapitulated.

July 13, 1892	(?)	August 1, 1914	$5,000
April 21, 1904	$1,600	March 4, 1915	5,000
March 3, 1905	6,000		
August 24, 1912	25,000	Total	42,600+

GILA RIVER.

Act February 15, 1897 (29 Stat., 527): An act to grant to the Hudson Reservoir and Canal Company, the right of way through the Gila River Indian Reservation.

Be it enacted by the Senate and House of Representatives of the United States of America in Congress assembled, That the Hudson Reservoir and Canal Company, a corporation created and existing under and by virtue of the laws of the Territory of Arizona, be, and the said corporation is hereby, authorized and empowered to locate, construct, own, maintain, and operate its main line of canal through and across the Indian reservation situated in the Territory of Arizona, known as the Gila River Reservation, occupied by the Pima, Maricopa, and Sacaton Indians, from a point on the northerly line of said reservation, running thence by the most practicable route to the southerly line of said reservation, and to construct, own, maintain, and operate such aqueducts, flumes, siphons, bridges, and other structures as may be necessary for the conveyance of water where the same can not be conveyed in the canal itself, and the development, utilization, and transmission of any power derived from the water so carried.

SEC. 2. That a right of way 50 feet in width on each side of said main canal is hereby granted to said Hudson Reservoir and Canal Company: *Provided*, That no part of the lands granted shall be used except in such manner and for such purposes only as shall be reasonably necessary for the construction and convenient operation of said canal and said other structures; but when any portion thereof shall cease to be so used, such portion shall revert to the tribe or tribes of Indians from which the same shall have been taken, or, in case they shall have ceased to occupy the same, to the United States: *And provided further*, That when any such lands shall be taken for the purposes aforesaid the consent of the occupants thereof shall be obtained in a manner satisfactory to the President of the United States.

SEC. 3. That before said canal or other structures shall be constructed through any lands held by individual occupants according to the laws, customs, and usages of any of the Indian tribes through which the same may be constructed, full compensation shall be made to such occupants for all property taken or damage done by reason of the construction of such canal or other structures, the amount of such compensation to be ascertained and determined in such manner as the Secretary of the Interior may direct, and to be subject to his final approval.

SEC. 4. That said company shall cause maps showing the route of its located line through said Indian reservation to be filed in the office of the Secretary of the Interior, and that said location shall be approved by the Secretary of the Interior before any grading or construction upon any section or part of said located line shall be begun: *Provided*, That said canal and other structures be located and constructed with a due regard for the rights of the Indians and especially so as not to interfere with their irrigating ditches.

SEC. 5. That the officers, servants, and employees of said company necessary to the construction, maintenance, management, and operation of the structures hereby authorized shall be allowed to reside while so engaged upon the lands herein granted, but subject to the provisions of the Indian intercourse laws, and such rules and regulations as may be established by the Secretary of the Interior in accordance with the said intercourse laws.

SEC. 6. That said company shall have the right to survey and locate its canal immediately after the passage of this act.

SEC. 7. That in connection with the said canal and its appurtenances said company shall have the right to erect, maintain, and use a telegraph or telephone line or both, and other appliances reasonably necessary or convenient for the construction, maintenance, and operation of the said canal and its appurtenances, but only within and upon the limits of the right of way hereby granted.

SEC. 8. That the said Hudson Reservoir and Canal Company shall accept this right of way upon the express condition, binding upon itself, its successors, and assigns, that they will neither aid, advise, nor assist in any effort looking toward changing or extinguishing the present tenure of the Indians in their lands, and will not attempt to secure from the Indian tribes any further grant of land or its occupancy than is hereinbefore provided: *Provided*, That the rights herein granted are upon the express condition that the grantee thereof, its successors or assigns shall at all times during the continuance of the grant furnish the Indians located under its canal along said right of way with water sufficient for all domestic and agricultural purposes, and purposes of irrigation on such just and reasonable terms and under such rules and regulations as shall be prescribed by the Secretary of the Interior.

SEC. 9. That Congress may at any time amend, alter, add to, or repeal this act.

Act July 1, 1898 (30 Stat., 594): For ascertaining the depth of the bedrock at a place on the Gila River in Gila County, Arizona, known as the Buttes, and particularly described in Senate Document numbered Twenty-seven, Fifty-fourth Congress, second session, and for ascertaining the feasibility, and estimating in detail the cost, of the construction of a dam across the river at that point for the purpose of irrigating the Sacaton Reservation, and for ascertaining the average daily flow of water in the river at that point, twenty thousand dollars, or so much thereof as may be necessary, the same to be expended by the Director of the United States Geological Survey, under the direction of the Secretary of the Interior: *Provided*, That nothing herein shall be construed as in any way committing the United States to the construction of said dam. And said director shall also ascertain and report upon the feasibility and cost of the Queen Creek project mentioned in said Senate Document.

Act March 3, 1905 (33 Stat., 1081): SEC. 10. For the construction of an irrigation system for developing and furnishing a water supply for the irrigation of the lands of the Pima Indians, in the vicinity of Sacaton, on the Gila River Indian Reservation, the sum of fifty thousand dollars to be expended under the direction of the Secretary of the Interior: *Provided*, That the total cost of the entire construction and installation of said irrigating system shall not exceed five hundred and forty thousand dollars: *Provided further*, That when said irrigation system is in successful operation and the Indians have become self-supporting the cost of operating the said system shall be equitably apportioned upon the lands irrigated and to the annual charge shall be added an amount sufficient to pay back into the Treasury the cost of the work within thirty years, suitable deduction being made for the amounts received from disposal of lands which now form a part of the said reservation.

Act June 21, 1906 (34 Stat., 333): For the construction of an irrigation system necessary for developing and furnishing a water supply for the irrigation of the lands of the Pima Indians in the vicinity of Sacaton, on the Gila River Indian reservation, two hundred and fifty thousand dollars, to be expended under the direction of the Secretary of the Interior: *Provided further*, That when said irrigation system is in successful operation and the Indians have become self-supporting, the cost of operating the said system shall be equitably apportioned upon the lands irrigated, and to the annual charge shall be added an amount sufficient to pay back into the Treasury the cost of the work within thirty years, suitable deduction being made for the amounts received from disposal of lands which now form a part of said reservation.

Act March 1, 1907 (34 Stat., 1022): That the Secretary of the Interior may, in his discretion, use such part of the three hundred thousand dollars heretofore appropriated for an irrigation system for the Pima Indians in the payment of such Indians' proportionate part of the construction of the Salt River project, and such funds may be transferred to the Reclamation fund, to be expended by that Service in accordance with its rules and regulations; the Indians to receive a credit upon the reclamation charge assessed against their lands under the Salt River project for the amount so transferred.

Act April 4, 1910 (36 Stat., 272) * * *: For continuing the work of constructing an irrigation system for the irrigation of the lands of the Pima Indians in the vicinity of Sacaton, in the Gila River Indian Reservation, seventy-five thousand dollars: *Provided*, That the amount hereby appropriated and all moneys heretofore, herein, or hereafter to be appropriated for this project, shall be repaid into the Treasury of the United States in accordance with the provisions of section ten of the act of March third, nineteen hundred and five. * * *

Act March 3, 1911 (36 Stat., 1062): For continuing the work of constructing an irrigation system for the irrigation of the lands of the Pima Indians in the vicinity of Sacaton, in the Gila River Indian Reservation, one hundred and twenty-five thousand dollars.

Act August 24, 1912 (37 Stat., 522): For maintenance, including purchase of electricity for irrigation wells already completed, and the completion of the lateral irrigating ditches thereunder in connection with the irrigation of the lands of the Pima Indians in the vicinity of Sacaton, in the Gila River Indian Reservation, fifteen thousand dollars: *Provided*, That the proportion of the cost of the irrigation project on the Gila River Indian Reservation heretofore and herein authorized to be paid from the public funds shall be repaid into the Treasury of the United States as and when funds may be available therefor: *Provided further*, That in the event any allottee shall receive a patent in fee to an allotment of land irrigated under this project before the United States shall have been wholly reimbursed as herein provided, then the proportionate cost of the project, to be apportioned equitably by the Secretary of the Interior, shall become a first lien on such allotment, and the fact of such lien shall be recited on the face of each patent in fee issued and the amount of the lien set forth therein, which said lien, however, shall not be enforced so long as the original allottee or his heirs shall own the allotment; and the receipt of the Secretary of the Interior, or of the officer, agent, or employee duly authorized by him for that purpose, for the payment of the amount assessed against any allotment as herein provided shall, when duly recorded by the recorder of deeds in the county wherein the land is located, operate as a satisfaction of such lien: *Provided*, That the Secretary of War be, and he hereby is, directed to convene a board of not less than three engineers of the Army of wide reputation and large experience to make the necessary examinations, borings, and surveys for the purpose of determining the reasonability and practicability of constructing a dam and reservoir at or in the vicinity of the Box Canyon, on the San Carlos Indian Reservation, known as the site of the proposed San Carlos Reservoir on the Gila River, Arizona, and the necessary irrigation works in connection therewith to provide for the irrigation of Indian, private, and public lands in the Gila River Valley, said board of engineers to submit to Congress the results of their examinations and surveys, together with an estimate of cost, with their recommendations thereon, at the earliest practicable date. The sum of fifteen thousand dollars, or so much thereof as may be necessary, is hereby appropriated, out of any money in the Treasury not otherwise appropriated, for the purpose of conducting said investigations.

Act June 30, 1913 (38 Stat., 84): For maintenance, care, and protection of machinery and irrigation wells already completed, in connection with the irrigation of the lands of the Pima Indians in the vicinity of Sacaton, in the Gila River Reservation, $5,000.

For continuing the investigation by the Secretary of War for the purpose of determining the feasibility and practicability of constructing a dam and reservoir at or in the vicinity of the Box Canyon on the San Carlos Indian Reservation and for other purposes, as authorized by the act of August twenty-fourth, nineteen hundred and twelve (Thirty-seventh Statutes at large, pages five hundred and eighteen to five hundred and twenty-two), $10,000, to be immediately available and to remain available until expended.

Act August 1, 1914 (38 Stat., 587): For maintenance, care, and protection of machinery and irrigation wells already completed, in connection with the irrigation of the lands of the Pima Indians in the vicinity of Sacaton, in the Gila River Reservation, $10,000, reimbursable from any funds of said Indians now or hereafter available.

For investigation recommended by the board of Engineer officers of the United States Army, as set forth in paragraph two hundred and seventeen of their report to the Secretary of War on February fourteenth, nineteen hundred and fourteen, House Document numbered seven hundred and ninety-one, Sixty-third Congress, second session, and report as to the supply of the legally available water, acreage available for irrigation and titles thereto, the maximum and minimum estimated cost of the San Carlos irrigation project, including dams and necessary canals, ditches, and laterals, with recommendations and reasons therefor and the probable cost of adjudicating the water rights along the Gila River necessary thereto, and to take the steps necessary to prevent the vesting of any water rights in addition to those, if any, now existing until further action by Congress, $50,000.

Joint resolution March 4, 1915 (38 Stat., 1228), reenacted the item of August 1, 1914, for the fiscal year 1916.

Act May 18, 1916 (39 Stat., 129): For continuing the work of constructing the irrigation system for the irrigation of the lands of the Pima Indians in the vicinity of Sacaton, on the Gila River Indian Reservation, within the limit of cost fixed by the act of March third, nineteen hundred and five, $10,000; and for maintenance and operation of the pumping plants and canal systems, $10,000; in all, $20,000, reimbursable as provided in section two of the act of August twenty-fourth, nineteen hundred and twelve (Thirty-seventh Statutes at Large, page five hundred and twenty-two), and to remain available until expended.

For beginning the construction by the Indian Service, of a dam with a bridge superstructure and the necessary controlling works for diverting water from the Gila River for the irrigation of Indian land and Indian allotments on the Gila River Indian Reservation, Arizona, as recommended by the Board of Engineers of the United States Army in paragraph two hundred and seventeen of its report to the Secretary of War of February fourteenth, nineteen hundred and fourteen (House Document numbered seven hundred and ninety-one), $75,000 to be immediately available and to remain available until expended, reimbursable as provided in section two of the act of August twenty-fourth, nineteen hundred and twelve (Thirty-seventh Statutes at Large, page five hundred and twenty-two), the total cost not to exceed $200,000.

For beginning the construction by the Indian Service of a diversion dam and necessary controlling works for diverting water from the Gila River at a site above Florence, Arizona, as estimated by the Board of Engineer Officers of the United States Army in paragraph one hundred and thirty-eight of its report to the Secretary of War of February fourteenth, nineteen hundred and fourteen (House Document numbered Seven hundred and ninety-one), $75,000 to remain available until expended, the total cost not to exceed $175,000: *Provided*, That said dam shall be constructed as a part of a project for the irrigation from the natural flow of the Gila River of Indian lands on the Gila River Indian Reservation and private and public lands in Pinal County, Arizona: *And provided further*, That the water diverted from the Gila River by said diversion dam shall be distributed by the Secretary of the Interior to the Indian lands of said reservation and to the private and public lands in said county in accordance with the respective rights and priorities of such lands to the beneficial use of said water as may be determined by agreement of the owners thereof with the Secretary of the Interior or by a court of competent jurisdiction: *And provided further*, That the construction charges for the actual cost of said diversion dam and other works and rights shall be divided equitably by the Secretary of the Interior between the Indian lands and the private and public lands in said county; and said cost as fixed for said Indian lands shall be reimbursable as provided in section two of the act of August twenty-fourth, nineteen hundred and twelve (Thirty-seventh Statutes at Large, page five hundred and twenty-two); but the construction charge as fixed for the private and public lands in said county shall be paid by the owner or entryman in accordance with the terms of an act extending the period of payment under reclamation projects, approved August thirteenth, nineteen hundred and fourteen (Thirty-eighth Statutes at Large, page six hundred and eighty-six): *And provided further*, That said project shall only be undertaken if the Secretary of the Interior shall be able to make or provide for what he shall deem to be satisfactory adjustments of the rights to the water to be diverted by said diversion dam or carried in canals, and satisfactory arrangements for the inclusion of lands within said project and the purchase of property rights which he shall deem necessary to be acquired, and shall determine and declare said project to be feasible.

That the Secretary of the Interior be, and he hereby is, authorized and directed to cause to be made by competent engineers the necessary examinations, investigations, and surveys for the purpose of determining the most suitable and practicable method or methods of constructing levees, revetments, or other suitable works sufficient to prevent the Gila River from further eroding and wearing and washing away its banks and from further overflowing its banks at any point in Graham County, Arizona. Said engineers shall also determine and report upon the most suitable, feasible, and practicable means of holding the said river within a fixed channel as it flows through said Graham County. Said Secretary shall submit to Congress the result of such examinations, investigations, and surveys, together with an estimate of the cost thereof, with recommendations thereon, at the earliest practicable date. The sum of $10,000, or so much thereof as may be necessary, is hereby appropriated, out of any money in the Treasury not otherwise appropriated, for the purpose of conducting said investigations, examinations, and surveys.

Act March 2, 1917 (39 Stat., 974): For continuing the work of constructing the irrigation system for the irrigation of the lands of the Pima Indians in the vicinity of Sacaton, on the Gila River Indian Reservation, within the limit of cost fixed by the act of March third, nineteen hundred and five, $10,000; and for maintenance and operation of the pumping plants and canal systems, $10,000; in all, $20,000, reimbursable as provided in section two of the act of August twenty-fourth, nineteen hundred and twelve (Thirty-seventh Statutes at Large, page five hundred and twenty-two), and to remain available until expended.

For completing the construction by the Indian Service of a dam with a bridge superstructure and the necessary controlling works for diverting water from the Gila River for the irrigation of Indian land and Indian allotments on the Gila River Indian Reservation, Arizona, as recommended by the Board of Engineers of the United

States Army in paragraph two hundred and seventeen of its report to the Secretary of War of February fourteenth, nineteen hundred and fourteen (House Document Numbered Seven hundred and ninety-one), $125,000, to be immediately available and to remain available until expended, reimbursable as provided in section two of the act of August twenty-fourth, nineteen hundred and twelve (Thirty-seventh Statutes at Large, page five hundred and twenty-two), the total cost not to exceed $200,000.

For completing the construction by the Indian Service of a diversion dam and necessary controlling works for diverting water from the Gila River at a site above Florence, Arizona, $100,000, to remain available until expended, the total cost not to exceed $175,000, and for beginning the construction of the necessary canals and structures to carry the natural flow of the Gila River to the Indian lands of the Gila River Indian Reservation and to public and private lands in Pinal County, as provided in the Indian appropriation act approved May eighteenth, nineteen hundred and sixteen, $75,000, to remain available until expended; in all, $175,000.

Act May 25, 1918 (40 Stat., 568): For continuing the work of constructing the irrigation system for the irrigation of the lands of the Pima Indians in the vicinity of Sacaton, on the Gila River Indian Reservation, within the limit of cost fixed by the act of March third, nineteen hundred and five, $5,000; and for maintenance and operation of the pumping plants and canal systems, $10,000; in all, $15,000, reimbursable as provided in section two of the act of August twenty-fourth, nineteen hundred and twelve (Thirty-seventh Statutes at Large, page five hundred and twenty-two), and to remain available until expended.

For completing the construction by the Indian Service of a dam with a bridge superstructure and the necessary controlling works for diverting water from the Gila River for the irrigation of Indian land and Indian allotments on the Gila River Indian Reservation, Arizona, as recommended by the Board of Engineers of the United States Army in paragraph two hundred and seventeen of its report to the Secretary of War of February fourteenth, nineteen hundred and fourteen (House Document Numbered Seven hundred and ninety-one), $50,000, to be immediately available and to remain available until expended, reimbursable as provided in section two of the act of August twenty-fourth, nineteen hundred and twelve (Thirty-seventh Statutes at Large, page five hundred and twenty-two): *Provided*, That the limit of cost of the said dam and bridge fixed by the act of May eighteenth, nineteen hundred and sixteen (Thirty-ninth Statutes at Large, page one hundred and thirty), is hereby changed from $200,000 to $250,000.

For continuing the construction of the necessary canals and structures to carry the natural flow of the Gila River to the Indian lands of the Gila River Indian Reservation and to public and private lands in Pinal County, reimbursable as provided in the Indian appropriation act approved May eighteenth, nineteen hundred and sixteen, $50,000, to remain available until expended.

Act of June 30, 1919 (41 Stat., 10): For continuing the work of constructing the irrigation system for the irrigation of the lands of the Pima Indians in the vicinity of Sacaton, on the Gila River Indian Reservation, within the limit of cost fixed by the act of March 3, 1905 (Thirty-third Statutes at Large, page 1081), $7,500; and for maintenance and operation of the pumping plants and canal systems, $7,500; in all, $15,000, reimbursable as provided in section two of the act of August 24, 1912 (Thirty-seventh Statutes at Large, page 522).

Date.	General.	Sacaton Dam.	Florence Dam.
July 1, 1898	$20,000		
Mar. 3, 1905	50,000		
June 21, 1906	250,000		
Apr. 4, 1910	75,000		
Mar. 3, 1911	125,000		
Aug. 24, 1912	15,000		
June 30, 1913	15,000		
Aug. 1, 1914	60,000		
Mar. 4, 1915	60,000		
May 18, 1916	30,000	$75,000	$75,000
Mar. 2, 1917	20,000	125,000	100,000
May 25, 1918	15,000	50,000	50,000
June 30, 1919	15,000		
Total	750,000	250,000	225,000

KAIBAB.

Act June 21, 1906 (34 Stat., 376): For the support and civilization of the Kaibab Indians in Utah, and for the purchase and acquiring of land and water, together with the necessary farming implements and machinery and live stock for their use, ten thousand five hundred dollars, to be immediately available.

Act March 1, 1907 (34 Stat., 1015), reappropriated the above sum for the fiscal year 1908.

NAVAJO (PARTLY IN NEW MEXICO).

Act July 4, 1884 (23 Stat., 90): For instruction, support, and civilization of the Navajo Indians, including the construction of ditches, reservoirs, and wells, the purchase of stock, pay of employees, and purchase of medicines, forty thousand dollars, to be paid from the funds now in the Treasury belonging to said Indians, and not exceeding one thousand two hundred dollars of this amount may be paid for a clerk.

Act March 3, 1885 (23 Stat. L., 378): For instruction, support, and civilization of the Navajo Indians, including the construction of ditches, reservoirs, and wells, the purchase of stock, pay of employees, and purchase of medicines, twenty-five thousand dollars, to be paid from the funds now in the Treasury belonging to said Indians; and not exceeding one thousand two hundred dollars of this amount may be paid for a clerk.

Act May 15, 1886 (24 Stat. L., 42): For support and civilization of the Navajo Indians, including pay of employees, $7,500; for expenses of constructing ditches and reservoirs, $7,500; in all, $15,000, to be taken from the funds now in the Treasury belonging to said Indians.

Act March 2, 1887 (24 Stat., 462): For expenses of constructing ditches and reservoirs for the Navajo Indians, $7,500, this sum to be taken from the funds now in the Treasury belonging to said Indians.

Act June 29, 1888 (25 Stat. L., 231): For continuing the work of constructing ditches and reservoirs for the Navajo Indians and for the purchase, maintenance, and operation of a portable sawmill for the use of said Indians, and for the purchase of nails and such other necessary materials as can not be obtained by the Indians for houses to be constructed by them, $15,000, to be taken from the funds now in the Treasury belonging to said Indians.

Act August 19, 1890 (26 Stat. L., 351): For construction of irrigation ditches on the Navajo Reservation, $7,500.

Act March 3. 1891 (26 Stat. L., 1005): For purposes of irrigation and purchase of a sawmill on the Navajo Reservation, $7,500.

Act July 13, 1892 (27 Stat., 135): For purposes of irrigation and running sawmill on the Navajo Reservation, $7,500; * * *

Act March 3, 1893 (27 Stat., 627): For the construction of irrigating ditches and the development of a water supply for agricultural, stock, and domestic purposes on the Navajo Indian Reservation, $40,000, to be expended in the discretion of the Secretary of the Interior.

Act March 3, 1909 (35 Stat., 787): To enable the Secretary of the Interior to purchase lands and water rights for the use of Navajo Indians who have lost title to their homes on the public domain in Arizona and New Mexico the sum of forty thousand dollars, or so much thereof as may be necessary, is hereby apportioned, out of any money in the Treasury not otherwise appropriated, the same to be immediately available.

Act August 24, 1912 (37 Stat., 522): For beginning the construction of the Ganado irrigation project on the Navajo Indian Reservation, in Arizona, in accordance with the plans submitted by the chief engineer of the Indian Service and approved by the Commissioner of Indian Affairs and the Secretary of the Interior, in conformity with section one of the act approved April fourth, nineteen hundred and ten, $35,000: *Provided*, That the total cost of the project shall not exceed sixty thousand one hundred dollars.

Act June 30, 1913 (38 Stat., 85): For continuing and completing the construction of the Ganado irrigation project, on the Navajo Indian Reservation, in Arizona, in accordance with the plans submitted by the chief engineer of the Indian Service and approved by the Commissioner of Indian Affairs and the Secretary of the Interior, in conformity with section one of the act approved April fourth, nineteen hundred and ten, $25,100: *Provided*, That the total cost of the project shall not exceed $60,100.

Act June 30, 1913 (38 Stat. L., 86): For the development of a water supply for the Navajo Indians, $15,000, to be immediately available and to remain available until expended.

Act August 1, 1914 (38 Stat., 588): For continuing the development of a water supply for the Navajo Indians on the Navajo Reservation, $25,000, to be immediately available and to remain available until expended, reimbursable out of any funds of said Indians now or hereafter available.

Joint resolution March 4, 1915 (38 Stat., 1228): Reenacted the last foregoing item for the fiscal year 1916.

Act May 18, 1916 (39 Stat., 130): For continuing the devolopment of a water supply for the Navajo Indians on the Navajo Reservation, $25,000, to be immediately available, reimbusable out of any funds of said Indians now or hereafter available.

Act May 18, 1916 (39 Stat., 131): For extension of the Ganado irrigation project on the Navajo Indian Reservation, in Arizona, for the irrigation of approximately six hundred acres of land in addition to the area to be irrigated by said project, as authorized in section two of the act of August twenty-fourth, nineteen hundred and twelve, $20,000; and for maintenance and operation of the project, $3,000; in all, $23,000, reimbursable and to remain available until expended.

Act March 2, 1917 (39 Stat., 974): For continuing the development of a water supply for the Navajo Indians on the Navajo Reservation, $25,000, to be immediately available, reimbursable out of any funds of said Indians now or hereafter available.

For the maintenance and operation of the Ganado irrigation project on the Navajo Indian Reservation in Arizona, $3,000, reimbursable under such rules and regulations as the Secretary of the Interior shall prescribe.

Act May 25, 1918 (40 Stat., 568): For continuing the development of a water supply for the Navajo and Hopi Indians on the Navajo, Moqui, Pueblo, San Juan, and Western Navajo Reservations, $25,000, to be immediately available, reimbursable out of any funds of said Indians now or hereafter available.

For repairs, betterments, and construction of the Ganado irrigation project, Arizona, $20,000; and for maintenance and operation, $3,000; in all, $23,000: *Provided*, That the limit of cost of $60,100 specified in the act of August twenty-fourth, nineteen hundred and twelve (Thirty-seventh Statutes at large, page five hundred and eighteen), is hereby changed to $80,100, reimbursable under such rules and regulations as the Secretary of the Interior shall prescribe.

Act June 30, 1919 (41 Stat., 3): For the construction, repair, and maintenance of irrigation systems, and for purchase or rental of irrigation tools and appliances, water rights, ditches, and lands necessary for irrigation purposes for Indian reservations and allotments: for operation of irrigation systems or appurtenances thereto, when no other funds are applicable or available for the purpose; for drainage and protection of irrigable lands from damage by floods or loss of water rights, upon the Indian irrigation projects named below:

Under the foregoing heading the acts of May 25, 1918 (40 Stat., 562), and June 30, 1919 (41 Stat., 3), provided for irrigation work on the Navajo Reservation, as follows:

San Juan:	
1918	$22,000
1919	20,000
Miscellaneous:	
1918	20,000
1919	18,200

Act June 30, 1919 (41 Stat., 10): * * * For continuing the development of a water supply for the Navajo and Hopi Indians on the Navajo, Moqui, Pueblo Bonito, San Juan, and Western Navajo Reservations, $30,000, reimbursable out of any funds of said Indians now or hereafter available.

For operation and maintenance of the Ganado irrigation project, reimbursable under such rules and regulations as the Secretary of the Interior may prescribe, $3,000: *Provided*, That any balance of the $20,000 appropriated by the act of May 25, 1918 (Fortieth Statutes at Large, p. 569), which shall be unexpended on June 30, 1919, is hereby appropriated.

PAPAGO.

Act January 1, 1889 (25 Stat., L. 639): An act granting to Citrous Water Company right of way across Papago Indian Reservation in Maricopa County, Arizona.

Be it enacted by the Senate and House of Representatives of the United States of American in Congress assembled, That the Citrous Water Company, a corporation organized under the laws of the State of California, and transacting business in the Territory of Arizona, is hereby granted the right of way, one hundred feet in width, across, through, and out of township south five, range west five, Gila and Salt River base and meridian, the said described land being a part of the Papago Indian reservation in Maricopa County, Arizona, for the sole purpose of constructing a ditch or canal, to be used in conveying water across said reservation for use in irrigating lands and supplying water to owners of land below: *Provided*, That so long as said reservation shall continue for the use and occupation of said Indians, said Indians shall, free of cost, be supplied with water from said ditch or canal in such quantity and under such regulations as shall be prescribed by the Secretary of the Interior, and that reasonable compensation only, subject at all times to the control of Congress, shall be charged to those supplied with water for use upon land held under the United States: *Provided further*, That said right of way herein granted shall not be mortgaged, sold, transferred, or assigned except for the purposes of construction: *And provided further*, That unless said canal for which this right of way is granted be completed within two years after the approval of this act the provisions of this act shall be null and void.

SEC. 2. This act, and all rights acquired under the same, shall be subject at all times to modification, revocation, amendment, or repeal by Congress.

(The reservation referred to in the foregoing is the Gila Bend Reservation.)

Act August 24, 1912 (37 Stat., L. 522): For the development of a water supply for domestic and stock purposes and for irrigation for nomadic Papago Indians in Pima County, Arizona, $5,000.

To enable the Secretary of the Interior to make an investigation of the conditions on the Papago Indian Reservation, in Arizona, with a view to determining the possibility of enlarging the irrigation system, for the protection and irrigation of the Indan lands, and the development of a water supply for domestic and stock purposes, $5,000: *Provided*, That the Secretary of the Interior shall cause surveys, plans, and reports to be made, together with an estimated limit of cost of said project, and shall submit his report thereon to Congress on the first Monday in December, nineteen hundred and twelve.

Act June 30, 1913 (38 Stat., 85): For the development of a water supply for domestic and stock purposes and for irrigation for nomadic Papago Indians in Pima County, Arizona, $5,000.

Act August 1, 1914 (38 Stat., 587): For the development of a water supply for domestic and stock purposes and for irrigation for nomadic Papago Indians in Pima County, Arizona, $5,000.

Act August 1, 1914 (38 Stat., 588): For improvement and sinking of wells, installation of pumping machinery, construction of tanks for domestic and stock water, and for the necessary structures for the development of a supply of water for domestic use for eight Papago villages in Southern Arizona, $20,000.

Joint Resolution March 4, 1915 (38 Stat., 1228): Reenacted the last foregoing item for the fiscal year 1916.

Act May 18, 1916 (39 Stat., 130): For improvement and sinking of wells, installation of pumping machinery, construction of tanks for domestic and stock water, and for the necessary structures for the development and distribution of a supply of water, and for maintenance and operation of constructed works, for Papago Indian villages in Southern Arizona, $20,000.

Act March 2, 1917 (39 Stat., 974): For improvement and sinking of wells, installation of pumping machinery, construction of tanks for domestic and stock water, and for the necessary structures for the development and distribution of a supply of water, and for maintenance and operation of constructed works, for papago Indian villages in Southern Arizona, $20,000.

Act May 25, 1918 (40 Stat., 568): For improvement and sinking of wells, installation of pumping machinery, construction of tanks for domestic and stock water, and for the necessary structures for the development and distribution of a supply of water, and for maintenance and operation of constructed works, for Papago Indian villages in Southern Arizona, $20,000.

Act June 30, 1919 (41 Stat., 10): For the construction of seven new pumping plants, including the sinking of wells, installation of pumping machinery, construction of tanks for domestic and stock water, and necessary structures for the development and distribution of a supply of water for Papago Indian villages in southern Arizona, $38,000; for operation and maintenance of constructed works for these villages, $14,000; in all, $52,000.

Act June 30, 1919 (41 Stat., 3): For the construction, repair, and maintenance of irrigation systems, and for purchase or rental of irrigation tools and appliances, water rights, ditches, and lands necessary for irrigation purposes for Indian reservations and allotments; for operation of irrigation systems or appurtenances thereto, when no other funds are applicable or available for the purpose; for drainage and protection of irrigable lands from damage by floods or loss of water rights, upon the Indian irrigation projects named below:

Under the foregoing heading the acts of May 25, 1918 (40 Stat., 562) and June 30, 1919 (41 Stat., 3) provided for Indian irrigation projects, as follows:

Ak Chin:	
1918	$800
1919	3,200
San Xavier, 1918	2,000

Act June 30, 1919 (41 Stat., 11): For operation and maintenance of the pumping plants on the San Xavier Indian Reservation, Arizona, $16,500, reimbursable out of any funds of the Indians of this reservation now or hereafter available.

Appropriations recapitulated.

Aug. 24, 1912	$10,000	Mar. 2, 1917	$20,000
June 30, 1913	5,000	May 25, 1918	22,800
Aug. 1, 1914	25,000	June 30, 1919	71,700
Mar. 4, 1915	25,000		
May 18, 1916	20,000	Total	199,500

PHOENIX.

Act March 3, 1893 (27 Stat., 636): * * * construction of water works, $2,000.

Act March 3, 1901 (31 Stat., 1081): For support and education of six hundred Indian pupils at the Indian School at Phoenix, Arizona * * * purchase of eighty acres of land, with water right, $4,800; * * *

SALT RIVER.

Act February 12, 1901 (31 Stat., L. 786): *Be it enacted by the Senate and House of Representatives of the United States of America in Congress assembled,* That the Arizona Water Company, its successors and assigns, be, and it hereby is, authorized to erect, construct, maintain, and operate a water-power plant at the place on the Indian reservation set apart for the Pima and Maricopa Indians by Executive order dated June fourteenth, eighteen hundred and seventy-nine, in the County of Maricopa, Territory of Arizona, where the Arizona Canal, by means of a cross-cut canal, drops a portion of the water back into the Salt River theretofore taken out by its dam and headgate. Said Arizona Water Company, its successors or assigns, is also authorized to erect, construct, and maintain the necessary poles and wires for the purpose of transmitting across said reservation, at the most practicable and convenient route, the electricity to be generated by such power plant: *Provided, however*, That said Arizona Water Company, its successors or assigns, shall at all times save and protect all persons on said Indian reservation from any and all damages which may be caused by the erection and maintenance of said power plant, pole line, and wires used in connection therewith.

Act May 18, 1916 (39 Stat., 130): That the Secretary of the Interior is hereby authorized and directed to provide for water rights in perpetuity for the irrigation of six hundred and thirty-one Salt River Indian allotments of ten acres each, to be designated by the Commissioner of Indian Affairs, water from works constructed under the provisions of the Reclamation act, and acts amendatory thereof or supplemental thereto: *Provided*, That the reclamation fund shall be reimbursed therefor upon terms the same as those provided in said act or acts for reimbursement by entrymen on lands irrigated by said works, and there is hereby appropriated $20,000, or so much thereof as may be necessary, to pay the initial installment of the charges when made for said water.

Act March 2, 1917 (39 Stat., 975): For additional installments of the charges for providing water rights for six thousand three hundred and ten acres of Salt River Indian allotments provided in the act of May eighteenth, nineteen hundred and sixteen, and for the extension of canals and laterals and for the construction of other necessary irrigation facilities to supply the said lands with water, $15,000.

Act May 25, 1918 (40 Stat., 569): For additional installments of the charges for providing water rights for six thousand three hundred and ten acres of Salt River Indian allotments reimbursable as provided in the act of May eighteenth, nineteen hundred and sixteen, and for the extension of canals and laterals and for the construction of other necessary irrigation facilities to supply the said lands with water, $15,000.

Act June 30, 1919 (41 Stat., 10): For additional installments of the charges for providing water rights for six thousand three hundred and ten acres of Salt River Indian allotments reimbursable as provided in the act of May 18, 1916, and for the extension of canals and laterals and for the construction of other necessary irrigation facilities to supply the said lands with water, $15,000.

Appropriations recapitulated.

May 18, 1916	$20,000	June 30, 1919	$15,000
March 2, 1917	15,000		
May 25, 1918	15,000	Total	65,000

SAN CARLOS.

Act March 3, 1885 (23 Stat., 463): * * * For this amount to pay claims for material furnished and labor performed on irrigating ditch and flume at the San Carlos Agency, Arizona, in eighteen hundred and eighty-one and eighteen hundred and eighty-two, being a deficiency for the fiscal year ending June thirtieth, eighteen hundred and eighty-two, and prior years, namely: To C. P. Schneider, balance due, one thousand eight hundred and fifty-nine dollars and seventy-six cents; to W. M. Breman, balance due, one thousand and nineteen dollars and forty-four cents; to James Thompson and Albert Baughman, balance due, seven hundred and eighty-seven dollars and ninety-four cents; in all, three thousand six hundred and sixty-seven dollars and fourteen cents.

Act August 24, 1912 (37 Stat., 522): * * * *Provided*, That the Secretary of War be, and he hereby is, directed to convene a board of not less than three engineers of the Army of wide reputation and large experience to make the necessary examinations, borings, and surveys for the purpose of determining the reasonability and practicability of constructing a dam and reservoir at or in the vicinity of the Box Canyon, on the San Carlos Indian Reservation, known as the site of the proposed San Carlos Reservoir, on the Gila River, Arizona, and the necessary irrigation works in connection therewith to provide for the irrigation of Indian, private and public lands in the Gila River Valley. Said board of engineers to submit to Congress the results of their examinations and surveys, together with an estimate of cost, with their recommendations thereon at the earliest practicable date. The sum of fifteen thousand dollars, or so much thereof as may be necessary, is hereby appropriated out of any money in the Treasury not otherwise appropriated, for the purpose of conducting said investigations.

Act June 30, 1913 (38 Stat., 85): For continuing the investigation by the Secretary of War for the purpose of determining the feasibility and practicability of constructing a dam and reservoir at or in the vicinity of the Box Canyon on the San Carlos Indian Reservation, and for other purposes, as authorized by the act of August twenty-fourth, nineteen hundred and twelve (Thirty-seventh Statutes at Large, pages five hundred and eighteen to five hundred and twenty-two), $10,000, to be immediately available and to remain available until expended.

Act August 1, 1914 (38 Stat., 588): For investigation recommended by the Board of Engineer Officers of the United States Army, as set forth in paragraph two hundred and seventeen of their report to the Secretary of War on February fourteenth, nineteen hundred and fourteen, House Document numbered Seven hundred and ninety-one, Sixty-third Congress, second session, and report as to the supply of the legally available water, acreage available for irrigation and titles thereto, the maximum and minimum estimated cost of the San Carlos irrigation project, including dams and necessary canals, ditches, and laterals, with recommendations and reasons therefor and the probable cost of adjudicating the water rights along the Gila River necessary thereto, and to take the steps necessary to prevent the vesting of any water rights in addition to those, if any, now existing until further action by Congress, $50,000.

Act June 30, 1919 (41 Stat., 11): The Secretary of the Interior is hereby authorized to withdraw from the Treasury of the United

States the sum of $17,500 of any tribal funds on deposit to the credit of the Indians of the San Carlos Reservation in Arizona, and to expend the same for the operation and maintenance of pumping plants for irrigating the lands of the Indians on the said reservation, and for the installation of a tank or tanks for the economical handling of fuel oil for said pumping plants: *Provided*, That the sum so used shall be reimbursed to the tribe by the Indians benefited, under such rules and regulations as the Secretary of the Interior may prescribe.

Appropriations recapitulated.

Mar. 3, 1885	$3,667.14	June 30, 1919	$17,500.00
Aug. 24, 1912	15,000.00		
June 30, 1913	10,000.00	Total	96,167.14
Aug. 1, 1914	50,000.00		

WALAPAI (TRUXTON CANYON).

Act March 3, 1903 (32 Stat., 1005): * * * at the Indian School at Truxton Canyon, Arizona, * * * for irrigation plant, ten thousand dollars.

Act March 1, 1907 (34 Stat., 1021): * * * at the Indian school at Truxton Canyon, Arizona, * * * maintaining irrigation plant, one thousand dollars.

Act March 3, 1909 (35 Stat., 787): For payment to James H. Owen, of Los Angeles, California, the amount found to be due him by the Secretary of the Interior under contract of May thirty-first, nineteen hundred and six, for the construction of buildings and irrigation works at the Truxton Canyon Indian School, Arizona, nine hundred and thirty dollars.

Appropriations recapitulated.

March 3, 1903	$10,000
March 1, 1907	1,000
March 3, 1909	930
Total	11,930

CALIFORNIA.

MISSION.

Act January 12, 1891 (26 Stat., 712): An act for the relief of the Mission Indians in the State of California. * * *

SEC. 8. That previous to the issuance of a patent for any reservation as provided in section three of this act the Secretary of the Interior may authorize any citizen of the United States, firm, or corporation to construct a flume, ditch, canal, pipe, or other appliances for the conveyance of water over, across, or through such reservation for agricultural, manufacturing, or other purposes, upon condition that the Indians owning or occupying such reservation or reservations shall, at all times during such ownership or occupation, be supplied with sufficient quantity of water for irrigating and domestic purposes upon such terms as shall be prescribed in writing by the

Secretary of the Interior, and upon such other terms as he may prescribe, and may grant a right of way for rail or other roads through such reservation: *Provided*, That any individual, firm, or corporation desiring such privilege shall first give bond to the United States in such sum as may be required by the Secretary of the Interior, with good and sufficient sureties, for the performance of such conditions and stipulations as said Secretary may require as a condition precedent to the granting of such authority: *And provided further*, That this act shall not authorize the Secretary of the Interior to grant a right of way to any railroad company through any reservation for a longer distance than ten miles. And any patent issued for any reservation upon which such privilege has been granted, or for any allotment therein, shall be subject to such privilege, right of way, or easement. Subsequent to the issuance of any tribal patent, or of any individual trust patent as provided in section five of this act, any citizen of the United States, firm, or corporation may contract with the tribe, band, or individual for whose use and benefit any lands are held in trust by the United States, for the right to construct a flume, ditch, canal, pipe, or other appliances for the conveyance of water over, across, or through such lands, which contract shall not be valid unless approved by the Secretary of the Interior under such conditions as he may see fit to impose.

Act March 3, 1903 (32 Stat. L., 999): That any part of the one hundred thousand dollars for the removal and support of the Mission Indians in California, appropriated by the act of May twenty-seventh, nineteen hundred and two, making appropriations for the Indian Service for the fiscal year nineteen hundred and three, not needed for the purposes specified in that act, may, in the discretion of the Secretary of the Interior, be used for the purchase of other tracts of land in California upon which to locate said Mission Indians and for the removal of such Indians to such purchased tract or tracts of land, and for acquiring, distributing, and developing water for the use of such Indians, and for the purchase of such building materials, agricultural implements, harness, wagons and horses, subsistence supplies, and other necessaries as may be required to properly establish such Indians in their new locations.

Act June 21, 1906 (34 Stat. 333): That the Secretary of the Interior be, and he is hereby, authorized to expend not to exceed one hundred thousand dollars to purchase for the use of the Indians in California now residing on reservations which do not contain land suitable for cultivation, and for Indians who are not now upon reservations in said State, suitable tracts or parcels of land, water, and water rights in said State of California, and have constructed the necessary ditches, flumes, and reservoirs for the purpose of irrigating said lands, and the irrigation of any lands now occupied by Indians in said State, and to construct suitable buildings upon said lands, and to fence the tracts of land so purchased, and fence, survey, and mark the boundaries of such Indian reservations in the State of California as the Secretary of the Interior may deem proper. One hundred thousand dollars, or so much thereof as may be necessary, is hereby appropriated out of any funds in the Treasury not otherwise appropriated for the purpose of carrying out the provisions of this act.

Act April 30, 1908 (35 Stat. 76): That the Secretary of the Interior be, and he is hereby, authorized to expend not to exceed fifty thousand dollars to purchase for the use of the Indians in California, now residing on reservations which do not contain land suitable for cultivation, and for Indians who are not now upon reservations in said State suitable tracts or parcels of land, water, and water rights in said State of California, and have constructed the necessary ditches, flumes, and reservoirs for the purpose of irrigating said lands and the irrigation of any lands now occupied by Indians in said State, and to construct suitable buildings upon said lands and to fence the tracts so purchased, and to fence, survey, and mark the boundaries of such Indian reservations in the State of California as the Secretary of the Interior may deem proper. And there is hereby appropriated, out of any money in the Treasury not otherwise appropriated, the sum of fifty thousand dollars, or so much thereof as may be necessary, for the purpose of carrying out the provisions of this act: *Provided*, That this appropriation shall be so expended as to make further appropriations for this purpose unnecessary.

Act June 30, 1919 (41 Stat., 3): For the construction, repair, and maintenance of irrigation systems, and for purchase or rental of irrigation tools and appliances, water rights, ditches, and lands necessary for irrigation purposes for Indian reservations and allotments; for operation of irrigation systems or appurtenances thereto, when no other funds are applicable or available for the purpose; for drainage and protection of irrigable lands from damage by floods or loss of water rights, upon the Indian irrigation projects named below:

Under the foregoing heading the acts of May 25, 1918 (40 Stat. 562) and June 30, 1919 (41 Stat., 3) provided for Indian irrigation projects in California, as follows:

Appropriations recapitulated.

	1918	1919		1918	1919
Agua Caliente Mission	$3,000	$3,000	Pauma Mission	$5,000	
La Jolla Mission		6,000	Rincon Mission	4,000	3,000
Martinez Mission		2,000	Big Pine		3,500
Morongo Mission	2,000	1,600	Grindstone Creek		1,300
Pala Mission	20,000	4,500	Owens Valley		1,000

Act February 28, 1919 (40 Stat., 1206): An act granting to the city of San Diego certain lands in the Cleveland National Forest and the Capitan Grande Indian Reservation for dam and reservoir purposes for the conservation of water, and for other purposes.

Be it enacted by the Senate and House of Representatives of the United States of America in Congress assembled, That the south half of the northeast quarter of the northwest quarter and the north half of the southwest quarter of section eight; the west half of the southwest quarter of the southwest quarter and the west half of the northeast quarter of the northwest quarter of section nine, all in township fifteen south, range two east, San Bernardino base and meridian, within the Cleveland National Forest; and the southeast quarter of the southwest quarter and the southwest quarter of the southeast quarter of section fifteen; the northeast quarter of the southeast quarter of section twenty one; the northwest quarter of the northeast quarter, the northwest quarter, the north half of the southwest quarter, and the southwest quarter of the southwest quarter of section twenty-two; the west half of the northwest quarter of section twenty-seven; and the east half of the northeast quarter, the southwest quarter of the northeast quarter, and the southeast quarter of section twenty-eight; and the northeast quarter, the west half of the southeast quarter, the east half of the southwest quarter, and the southeast quarter of the northwest quarter of section thirty-three, all in township fourteen south, range two east, San Bernardino base and meridian; also the north half of the southwest quarter and the southwest quarter of the southwest quarter of section three, and lots two, three, six, seven, eight, nine, ten, eleven, and the south half of section four, all in township fifteen south, range two east, San Bernardino base and meridian, within the Capitan Grande Indian Reservation, and all within the county of San Diego and State of California, are hereby granted to the city of San Diego, a municipal corporation in said county and State, for dam and reservoir purposes for the conservation and storage of water, whenever said city shall have provided compensation as hereinafter specified for all property rights and interests and damages done to Mission Indians located upon the Capitan Grande Indian Reservation: *Provided*, That the lands herein granted shall not be sold, assigned, transferred, or conveyed to any private person, corporation, or association; and in case of any attempt to sell, assign, transfer, or convey, or upon a failure to use and apply said lands exclusively to the purposes herein specified, this grant shall revert to the United States.

SEC. 2. That the lands herein granted are and shall be subject to all legal rights heretofore acquired by any person, persons, or corporation in or to the above described premises, or any part thereof, and now existing under and by virtue of the laws of the United States, and no private right, title, interest, or claim of any person, persons, or corporation in or to any of such lands shall be interfered with or abridged, except with the consent of the owner or owners, or claimant or claimants thereof, or by due process of law and just compensation paid to such owner or claimant: *Provided*, That the rights and claims of the Mission Indians of the Capitan Grande Indian Reservation, located upon the lands herein described and affected by the grant herein, shall be protected and provided for as hereafter set forth in section three of this act.

SEC. 3. That the law of eminent domain of the State of California is hereby extended over and made to apply to said lands, and the Secretary of the Interior or his duly authorized representative is hereby directed to appear on behalf of, in the name of, and to represent the Capitan Grande Band of Indians and the United States in any proceedings instituted by the city of San Diego to condemn the interest of said Indians in said lands: *Provided*, That any judgment or order of condemnation entered in such proceeding shall be binding upon said Capitan Grande Band of Indians only upon the approval by the Secretary of the Interior of the terms of said judgment: *Provided further*, That the Secretary of the Interior shall require from the City of San Diego in addition to the award of condemnation such further sum which, in his opinion, when added to said award, will be sufficient in the aggregate to provide for the purchase of additional lands for the Capitan Grande Band of Indians, the erection of suitable homes for the Indians on the lands so purchased, the erection of such schools, churches, and administrative buildings, the sinking of such wells and the construction of such roads and ditches, and providing water and water rights and for such other expenses as may be deemed necessary by the Secretary of the Interior to properly establish these Indians permanently on the lands purchased for them; and the Secretary of the Interior is hereby authorized to expend the proceeds or any part thereof, derived from this grant for the purposes above enumerated, for the exclusive use and benefit of said Indians: *And provided further*, That the grant made in this act shall not become effective until payment has been made of the sums herein provided for.

SEC. 4. That within one year after the approval of this act the city of San Diego shall commence condemnation proceedings to acquire the lands herein described and shall diligently prosecute such proceedings to a final judgment. Within two years after the approval by the Secretary of the Interior of any such judgment of condemnation the city of San Diego shall institute, and thereafter shall diligently prosecute, proceedings for the issuance and sale of municipal bonds to defray the amount necessary to satisfy any such judgment of condemnation, paying such additional sum as the Secretary of the Interior may require, as provided for in section three, and providing for the acquisition, construction, and completion of a dam, reservoir, pipe line, and appurtenances thereto necessary or convenient to the storage and conservation of water upon the lands herein described for the purposes set forth in this bill. Within six months from the time of payment into the city treasury of the moneys realized from the sale of municipal bonds issued as herein provided the city of San Diego shall commence the construction of said dam and reservoir, and the same shall be prosecuted diligently, and in the event that the Secretary of the Interior shall find and determine that there has not been diligent prosecution of the work, or that said condemnation proceedings have not been commenced and diligently prosecuted, or that municipal bonds have not been issued and sold as herein provided, then he may declare forfeited all rights of the grantees herein and request the Attorney General, on behalf of the United States, to commence suits or proceedings in the proper court having jurisdiction thereof for the purpose of procuring a judgment declaring all rights to be forfeited to the United States, and upon such request it shall be the duty of said Attorney General to cause to be commenced and prosecuted to a final judgment such suits or proceedings: *Provided*, That the Secretary of the Interior shall make no such findings and take no such action if he shall find that the issuance or sale of municipal bonds or the construction or progress of the dam or reservoir has been delayed or prevented by the act of God or the public enemy or by legal, engineering, or other difficulties that could not have been reasonably foreseen and overcome, or by other special or peculiar difficulties beyond the control of said grantee: *Provided further*, That in the exercise of the rights granted by this act the grantee shall at all times comply with the regulations herein authorized, and in the event of any material departure therefrom the Secretary of the Interior or the Secretary of Agriculture, respectively, may take such action as may be necessary in the courts or otherwise to enforce such regulations: *Provided further*, That if such dam be built the Indians of the Capitan Grande Reservation shall be permitted to reside on, occupy, and cultivate the lands of their present reservation up until within ninety days of the time when water for storage purposes will be turned into the reservoir to be constructed hereunder, provided such occupancy by the Indians will not materially hinder the construction of the dam and storage work, which fact is to be determined by the Secretary of the Interior.

Sec. 5. That said reservoir, when constructed, shall be maintained and controlled by the city of San Diego for the use and benefit of said city and the inhabitants thereof and of such other municipalities within the county of San Diego, State of California, as may be now or hereafter furnished with water by said city of San Diego, and for the use and benefit of riparian owners along the San Diego River below the lands herein described and for the benefit of persons, corporations, or municipalities situated along or adjacent to the pipe lines of said city of San Diego for the conservation and storage of water for domestic, irrigation, or municipal uses: *Provided*, That the city of San Diego shall sell to the United States for the use of the War and Navy Departments such water as the War and Navy Departments, or either of them, may elect to take, and shall deliver the same through its system in or near the city of San Diego to the mains or systems of such military or naval reservations in that vicinity as may be designated by the Secretary of War or the Secretary of the Navy, or both, under such rules and regulations as they or either of them may prescribe. In payment of such water and the delivery thereof the United States shall pay to said city of San Diego a rental to be calculated at a fixed rate per one thousand gallons, said rate not to exceed the actual cost of such water to said city for all water so furnished as determined by meter measurements: *Provided, however*, That the grantee shall at all times comply with and observe on its part all of the conditions specified in this act, and in the event that the sums are not reasonably complied with and carried out by the grantee upon written request by the Secretary of the Interior it is made the duty of the Attorney General, in the name of the United States, to commence all necessary suits or proceedings in the proper court having jurisdiction thereof for the purpose of enforcing and carrying out the provisions of this act: *Provided*, That the city of San Diego is authorized to assign all its rights, powers, and privileges under this act to any public water district formed under the laws of California.

Sec. 6. That this act is a grant upon certain express conditions specifically set forth herein, and nothing herein contained shall be construed as affecting or intending to affect or in any way to interfere with the laws of the State of California relating to the control, appropriation, use, or distribution of water used in irrigation, or for municipal or other uses or any vested rights acquired thereunder, and the Secretary of the Interior and the city of San Diego in carrying out the provisions of this act shall proceed in conformity with the laws of said State.

SEC. 7. That the grantee shall file with the Secretary of the Interior, within six months after the approval of this act, its acceptance of the terms and conditions of this grant.

Approved, February 28, 1919.

ROUND VALLEY.

Act June 21, 1906 (34 Stat., 333): For the purpose of removing obstructions from the bed of the stream which drains into the Eel River in the Round Valley Reservation, Mendocino County, California, $8,000.

Act March 1, 1907 (34 Stat., 1022): That the paragraph in the Indian appropriation act, approved June twenty-first, nineteen hnudred and six (Thirty-fourth Statutes at Large, pages three hundred and twenty-five to three hundred and thirty-three), relating to the removal of obstructions from the bed of a stream in the Round Valley Reservation, California, be amended as follows: Insert after the word "obstructions" the words "both within and without the reservation"; strike out the words "drains into the Eel River in" and insert the words "flows through" and insert after the word "California" the words "and drains into the Eel River."

Act April 30, 1908 (35 Stat., L. 77): That one thousand dollars of the unexpended balance of eight thousand dollars appropriated by the act of June twenty-first, nineteen hundred and six (Thirty-fourth Statutes, page three hundred and thirty-three), and March first, nineteen hundred and seven (Thirty-fourth Statutes, page one thousand and twenty-two), for the purpose of removing obstructions both within and without the reservation from the bed of the stream which flows through the Round Valley Reservation, Mendocino County, California, and drains into the Eel River be, and the same is hereby, reappropriated and made available for use during the fiscal year ending June thirtieth, nineteen hundred and nine.

Act June 30, 1919 (41 Stat., 3): For the construction, repair, and maintenance of irrigation systems, and for purchase or rental of irrigation tools and appliances, water rights, ditches, and lands necessary for irrigation purposes for Indian reservations and allotments; for operation of irrigation systems or appurtenances thereto, when no other funds are applicable or available for the purpose; for drainage and protection of irrigable lands from damage by floods or loss of water rights, upon the Indian irrigation projects named below:

Under the foregoing heading the act of June 30, 1919, provided $2,000 for irrigation work in the Round Valley Reservation.

SHERMAN INSTITUTE.

Act March 3, 1893 (27 Stat., 638): * * * fencing, irrigation, and general repairs, $4,000 (formerly Perris Indian School).

Act April 21, 1904 (33 Stat. L., 214): * * * At the Indian School, Riverside, California, * * * for additional water irrigation and sewer systems, $6,000 * * *: *Provided*, That so much of said amounts as may be necessary in the judgment of the

Commissioner of Indian Affairs may be used for the education and support of pupils and repairs to the plant at the Indian School, Perris, California.

YUMA.

Act January 20, 1893 (27 Stat. L., 420): An act granting to the Yuma Pumping Irrigation Company the right of way for two ditches across that part of the Yuma Indian Reservation lying in Arizona.

Be it enacted by the Senate and House of Representatives of the United States of America in Congress assembled, That there is hereby granted unto the Yuma Pumping Irrigation Company, incorporated under the laws of Arizona, its successors and assigns, a right of way one hundred feet wide, the center line of which right of way shall commence on the bank of the Colorado River, three hundred feet west of the east line of the Yuma Indian Reservation, in Arizona (formerly the Fort Yuma Military Rerservation); thence running westerly along said bank to the center of the angle of the flume of said company; thence following the center of the ditch of said company to the boundary line of said reservation. Also there is hereby granted unto said corporation, its successors and assigns, a right of way two hundred feet wide across said reservation in Arizona, the center line of which shall commence at low water of the Colorado River, one hundred and fifty feet westerly of the east line of the said reservation; thence running in a southerly direction to and crossing the west line of said reservation one hundred and fifty feet, more or less, north of the southwest corner of said reservation: *Provided*, That for the distance of two hundred and fifty feet from the point of beginning on said river said right of way shall be three hundred feet in width. The plats of the ditches of said company through said reservation shall be subject to the approval of the Secretary of the Interior, and such ditches shall not be so located or the rights of way herein granted so used as to in any manner interfere with any permanent building upon said reservation, except with the express assent of said Secretary of the Interior.

SEC. 2. That the rights herein granted are upon the express condition that the grantee or grantees thereof shall, at all times during the continuance thereof, furnish the Indian occupants of the lands situated south of and under either of said ditches, and within said reservation as now bounded, water sufficient for all domestic and agricultural purposes, and purposes of irrigation, on such terms and under such rules and regulations as shall be prescribed by the Secretary of the Interior.

SEC. 3. That this act shall take effect and be in force from and after its passage, but the right to amend or repeal it at any time is hereby reserved to Congress.

Act February 15, 1893 (27 Stat. L., 456): An act granting right of way to the Colorado River Irrigation Company through the Yuma Indian Reservation in California.

Be it enacted by the Senate and House of Representatives of the United States of America in Congress assembled, That there is hereby granted unto the Colorado River Irrigation Company, incorporated under the laws of the State of Colorado, its successors and assigns, a right of way for an irrigating canal through the Yuma Indian Reservation in California to the extent of the ground occupied by the water of the canal and its adits and laterals, and fifty feet on each side of the marginal limits thereof, beginning at a point near where the northeast boundary line of the said reservation joins the Colorado River, and running thence south and west through the said reservation to and beyond the limits thereof. The plats of the ditches of said company through said reservation shall be subject to the approval of the Secretary of the Interior, and such ditches shall be so located, or the rights of way herein granted so used, as to not in any way interfere with any permanent buildings upon said reservation, except with the express consent of the Secretary of the Interior.

SEC. 2. That the rights herein granted are upon the express condition that the grantee or grantees hereof shall at all times during the continuance thereof furnish the Indian occupants of the land situated on the lower side of the canal with water sufficient for all domestic and agricultural purposes and purposes of irrigation on such terms and under such rules and regulations as shall be prescribed by the Secretary of the Interior.

SEC. 3. That this act shall take effect and be in force from and after its passage; but the right to amend or repeal it at any time is hereby reserved to Congress.

Act August 15, 1894 (28 Stat. L., 333): Agreement with Yuma Indians.

ART. III. That the allotments provided for in this agreement shall be made * * *; and when all of said allotments are made and approved, then all the residue of said reservation which may be subject to irrigation, except as hereinafter stated, shall be disposed of as follows: The Secretary of the Interior shall cause the said lands to be regularly surveyed * * * and shall cause the lands to be appraised * * * and when the appraisement has been approved the Secretary of the Interior shall cause the said lands to be sold * * *.

ART. IV. That the money realized by the sale of the aforesaid lands shall be placed in the Treasury of the United States to the credit of the said Yuma Indians, and the same, with interest thereof at five per centum per annum, shall be at all times subject to appropriation by Congress, or to application, by order of the President, for the payment of water rents, building levees, irrigating ditches, laterals, the erection and repair of buildings, purchase of tools, farming implements and seeds, and for the education and civilization of said Yuma Indians.

* * * * * * *

ART. VI. All lands upon said reservation that can not be irrigated are to be open to settlement under the general land laws of the United States.

* * * * * * *

Therefore be it enacted by the Senate and House of Representatives of the United States of America in Congress assembled, That the said agreement be, and the same hereby is, accepted, ratified, and confirmed.

* * * * * * *

The Secretary of the Interior is hereby authorized and directed to cause all the lands ceded by said agreement which may be susceptible of irrigation, after said allotments have been made and approved and said lands have been surveyed and appraised, and the appraisal approved, to be sold at public sale by the officers of the land office in the district wherein said lands are situated, to the highest bidder for cash, at not less than the appraised value thereof, after first having given at least sixty days' public notice of the time, place, and terms of sale immediately prior to such sale, by publication in at least two newspapers of general circulation, and any lands or subdivisions remaining unsold may be reoffered for sale at any subsequent time in the same manner at the discretion of the Secretary of the Interior, and if not sold at such second offering for want of bidders, then the Secretary may cause the same to be sold at private sale at not less than the appraised value. The money realized from the sale of said lands, after deducting the expenses of the sale of said lands, and the other money for which provision is made for the reimbursement of the United States, shall be placed in the Treasury of the United States to the credit of said Yuma Indians and shall draw interest at the rate of five per centum per annum, and said principal and interest shall be subject to appropriation by Congress, or to application by the President of the United States for the payment of water rents, the building of levees, irrigating ditches and laterals, the purchase of tools, farming implements, and seeds, and for the education and civilization of said Indians: *Provided, however*, That none of said money realized from the sale of said lands, or any of the interest thereon, shall be applied to the payment of any judgment that has been or may hereafter be rendered on claims for damages because of depredations committed by said Indians prior to the date of the agreement herein ratified.

That all of the lands ceded by said agreement which are not susceptible of irrigation shall become a part of the public domain, and shall be opened to settlement and sale by proclamation of the President of the United States, and be subject to disposal under the provisions of the general land laws.

That the Colorado River Irrigating Company, which was granted a right of way for an irrigating canal through the said Yuma Indian Reservation by the act of Congress approved February fifteenth, eighteen hundred and ninety-three, shall be required to begin the construction of said canal through said reservation within three years from the date of the passage of this act, otherwise the rights granted by the act aforesaid shall be forfeited.

That the Secretary of the Interior shall have authority from time to time to fix the rate of water rents to be paid by said Indians for all domestic, agricultural, and irrigation purposes, and in addition thereto each male adult Indian of the Yuma Tribe shall be granted water for one acre of the land which shall be allotted to him, if he utilizes the same in growing crops, free of all rent charges during the period of ten years, to be computed from the date when said irrigation company begins the delivery of water on said reservation.

Act April 21, 1904 (33 Stat. L., 224): SEC. 25. That in carrying out any irrigation enterprise which may be undertaken under the provisions of the reclamation act of June seventeenth, nineteen hundred and two, and which may make possible and provide for, in connection with the reclamation of other lands, the reclamation of all or any portion of the irrigable lands on the Yuma and Colorado River Indian Reservations in California and Arizona, the Secretary of the Interior is hereby authorized to divert the waters of the Colorado River and to reclaim, utilize, and dispose of any lands in said reservations which may be irrigable by such works in like manner as though the same were a part of the public domain: *Provided*, That there shall be reserved for and allotted to each of the Indians belonging on the said reservation five acres of the irrigable lands. The remainder of the lands irrigable in said reservations shall be disposed of to settlers under the provisions of the reclamation act: *Provided further*, That there shall be added to the charges required to be paid under said act by settlers upon the unallotted Indian lands such sum per acre as in the opinion of the Secretary of the Interior shall fairly represent the value of the unallotted lands in said reservations before reclamation; said sum to be paid in annual installments in the same manner as the charges under the reclamation act. Such additional sum per acre, when paid, shall be used to pay into the reclamation fund the charges for the reclamation of the said allotted lands, and the remainder thereof shall be placed to the credit of said Indians and shall be expended from time to time, under the direction of the Secretary of the Interior, for their benefit.

Act March 3, 1911 (26 Stat. L., 1063): The first proviso in section twenty-five of the Indian appropriation act, approved April twenty-first, nineteen hundred and four (33 Stat. L., 224), is hereby amended so that the first sentence in said proviso shall read as follows: "*Provided*, That there shall be reserved for and allotted to each of the Indians belonging on the said reservations ten acres of the irrigable lands;" and there is hereby appropriated the sum of eighteen thousand dollars, or so much thereof as may be necessary, to defray the cost of the irrigation of the increased allotments, for the fiscal year nineteen hundred and twelve: *Provided*, That the entire cost of irrigation of the allotted lands shall be reimbursed to the United States from any funds received from the sale of the surplus lands of the reservations or from any other funds that may become available for such purpose: *Provided further*, That in the event any allottee shall receive a patent in fee to an allotment of land irrigated under this project before the United States shall have been wholly reimbursed as herein provided, then the proportionate cost of the project to be apportioned equitably by the Secretary of the Interior shall become a first lien on such allotment, and the fact of such lien shall be recited on the face of each patent in fee issued and the amount of the lien set forth thereon, which said lien, however, shall not be enforced so long as the original allottee, or his heirs, shall actually occupy the allotment as a homestead, and the receipt of the Secretary of the Interior or of the officer, agent, or employee duly authorized by him for that purpose, for the payment of the amount assessed against any allotment as herein provided shall, when duly recorded by the recorder of deeds in the county wherein the land is located, operate as a satisfaction of such lien.

Act August 24, 1912 (37 Stat. L., 523): For the balance of the first annual reclamation and maintenance charge on Yuma allotments and for the second annual charge and maintenance, fifty-two thousand three hundred and sixty-two dollars and sixty-two cents, or so much thereof as may be required to be reimbursed from the sale of surplus lands or from other funds that may be available, in accordance with the provisions of the act of March third, nineteen hundred and eleven.

Act June 30, 1913 (38 Stat. L., 86): For reclamation and maintenance charge on Yuma allotments, $40,000, to be reimbursed from the sale of surplus lands or from other funds that may be available, in accordance with the provisions of the act of March third, nineteen hundred and eleven.

Act August 1, 1914 (38 Stat. L., 589): For reclamation and maintenance charge on Yuma allotments, $40,000, to be reimbursed from the sale of surplus lands or from other funds that may be available, in accordance with the provisions of the act of March third, nineteen hundred and eleven.

Joint resolution of March 4, 1915 (38 Stats., 1228): Reenacted the last foregoing item for the fiscal year 1916.

Act May 18, 1916 (39 Stat. L., 132): For reclamation and maintenance charge on Yuma allotments, $10,000, to remain available until expended and to be reimbursed from the sale of surplus lands or from other funds that may be available, in accordance with the provisions of the act of March third, nineteen hundred and eleven.

Act March 2, 1917 (39 Stat. L., 975): For reclamation and maintenance charge on Yuma allotments, $15,000, to remain available until expended and to be reimbursed from the sale of surplus lands or from other funds that may be available, in accordance with the provisions of the act of March third, nineteen hundred and eleven.

Act May 25, 1918 (40 Stat. L., 570): For reclamation and maintenance charge on Yuma allotments, $15,000, to remain available until expended and to be reimbursed from the sale of surplus lands or from other funds that may be available, in accordance with the provisions of the act of March third, nineteen hundred and eleven.

Act June 30, 1919 (41 Stat. L., 12): For reclamation and maintenance charge on Yuma allotments, $131,564.94, to be reimbursed from the sale of surplus lands or from other funds that may be available, in accordance with the provisions of the act of March 3, 1911 (Thirty-sixth Statutes at Large, page 1063).

GRAND JUNCTION.

Act March 3, 1885 (23 Stat., 382): To enable the Secretary of the Interior to erect buildings for a school for the Indians near Grand Junction, Colorado, fifteen thousand dollars, to be paid from any money due the confederated bands of Ute Indians; and in addition thereto he is authorized to use the sum of eight thousand dollars out of any money available for that purpose heretofore appropriated: *Provided*, That before such school shall be established there shall be donated to the Government for the purpose of said school not less than one hundred and sixty acres of land, together with a sufficient amount of water for the cultivation thereof, on which land the said school buildings shall be erected; to be immediately available.

Act August 19, 1890 (26 Stat., 359): For support of Indian pupils at one hundred and seventy-five dollars per annum each; for the erection of a new building at a cost not to exceed twelve thousand dollars; for the erection of a barn, shops, out-houses; for securing a proper water supply; for necessary repairs, furnishings, tools, and farm implements; and for pay of superintendent at the Indian school, Grand Junction, Colorado, at one thousand five hundred dollars per annum, thirty-five thousand dollars.

Act July 13, 1892 (27 Stat., 141): For support of Indian pupils * * *; for necessary repairs * * *; cost of water for irrigating purposes, and for pay of superintendent at the Indian School, Grand Junction, Colorado, at one thousand five hundred dollars per annum, twenty-nine thousand dollars: *Provided*, That not more than ten thousand dollars of this amount shall be used for erecting and repairing buildings, heating, and furnishing school.

(Turned over to State of Colorado pursuant to acts of March 3, 1909, and April 4, 1910).

SOUTHERN UTE.

Act February 20, 1895 (28 Stat., 677): An act to disapprove the treaty heretofore made with the Southern Ute Indians to be removed to the Territory of Utah, and providing for settling them down in severally where they may so elect and are qualified, and to settle all those not electing to take lands in severalty on the west forty miles of present reservation and in portions of New Mexico, and for other purposes, and to carry out the provisions of the treaty with said Indians June fifteenth, eighteen hundred and eighty.

* * * * * * *

SEC. 3. That for the sole and exclusive use and occupany of such of said Indians as may not elect or be deemed qualified to take allotments of land in severalty, as provided in the preceding section, there shall be, and is hereby, set apart, and reserved all that portion of their present reservation lying west of the range line between ranges thirteen and fourteen west of the New Mexico principal meridian, and also all of townships thirty-one and thirty-two of ranges fourteen, fifteen, and sixteen west of the New Mexico principal meridian and lying in the Territory of New Mexico, subject, however, to the right of the Government to erect and maintain agency buildings thereon, and to grant rights of way through the same for railroads, irrigation ditches, highways, and other necessary purposes; and the Government shall maintain an agency at some suitable place on said lands so reserved.

Act June 7, 1897 (30 Stat., 76): The Secretary of the Interior is hereby directed to confer with the owners of the Montezuma Valley Canal, in the county of Montezuma and State of Colorado, or any other parties, for the purpose of securing by the Government water rights, or for the supply of so much water, or both, as he may deem necessary for the irrigation of that part of the Montezuma Valley lying within the boundaries of the Southern Ute Indian Reservation in said State, and for the domestic use of the Indians thereon; and he shall report to Congress at its next regular session the amount of water necessary to be secured for said purpose and the cost of the same, and such recommendations as he shall deem proper.

Act July 1, 1898 (30 Stat., 593): That the Secretary of the Interior shall make investigation as to the practicability of providing a water supply for irrigation purposes, to be used on a portion of the reservation of the Southern Utes in Colorado, and he is authorized, in his discretion, to contract for, and to expend from the funds of said Southern Utes in the purchase of perpetual water rights sufficient to irrigate not exceeding ten thousand acres on the western part of the Southern Ute Reservation, and for annual charges for maintenance of such water thereon, such amount and upon such terms and conditions as to him may seem just and reasonable, not exceeding one hundred and fifty thousand dollars for the purchase of such perpetual water rights, and not exceeding a maximum of fifty cents per acre per annum for the maintenance of water upon land irrigated, provided that after such an investigation he shall find all the essential conditions relative to the water supply and to the perpetuity of its availability for use upon said lands, such as in his judgment will justify a contract for its perpetual use: *Provided*, That the Secretary of the Interior, upon making all such contracts, shall require from the person or persons entering into such contract a bond of indemnity, to be approved by him, for the faithful and continuous execution of such contract as provided therein.

Act March 1, 1899 (30 Stat., 941): That the provision in the Indian appropriation act approved July first, eighteen hundred and ninety-eight, relating to a water supply for irrigation purposes to be used on a portion of the reservation of the Southern Utes in Colorado, is hereby continued in force for and during the fiscal year nineteen hundred, and is hereby amended so as to read as follows:

"That the Secretary of the Interior shall make investigations as to the practicability of providing a water supply for irrigation purposes, to be used on a portion of the reservation of the Southern Utes in Colorado, and he is authorized, in his discretion, to contract for, and to expend from the funds of said Southern Utes in the purchase of, perpetual water rights sufficient to irrigate not exceeding ten thousand acres on the western part of the Southern Ute Reservation, and for annual charges for maintenance of such water thereon, such amount and upon such terms and conditions as to him may seem just and reasonable, not exceeding one hundred and fifty thousand dollars for the purchase of such perpetual water rights, and not exceeding a maximum of fifty cents per acre per annum for the maintenance of water upon the land to be irrigated: *Provided*, That after such an investigation he shall find all the essential conditions relative to the water supply and to the perpetuity of its availability for use upon said lands, such as in his judgment will justify a contract for its perpetual use: *Provided*, That the Secretary of the Interior, upon making all such contracts, shall require from the person or persons entering into such contract a bond of indemnity, to be approved by him, for the faithful and continuous execution of such contract as provided therein.

Act May 27, 1902 (32 Stat., 266): That the Secretary of the Interior be, and he is hereby, authorized and empowered, under general regulations to be fixed by him, to permit the use of the right of way through the allotted lands of the Southern Ute Indians in Colorado for irrigating ditches to the extent of the ground occupied by the water in said ditches and such number of feet on each side of the marginal limits thereof as may be necessary in maintaining and operating the ditches: *Provided*, That no application for such right of way shall be granted unless accompanied by the consent, in writing, of the allottee or allottees whose land may be affected thereby.

That the Secretary of the Interior shall make investigations as to the practicability of providing a water supply for irrigation purposes to be used on a portion of the reservation of the Southern Utes in Colorado, and he is authorized, in his discretion, to contract for and to expend from the funds of the said Southern Utes in the purchase of perpetual water rights sufficient to irrigate not exceeding ten thousand acres on the western part of the Southern Ute Reservation and for annual charges for maintenance of such water thereon such amount and upon such terms and conditions as to him may seem just and reasonable, not exceeding one hundred and fifty thousand dollars for the purchase of such perpetual water rights and not exceeding a maximum of fifty cents per acre per annum for the maintenance of water upon the land to be irrigated. *Provided*, That after such an investigation he shall find all the essential conditions relative to the water supply and to the perpetuity of its availability for use upon said lands such as in his judgment will justify a contract for its perpetual use: *Provided further*, That the Secretary of the Interior, upon making all such contracts, shall require from the person or persons entering upon such contract a bond of indemnity, to be approved by him, for the faithful and continuous execution of such contract as provided therein.

Act March 3, 1905 (33 Stat., 1080): Sec. 8. That the Secretary of the Interior shall make an investigation as to the practicability of providing a water supply for irrigation purposes to be used on a portion of the reservation of the Southern Utes in Colorado, and he is authorized to contract for and to expend from the funds of said Southern Utes in the purchase of perpetual water rights sufficient to irrigate not exceeding ten thousand acres on the western part of the Southern Ute Reservation and for annual charges for maintenance of such water thereon such amount and upon such terms and conditions as to him may seem just and reasonable, not exceeding one hundred and fifty thousand dollars, for the purchase of such perpetual water rights and not exceeding a maximum of fifty cents per acre per annum for the maintenance of water upon the land to be irrigated: *Provided*, That after such an investigation he shall find all the essential conditions relative to the water supply and to the perpetuity of its availability for use upon said lands as will justify a contract for its perpetual use the contract for such water shall be for a specific number of inches: *Provided*, That the Secretary of the Interior, upon making all such contracts, shall require from the company, person, or persons entering into such contract a bond of indemnity, to be approved by him, for the faithful and continuous execution of such contract as provided therein.

Act March 3, 1909 (35 Stat., 788): That the Secretary of the Interior is hereby authorized to expend from the funds of the Southern Ute Indians in the Treasury of the United States sufficient moneys, not exceeding one hundred and fifty thousand dollars, to purchase a perpetual water right for the purpose of irrigating not less than ten thousand acres of land in the Southern Ute Indian Reservation in Colorado.

Act June 30, 1919 (41 Stat., 3): For the construction, repair, and maintenance of irrigation systems, and for purchase or rental of irrigation tools and appliances, water rights, ditches, and lands necessary for irrigation purposes for Indian reservations and allotments; for operation of irrigation systems or appurtenances thereto, when no other funds are applicable or available for the purpose; for drainage and protection of irrigable lands from damage by floods or loss of water rights, upon the Indian irrigation projects named below.

Under the foregoing heading the acts of May 18, 1916 (40 Stat., 562), and June 30, 1919 (41 Stat., 3), provide the sums of $9,000 and $8,000, respectively, for irrigation work on the Southern Ute Reservation.

IDAHO.

FORT HALL.

Act September 1, 1888 (25 Stat., 453): SEC. 2. That the Secretary of the Interior be, and he hereby is, authorized to cause to be surveyed and laid out into lots and blocks so much of the Fort Hall Reservation in the Territory of Idaho, at or near Pocatello Station, on the Utah and Northern Railway, as when the sectional and subdivisional lines are run and established shall be found to be within the following descriptions, to wit: The west half of section twenty-five, all of section twenty-six, the east half of section twenty-seven, the northeast quarter of section thirty-six, the north half of section thirty-five, the northeast quarter of the southwest quarter of section thirty-five, and the northeast quarter of the northeast quarter of section thirty-four, all in township six south of range thirty-four east, of Boise Meridian, in the Territory of Idaho, and containing an area of one thousand eight hundred and forty acres, or thereabouts; saving and excepting thereout so much of the above described tracts as has heretofore been, or is hereby, granted for the use of the Utah and Northern Railway Company.

SEC. 10. That the citizens of the town hereinbefore provided for shall have the free and undisturbed use in common with the said Indians of the waters of any river, creek, stream, or spring flowing through the Fort Hall Reservation in the vicinity of said town, with right of access at all times thereto, and the right to construct, operate, and maintain all such ditches, canals, works, or other aqueducts, drain, and sewerage pipes, and other appliances on the reservation, as may be necessary to provide said town with proper water and sewerage facilities.

Act March 3, 1891 (26 Stat., 1011): That the Secretary of the Interior is authorized to grant rights of way into and across the Fort Hall Reservation in Idaho to canal, ditch, or reservoir companies for the purpose of enabling the citizens of Pocatello to thereby receive the water supply, contemplated by section ten (10) of an act to accept and ratify an agreement made with the Shoshone and Bannock Indians, and for other purposes, being chapter nine hundred and thirty-six, laws of eighteen hundred and eighty-eight, and may also attach conditions as to the supply of surplus water to Indians on said Fort Hall Reservation as may be reasonable and prescribe rules and regulations for the same.

Act August 15, 1894 (28 Stat., 305): The Secretary of the Interior is directed to contract with responsible parties for the construction of irrigating canals and the purchase, or securing of water supply on the Fort Hall Indian Reservation, in the State of Idaho, for the purpose of irrigating the lands of said reservation: *Provided*, That the expense of constructing said canals and the purchase, or securing of water supply shall be paid out of moneys belonging to the said Fort Hall Indians now in the Treasury of the United States and subject to the disposal of the Secretary of the Interior for the benefit of said Indians.

Act June 6, 1900 (31 Stat., 674), ratifying Fort Hall agreement.

ART. VIII. The water from streams on that portion of the reservation, now sold, which is necessary for irrigating on land actually cultivated and in use shall be reserved for the Indians now using the same, so long as said Indians remain where they now live.

SEC. 5. That on the completion of the allotments and the preparation of the schedule provided for in the preceding section, and the classification of the lands as provided for herein, the residue of said ceded lands shall be opened to settlement by the proclamation of the President, and shall be subject to disposal under the homestead, townsite, stone and timber, and mining laws of the United States only, excepting as to price and excepting the sixteenth and thirty-sixth sections in each congressional township, which shall be reserved for common-school purposes and be subject to the laws of Idaho: *Provided*, That all purchasers of lands lying under the canal of the Idaho Canal Company, and which are susceptible of irrigation from the water from said canal, shall pay for the same at the rate of ten dollars per acre; all agricultural lands not under said canal shall be paid for at the rate of two dollars and fifty cents per acre and grazing lands at the rate of one dollar and twenty-five cents per acre, one-fifth of the respective sums to be paid at time of original entry and four-fifths thereof at the time of making final proof; but no purchaser shall be permitted in any manner to purchase more than one hundred and sixty acres of the land hereinbefore referred to; * * *.

Act June 21, 1906 (34 Stat., 334): That there be appropriated from the moneys of the United States Treasury not otherwise appropriated, the sum of twenty-five thousand dollars for completing the survey on the Fort Lemhi and Fort Hall Indian Reservations, in Idaho; including expenses in the office of the surveyor general for Idaho, and for the examination of said surveys; and for a reconnaissance survey and preparation of plans for an irrigation system and storage system for Indian lands and lands ceded by the act of June sixth, nineteen hundred, on the Fort Hall Reservation, in Idaho.

Act March 1, 1907 (34 Stat., 1024): That the Secretary of the Interior be, and he is hereby, authorized to acquire by purchase or condemnation on behalf of the United States all land in townships four, five, six, and seven south, range forty, forty-one, and forty-two east, Boise meridian in Idaho, that he shall deem necessary in constructing a reservoir for storing water for the purpose of irrigating lands on the Fort Hall Indian Reservation and those ceded by the Indians of the said reservation and also the lands, rights, and property which he may determine to be necessary to the success of any plan or project for the said purpose; or he may cause the enlargement to be made of any irrigating system in accordance with the laws of Idaho that circumstances may require.

Upon acquiring the site, as herein provided, the Secretary may cause the system determined on to be constructed by contract or otherwise, in sections or as a whole, as he may determine, and may sell the water right for lands in private ownership at six dollars an acre, but no such right shall permanently attach until all payments therefor are made. The amount at which such water rights shall be sold shall be payable in five equal annual installments, to be paid to the receiver of the local land office, and the failure to make any two payments shall work a forfeiture of the rights acquired by the purchaser, and he shall lose the money previously paid and the water right for the land, but it may be purchased by another person who shall thereafter acquire the land in question at such price and upon such conditions as the Secretary of the Interior may determine, but not less than the cost originally determined. In addition, the same fee shall be paid to the register and receiver as though the land was entered as a part of the public domain at one dollar and twenty-five cents an acre; the money so paid, less the fee, shall reimburse the United States for the expenditures made thereunder.

The land susceptible of irrigation under the system herein provided and owned by Indians in severalty or in common shall be deemed to have a right to so much water as may be required to irrigate said lands, without cost to the Indians so long as the title remains in said Indians or tribe, but any such lands leased for a longer term than three years shall bear their pro rata part of the cost of the maintenance of the system that may be constructed, and when the Indian title is extinguished these lands shall also bear their pro rata cost of maintenance. When the payments required by this act are made for the major part of the lands that can be irrigated from the system, the management and operation of such irrigation work shall pass to the owners of the lands irrigated thereby, to be maintained at their expense under such form of organization and under such rules and regulations as may be acceptable to the Secretary of the Interior, in accordance with the statute of the

State of Idaho. The title to and management and operation of the reservoir and the works necessary to its protection and operation shall remain in the Government until otherwise provided by Congress. The Government institutions established for the administration of the affairs of the Fort Hall Reservation including the school plant and farm, shall have sufficient water for their needs without cost, and any town or city embraced within the project may acquire water rights sufficient for its needs on such terms and conditions as the Secretary of the Interior may impose.

The water rights acquired or provided for in this measure shall be appurtenant to the lands irrigated, and there is hereby appropriated for the purpose of carrying out the provisions of this act, three hundred and fifty thousand dollars, which shall be reimbursed the United States from the moneys obtained from the sale of water rights, and the Secretary of the Interior shall have full power to do all acts or make all rules and regulations necessary to carry out the provisions of this act relating to the foregoing irrigation system.

Act April 30, 1908 (35 Stat., 78): For carrying out the provisions of the act of March first, nineteen hundred and seven (thirty-fourth Statutes at Large, page one thousand and four), authorizing the Secretary of the Interior to acquire lands and other property necessary in constructing a reservoir for storing water for the purpose of irrigating lands on the Fort Hall Reservation in Idaho and those ceded by the Indians of said reservation, and for construction of the system determined on, one hundred thousand dollars.

Act March 3, 1909 (35 Stat., 790): For carrying out the provisions of the act of March first, nineteen hundred and seven (Thirty-fourth Statutes at Large, page one thousand and twenty-four), authorizing the Secretary of the Interior to acquire lands and other property necessary in constructing a reservoir for storing water for the purpose of irrigating lands on the Fort Hall Reservation in Idaho and those ceded by the Indians of said reservation, and for construction of the system determined on, one hundred thousand dollars, reimbursable.

That the Secretary of the Interior be, and he is hereby, authorized to investigate and settle the equitable claims of Neils Anderson, William Winchell, and others whose lands or improvements, held under possessory claims, have been or will be damaged by reason of the construction of said reservoir, for which purpose the sum of twenty-five thousand dollars, or so much thereof as may be necessary, is hereby appropriated.

Act April 4, 1910 (36 Stat., 274): For continuing the work of constructing an irrigation system for the irrigation of lands on the Fort Hall Reservation, Idaho, and lands ceded by the Indians of said reservation, one hundred thousand dollars: *Provided*, That the amount hereby appropriated, and all moneys heretofore or hereafter to be appropriated for this project, shall be repaid into the Treasury of the United States in accordance with the provisions of the act of March first, nineteen hundred and eleven: *Provided further*, That lands in private ownership shall pay only six dollars per acre for water rights, including construction charges, in accordance with the act of March first, nineteen hundred and seven: *Provided however*, That in case of any forfeiture of the rights acquired by the purchaser he shall lose the money previously paid and the water right for the land, but it may be purchased by another person who shall thereafter acquire the land in question at such price and on such conditions as the Secretary of the Interior may determine, but not less than the cost originally determined. * * *

For the twelfth to the twentieth, inclusive, of the twenty installments, as provided in the agreement with the Indians of the Fort Hall and Lemhi agencies, Idaho, approved February twenty-third, eighteen hundred and eighty-nine, to be used for the benefit of the Indians removed to Fort Hall Reservation from Lemhi agency, Idaho, insuch manner as the President may direct, thirty-six thousand dollars.

Provided, That it shall be optional with those Indians entitled to allotments on the Fort Hall Reservation whether they accept a portion of their allotment within the irrigated portion of the reservation or shall avail themselves of the provisions of the act of February twenty-third, eighteen hundred and eighty-nine, entitled "An act to accept and ratify the agreement submitted by the Shoshones, Bannocks, and the Sheepeaters of the Fort Hall and Lemhi Reservation in Idaho, May fourteenth, eighteen hundred and eighty, and for other purposes."

Act June 25, 1910 (36 Stat., 744): That twenty-five thousand dollars of the amount heretofore appropriated for continuing the work of constructing an irrigation system for the irrigation of lands on the Fort Hall Reservation, in Idaho, and lands ceded by the Indians of said reservation, as provided in the act approved April fourth, nineteen hundred and ten, be, and the same is hereby made immediately available for the purpose therein mentioned.

Act March 3, 1911 (36 Stat., 1063): To complete the work of constructing an irrigation system for the irrigation of lands on the Fort Hall Reservation, Idaho, and lands ceded by the Indians of said reservation, eighty-five thousand dollars, including ten thousaid dollars for maintenance, to be immediately available. * * *

The Secretary of the Interior is hereby authorized to cause allotments to be made of the lands on the Fort Hall Indian Reservation in Idaho in areas as follows: To each head of a family whose consort is dead, forty acres of irrigable land and three hundred and twenty acres of grazing land, and to each other Indian belonging on the reservation or having rights thereon, twenty acres of irrigable land and one hundred and sixty acres of grazing land.

Act August 24, 1912 (37 Stat., 524): For maintenance and operation of the Fort Hall irrigation system, twenty thousand dollars.

Act June 30, 1913 (38 Stat., 87): For maintenance and operation of the Fort Hall irrigation system, $20,000.

Act August 1, 1914 (38 Stat., 589): For maintenance and operation of the Fort Hall irrigation system, $25,000, reimbursable to the United States out of any funds of the Indians occupying the Fort Hall Reservation now or hereafter available.

Joint resolution March 4, 1915 (38 Stat., 1228), reenacted the item of August 1, 1914, for the fiscal year 1916.

Act May 18, 1916 (39 Stat., 132): For improvement and maintenance and operation of the Fort Hall irrigation system, $25,000, reimbursable to the United States out of any funds of the Indians occupying the Fort Hall Reservation now or hereafter available.

Act March 2, 1917 (39 Stat., 976): For improvement and maintenance and operation of the Fort Hall irrigation system, $25,000: *Provided*, That expenditures hereunder for improvements shall be reimbursable to the United States in accordance with the provisions of the act of March first, nineteen hundred and seven.

Act May 25, 1918 (40 Stat., 571); For improvement and maintenance and operation of the Fort Hall irrigation system, $50,000, to be immediately available: *Provided*, That expenditures hereunder for improvements shall be reimbursable to the United States in accordance with the provisions of the act of March first, nineteen hundred and seven.

Act June 30, 1919 (41 Stat., 13): For improvement and maintenance and operation of the Fort Hall irrigation system, $50,000: *Provided*, That expenditures hereunder for improvements shall be reimbursable to the United States in accordance with the provisions of the act of March 1, 1907.

Appropriations recapitulated.

Date	Amount	Date	Amount
To June 21, 1906	(?)	June 30, 1913	$20,000
June 21, 1906	$25,000	Aug. 1, 1914	25,000
Mar. 1, 1907	350,000	Mar. 4, 1915	25,000
Apr. 30, 1908	100,000	May 18, 1916	25,000
Mar. 3, 1909	100,000	Mar. 2, 1917	25,000
Mar. 3, 1909	25,000	May 25, 1918	50,000
Apr. 4, 1910	100,000	June 30, 1919	50,000
Apr. 4, 1910	36,000		
Mar. 3, 1911	85,000	Total	1,061,000+
Aug. 24, 1912	20,000		

KANSAS.

HASKELL INSTITUTE.

Act June 21, 1906 (34 Stat., 347): For draining and ditching, four thousand five hundred dollars, to be immediately available.

Act April 4, 1910 (36 Stat., 275): SEC. 8. * * * for drainage, ten thousand dollars.

Act May 25, 1918 (40 Stat., 571): For completing the construction of a drainage system on the Haskell Indian School Reservation, Lawrence, Kansas, $10,000, to be immediately available.

Appropriations recapitulated.

June 21, 1906	$4,500
Apr. 4, 1910	10,000
May 25, 1918	10,000
Total	24,500

MINNESOTA.

DRAINAGE.

Act July 1, 1898 (30 Stat., 576): For completing the necessary surveys within the Chippewa Indian Reservation in Minnesota, including expenses of examining and appraising pine lands, under the provisions of the act approved January fourteenth, eighteen hundred and eighty-nine, to be reimbursed to the United States out of proceeds of the sales of their lands, $50,000: *Provided*, That all lands heretofore or hereafter acquired and sold by the United States under the "Act for the relief and civilization of the Chippewa Indians in the State of Minnesota," approved January fourteenth, eighteen hundred and eighty-nine, shall be subject to the right of the United States to construct and maintain dams for the purpose of creating reservoirs in aid of navigation, and no claim or right of compensation shall accrue from the overflowing of said lands on account of the construction and maintenance of such dams or reservoirs. And the Secretary of War shall furnish the Commissioner of the General Land Office a list of such lands, with the particular tracts appropriately described, and in the disposal of each and every one of said tracts, whether by sale, by allotment in severalty to individual Indians, or otherwise, under said act, the provisions of this paragraph shall enter into and form a part of the contract of purchase or transfer of title.

(See also act of June 30, 1897 (30 Stat., 67).)

Act June 21, 1906 (34 Stat. L., 352): That the Secretary of the Interior is hereby authorized to cause to be made a drainage survey of the lands ceded by the Chippewa Indians in the State of Minnesota under the act of Congress entitled "An act for the relief and civilization of the Chippewa Indians in the State of Minnesota," approved January fourteenth, eighteen hundred and eighty-nine, and an act entitled "An act to authorize the sale of a part of what is known as the Red Lake Indian Reservation, in the State of Minnesota," approved February twentieth, nineteen hundred and four, which remain unsold, and are wet, overflowed, or swampy in character, with a view to determining what portions thereof may be profitably and economically reclaimed by drainage, the number, location, cost, and extent of drainage ditches, canals, or improved natural watercourses required to afford drainage outlets; and whether a sufficient fund for such improvement could be provided by an increase in the price at which such unsold ceded lands should be sold in the future, and the sum of fifteen thousand dollars, or so much thereof as may be necessary, is hereby appropriated, out of any money in the Treasury not otherwise appropriated, for the purpose of paying for the expenses of said survey and carrying the foregoing provision into effect: *Provided*, That said amount shall be reimbursable from any funds in the Treasury belonging to said Indians derived from the sale of lands under said act: *Provided further*, That the Secretary of the Interior in his discretion may withdraw said unsold ceded lands, or any portion thereof, from sale and entry pending the survey herein provided for or pending the improvements contemplated thereby.

Act March 1, 1907 (34 Stat., 1033): That the lands withdrawn by the Secretary of the Interior under the provisions of chapter thirty-five hundred and four, Fifty-ninth Congress, first session, approved June twenty-first, nineteen hundred and six, authorizing a drainage survey of the lands ceded by the Chippewa Indians, shall be subject to entry in the same manner as other lands so ceded, subject to the condition, however, that the entrymen shall be required in addition to the fees and charges now authorized by law, to pay a pro rata charge for the examination and investigation of the swampy and overflowed character of the land, and for the drainage and reclamation thereof.

Act March 1, 1907 (34 Stat., 1033): To carry out and complete the survey provided for in the act of Congress approved June twenty-first, nineteen hundred and six, of the lands ceded by the Chippewa Indians in the State of Minnesota under the act of Congress entitled "An act for the relief and civilization of the Chippewa Indians in the State of Minnesota," approved January fourteenth, eighteen hundred and eighty-nine, and an act entitled "An act to authorize the sale of a part of what is known as the Red Lake Indian Reservation, in the State of Minnesota," approved February twentieth, nineteen hundred and four, which remains unsold, and are wet, overflowed or swampy in character, with a view of determining what portion thereof may be profitably and economically reclaimed by drainage, the sum of ten thousand dollars, or so much thereof as may be necessary, is hereby appropriated, out of any money in the Treasury not otherwise appropriated. for the purpose of paying for the expense of said survey: *Provided*, That said amount shall be reimbursable from any funds in the Treasury belonging to said Indians and derived from the sale of the lands under said act. The said survey shall be continued under the direction of the Secretary of the Interior.

Act April 30, 1908 (35 Stat., 82): To complete the drainage survey provided for under the act of June twenty-first, nineteen hundred and six, $10,000: *Provided*, That said amount shall be reimbursed to the Treasury of the United States from the funds in the Treasury belonging to said Indians derived from the sale of lands under the act of January fourteenth, eighteen hundred and eighty-nine

Act May 20, 1908 (35 Stat., 171): SEC. 8. That hereafter homestead entries and final proofs may be made upon all ceded Chippewa Indian lands in Minnesota embraced in the withdrawal under the act of June twenty-first, nineteen hundred and six, entitled "An act making appropriations for the current and contingent expenses of the Indian Department" (Thirty-fourth Statutes at Large, page three hundred and twenty-five), and patents may issue thereon as in other homestead cases, upon the payment by the entryman of the price prescribed by law for such land and on entries on the ceded Red Lake Reservation, in addition thereto the sum of three cents per acre to repay the cost of the drainage survey thereof, which addition shall be disposed of the same as the other proceeds of said land.

(Entire act to which reference is made may be applicable to some extent.)

Act June 30, 1913 (38 Stat., 88): That the unexpended balance of the appropriation for the completion of the drainage survey of ceded Indian lands made by the act of May thirtieth, nineteen hundred and eight, is hereby reappropriated and made immediately available for an extension of the drainage survey, together with an estimate of the cost of the project, to cover the Red Lake Diminished Reservation in Minnesota, with a view to determining what portions thereof may be profitably and economically reclaimed by drainage to make the same suitable for agricultural purposes.

Act August 1, 1914 (38 Stat., 591): That the Secretary of the Interior be, and he is hereby authorized, in his discretion, to approve the assessments, together with maps showing right of way and definite location of proposed drainage ditches made under the laws of the State of Minnesota upon the tribal and allotted lands of the Fond du Lac Indian Reservation, Minnesota, in Carlton County, judicial ditch number one. That the Secretary of the Interior be, and he is hereby authorized, in his discretion, to pay the amount assessed against said allotted and tribal lands. There is hereby appropriated out of any money in the Treasury not otherwise appropriated the sum of $13,080, to be reimbursable from any funds belonging to the individual allottees or their heirs or from any funds belonging to the tribe subject to be prorated in the discretion of the Secretary of the Interior. That the Secretary of the Interior be, and he is hereby authorized, to approve deeds for right of way from such said allottees or their heirs as may be necessary to permit the construction and maintenance of said drainage ditch upon the payment of adequate damages therefor: *Provided*, That no patent in fee shall be issued for any tract of land under the terms of this paragraph until the United States shall have been wholly reimbursed for all assessments paid, or to be paid on such tract, under the terms hereof. That the Secretary of the Interior is hereby authorized to do and perform any and all acts and to make such rules and regulations as may be necessary and proper for the purpose of carrying the provisions hereof into force and effect.

Act March 2, 1917 (39 Stat., 978): That the Secretary of the Interior be, and he is hereby, authorized, in his discretion, to approve the assessments, together with maps showing right of way and definite location of proposed drainage ditches made under the laws of the State of Minnesota upon the tribal and allotted lands of the Indian reservations in the State of Minnesota. That the Secretary of the Interior be, and he is hereby, authorized, in his discretion, to pay the amounts assessed against said tribal and allotted lands, on account of benefits accruing to said lands by reason of the construction of a drainage ditch or ditches under the laws of the State of Minnesota.

That for the purposes specified in this section there is hereby appropriated, out of any money in the Treasury not otherwise appropriated, the sum of $60,000, to be reimbursable from any funds in the possession of the United States belonging to the individual allottees whose lands are benefited, or their heirs, in case of their decease, when the payment relates to allotted lands, and from any funds belonging to the tribes subject to be prorated, when the payment relates to tribal lands. That the Secretary of the Interior be, and he is hereby, authorized to approve deeds for right of way from such said allottees, or their heirs, as may be necessary to permit the construction and maintenance of said drainage ditches upon the payment of adequate damages therefor: *Provided*, That no patent in fee shall be issued for any tract of land under the terms of this paragraph until the United States shall have been wholly reimbursed for all assessments paid or to be paid on such tract under the terms hereof. That the Secretary of the Interior is hereby authorized to do and perform any and all acts and to make such rules and regulations as may be necessary and proper for the purpose of carrying the provisions hereof into force and effect.

Act June 30, 1919 (41 Stat., 15): That the Secretary of the Interior be, and he is hereby, authorized, in his discretion, to pay the amounts assessed against tribal and allotted lands of the Indian reservations of Minnesota on account of benefits accruing to said lands by reason of the construction of a drainage ditch or ditches under the laws of Minnesota. There is hereby appropriated, out of any money in the Treasury of the United States not otherwise appropriated, the sum of $60,000, or so much thereof as may be necessary, to be reimbursed from any funds in the possession of the United States belonging to the individual allottees whose lands are benefited, or their heirs, in case of their decease, when the payment relates to allotted lands, and from any funds belonging to the tribe subject to be prorated, when the payment relates to tribal lands: *Provided*, That no patent in fee shall be issued for any tract of land under the terms of this paragraph until the United States shall have been wholly reimbursed for all assessments paid or to be paid on such tract under the terms hereof.

MONTANA.

BLACKFEET.

Act June 10, 1896 (29 Stat., 354), Article II: For and in consideration of the conveyance, cession, and relinquishment hereinbefore made the United States hereby covenants and agrees to advance and expend during the period of ten years beginning from and after the expiration of the payments provided for in the agreement made between the parties hereto on the eleventh day of February, A. D., eighteen hundred and eighty-seven, and ratified by Congress on the first day of May, A. D. eighteen hundred and eighty-eight, under the direction of the Secretary of the Interior for the Indians, both full bloods and mixed bloods, now attached to and receiving rations and annuities at the Blackfeet Agency, and all who shall hereafter be declared by the tribes located upon said reservation, with the approval of the Secretary of the Interior, entitled to membership in those tribes, the sum of one million five hundred thousand ($1,500,000.00) dollars.

It is agreed that said money shall be paid as follows: The first year after the expiration of payments under the agreement of eighteen hundred and eighty-seven (1887), three hundred thousand ($300,000.00) dollars, one-half of which shall be deposited in the United States Treasury and bear interest at four per centum per annum, and one-half, or so much thereof as shall be necessary, shall be expended as hereinafter provided; and annually thereafter for eight years the sum of one hundred and fifty thousand ($150,000.00) dollars: *Provided*, That any surplus accumulated under and remaining at the expiration of the agreement of 1887, and any surplus that may remain from any annual payment provided for herein, shall also be placed in the United States Treasury to the credit of said Indians, and shall bear interest at the rate of four per centum per annum. Such sums, or so much thereof as may be necessary in any one year, shall be expended in the purchase of cows, bulls, and other live stock, goods, clothing, subsistence, agricultural implements, in providing employees, in the education of Indian children, in procuring medicine and medical attendance, in the care and support of the aged, sick, and infirm, and of helpless orphans, in the erection and keeping in repair of such new agency and school buildings, mills, blacksmith, carpenter, and wagon shops as may be necessary, in assisting the Indians to build and keep in repair their houses, inclose and irrigate their farms, and in such other ways as may best promote their civilization and improvement.

ARTICLE VII. It is further agreed that whenever, in the opinion of the President, the public interests require the construction of railroads or other highways, telegraph or telephone lines, canals and irrigation ditches, through any portion of this reservation, right of way shall be and is hereby granted for such purposes, under such rules, regulations, limitations, and restrictions as the Secretary of the Interior may prescribe; the compensation to be fixed by said Secretary and by him expended for the benefit of the Indians.

Act March 1, 1907 (34 Stat., 1035): That the Secretary of the Interior is hereby authorized and directed to immediately cause to be surveyed all of the lands embraced within the limits of the Blackfeet Indian Reservation, in the State of Montana.

That so soon as all the lands embraced within the said Blackfeet Indian reservation shall have been surveyed the Commissioner of Indian Affairs shall cause allotments of the same to be made under the provisions of the allotment laws of the United States to all persons having tribal rights or holding tribal relations and who may rightfully belong on said reservation. That there shall be allotted to each member forty acres of irrigable land and two hundred and eighty acres of additional land valuable only for grazing purposes; or, at the option of the allottee, the entire three hundred and twenty acres may be taken in land valuable only for grazing purposes, respectively, and for constructing irrigating systems to irrigate the aforesaid allotted lands, three hundred thousand dollars, one hundred thousand dollars of which shall be immediately available, the cost of said entire work to be reimbursed from the proceeds of the sale of the lands within said reservation: *Provided*, That the Indians and the settlers on the surplus land, in the order named, shall have a preference right for one year from the date of the President's proclamation opening the reservation to settlement to appropriate the waters of the reservation, which shall be filed on and appropriated under the laws of the State of Montana by the Commissioner of Indian Affairs on behalf of the Indians taking irrigable allotments and by the settlers under the same law. At the expiration of the one year aforesaid the irrigation system constructed and to be constructed shall be operated under the laws of the State of Montana, and the title to such systems as may be constructed under this act, until otherwise provided by law, shall be in the Secretary of the Interior in trust for the said Indians, and he may sue and be sued in matters relating thereto: *And provided further*, That the ditches and canals of such irrigation systems may be used, extended, or enlarged for the purpose of conveying water by any person, association, or corporation under and upon compliance with the provisions of the laws of the State of Montana: *And provided further*, That when said irrigation systems are in successful operation the cost of operating the same shall be equitably apportioned upon the lands irrigated, and when the Indians have become self-supporting to the annual charge shall be added an amount sufficient to pay back into the Treasury the cost of the work done in their behalf within thirty years, suitable deduction being made for the amounts received from the disposal of the lands within the reservation aforesaid: *Provided*, That the right to the use of water acquired under the provisions of this act shall be appurtenant to the land irrigated, and beneficial use shall be the basis, the measure, and the limit of the right: * * *

That if, after the approval of the classification and appraisement, as provided for herein, there shall be found lands within the limits of the reservation under irrigation projects deemed practicable under the provisions of the act of Congress approved June seventeenth, nineteen hundred and two, known as the reclamation act, said lands shall be subject to withdrawal and be disposed of under the provisions of said act, and settlers shall pay, in addition to the cost of construction and maintenance provided therein, the appraised value, as provided in this act, to the proper officers, to be covered into the Treasury of the United States to the credit of the Indians: * * *

Act April 4, 1910 (36 Stat., 277): For construction of irrigation systems to irrigate the allotted lands of the Indians of the Blackfeet Indian Reservation in Montana and the unallotted irrigable lands to be disposed of under authority of law, including the necessary surveys, plans, and estimates, two hundred thousand dollars: *Provided*, That the amount hereby appropriated, and all moneys heretofore or hereafter to be appropriated for this project shall be repaid into the Treasury of the United States in accordance with the provisions of the act of March first, nineteen hundred and seven.

Act March 3, 1911 (36 Stat., 1066): For continuing construction of the first unit of irrigation system to irrigate the allotted lands of the Indians of the Blackfeet Indian Reservation in Montana and the unallotted irrigable lands to be disposed of under authority of law, including the necessary surveys, plans, and estimates, one hundred and fifty thousands dollars.

Act August 24, 1912 (37 Stat., 526): For continuing the construction of irrigation systems to irrigate the allotted lands of the Indians of the Blackfeet Indian Reservation in Montana, and the unallotted irrigable lands to be disposed of under authority of law, including the necessary surveys, plans, and estimates, one hundred thousand dollars, reimbursable in accordance with the provision of the act of March first, nineteen hundred and seven.

Act June 30, 1913 (38 Stat., 90): For continuing the construction or irrigation systems to irrigate the allotted lands of the Indians of the Blackfeet Indian Reservation, in Montana, and the unallotted irrigable lands to be disposed of under authority of law, including the necessary surveys, plans, and estimates, $150,000, reimbursable in occordance with the provisions of the act of March first, nineteen hundred and seven.

Act August 1, 1914 (38 Stat., 593): For continuing the construction of irrigation systems to irrigate the lands of the Indians of the Blackfeet Indian Reservation, in Montana, including the necessary surveys, plans, and estimates, $50,000, reimbursable in accordance with the provisions of the act of March first, nineteen hundred and seven, and to remain available until expended.

Joint Resolution March 4, 1915 (38 Stat., 1228) reenacted the item of August 1, 1914, for the fiscal year 1916.

Act May 18, 1916 (39 Stat., 140): For continuing construction of the irrigation systems on the Blackfeet Indian Reservation, in Montana, $25,000 (reimbursable), which shall be immediately available: *Provided*, that the entryman upon the surplus unallotted lands to be irrigated by such systems shall, in addition to compliance with the homestead laws, before receiving patents for the lands covered by his entry, pay the charges apportioned against such tract as herein authorized, and a failure to make any two payments when due shall render the entry subject to cancellation, with the forfeiture to the United States of all rights acquired under the provisions of this act, as well as of any moneys paid on account thereof. The purchaser of any Indian allotment to be irrigated by such systems, purchased upon approval of the Secretary of the Interior, before the charges against said allotment herein authorized shall have been paid, shall pay all charges remaining unpaid at the time of such purchase and in all patents or deeds for such purchased allotments, and also in all patents in fee to allottees or their heirs issued before payment, of all such charges herein authorized to be made against their allotments, there shall be expressed that there is reserved upon the lands therein described a lien for such charges, and such lien may be enforced; or, upon payment of the delinquent charges, may be released by the Secretary of the Interior.

The work to be done with the amounts herein appropriated for the completion of the Blackfeet, Flathead, and Fort Peck projects may be done by the Reclamation Service on plans and estimates furnished by that service and approved by the Commissioner of Indian Affairs: *Provided*, That not to exceed $15,000 of applicable appropriations made for the Flathead, Blackfeet, and Fort Peck irrigation projects shall be available for the maintenance, repair, and operation of motor-propelled and horse-drawn passenger-carrying vehicles for official use upon the aforesaid irrigation projects: *Provided further*, That not to exceed $7,500 may be used for the purchase of horse-drawn passenger-carrying vehicles, and that not to exceed $1,500 may be used for the purchase of motor-propelled passenger-carrying vehicles.

That the Secretary of the Interior be, and he is hereby, authorized and directed to announce, at such time as in his opinion seems proper, the charge for construction of irrigation systems on the Blackfeet, Flathead, and Fort Peck Indian Reservations in Montana, which shall be made against each acre of land irrigable by the systems on each of said reservations. Such charges shall be assessed against the land irrigable by the systems on each said reservation in the proportion of the total construction cost which each acre of such land bears to the whole area of irrigable land thereunder.

On the first day of December after the announcement by the Secretary of the Interior of the construction charge the allottee, entryman, purchaser, or owner of such irrigable land which might have been furnished water for irrigation during the whole of the preceding irrigation season, from ditches actually constructed, shall pay to the superintendent of the reservation where the land is located, for deposit to the credit of the United States as a reimbursement of the appropriations made or to be made for construction of said irrigation systems, five per centum of the construction charge fixed for his land, as an initial installment, and shall pay the balance of the charge in fifteen annual installments, the first five of which shall each be five per centum of the construction charge and the remainder shall each be seven per centum of the construction charge. The first of the annual installments shall become due and payable on December first of the fifth calendar year after the initial installment: *Provided*, That any allottee, entryman, purchaser, or owner may, if he so elects, pay the whole or any part of the construction charges within any shorter period: *Provided further*, That the Secretary of the Interior may, in his discretion, grant such extension of the time for payments herein acquired from Indian allottees or their heirs as he may determine proper and necessary, so long as such land remains in Indian title.

That the tribal funds heretofore covered into the Treasury of the United States in partial reimbursement of appropriations made for constructing irrigation systems on said reservations shall be placed to the credit of the tribe and be available for such expenditure for the benefit of the tribe as Congress may hereafter direct.

The cost of constructing the irrigation systems to irrigate allotted lands of the Indians on these reservations shall be reimbursed to the United States as herein before provided, and no further reimbursements from the tribal funds shall be made on account of said irrigation works except that all charges against Indian allottees or their heirs herein authorized, unless otherwise paid, may be paid from the individual shares in the tribal funds, when the same is available for distribution, in the discretion of the Secretary of the Interior.

That in addition to the construction charges every allottee, entryman, purchaser, or owner shall pay to the superintendent of the reservation a maintenance and operation charge based upon the total cost of maintenance and operation of the systems on the several reservations, and the Secretary of the Interior is hereby authorized to fix such maintenance and operation charge upon such basis as shall be equitable to the owners of the irrigable land. Such charges when collected shall be available for expenditure in the maintenance and operation of the systems on the reservation where collected: *Provided*, That delivery of water to any tract of land may be refused on account of nonpayment of any charges herein authorized, and the same may, in the discretion of the Secretary of the Interior, be collected by a suit for money owed: *Provided further*, That the rights of the United States heretofore acquired, to water for Indian lands referred to in the foregoing provision, namely, the Blackfeet, Fort Peck, and Flathead Reservation land, shall be continued in full force and effect until the Indian title to such land is extinguished.

That the Secretary of the Interior be, and he is hereby, authorized to prescribe such rules and regulations and issue such notices as may be necessary to carry into effect the provisions of this act, and he is hereby authorized and directed to determine the area of land on each reservation which may be irrigated from constructed ditches, and to determine what allowance, if any, shall be made for ditches constructed by individuals for the diversion and distribution of a partial or total water supply for allotted or surplus unallotted land: *Provided*, That if water be available prior to the announcement of the charge herein authorized, the Secretary of the Interior may furnish water to land under the systems on the said reservations, making a reasonable charge therefor, and such charges when collected may be used for construction or maintenance of the systems through which such water shall have been furnished.

Act March 2, 1917 (39 Stat., 980): For continuing construction of the irrigation systems of the Blackfeet Indian Reservation, in Montana, $25,000 (reimbursable), which shall be immediately available and remain available until expended: *Provided*, That not to exceed $15,000 of applicable appropriations made for the Flathead, Blackfeet, and Fort Peck irrigation projects shall be available for the maintenance, repair, and operation of motor-propelled and horse-drawn passenger-carrying vehicles for official use upon the aforesaid irrigation projects: *Provided further*, That not to exceed $9,000 may be used for the purchase of horse-drawn passenger-carrying vehicles, and that not to exceed $2,000 may be used for the purchase of motor-propelled passenger-carrying vehicles.

Act May 25, 1918 (40 Stat., 574): For continuing construction, maintenance, and operation of the irrigation systems on the Blackfeet Indian Reservation, in Montana, $50,000 (reimbursable), which shall be immedately available, and remain available until expended: *Provided*, That not to exceed $15,000 of applicable appropriations made for the Flathead, Blackfeet, and Fort Pack irrigation projects shall be available for the maintenance, repair, and operation of motor-propelled and horsedrawn passenger-carrying vehicles for official use upon the aforesaid irrigation project: *Provided further*, That not to exceed $3,500 may be used for the purchase of horse-drawn passenger-carrying vehicles, and that not to exceed $4,000 may be used for the purchase of motor-propelled passenger-carrying vehicles.

Act June 30, 1919 (41 Stat., 16): For continuing construction, maintenance, and operation of the irrigation systems on the Blackfeet Indian Reservation, in Montana, $50,000 (reimbusable): *Provided*, That not to exceed $15,000 of applicable appropriations made for the Flathead, Blackfeet, and Fort Peck irrigation projects shall be available for the maintenance, repair, and operation of motor-propelled and horsedrawn passenger-carrying vehicles for official use upon the aforesaid irrigation project: *Provided further*, That not to exceed $3,500 may be used for the purchase of horse-drawn passenger-carrying vehicles, and that not to exceed $4,000 may be used for the purchase of motor-propelled passenger-carrying vehicles.

Act June 30, 1919 (41 Stat., 16): That so much of the Indian appropriation act of March 1, 1907 (Thirty-fourth Statutes at Large, pages 1015 and 1035), as relates to the disposal of surplus unallotted lands within the Blackfeet Indian Reservation, in Montana, is hereby repealed, and the Secretary of the Interior is authorized to make allotments under existing laws within the said reservation to any Indians of said Blackfeet Tribe not heretofore allotted, living six months after the approval of this act, and thereafter to prorate all unallotted and otherwise unreserved lands therein among the Indians who have been allotted or may be entitled to rights within said reservation: *Provided*, That of the lands so allotted eighty acres of each allotment shall be designated as a homestead by the allottee and be evidenced by a trust patent and shall remain inalienable and non-taxable until Congress shall otherwise direct: *Provided further*, That the Blackfeet tribal rolls shall close six months after the approval of this act and thereafter no additional names shall be added to said rolls: *Provided*, That nothing herein shall be construed to repeal the grants of land made by the act of March 1, 1907, to religious institutions and to the State of Montana for school purposes, nor repeal the authority of the Secretary of the Interior to dispose of any land within said reservation suitable for townsite purposes, as provided by that act: *Provided*, That the State of Montana, in making indemnity school selections, shall be confined to nonmineral and nonirrigable lands: *Provided further*, That the provisions of the act of March 1, 1907, which require a division of the funds received from the sale of the surplus lands immediately upon the date of the approval of the allotments of land are hereby repealed: *Provided further*, That the lands within said reservation, whether allotted, unallotted, reserved, set aside for townsite purposes, granted to the State of Montana for school purposes, or otherwise disposed of, shall be subject to all the laws of the United States prohibiting the introduction of intoxicants into the Indian country until otherwise provided by Congress: *Provided further*, That any and all minerals, including coal, oil, and gas, are hereby reserved for the benefit of the Blackfeet Tribe of Indians until Congress shall otherwise direct, and patents hereafter issued shall contain a reservation accordingly: *Provided*, That the lands containing said minerals may be leased under such rules and regulations, and upon such terms and conditions as the Secretary of the Interior may prescribe: *And provided further*, That allotments herein provided for shall be made under such rules and regulations as the said Secretary may prescribe, and trust patents shall be issued therefor as provided by the aforesaid act of March 1, 1907, except as to the homestead hereinbefore mentioned.

Appropriations recapitulated.

June 10, 1896	(?)	Mar. 4, 1915	$50,000
Mar. 1, 1907	$300,000	May 18, 1916	25,000
Apr. 4, 1910	200,000	Mar. 2, 1917	25,000
Mar. 3, 1911	150,000	May 25, 1918	50,000
Aug. 24, 1912	100,000	June 30, 1919	50,000
June 30, 1913	150,000		
Aug. 1, 1914	50,000	Total	1,150,000+

CROW.

Crow agreement, March 3, 1891 (26 Stat., 1040): That, in consideration of the cession of territory herein made by us as individual Indians and heads of families of the Crow tribe to the Government of the United States, the said Government of the United States, in addition to the annuities and sums for provisions and clothing stipulated and provided for in existing treaties and laws, hereby agrees to pay the sum of nine hundred and forty-six thousand dollars, lawful money of the United States, in the manner hereinafter described:

First: That, of the above-named sum, there is hereby appropriated and set apart two hundred thousand dollars to be expended under the direction of the Secretary of the Interior in the building of dams, canals, ditches, and laterals for the purpose of irrigation in the valleys of the Big Horn and Little Big Horn Rivers, and on Pryor Creek, and such other streams as the Secretary of the Interior may deem proper: *Provided*, That not to exceed fifty thousand dollars shall be expended annually in performing this work: *And provided further*, That the superintendent in charge of said works shall, in the employment of laborers, be required to give preference to such Indians of the Crow tribe as are competent and willing to work at the average wages paid to common laborers for the same kind of work, and the labor so employed shall be paid in cash.

That the sum of seventy-five thousand dollars is hereby appropriated and set apart as an irrigating fund, to be expended under the direction of the Secretary of the Interior for the maintenance and management of the system of irrigation provided for in this agreement.

Act March 1, 1899 (30 Stat. 947): * * * *Provided*, That, with the consent of the Crow Indians in Montana, to be obtained in the usual way, the Secretary of the Interior, in his discretion, may use the annuity money due, or to become due, the said Indians to complete the irrigation system heretofore commenced on said Crow Indian Reservation.

Act May 31, 1900 (31 Stat., 247): * * * *Provided*, That with the consent of the Crow Indians in Montana, to be obtained in the usual way, the Secretary of the Interior, in his discretion, may use the annuity money due, or to become due, said Indians to complete the irrigation system heretofore commenced on said Crow Indian Reservation.

Crow agreement, act April 27, 1904 (33 Stat., 357):

ART. II. * * * Ninety thousand dollars, or so much thereof as may be necessary, shall be expended, under the direction of the Secretary of the Interior, in the extension and completion, including the necessary laterals, of the system of irrigation now being constructed on said reservation.

One hundred thousand dollars shall be placed in the Treasury of the United States to the credit of the Crow Indians as a trust fund, the same to remain in the Treasury for fifteen years and shall draw interest at the rate of four per centum per annum, said interest to be expended by the Secretary of the Interior in maintaining and managing said irrigation system: *Provided, further*, That at the expiration of the fifteen years above mentioned such disposition shall be made of said fund as the Indians, with the consent of the Secretary of the Interior, may determine.

* * * It is further agreed that in the construction of ditches, dams, canals, and fences no contract shall be awarded nor employment given to other than Crow Indians or whites intermarried with them, except that any Indian employed in construction may hire white men to work for him if he so desires: *Provided, further*, That nothing herein contained shall be construed to prevent the employment of such engineers or other skilled employees, or to prevent the employment of white labor where it is impracticable for the Crows to perform the same.

ART. V. The water from streams on that portion of the reservation now sold which is necessary for irrigating land actually cultivated and in use shall be reserved for the Indians now using the same so long as said Indians remain where they now live.

ART. VIII. The right to take out water upon the diminished reservation subject to any prior claim of the Indians thereto by reason of previous appropriation, and the right to construct, maintain, and operate dams, flumes, and canals upon and across the said diminished reservation for the purpose of irrigating lands within any portion of the ceded tract are hereby granted, such rights to be exercised by persons, companies, or corporations under such rules, regulations, and requirements as may be prescribed by the Secretary of the Interior.

SEC. 5. * * * the residue of such ceded lands except sections sixteen and thirty-six, or lands in lieu thereof, which shall be reserved for common-school purposes, and are hereby granted to the State of Montana for such purpose, shall be subject to withdrawal and disposition under the reclamation act of June seventeenth, nineteen hundred and two, so far as feasible irrigation projects may be found therein. The charges provided for by said reclamation act shall be in addition to the charge of four dollars per acre for the land, and shall be paid in annual installments as required under the reclamation act; and the amounts to be paid for the land shall be credited to the funds herein established for the benefit of the Crow Indians. If any lands in sections sixteen and thirty-six are included in an irrigation project under the reclamation act, the State of Montana may select in lieu thereof, as herein provided, other lands not included in any such project, in accordance with the provisions of existing law concerning school-land selections. In any construction work upon the ceded lands performed directly by the United States under the reclamation act, preference shall be given to the employment of Crow Indians, or whites intermarried with them, as far as may be practicable: *Provided, however*, That if the lands withdrawn under the reclamation act are not disposed of within five years after the passage of this act, then all of said lands so withdrawn shall be disposed of as other lands provided for in this act. That the lands not withdrawn for irrigation under said reclamation act, which lands shall be determined under the direction of the Secretary of the Interior at the earliest practicable date, shall be disposed of under the homestead, town site, and mineral-land laws of the United States, and shall be opened to settlement and entry by proclamation of the President, which proclamation shall prescribe the manner in which these lands may be settled upon, occupied, and entered by persons entitled to make entry thereof; and no person shall be permitted to settle upon, occupy, or enter any of said lands, except as prescribed in such proclamation, until after the expiration of sixty days from the time when the same are opened to settlement and entry.

Act March 3, 1909 (35 Stat., 797): That any of the lands withdrawn under the reclamation act in pursuance of the provisions of section five of the act of Congress approved April twenty-seventh, nineteen hundred and four, entitled, "An act to ratify and amend an agreement with the Indians of the Crow Reservation, in Montana, and making appropriations to carry the same into effect," which are not disposed of within five years from the date of the passage of said act shall remain subject to disposal under the provisions of the reclamation act until otherwise directed by the Secretary of the Interior.

Act May 25, 1918 (40 Stat., 574): That the Secretary of the Interior be, and he is hereby, authorized to withdraw from the Treasury of the United States the sum of $200,000 of any tribal funds on deposit to the credit of the Crow Indians in the State of Montana, and to expend the same for making necessary improvements to the irrigation systems in the Big Horn Valley on the Crow Reservation in Montana, said sum, or such part thereof as may be used for the purpose indicated, to be reimbursed to the tribe under such rules and regulations as may be prescribed by the Secretary of the Interior.

Act June 30, 1919 (41 Stat., 16): That the Secretary of the Interior be, and he is hereby, authorized to withdraw from the Treasury of the United States the sum of $150,000 of any tribal funds on deposit to the credit of the Crow Indians, in the State of Montana, and to expend the same for making necessary improvements to the irrigation systems in the Big Horn Valley on the Crow Reservation in Montana, said sum, or such part thereof as may be used for the purpose indicated, to be reimbursed to the tribe under such rules and regulations as may be prescribed by the Secretary of the Interior.

Act July 19, 1919 (41 Stat., 196): Of the sum of $150,000, which the Secretary of the Interior is authorized by the Indian appropriation act for the fiscal year 1920 to withdraw from the tribal funds of the Crow Indians in the State of Montana to be expended for making necessary improvements to the irrigation systems in the Big Horn Valley on the Crow Reservation in Montana, said sum, or such part thereof as may be used for the purpose indicated, to be reimbursed to the tribe under such rules and regulations as may be prescribed by the Secretary of the Interior, not to exceed $25,000 of this amount shall be available for expenses incurred during the fiscal year ending June 30, 1919.

FLATHEAD.

Act April 23, 1904 (33 Stat., 305): SEC. 14. That the proceeds received from the sale of said lands in conformity with this act shall be paid into the Treasury of the United States, and after deducting the expenses of the commission, of classification and sale of lands, and such other incidental expenses as shall have been necessarily incurred, and expenses of the survey of the lands, shall be expended or paid, as follows: One-half shall be expended from time to time by the Secretary of the Interior as he may deem advisable for the benefit of the said Indians and such persons having tribal rights on the reservation, including the Lower Pend d'Oreille or Kalispel thereon at the time that this act shall take effect, in the construction of irrigation ditches, the purchase of stock cattle, farming implements, or other necessary articles to aid the Indians in farming and stock raising, and in the education and civilization of said Indians, and the remaining half to be paid to the said Indians and such persons having tribal rights on the reservation, including the Lower Pend d'Oreille or Kalispel thereon at the date of the proclamation provided for in section nine hereof, or expended on their account, as they may elect.

Act June 21, 1906 (34 Stat., 354): That the act of April twenty-third, nineteen hundred and four (Thirty-third Statutes at Large, page three hundred and two), entitled "An act for the survey and allotment of lands now embraced within the limits of the Flathead Indian Reservation, in the State of Montana, and the sale and disposal of all surplus lands after allotment," as amended by section nine of the act of March third, nineteen hundred and five (Thirty-third Statutes at Large, page one thousand and forty-eight), be amended by adding the following sections:

SEC. 19. That nothing in this act shall be construed to deprive any of said Indians, or said persons or corporations to whom the use of land is granted by this act, of the use of water appropriated and used by them for the necessary irrigation of their lands or for domestic use or any ditches, dams, flumes, reservoirs constructed and used by them in the appropriation and use of said water.

Act April 30, 1908 (35 Stat., 83): For preliminary surveys, plans, and estimates of irrigating systems to irrigate the allotted lands of the Indians of the Flathead Reservation in Montana and the unallotted irrigable lands to be disposed of under the act of April twenty-third, nineteen hundred and four, entitled "An act for the survey and allotment of lands now embraced within the limits of the Flathead Indian Reservation, in the State of Montana, and the sale and disposal of all surplus lands after allotment," and to begin the construction of the same, fifty thousand dollars, the cost of said entire work to be reimbursed from the proceeds of the sale of the lands within said reservation.

Act May 29, 1908 (35 Stat., 448): Sec. 15. That section nine, chapter fourteen hundred and ninety-five, Statutes of the United States of America, entitled "An act for the survey and allotment of lands now embraced within the limits of the Flathead Indian Reservation, in the State of Montana, and the sale and disposal of all surplus lands after allotment," be, and the same is hereby, amended to read as follows:

"Sec. 9. That said lands shall be opened to settlement and entry by proclamation of the President, which proclamation shall prescribe the time when and the manner in which these lands may be settled upon, occupied, and entered by persons entitled to make entry thereof, and no person shall be permitted to settle upon, occupy, or enter any of said lands, except as prescribed in such proclamation: *Provided*, That the rights of honorably discharged Union soldiers and sailors of the late Civil and Spanish Wars, as defined and prescribed in section twenty-three hundred and four and twenty-three hundred and five of the Revised Statutes, as amended by the act of March first, nineteen hundred and one, shall not be abridged: *Provided further*, That the price of said lands shall be the appraised value thereof, as fixed by the said commission, but settlers under the homestead law who shall reside upon and cultivate the land entered in good faith for the period required by existing law shall pay one-third of the appraised value in cash at the time of entry, and the remainder in five equal annual installments, to be paid one, two, three, four, and five years, respectively, from and after the date of entry, and shall be entitled to a patent for the lands so entered upon the payment to the local land officers of said five annual payments, and in addition thereto the same fees and commissions at the time of commutation or final entry as now provided by law where the price of the land is one dollar and twenty-five cents per acre, and no other and further charge of any kind whatsoever shall be required of such settler to entitle him to a patent for the land covered by his entry: *Provided*, That if any entryman fails to make such payments, or any of them, within the time stated, all rights in and to the land covered by his or her entry shall at once cease, and any payments theretofore made shall be forfeited, and the entry shall be forfeited and canceled: *And provided*, That nothing in this act shall prevent homestead settlers from commuting their entries under section twenty-three hundred and one, Revised Statutes, by paying for the land entered the price fixed by said commission, receiving credit for payments previously made: *Provided, however*, That the entryman or owner of any land irrigable by any system hereunder constructed under the provisions of section fourteen of this act shall in addition to the payment required by section nine of said act be required to pay for a water right the proportionate cost of the construction of said system in not more than fifteen annual installments, as fixed by the Secretary of the Interior, the same to be paid at the local land office, and the register and receiver shall be allowed the usual commissions on all moneys paid.

"The entryman of lands to be irrigated by said system shall in addition to compliance with the homestead laws reclaim at least one-half of the total irrigable area of his entry for agricultural purposes, and before receiving patent for the lands covered by his entry shall pay the charges apportioned against such tract. No right to the use of water shall be disposed of for a tract exceeding one hundred and sixty acres to any one person, and the Secretary of the Interior may limit the areas to be entered at not less than forty nor more than one hundred and sixty acres each.

"A failure to make any two payments when due shall render the entry and water-right application subject to cancellation, with the forfeiture of all rights under this act, as well as of any moneys paid thereon. The funds arising hereunder shall be paid into the Treasury of the United States and be added to the proceeds derived from the sale of the lands. No right to the use of water for lands in private ownership shall be sold to any landowner unless he be an actual bona fide resident on such land or occupant thereof residing in the neighborhood of such land, and no such right shall permanently attach until all payments therefor are made.

"All applicants for water rights under the systems constructed in pursuance of this act shall be required to pay such annual charges for operation and maintenance as shall be fixed by the Secretary of the Interior, and the failure to pay such charges when due shall render the water-right application and the entry subject to cancellation, with the forfeiture of all rights under this act as well as of any moneys already paid thereon.

"The Secretary of the Interior is hereby authorized to fix the time for the beginning of such payments and to provide such rules and regulations in regard thereto as he may deem proper. Upon the cancellation of any entry or water-right application, as herein provided, such lands or water rights may be disposed of under the terms of this act and at such price and upon such conditions as the Secretary of the Interior may determine, but not less than the cost originally fixed.

"The land irrigable under the systems herein provided, which has been allotted to Indians in severalty, shall be deemed to have a right to so much water as may be required to irrigate such lands without cost to the Indians for construction of such irrigation systems. The purchaser of any Indian allotment, purchased prior to the expiration of the trust period thereon, shall be exempt from any and all charge for construction of the irrigation system incurred up to the time of such purchase. All lands allotted to Indians shall bear their pro rata share of the cost of the operation and maintenance of the system under which they lie.

"When the payments required by this act have been made for the major part of the unallotted lands irrigable under any system and subject to charges for construction thereof, the management and operation of such irrigation works shall pass to the owners of the lands irrigated thereby, to be maintained at their expense under such form of organization and under such rules and regulations as may be acceptable to the Secretary of the Interior.

"The Secretary of the Interior is hereby authorized to perform any and all acts and to make such rules and regulations as may be necessary and proper for the purpose of carrying the provisions of this act into full force and effect."

That section fourteen of said act be, and the same is hereby, amended to read as follows:

"SEC. 14. That the proceeds received from the sale of said lands in conformity with this act shall be paid into the Treasury of the United States, and after deducting the expenses of the commission, of classification and sale of lands, and such other incidental expenses as shall have been necessarily incurred, and expenses of the survey of the land, shall be expended or paid, as follows: So much thereof as the Secretary of the Interior may deem advisable in the construction of irrigation systems, for the irrigation of the irrigable lands embraced within the limits of said reservation; one-half of the money remaining after the construction of said irrigation systems to be expended by the Secretary of the Interior as he may deem advisable for the benefit of such Indians in the purchase of live stock, farming implements, or the necessary articles to aid such Indians in farming and stock raising and in the education and civilization of said Indians, and the remaining half of said money to be paid to said Indians and persons holding tribal rights on said reservation, semiannually as the same shall become available, share and share alike: *Provided*, That the Secretary of the Interior may withhold from any Indian a sufficient amount of his pro rata share to pay any charge assessed against land held in trust for him for operation and maintenance of irrigation systems." * * *

Act March 3, 1909 (35 Stat., 795): For construction of irrigation systems to irrigate the allotted lands of the Indians of the Flathead Reservation in Montana and the unallotted irrigable lands to be disposed of under the act of April twenty-third, nineteen hundred and four, entitled "An act for the survey and allotment of lands now embraced within the limits of the Flathead Indian Reservation in the State of Montana, and the sale and disposal of all surplus lands after allotment," including the necessary surveys, plans, and estimates, two hundred and fifty thousand dollars, one hundred thousand dollars thereof to be immediately available, the cost of said entire work to be reimbursed from the proceeds of the sale of the lands and timber within said reservation.

That the act of April twenty-third, nineteen hundred and four (Thirty-third Statutes at Large, page three hundred and two), entitled "An act for the survey and allotment of lands now embraced within the limits of the Flathead Indian Reservation, in the State of Montana, and the sale and disposal of all surplus lands after allotment," as amended by the act of June twenty-first, nineteen hundred and six, and the act of May twenty-ninth, nineteen hundred and eight, be amended by adding thereto the following sections:

* * * * * * *

"SEC. 22. That the Secretary of the Interior be, and he is hereby, authorized, in his discretion, to reserve from location, entry, sale, or other appropriation all lands within said Flathead Indian Reservation chiefly valuable for power sites or reservoir sites, and he shall report to Congress such reservations."

Act April 4, 1910 (36 Stat., 277): For the construction of irrigation systems to irrigate the allotted lands of the Indians of the Flathead Reservation, in Montana, and the unallotted irrigable lands to be disposed of under authority of law, including the necessary surveys, plans, and estimates, two hundred and fifty thousand dollars, one hundred thousand dollars of which shall be immediately available: *Provided*, That the amount hereby appropriated, and all moneys heretofore or hereafter to be appropriated for this project shall be repaid into the Treasury of the United States in accordance with the provisions of the act of April thirtieth, nineteen hundred and eight, and the act of March third, nineteen hundred and nine.

Act April 12, 1910 (36 Stat., 296): An act to amend the act of April twenty-third, nineteen hundred and four (33 Stat. L., 302), entitled "An act for the survey and allotment of lands now embraced within the limits of the Flathead Indian Reservation, in the State of Montana, and the sale and disposal of all surplus lands after allotment," and all amendments thereto.

SEC. 24. That where allotments of land have been made in severalty to said Indians from the lands embraced within the area of said Flathead Indian Reservation, which are or may be irrigable lands, the Secretary of the Interior may, upon application of the Indian allottee, sell and dispose of not to exceed sixty acres of such individual allotment of land under such terms and conditions of sale as the Secretary of the Interior may prescribe, one-half of the proceeds of the sale of said individual allotment to be paid to the Indian allottee and the remaining half of the proceeds of sale to be held in trust for the said Indian allottee, upon which he shall be paid annually not less than three per centum interest, the remaining principal sum to be paid to said allottee or his heirs when the full period of his trust patent for the remaining lands covered by his allotment shall have expired, or sooner, should the Secretary of the Interior, in his judgment, deem it best for said Indian allottee.

SEC. 25. That the Secretary of the Interior is hereby authorized to set aside and reserve so much of the surplus unallotted and otherwise unreserved lands of the Flathead Indian Reservation as may be necessary to provide an allotment to each Indian having an allotment on any of the lands set aside and reserved for power or reservoir sites, as authorized by section twenty-two of the act of March third, nineteen hundred and nine (35 Stat. L., 796), who may relinquish his allotment within such power or reservoir sites.

And in the event of the failure, neglect, or refusal of any such allottee to relinquish any allotment made to him on any land reserved or necessary for reservoir sites, as aforesaid, the Secretary of the Interior is authorized to bring action under the provision of the laws of the State of Montana to condemn and acquire title to any and all lands necessary or useful for said reservoir sites that have heretofore been allotted on said Flathead Indian Reservation lands.

Act March 3, 1911 (36 Stat., 1066): For the construction of irrigation systems to irrigate the allotted lands of the Indians of the Flathead Reservation, in Montana, and the unallotted irrigable lands to be disposed of under authority of law, including the necessary surveys, plans, and estimates, four hundred thousand dollars.

* * * * * * *

In the issuance of patents for all tracts of land bordering upon Flathead Lake, Montana, it shall be incorporated in the patent that "this conveyance is subject to an easement of one hundred linear feet back from a contour of elevation nine feet above the high-water mark of the year nineteen hundred and nine of Flathead Lake, to remain in the Government for purposes connected with the development of water power."

Act August 24, 1912 (37 Stat., 526): For continuing the construction of irrigation systems to irrigate the allotted lands of the Indians of the Flathead Reservation, in Montana, and the unallotted irrigable lands to be disposed of under authority of law, including the necessary surveys, plans, and estimates, two hundred thousand dollars, reimbursable in accordance with the provisions of the act of April fourth, nineteen hundred and ten.

* * * * * * *

That so much of the act of Congress approved March third, nineteen hundred and eleven (Thirty-sixth Statutes at Large, page one thousand sixty-six), which provides for the reservation of an easement over tracts of land bordering Flathead Lake, Montana, be, and the same hereby is, amended to read as follows: "That an easement in, to, and over all lands bordering on or adjacent to Flathead Lake, Montana, which lie below an elevation of nine feet above the high-water mark of said lake for the year nineteen hundred and nine, is hereby reserved for uses and purposes connected with storage for irrigation or development of water power, and all patents hereafter issued for any such lands shall recite such reservation.

Act June 30, 1913 (38 Stat., 90): For continuing the construction of irrigation systems to irrigate the allotted lands of the Indians of the Flathead Reservation, in Montana, and the unallotted irrigable lands to be or which have been heretofore disposed of under authority of law, including the necessary surveys, plans, and estimates. $325,000, to be immediately available, reimbursable in accordance with the provisions of the act of April fourth, nineteen hundred and ten.

Act July 17, 1914 (38 Stat., 510): * * * That the provisions of the act of June twenty-third, nineteen hundred and ten (36 Stat. L., 592), authorizing the assignment under certain conditions of homesteads within reclamation projects, and of the act of August ninth, nineteen hundred and twelve (37 Stat. L., 265), authorizing under certain conditions the issuance of patents on reclamation entries, and for other purposes, be, and the same are hereby, extended and made applicable to lands within the Flathead irrigation project, in the former Flathead Indian Reservation, Montana, but such lands shall otherwise be subject to the provisions of the act of Congress approved April twenty-third, nineteen hundred and four (33 Stat. L., 302), as amended by the act of Congress approved May twenty-ninth, nineteen hundred and eight (35 Stat. L., 448): *Provided*, That the lien reserved to the United States on the land patented, as provided for in section two of said act of August ninth, nineteen hundred and twelve, shall include all sums due or to become due to the United States on account of the Indian price of such land.

Act August 1, 1914 (38 Stat., 593): For continuing the construction of irrigation systems to irrigate the allotted lands of the Indians of the Flathead Reservation, in Montana, and the unallotted irrigable lands to be or which have been heretofore disposed of under authority of law, including the necessary surveys, plans, and estimates, $200,000, reimbursable in accordance with the provisions of the act of April fourth, nineteen hundred and ten, and to remain available until expended.

Joint resolution March 4, 1915 (38 Stat., 1228) reenacted the item of August 1, 1914, for the fiscal year 1916.

Act May 18, 1916 (39 Stat., 139): For continuing construction of the irrigation systems on the Flathead Indian Reservation, in Montana, $750,000 (reimbursable), which shall be immediately available and remain available until expended: *Provided*, That the payments for the proportionate cost of the construction of said systems required of settlers on the surplus unallotted land by section nine, chapter fourteen hundred ninety-five, Statutes of the United States of America, entitled "An act for the survey and allotment of lands now embraced within the limits of the Flathead Indian Reservation in the State of Montana, and the sale and disposal of all surplus lands after allotment," as amended by section fifteen of the act of May twenty-ninth, nineteen hundred and eight (Thirty-fifth Statutes at Large, page four hundred and forty-eight), shall be made as herein provided: *Provided further*, That nothing contained in the act of May twenty-ninth, nineteen hundred and eight (Thirty-fifth Statutes at Large, page four hundred and forty-four), shall be construed to exempt the purchaser of any Indian allotment purchased prior to the expiration of the trust period thereon from any charge for construction of the irrigation system incurred up to the time of such purchase, except such charges as shall have accrued and become due in accordance with the public notices herein provided for, or to relieve the owners of any or all land allotted to Indians in severalty from payment of the charges herein required to be made against said land on account of construction of the irrigation systems; and in carrying out the provisions of said section the exemption therein authorized from charges incurred against allotments purchased prior to the expiration of the trust period thereon shall be the amount of the charges or installments thereof due under public notice herein provided for up to the time of such purchase.

Act May 18, 1916 (39 Stat., 141): * * * The work to be done with the amounts herein appropriated for the completion of the Blackfeet, Flathead, and Fort Peck projects may be done by the Reclamation Service on plans and estimates furnished by that service and approved by the Commissioner of Indian Affairs: *Provided*, That not to exceed $15,000 of applicable appropriations made for the Flathead, Blackfeet, and Fort Peck irrigation projects shall be available for the maintenance, repair, and operation of motor-propelled and horse-drawn passenger-carrying vehicles for official use upon the aforesaid irrigation projects: *Provided further*, That not to exceed $7,500 may be used for the purchase of horse-drawn passenger-carrying vehicles, and that not to exceed $1,500 may be used for the purchase of motor-propelled passenger-carrying vehicles.

That the Secretary of the Interior be, and he is hereby, authorized and directed to announce at such time as in his opinion seems proper the charge for construction of irrigation systems on the Blackfeet, Flathead, and Fort Peck Indian Reservations in Montana, which shall be made against each acre of land irrigable by the systems on each of said reservations. Such charges shall be assessed against the land irrigable by the systems on each said reservation in the proportion of the total construction cost which each acre of such land bears to the whole area of irrigable land thereunder.

On the first day of December after the announcement by the Secretary of the Interior of the construction charge the allottee, entryman, purchaser, or owner of such irrigable land which might have been furnished water for irrigation during the whole of the preceding irrigation season from ditches actually constructed shall pay to the superintendent of the reservation where the land is located for deposit to the credit of the United States as a reimbursement of the appropriations made or to be made for construction of said irrigation systems five per centum of the construction charge fixed for his land as an initial installment, and shall pay the balance of the charge in fifteen annual installments, the first five of which shall each be five per centum of the construction charge and the remainder shall each be seven per centum of the construction charge. The first of the annual installments shall become due and payable on December first of the fifth calendar year after the initial installment: *Provided*, That any allottee, entryman, purchaser, or owner may, if he so elects, pay the whole or any part of the construction charges within any shorter period: *Provided further*, That the Secretary of the Interior may, in his discretion, grant such extension of the time for payments herein required from Indian allottees or their heirs as he may determine proper and necessary, so long as such land remains in Indian title.

That the tribal funds heretofore covered into the Treasury of the United States in partial reimbursement of appropriations made for constructing irrigation systems on said reservations shall be placed to the credit of the tribe and be available for such expenditure for the benefit of the tribe as Congress may hereafter direct.

The cost of constructing the irrigation systems to irrigate allotted lands of the Indians on these reservations shall be reimbursed to the United States as hereinbefore provided, and no further reimbursements from the tribal funds shall be made on account of said irrigation works except that all charges against Indian allottees or their heirs herein authorized, unless otherwise paid, may be paid from the individual shares in the tribal funds, when the same is available for distribution, in the discretion of the Secretary of the Interior.

That in addition to the construction charges every allottee, entryman, purchaser, or owner shall pay to the superintendent of the reservation a maintenance and operation charge based upon the total cost of maintenance and operation of the systems on the several reservations, and the Secretary of the Interior is hereby authorized to fix such maintenance and operation charge upon such basis as shall be equitable to the owners of the irrigable land. Such charges when collected shall be available for expenditure in the maintenance and operation of the systems on the reservation where collected: *Provided*, That delivery of water to any tract of land may be refused on account of nonpayment of any charges herein authorized, and the same may, in the discretion of the Secretary of the Interior, be collected by a suit for money owed: *Provided further*, That the rights of the United States heretofore acquired, to water for Indian lands referred to in the foregoing provision, namely, the Blackfeet, Fort Peck, and Flathead reservation land, shall be continued in full force and effect until the Indian title to such land is extinguished.

That the Secretary of the Interior be, and he is hereby authorized to prescribe such rules and regulations and issue such notices as may be necessary to carry into effect the provisions of this act, and he is hereby authorized and directed to determine the area of land on each reservation which may be irrigated from constructed ditches, and to determine what allowance, if any, shall be made for ditches constructed by individuals for the diversion and distribution of a partial or total water supply for allotted or surplus unallotted land: *Provided*, That if water be available prior to the announcement of the charge herein authorized, the Secretary of the Interior may furnish water to land under the systems on the said reservations, making a reasonable charge therefor, and such charges when collected may be used for construction or maintenance of the systems through which such water shall have been furnished.

Act March 2, 1917 (39 Stat., 980): For continuing construction of the irrigation systems on the Flathead Indian Reservation, in Montana, $750,000 (reimbursable), which shall be immediately available and remain available until expended * * * *Provided*, That not to exceed $15,000 of applicable appropriations made for the Flathead, Blackfeet, and Fort Peck irrigation projects shall be available for the maintenance, repair, and operation of motor-propelled and horse-drawn passenger-carrying vehicles for official use upon the aforesaid irrigation projects: *Provided further*, That not to exceed $9,000 may be used for the purchase of horse-drawn passenger-carrying vehicles, and that not to exceed $2,000 may be used for the purchase of motor-propelled passenger-carrying vehicles.

Act May 25, 1918 (40 Stat., 574): For continuing construction, maintenance, and operation of the irrigation systems on the Flathead Indian Reservation, in Montana, $375,000 (reimbursable), which shall be immediately available and remain available until expended * * *: *Provided*, That not to exceed $15,000 of applicable appropriations made for the Flathead, Blackfeet, and Fort Peck irrigation projects shall be available for the maintenance, repair, and operation of motor-propelled and horse-drawn passenger-carrying vehicles for official use upon the aforesaid irrigation project: *Provided further*, That not to exceed $3,500 may be used for the purchase of horse-drawn, passenger-carrying vehicles, and that not to exceed $4,000 may be used for the purchase of motor-propelled, passenger-carrying vehicles.

Act of June 30, 1919 (41 Stat., 16): For continuing construction, maintenance, and operation of the irrigation systems on the Flathead Indian Reservation, in Montana, $375,000 (reimbursable), to remain available until expended * * *: *Provided*, That not to exceed $15,000 of applicable appropriations made for the Flathead, Blackfeet, and Fort Peck irrigation projects shall be available for the maintenance, repair, and operation of motor-propelled and horse-drawn passenger-carrying vehicles for official use upon the aforesaid irrigation project: *Provided further*, That not to exceed $3,500 may be used for the purchase of horse-drawn, passenger-carrying vehicles, and that not to exceed $4,000 may be used for the purchase of motor-propelled, passenger-carrying vehicles.

Appropriations recapitulated.

Date	Amount	Date	Amount
To Apr. 23, 1904	(?)	Mar. 4, 1915	$200,000
Apr. 30, 1908	$50,000	May 18, 1916	750,000
Mar. 3, 1909	250,000	Mar. 2, 1917	750,000
Apr. 4, 1910	250,000	May 25, 1918	375,000
Mar. 3, 1911	400,000	June 30, 1919	375,000
Aug. 24, 1912	200,000		
June 30, 1913	325,000	Total	4,125,000+
Aug. 1, 1914	200,000		

FORT BELKNAP.

Act June 10, 1896 (29 Stat. L., 351): Fort Belknap agreement: * * * Such sums, or so much thereof as may be necessary, in any one year, shall be expended * * * in assisting the Indians to build and keep in repair their houses, enclose and irrigate their farms, and in such other ways as may best promote their civilization and improvement.

Act April 30, 1908 (35 Stat. L., 83): For completion and extension of the Milk River irrigation system on the Fort Belknap Reservation in Montana, $25,000.

Act March 3, 1909 (35 Stat. L., 795): For completion and extension of the Milk River irrigation system on the Fort Belknap Reservation in Montana, $25,000, reimbursable.

Act April 4, 1910 (36 Stat., 277): For the Milk River irrigation system on the Fort Belknap Reservation, in Montana, $25,000: *Provided*, That the amount hereby appropriated and all moneys appropriated in the acts of May thirtieth, nineteen hundred and eight, and March third, nineteen hundred and nine, shall be repaid into the Treasury of the United States from Indian funds applicable for such purpose.

Act March 3, 1911 (36 Stat., 1066): For the Milk River irrigation system on the Fort Belknap Reservation, in Montana, $15,000: *Provided*, That the portion of the cost of this project paid from public funds shall be repaid into the Treasury of the United States as and when funds may be available therefor: *Provided further*, That in the event any allottee shall receive a patent in fee to an allotment of land irrigated under this project, before the United States shall have been wholly reimbursed as herein provided, then the proportionate cost of the project, to be apportioned equitably by the Secretary of the Interior, shall become a first lien on such allotment, and the fact of such lien shall be recited on the face of each patent in fee issued and the amount of the lien set forth thereon, which said lien, however, shall not be enforced so long as the original allottee or his heirs shall actually occupy the allotment as a homestead, and the receipt of the Secretary of the Interior, or of the officer, agent, or employee duly authorized by him for that purpose, for the payment of the amount assessed against any allotment as herein provided shall, when duly recorded by the recorder of deeds in the county wherein the land is located, operate as a satisfaction of such lien.

Act August 24, 1912 (37 Stat. L., 526): For extending the construction and maintaining the Milk River irrigation system on the Fort Belknap Reservation, in Montana, $15,000, reimbursable in accordance with the provisions of the act of April fourth, nineteen hundred and ten.

Act August 26, 1912 (37 Stat. L, 621): For irrigation system, Milk River, Fort Belknap Reservation, Montana (reimbursable), $22.45.

Act June 30, 1913 (38 Stat. L., 90): For extending the construction and maintaining the Milk River irrigation system on the Fort Belknap Reservation in Montana, $15,000, reimbursable in accordance with the provisions of the act of April fourth, nineteen hundred and ten.

Act August 1, 1914 (38 Stat. L., 593): For maintenance and operation, including repairs, of the Milk River irrigation system on the Fort Belknap Reservation, in Montana, $20,000, reimbursable in accordance with the provisions of the act of April fourth, nineteen hundred and ten.

Joint resolution March 4, 1915 (38 Stat., 1228) reenacted the item of August 1, 1914, for the fiscal year 1916.

Act May 18, 1916 (39 Stat., 139): For maintenance and operation, including repairs, of the irrigation systems on the Fort Belknap Reservation, in Montana, $20,000, reimbursable in accordance with the provisions of the act of April fourth, nineteen hundred and ten.

Act March 2, 1917 (39 Stat. L., 980): For maintenance and operation, including repairs, of the irrigation systems on the Fort Belknap Reservation, in Montana, $30,000, reimbursable in accordance with the provisions of the act of April fourth, nineteen hundred and ten.

Act May 25, 1918 (40 Stat., 573): For maintenance and operation, including repairs, of the irrigation systems on the Fort Belknap Reservation, in Montana, $30,000, reimbursable in accordance with the provisions of the act of April fourth, nineteen hundred and ten.

Act June 30, 1919 (41 Stat., 16): For maintenance and operation, including repairs, of the irrigation systems on the Fort Belknap Reservation, in Montana, $30,000, reimbursable in accordance with the provisions of the act of April 4, 1910.

Appropriations recapitulated.

Apr. 30, 1908	$25,000.00	Mar. 4, 1915	$20,000.00
Mar. 3, 1909	25,000.00	May 18, 1916	20,000.00
Apr. 4, 1910	25,000.00	Mar. 2, 1917	30,000.00
Mar. 3, 1911	15,000.00	May 25, 1918	30,000.00
Aug. 24, 1912	15,000.00	June 30, 1919	30,000.00
Aug. 26, 1912	22.45		
June 30,	15,000.00	Total	270,022.45
Aug. 1,	20,000.00		

FORT PECK.

Act May 30, 1908 (35 Stat., 558): An act for the survey and allotment of lands now embraced within the limits of the Fort Peck Indian Reservation, in the State of Montana, and the sale and disposal of all the surplus lands after allotment.

Be it enacted by the Senate and House of Representatives of the United States of America in Congress assembled, That the Secretary of the Interior be, and he is hereby, authorized and directed to cause to be surveyed all the lands embraced within the limits of the Fort Peck Indian Reservation, in the State of Montana, and to cause an examination of the lands within such reservation to be made by the Reclamation Service and by experts of the Geological Survey, and if there be found any lands which it may be deemed practicable to bring under an irrigation project, or any lands bearing lignite coal, the Secretary of the Interior is hereby authorized to construct such irrigation projects and reserve such lands as may be irrigable therefrom, or necessary for irrigation works, and also coal lands as may be necessary to the construction and maintenance of any such projects.

SEC. 2. That as soon as all the lands embraced within the said Fort Peck Indian Reservation shall have been surveyed the Commissioner of Indian Affairs shall cause allotments of the same to be made, under the provisions of the allotment laws of the United States, to all Indians belonging and having tribal rights on said reservation; and there shall be allotted to each such Indian three hundred and twenty acres of grazing land, and there shall also be made an additional allotment of not less than two and one-half acres nor more than twenty acres of timber land to heads of families and single adult members of the tribe over eighteen years of age: *Provided*, That should it be determined as feasible, after examination, to irrigate any of said lands, the irrigable land shall be allotted in equal proportions to such only of the members of said tribe as shall be living at the day of the beginning of the work of allotment on said reservation by the special allotting agent, and such allotment of irrigable land shall be in addition to the allotment of grazing and timber lands aforesaid, but no member shall receive more than forty acres of such irrigable land; and to pay the costs of examination provided for herein and for the construction of irrigation systems to irrigate lands which may be found susceptible of irrigation, there is hereby appropriated two hundred thousand dollars, to be immediately available, the said sum and any and all additional sums hereafter appropriated to pay the cost of such examination and irrigation systems to be reimbursed from proceeds from sales of lands within said reservation: *Provided, however*, That any land irrigable by any system constructed under the provisions of this act may be disposed of, subject to the following conditions: The entryman or owner shall, in addition to the payments required by section eight of this act, be required to pay for a water right the proportionate cost of the construction of said system in not more than fifteen annual installments, as fixed by the Secretary of the Interior, with a view to the return of all moneys expended thereon, the same to be paid at the local land office, and the register and receiver shall be allowed the usual commissions on all moneys paid.

The entryman of lands to be irrigated by said system shall, in addition to compliance with the homestead laws, reclaim at least one-half of the total irrigable area of his entry for agricultural purposes, and before receiving patent for the lands covered by his entry shall pay the charges apportioned against such tract, nor shall any such lands be subject to mineral entry or location. No right to the use of water shall be disposed of for a tract exceeding one hundred and sixty acres to any one person, and the Secretary of the Interior may limit the areas to be entered at not less than forty nor more than one hundred and sixty acres each.

A failure to make any two payments when due shall render the entry and water-right application subject to cancellation, with the forfeiture of all rights under this act, as well as of any moneys paid thereon. The funds arising hereunder shall be paid into the Treasury of the United States and be added to the proceeds derived from the sale of the lands. No right to the use of water for lands in private ownership shall be sold to any landowner unless he be an actual bona fide resident on such land or occupant thereof residing in the neighborhood of such land, and no such right shall permanently attach until all payments therefor are made.

All applicants for water rights under the systems constructed in pursuance of this act shall be required to pay such annual charges for operation and maintenance as shall be fixed by the Secretary of the Interior, and the failure to pay such charges when due shall render the water-right application and the entry subject to cancellation, with the forfeiture of all rights under this act as well as of any moneys already paid thereon.

The Secretary of the Interior is hereby authorized to fix the time for the beginning of such payments and to provide such rules and regulations in regard thereto as he may deem proper. Upon the cancellation of any entry or water-right application, as herein provided, such land or water rights may be disposed of under the terms of this act and at such price and upon such conditions as the Secretary of the Interior may determine, but not less nor more than the cost as originally fixed.

In every case in which a forfeiture is enforced and the land and rights of an entryman are made the subject of resale then, after the payment of the balance due from the entryman and the cost and charges, if any attendant on the forfeiture and resale, any surplus remaining out of the proceeds of such sale shall be refunded to said entryman or his heirs.

The land irrigable under the systems herein provided which has been allotted to Indians in severalty shall be deemed to have a right to so much water as may be required to irrigate such land without cost to the Indians for the construction of such irrigation systems. The purchaser of any Indian allotment purchased prior to the expiration of the trust period thereon shall be exempt from any and all charge for construction of the irrigation system incurred up to the time of such purchase. All lands allotted to Indians shall bear their pro rata share of the cost of operation and maintenance of the irrigation system under which they lie; and the Secretary of the Interior may withhold from any Indian a sufficient amount of his pro rata share of any moneys subject to distribution to pay any charge assessed against land held in trust for him for operation and maintenance of the irrigation system.

When the payments required by this act have been made for the major part of the unallotted lands irrigable under any system, and subject to charges for construction thereof, the management and operation of such irrigation works shall pass to the owners of the lands irrigated thereby, to be maintained at their expense, under such form of organization and under such rules and regulations as may be acceptable to the Secretary of the Interior.

All appropriations of the waters of the reservation shall be made under the provisions of the laws of the State of Montana.

SEC. 3. * * * The Secretary of the Interior is hereby authorized and directed, when the said lands are surveyed, to issue to the Great Northern Railway Company a patent or patents conveying for railroad purposes such lands at such point or points as in the judgment of the said Secretary are necessary for the use of said railway company in the construction and maintenance of water reservoirs, dam sites, and for right of way for water pipe lines for use by said railway company in operating its line of railroad over and across said reservation; * * *

SEC. 10. That if, after the approval of the classification and appraisement, as provided herein, there shall be found lands within the limits of the reservation deemed practicable for irrigation projects deemed practicable under the provisions of the act of Congress approved June seventeenth, nineteen hundred and two, known as the reclamation act, said lands shall be subject to withdrawal and be disposed of under the provisions of said act, and settlers shall pay, in addition to the cost of construction and maintenances provided therein, the appraised value as provided in this act, to the proper officers, to be covered into the Treasury of the United States to the credit of the Indians.

Act August 24, 1912 (37 Stat., 526): For continuing construction of irrigation systems to irrigate allotted lands of the Indians of the Fort Peck Indian Reservation in Montana, including necessary surveys, plans, and estimates, one hundred thousand dollars, the same to be reimbursable.

Act June 30, 1913 (38 Stat., 90): For continuing construction of irrigation systems to irrigate allotted lands of the Indians of the Fort Peck Indian Reservation, in Montana, including necessary surveys, plans, and estimates, $150,000, the same to be reimbursable.

Act August 1, 1914 (38 Stat., 593): For continuing construction of irrigation systems to irrigate allotted lands of the Indians of the Fort Peck Indian Reservation, in Montana, including necessary surveys, plans, and estimates, $50,000, the same to be reimbursable, and to remain available until expended: *Provided*, That the Secretary of the Interior is hereby authorized to make allotments in accordance with the provisions of the act of May thirtieth, nineteen hundred and eight (35 Stat. L., 558), to children on the Fort Peck Reservation who have not received, but who are entitled to, allotments as long as any of the surplus lands within said reservation remain undisposed of, such allotments to be made under such rules and regulations as the Secretary of the Interior may prescribe.

Joint resolution March 4, 1915 (38 Stat., 1228). Reenacted the item of August 1, 1914, for the fiscal year 1916.

Act May 18, 1916 (39 Stat., 140): For continuing construction of the irrigation systems on the Fort Peck Indian Reservation, in Montana, $100,000 (reimbursable), which shall be immediately available: *Provided*, That the proportionate cost of the construction of said systems required of settlers and entrymen on the surplus unallotted irrigable land by section two of the act of May thirtieth, nineteen hundred and eight (Thirty-fifth Statutes at Large, page five hundred and fifty-eight), shall be paid as herein provided: *Provided further*, That nothing contained in said act of May thirtieth, nineteen hundred and eight, shall be construed to exempt the purchaser of any Indian allotment purchased prior to the expiration of the trust period thereon from any charge for construction of the irrigation system incurred up to the time of such purchase, except such charges as shall have accrued and become due in accordance with the public notices herein provided for, and the purchaser of any Indian allotment to be irrigated by said systems purchased upon approval of the Secretary of the Interior before the charges against said allotment herein authorized shall have been paid shall pay all charges remaining unpaid at the time of such purchase, and in all patents or deeds for such purchased allotments, and also in all patents in fee to allottees or their heirs issued before payment shall have been made of all such charges herein authorized to be made against their allotments, there shall be expressed that there is reserved upon the lands therein described a lien for such charges, and such lien may be enforced, or upon payment of the delinquent charges may be released by the Secretary of the Interior. * * *

The work to be done with the amounts herein appropriated for the completion of the Blackfeet, Flathead, and Fort Peck projects may be done by the Reclamation Service on plans and estimates furnished by that service and approved by the Commissioner of Indian Affairs: *Provided*, That not to exceed $15,000 of applicable appropriations made for the Flathead, Blackfeet, and Fort Peck irrigation projects shall be available for the maintenance, repair, and operation of motor-propelled and horse-drawn passenger-carrying vehicles for official use upon the aforesaid irrigation projects: *Provided further*, That not to exceed $7,500 may be used for the purchase of horse-drawn passenger-carrying vehicles, and that not to exceed $1,500 may be used for the purchase of motor-propelled passenger-carrying vehicles.

That the Secretary of the Interior be, and he is hereby, authorized and directed to announce, at such time as in his opinion seems proper, the charge for construction of irrigation systems on the Blackfeet, Flathead, and Fort Peck Indian Reservations in Montana, which shall be made against each acre of land irrigable by the systems on each of said reservations. Such charges shall be assessed against the land irrigable by the systems on each said reservation in the proportion of the total construction cost which each acre of such land bears to the whole area of irrigable land thereunder.

On the first day of December after the announcement by the Secretary of the Interior of the construction charge the allottee, entryman, purchaser, or owner of such irrigable land which might have been furnished water for irrigation during the whole of the preceding irrigation season, from ditches actually constructed, shall pay to the superintendent of the reservation where the land is located, for deposit to the credit of the United States as a reimbursement of the appropriations made or to be made for construction of said irrigation systems, five per centum of the construction charge fixed for his land, as an initial installment, and shall pay the balance of the charge in fifteen annual installments, the first five of which shall each be five per centum of the construction charge, and the remainder shall each be seven per centum of the construction charge. The first of the annual installments shall become due and payable on December first of the fifth calendar year after the initial installment: *Provided*, That any allottee, entryman, purchaser, or owner may, if he so elects, pay the whole or any part of the construction charges within any shorter period: *Provided further*, That the Secretary of the Interior may, in his discretion, grant such extension of the time for payments herein required from Indian allottees or their heirs as he may determine proper and necessary, so long as such land remains in Indian title.

That the tribal funds heretofore covered into the Treasury of the United States in partial reimbursement of appropriations made for constructing irrigation systems on said reservations shall be placed to the credit of the tribe and be available for such expenditure for the benefit of the tribe as Congress may hereafter direct.

The cost of constructing the irrigation systems to irrigate allotted lands of the Indians on these reservations shall be reimbursed to the United States as hereinbefore provided, and no further reimbursements from the tribal funds shall be made on account of said irrigation works except that all charges against Indian allottees or their heirs herein authorized, unless otherwise paid, may be paid from the individual shares in the tribal funds, when the same is available for distribution, in the discretion of the Secretary of the Interior.

That in addition to the construction charges every allottee, entryman, purchaser, or owner shall pay to the superintendent of the reservation a maintenance and operation charge based upon the total cost of maintenance and operation of the systems on the several reservations, and the Secretary of the Interior is hereby authorized to fix such maintenance and operation charge upon such basis as shall be equitable to the owners of the irrigable land. Such charges when collected shall be available for expenditure in the maintenance and operation of the systems on the reservation where collected: *Provided*, That delivery of water to any tract of land may be refused on account of nonpayment of any charges herein authorized, and the same may, in the discretion of the Secretary of the Interior, be collected by a suit for money owed: *Provided further*, That the rights of the United States heretofore acquired to water for Indian lands referred to in the foregoing provision, namely, the Blackfeet, Fort Peck, and Flathead reservation land, shall be continued in full force and effect until the Indian title to such land is extinguished.

That the Secretary of the Interior be, and he is hereby, authorized to prescribe such rules and regulations and issue such notices as may be necessary to carry into effect the provisions of this act, and he is hereby authorized and directed to determine the area of land on each reservation which may be irrigated from constructed ditches, and to determine what allowance, if any, shall be made for ditches constructed by individuals for the diversion and distribution of a partial or total water supply for allotted or surplus unallotted land: *Provided*, That if water be available prior to the announcement of the charge herein authorized, the Secretary of the Interior may furnish water to land under the systems on the said reservations, making a reasonable charge therefor, and such charges when collected may be used for construction or maintenance of the systems through which such water shall have been furnished.

Act March 2, 1917 (39 Stat., 980): For continuing construction of the irrigation systems on the Fort Peck Indian Reservation, in Montana, $100,000 (reimbursable), which shall be immediately available and remain available until expended *. * * : *Provided*, That not to exceed $15,000 of applicable appropriations made for the Flathead, Blackfeet, and Fort Peck irrigation projects shall be available for the maintenance, repair, and operation of motor-propelled and horse-drawn passenger-carrying vehicles for official use upon the aforesaid irrigation projects: *Provided further*, That not to exceed $9,000 may be used for the purchase of horse-drawn passenger-carrying vehicles, and that not to exceed $2,000 may be used for the purchase of motor-propelled, passenger-carrying vehicles.

Act May 25, 1918 (40 Stat., 574): For continuing construction, maintenance, and operation of the irrigation systems on the Fort Peck Indian Reservation, in Montana, $50,000 (reimbursable), which shall be immediately available and remain available until expended * * *: *Provided*, That not to exceed $15,000 of applicable appropriations made for the Flathead, Blackfeet, and Fort Peck irrigation projects shall be available for the maintenance, repair, and operation of motor-propelled and horse-drawn passenger-carrying vehicles for official use upon the aforesaid irrigation project: *Provided further*, That not to exceed $3,500 may be used for the purchase of horse-drawn passenger-carrying vehicles, and that not to exceed $4,000 may be used for the purchase of motor-propelled passenger-carrying vehicles.

Act June 30, 1919 (41 Stat., 16): For continuing construction, maintenance, and operation of the irrigation systems on the Fort Peck Indian Reservation, in Montana, $100,000 (reimbursable) * * *: *Provided*, That not to exceed $15,000 of applicable appropriations made for the Flathead, Blackfeet, and Fort Peck irrigation projects shall be available for the maintenance, repair, and operation of motor-propelled and horse-drawn passenger-carrying vehicles for official use upon the aforesaid irrigation project: *Provided further*, That not to exceed $3,500 may be used for the purchase of horse-drawn passenger-carrying vehicles, and that not to exceed $4,000 may be used for the purchase of motor-propelled passenger-carrying vehicles.

Appropriations recapitulated.

May 30, 1908	$200,000	Mar. 2, 1917	100,000
Aug. 24, 1912	100,000	May 25, 1918	50,000
June 30, 1913	150,000	June 30, 1919	100,000
Aug. 1, 1914	50,000		
Mar. 4, 1915	50,000	Total	900,000
May 18, 1916	100,000		

FORT SHAW.

Act March 2, 1895 (28 Stat., 905): That any unexpended balance of the amount appropriated for buildings and repairs of buildings for Fort Shaw Reservation and Indian Industrial School, Montana, for the fiscal year eighteen hundred and ninety-five, not needed for that purpose, may be used for purchase of seed, agricultural implements, irrigation, and for water and sewer system for said school, and shall be available during the fiscal year eighteen hundred and ninety-six.

ROCKY BOY.

Act April 30, 1908 (35 Stat., 84): That the Secretary of the Interior be, and he is hereby, authorized to expend not to exceed thirty thousand dollars for the purpose of settling Chief Rocky Boy's band of Chippewa Indians, now residing in Montana, upon public lands, if available, in the judgment of the Secretary of the Interior, or upon some suitable existing Indian reservation in said State, and to this end he is authorized to negotiate and conclude an agreement with any Indian tribe in said State, or, in his discretion, to purchase suitable tracts of lands, water, and water rights, in said State of Montana and to construct suitable buildings upon said lands and to purchase for them such necessary live stock and implements of agriculture as he may deem proper. And there is hereby appropriated, out of any money in the Treasury not otherwise appropriated, the sum of thirty thousand dollars, or so much thereof as may be necessary, for the purpose of carrying out the provisions of this section.

TONGUE RIVER.

Act March 1, 1907 (34 Stat., 1035): For an irrigation system on the Tongue River Reservation in Montana, $40,000.

Act June 30, 1919 (41 Stat., 3): For the construction, repair, and maintenance of irrigation systems, and for purchase or rental of irrigation tools and appliances, water rights, ditches, and lands necessary for irrigation purposes for Indian reservations and allotments; for operation of irrigation systems or appurtenances thereto, when no other funds are applicable or available for the purpose; for drainage and protection of irrigable lands from damage by floods or loss of water rights upon the Indian irrigation projects named below:

The foregoing act provided $2,000 for the irrigation project on the Tongue River Reservation.

NEBRASKA.

DRAINAGE.

OMAHA AND WINNEBAGO.

Act February 18, 1909 (35 Stat. L., 628): *Be it enacted by the Senate and House of Representatives of the United States of America in Congress assembled*, That the Secretary of the Interior be, and he is hereby, authorized, in his discretion, to pay from the funds remaining to the credit of the Omaha and Winnebago tribes of Indians any assessments which may be made by any drainage districts in the State of Nebraska on the tribal lands of said Indians to protect such lands from overflow, not exceeding an average of eight dollars per acre.

SEC. 2. That the Secretary of the Interior be, and he is hereby, authorized, in his discretion, under such regulations as he may prescribe, to pay per capita to the Indians of the Omaha and Winnebago tribes who have allotted lands within any such drainage district the proportionate share of such Indians in the funds remaining to the credit of said tribe after the payment provided for in section one of this act: *Provided*, That no assessment made by such drainage district on the allotment of any Indian while the same is held in trust by the United States for the use and benefit of the allottee shall be valid or constitute a lien on the land, but the Secretary of the Interior shall retain not exceeding two hundred and forty dollars of the per capita share of any such allottee and expend the same for the payment or partial payment of the sum found by such drainage district to be due from such allottee for the purpose of protecting his lands embraced in the drainage district from overflow. Such payment shall be credited on any assessment which may be made on the allotment of said Indian after the termination of the trust by expiration of the period, issuance of a fee-simple patent, or by a conveyance under existing law, duly approved by the Secretary of the Interior.

SEC. 3. That any such drainage district be, and is hereby, authorized to assess the cost of reclaiming the tribal lands of the Omaha and Winnebago Indians and all lands allotted to Indians in severalty and held by patents containing restrictions as to alienation and taxation within such districts, subject to the limitation contained in the preceding section, and to condemn any of such lands necessary for the purpose of reclamation in the same manner as such district may condemn other lands: *Provided*, That the payments to be made or the taking of lands under the provisions of this section shall be subject to the approval of the Secretary of the Interior.

SEC. 4. That the Secretary of the Interior be, and he is hereby, authorized, in his discretion, upon application of the allottee, or his heirs, to issue a fee-simple patent to any Omaha and Winnebago Indian for the lands allotted to him within any such drainage district, and the issuance of such patent shall operate as a removal of all restrictions as to the sale, incumbrance, and taxation of the lands covered thereby.

Act May 18, 1916 (39 Stat., 142): That the Secretary of the Interior be, and he is hereby, authorized, in his discretion, to approve the assessments, together with maps showing right of way and definite location of proposed drainage ditches to be made under the laws of the State of Nebraska upon the allotments of certain Omaha and Winnebago Indians in Wakefield drainage district, in Dixon, Wayne, and Thurston counties in Nebraska.

That the Secretary of the Interior be, and he is hereby, authorized to pay the amount assessed against each of said allotments: *Provided*, That said assessment shall not exceed $10 per acre on any allotment or portion thereof; and there is hereby appropriated for said purpose, out of any money in the Treasury not otherwise appropriated, the sum of $30,000, to be immediately available, the said sum to be reimbursable from the rentals of said allotments, not to exceed fifty per centum of the amount of rents received annually, or from any funds belonging to the said allottees, in the discretion of the Secretary of the Interior.

That the Secretary of the Interior be, and he is hereby, authorized, in his discretion, to approve deeds for right of way from such said allottees or their heirs as may be necessary to permit the construction and maintenance of said drainage ditch upon the payment of adequate damages therefor.

That the Secretary of the Interior is hereby authorized to approve the assessments upon all other restricted allotments located within any proposed drainage district located and made under the laws of the State of Nebraska.

That in the event any allottees shall receive a patent in fee to any allotment of land in any lawfully constituted drainage district within the State of Nebraska before the United States shall have been wholly reimbursed as herein provided, the amount remaining unpaid shall become a first lien on such allotment, and the fact of such lien shall be recited on the face of each patent in fee issued and the amount of the lien set forth thereon, and the receipt of the Secretary of the Interior, or of the officer, agent, or employee duly authorized by him for that purpose, for the payment of the amount assessed against any allotment as herein provided shall, when duly recorded by the recorder of deeds in the county wherein the land is located, operate as a satisfaction of such lien.

That the Secretary of the Interior is hereby authorized to perform any and all acts and to make such rules and regulations as may be necessary and proper for the purpose of carrying these provisions into full force and effect.

NEBRASKA.

SAC AND FOX.

Act June 14, 1906 (34 Stat. L., 262): An act to enable the Indians allotted lands in severalty within the boundaries of drainage district numbered one, in Richardson County, Nebraska, to protect their lands from overflow, and for the segregation of such of said Indians from their tribal relations as may be expedient, and for other purposes.

Be it enacted by the Senate and House of Representatives of the United States of America in Congress assembled, That the Secretary of the Interior be, and he is hereby authorized, in his discretion, under such rules and regulations as he may prescribe, to pay per capita to the Indians of the Sac and Fox tribe, of Missouri, allotted lands in severalty within the boundaries of drainage district numbered one, in Richardson County, Nebraska, the proportionate share of such Indians in the one hundred and fifty-seven thousand dollars "paper principal" remaining to the credit of said tribe under the second article of the treaty of October twenty-first, eighteen hundred and thirty-seven: *Provided*, That sufficient of the amount due said Indians shall be retained and expended by the

Secretary of the Interior in paying the assessments that may be made by the said drainage district on the allotments of said Indians for the purpose of protecting the lands embraced in the drainage district from overflow, not exceeding seven dollars per acre, and there is hereby appropriated the sum of fifty thousand dollars, or so much thereof as may be necessary to enable the Secretary of the Interior to make the per capita payments herein provided. If any surplus remain, it shall be credited to the remainder of the tribe.

SEC. 2. That the Secretary of the Interior be, and he is hereby, authorized, in his discretion, to pay the assessments that may be made on the Sac and Fox tribal lands by said drainage district, not exceeding seven dollars per acre, and there is hereby appropriated for this purpose seven thousand dollars to be deducted from the "paper principal" of one hundred and fifty-seven thousand dollars: *Provided*, That the amount disbursed under the provisions of this section shall be reimbursed from the proceeds derived from the sale of said tribal lands.

SEC. 3. That the Secretary of the Interior be, and he is hereby, authorized, in his discretion, to pay the assessments on lands allotted to the Iowa Indians that may be made by said drainage district, not exceeding seven dollars per acre, and there is hereby appropriated for such purpose two thousand six hundred dollars.

SEC. 4. That the said drainage district be, and it is hereby, authorized to assess the cost of reclaiming the tribal lands of the Sac and Fox Indians, and all lands allotted to the Indians in severalty and held by patents containing restrictions as to sale, taxation, and alienation within said district, and to condemn any of said lands necessary for the purpose of reclamation in the same manner as said district may condemn other lands: *Provided*, That the payments to be made or the taking of lands under the provisions of this section shall be subject to the approval of the Secretary of the Interior.

SEC. 5. That the Secretary of the Interior be, and he is hereby, authorized, in his discretion, upon application, to issue a fee-simple patent to any Indian for the lands allotted to him within said drainage district, and the issuance of such patent shall operate as a removal of all restrictions as to the sale, encumbrance, or taxation of the lands covered thereby.

Act May 13, 1910 (36 Stat. L., 368): *Be it enacted by the Senate and House of Representatives of the United States of America in Congress assembled*, That sections one, two, and three of chapter thirty-two hundred and ninety-eight (thirty-fourth United States Statutes at Large), entitled "An act to enable the Indians allotted lands in severalty within the boundaries of drainage district numbered one, in Richardson County, Nebraska, to protect their lands from overflow, and for the segregation of such of said Indians from their tribal relations as may be expedient, and for other purposes," approved June fourteenth, nineteen hundred and six, be amended so as to read as follows:

"That the Secretary of the Interior be, and he is hereby, authorized, in his discretion, under such rules and regulations as he may prescribe, to pay per capita to the Indians of the Sac and Fox Tribe, of Missouri, allotted lands in severalty within the boundaries of drainage district numbered one, in Richardson County, Nebraska, the proportionate share of such Indians in the one hundred and fifty-seven thousand dollars 'paper principal' remaining to the credit of said tribe under the second article of the treaty of October twenty-first, eighteen hundred and thirty-seven: *Provided*, That sufficient of the amount due said Indians shall be retained and expended by the Secretary of the Interior in paying the assessments that may be made by said drainage district on the allotments of said Indians for the purpose of protecting the lands embraced in the drainage district from overflow, not exceeding nine dollars and fifty cents per acre, and there is hereby appropriated the sum of fifty thousand dollars, or so much thereof as may be necessary, to enable the Secretary of the Interior to make the per capita payments herein provided. If any surplus remain, it shall be credited to the remainder of the tribe.

SEC. 2. That the Secretary of the Interior be, and he is hereby, authorized, in his discretion, to pay the assessments that may be made on the Sac and Fox tribal lands by said drainage district, not exceeding nine dollars and fifty cents per acre, and there is hereby appropriated for this purpose nine thousand five hundred dollars, to be deducted from the 'paper principal' of one hundred and fifty-seven thousand dollars: *Provided*, That the amount disbursed under the provisions of this section shall be reimbursed from the proceeds derived from the sale of said tribal lands.

SEC. 3. That the Secretary of the Interior be, and he is hereby, authorized, in his discretion, to pay the assessments on lands allotted to the Iowa Indians that may be made by said drainage district, not exceeding nine dollars and fifty cents per acre, and there is hereby appropriated for such purpose three thousand five hundred and twenty-nine dollars."

Act. August 1, 1914 (38 Stat., 594): That the Secretary of the Interior be, and he is hereby, authorized, in his discretion, under such rules and regulations as he may prescribe, after the assessments made on Sac and Fox tribal lands by drainage district numbered one, in Richardson County, Nebraska, shall have been paid, and after the Indians, whose allotments are within the drainage district, shall have received their proportionate shares of the tribal funds as authorized by the act of May thirteenth, nineteen hundred and ten (36 Stat. L., 368), to distribute and pay per capita to the remaining members of the tribe entitled thereto the tribal funds on deposit in the Treasury of the United States to the credit of the Sac and Fox of the Missouri tribe, under the above act, in the same manner as provided by the act of April twenty-first, nineteen hundred and four (33 Stat. L., 201).

NEVADA.

DUCK VALLEY (WESTERN SHOSHONE).

See Miscellaneous.

MOAPA RIVER.

See Miscellaneous, pages 258 and 259.

NONRESERVATION INDIANS.

Act May 18, 1916 (39 Stat., 143): For the purpose of procuring home and farm sites with adequate water rights, and providing agricultural equipment and instruction and other necessary supplies for the nonreservation Indians in the State of Nevada, $15,000: *Provided*, That no part of this appropriation shall be expended for mileage, salaries, or expenses of employees.

PYRAMID LAKE.

Act April 21, 1904 (33 Stat., 225): Sec. 26. That in carrying out any irrigation enterprise which may be undertaken under the provisions of the reclamation act of June seventeenth, nineteen hundred and two, and which may make possible and provide for, in connection with the reclamation of other lands, the reclamation of all or any portion of the irrigable lands on the Pyramid Lake Indian Reservation, Nevada, the Secretary of the Interior is hereby authorized to reclaim, utilize, and dispose of any lands in said reservation which may be irrigable by such works in like manner as though the same were a part of the public domain: *Provided*, That there shall be reserved for and allotted to each of the Indians belonging on the said reservation five acres of the irrigable lands. The remainder of the lands irrrigable in said reservation shall be disposed of to settlers under the provisions of the reclamation act: *Provided further*, That there shall be added to the charges required to be paid under said act by settlers upon the unallotted Indian lands such sum per acre as in the opinion of the Secretary of the Interior shall fairly represent the value of the unallotted lands in said reservation before reclamation, said sum to be paid in annual installments in the same manner as the charges under the reclamation act. Such additional sum per acre, when paid, shall be used to pay into the reclamation fund the charges for the reclamation of the said allotted lands, and the remainder thereof shall be placed to the credit of said Indians and shall be expended from time to time, under the direction of the Secretary of the Interior, for their benefit.

Act May 18, 1916 (39 Stat., 143): For the improvement, enlargement and extension of the irrigation diversions and distribution system to irrigate approximately three thousand three hundred acres of Indian land on the Pyramid Lake Reservation, Nevada, $30,000, reimbursable, from any funds of said Indians now or hereinafter available, and to remain available until expended: *Provided*, That the cost of said entire work shall not exceed $85,000.

Act March 2, 1917 (39 Stat., L. 981): For the improvement, enlargement, and extension of the irrigation diversion and distribution system to irrigate approximately three thousand three hundred acres of Indian land on the Pyramid Lake Reservation, Nevada, $30,000, reimbursable from any funds of said Indians now or hereafter available, and to remain available until expended: *Provided*, That the cost of said entire work shall not exceed $85,000.

Act May 25, 1918 (40 Stat. 575): For the improvement, enlargement, and extension of the irrigation diversion and distribution system to irrigate approximately three thousand three hundred acres of Indian land on the Pyramid Lake Reservation, Nevada, $25,000, to be immediately available: *Provided*, That the cost of said entire work shall not exceed $85,000; and for maintenance and operation of the improved system, $5,000; in all, $30,000, to remain available until expended, reimbursable from any funds of said Indians now or hereafter available.

Act June 30, 1919 (41 Stat., 17): For maintenance and operation of the irrigation system on the Pyramid Lake Reservation, Nevada, $5,400, reimbursable from any funds of the Indians of this reservation now or hereafter available.

TRUCKEE-CARSON ALLOTMENTS.

Pursuant to the provisions of the act of April 30, 1908 (35 Stat., 85. See Miscellaneous, p. —), arrangements were made with the Reclamation Service for acquiring water for 4,640 acres of Indian land, of which 3,730 acres have been allotted to 369 Paiute Indians.

CARSON SCHOOL.

Act June 30, 1919 (41 Stat., 17): For support and education of three hundred and fifty Indian pupils at the Indian school at Carson City, Nevada, including pay of superintendent, $75,750; for general repairs and improvements, $10,000; for enlarging and improving sewerage system, $8,000; for enlarging and improving irrigation system and placing additional land under cultivation, $5,000; in all, $98,750.

WALKER RIVER.

Act May 27, 1902 (32 Stat., 260): That the Secretary of the Interior be, and he is hereby, directed to allot from the land on the Walker River Reservation in Nevada susceptible of irrigation by the present ditches or extensions thereof, twenty acres to each head of a family residing on said reservation, the remainder of such irrigable land to be allotted to such Indians on said reservation as the Secretary of the Interior may designate, not exceeding twenty acres each; and when a majority of the heads of families on said reservation shall have accepted such allotments and consented to the relinquishment of the right of occupancy to land on said reservation which can not be irrigated from existing ditches and extensions thereof and land which is not necessary for dwellings, school buildings, or habitations for the members of said tribe, such allottees who are heads of families shall receive the sum of three hundred dollars each to enable them to commence the business of agriculture, to be paid in such manner and at such times as may be agreed upon between such allottees and the Secretary of the Interior. * * *

Joint resolution June 19, 1902 (32 Stat., 744): In addition to the allotment in severalty of lands in the Walker River Indian Reservation in the State of Nevada, the Secretary of the Interior shall, before any of said lands are opened to disposition under any public-land law, select and set apart for the use in common of the Indians of that reservation such an amount of nonirrigable grazing lands therein at one or more places as will subserve the reasonable requirements of said Indians for the grazing of live stock.

For the construction, repair and maintenance of irrigation systems, and for purchase or rental of irrigation tools and appliances, water rights, ditches, and lands necessary for irrigation purposes for Indian reservations and allotments; for operation of irrigation systems or appurtenances thereto, when no other funds are applicable or available for the purpose; for drainage and protection of irrigable lands from damage by floods or loss of water rights, upon the Indian irrigation projects named below:

Under the foregoing heading the acts of May 25, 1918 (40 Stat., 562), and June 30, 1919 (41 Stat., 3), provided $6,800 and $8,500, respectively, for irrigation work on the Walker River Reservation.

WASHOES.

Act May 18, 1916 (39 Stat., 143): For the purchase of land and water rights for the Washoe Tribe of Indians, the title to which is to be held in the United States for the benefit of said Indians, $10,000, to be immediately available; for the support and civilization of said Indians, $5,000; in all, $15,000.

Act May 25, 1918 (40 Stat., 575): That the unexpended balance of $11,996.13 of the appropriation of $15,000 for procuring home and farm sites and providing agricultural equipment and instruction for nonreservation Indians in Nevada, and the unexpended balance of $7,611.23 of the appropriation of $15,000 for the purchase of land and water rights for the Washoe Tribe of Indians in said State and for their support and civilization, contained in the Indian appropriation act for the fiscal year nineteen hundred and seventeen (Thirty-ninth Statutes at Large, page one hundred and forty-three), are hereby reappropriated and made immediately available for the purchase of agricultural equipment, building material, and other supplies necessary for said Indians in utilizing the land purchased for them, and also for the expense of locating the Indians upon such land, including pay of employees where necessary.

NEW MEXICO.

PUEBLOS.

Act June 30, 1919 (41 Stat., 3): For the construction, repair, and maintenance of irrigation systems, and for purchase or rental of irrigation tools and appliances, water rights, ditches, and lands necessary for irrigation purposes for Indian reservations and allotments for operation of irrigation systems of appurtenances thereto, when no other funds are applicable or available for the purpose; for drainage and protection of irrigable lands from damage by floods or loss of water rights, upon the Indian irrigation projects named below:

Under the foregoing heading the acts of May 25, 1918 (40 Stat., 562) and June 30, 1919 (41 Stat., 3) provided for Indian irrigation projects in New Mexico, as follows:

Pueblos:	
1918	$12,000
1919	11,000

Act June 30, 1919 (41 Stat., 10): For enlarging and improving the reservoir and ditch system for the Laguna Indians of the Laguna Pueblo, New Mexico, $5,000.

Act June 30, 1919 (41 Stat., 18): For constructing ditches to irrigate three hundred additional acres near Jemez and Zia Pueblos, New Mexico, $15,000, and for the survey of proposed irrigation system to irrigate one thousand six hundred acres at San Juan Pueblo, New Mexico, $1,000; for sinking wells on Pueblo Indian land for domestic supply and for stock, $15,000; in all, $31,000.

SANTA FE.

Act March 3, 1891 (26 Stat., 1012): For support of Indian pupils at one hundred and seventy-five dollars per annum each; necessary buildings, repairs, and fencing, and irrigation at the Indian school at Santa Fe, New Mexico, and for pay of superintendent of said school, at one thousand five hundred dollars per annum, forty thousand dollars.

Act March 3, 1893 (27 Stat., 635): (Support, etc., Santa Fe School.) * * * for irrigation and water supply, one thousand five hundred dollars.

Act August 15, 1894 (28 Stat., 311): For support and education of one hundred and fifty pupils at Santa Fe * * * water supply for irrigation and fire protection, one thousand five hundred dollars. * * *.

Act March 2, 1895 (28 Stat., 906): Sante Fe, New Mexico. * * * for water supply for irrigation and fire protection, one thousand five hundred dollars.

Act June 10, 1896 (29 Stat., 348): Santa Fe School. * * * for water supply for irrigation and fire protection, one thousand five hundred dollars,

Act March 3, 1903 (32 Stat., 1005): * * * At the Indian School at Santa Fe, New Mexico, * * * For water supply, one thousand five hundred dollars; * * * artesian well, five thousand dollars.

Appropriations recapitulated.

Mar. 3, 1891	(?)	Mar. 3, 1903	$1,500
Mar. 3, 1893	$1,500	Mar. 3, 1903	5,000
Aug. 15, 1894	1,500		
Mar. 2, 1895	1,500	Total	12,500+
June 10, 1896	1,500		

ZUNI.

Act March 1, 1907 (34 Stat. L., 1041): For the completion of the Zuni dam and irrigation project in New Mexico, $30,000.

Act April 30, 1908 (35 Stat., 86): For the completion of the Zuni irrigation project in New Mexico, $25,000.

Act March 3, 1909 (35 Stat., 799): For completion of the irrigation system on the Zuni Reservation in New Mexico, $25,000, to be immediately available.

Work initiated and balance of cost paid from general appropriation for irrigation work.

Act June 30, 1919 (41 Stat., 3): For the construction, repair, and maintenance of irrigation systems, and for purchase or rental of irrigation tools and appliances, water rights, ditches, and lands necessary for irrigation purposes for Indian reservations and allotments for operation of irrigation systems or appurtenances thereto, when no other funds are applicable or available for the purpose; for drainage and protection of irrigable lands from damage by floods or loss of water rights, upon the Indian irrigation projects named below:
Under the foregoing heading the acts of May 25, 1918 (40 Stat., 562), and June 30, 1919 (41 Stat., 3), provided for Indian irrigation projects in New Mexico, as follows:

Zuni:	
1918	$5,000
1919	18,200

North and South Dakota.

FORT BERTHOLD.

Act June 1, 1910 (36 Stat., 455): An act to authorize the survey and allotment of lands embraced within the limits of the Fort Berthold Indian Reservation, in the State of North Dakota, and the sale and disposition of a portion of the surplus lands after allotments, and making appropriation and provision to carry the same into effect.
Sec. 5. That the Secretary of the Interior is hereby authorized to set aside and reserve from location, entry, sale, allotment, or other appropriation such tracts as are found to be chiefly valuable for power sites or reservoir sites: *Provided*, That the Secretary of the Interior is hereby authorized to cancel, after notice and a hearing, all trust patents issued to Indian allottees for allotments within any such power or reservoir site: *Provided further*, That the Secretary of the Interior shall report to Congress all lands so withdrawn for power or reservoir sites.

PIERRE.

Act June 21, 1906 (34 Stat., 370): For artesian well, water system, and irrigation plant, ten thousand dollars.

Act March 1, 1907 (34 Stat., 1047): For completing irrigation plant, five thousand dollars.

Act February 15, 1908 (35 Stat., 19): * * * The act of March first, nineteen hundred and seven (Thirty-fourth Statutes at Large, page one thousand and forty-seven), appropriating the sum of five thousand dollars for completing the irrigation plant at the Pierre Indian School, South Dakota, is hereby so modified as to permit the expenditure of so much of said amount as may be necessary in completing the work on the artesian well appropriated for by the act of June twenty-first, nineteen hundred and six (Thirty-fourth Statutes at Large, page three hundred and seventy), at said school.

Act March 3, 1911 (36 Stat., 1071), to complete irrigation plant, seventeen thousand dollars.

Act August 24, 1912 (37 Stat., 536): * * * Indian school at Pierre, South Dakota, * * * eleven thousand dollars; * * * *Provided*, That four thousand dollars of this amount shall be used in the construction and maintenance of an irrigation system for the use of said school; * * *

The Secretary of the Treasury is hereby authorized and directed to pay to A. C. Brink, of Pierre, South Dakota, the sum of one hundred and twenty-eight dollars and sixty-eight cents, on account of repairs to a gas engine, made while said engine was rented by him to the superintendent of the Pierre Indian School and being used during September and October, nineteen hundred and eleven, in digging a test well for the purpose of securing a water supply for that school, and to charge said amount to the appropriation for "Indian School, Pierre, South Dakota, Water Supply."

Act August 1, 1914 (38 Stat., 602): * * * at the Indian School at Pierre, South Dakota, * * * for completion of irrigation system, $7,000.

RAPID CITY.

Act March 3, 1903 (32 Stat., 1004): For * * * Rapid City, South Dakota, * * * for water plant, six thousand dollars; for additional buildings and improvements to complete plant, sixteen thousand dollars, to be immediately available; for the purchase of additional land with perpetual water right for the irrigation thereof, not exceeding one hundred and sixty-two acres, eleven thousand seven hundred and forty-five dollars, to be immediately available: *Provided*, That in the purchase of said land, not more than seventy-two dollars and fifty cents per acre shall be paid; in all, sixty-two thousand seven hundred and ninety-five dollars.

Act June 21, 1906 (34 Stat., 370): For the purchase of one thousand acres of land and springs and water right for a permanent water supply for the Indian school at Rapid City, South Dakota, eight thousand six hundred and fifty dollars.

Act March 2, 1917 (39 Stat., 987): * * * At the Indian school, Rapid City, South Dakota, * * * for irrigation, drainage, and improving school farm, $3,000.

Act May 25, 1918 (40 Stat., 585): For irrigation, drainage, and improving school farm, to remain available until expended, $3,000.

SIOUX.

Act April 30, 1888 (25 Stat., 99): SEC. 14. That in cases where the use of water for irrigation is necessary to render the lands within any Indian reservation created by this act available for agricultural purposes, the Secretary of the Interior be, and he is hereby, authorized to prescribe such rules and regulations as he may deem necessary to secure a just and equal distribution thereof among the Indians residing upon any such Indian reservation created by this act; and no other appropriation or grant of water by any riparian proprietor shall be authorized or permitted to the damage of any other riparian proprietor.

Act March 2, 1889 (25 Stat., 893) contains the same provision as that above.

Act March 3, 1893 (27 Stat., 631): Irrigation, Indian Reservations: For the construction, purchase and use of irrigating machinery and appliances on Indian reservations in the discretion of the Secretary of the Interior, forty thousand dollars: *Provided*, That of this sum a sufficient amount may be used to sink one artesian well at each of the following places, namely: Rosebud Reservation, Standing Rock Reservation, and Pine Ridge Reservation, in South Dakota, neither of said wells to cost more than five thousand dollars.

YANKTON.

Act June 10, 1896 (29 Stat., 343): To enable the Secretary of the Interior to put down an artesian well or wells at or near Lake Andes, on the Yankton Indian Reservation, South Dakota, at such place or places as he may determine, for the purpose of supplying said Indians with water for domestic purposes, for stock, and for irrigation purposes, five thousand dollars.

Act June 21, 1906 (34 Stat., 371): That the sum of five thousand dollars be, and the same is hereby, appropriated, out of any money in the Treasury not otherwise appropriated, to enable the Secretary of the Interior to put down an artesian well or wells at or near Lake Andes, on the Yankton Indian Reservation, South Dakota, at such place or places as he may determine, for the purpose of supplying said Indians with water for domestic purposes, for stock, and for irrigation purposes.

OKLAHOMA.

DRAINAGE.

Act July 19, 1912 (37 Stat., 194): An act to provide for the payment of drainage assessments on Indian lands in Oklahoma.

Be it enacted by the Senate and House of Representatives of the United States of America in Congress assembled, That the Secretary of the Interior be, and he is hereby, authorized, in his discretion, to approve the assessments, together with maps showing right of way and definite location of proposed drainage ditches made under the laws of the State of Oklahoma upon the allotments of certain Absentee Shawnee and Citizen Pottawatomie allottees in Little River drainage district, in Pottawatomie County, Oklahoma, and upon the allotments of certain Sac and Fox allottees in Deep Fork drainage districts, in Lincoln County, Oklahoma.

SEC. 2. That the Secretary of the Interior be, and he is hereby, authorized, in his discretion, to pay the amount assessed against each of said allotments: *Provided*, That said assessment shall not exceed fifteen dollars per acre on any allotment or portion thereof; and there is hereby appropriated for said purpose, out of any money in the Treasury not otherwise appropriated, the sum of forty thousand dollars, to be immediately available, the said sum to be reimbursable from the rentals of said allotments, not to exceed fifty per centum of the amount of rents received annually, or from any funds belonging to the said allottees, in the discretion of the Secretary of the Interior.

SEC. 3. That the Secretary of the Interior be, and he is hereby, authorized, in his discretion, to approve deeds for right of way from such said allottees or their heirs as may be necessary to permit the construction and maintenance of said drainage ditch upon the payment of adequate damages therefor.

That the Secretary of the Interior is hereby authorized to approve the assessments upon all other restricted allotments located within any proposed drainage district located and made under the laws of the State of Oklahoma.

That in the event any allottee shall receive a patent in fee to an allotment of land in any lawfully constituted drainage district within the State of Oklahoma, before the United States shall have been wholly reimbursed as herein provided, the amount remaining unpaid shall become a first lien on such allotment, and the fact of such lien shall be recited on the face of each patent in fee issued and the amount of the lien set forth thereon, and the receipt of the Secretary of the Interior, or of the officer, agent, or employee duly authorized by him for that purpose, for the payment of the amount assessed against any allotment as herein provided shall, when duly recorded by the recorder of deeds in the county wherein the land is located, operate as a satisfaction of such lien.

SEC. 4. That the Secretary of the Interior is hereby authorized to perform any and all acts and to make such rules and regulations as may be necessary and proper for the purpose of carrying the provisions of this act into full force and effect.

Act June 30, 1913 (38 Stat., 97): That the Secretary of the Interior be, and he is hereby, authorized, in his discretion, to approve the assessments, together with maps showing right of way and definite location of proposed drainage ditches and levees made under the laws of the State of Oklahoma upon the allotments of restricted allottees of the Creek Nation in the Verdigris drainage district numbered one, in Wagoner County, Oklahoma.

That the Secretary of the Interior be, and he is hereby, authorized, in his discretion, to pay amounts assessed against each of said allotments: *Provided*, That said assessment shall not exceed $5 per acre on any allotment or portion thereof, and there is appropriated for said purposes, out of any money in the Treasury not otherwise appropriated, the sum of $20,000, to be immediately available, said sum to be reimbursable from rentals from said allotments, not to exceed twenty-five per centum of the amount of rents received annually, or from any funds belonging to said allottees, in the discretion of the Secretary of the Interior.

That the Secretary of the Interior be, and he is hereby, authorized, in his discretion, to approve such deeds for right of way from said allottees or their heirs as may be necessary to permit the construction and maintenance of said drainage ditches and levees upon the payment of adequate damages therefor.

That the Secretary of the Interior be, and he is hereby, authorized to perform all acts and make such rules and regulations as may be necessary and proper for the purpose of carrying the provisions of this act into full force and effect.

Act March 27, 1914 (38 Stat., 310): *Be it enacted by the Senate and House of Representatives of the United States of America in Congress assembled*, That whenever a drainage district is organized in any county in the Five Civilized Tribes of the State of Oklahoma, under the laws of that State, for the purpose of draining the lands within such district, the Secretary of the Interior is authorized, in his discretion, to pay from the funds or moneys arising from any source under his control or under the control of the United States, and which would be prorated to such allottee, the assessment for drainage purposes against any Indian allottee or upon the lands of any allottee who is not subject to taxation or whose lands are exempt from taxation or from assessment for taxation under the treaties or agreements with the tribe to which such allottee may belong, or under any act of Congress; and such amount so paid out shall be charged against such allottee's prorata share of any funds to his credit under the control of the Secretary of the Interior or the United States: *Provided*, That the Secretary of the Interior, before paying out such funds, shall designate some person with a knowledge of the subject of drainage, to review the schedules of assessment against each tract of land and to review the land assessed to ascertain whether such Indian allottee, or his lands not subject to taxation, have been assessed more than their prorata share as compared with other lands located in said district similarly situated and deriving like benefits. And if such Indian lands have been assessed justly when compared with other assessments, then, in that event, said funds shall be paid to the proper county in which such drainage district may be organized, or, in the option of the Secretary of the Interior, to the construction company or bond-holder shown to be entitled to the funds arising from such assessment: *Provided further*, That in any event such assessment on any Indian allotment shall not exceed $15 per acre, and no such assessment shall be made unless the Indian allottee affected, or his legal guardian, shall consent thereto: *And provided further*, That nothing in this act shall be so construed as to deprive any allottee of any right which he might otherwise have individually to apply to the courts for the purpose of having his rights adjudicated.

Act July 21, 1914 (38 Stat., 553): An act for the approving and payment of the drainage assessments on Indian lands in Salt Creek drainage district numbered two, in Pottawatomie County, Oklahoma.

Be it enacted by the Senate and House of Representatives of the United States of America in Congress assembled, That the Secretary of the Interior be, and he is hereby, authorized, in his discretion, to approve the assessments, together with maps showing right of way and definite location of proposed drainage ditches, made under the laws of the State of Oklahoma upon the allottees in Salt Creek drainage district numbered two, in Pottawatomie County, Oklahoma.

SEC. 2. That the Secretary of the Interior be, and he is hereby, authorized, in his discretion, to pay the amount assessed against each of said allotments: *Provided*, That said assessment shall not exceed $15 per acre on any allotment or portion thereof; and there is hereby appropriated for said purpose, out of any money in the Treasury not otherwise appropriated, the sum of $21,183.39, or so much thereof as may be necessary, to be immediately available, the said sum to be reimbursable from the rentals of said allotments, not to exceed fifty per centum of the amount of rents received annually, or from any funds belonging to the said allottees, in the discretion of the Secretary of the Interior.

SEC. 3. That in the event any allottee shall receive a patent in fee to an allotment of land in any lawfully constituted drainage district within the State of Oklahoma before the United States shall have been wholly reimbursed as herein provided, the amount remaining unpaid shall become a first lien on such allotment, and the fact of such lien shall be recited on the face of each patent in fee issued and the amount of the lien set forth thereon, and the receipt of the Secretary of the Interior, or of the officer, agent, or employee duly authorized by him for that purpose, for the payment of the amount assessed against any allotment as herein provided shall, when duly recorded by the recorder of deeds in the county wherein the land is located operate as a satisfaction of such lien.

SEC. 4. That the Secretary of the Interior is hereby authorized to perform any and all acts and to make such rules and regulations as may be necessary and proper for the purpose of carrying the provisions of this act into full force and effect.

Act August 31, 1916 (39 Stat., 673): An act to amend an act entitled, "An act to provide for the payment of drainage assessments on Indian lands in Oklahoma."

Be it enacted by the Senate and House of Representatives of the United States of America in Congress assembled, That an act entitled, "An act to provide for the payment of drainage assessments on Indian lands in Oklahoma," approved July nineteenth, nineteen hundred and twelve (Thirty-seventh Statutes at Large, page one hundred and ninety-four), be, and the same is hereby, amended so as to confer upon the Secretary of the Interior authority to subject Government lands of the Sac and Fox Indian Agency or the lands of the Sac and Fox Indian School or Agency in the Sac and Fox Agency of Lincoln County, Oklahoma, to all of the provisions touching the organization of drainage districts and the construction of drain ditches and canals across said lands, or assessment for benefits conferred by the construction of said canals or ditches of the Deep Fork drainage district of Lincoln County, Oklahoma, and that the provisions of said act shall apply in all particulars to the Sac and Fox Indian School lands and the lands of the Sac and Fox Indian Agency of said Lincoln County, Oklahoma.

KIOWA.

Act March 3, 1903 (32 Stat., 1001): Whenever the Secretary of the Interior shall determine the same to be necessary for the purposes intended, the city of Lawton, in the Territory of Oklahoma, is hereby authorized and permitted, upon such conditions as the Secretary of the Interior may prescribe, to erect, maintain, and operate on section twenty-nine, township two north, range eleven west, in said Territory, and within the limits of the reservation created for the Fort Sill Boarding School, a pumping station, collecting gallery, reservoir, and such other appurtenant and necessary structures and pipe lines as may be required to furnish said city with a sufficient water supply.

Act August 1, 1914 (38 Stat., 597): That the Secretary of the Interior be, and he is hereby, authorized to contract for water rights for the irrigation of not to exceed six hundred acres of land in the Fort Sill Indian School Reservation, in the State of Oklahoma, within the proposed Lawton reclamation project for the irrigation of not to exceed two thousand five hundred acres of Indian and private lands, upon the same terms and conditions as those prescribed for the acquisition of water rights for other lands to be irrigated by said project: *Provided*, That operation and maintenance charges shall not be assessed against said Indian land prior to the completion of the lateral system so as to provide for actual delivery of water thereto, and the project shall include lateral construction for the Indian lands down to each legal subdivision thereof equal in area to the size of the farm unit for lands in private ownership within said project.

Act March 4, 1915 (38 Stat., 1116): The north half of the south half of section nineteen, township two north, range eleven west, Indian meridian, Oklahoma, formerly a part of the Kiowa, Comanche, and Apache Indian Reservation, is hereby set aside for use of the Department of Agriculture for a dry farming or subhumid station; and the sum of $200 is hereby appropriated to pay the Indians therefor, which sum shall be placed on deposit in the Treasury of the United States to the credit of the fund "Interest on Apache, Kiowa, and Comanche four per cent fund (benefits)."

(This land was to have been included in the Indian lands of the Fort Sill project.)

OREGON.

KLAMATH.

Act June 21, 1906 (34 Stat., 367): (Klamath Agreement).

ARTICLE III. It is agreed that of the amount to be paid to the said Klamath and other Indians, as stipulated in Article II of this agreement, the sum of twenty-five thousand dollars shall be paid in cash pro rata, share and share alike, to each man, woman, and child belonging to said Klamath and other tribes under the jurisdiction of the Klamath Indian Agency, within one hundred and fifty days from and after the date of the ratification of this agreement, and the sum of three hundred and fifty thousand dollars shall be deposited in the Treasury of the United States to the credit of said

Indians, and shall draw interest at the rate of five per centum per annum, which interest shall be paid to said Indians annually per capita in cash, and that the remainder of said sum of five hundred and thirty-seven thousand and seven dollars and twenty cents, after the payment of the legal fees of attorneys having duly approved contracts, shall be expended for the benefit of said Indians, under the direction of the Secretary of the Interior, upon requisition of the Indians through the U. S. Indian agent, in the drainage and irrigation of their lands, and the purchase of stock cattle for issue to said Indians, and for such other purposes as may in his opinion best promote their welfare: *Provided*, That beneficiaries whose allotments will not be benefited by the irrigation systems constructed under this provision shall not bear any of the expense of such irrigation construction, and shall, as nearly as practicable, receive an equivalent in value of the stock cattle or other articles herein contemplated, that each beneficiary may thus receive his or her proportionate share of the benefits of this provision. * * *

SEC. 5. * * * For the purpose of carrying into effect the foregoing agreement the sum of five hundred and thirty-seven thousand and seven dollars and twenty cents is hereby appropriated out of any money in the Treasury not otherwise appropriated, and the said agreement is hereby ratified and confirmed. Of the said sum so appropriated, three hundred and fifty thousand dollars shall be deposited in the Treasury of the United States to the credit of said Indians and the remainder shall be expended as provided in the third article of said agreement.

Act March 3, 1911 (36 Stat., 1071): For continuing the construction of the Modoc Point irrigation project, including drainage and canal systems, within the Klamath Indian Reservation, in the State of Oregon, in accordance with the plans and specifications submitted by the chief engineer in the Indian Service and approved by the Commissioner of Indian Affairs and the Secretary of the Interior in conformity with a provision in section one of the Indian appropriation act for the fiscal year nineteen hundred and eleven, $50,000: *Provided*, That the total cost of this project shall not exceed one hundred and fifty-five thousand dollars, including the sum of thirty-five thousand one hundred and forty-one dollars and fifty-nine cents expended on this project to June thirtieth, nineteen hundred and ten, and that the entire cost of the project shall be repaid into the Treasury of the United States from the proceeds from the sale of timber or lands on the Klamath Indian Reservation.

Act August 24, 1912 (37 Stat., 534): For continuing the construction of the Modoc Point irrigation project, including drainage and canal systems within the Klamath Indian Reservation, in the State of Oregon, in accordance with the plans and specifications submitted by the chief engineer in the Indian Service and approved by the Commissioner of Indian Affairs and the Secretary of the Interior in conformity with a provision in section one of the Indian appropriation act for the fiscal year nineteen hundred and eleven, fifty thousand dollars appropriated in the act of March third, nineteen hundred and eleven, is hereby reappropriated: *Provided*, That the total cost of this project shall not exceed one hundred and fifty-five thousand dollars, excluding the sum of thirty-five thousand one hundred and forty-one dollars and fifty-nine cents, expended on this reservation to June thirtieth, nineteen hundred and ten, and that the entire cost of the project shall be repaid in to the Treasury of the United States from the proceeds from the sale of timber or lands on the Klamath Indian Rerservation.

Act June 30, 1913 (38 Stat., 98): For completion of the construction of the Modoc Point irrigation project, including drainage and canal systems within the Klamath Indian Reservation, in the State of Oregan, in accordance with the plans and specifications submitted by the chief engineer in the Indian Service and approved by the Commissioner of Indian Affairs and the Secretary of the Interior in conformity with a provision in section one of the Indian appropriation act for the fiscal year nineteen hundred and eleven, $105,-000, to remain available until expended.

Act August 1, 1914 (38 Stat., 602): For maintenance and operation of the Modoc Point irrigation system within the Klamath Indian Reservation, in the State of Oregon, $4,740, reimbursable in accordance with the provisions of the act of March third, nineteen hundred and eleven.

Joint resolution March 4, 1915 (38 Stat., 1228). Reenacted the last foregoing item for the fiscal year 1916.

Act May 18, 1916 (39 Stat., 150): For construction, maintenance, and operation of the Modoc Point irrigation system within the Klamath Indian Reservation, in the State of Oregon, $20,000, reimbursable in accordance with the provisions of the act of March third, nineteen hundred and eleven: *Provided*, That the limit of cost of said project fixed by the act of August twenty-fourth, nineteen hundred and twelve, is hereby changed from $155,000 to $170,000.

OREGON.

Act March 2, 1917 (39 Stat., 986): For maintenance and operation of the Modoc Point irrigation system within the Klamath Indian Reservation, in the State of Oregon, $4,000, reimbursable in accordance with the provisions of the act of March third, nineteen hundred and eleven.

Act May 25, 1918 (40 Stat. L., 584): For maintenance and operation of the Modoc Point irrigation system within the Klamath Indian Reservation, in the State of Oregon, $4,000, reimbursable in accordance with the provisions of the act of March third, nineteen hundred and eleven, and for completing construction of the Modoc Point irrigation system within the Klamath Indian Reservation, in the State of Oregon, $3,000, to be immediately available and to remain available until expended, reimbursable in accordance with the provisions of the act of March third, nineteen hundred and eleven: *Provided*, That the limit of cost of said project fixed by the act of May eighteenth, nineteen hundred and sixteen, is hereby changed from $170.000 to $172,000; in all, $7,000.

Act June 30, 1919 (41 Stat., 25): For maintenance and operation of the Modoc Point irrigation system within the Klamath Indian

Reservation, in the State of Oregon, $5,000, reimbursable in accordance with the provisions of the act of March 3, 1911:

Act June 30, 1919 (41 Stat., 3): For the construction, repair, and maintenance of irrigation systems, and for purchase or rental of irrigation tools and appliances, water rights, ditches, and lands necessary for irrigation purposes for Indian reservations and allotments; for operation of irrigation systems or appurtenances thereto, when no other funds are applicable or available for the purpose; for drainage and protection of irrigable lands from damage by floods or loss of water rights, upon the Indian irrigation projects named below:

Under the foregoing $20,000 was appropriated for irrigation work on the Sand Creek and Agency projects, Klamath Reservation, Oregon.

KLAMATH.

Appropriations recapitulated.

June 30, 1910	(?)	May 18, 1916	$20,000
Mar. 3, 1911	$50,000	Mar. 2, 1917	4,000
Aug. 24, 1912	50,000	May 25, 1918	7,000
June 30, 1913	105,000	June 30, 1919	25,000
Aug. 1, 1914	4,740		
Mar. 4, 1915	4,740	Total	270,480+

SILETZ.

Act May 13, 1910 (36 Stat., 367): *Be it enacted by the Senate and House of Representatives of the United States of America in Congress assembled*, That the Secretary of the Interior be, and he is hereby, authorized to dispose of the lands reserved under the provisions of article four of the agreement concluded with the Indians of the Siletz Reservation on October thirty-first, eighteen hundred and ninety-two, and ratified by the Act of Congress approved August fifteenth, eighteen hundred and ninety-four (Twenty-eighth statutes at Large, page three hundred and twenty-five), at public auction, in such areas and on such terms and conditions as he may prescribe.

SEC. 2. That he is also authorized to cause the lands reserved for administrative purposes in connection with the affairs of the Siletz Indians and those reserved for educational and missionary purposes to be surveyed, platted, appraised without considering any improvements located thereon, and sold for town lots, or for such other purposes as he may deem advisable: *Provided*, That he shall reserve from sale any water-power sites that may be located on the lands so reserved. * * *

SEC. 3. That when such lands are surveyed and platted they shall be appraised and sold, except land reserved for water-power sites as provided in section two of this act, under the provisions of the Revised Statutes covering the sale of town sites located on the public domain. The proceeds derived from the sale of any lands as herein provided shall first be devoted to reimbursing the United States for the expenses incurred in carrying out the provisions of this act, and those derived from the sale of the lands reserved for administrative, educational, and missionary purposes, after making the deductions as herein provided, shall be used for the purpose of purchasing sites for day schools, erecting the necessary buildings, and equipping, supporting, and maintaining the same.

Act June 22, 1910 (36 Stat., 582): An act granting to the Siletz Power and Manufacturing Company a right of way for a water ditch or canal through the Siletz Indian Reservation, in Oregon.

Be it enacted by the Senate and House of Representatives of the United States of America in Congress assembled, That the right of way is hereby granted, as hereinafter set forth, to the Siletz Power and Manufacturing Company, a corporation organized and existing under the laws of the State of Oregon, and its successors and assigns, for the construction, operation, and maintenance of a water ditch or canal through the lands of the United States in the Siletz Indian Reservation, in Oregon, beginning at a point on the right bank of the Siletz River, in lot thirteen of section nine, township ten south, range ten west of Willamette meridian; running thence in a northeasterly direction through said section and terminating at a point on the right bank of the Siletz River, in lot thirty of section four, township ten south, range ten west of Willamette meridian: *Provided*, That no rights hereunder shall attach until the Secretary of the Interior shall have determined to his satisfaction that the interests of the Indians and the public will be promoted thereby.

SEC. 2. That the right of way hereby granted shall be fifty feet in width on each side of the central line of such water ditch or canal.

SEC. 3. That before the grant of such right of way shall become effective a map showing the definite location of such water ditch or canal must be filed with and approved by the Secretary of the Interior, and the company shall make payment to the Secretary of the Interior for the benefit of the allottees of full compensation for such right of way through their allotments, including all damage to their improvements and lands, and for damage to lands reserved for agency purposes, which compensation shall be determined and paid under the direction of the Secretary of the Interior in such manner as he may prescribe: *Provided further*, That the Siletz Power and Manufacturing Company, its successors or assigns, where not otherwise provided, shall, at its own expense, construct and maintain sufficient and suitable bridges across the water ditch or canal the right of way for which is hereby granted at the crossing of public roads, and be designated by the county court of the county in which they may be, failing in which the rights herein granted shall be forfeited.

SEC. 4. That the rights herein granted shall be forfeited by said corporation unless the water ditch or canal shall be constructed through the said lands within three years from the passage of this act.

SEC. 5. That it is hereby expressly provided that Congress may at any time alter, amend, or repeal this act or any part thereof.

Act May 18, 1916 (39 Stat., 149): * * * *Provided*, That section three of an act entitled "An act to authorize the sale of certain lands belonging to the Indians of the Siletz Indian Reservation in the State of Oregon," approved May thirteenth, nineteen hundred and ten, be, and the same is hereby, amended by striking out all of said section and inserting in lieu thereof the following:

"SEC. 3. That when such lands are surveyed and platted they shall be appraised and sold, except land reserved for water-power sites as provided in section two of this act, under the provisions of the Revised Statutes covering the sale of town sites located on the public domain. That the proceeds derived from the sale of any lands hereunder, after reimbursing the United States for the expense incurred in carrying out the provisions of this act, shall be paid share and share alike to the enrolled members of the tribe."

UMATILLA.

Act February 10, 1891 (26 Stat., 745): An act granting to the Umatilla Irrigation Company a right of way through the Umatilla Indian Reservation in the State of Oregon.

Be it enacted by the Senate and House of Representatives of the United States of America in Congress assembled, That the right of way is hereby granted, as hereinafter set forth, to the Umatilla Irrigation Company, a corporation organized and existing under the laws of the State of Oregon, for the construction and maintenance of a water ditch or canal for irrigation purposes from any convenient point on the Umatilla Indian Reservation, in Umatilla County, State of Oregon, near the headwaters of the Umatilla River, across said reservation to Wild Horse Creek, its northwestern boundary, at any convenient point, with the right to divert the waters of said Umatilla River and tributary streams from their beds, and for such purpose to construct and maintain reservoirs, dams, flumes, ditches, and such other structures and devices as may be necessary for storing, conveying, and distributing water at such points as such company may desire to use the same. The rights herein granted are upon the express condition that, during their continuance, the grantees or their assigns shall furnish all occupants of lands of said reservation, so situated as to be capable of irrigation from any ditches constructed by them hereunder, with water sufficient for purposes of agricultural and domestic uses and irrigation under such rules and regulations and on such terms as the Secretary of the Interior shall prescribe; and shall not divert or diminish the volume of water in said streams or exhaust either of them, so far as to impair vested rights, or to hinder or prevent the occupants of lands on said reservation the full enjoyment of said streams either for power, irrigation, or domestic purposes.

SEC. 2. That the right of way hereby granted to said company shall be fifty feet in width on each side of the center line of said ditch or canal, together with ground adjacent to such right of way for dams, reservoirs, and distributing ditches, not exceeding ten acres in the aggregate for every ten miles of said ditch or canal; and said company shall also have the right to enter upon lands adjacent to the line of said ditch or canal and to take therefrom material, stone, earth, and timber necessary for the construction of said ditch or canal.

SEC. 3. That whereas E. J. Summerville, J. P. Bushee, and J. B. Eddy have been appointed by the Secretary of the Interior as commissioners to appraise the lands of said reservation for the purpose of carrying into effect the provisions of the act of Congress entitled "An act providing for allotment of lands in severalty to the Indians residing upon the Umatilla Reservation, in the State of Oregon, and granting patents therefor, and for other purposes," approved March third, eighteen hundred and eighty-five, and are now acting as such commissioners, they are hereby appointed commissioners to fix the amount of compensation to be paid the Indians for such right of way and other grounds, estimating the same by the smallest legal subdivisions in accordance with the public surveys; and also to ascertain and fix the amount of compensation to be made individual members of the confederated tribes of Umatilla, Walla Walla, and Cayuse Indians for damages sustained by them by reason of said ditch or canal crossing lands now inclosed or improved by them; and said compensation and damages shall be ascertained and adjusted, and all surveys made pursuant to such regulations as the Secretary of the Interior shall prescribe, and shall be subject to his approval. In case of the inability or refusal of said commissioners, or any of them, to act, the Secretary of the Interior shall, by appointment, supply the vacancy or vacancies so caused. The compensation of said commissioners shall be the same as that now received for the services rendered by them under their aforesaid appointment, and shall be paid by said company: *Provided*, That the consent of the Indians to said diversion of water, compensation, and right of way shall be obtained by said irrigation company in such manner as the Secretary of the Interior shall prescribe before any right under this act shall accrue to said company.

SEC. 4. That said company shall not assign, or transfer, or mortgage its right of way for any purpose whatever until said canal shall be completed; except, however, that the company may mortgage said franchise for the purpose of raising money to construct and build said canal: *And provided further*, That the right herein granted shall be lost and forfeited by said company unless the canal is constructed across said reservation within three years from the passage of this act.

SEC. 5. That the right of immediate entry upon the lands of said reservation for the purpose of making surveys of the line of the ditch or canal of said company is hereby granted, but no right of any kind in or to any part of the right of way or other grounds above mentioned shall vest in said company until plats thereof, made upon actual survey for the definite location of said ditch or canal, including the points for dams, reservoirs, and distributing ditches, with the amount of ground requisite for such purposes, shall be filed with the Secretary of the Interior, and until the compensation for said lands and for the services of said commissioners has been fixed and paid.

SEC. 6. That whereas, under the provisions of the act of Congress above mentioned the lands of said reservation are soon to be allotted to the Indians belonging thereto in severalty, the Secretary of the Interior shall hold the moneys paid to him by said company for right of way and other grounds, as above provided, until such allotment in severalty shall have been perfected, and thereupon he shall pay over to the Indians to whom shall be allotted the lands traversed by said ditch or canal the amount of compensation assessed by the commissioners as properly appertaining to the tract of land to each Indian allotted. Payments for improved or inclosed lands held by Indians prior to such allotment and damaged by the construction of said ditch or canal shall be made to the several Indians affected thereby immediately upon the appraisement of said commissioners being made, and vouchers for such payments, attested by the agent in charge of the reservation, shall be filed by said company with the Secretary of the Interior at the time of filing its plat of location of said ditch or canal.

SEC. 7. That any failure in the performance of the conditions prescribed in this act shall be taken and deemed to work a forfeiture of the rights herein granted, without any act of Congress or judgment of court declaring the same.

SEC. 8. That the right to alter, amend, or repeal this act is hereby reserved.

Act January 12, 1893 (27 Stat., 417): An act granting to the Blue Mountain Irrigation and Improvement Company a right of way for reservoir and canals through the Umatilla Indian Reservation in the State of Oregon.

Be it enacted by the Senate and House of Representatives of the United States of America in Congress assembled, That the Blue Mountain Irrigation and Improvement Company, a corporation organized and existing under the laws of the State of Oregon, may purchase so much of sections one (1) and two (2) in township one (1), south of range thirty-three (33), east Willamette meridian, in the Umatilla Indian Reservation in the State of Oregon, as may be required by said company for the purpose of a reservoir, dam, and grounds accompanying, out of lands allotted to or which may have been selected for allotment by any Indians, if said company shall be able to agree with the Indian owners or allottees thereof upon the terms of such sale and the Secretary of the Interior shall approve and ratify the same; but the said company shall have no right to compel the sale by any Indian owner or allottee of any lands for the purposes of reservoir or dam, or accompanying grounds. And said company may also take of the lands in said sections one and two in said reservation which have not yet been allotted, so much additional land as shall be required for the purposes of a reservoir and dam and necessary grounds appurtenant thereto, upon making payment as hereafter provided in respect to the right of way. And upon and after acquiring by purchase, as aforesaid, with the approval of the Secretary of the Interior, the necessary grounds for reservoir and dam, the right of way is hereby granted to said Blue Mountain Irrigation and Improvement Company for a main ditch or canal, to commence at a point on McKay Creek north, six degrees west of corner to sections one, two, eleven, and twelve, township one south, range thirty-three east, Willamette meridian, thence running across said Indian reservation to the city of Pendleton and to the Umatilla River, with the right to divert the waters of McKay Creek and its tributaries, and for such other purposes to construct and maintain reservoirs, dams, flumes, ditches, and such other structures and devices as may be necessary for storing, conveying, and distributing water at such points as said company may desire to use the same. But all the rights herein granted are upon the express condition that during their continuance the grantees or their assigns shall furnish to occupants of said lands on said reservation, so situated as to be capable of irrigation or supply from any ditch constructed by them hereunder, water sufficient for purposes of agricultural and domestic uses and irrigation, under such rules and regulations and on such terms as the Secretary of the Interior shall prescribe, and shall not divert or diminish the volume of water in said streams or exhaust either of them, so far as to impair vested rights, or to hinder or prevent the occupants of lands on said reservation from the full enjoyment of said streams, either for power, irrigation, or domestic purposes. For the purpose of determining the fairness of any agreement of sale negotiated with any of said Indian owners or allottees, and the wisdom of their making such sale to said company, the Secretary of the Interior shall appoint such commissioners, not exceeding three in number, as he shall think fit to personally inquire into and report to him the facts in respect to said matter, and he shall approve and ratify or disapprove any such agreement as he shall think the best interests of the Indians may require; and all expenses attending such inquiry shall be paid by the said Blue Mountain Irrigation and Improvement Company, security for the payment of which may be required in advance by the Secretary of the Interior.

SEC. 2. That the right of way to said company shall be fifty feet in width on each side of the center line of said ditch or canal, together with the ground adjacent to the said right of way for distributing ditches not exceeding ten acres in the aggregate for every ten miles of said ditch or canal. The company shall also have the right to enter upon lands adjacent to said canal or reservoir to take therefrom material, stone, earth, or timber necessary for the construction of said dam, ditch, or canal. But no land belonging to any Indian owner in severalty, or which shall have been selected for allotment by any Indian, shall be taken by the said company, nor shall the company have a right to take therefrom any material, stone, earth, or timber except by agreement with the said Indian owner approved by the Secretary of the Interior, or by first making compensation for the same, and any injury thereby caused to other lands of such Indian owner or allottee, to be determined by the Secretary of the Interior, after appraisal in the manner provided in section one of this act.

SEC. 3. That the Secretary of the Interior may appoint three commissioners to fix the amount of compensation to be paid the Indian owners or allottees for right of way for the said main ditch or canal of the said company, which shall include the value of the land taken therefor and all damages to other lands of such owner of allottee caused by such taking; and also to fix the amount of compensation to be paid for any lands of the tribe, not allotted or selected for allotment by individuals which may be required by said company for reservoir and dam and adjacent grounds or for right of way or for distributing ditches, which shall be fixed upon the same principle; and such compensation and damages shall be ascertained and adjusted and all surveys made pursuant to such regulations as the Secretary of the Interior shall prescribe, and shall be in all cases subject to his approval. In case of inability or refusal of any commissioner to act or continue in service, after appointment, the Secretary of the Interior shall by appointment supply such vacancy or vacancies so caused. The Secretary of the Interior shall fix the compensation of such commissioners, not exceeding that allowed to the commissioners appointed under the provisions of an act of Congress entitled "An act providing for the allotment of lands in severalty to the Indians residing upon the Umatilla Indian Reservation in the State of Oregon, and granting patents therefor, and for other purposes," approved March third, eighteen hundred and eight-five, and the same shall be paid by the said Blue Mountain Irrigation and Improvement Company, and the Secretary of the Interior may require security for the payment thereof in advance of their appointment. The consent of the Indians upon said reservation to the granting of this right of way and the diversion of the water necessary to the accomplishment of the purposes of said company shall be obtained by the said company in such manner as the Secretary of the Interior shall prescribe, before any right of way under this act shall accrue to this company. In all cases, all lands which have been selected by any individual Indians upon said reservation for allotment, shall be treated and regarded for the purposes of this act as belonging to such Indian allottee; but the Secretary of the Interior may hold any moneys agreed to be paid, or awarded to him, in compensation for lands sold or taken, or injuries resulting, until the approval by him of the allotment and the issuance of patent therefor; but the same shall then be paid over to, or invested for, such Indian owner as the Secretary of the Interior in his discretion may see fit. Payment for land in said reservation held by the Indians of said tribe in common, and of all damages awarded to them by reason of the construction of the dam and reservoir, ditch or canal, are to be made to the confederated tribe in common occupying the reservation under the direction of the Secretary of the Interior.

SEC. 4. That said company shall not assign, transfer, or mortgage its rights of way for any purpose whatever until the said canal shall be completed; except, however, that the company may mortgage said franchise for the purpose of raising money to construct said reservoir and canals: *Provided*, That the right herein granted shall be lost and forfeited by said company unless the canal is constructed across the reservation within three years from the passage of this act.

SEC. 5. That the right of immediate entry upon the lands of said reservation for the purpose of making surveys of the line of the ditch or canal of said company is hereby granted, but no right of any kind in or to any part of the right of way or other grounds above mentioned shall vest in said company until plats thereof, made upon actual survey for the definite location of said ditch or canal, including the points for dams, reservoirs, and distributing ditches, with the amount of ground requisite for such purposes, shall be filed with the Secretary of the Interior, and until the compensation for said lands and for the services of said commissioners has been fixed and paid.

SEC. 6. That any failure in the performance of the conditions prescribed in this act shall be taken and deemed to work a forfeiture of the rights herein granted, without any act of Congress or judgment of conrt declaring the same.

Representative JOHNSON. Well, of course, we would have to debate that. It is the only road that serves several coal mines.

Now, it appears to me that the road has been operating for some time and that this is a poor time to requistiion the road, especially without the regular procedure of a hearing and an opportunity for the real facts to be determined. It has been my view all the time that in time of war, one of the important things was to keep all lines of communication open, and especially the railroads.

Now, with the rubber shortage, with the lack of transportation, trucks, and such, many of the people in many of the communities are worried considerably how they are going to get supplies in and out, if the railroad is abandoned.

Senator REED. You think the need of a railroad perhaps is emphasized by the uncertainty of being able to buy any more motortrucks and the uncertainty as to whether they will be able to get tires for their trucks that they now own?

Representative JOHNSON. That is right.

Senator REED. Or might acquire in the future?

Representative JOHNSON. That is right.

Senator REED. There is uncertainty on both of those points.

Representative JOHNSON. Exactly. And, if the railroad is requisitioned, they will be wholly dependent upon a new form of transportation to and from their communities, for their produce, and that applies particularly to the people in these towns and to the elevators. I do not have the data as to the number of cars each elevator ships, the number of cars of coal that are shipped or the amount of traffic that it supplies to and from the Harrison Steel Castings Co. plant, but undoubtedly they have been oprating all of the time, and it seems peculiar right at this particluar time, when the need for the continuance of the road is greatest, that it should be proposed to requisition it without a hearing.

Senator REED. Congressman Johnson, in all fairness to all interests, let me say that there is an urgent need for steel rail for war industrial purposes and the various munitions plants, air bases, and ordnance plants, navy yards, and things of that kind. I think there is no reasonable doubt about that.

Representative JOHNSON. I am wholeheartedly with that.

Senator REED. The whole question involved here is the supply of steel rail that is available to fill that demand without taking up branch lines or, as in this case, perhaps the whole system, being a small system, without a careful examination of all the facts and circumstances surrounding the operation of such lines in the communities which they serve.

Representative JOHNSON. I agree with that.

Senator REED. If there is a vital war need that can be filled in no other way, I think, of course, we would all bow to the inevitable, but being the author of the resolution, I never was satisfied that sufficient consideration had been given to the needs of these communities and the ultimate possibility of obtaining rail from some other source.

Representative JOHNSON. I agree with your views completely. I don't know what effort has been made to find rails.

Now, for instance, driving from Washington to my home, I cross quite a few railroad tracks that are rusty, that have been abandoned, to be allotted to each head of a family eighty acres of agricultural land which can be irrigated and forty acres of such land to each other member of said tribes, said allotments to be made prior to October first, nineteen hundred and three, on which date all the unallotted lands within said reservation shall be restored to the public domain: *Provided*, That persons entering any of said land under the homestead law shall pay therefor at the rate of one dollar and twenty-five cents per acre: *And provided further*, That nothing herein contained shall impair the rights of any mineral lease. * * *

Act June 19, 1902 (32 Stat., 744): In addition to the allotments in severalty to the Uintah and White River Utes of the Uintah Indian Reservation in the State of Utah, the Secretary of the Interior shall, before any of said lands are opened to disposition under any public-land law, select and set apart for the use in common of the Indians of that reservation such an amount of nonirrigable grazing lands therein at one or more places as will subserve the reasonable requirements of said Indians for the grazing of live stock.

All allotments hereafter made to Uncompahgre Indians of lands in said Uintah Indian Reservation shall be confined to agricultural land which can be irrigated, and shall be on the basis of eighty acres to each head of a family and forty acres to each other Indian, and no more. The grazing land selected and set apart as aforesaid in the Uintah Indian Reservation for the use in common of the Indians of that reservation shall be equally open to the use of all Uncompahgre Indians receiving allotments in said reservation of the reduced area here named.

Act March 3, 1905 (33 Stat., 1070): That before the opening of the Uintah Indian Reservation the President is hereby authorized to set apart and reserve as an addition to the Uintah Forest Reserve, subject to the laws, rules, and regulations governing forest reserves, and subject to the mineral rights granted by the act of Congress of May tweny-seventh, nineteen hundred and two, such portions of the lands within the Uintah Indian Reservation as he considers necessary, and he may also set apart and reserve any reservoir site or other lands necessary to conserve and protect the water supply for the Indians or for general agricultural development, and may confirm such rights to water thereon as have already accrued. * * *

Act June 21, 1906 (34 Stat., 375): For constructing irrigation systems to irrigate the allotted lands of the Uncompahgre, Uintah, and White River Utes in Utah, the limit of cost of which is hereby fixed at six hundred thousand dollars, one hundred and twenty-five thousand dollars which shall be immediately available, the cost of said entire work to be reimbursed from the proceeds of the sale of the lands within the former Uintah Reservation: *Provided*, That such irrigation systems shall be constructed and completed and held and operated, and water therefor appropriated under the laws of the State of Utah, and the title thereto until otherwise provided by law shall be in the Secretary of the Interior in trust for the Indians, and he may sue and be sued in matters relating thereto: *And provided further*, That the ditches and canals of such irrigation systems may be used, extended, or enlarged for the purpose of conveying water by any person, association, or corporation under and upon compliance with the provisions of the laws of the State of Utah: *And provided further*, That when said irrigation systems are in successful operation the cost of operating same shall be equitably apportioned upon the lands irrigated, and, when the Indians have become self-supporting, to the annual charge shall be added an amount sufficient to pay back into the Treasury the cost of the work done, in their behalf, within thirty years, suitable deduction being made for the amounts received from disposal of the lands within the former Uintah Reservation.

Act March 1, 1907 (34 Stat., 1049): For constructing irrigation system, to irrigate the allotted lands of the Uncompahgre, Uintah, and White River Utes in Utah, as provided by the act of June twenty-first, nineteen hundred and six, one hundred and fifty thousand dollars.

Act April 30, 1908 (35 Stat., 95): For constructing irrigation system, to irrigate the allotted lands of the Uncompahgre, Uintah, and White River Utes in Utah, as provided by the act of June twenty-first, nineteen hundred and six, two hundred thousand dollars. * * *
That whenever it shall appear to the satisfaction of the Secretary of the Interior that the allotted lands of any Indian of the former Uintah and Uncompahgre reservations in Utah are susceptible of irrigation and that the allottee is unable to cultivate the same or any portion thereof, such lands or such portion thereof may be leased by the Secretary of the Interior with the consent of the allottee for a period not exceeding ten years, under such rules and regulations as he may establish.

Act March 3, 1909 (35 Stat., 811): For constructing irrigation system, to irrigate the allotted lands of the Uncompahgre, Uintah, and White River Utes in Utah, as provided by the act of June twenty-first, nineteen hundred and six, one hundred and twenty-five thousand dollars, reimbursable. * * *
To enable the Commissioner of Indian Affairs to perfect and protect the rights of the Uncompahgre, Uintah, and White River Utes in Utah in and to the waters appropriated under the laws of the State of Utah for the irrigation systems authorized by the act of June twenty-first, nineteen hundred and six, two hundred thousand dollars, or so much thereof as may be necessary, the amount expended hereunder to be reimbursed from the proceeds of the sale of lands within the former Uintah Reservation: *Provided*, That said sum, or any part thereof, shall be used only in the event of failure to procure from the State of Utah or its officers an extension of time in which to make final proof for waters appropriated for the benefit of the Indians, and any sum expended hereunder shall be reimbursed from the proceeds of the sale of the lands within the former Uintah Reservation.

Act April 4, 1910 (36 Stat., 285): For straightening the Duchesne River within the limits of the town site of Duchesne, now Theodore, in the State of Utah, five thousand dollars, to be immediately available and to be reimbursed to the United States out of the proceeds of the sale of lands within the ceded Uintah Indian Reservation opened to entry under the act of May twenty-seventh, nineteen hundred and two, including the sales of lots within said town site of Theodore.

That the Secretary of the Interior is hereby authorized to pay from the reclamation fund for the benefit of the Uintah Indians the sum of one dollar and twenty-five cents per acre for the lands in the former Uintah Indian Reservation, in the State of Utah, which were set apart by the President for reservoir and other purposes under the provisions of the act approved March third, nineteen hundred and five, chapter fourteen hundred and seventy-nine, and which were by the Secretary of the Interior withdrawn for irrigation works under the provisions of the reclamation act of June seventeenth, nineteen hundred and two, in connection with the reservoir for the Strawberry Valley project. Such payment shall be made in five annual installments, and the moneys paid shall be subject to the same disposition as the proceeds of the sales of lands in the former Indian reservation. All such payments shall be included in the cost of construction of said Strawberry Valley project to be reimbursed by the owners of lands irrigated therefrom, all receipts from said lands, as rentals or otherwise, being credited to the said owners. All right, title, and interest of the Indians in the said lands are hereby extinguished, and the title, management, and control thereof shall pass to the owners of the lands irrigated from said project whenever the management and operation of the irrigation works shall so pass under the terms of the reclamation act.

To complete the irrigation systems to irrigate the allotted lands of the Uncompahgre, Uintah, and White River Utes, in Utah, authorized under the act of June twenty-first, nineteen hundred and six, to be expended under the terms thereof and reimbursable as therein provided, seventy-five thousand dollars.

Act March 3, 1911 (36 Stat., 1074): For continuing the construction of irrigation systems to irrigate the allotted lands of the Uncompahgre, Uintah, and White River Utes, in Utah, authorized under the act of June twenty-first, nineteen hundred and six, to be expended under the terms thereof, and reimbursable as therein provided, seventy-five thousand dollars.

Act August 24, 1912 (37 Stat., 537): For continuing the construction of lateral distributing systems to irrigate the allotted lands of the Uncompahgre, Uintah, and White River Utes, in Utah, and to maintain existing irrigation systems authorized under the act of June twenty-first, nineteen hundred and six, to be expended under the terms thereof and reimbursable as therein provided, seventy-five thousand dollars.

The Secretary of the Interior is hereby authorized to expend the unexpended balance, which is hereby reappropriated, of the appropriation of fifteen thousand dollars, or so much thereof as may be necessary, appropriated by the act approved March third, nineteen hundred and eleven (Thirty-sixth Statutes at Large, page one thousand and seventy-four), "for the purpose of constructing a bridge across the Duchesne River at or near the town of Theodore, Utah," for the purpose of straightening the said Duchesne River at or near said bridge, with a view to protecting said bridge.

Act August 1, 1914 (38 Stat., 604): For continuing the construction of lateral distributing systems to irrigate the allotted lands of the Uncompahgre, Uintah, and White River Utes, in Utah, and to maintain existing irrigation systems, authorized under the act of June twenty-first, nineteen hundred and six, to be expended under the terms thereof and reimbursable as therein provided, $10,000, to remain available until expended.

To enable the Secretary of the Interior to protect the north abutment of the bridge at Myton, on the Uintah Indian Reservation, Utah, from high water, $200.

Joint resolution March 4, 1915 (38 Stat., 1228), reenacted the item of August 1, 1914, for the fiscal year 1916.

Act May 18, 1916 (39 Stat., 153): For continuing the construction of lateral distributing systems to irrigate the allotted lands of the Uncompahgre, Uintah, and White River Utes, in Utah, and to maintain existing irrigation systems, authorized under the act of June twenty-first, nineteen hundred and six, reimbursable as therein provided, $40,000, to remain available until expended.

* * * * * * *

The Secretary of the Interior is hereby authorized to withdraw from the Treasury of the United States the sum of $1,000, or so much thereof as may be necessary, of the funds on deposit to the credit of the Uintah Tribe of Indians, in the State of Utah, and to use the same to protect the north abutment of the Government bridge at Myton, Utah, under such rules and regulations as he may prescribe, said sum to be immediately available.

Act March 2, 1917 (39 Stat., 989): For continuing the construction of lateral distributing systems to irrigate the allotted lands of the Uncompahgre, Uintah, and White River Utes, in Utah, and to maintain existing irrigation systems, authorized under the act of June twenty-first, nineteen hundred and six, reimbursable as therein provided, $40,000, to remain available until expended.

Act May 25, 1918 (40 Stat., 587): The Secretary of the Interior is hereby authorized to withdraw from the Treasury of the United States, within his discretion, the sum of $150,000 of the principal funds to the credit of the Confederated Band of Ute Indians and to expend same for continuing the construction of lateral distributing systems to irrigate the allotted lands of the Uncompahgre, Uintah, and White River Utes, in Utah, and to maintain existing irrigation systems authorized under the act of June twenty-first, nineteen hundred and six, to be immediately available and to remain available until expended.

Act June 30, 1919 (41 Stat., 27): The Secretary of the Interior is hereby authorized to withdraw from the Treasury of the United States, within his discretion, the sum of $100,000 of the principal funds to the credit of the Confederated Bands of Ute Indians and to expend same for continuing the construction of lateral distributing systems to irrigate the allotted lands of the Uncompahgre, Uintah, and White River Utes, in Utah, and to maintain existing irrigation systems authorized under the act of June 21, 1906.

WASHINGTON.

COLVILLE.

Act April 28, 1904 (33 Stat., 567). *Be it enacted by the Senate and House of Representatives of the United States of America, in Congress assembled*, That the Secretary of the Interior be, and he is hereby, authorized and directed to permit the Kellar and Indiana Consolidated Smelting Company, a corporation organized under the laws of the State of Washington, to construct a smelter in the immediate vicinity of the San Poil River, in the south half of the Colville Indian Reservation; that the smelter shall be located on the San Poil River, and that permission be granted to construct a flume from the site of the smelter to a point on the San Poil River, where a water supply can be made available; that six acres of land be set aside for the site of the smelter, and strip of land of sufficient width allowed for the erection and construction of the flume; that permission shall be given to the Kellar and Indiana Consolidated Smelting Company to purchase timber and stone necessary for the work of construction; that the Secretary of the Interior shall permit the work to be done under such rules and regulations as he may prescribe, and he shall also prescribe the prices the said Kellar and Indiana Consolidated Smelting Company shall pay for the land, the stone, and the timber used in the construction work: *Provided*, That the laws regulating intercourse with Indians shall be applicable to the lands set aside under this Act, so long as the south half of the Colville Reservation remains as an Indian reservation.

Act March, 22, 1906 (34 Stat., 80): *Be it enacted by the Senate and House of Representatives of the United States of America in Congress assembled*, That the Secretary of the Interior be, and he is hereby, authorized and directed, as hereinafter provided, to sell or dispose of unallotted lands in the diminished Colville Indian reservation, in the State of Washington.

SEC. 2. That as soon as the lands embraced within the diminished Colville Indian Reservation shall have been surveyed, the Secretary of the Interior shall cause allotments of the same to be made to all persons belonging to or having tribal relations on said Colville Indian Reservation, to each man, woman, and child eighty acres, and, upon the approval of such allotments by the Secretary of the Interior, he shall cause patents to issue therefor under the provisions of the general allotment law of the United States.

SEC. 3. That upon the completion of said allotments to said Indians, the residue or surplus lands—that is, lands not allotted or reserved for Indian school, agency, or other purposes—of the said diminished Colville Indian Reservation shall be classified under the direction of the Secretary of the Interior as irrigable lands, grazing lands, timber lands, mineral lands, or arid lands, and shall be appraised under their appropriate classes by legal subdivisions, with the exception of the lands classed as mineral lands, which need not be appraised, and which shall be disposed of under the general mining laws of the United States, and, upon completion of the classification and appraisement, such surplus lands shall be open to settlement and entry under the provisions of the homestead laws at not less than their appraised value in additon to the fees and commissions now prescribed by law for the disposition of lands of the value of one dollar and twenty-five cents per acre by proclamation of the President, which proclamation shall prescribe the manner in which these lands shall be settled upon, occupied, and entered by persons entitled to make entry thereof: *Provided*, That the price of said lands when entered shall be fixed by the appraisement, as herein provided for, which shall be paid in accordance with rules and regulations to be prescribed by the Secretary of the Interior upon the following terms: One-fifth of the purchase price to be paid in cash at the time of entry and the balance in five equal annual installments to be paid in one, two, three, four, and five years, respectively, from and after the date of entry, and in case any entryman fails to make the annual payments, or any of them, promptly when due all rights in and to the land covered by his or her entry shall cease, and any payments theretofore made shall be forfeited and the entry canceled, and the lands shall be reoffered for sale and entry: *Provided further*, That the lands remaining undisposed of at the expiration of five years from the opening of the said lands to entry shall be sold to the highest bidder for cash, at not less than one dollar per acre, under rules and regulations to be prescribed by the Secretary of the Interior, and that any lands remaining unsold ten years after the said lands shall have been opened to entry may be sold to the highest bidder for cash without regard to the above minimum limit of price.

SEC. 4. That the said lands shall be opened to settlement and entry by proclamation of the President, which proclamation shall prescribe the time when and the manner in which these lands may be settled upon, occupied, and entered by persons entitled to make entry thereof, and no person shall be permitted to settle upon, occupy and enter any of said lands except as prescribed in such proclamation: *Provided*, That the rights of honorably discharged Union soldiers and sailors of the late civil and Spanish wars, as defined and described in sections twenty-three hundred and four and twenty-three hundred and five of the Revised Statutes, as amended by the Act of March first, nineteen hundred and one, shall not be abridged.

SEC. 5. That all of said lands returned and classified as timber lands shall be sold and disposed of by the Secretary of the Interior under sealed bids to the highest bidder for cash or at public auction, as the Secretary of the Interior may determine, and under such rules and regulations as he may prescribe.

SEC. 6. That the proceeds not including fees and commissions arising from the sale and disposition of the lands aforesaid, including the sums paid for mineral and town-site lands shall be, after deducting the expenses incurred from time to time in connection with the allotment, appraisement, and sales, and surveys, herein provided, deposited in the Treasury of the Unted States to the credit of the Colville and confederated tribes of Indians belonging and having tribal rights on the Colville Indian reservation, in the State of Washington, and shall be expended for their benefit, under the direction of the Secretary of the Interior, in the education and improvement of said Indians, and in the purchase of stock, cattle, horse teams, harness, wagons, mowing machines, horserakes, thrashing machines, and other agricultural implements for issue to said Indians, and also for the purchase of material for the construction of houses or other necessary buildings, and a reasonable sum may also be expended by the secretary, in his discretion, for comfort, benefit, and improvement of said Indians: *Provided*, That a portion of the proceeds may be paid to the Indians in cash per capita, share and share alike, if, in the opinion of the Secretary of the Interior, such payments will further tend to improve the condition and advance and progress of said Indians, but not otherwise.

SEC. 7. That any of said lands necessary for agency, school, and religious purposes, and any lands now occupied by the agency buildings, and the site of any sawmill, gristmill, or other mill property, on said lands are hereby reserved from the operation of this act: *Provided*, That all such reserved lands shall not exceed in the aggregate three sections and must be selected in legal subdivisions conformable to the public surveys, such selection to be made by the Indian agent of the Colville Agency, under the direction of the Secretary of the Interior and subject to his approval.

SEC. 8. That the Secretary of the Interior is hereby vested with full power and authority to make all needful rules and regulations as to the manner of sale, notice of same, and other matters incident to the carrying out of the provisions of this act, and with authority to reappraise and reclassify said lands if deemed necessary from time to time, and to continue making sales of the same, in accordance with the provisions of this act, until all of the lands shall have been disposed of.

SEC. 9. That nothing in this act contained shall be construed to bind the United States to find purchasers for any of said lands, it being the purpose of this act merely to have the United States to act as trustee for said Indians in the disposition and sale of said lands and to expend or pay over to them the net proceeds derived from the sales as herein provided.

SEC. 10. That to enable the Secretary of the Interior to survey, allot, classify, appraise, and conduct the sale and entry of said lands as in this act provided the sum of seventy-five thousand dollars, or so much thereof as may be necessary, is hereby appropriated, from any money in the Treasury not otherwise appropriated, the same to be reimbursed from the proceeds of the sales of the aforesaid lands: *Provided*, That when funds shall have been procured from the first sales of the land the Secretary of the Interior may use such portion thereof as may be actually necessary in conducting future sales and otherwise carrying out the provisions of this act.

SEC. 11. That nothing contained in this act shall prohibit the Secretary of the Interior from reserving from said lands, whether surveyed or unsurveyed, such tracts for town-site purposes, as in his opinion may be required for the future public interests, and he may cause any such reservations, or parts thereof, to be surveyed into blocks and lots of suitable size, and to be appraised and disposed of under such regulations as he may prescribe, and the net proceeds derived from the sale of such lands shall be paid to said Indians, as provided in section six of this act.

SEC. 12. That if any of the lands of said diminished Colville Indian Reservation can be included in any feasible irrigation project under the reclamation act of June seventeenth, nineteen hundred and two, the Secretary of the Interior is authorized to withhold said lands from disposition under this act and to dispose of them under the said reclamation act, and the charges provided for by said reclamation act shall be in addition to the appraised value of said lands fixed as hereinbefore provided and shall be paid in annual installments as required under the said reclamation act, and the amounts to be paid for the land, according to appraisement shall be credited to the fund herein established for the benefit of the Colville Indians.

Act September 17, 1913 (38 Stat. L. 111): An act for the acquiring of station grounds by the Great Northern Railway Company in the Colville Indian Reservation in the State of Washington. * * *

Provided, That if any of the lands to be acquired by the railway company under the provisions of this act shall have been tentatively selected by Indians as a part of their allotments, they shall be entitled to receive upon the approval of their allotments the compensation for damages to said lands and improvements thereon paid by the said railway company: *And provided further*, That such station grounds are granted subject to the right of the United States to cross the same and the works constructed thereon with canals or water conduits of any kind, or with roadways, or with transmission lines for telephone, telegraph, or electric power, or with any other public improvements which may now or in the future be built by or under authority of the United States across such grounds; and the said company shall build and maintain at its own expense all structures that may be required at such crossing, and in accepting this grant shall release the United States from all damages which may result from the construction and use of such crossings, canals, conduits, transmission lines, and other improvements.

Act May 18, 1916 (39 Stat., 155): That there is hereby appropriated, out of any funds in the Treasury not otherwise appropriated, $95,000, to be used by the Commissioner of Indian Affairs under the direction of the Secretary of the Interior, in the acquisition of water rights for lands heretofore allotted to Indians, situated within the boundaries of the West Okanogan Valley irrigation district, Okanogan County, Washington, and for the payment of the proportionate operation and maintenance charges of the said district. The Secretary of the Interior is authorized to negotiate for said water rights and to pay therefor as he may deem appropriate, such part of the sum herein appropriated as he may determine to be necessary for the best interests of the Indians: *Provided*. That nothing herein contained shall be construed to authorize any lien or claims upon or against said allotted lands not herein specifically appropriated for: *Provided further*: That the amounts expended under this appropriation shall be reimbursed to the United States by the owners of the land on behalf of which such expenditure is made, upon such terms as the Secretary may prescribe, which shall be not less favorable to the Indians than the reimbursement required of settlers upon lands irrigated under the provisions of the reclamation act of June seventeenth, nineteen hundred and two (Thirty-second Statutes at Large, page three hundred and eighty-eight), and acts amendatory thereof or supplementary thereto; and if any Indian shall sell his allotment or part thereof, or receive a patent in fee for the same, any amount of the charge made to secure reimbursement remaining unpaid at the time of such sale or issuance of patent shall be a lien on the land, and patents issued therefor shall recite the amount of such item.

Act June 30, 1919: For the construction, repair, and maintenance of irrigation systems and for purchase or rental of irrigation tools and appliances, water rights, ditches, and lands necessary for irrigation purposes for Indian reservations and allotments; for operation of irrigation systems or appurtenances thereto, when no other funds are applicable or available for the purpose; for drainage and protection of irrigable lands from damage by floods or loss of water rights, upon the Indian irrigation projects named below:

Under the foregoing heading the acts of May 25, 1918 (40 Stat., 562) and June 30, 1919 (41 Stat., 3), provided the sums of $5,200 and $10,000, respectively, for irrigation work on the Colville Reservation, Washington.

KALISPEL.

Act April 21, 1904 (33 Stat., 219): SEC. 12. That the Indians living along and near the Colville River in Stevens County, State of Washington, to whom trust patents have been issued containing restrictions upon alienation, may sell and convey, for drainage purposes, so much of such allotments as may be necessary for right of way for drainage canals, but such conveyances shall be subject to the approval of the Secretary of the Interior, and when so approved shall convey, for said purposes, a full title to the purchasers the same as if final patent, without restrictions, had been issued to the allottees.

SPOKANE.

Act of June 21, 1906 (34 Stat., 377): That the Secretary of the Interior be, and he is hereby, authorized, in his discretion, to sell and convey by patent, with such reservations as to flowage rights, dam sites, and mill sites appurtenant to water powers, as he may prescribe, such tract or tracts of lands of the Spokane Indian Reservation, State of Washington, lying at or near the junction of the Columbia and Spokane Rivers, not exceeding three hundred and sixty acres in extent, for town-site and terminal purposes, upon the payment of such price as may be fixed by him, and that the money received therefrom shall be deposited in the Treasury of the United States, to the credit of the Spokane Indians.

Act March 3, 1911 (36 Stat., 1075): The Secretary of the Interior is authorized to sell and convey the lands, buildings, and other appurtenances of the old Fort Spokane * * * *Provided*, That the Secretary of the Interior is authorized, in his discretion, to reserve from sale, or other disposition, any part of said reservation chiefly valuable for power sites and reservoir sites. * * *

YAKIMA.

Act October 1, 1890 (26 Stat., L. 661): An act granting to the Northern Pacific and Yakima Irrigation Company a right of way through the Yakima Indian Reservation, in Washington.

Be it enacted by the Senate and House of Representatives of the United States of America, in Congress assembled, That the right of way is hereby granted, as hereinafter set forth, to the Northern Pacific and Yakima Irrigation Company, a corporation organized and existing under the laws of the State of Washington, for the construction of an irrigating canal through the Yakima Indian Reservation, from a point on the boundary of said reservation in either sections four, eight, nine, or ten, township twelve north, range eighteen east, of the Willamette meridian, in Yakima County, in the State of Washington; thence extending, in a southeasterly direction, to a point on the boundary of said reservation, at section seventeen, township twelve north, range nineteen east, of the said meridian.

SEC. 2. That the right of way hereby granted to said company shall be seventy-five feet in width on each side of the central line of said canal, as aforesaid; and said company shall also have the right to take from said lands adjacent to the line of said canal material, stone, earth, and timber necessary for the construction of said canal.

SEC. 3. That it shall be the duty of the Secretary of the Interior to fix the amount of compensation to be paid the Indians for such right of way, and for whatever property of said Indians may be taken in the construction of said canal, and provide the time and manner for the payment thereof, and also to ascertain and fix the amount of compensation to be made individual members of the tribe for damages sustained by them by reason of the construction of said canal; but no right of any kind shall vest in said irrigation company in, or to any part of, the right of way, herein provided for, until plats thereof, made upon actual surveys for the definite location of such canal, shall be filed with, and approved by, the Secretary of the Interior, which approval shall be made in writing, and be opened for the inspection of any party interested therein, and until the compensation aforesaid has been fixed and paid; and the surveys, construction, and operation of such canal shall be conducted with due regard for the rights of the Indians, and in accordance with such rules and regulations as the Secretary of the Interior may make to carry out this provision: *Provided*, That the consent of the Indians to said right of way and compensation shall be obtained by said irrigation company, in such manner as the Secretary of the Interior shall prescribe, before any right under this act shall accrue to said company.

SEC. 4. That said company shall not assign, or transfer, or mortgage this right of way for any purpose whatever until said canal shall be completed: *Provided*, That the company may mortgage said franchise for money to construct and complete said canal: *And provided further*, That the right herein granted shall be lost and forfeited by said company unless the canal is constructed across said reservation within two years from the passage of this act.

SEC. 5. That said irrigation company shall accept this right of way upon the express condition, binding upon itself, its successors, or assigns, that they will neither aid, advise, nor assist in any effort looking toward the changing or extinguishing the present tenure of the Indians in their land, and will not attempt to secure from the Indian tribes any further grant of land or its occupancy than is hereinbefore provided: *Provided*, That any violation of the condition mentioned in this section shall operate as a forfeiture of all the rights and privileges of said irrigation company under this act.

SEC. 6. That Congress may at any time amend, add to, alter, or repeal this act.

Act July 23, 1894 (28 Stat. L., 118): *Be it enacted by the Senate and House of Representatives of the United States of America in Congress assembled*, That the right of way is hereby granted, as is hereinafter set forth, to the Columbia Irrigation Company, a corporation organized and existing under the laws of the State of Washington, for the construction of an irrigation canal through the Yakima Indian Reservation, from a point about one-half mile below where the Ahtanum Creek empties into the Yakima River, on said reservation, in Yakima County, in the State of Washington; thence extending in a southerly direction to a point where said canal crosses the Toppenish Creek; thence in a southeasterly direction, by the most practical route, to a point on the east boundary of said reservation, at or near section nineteen (19), township eight (8) north, range twenty-three (23) east of the Willamette meridian.

SEC. 2. That said irrigation company shall have the right to appropriate and use any and all water necessary for their use from the Yakima River, not otherwise appropriated and in actual use at the time of the passage of this act, or that may not be necessary for the domestic and irrigating purposes of any Indian to whom an allotment has been made, or shall hereafter be made, upon or along said Yakima River.

SEC. 3. That the said irrigation company is hereby granted sufficient land on said reservation for reservoirs for the storage of water to be used during the dry season, and for right of way connecting said storage reservoirs with said irrigation canal, and shall have the right to locate, construct, and maintain the same under the same terms and restrictions provided herein for the right of way of said canal.

SEC. 4. That the right of way hereby granted to said company shall be seventy-five (75) feet in width on each side of the central line of said canal as aforesaid; and said company shall also have the right to take from said lands adjacent to the line of said canal material, stone, earth, and timber necessary for the construction of said canal.

SEC. 5. That it shall be the duty of the Secretary of the Interior to fix the amount of compensation to be paid individual members of the tribe for damages sustained by them by reason of the construction of said canal, and to provide the time and manner for the payment thereof; but no right of any kind shall vest in said irrigation company in or to any part of the right of way herein provided for until plats thereof made upon actual survey for the definite location of such canal shall be filed with and approved by the Secretary of the Interior, which approval shall be made in writing and be open for the inspection of any party interested therein; and the survey, construction, and operation of such canal shall be conducted with due regard for the rights of the Indians, and in accordance with such rules and regulations as the Secretary of the Interior may make to carry out this provision.

SEC. 6. That said company shall not assign or transfer or mortgage this right of way for any purpose whatever until said canal shall be completed: *Provided*, That the company may mortgage said franchise for money to construct and complete said canal: *And provided further*, That the right herein granted shall be lost and forfeited by said company to any portion of said canal not completed within five years from the passage of this act: *Provided further*, That one-fourth of said canal shall be completed in two years.

SEC. 7. That said irrigation company shall accept this right of way upon the express condition, binding upon itself, its successors, or assigns, that they will not attempt to secure from the Indian tribe any further grant of land or its occupancy than is hereinbefore provided: *Provided*, That any violation of the conditions mentioned in this section shall operate as a forfeiture of all the rights and privileges of said irrigation company under this act: *Provided further*, That the rights herein granted are upon the express condition that the grantee or grantees thereof shall at all times during the continuance thereof furnish the Indian allottees along said right of way with water sufficient for all domestic and agricultural purposes and purposes of irrigation, on such terms and under such rules and regulations as shall be prescribed by the Secretary of the Interior: *Provided further*, That Indians who have or may have allotments along said right of way shall have water for irrigation and domestic purposes free.

SEC. 8. The right to alter, amend, or repeal this act is hereby expressly reserved.

Act June 10, 1896 (29 Stat., 342): * * * That the time for the completion of the canal, or any part thereof, authorized by an act entitled "An act granting to the Columbia Irrigation Company a right of way through the Yakima Indian Reservation, in Washington" be, and is hereby, extended two years from July twenty-fourth, eighteen hundred and ninety-six.

Act July 1, 1898 (30 Stat., 591): * * * *Provided*, That the time for the completion of the canal, or any part thereof, authorized by an act entitled "An act granting to the Columbia Irrigation Company a right of way through the Yakima Indian Reservation, in Washington" be, and is hereby, extended two years from July twenty-fourth, eighteen hundred and ninety-eight.

Act December 21, 1904 (33 Stat. L., 595): An act to authorize the sale and disposition of surplus or unallotted lands of the Yakima Indian Reservation, in the State of Washington.

Be it enacted by the Senate and House of Representatives of the United States of America in Congress assembled, That the Secretary of the Interior be, and he is hereby, authorized and directed, as hereinafter provided, to sell or dispose of unallotted lands embraced in the Yakima Indian Reservation proper, in the State of Washington, set aside and established by treaty with the Yakima Nation of Indians, dated June eighth, eighteen hundred and fifty-five: *Provided*, That the claim of said Indians to the tract of land adjoining their present reservation on the west, excluded by erroneous boundary survey and containing approximately two hundred and ninety-three thousand eight hundred and thirty-seven acres, according to the findings, after examination, of Mr. E. C. Barnard, topographer of the Geological Survey, approved by the Secretary of the Interior April seventh, nineteen hundred, is hereby recognized, and the said tract shall be regarded as a part of the Yakima Indian Reservation for the purposes of this act: *Provided further*, That where valid rights have been acquired prior to March fifth, nineteen hundred and four, to lands within said tract by bona fide settlers or purchasers under the public-land laws, such rights shall not be abridged, and any claim of said Indians to these lands is hereby declared to be fully compensated for by the expenditure of money heretofore made for their benefit and in the construction of irrigation works on the Yakima Indian Reservation.

SEC. 2. That allotments of land shall be made, under the direction of the Secretary of the Interior, to any Indians entitled thereto, including children now living born since the completion of the existing allotments who have not heretofore received such allotments. The Secretary of the Interior is also authorized to reserve such lands as he may deem necessary or desirable in connection with the construction of contemplated irrigation systems or lands crossed by existing irrigation ditches; also lands necessary for agency, school, and religious purposes; also such tract or tracts of grazing and timber lands as may be deemed expedient for the use and benefit of the Indians of said reservation in common: *Provided*, That such reserved lands, or any portion thereof, may be classified, appraised, and disposed of from time to time under the terms and provisions of this act.

SEC. 3. That the residue of the lands of said reservation—that is, the lands not allotted and not reserved—shall be classified under the direction of the Secretary of the Interior as irrigable lands, grazing lands, timber lands, mineral lands, or arid lands, and shall be appraised under their appropriate classes by legal subdivisions, with the exception of the mineral lands, which need not be appraised, and the timber on the lands classified as timber lands shall be appraised separately from the land. The basis for the appraisal of the timber shall be the amount of standing merchantable timber thereon, which shall be ascertained and reported.

Upon completion of the classification and appraisements the irrigable, grazing, and arid lands, and the timbered lands upon the completion of the classification, appraisement, and the sale and removal of the timber therefrom, shall be disposed of under the general provisions of the homestead laws of the United States, and shall be opened to settlement and entry at not less than their appraised value by proclamation of the President, which proclamation shall prescribe the manner in which these lands shall be settled upon, occupied, and entered by persons entitled to make entry thereof, and no person shall be permitted to settle upon, occupy, or enter any of said lands, except as prescribed in such proclamation, until after the expiration of sixty days from the time when the same are opened to settlement and entry: *Provided*, That the rights of honorably discharged Union soldiers and sailors of the late Civil and Spanish Wars and the Philippine insurrection, as defined and described in sections twenty-three hundred and four and twenty-three hundred and five of the Revised Statutes, as amended by the act of March first, nineteen hundred and one, shall not be abridged: *Provided further*, That the price of said lands when entered shall be that fixed by the appraisement or by the President, as herein provided for, which shall be paid in accordance with rules and regulations to be prescribed by the Secretary of the Interior upon the following terms: One-fifth of the purchase price to be paid in cash at the time of entry, and the balance in five equal annual installments, to be paid in one, two, three, four, and five years, respectively, from and after the date of entry. In case any entryman fails to make the annual payments, or any of them, promptly when due, all rights in and to the land covered by his entry shall cease, and any payments theretofore made shall be forfeited and the entry canceled, and the lands shall be reoffered for sale and entry: *And provided further*, That the lands embraced within such canceled entry shall, after the cancellation of such entry, be subject to entry under the provisions of the homestead law, at the appraised value until otherwise directed by the President, as herein provided.

When the entryman shall have complied with all the requirements and terms of the homestead laws as to settlement and residence and shall have made all the required payments aforesaid, he shall be entitled to a patent for the lands entered: *Provided*, That the entryman shall make his final proofs in accordance with the homestead laws within six years; and that aliens who have declared their intention to become citizens of the United States may become such entrymen, but before making final proof and receiving patent they must have received their full naturalization papers: *Provided further*, That the fees and commissions to be paid in connection with such entries and final proofs shall be the same as those now provided by law where the price of the land is one dollar and twenty-five cents per acre: *And provided further*, That the Secretary of the Interior may, in his discretion, limit the quantity of irrigable land that may be taken by an entryman to eighty acres, but not to less than that quantity: *And provided further*, That when, in the judgment of the President, no more of the said land can be disposed of at the appraised price, he may, by proclamation, to be repeated at his discretion, sell from time to time the remaining lands subject to the provisions of the homestead law, or otherwise as he may deem most advantageous, at such price or prices, in such manner, upon such conditions, with such restrictions, and upon such terms as he may deem best for all the interests concerned.

The timber on lands classified as timberlands shall be sold at not less than its appraised value, under sealed proposals in accordance with such rules and regulations as the Secretary of the Interior may prescribe.

The lands classified as mineral lands shall be subject to location and disposal under the mineral land laws of the United States: *Provided*, That lands not classified as mineral may also be located and entered as mineral land, subject to approval by the Secretary of the Interior and conditioned upon the payment, within one year from the date when located, of the appraised value of the lands per acre fixed prior to the date of such location, but at not less than the price fixed by existing law for mineral lands: *Provided further*, That no such mineral locations shall be permitted on any lands allotted to Indians in severalty or reserved for any purpose as herein authorized.

SEC. 4. That the proceeds arising from the sale and disposition of the lands aforesaid, including the sums paid for mineral lands, exclusive of the customary fees and commissions, shall, after deducting the expenses incurred from time to time in connection with the appraisements and sales, be deposited in the Treasury of the United States to the credit of the Indians belonging and having tribal rights on the Yakima Reservation, and shall be expended for their benefit under the direction of the Secretary of the Interior in the construction, completion, and maintenance of irrigation ditches, purchase of wagons, horses, farm implements, materials for houses, and other necessary and useful articles, as may be deemed best to promote their welfare and aid them in the adoption of civilized pursuits and in improving and building homes for themselves on their allotments: *Provided*, That a portion of the proceeds may be paid to the Indians in cash per capita, share and share alike, if in the opinion of the Secretary of the Interior such payments will further tend to improve the condition and advance the progress of said Indians, but not otherwise.

SEC. 5. That the Secretary of the Interior is hereby authorized, in the cases of entrymen and purchasers of lands now irrigated or that may be hereafter irrigated from systems constructed for the benefit of the Indians, to require such annual proportionate payments to be made as may be just and equitable for the maintenance of said systems: *Provided*, That in appraising the value of irrigable lands, such sum per acre as the Secretary of the Interior may deem proper, to be determined as nearly as may be by the total cost of the irrigation system or systems, shall be added as the proportionate share of the cost of placing water on said lands, and when the entryman or purchaser shall have paid in full the appraised value of the land, including the cost of providing water therefor, the Secretary of the Interior shall give to him such evidence of title in writing to a perpetual water right as may be deemed suitable: *Provided*, That the Secretary of the Interior shall have power to determine and direct when the management and operation of such irrigation works shall pass to the owners of the lands irrigated thereby, to be maintained at their expense, under such forms of organization and under such rules and regulations as may be acceptable to him: *Provided also*, That the title to and management and operation of the reservoirs, and the work necessary for their protection and operation, shall remain in the Government until otherwise provided by Congress.

SEC. 6. That the Secretary of the Interior is hereby vested with full power and authority to make all needful rules and regulations as to manner of sale, notice of same, and other matters incident to the carrying out of the provisions of this act, and with authority to reappraise and reclassify said lands, if deemed necessary from time to time, and to continue making sales of the same, in accordance with the provisions of this act, until all of the lands shall have been disposed of.

SEC. 7. That nothing in this act contained shall be construed to bind the United States to find purchasers for any of said lands, it being the purpose of this act merely to have the United States to act as trustee for said Indians in the disposition and sales of said lands, and to expend or pay over to them the proceeds derived from the sales as herein provided.

SEC. 8. That to enable the Secretary of the Interior to classify and appraise the aforesaid lands as in this act provided, and to conduct the sales thereof, and to define and mark the boundaries of the western portion of said reservation, including the adjoining tract of two hundred and ninety-three thousand eight hundred and thirty-seven acres, to which the claim of the Indians is, by this act, recognized, as above set out, and to complete the surveys thereof, the sum of fifty-three thousand dollars, or so much thereof as may be necessary, is hereby appropriated from any moneys in the Treasury not otherwise appropriated, the same to be reimbursed from the proceeds of the sales of the aforesaid lands: *Provided*, That when funds shall have been procured from the first sales of the land the Secretary of the Interior may use such portion thereof as may be actually necessary in conducting future sales and otherwise carrying out the provisions of this act.

Act March 6, 1906 (34 Stat., L. 53): *Be it enacted by the Senate and House of Representatives of the United States of America, in Congress assembled*, That if within the limits of the Yakima Indian Reservation, in the State of Washington, as described in the act approved December twenty-first, nineteen hundred and four, entitled "An act to authorize the sale and disposition of surplus or unallotted lands of the Yakima Indian Reservation, in the State of Washington," there shall be found surplus or unallotted lands under irrigation projects deemed practicable and undertaken under the provisions of the act of Congress approved June seventeenth, nineteen hundred and two, known as the reclamation act, the Secretary of the Interior is hereby authorized to exclude from the provisions of said act of December twenty-first, nineteen hundred and four, such surplus or unallotted lands which can be irrigated under such project, and to dispose of the same in the manner hereinafter provided, and he is further authorized to make withdrawals of such lands for the purposes provided in said reclamation act.

SEC. 2. That the irrigable surplus and unallotted lands in any such project shall be subject to homestead entry under all the provisions of the reclamation act at such time as may be fixed by the Secretary of the Interior and at a price determined by appraisal as provided in said act of December twenty-first, nineteen hundred and four. Payments for the land shall be made in annual installments, the number and time of beginning being fixed by the Secretary of the Interior, and shall be deposited in the Treasury of the United States and credited to the Yakima Indian fund, and disposed of as provided by section four of the said act of December twenty-first, nineteen hundred and four. Such payments shall be in addition to the charges for construction and maintenance of the irrigation system made payable into the reclamation fund by the provisions of the reclamation act. In case of failure to make any payment for such lands when due, the Secretary of the Interior shall have power to cancel the entry and the corresponding water right and declare forfeited to the said Yakima Indian fund and the reclamation fund, respectively, the amounts paid on such entry and water right. The lands embraced within such canceled entry shall be subject to further entry under the reclamation act at the appraised value until otherwise directed by the President, who may by proclamation, as provided by said act of December twenty-first, nineteen hundred and four, from time to time fix such price as he may deem most advantageous upon all lands within such project not disposed of.

SEC. 3. That if any lands heretofore allotted or patented to Indians on said Yakima Indian reservation shall be found irrigable under any project, the Secretary of the Interior is hereby authorized, upon the request or with the consent of such allottee or patentee, to dispose of all land in excess of twenty acres in each case, in tracts of an area approved by him and subject to all the provisions of the reclamation act to any person qualified to acquire water rights under the provisions of the reclamation act at a price satisfactory to the allottee or patentee and approved by the Secretary of the Interior, or at public sale to the highest bidder. The payments shall be made in annual installments, the number and terms being approved by the Secretary of the Interior. Such payments shall be in addition to the charges for construction and maintenance of the irrigation system, made payable into the reclamation fund by the provisions of the reclamation act. In case of failure to make any payment for such lands when due or the charges under the reclamation act, the Secretary of the Interior shall have power to cancel the entry and the corresponding water right and again dispose of the land in the manner hereinbefore provided.

SEC. 4. That from the payments received from the sale of such individual Indian lands there shall be covered into the reclamation fund the amounts fixed by the Secretary of the Interior as the annual charges on account of the land retained by such Indian for the construction and maintenance of the irrigation system, as required under the reclamation act. The balance, if any, shall be deposited in the Treasury of the United States to the credit of the individual Indians, and may be paid to any of them if, in the opinion of the Secretary of the Interior, such payments will tend to improve the condition and advance the progress of said Indians, but not otherwise.

SEC. 5. That the Secretary is hereby authorized to cover into the reclamation fund from the money of any such Indian, either from his individual credit or from the general Yakima Indian fund, for the payment of charges for construction and maintenance for the water rights appurtenant to the land retained by him or for the annual maintenance charges payable on account of such water rights after the construction charge thereon has been paid in full. After unconditional title in fee has passed from the United States for any lands retained by such Indians the water for irrigating such lands shall be furnished under the same conditions in all respects as for other lands under the project: *Provided*, That any Indian taking advantage of this act shall have a perpetual water right so long as the maintenance charges are paid, whether he uses the water or not, and the Secretary of the Interior is hereby authorized to use the funds of the tribe to pay such maintenance charges which, in his discretion, it is necessary to preserve said water right: *Provided further*, That he may, in his discretion, use said funds to pay for water rights and the maintenance charges on twenty acres of any Indian allotment if the sum obtained from the sale of the allottee's land in excess of twenty acres and his interest in the tribal funds be insufficient for those purposes.

SEC. 6. That the Secretary of the Interior shall be authorized, upon compliance with the provisions of this act and of the reclamation act, by any party having purchased such allotted or patented lands as herein provided, to issue patent passing unconditional title in fee by the United States as trustee for the allottee or patentee and shall cancel any allotment as to the lands disposed of under this act.

SEC. 7. That the irrigation works heretofore constructed for the Yakima Indian Reservation may be at a cost to be determined by the Secretary of the Interior included in any project developed under the provisions of the reclamation act and of this act and become a part of said project for all purposes of the reclamation act, and the cost of same shall be included in the cost of such project and be paid into the Yakima Indian fund out of the proceeds arising from the sale of water rights from time to time as payments on account thereof are received. The provisions of this act shall be construed as superseding or amending any provisions of the said act of December twenty-first, nineteen hundred and four, so far as any conflict may appear.

SEC. 8. That the Secretary of the Interior is hereby authorized to perform any and all acts and to make such rules and regulations as may be necessary and proper for the purpose of carrying the provisions of this act into full force and effect.

Act June 21, 1906 (34 Stat., L. 377): For the extension of the irrigation system on lands allotted to Yakima Indians in Washington, $15,000, to be reimbursed from the proceeds of the sale of surplus lands as provided by the act of December twenty-first, nineteen hundred and four, entitled "An act to authorize the sale and disposition of surplus or unallotted lands of the Yakima Indian Reservation, in the State of Washington;" in all, $15,000.

Act March 1, 1907 (34 Stat., 1050): For the extension of the irrigation system on lands allotted to Yakima Indians in Washington, $15,000, to be reimbursed from the proceeds of the sale of surplus lands, as provided by the act of December twenty-first, nineteen hundred and four, entitled "An act to authorize the sale and disposition of surplus or unallotted lands of the Yakima Indian Reservation in the State of Washington;" in all, $15,000.

Act April 30, 1908 (35 Stat., 96): For the extension of the irrigation system on lands allotted to Yakima Indians in Washington, $15,000, to be reimbursed from the proceeds of the sale of surplus lands, as provided by the act of December twenty-first, nineteen hundren and four, entitled "An act to authorize the sale and disposition of surplus or unallotted lands of the Yakima Indian Reservation in the State of Washington;" in all, $15,000.

Act March 3, 1909 (35 Stat., 813): For the extension of the irrigation system on lands allotted to Yakima Indians in Washington, $15,000, to be reimbursed from the proceeds of the sale of surplus lands, as provided by the act of December twenty-first, nineteen hundred and four, entitled "An act to authorize the sale and disposition of surplus or unallotted lands of the Yakima Indian Reservation in the State of Washington."

Act April 4, 1910 (36 Stat., 286): For the extension of the irrigation system on lands allotted to Yakima Indians in Washington, $15,000, and the construction of drainage system, $250,000, of which sum of two hundred and fifty thousand dollars, twenty-five thousand dollars shall be immedately available; in all, $265,000: *Provided*, That the amount hereby appropriated and all moneys heretofore or hereafter to be appropriated for these purposes, shall be repaid into the Treasury of the United States in accordance with the provisions of the act of December twenty-first, nineteen hundred and four.

Act March 3, 1911 (36 Stat., 1075): For extension and maintenance of the irrigation system on lands allotted to Yakima Indians in Washington, $15,000: *Provided*, That the amount hereby appropriated, and all moneys heretofore or hereafter to be appropriated, for this project shall be repaid into the Treasury of the United States in accordance with the provisions of the act of March first, nineteen hundred and seven.

Act August 24, 1912 (37 Stat., 538): For extension and maintenance of the irrigation system on lands allotted to Yakima Indians in Washington, $15,000, reimbursable in accordance with the provisions of the act of March first, nineteen hundred and seven. * * *

* * * That the Secretary of the Interior be, and he is hereby, authorized and directed to investigate the conditions on the Yakima Indian Reservation in the State of Washington, with a view to determine the best, most practicable, and most feasible plan for providing water for such lands of said reservation as may be irrigated and to cause surveys, plans, and reports to be made thereon, together with an estimated limit of cost of such irrigation project and to submit his report thereon to Congress on the first Monday in December, nineteen hundred and twelve, together with such facts and reasons in support of the same as may be necessary to advise Congress fully in regard thereto.

Act June 30, 1913 (38 Stat., 100): For extension and maintenance of the irrigation system on lands allotted to Yakima Indians in Washington, $15,000, reimbursable in accordance with the provisions of the act of March first, nineteen hundred and seven.

Act June 30, 1913 (38 Stat., 100): A commission consisting of two members of the Senate Committee on Indian Affairs, to be appointed by the chairman of said committee, and two members of the House of Representatives to be appointed by the Speaker, is hereby created for the purpose of investigating * * * the necessity and feasibility of procuring impounded waters for the Yakima Indian Reservation or the construction of an irrigation system upon said reservation, to impound the waters of the Yakima River, Washington, for the reclamation of the lands on said reservation, and for the use and benefit of the Indians of said reservation. That said commission shall have full power to make the investigations herein provided for, and shall have authority to subpœna and compel the attendance of witnesses, administer oaths, take testimony, incur expenses, employ clerical help, and do and perform all acts necessary to make a thorough and complete investigation of the subject herein mentioned, and that said commission shall report to Congress on or before January first, nineteen hundred and fourteen * * *.

Act August 1, 1914 (38 Stat., 604): It appearing by the report of the Joint Congressional Commission, created under section twenty-three of the Indian appropriation act, approved June thirtieth, nineteen hundred and thirteen (Senate Document Numbered three hundred and thirty-seven, Sixty-third Congress, second session), that the Indians of the Yakima Reservation in the State of Washington, have been unjustly deprived of the portion of the natural flow of the Yakima River to which they are equitably entitled for the purpose of irrigation, having only been allowed one hundred and forty-seven cubic feet per second, the Secretary of the Interior is hereby authorized and directed to furnish at the northern boundary of said Yakima Indian Reservation, in perpetuity, enough water, in addition to the one hundred and forty-seven cubic feet per second heretofore allotted to said Indians, so that there shall be, during the low-water irrigation season, at least seven hundred and twenty cubic feet per second of water available when needed for irrigation, this quantity being considered as equivalent to and in satisfaction of the rights of the Indians in the low-water flow of Yakima River and adequate for the irrigation of forty acres on each Indian allotment; the apportionment of this water to be made under the direction of the Secretary of the Interior; and there is hereby authorized to be appropriated the sum of $635,000 to pay for said water to be covered into the reclamation fund; the amount to be appropriated annually in installments upon estimates certified to Congress by the Secretary of the Treasury. One hundred thousand dollars is hereby appropriated to pay the first installment of the amount herein authorized to be expended, and the Secretary of the Interior is hereby directed to prepare and submit to Congress the most feasible and economical plans for the distribution of said water upon the lands of said Yakima Reservation, in connection with the present system and with a view to reimbursing the Government for any sum it may have expended or may expend for a complete irrigation system for said reservation.

For operation and maintenance of the irrigation system on lands allotted to Yakima Indians in Washington, $15,000, reimbursable in accordance with the provisions of the act of March first, nineteen hundred and seven.

Joint resolution of March 4, 1915 (38 Stat., 1228): Reenacted the last foregoing provisions for the fiscal year 1916.

Act May 18, 1916 (39 Stat., 153): For operation and maintenance of the irrigation system on lands allotted to Yakima Indians in Washington, $15,000, reimbursable in accordance with the provisions of the act of March first, nineteen hundred and seven: *Provided*, That money received under agreements for temporary water supply may be expended under the direction of the Secretary of the Interior for maintenance and improvement of the irrigation system on said lands. * * *

For construction of a dam across the Yakima River for the diversion and utilization of water provided for forty acres of each Indian allotment on the Yakima Reservation, Washington, and such other water supply as may be available or obtainable for the irrigation of a total of one hundred and twenty thousand acres of allotted Indian land on said reservation, and for beginning the enlargement and extension of the distribution and drainage system on said reservation, $200,000, to be immediately available and to remain available until expended: *Provided*, That the cost of the entire diversion works and distribution and drainage system shall be reimbursed to the United States by the owners of the lands irrigable thereunder in not to exceed twenty annual payments, and the Secretary of the Interior may fix operation and maintenance charges, which shall be paid as he may direct.

In the apportionment of charges against Indians, due allowance shall be made for such amounts as may have been repaid the United States on account of reimbursable appropriations heretofore made for this project and for the construction of the irrigation system prior to the passage of the act of December twenty-first, nineteen hundred and four (Thirty-third Statutes at Large, page five hundred and ninety-five), as therein provided. All charges against Indian allottees herein authorized, unless otherwise paid, may be paid from individual shares in the tribal fund when the same is available for distribution, and if any allottee shall receive patent in fee to his allotment before the amount so charged against him has been paid to the United States, then such amount remaining unpaid shall be and become a lien upon his allotment, and the fact of such lien shall be recited in such patent and may be enforced by the Secretary of the Interior by foreclosure as a mortgage; and should any Indian sell any part of his allotment with the approval of the Secretary of the Interior, the amount of any unpaid charges against the land sold shall be and become a first lien thereon and may be enforced by Secretary of the Interior by foreclosure as a mortgage, and delivery of water to such land may be refused within the discretion of the Secretary of the Interior until all dues are paid: *Provided further*, That no right to water or to the use of any irrigation ditch or other structure on said reservation shall vest or be allowed until the owner of the land to be irrigated as herein provided shall comply with such rules and regulations as the Secretary of the Interior may prescribe, and he is hereby authorized to prescribe such rules and regulations as he may determine proper for making effective the foregoing provisions, and to require of owners of lands in fee such security for the reimbursement herein required as he may determine necessary, and to refuse delivery of water to any tract of land until the owners thereof shall have complied therewith.

For the third installment in payment of $635,000 for water supply for irrigation of forty acres of each Indian allotment on the Yakima Indian Reservation irrigation system, in the State of Washington, provided by the act of August first, nineteen hundred and fourteen (Thirty-eighth Statutes at Large, page six hundred and four), $100,000 to be covered into the reclamation fund.

Act March 2, 1917 (39 Stat., 989): For operation and maintenance of the irrigation system on lands allotted to Yakima Indians in Washington, $15,000, reimbursable in accordance with the provisions of the act of March first, nineteen hundred and seven: *Provided*, That money received under agreements for temporary water supply may be expended under the direction of the Secretary of the Interior for maintenance and improvement of the irrigation system on said lands.

For the fourth installment in payment of $635,000 for water supply for irrigation of forty acres of each Indian allotment on the Yakima Indian Reservation irrigation system in the State of Washington, provided by the act of August first, nineteen hundred and fourteen (Thirty-eighth Statutes at Large, page six hundred and four), $100,000 to be covered into the reclamation fund.

For continuing construction and enlargement of the irrigation and drainage system, to make possible the utilization of the water supply provided for forty acres of each Indian allotment on the Yakima Indian Reservation, Washington, and such other water supply as may be available or obtainable for the irrigation of a total of one hundred and twenty thousand acres of allotted Indian lands on said reservation, $200,000, to remain available until expended: *Provided*, That the entire cost of said irrigation and drainage system shall be reimbursed to the United States under the conditions and terms of the act of May eighteenth, nineteen hundred and sixteen.

Act May 25, 1918 (40 Stat., 587): For operation and maintenance of the irrigation system on lands allotted to Yakima Indians in Washington, $15,000, reimbursable in accordance with the provisions of the act of March first, nineteen hundred and seven: *Provided*, That money received under agreements for temporary water supply may be expended under the direction of the Secretary of the Interior for maintenance and improvement of the irrigation system on said lands.

For the fifth installment in payment of $635,000 for water supply or irrigation of forty acres of each Indian allotment on the Yakima Indian Reservation irrigation system in the State of Washington provided by the act of August first, nineteen hundred and fourteen (Thirty-eighth Statutes at Large, page six hundred and four), $100,000 to be covered into the reclamation fund: *Provided*, That the land for which the aforesaid water supply was purchased shall be understood to be included within the Wapato irrigation project.

For continuing construction and enlargement of the Wapato irrigation and drainage system, to make possible the utilization of the water supply provided by the act of August first, nineteen hundred and fourteen (Thirty-eighth Statutes at Large, page six hundred and four), for forty acres of each Indian allotment under the Wapato irrigation project on the Yakima Indian Reservation, Washington, and such other water supply as may be available or obtainable for the irrigation of a total of one hundred and twenty thousand acres of allotted Indian lands on said reservation, $500,000, to be immediately available, and to remain available until expended: *Provided*, That the entire cost of said irrigation and drainage sys-[illegible]ll be reimbursed to the United States under the conditions and terms of the act of May eighteenth, nineteen hundred and sixteen: *Provided further*, That out of the sum herein appropriated the Secretary of the Interior is hereby authorized to pay to Violetta Stone and W. D. Stone, husband and wife, the sum of $629.48 for lands purchased of them for use in connection with the construction of the diversion dam across the Yakima River, as provided for in the act of May eighteenth, nineteen hundred and sixteen (Thirty-ninth Statutes at Large, page one hundred and fifty-four), and the sum herein appropriated shall be available for the purchase of such other lands as may be required in connection with the construction of the aforesaid irrigation project.

Act June 30, 1919 (41 Stat., 27): For operation and maintenance of the irrigation system on lands allotted to Yakima Indians in Washington, $15,000, reimbursable in accordance with the provisions of the act of March 1, 1907: *Provided*, That money received under agreements for temporary water supply may be expended under the direction of the Secretary of the Interior for maintenance and improvement of the irrigation system on said lands.

For the sixth installment in payment of $635,000 for water supply for irrigation of forty acres of each Indian allotment on the Yakima Indian Reservation irrigation system in the State of Washington, provided by the act of August 1, 1914 (Thirty-eighth Statutes at Large, page 604), $100,000 to be covered into the reclamation fund: *Provided*, That the land for which the aforesaid water supply was purchased shall be understood to be included within the Wapato irrigation project.

For continuing construction and enlargement of the Wapato irrigation and drainage system, to make possible the utilization of the water supply provided by the act of August 1, 1914 (Thirty-eighth Statutes at Large, page 604), for forty acres of each Indian allotment under the Wapato irrigation project on the Yakima Indian Reservation, Washington, and such other water supply as may be available or obtainable for the irrigation of a total of one hundred and twenty thousand acres of allotted Indian lands on said reservation, $500,000: *Provided*, That the entire cost of said irrigation and drainage system shall be reimbursed to the United States under the conditions and terms of the act of May 18, 1916: *Provided further*, That the funds hereby appropriated shall be available for the reimbursement of Indian and white landowners for improvements and crops destroyed by the Government in connection with the construction of irrigation canals and drains of this project. * * *

For beginning the construction of diversion dams and canal systems for irrigating twelve thousand acres of Indian land adjacent to Toppenish and Simcoe Creeks, Yakima Indian Reservation, $75,000, the total cost not to exceed $150,000: *Provided*, That the cost of the diversion dams and distributing systems shall be reimbursed to the United States by the owners of the lands irrigable thereunder in not to exceed twenty annual payments, and the Secretary of the Interior may fix operation and maintenance charges, which shall be paid as he may direct: *Provided*, That if any allottee shall receive patent in fee to his allotment before the amounts so charged against him shall have been paid to the United States, then such amount remaining unpaid shall be and become a lien upon his allotment, and the fact of such lien shall be recited in such patent and may be enforced by the Secretary of the Interior by foreclosure as a mortgage, and should any Indian sell any part of his allotment with the approval of the Secretary of the Interior, the amount of any unpaid charges against the land sold shall be and become a first lien thereon and may be enforced by the Secretary of the Interior by foreclosure as a mortgage, and delivery of water to such land may be refused within the discretion of the Secretary of the Interior until all dues are paid: *Provided further*, That no right to water or to the use of any irrigation ditch or other structure on said reservation shall rest or be allowed until the owner of the land to be irrigated as herein provided shall comply with such rules and regulations as the Secretary of the Interior may prescribe, and he is hereby authorized to prescribe such rules and regulations as he may determine proper for making effective the foregoing provisions, and to require of owners of lands in fee such security for the reimbursement herein required as he may determine necessary, and to refuse delivery of water to any tract of land until the owners thereof shall have complied therewith.

For the construction, repair, and maintenance of irrigation systems, and for purchase or rental of irrigation tools and appliances, water rights, ditches, and lands necessary for irrigation purposes for Indian reservations and allotments; for operation of irrigation systems or appurtenances thereto, when no other funds are applicable or available for the purpose; for drainage and protection of irrigable lands from damage by floods or loss of water rights upon the Indian irrigation projects named below:

Under the foregoing heading the act of May 25, 1918 (40 Stat., 562), provided $23,000 for the Ahtanum project and $3,000 for the Satus, Toppenish, and Simcoe projects.

Appropriations recapitulated.

Date.	Amount.	Amount.	Date.	Amount.	Amount.
Dec. 21, 1904	(?)		Aug. 1, 1914	$15,000	[1] $100,000
June 21, 1906	$15,000		Mar. 4, 1915	15,000	[1] 100,000
Mar. 1, 1907	15,000		May 18, 1916	215,000	[1] 100,000
Apr. 30, 1908	15,000		Mar. 2, 1917	215,000	[1] 100,000
Mar. 3, 1909	15,000		May 25, 1918	541,000	[1] 100,000
Apr. 4, 1910	265,000		June 30, 1919	590,000	[1] 100,000
Mar. 3, 1911	15,000				
Aug. 24, 1912	15,000		Total	1,961,000+	600,000
June 30, 1913	15,000				

[1] To pay Reclamation Service for stored water.

WISCONSIN.

BAD RIVER.

Act August 1, 1914 (38 Stat., 607): For improving sanitary conditions among the Chippewa Indians of the Bad River Reservation and for diking the Bad River to prevent the overflow of said river and damage to Indian homes on tribal lands, $8,000, said sum to be reimbursed to the United States from any moneys which are now or which may hereafter be placed to the credit of the Bad River band of Wisconsin Chippewa Indians.

LAC COURTE OREILLE.

Act May 18, 1916 (39 Stat., 157): With the consent of the Indians of the Lac Courte Oreilles Tribe, to be obtained in such manner as the Secretary of the Interior may require, flowage rights on the unallotted tribal lands, and, with the consent of the allottee or of the heirs of any deceased allottee and under such rules and regulations as the Secretary of the Interior may prescribe, flowage rights on any allotted lands in the Lac Courte Oreilles Reservation, in the State of Wisconsin, may be leased or granted for storage-reservoir purposes. The tribe, as a condition to giving its consent to the granting or leasing of flowage rights on tribal lands, and any allottee or the heirs of any deceased allottee, as a condition to giving his or their consent to the leasing or granting of flowage rights on their respective allotments, may determine, subject to the approval of the Secretary of the Interior, what consideration or rental shall be received for such flowage rights, and in what manner and for what purposes such consideration or rental shall be paid or expended and the consideration or rental shall be paid or expended under such rules and regulations as the Secretary of the Interior may prescribe.

TOMAH.

Act June 30, 1919 (41 Stat., 29): For support and education of two hundred and seventy-five Indian pupils at the Indian school, Tomah, Wisconsin, including pay of superintendent, $63,875; for general repairs and improvements, $8,000; for drainage of school land, $2,500; in all, $74,375.

WYOMING.

WIND RIVER (SHOSHONE).

Act March 3, 1905 (33 Stat. L., 1016): An act to ratify and amend an agreement with the Indians residing on the Shoshone or Wind River Reservation in the State of Wyoming and to make appropriations for carrying the same into effect.

ARTICLE IV. It is further agreed that of the moneys derived from the sale of said lands the sum of one hundred and fifty thousand dollars, or so much thereof as may be necessary, shall be expended under the direction of the Secretary of the Interior for the construction and extension of an irrigation system within the diminished reservation for the irrigation of the lands of said Indians: *Provided*, That in the employment of persons for the construction, enlargement, repair, and management of such irrigation system members of the said Shoshone and Arapahoe Tribes shall be employed wherever practicable.

ARTICLE III. As amended, it is further agreed that of the amount to be derived from the sale of said lands, as stipulated in Article II of this agreement, the sum of eighty-five thousand dollars shall be devoted to making a per capita payment to the said Indians of fifty dollars each in cash within sixty days after the opening of the ceded lands to settlement, or as soon thereafter as such sum shall be available: *And provided further*, That upon the completion of the said fifty dollars per capita payment any balance remaining in the said fund of eighty-five thousand dollars shall at once become available and shall be devoted to surveying, platting, making of maps, payment of the fees, and the performance of such acts as are required by the statutes of the State of Wyoming in securing water rights from said State for the irrigation of such lands as shall remain the property of said Indians, whether located within the territory intended to be ceded by this agreement or within the diminished reserve.

SEC. 3. That there is hereby appropriated, out of any money in the Treasury of the United States not otherwise appropriated, the sum of eighty-five thousand dollars to make the per capita payment provided in article three of the agreement herein ratified, the same to be reimbursed from the first money received from the sale of the lands herein ceded and relinquished. And the sum of thirty-five thousand dollars, or so much thereof as may be necessary, is hereby appropriated, out of any money in the Treasury of the United States not otherwise appropriated, the same to be reimbursed from the proceeds of the sale of said lands, for the survey and field and office examination of the unsurveyed portion of the ceded lands, and the survey and marking of the outboundaries of the diminished reservation, where the same is not a natural water boundary; and the sum of twenty-five thousand dollars is hereby appropriated out of any money in the Treasury of the United States not otherwise appropriated, the same to be reimbursed from the proceeds of the sale of said lands, to be used in the construction and extension of an irrigation system on the diminished reserve, as provided in article four of the agreement.

Act June 21, 1906 (34 Stat., 384): For the purpose of carrying out the provisions of article four of the agreement ratified by the act of March third, nineteen hundred and five, entitled "An act to ratify and amend an agreement with the Indians residing on the Shoshone or Wind River Indian Reservation, in the State of Wyoming, and making appropriation for carrying the same into effect," one hundred thousand dollars; of the amount specified by said fourth article to be imediately available and to be reimbursed from the proceeds derived from the sale of surplus lands, as provided by said act.

Act March 1, 1907 (34 Stat., 1052): For the purpose of carrying out the provisions of article four of the agreement ratified by the act of March third, nineteen hundred and five, entitled "An act to ratify and amend an agreement with the Indians residing on the Shoshone or Wind River Indian Reservation, in the State of Wyoming, and making appropriation for carrying the same into effect," one hundred thousand dollars of the amount specified by said fourth article twenty-five thousand dollars to be immediately available and to be reimbursed from the proceeds derived from the sale of surplus lands, as provided by said act.

Act April 30, 1908 (35 Stat., 97): For continuing the work of constructing an irrigation system within the diminished Shoshone or Wind River Reservation in Wyoming, $125,000: *Provided*, That said sum be reimbursed to the Treasury of the United States from the sale of lands made under the provisions of the act of March third, nineteen hundred and five (33 Stat. L., 1016).

Act March 3, 1909 (35 Stat., 815): For continuing the work of constructing an irrigation system within the diminished Shoshone or Wind River Reservation, in Wyoming, $100,000; *Provided*, That said sum be reimbursed to the Treasury of the United States from the sale of lands made under the provisions of the act of March third, nineteen hundred and five (Thirty-third Statutes at Large, page one thousand and sixteen).

Act April 4, 1910 (36 Stat., 288): For continuing the work of constructing an irrigation system within the diminished Shoshone or Wind River Reservation, in Wyoming, $75,000: *Provided*, That the amount hereby appropriated and all moneys heretofore or hereafter to be appropriated for this project, shall be repaid into the Treasury of the United States in accordance with the provision of the act of March third, nineteen hundred and five.

Act March 3, 1911 (36 Stat. L., 1076): For continuing the work of constructing an irrigation system within the diminished Shoshone or Wind River Reservation in Wyoming, $50,000.

Act April 27, 1912 (37 Stat., L. 91): An act providing for patents to homesteads on the ceded portion of the Wind River Reservation in Wyoming.

Be it enacted by the Senate and House of Representatives of the United States of America in Congress assembled, That any person who, prior to December sixteenth, nineteen hundred and eleven, made homestead entry on the ceded portion of the Wind River Reservation in Wyoming, and has not abandoned the same, and who has been unable to secure water for the irrigation of the lands covered by his entry, may secure title to the same upon the submission of satisfactory proof that he has established and maintained actual bona fide residence upon his land for a period of not less than eight months and upon payment of all sums remaining due on said land as provided for by the act of March third, nineteen hundred and five.

Act August 24, 1912 (37 Stat., 539): For continuing the work of constructing an irrigation system within the diminished Shoshone or Wind River Reservation, in Wyoming, including the maintenance and operation of completed canals, $50,000, reimbursable in accordance with the provisions of the act of March third, nineteen hundred and five.

Act June 30, 1913 (38 Stat., 102): For continuing the work of constructing an irrigation system within the diminished Shoshone or Wind River Reservation, in Wyoming, including the maintenance and operation of completed canals, $50,000, reimbursable in accordance with the provisions of the act of March third, nineteen hundred and five: *Provided*, That the Secretary of the Interior is hereby authorized and directed to use not to exceed $1,000 of the sum herein appropriated for the purpose of making an investigation of the condition of the roads and bridges on the said Wind River Reservation and shall submit a report thereon, together with maps and plans of said roads, together with an estimate of the cost of construction of suitable and necessary roads and bridges on said reservation.

Act August 1, 1914 (38 Stat., 608): For continuing the work of constructing an irrigation system within the diminished Shoshone or Wind River Reservation, in Wyoming, including the maintenance and operation of our completed canals, $25,000, reimbursable in accordance with the provisions of the act of March third, nineteen hundred and five, and to remain available until expended.

Joint resolution March 4, 1915 (38 Stat., 1228). Reenacted the last foregoing item for the fiscal year 1916.

Act May 18, 1916 (39 Stat., 158): For continuing the work of constructing an irrigation system within the diminished Shoshone or Wind River Reservation, in Wyoming, including the maintenance and operation of completed canals, $50,000, reimbursable in accordance with the provisions of the act of March third, nineteen hundred and five, and to remain available until expended.

To enable the Secretary of the Interior to have prepared and submitted to Congress at the beginning of the next regular session plans and estimates of the character and cost of structures necessary for completing the irrigation of all of the irrigable lands of the Shoshone or Wind River Reservation, including the ceded lands of said reservation, in Wyoming, $5,000.

Act March 2, 1917 (39 Stat., 993): For continuing the work of constructing an irrigation system within the diminished Shoshone or Wind River Reservation, in Wyoming, including the Big Wind River and Dry Creek Canals, and including the maintenance and operation of completed canals, $150,000, and to enable the Secretary of the Interior to make such additional surveys and examinations as may be required for the purpose of preparing and submitting with the estimates to be submitted before the first regular session of the Sixty-fifth Congress of an estimate for the beginning of construction of a project for the watering of a portion of the conditionally ceded lands of the Wind River Reservation, in substantial accordance with the plan outlined in House Document numbered seventeen hundred and sixty-seven of the Sixty-fourth Congress, second session, or such modification of such plan as the said Secretary may approve, $5,000, reimbursable in accordance with the provisions of the act of March third, nineteen hundred and five, and to remain available until expended.

Act May 25, 1918 (40 Stat., 590): For continuing the work of constructing an irrigation system within the diminished Shoshone or Wind River Reservation, in Wyoming, including the Big Wind River and Dry Creek Canals, and including the maintenance and operation of completed canals, $50,000, reimbursable in accordance with the provisions of the act of March third, nineteen hundred and five, and to remain available until expended.

For continuation of investigations, beginning of construction, and incidental operations on a project for the irrigation of a portion of the conditionally ceded lands of the Wind River Reservation, Wyoming, $100,000, reimbursable in accordance with the provisions of the act of March third, nineteen hundred and five, and to remain available until expended: *Provided*, That the construction charge for the actual cost of said project shall be fixed by the Secretary of the Interior and divided equitably between the Indian land and public and private land irrigated by such project, and that the charge as fixed for said Indian lands shall be reimbursable in accordance with the provisions of the act of March third, nineteen hundred and five, and that the charges as fixed for private and public land irrigated under such project shall be paid by the owner or entryman in accordance with the terms of payment of construction and maintenance charges as provided by the reclamation law and amendments thereto.

Act June 30, 1919 (41 Stat., 30): For continuing the work of constructing an irrigation system within the diminished Shoshone or Wind River Reservation, in Wyoming, including the Big Wind River and Dry Creek Canals, and including the maintenance and operation of completed canals, $100,000, reimbursable in accordance with the provisions of the act of March 3, 1905.

For continuation of investigations, construction, operation, and maintenance and incidental operations on a project for the irrigation of a portion of the conditionally ceded lands of the Wind River Reservation, Wyoming, to be known as the Riverton Project, $200,000, reimbursable in accordance with the provisions of the act of March 3, 1905: *Provided*, That the construction charge for the actual cost of said project shall be fixed by the Secretary of the Interior and divided equitably between the Indian land and public and private land irrigated by such project, and that the charge as fixed for said Indian lands shall be reimbursable in accordance with the provisions of the act of March 3, 1905, and that the charges as fixed for private and public land irrigated under such project shall be paid by the owner or entryman in accordance with the terms of payment of construction and maintenance charges as provided by the reclamation law and amendments thereto.

For the proportionate share of the cost of constructing a diversion dam and for the construction of canals and laterals for the irrigation of Indian land on the ceded portion of the Wind River Reservation, Wyoming, $50,000, reimbursable under such rules and regulations as the Secretary of the Interior may prescribe.

MISCELLANEOUS.

PURCHASE OF SUPPLIES.

Act May 15, 1886 (24 Stat. L., 46): SEC. 3. That no purchase of supplies for which appropriations are herein made, exceeding in the aggregate five hundred dollars in value at any one time, shall be made without first giving at least three weeks' public notice by advertisement, except in cases of exigency, when, in the discretion of the Secretary of the Interior, who shall make official record of the facts constituting the exigency and shall report the same to Congress at its next session, he may direct that purchases may be made in open market in amount not exceeding three thousand dollars: *Provided*, That funds herein and heretofore appropriated for construction of ditches and other works for irrigating may, in the discretion of the Secretary of the Interior, be expended in open market: *Provided further*, That purchases in open market may be made from Indians, under the direction of the Secretary of the Interior, to an amount not exceeding three thousand dollars.

With but slight alterations the above item appears in the following acts:

March 2, 1887, 24 Stat. L., 466.
June 29, 1888, 25 Stat. L., 237.
March 2, 1889, 25 Stat. L., 1002.
August 19, 1890, 26 Stat. L., 360.
March 3, 1891, 26 Stat. L., 1015.
July 13, 1892, 27 Stat. L., 144.
March 3, 1893, 27 Stat. L., 639.
August 15, 1894, 28 Stat. L., 312.
March 2, 1895, 28 Stat. L., 907.
June 10, 1896, 29 Stat. L., 348.
June 7, 1897, 30 Stat. L., 90.
July 1, 1898. 30 Stat. L., 595.
March 1, 1899, 30 Stat. L., 946.
June 6, 1900, 31 Stat. L., 246.
March 3, 1901, 31 Stat. L., 1083.
May 27, 1902, 32 Stat. L., 273.
March 3, 1903, 32 Stat. L., 1006.
April 21, 1904, 33 Stat. L., 216.
March 3, 1905, 33 Stat. L., 1077.
June 21, 1906, 34 Stat. L., 326.
March 1, 1907, 34 Stat. L., 1015.

* * *

Act April 30, 1908 (35 Stat. L., 71): That no purchase of supplies for which appropriations are herein or hereinafter made for the Indian Service, exceeding in the aggregate five hundred dollars in value at any one time, shall be made without first giving at least three weeks' public notice by advertisement, except in case of exigency, when, in the discretion of the Secretary of the Interior, who shall make official record of the facts constituting the exigency, and shall report the same to Congress at its next session, he may direct that purchases may be made in open market in amount not exceeding three thousand dollars at any one purchase: *Provided*, That hereafter supplies may be purchased, contracts let, and labor employed for the construction of artesian wells, ditches, and other works for irrigation, not to exceed the sum of five thousand dollars in any one purchase or contract, in the discretion of the Secretary of the Interior, without advertising as hereinbefore provided: *Provided further*, That so far as practicable Indian labor shall be employed and purchase in the open market made from Indians, under the direction of the Secretary of the Interior.

MISCELLANEOUS.

APPROPRIATIONS.

Act July 4, 1884 (23 Stat. L., 94): For the purpose of constructing irrigating ditches on Indian reservations, and instructing Indians in farming in connection therewith, fifty thousand dollars.

Act March 3, 1891 (26 Stat. L., 1011): For the construction, purchase, and use of irrigating machinery and appliances in Arizona, Montana, and Nevada for the uses of Indian reservations, in the discretion of the Secretary of the Interior and subject to his control, thirty thousand dollars, to be immediately available.

Act July 13, 1892 (27 Stat. L., 137): Irrigation, Indian Reservations: For the construction, purchase, and use of irrigating machinery and appliances, on Indian reservations, in the discretion of the Secretary of the Interior and subject to his control, forty thousand dollars.

Act March 3, 1893 (27 Stat. L., 631): Irrigation, Indian Reservations: For the construction, purchase, and use of irrigating machinery and appliances on Indian reservations in the discretion of the Secretary of the Interior forty thousand dollars: *Provided*, That of this sum a sufficient amount may be used to sink one artesian well at each of the three following places, namely, Rosebud Reservation, Standing Rock Reservation, and Pine Ridge Reservation, in South Dakota, neither of said wells to cost more than five thousand dollars.

Act August 15, 1894 (28 Stat. L., 305): For the construction, purchase, and use of irrigating machinery and appliances on Indian reservations, in the discretion of the Secretary of the Interior and subject to his control, thirty thousand dollars.

Act March 2, 1895 (28 Stat. L., 900): For the construction, purchase, and use of irrigating machinery and appliances on Indian reservations, in the discretion of the Secretary of the Interior, and subject to his control, thirty thousand dollars.

Act June 10, 1896 (29 Stat. L., 341): For the construction, purchase, and use of irrigating tools and appliances on Indian reservations, in the discretion of the Secretary of the Interior, and subject to his control, thirty thousand dollars; and of this amount not exceeding two thousand seven hundred dollars may be used for the temporary employment of persons of practical experience in irrigation work at a compensation not to exceed seventy-five dollars per month each, and not exceeding one thousand five hundred dollars for necessary traveling and incidental expenses of such persons.

Act June 7, 1897 (30 Stat. L., 85): For construction of ditches and reservoirs, purchase and use of irrigation tools, and appliances on Indian reservations, in the discretion of the Secretary of the Interior and subject to his control, thirty thousand dollars; and of this amount not exceeding two thousand seven hundred dollars may be used for the temporary employment of persons of practical experience in irrigation work, at a compensation not to exceed one hundred dollars per month each, and not exceeding one thousand five hundred dollars for necessary traveling and incidental expenses of such persons.

Act July 1, 1898 (30 Stat. L., 591): For construction of ditches and reservoirs, purchase and use of irrigation tools and appliances, and purchase of water rights on Indian reservations, in the discretion of the Secretary of the Interior and subject to his control, forty thousand dollars. * * *

Act March 1, 1899 (30 Stat. L., 940): For construction of ditches and reservoirs, purchase and use of irrigating tools and appliances, and purchase of water rights on Indian reservations, in the discretion of the Secretary of the Interior and subject to his control, forty thousand dollars.

Act June 6, 1900 (31 Stat. L., 239): For construction of ditches and reservoirs, purchase, and use of irrigating tools and appliances, and purchase of water rights on Indian reservations, in the discretion of the Secretary of the Interior, and subject to his control, fifty thousand dollars: *Provided*, That the Secretary of the Interior may employ superintendents of irrigation, who shall be skilled irrigation engineers, not to exceed two, as in his judgment may be necessary to secure the construction of ditches and other irrigation works in a substantial and workmanlike manner; and also one clerk in the Office of Indian Affairs, at a salary of one thousand dollars per annum.

Act March 3, 1901 (31 Stat. L., 1060): For pay of eight Indian inspectors, one of whom shall be an engineer competent in the location, construction, and maintenance of irrigation works, at two thousand five hundred dollars per annum each. * * *

For traveling expenses of eight Indian inspectors, at three dollars per day when actually employed on duty in the field, exclusive of transportation and sleeping-car fare, in lieu of all other expenses now authorized by law, and for incidental expenses of inspection and investigation, including telegraphing and expenses of going to and going from the seat of government, and while remaining there under orders and direction of the Secretary of the Interior, for a period not to exceed twenty days, twelve thousand eight hundred dollars.

Act March 3, 1901 (31 Stat. L., 1075): For construction of ditches and reservoirs, purchase and use of irrigating tools and appliances, and purchase of water rights on Indian reservations, in the discretion of the Secretary of the Interior, and subject to his control, one hundred thousand dollars: *Provided*, That the Secretary of the Interior may employ such number of superintendents of irrigation, who shall be skilled irrigation engineers, not to exceed two, as in his judgment may be necessary to secure the construction of ditches and other irrigation works in a substantial and workmanlike manner; and also one clerk in the Office of Indian Affairs, at a salary of one thousand dollars per annum.

Act May 27, 1902 (32 Stat. L., 247): For pay of eight Indian inspectors, one of whom shall be an engineer competent in the location, construction, and maintenance of irrigation works, at two thousand five hundred dollars per annum each, twenty thousand dollars: * * *

For traveling expenses of eight Indian inspectors, at three dollars per day when actually employed on duty in the field, exclusive of transportation and sleeping-car fare, in lieu of all other expenses now authorized by law, and for incidental expenses of inspection and investigation, including telegraphing and expenses of going to and going from the seat of government, and while remaining there under orders and direction of the Secretary of the Interior for a period not to exceed twenty days, twelve thousand eight hundred dollars.

Act May 27, 1902 (32 Stat. L., 261): For construction of ditches and reservoirs, purchase and use of irrigating tools and appliances, and purchase of water rights on Indian reservations, in the discretion of the Secretary of the Interior and subject to his control, one hundred and fifty thousand dollars: *Provided*, That the Secretary of the interior may employ such number of superintendents of irrigation, who shall be skilled irrigation engineers, not to exceed two, as in his judgment may be necessary to secure the construction of ditches and other irrigation works in a substantial and workmanlike manner.

Act March 3, 1903 (32 Stat. L., 983): For pay of eight Indian inspectors, one of whom shall be an engineer competent in the location, construction, and maintenance of irrigation works, at two thousand five hundred dollars per annum each, twenty thousand dollars.

For traveling expenses of eight Indian inspectors, at three dollars per day when actually employed on duty in the field, exclusive of transportation and sleeping-car fare, in lieu of all other expenses now authorized by law, and for incidental expenses of negotiation, inspection, and investigation, including telegraphing and expenses of going to and going from the seat of government, and while remaining there under orders and direction of the Secretary of the Interior, for a period not to exceed twenty days, twelve thousand eight hundred dollars.

Act March 3, 1903 (32 Stat. L., 997): For construction of ditches and reservoirs, purchase and use of irrigating tools and appliances, and purchase of water rights on Indian reservations in the discretion of the Secretary of the Interior and subject to his control, one hundred and fifty thousand dollars: *Provided*, That the Secretary of the Interior may employ such number of superintendents of irrigation, who shall be skilled irrigation engineers, not to exceed four, as in his jurgment may be necessary to secure the construction of ditches and other irrigation works in a substantial and workmanlike manner.

Act April 21, 1904 (33 Stat. L., 191): For pay of eight Indian inspectors, one of whom shall be an engineer competent in the location, construction, and maintenance of irrigation works, at two thousand five hundred dollars per annum each, twenty thousand dollars.

For traveling expenses of eight Indian inspectors, at three dollars per day when actually employed on duty in the field, exclusive of transportation and sleeping-car fare, in lieu of all other expenses now authorized by law, and for incidental expenses of inspection and investigation, including telegraphing and expenses of going to and going from the seat of government, and while remaining there under orders and direction of the Secretary of the Interior, for a period not to exceed twenty days, twelve thousand eight hundred dollars.

Act April 21, 1904 (33 Stat. L., 206): For construction of ditches and reservoirs, purchase and use of irrigating tools and appliances, and purchase of water rights on Indian reservations, in the discretion of the Commissioner of Indian Affairs, under the direction of the Secretary of the Interior, one hundred and eighty-five thousand dollars, of which thirty-five thousand dollars shall be immediately available: *Provided*, That the Commissioner of Indian Affairs, under the direction of the Secretary of the Interior, may employ superintendents of irrigation, who shall be skilled irrigation engineers, not to exceed four, as in his judgment may be necessary, to secure the construction of ditches and other irrigation works in a substantial and workmanlike manner.

Act March 3, 1905 (33 Stat. L., 1049): For pay of eight Indian inpsctors, two of whom shall be engineers, one to be designated as chief, competent in the location, construction, and maintenance of irrigation works, at two thousand five hundred dollars per annum each, except the chief engineer, who shall receive three thousand five hundred dollars, twenty-one thousand dollars: *Provided*, That the requirement of two engineers skilled in irrigation shall become immediately operative.

For traveling expenses of eight Indian inspectors, at three dollars per day when actually employed on duty in the field, exclusive of transportation and sleeping-car fare, in lieu of all other expenses now authorized by law, and for incidental expenses of negotiation, inspection, and investigation, including telegraphing and expenses of going to and going from the seat of government, and while remaining there under orders and direction of the Secretary of the Interior, for a period not to exceed twenty days, twelve thousand eight hundred dollars.

Act March 3, 1905 (33 Stat. L., 1060): For construction of ditches and reservoirs, purchase and use of irrigating tools and appliances, and purchase of water rights on Indian reservations, in the discretion of the Commissioner of Indian Affairs, under the direction of the Secretary of the Interior and subject to his control, one hundred and eighty-five thousand dollars, of which twenty-five thousand dollars shall be made immediately available: *Provided*, That the Commissioner of Indian Affairs, under the direction of the Secretary of the Interior, may employ such superintendents of irrigation, who shall be skilled irrigation engineers, not to exceed four, as in his judgment may be necessary to secure the construction of ditches and other irrigation works in a substantial and workmanlike manner.

Act June 21, 1906 (34 Stat. L., 328): For construction of ditches and reservoirs, purchase and use of irrigating tools and appliances, and purchase of water rights on Indian reservations, in the discretion of the Commissioner of Indian Affairs, under the direction of the

Secretary of the Interior and subject to his control, one hundred and fifty-five thousand dollars, of which twenty-five thousand dollars shall be made immediately available: *Provided*, That the Commissioner of Indian Affairs, under the direction of the Secretary of the Interior, may employ superintendents of irrigation, who shall be skilled irrigation engineers, not to exceed four, as in his judgment may be necessary to secure the construction of ditches and other irrigation works in a substantial and workmanlike manner.

Act June 21, 1906 (34 Stat. L., 330): For pay of eight Indian inspectors, two of whom shall be engineers, one to be designated as chief, competent in the location, construction, and maintenance of irrigation works, at two thousand five hundred dollars per annum each, except the chief engineer, who shall receive three thousand five hundred dollars, twenty-one thousand dollars.

For traveling expenses of eight Indian inspectors, at three dollars per day when actually employed on duty in the field, exclusive of transportation and sleeping-car fare, in lieu of all other expenses now authorized by law, and for incidental expenses of negotiation, inspection, and investigation, including telegraphing and expenses of going to and going from the seat of government, and while remaining there under orders and direction of the Secretary of the Interior, for a period of not to exceed twenty days, twelve thousand eight hundred dollars.

Act March 1, 1907 (34 Stat. L., 1017): For construction of ditches and reservoirs, purchase and use of irrigating tools and appliances, and purchase of water rights on Indian reservations, in the discretion of the Commissioner of Indian Affairs, under the direction of the Secretary of the Interior and subject to his control, one hundred and twenty-five thousand dollars: *Provided*, That the Commissioner of Indian Affairs, under the direction of the Secretary of the Interior, may employ superintendents of irrigation, who shall be skilled irrigation engineers, not to exceed five, as in his judgment may be necessary to secure the construction of ditches and other irrigation works in a substantial and workmanlike manner.

Act March 1, 1907 (34 Stat. L., 1019): For pay of eight Indian inspectors, two of whom shall be engineers, one to be designated as chief, competent in the location, construction, and maintenance of irrigation works, at two thousand five hundred dollars per annum each, except the chief engineer, who shall receive three thousand five hundred dollars, twenty-one thousand dollars.

For traveling expenses of eight Indian inspectors, at three dollars per day when actually employed on duty in the field, exclusive of transportation and sleeping-car fare, in lieu of all other expenses now authorized by law, and for incidental expenses of negotiation, inspection, and investigation, including telegraphing and expenses of going to and going from the seat of government, and while remaining there under orders and direction of the Secretary of the Interior, for a period not to exceed twenty days, twelve thousand eight hundred dollars.

Act April 30, 1908 (35 Stat. L., 71): For construction of ditches and reservoirs, purchase and use of irrigating tools and appliances and water rights, including lands necessary for canals, pipe lines, and reservoirs, for Indian reservations, in the discretion of the Commissioner of Indian Affairs, under the direction of the Secretary of the Interior and subject to his control, two hundred thousand dollars, of which twenty-five thousand dollars shall be immediately available: *Provided*, That the Commissioner of Indian Affairs, under the direction of the Secretary of the Interior, may employ superintendents of irrigation, who shall be skilled irrigation engineers, not to exceed five, as in his judgment may be necessary to secure the construction of ditches and other irrigation works in a substantial and workmanlike manner.

Act April 30, 1908 (35 Stat. L., 74): For pay of eight Indian inspectors, two of whom shall be engineers, one to be designated as chief, competent in the location, construction, and maintenance of irrigation works, at two thousand five hundred dollars per annum each, except the chief engineer, who shall receive three thousand five hundred dollars, twenty-one thousand dollars.

For traveling expenses of eight Indian inspectors, at three dollars per day when actually employed on duty in the field, exclusive of transportation and sleeping-car fare, in lieu of all other expenses now authorized by law, and for incidental expenses of negotiation, inspection, and investigation, including telegraphing and expenses of going to and going from the seat of government, and while remaining there under orders and direction of the Secretary of the Interior, for a period not to exceed twenty days, twelve thousand eight hundred dollars.

Act March 3, 1909 (35 Stat. L., 782): For construction of ditches and reservoirs, purchase and use of irrigating tools and appliances and water rights, including lands necessary for canals, pipe lines, and reservoirs, for Indian reservations and allotments, and for drainage and protection of irrigable lands from damage by floods, in the discretion of the Commissioner of Indian Affairs, under the direction of the Secretary of the Interior and subject to his control, two hundred thousand dollars, to be immediately available and to remain available until expended: *Provided*, That the Commissioner of Indian Affairs, under the direction of the Secretary of the Interior, may employ superintendents of irrigation, who shall be skilled irrigation engineers, not to exceed five, as in his judgment may be necessary to secure the construction of ditches and other irrigation works in a substantial and workmanlike manner.

Act March 3, 1909 (35 Stat. L., 785): For pay of two Indian inspectors, who shall be engineers, one to be designated as chief, competent in the location, construction, and maintenance of irrigation works, one at two thousand five hundred dollars per annum and one at three thousand five hundred dollars per annum; in all, six thousand dollars. For traveling expenses of two Indian inspectors, at three dollars per day when actually employed on duty in the field, exclusive of transportation and sleeping-car fare, in lieu of all other expenses now authorized by law, for incidental expenses of negotiation, inspection, and investigation, including telegraphing and expense of going to and coming from the seat of government and while remaining there under orders and direction of the Secretary of the

Interior, for a period not to exceed twenty days, three thousand eight hundred dollars.

Act April 4, 1910 (36 Stat. L., 270): For the construction, repair, and maintenance of ditches, reservoirs, and dams, purchase and use of irrigation tools and appliances, water rights, lands necessary for canals, pipe lines and reservoirs for Indian reservations and allotments, and for drainage and protection of irrigable lands from damage by floods, two hundred and forty-nine thousand one hundred dollars, of which twenty-five thousand dollars shall be immediately available, and the balance of the appropriation shall remain available until expended: *Provided*, That no part of this appropriation shall be expended on any irrigation system or reclamation project for which specific appropriation is made in this act or for which public funds are or may be available under any other act of Congress. * * *

For pay of one chief inspector of irrigation, who shall be a skilled irrigation engineer, four thousand dollars; one assistant inspector of irrigation, who shall be a skilled irrigation engineer, two thousand five hundred dollars; for traveling expenses of two inspectors of irrigation, at three dollars per diem when actually employed on duty in the field, exclusive of transportation and sleeping-car fare, in lieu of all other expenses authorized by law, and for incidental expenses of negotiations, inspection, and investigation, including telegraphing and expense of going to and from the seat of government and while remaining there under orders, four thousand two hundred dollars; in all, two hundred fifty-nine thousand eight hundred dollars: *Provided*, That the Commissioner of Indian Affairs, under the direction of the Secretary of the Interior, may employ superintendents of irrigation, who shall be skilled irrigation engineers, not to exceed seven in number.

Act April 4, 1910 (36 Stat., 272): *Provided further*, That the Secretary of the Interior shall transmit to Congress on the first Monday in December, nineteen hundred and ten, a statement showing the original estimated cost, the present estimated cost, and the total amount of all moneys, from whatever source derived, expended thereon, of each irrigation project for which specific appropriation is made in this act, to and including June thirtieth, nineteen hundred and ten, and annually thereafter the Secretary of the Interior shall transmit to Congress a cost account of all moneys, from whatever source derived, expended on each such irrigation project for the preceding fiscal year.

Act March 3, 1911 (36 Stat. L., 1059): For the construction, repair, and maintenance of ditches, reservoirs, and dams, purchase and use of irrigation tools and appliances, water rights, ditches, lands necessary for canals, pipe lines, and reservoirs for Indian reservations and allotments, and for drainage and protection of irrigable lands from damage by floods, three hundred and fourteen thousand three hundred dollars, to remain available until expended: *Provided*, That no part of this appropriation shall be expended on any irrigation system or reclamation project for which specific appropriation is made in this act or for which public funds are or may be available under any other act of Congress: *Provided further*, That nothing herein contained shall be construed to prohibit reasonable expenditures from this appropriation for preliminary surveys and investigations to determine the feasibility and estimated cost of new projects, for investigations and surveys for power and reservoir sites on Indian reservations in accordance with the provisions of section thirteen of the act of June twenty-fifth, nineteen hundred and ten, or to prevent the Bureau of Indian Affairs from having the benefit of consultation with engineers in other branches of the public service or carrying out existing agreements with the Reclamation Service; for pay of one chief inspector of irrigation, who shall be a skilled irrigation engineer, four thousand dollars; one assistant inspector of irrigation, who shall be a skilled irrigation engineer, two thousand five hundred dollars; for traveling expenses of two inspectors of irrigation, at three dollars per diem when actually employed on duty in the field, exclusive of transportation and sleeping-car fare, in lieu of all other expenses authorized by law, and for incidental expenses of negotiation, inspection, and investigation, including telegraphing and expense of going to and from the seat of government and while remaining there under orders, four thousand two hundred dollars; in all, three hundred and twenty-five thousand dollars: *Provided, also*, That not to exceed seven superintendents of irrigation, who shall be skilled irrigation engineers, may be employed.

Act August 24, 1912 (37 Stat. L., 518): For the construction, repair, and maintenance of ditches, reservoirs, and dams, purchase and use of irrigation tools and appliances, water rights, ditches, lands necessary for canals, pipe lines, and reservoirs for Indian reservations and allotments, and for drainage and protection of irrigable lands from damage by floods, three hundred and twenty-five thousand dollars, to remain available until expended: *Provided*, That no part of this appropriation shall be expended on any irrigation system or reclamation project for which specific appropriation is made in this act or for which public funds are or may be available under any other act of Congress: *Provided further*, That nothing herein contained shall be construed to prohibit reasonable expenditures from this appropriation for preliminary surveys and investigations to determine the feasibility and estimated cost of new projects, for investigations and surveys for power and reservoir sites on Indian reservations in accordance with the provisions of section thirteen of the act of June twenty-fifth, nineteen hundred and ten, or to prevent the Bureau of Indian Affairs from having the benefit of consultation with engineers in other branches of the public service or carrying out existing agreements with the Reclamation Service; for pay of one chief inspector of irrigation, who shall be a skilled irrigation engineer, four thousand dollars; one assistant inspector of irrigation, who shall be a skilled irrigation engineer, two thousand five hundred dollars; for traveling expenses of two inspectors of irrigation, at three dollars per diem when actually employed on duty in the field, exclusive of transportation and sleeping-car fare, in lieu of all other expenses authorized by law, and for incidental expenses of negotiation, inspection, and investigation, including telegraphing and expense of going to and from the seat of government and while remaining there under orders, four thousand two hundred dollars; in all, three hundred and thirty-five thousand seven hundred dollars: *Provided also*, That not to exceed seven superintendents of irrigation, who shall be [illegible]gation engineers, may be employed.

Act June 30, 1913 (38 Stat. L., 78): For the construction, repair, and maintenance of ditches, reservoirs, and dams, purchase and use of irrigation tools and appliances, water rights, ditches, lands necessary for canals, pipe lines, and reservoirs for Indian reservations and allotments, and for drainage and protection of irrigable lands from damage by floods, $335,000, to remain available until expended: *Provided*, That no part of this appropriation shall be expended on any irrigation system or reclamation project for which specific appropriation is made in this act or for which public funds are or may be available under any other act of Congress: *Provided further*, That nothing herein contained shall be construed to prohibit reasonable expenditures from this appropriation for preliminary surveys and investigations to determine the feasibility and estimated cost of new projects, for investigations and surveys for power and reservoir sites on Indian reservations in accordance with the provisions of section thirteen of the act of June twenty-fifth, nineteen hundred and ten, or to prevent the Bureau of Indian Affairs from having the benefit of consultation with engineers in other branches of the public service or carrying out existing agreements with the Reclamation Service; for pay of one chief inspector of irrigation, who shall be a skilled irrigation engineer, $4,000; one assistant inspector of irrigation, who shall be a skilled irrigation engineer, $2,500; for traveling expenses of two inspectors of irrigation, at $3 per diem when actually employed on duty in the field, exclusive of transportation and sleeping car fare, in lieu of all other expenses authorized by law, and for incidental expenses of negotiation, inspection, and investigation, including telegraphing and expense of going to and from the seat of government and while remaining there under orders, $4,200; in all, $345,700: *Provided, also*, That not to exceed seven superintendents of irrigation who shall be skilled irrigation engineers may be employed.

Act August 1, 1914 (38 Stat. L., 582): For the construction, repair, and maintenance of ditches, reservoirs, and dams, purchase and use of irrigation tools and appliances, water rights, ditches, lands necessary for canals, pipe lines, and reservoirs for Indian reservations and allotments, and for drainage and protection of irrigable lands from damage by floods, or loss of water rights, including expenses of necessary surveys and investigations to determine the feasibility and estimated cost of new projects and power and reservoir sites on Indian reservations in accordance with the provisions of section thirteen of the act of June twenty-fifth, nineteen hundred and ten, $335,000, to remain available until expended: *Provided*, That no part of this appropriation shall be expended on any irrigation system or reclamation project for which specific appropriation is made in this act or for which public funds are or may be available under any other act of Congress; for pay of one chief inspector of irrigation, who shall be a skilled irrigation engineer, $4,000; one assistant inspector of irrigation, who shall be a skilled irrigation engineer, $2,500; for traveling and incidental expenses of two inspectors of irrigation, including sleeping-car fare and a per diem of $3 in lieu of subsistence when actually employed on duty in the field and away from designated headquarters, $4,200; in all, $345,700: *Provided also*, That not to exceed seven superintendents of irrigation, six of whom shall be skilled irrigation engineers and one competent to pass upon water rights, and one field-cost accountant, may be employed: * * *

Joint resolution March 4, 1915 (38 Stat., 1228) making appropriations for current and contingent expenses of the Bureau of Indian Affairs, for fulfilling treaty stipulations with various Indian tribes, and for other purposes, for the fiscal year ending June thirtieth, nineteen hundred and sixteen.

Resolved, by the Senate and House of Representatives of the United States of America in Congress assembled, That all appropriations for the current and contingent expenses of the Bureau of Indian Affairs and for fulfilling treaty stipulations with various Indian tribes, which shall remain unprovided for on June thirtieth, nineteen hundred and fifteen, are continued and made available for and during the fiscal year nineteen hundred and sixteen to the same extent, in detail, and under the same conditions, restrictions, and limitations for the fiscal year nineteen hundred and sixteen as the same were provided for on account of the fiscal year nineteen hundred and fifteen in the Indian appropriation act for that fiscal year. For all of such purposes a sufficient sum is appropriated, out of any money in the Treasury not otherwise appropriated, or out of funds to the credit of Indians as the same were respectively provided in the Indian appropriation Act for the fiscal year nineteen hundred and fifteen: *Provided*, That the appropriations from the Treasury of the United States or from Indian funds shall not exceed in the aggregate the amounts of such appropriations for the fiscal year nineteen hundred and fifteen: *Provided further*, That this joint resolution shall not be construed as providing for or authorizing the duplication of any special payment or for the execution of any purpose provided for in said appropriation act that was intended to be paid only once or done solely on account of the fiscal year nineteen hundred and fifteen: *Provided further*, That appropriations continued hereunder shall be available for the maintenance, repair, and operation of motor-propelled and horse-drawn passenger-carrying vehicles in the same manner as appropriations were available for those purposes during the fiscal year nineteen hundred and fifteen.

Act May 18, 1916 (39 Stat. L., 124): For the construction, repair, and maintenance of ditches, reservoirs, and dams, purchase and use of irrigation tools and appliances, water rights, ditches, lands necessary for canals, pipe lines, and reservoirs for Indian reservations and allotments and for drainage and protection of irrigable lands from damage by floods or loss of water rights, including expenses of necessary surveys and investigations to determine the feasibility and estimated cost of new projects and power and reservoir sites on Indian reservations in accordance with the provisions of section thirteen of the act of June twenty-fifth, nineteen hundred and ten, $235,000, reimbursable as provided in the act of August first, nineteen hundred and fourteen, and to remain available until expended: *Provided*, That no part of this appropriation shall be expended on any irrigation system or reclamation project for which specific appropriation is made in this act or for which public funds are or may be available under any other act of Congress; for pay of one chief inspector of irrigation, who shall be a skilled irrigation engineer, $4,000; one assistant inspector of irrigation, who shall be a skilled irrigation engineer, $2,500; for traveling and incidental expenses of two inspectors of irrigation, including sleeping-car fare and a per diem of $3 in lieu of subsistence when actually employed on duty in the field and away from designated headquarters, $3,200; in all, $244,700: *Provided also*, That not to exceed seven superintendents of irrigation, six of whom shall be skilled irrigation engineers and one competent to pass upon water rights, and one field-cost accountant may be employed.

Act March 2, 1917 (39 Stat. L., 969): For the construction, repair, and maintenance of ditches, reservoirs, and dams, purchase and use of irrigation tools and appliances, water rights, ditches, lands necessary for canals, pipe lines, and reservoirs for Indian reservations and allotments and for drainage and protection of irrigable lands from damage by floods, or loss of water rights, including expenses of necessary surveys and investigations to determine the feasibility and estimated cost of new projects and power and reservoir sites on Indian reservations in accordance with the provisions of section thirteen of the act of June twenty-fifth, nineteen hundred and ten, $235,000, reimbursable as provided in the act of August first, nineteen hundred and fourteen, and to remain available until expended: *Provided*, That no part of this appropriation shall be expended on any irrigation system or reclamation project for which specific appropriation is made in this act or for which public funds are or mav be available under any other act of Congress; for pay of one chief inspector of irrigation, who shall be a skilled irrigation engineer, $4,000; one assistant inspector of irrigation who shall be a skilled irrigation engineer, $2,500; for traveling and incidental expenses of two inspectors of irrigation, including sleeping-car fare and a per diem of $3 in lieu of subsistence when actually employed on duty in the field and away from designated headquarters, $3,200; in all, $244,700: *Provided also*, That not to exceed seven superintendents of irrigation, six of whom shall be skilled irrigation engineers and one competent to pass upon water rights, and one field-cost accountant, may be employed.

Act May 25, 1918 (40 Stats. L., 562): For the construction, repair, and maintenance of irrigation systems, and for purchase or rental of irrigation tools and appliances, water rights, ditches, and lands necessary for irrigation purposes for Indian reservations and allotments; for operation of irrigation systems or appurtenances thereto, when no other funds are applicable or available for the purpose; for drainage and protection of irrigable lands from damage by floods or loss of water rights, upon the Indian irrigation projects named below.

Irrigation district one: Ahtanum project, $23,000; Satus, Toppenish, and Simcoe projects, Yakima Reservation, $3,000; Stranger Marsh project, Colville Reservation, $5.200; total, $31.200.

Irrigation district two: Shivwitz Reservation, $1,200; Moapa River Reservation, $1,000; Western Shoshone, $9.500; Walker River Reservation, $6,800; total, $18,500.

Irrigation district four: Agua Caliente Reservation, $3,000; Morongo Reservation, $2,000; Pala Reservation, $20,000; Pauma Reservation, $5,000; Rincon Reservation, $4,000; Ak Chin Reservation, $800; Papago Reservation, San Xavier, $2,000; miscellaneous projects, $10,000; total, $46,800.

Irrigation district five: Southern Ute Reservation, Pine River project, $9,000; San Juan Reservation, $22,000; New Mexico Pueblos, $12,000: Zuni Reservation, $5,000; Navajo, miscellaneous projects, including Tes-nos-pos, Moencopi Wash, Captain Tom Wash, and Red Lake, $20,000; total, $68,000.

For necessary miscellaneous expenses incident to the general administration of Indian irrigation projects, including salaries of not to exceed five supervising engineers:

In Indian irrigation district one: Oregon, Washington, northern California, and northern Idaho, $10.000;

In Indian irrigation district two: Southern Idaho, Nevada, and Utah, $10,000;

In Indian irrigation district three: Montana, Wyoming, and South Dakota, $8,000;

In Indian irrigation district four: Central and southern California and southern Arizona, $15,000;

In Indian irrigation district five: Northern Arizona, New Mexico, and Colorado, $12,000;

For cooperative stream gauging with the United States Geological Survey, $4,000;

For necessary surveys and investigations to determine the feasibility and estimated cost of new projects and power and reservoir sites on Indian reservations in accordance with the provisions of section thirteen of the act of June twenty-fifth, nineteen hundred and ten, $10,000;

For pay of one chief irrigation engineer, $4,000;

One assistant chief irrigation engineer, $2,500;

One superintendent of irrigation competent to pass upon water rights, $2,500;

One field-cost accountant, $2,250;

And for traveling and incidental expenses of officials and employees of the Indian irrigation service, including sleeping-car fare, and a per diem not exceeding $3.50 in lieu of subsistence when actually employed in the field and away from designated headquarters, $6,000;

In all, for irrigation on Indian reservations, $250,750, reimbursable as provided in the act of August first, nineteen hundred and fourteen, and to remain available until expended: *Provided*, That no part of this appropriation shall be expended on any irrigation system or reclamation project for which public funds are or may be otherwise available: *Provided further*, That the foregoing amounts appropriated for such purposes shall be available interchangeably in the discretion of the Secretary of the Interior for the necessary expenditures for damage by floods and other unforeseen exigencies: *Provided, however*, That the amount so interchanged shall not exceed in the aggregate ten per centum of all the amounts so appropriated.

Act June 30, 1919 (40 Stat. L., 3): For the construction, repair, and maintenance of irrigation systems, and for purchase or rental of irrigation tools and appliances, water rights, ditches, and lands necessary for irrigation purposes for Indian reservations and allotments; for operation of irrigation systems or appurtenances thereto, when no other funds are applicable or available for the purpose; for drainage and protection of irrigable lands from damage by floods or loss of water rights, upon the Indian irrigation projects named below:

Irrigation district one: Sand Creek and Agency projects, Klamath Reservation, $20,000; Round Valley Reservation, California, $2,000; Colville Reservation, $10,000; total, $32,000.

Irrigation district two: Moapa River, $1,200; Shivwits, $1,200; Walker River, $8,500; Western Shoshone, $5,000; total, $15,900.

Irrigation district three: Tongue River, Montana, $2,000.

Irrigation district four: Agua Caliente Reservation, $3,000; Ak Chin, Maricopa Reservation, $3,200; Big Pine Reservation, $3,500; Grindstone Creek Reservation, $1,300; La Jolla Reservation, $6,000; Martinez pumping plant, $2,000; Morongo Reservation, $1,600; Owens Valley Reservation, $1,000; Pala Reservation, $4,500; Rincon Reservation, $3,000; miscellaneous projects, $7,600; total, $36,700.

Irrigation district five: Southern Ute Reservation, Pine River project, $8,000; San Juan Reservation, $20,000; New Mexico Pueblos, $11,000; Zuni Reservation, $18,200; Navajo and Hopi miscellaneous projects, including Tes-nos-pos, Moencopi Wash, Captain Tom Wash, and Red Lake, $18,200; total, $75,400;

For necessary miscellaneous expenses incident to the general administration of Indian irrigation projects, including salaries of not to exceed five supervising engineers:

In Indian irrigation district one: Oregon, Washington, northern California, and northern Idaho, $10,000;

In Indian irrigation district two: Southern Idaho, Nevada, and Utah, $12,500;

In Indian irrigation district three: Montana, Wyoming, and South Dakota, $11,000;

In Indian irrigation district four: Central and southern California and southern Arizona, $15,000;

In Indian irrigation district five: Northern Arizona, New Mexico, and Colorado, $12,000;

For cooperative stream gauging with the United States Geological Survey, $4,000;

For necessary surveys and investigations to determine the feasibility and estimated cost of new projects and power and reservoir sites on Indian reservations in accordance with the provisions of section 13 of the act of June 25, 1910, $10,000;

For pay of one chief irrigation engineer, $4,000; one assistant chief irrigation engineer, $2,500; one superintendent of irrigation competent to pass upon water rights, $2,500; one field-cost accountant, $2,250; and for traveling and incidental expenses of officials and employees of the Indian irrigation service, including sleeping-car fare, and a per diem not exceeding $3.50 in lieu of subsistence when actually employed in the field and away from designated headquarters, $6,000;

In all, for irrigation on Indian reservations, $253,750, reimbursable as provided in the act of August 1, 1914: *Provided*, That no part of this appropriation shall be expended on any irrigation system or reclamation project for which public funds are or may be otherwise available: *Provided further*, That the foregoing amounts appropriated for such purposes shall be available interchangeably in the discretion of the Secretary of the Interior for the necessary expenditures for damage by floods and other unforeseen exigiencies: *Provided, however*, That the amount so interchanged shall not exceed in the aggregate 10 per centum of all the amounts so appropriated.

Act June 30, 1919 (41 Stat., 9): For improving springs, drilling wells, and otherwise developing and conserving water for the use of stock, including the purchase, construction, and installation of pumping machinery, tanks, troughs, and other necessary equipment, and for necessary investigations and surveys, for the purpose of increasing the available grazing range on unallotted lands on Indian reservations, $50,000.

MISCELLANEOUS.

SUBSTANTIVE LEGISLATION.

Act February 8, 1887 (24 Stat., 390): SEC. 7. That in cases where the use of water for irrigation is necessary to render the lands within any Indian reservation availabe for agricultural purposes, the Secretary of the Interior be, and he is hereby, authorized to prescribe such rules and regulations as he may deem necessary to secure a just and equal distribution thereof among the Indians residing upon any such reservations; and no other appropriation or grant of water by any raparian proprietor shall be authorized or permitted to the damage of any other riparian proprietor.

Act March 3, 1891 (26 Stat., 1101): SEC. 18. That the right of way through the public lands and reservations of the United States is hereby granted to any canal or ditch company formed for the purpose of irrigation, and duly organized under the laws of any State or Territory, which shall have filed or may hereafter file with the Secretary of the Interior a copy of its articles of incorporation and due proofs of its organization under the same to the extent of the ground occupied by the water of the reservoir and of the canal and its laterals, and fifty feet on each side of the marginal limits thereof; also the right to take from the public lands adjacent to the line of the canal or ditch material, earth, and stone necessary for the construction of such canal or ditch: *Provided*, That no such right of way shall be so located as to interfere with the proper occupation by the Government of any such reservation, and all maps of location shall be subject to the approval of the department of the Government having jurisdiction of such reservation, and the privilege herein granted shall not be construed to interfere with the control of water for irrigation and other purposes under authority of the respective States or Territories.

SEC. 19. That any canal or ditch company desiring to secure the benefits of this act shall, within twelve months after the location of ten miles of its canal, if the same be upon surveyed lands, and if upon unsurveyed lands within twelve months after the survey thereof by the United States, file with the register of the land office for the district where such land is located a map of its canal or ditch and reservoir; and upon the approval thereof by the Secretary of the Interior the same shall be noted upon the plats in said office, and thereafter all such lands over which such rights of way shall pass shall be disposed of subject to such right of way. Whenever any person or corporation, in the construction of any canal, ditch, or reservoir injures or damages the possession of any settler on the public domain, the party committing such injury or damage shall be liable to the party injured for such injury or damage.

Sec. 20. That the provisions of this act shall apply to all canals, ditches, or reservoirs heretofore or hereafter constructed, whether constructed by corporations, individuals, or association of individuals, on the filing of the certificates and maps herein provided for. If such ditch, canal, or reservoir has been or shall be constructed by an individual or association of individuals, it shall be sufficient for such individual or association of individuals to file with the Secretary of the Interior and with the register of the land office where said land is located a map of the line of such canal, ditch, or reservoir, as in case of a corporation, with the name of the individual owner or owners thereof, together with the articles of association, if any there be. Plats heretofore filed shall have the benefits of this act from the date of their filing, as though filed under it: *Provided*, That if any section of said canal or ditch shall not be completed within five years after the location of said section, the rights herein granted shall be forfeited as to any uncompleted section of said canal, ditch, or reservoir, to the extent that the same is not completed at the date of the forfeiture.

Sec. 21. That nothing in this act shall authorize such canal or ditch company to occupy such right of way except for the purpose of said canal or ditch, and then only so far as may be necessary for the construction, maintenance, and care of said canal or ditch.

Act February 26, 1897 (29 Stat., 599): *Be it enacted by the Senate and House of Representatives of the United States of America in Congress assembled*, That all reservoir sites, reserved or to be reserved, shall be open to use and occupation under the right-of-way act of March third, eighteen hundred and ninety-one. And any State is hereby authorized to improve and occupy such reservoir sites to the same extent as an individual or private corporation, under such rules and regulations as the Secretary of the Interior may prescribe: *Provided*, That the charges for water coming in whole or part from reservoir sites used or occupied under the provisions of this act shall always be subject to the control and regulation of the respective States and Territories in which such reservoirs are in whole or part situate.

Act May 11, 1898 (30 Stat., 404): Sec. 2. That rights of way for ditches, canals, or reservoirs heretofore or hereafter approved under the provisions of sections eighteen, nineteen, twenty, and twenty-one of the act entitled "An act to repeal timber-culture laws, and for other purposes," approved March third, eighteen hundred and ninety-one, may be used for purposes of a public nature; and said rights of way may be used for purposes of water transportation, for domestic purposes, or for the development of power, as subsidiary to the main purpose of irrigation.

Act February 15, 1901 (31 Stat., 790): *Be it enacted by the Senate and House of Representatives of the United States of America in Congress assembled*, That the Secretary of the Interior be, and hereby is, authorized and empowered, under general regulations to be fixed by him, to permit the use of rights of way through the public lands, forest, and other reservations of the United States, and the Yosemite, Sequoia, and General Grant National Parks, California, for electrical plants, poles, and lines for the generation and distribution of electrical power, and for telephone and telegraph purposes, and for canals, ditches, pipes, and pipe lines, flumes, tunnels, or other water conduits, and for water plants, dams, and reservoirs used to promote irrigation or mining or quarrying, or the manufacturing or cutting of timber or lumber, or the supplying of water for domestic, public, or any other beneficial uses to the extent of the ground occupied by such canals, ditches, flumes, tunnels, reservoirs, or other water conduits or water plants, or electrical or other works permitted hereunder, and not to exceed fifty feet on each side of the marginal limits thereof, or not to exceed fifty feet on each side of the center line of such pipes and pipe lines, electrical, telegraph, and telephone lines and poles, by any citizen, association, or corporation of the United States, where it is intended by such to exercise the use permitted hereunder or any one or more of the purposes herein named: *Provided*, That such permits shall be allowed within or through any of said parks or any forest, military, Indian, or other reservation only upon the approval of the chief officer of the department under whose supervision such park or reservation falls and upon a finding by him that the same is not incomparable with the public interest: *Provided further*, That all permits given hereunder for telegraph and telephone purposes shall be subject to the provision of title sixty-five of the Revised Statutes of the United States, and amendments thereto, regulating rights of way for telegraph companies over the public domain: *And provided further*, That any permission given by the Secretary of the Interior under the provisions of this act may be revoked by him or his successor in his discretion, and shall not be held to confer any right, or easement, or interest in, to, or over any public land, reservation, or park.

Act June 21, 1906 (34 Stat., 327): That any Indian allotted lands under any law or treaty without the power of alienation, and within a reclamation project approved by the Secretary of the Interior, may sell or convey any part thereof, under rules and regulations prescribed by the Secretary of the Interior, but such conveyance shall be subject to his approval, and when so approved shall convey full title to the purchaser the same as if final patent without restrictions had been issued to the allottee: *Provided*, That the consideration shall be placed in the Treasury of the United States, and used by the Commissioner of Indian Affairs to pay the construction charges that may be assessed against the unsold part of the allotment, and to pay the maintenance charges thereon during the trust period, and any surplus shall be a benefit running with the water right to be paid to the holder thereof.

Act April 30, 1908 (35 Stat., 85): That in carrying out any irrigation project which may be undertaken under the provisions of the act of June seventeenth, nineteen hundred and two (Thirty-second

Statutes, page three hundred and eighty-eight), known as the reclamation act, and which may make possible and provide for in connection with the reclamation of other lands the irrigation of all or any part of the irrigable lands heretofore included in allotments made to Indians under the fourth section of the general allotment act, the Secretary of the Interior be, and he hereby is, authorized to make such arrangement and agreement in reference thereto as said Secretary deems for the best interest of the Indians: *Provided*, That no lien or charge for construction, operation, or maintenance shall thereby be created against any such reserved lands: *And provided further*, That to meet the necessary cost of carrying out this legislation the Secretary of the Interior is authorized to expend, out of the sum appropriated in this act for irrigation, an amount not exceeding thirteen thousand dollars.

Act March 3, 1909 (35 Stat., 798): That in carrying out any irrigation project which may be undertaken under the provisions of the act of June seventeenth, nineteen hundred and two (Thirty-second Statutes, page three hundred and eighty-eight), known as "the reclamation act," and which may make possible and provide for in connection with the reclamation of other lands, the irrigation of all or any part of the irrigable lands heretofore included in allotments made to the Indians under the fourth section of the general allotment act, the Secretary of the Interior be, and he hereby is, authorized to make such arrangement and agreement in reference thereto as said Secretary deems for the best interest of the Indians: *Provided*, That no lien or charge for construction, operation, or maintenance shall thereby be created against any such lands: *Provided further*, That to meet the necessary cost of carrying out this legislation the Secretary of the Interior is authorized to expend, out of the sum appropriated in this act for irrigation, an amount not exceeding thirteen thousand dollars.

Act April 4, 1910 (36 Stat., 270): * * * and hereafter no new irrigation project on any Indian reservation, allotments, or lands, shall be undertaken until it shall have been estimated for and a maximum limit of cost ascertained from surveys, plans, and reports submitted by the chief irrigation engineer in the Indian Service and approved by the Commissioner of Indian Affairs and the Secretary of the Interior, and such limit of cost shall in no case be exceeded without express authorization of Congress, and hereafter no new project to cost in the aggregate to exceed thirty-five thousand dollars shall be undertaken on any Indian reservation or allotment without specific authority of Congress; and the Secretary of the Interior shall transmit to Congress on the first Monday in December, nineteen hundred and ten, a statement by systems or projects, showing the original estimated cost, the present estimated cost, and the total amount of all moneys, from whatever source derived, expended thereon for construction, extension, repair, or maintenance of each irrigation system or reclamation project on Indian reservations, allotments, or lands to and including June thirtieth, nineteen hundred and ten; and annually thereafter the Secretary of the Interior shall transmit to Congress a cost account of all moneys, from whatever source derived, expended on each such irrigation project for the preceding fiscal year: *Provided further*, That nothing herein contained shall be construed to prohibit reasonable expenditures from this appropriation for preliminary surveys and investigations to determine the feasibility and estimated cost of new projects, or to prevent the Bureau of Indian Affairs from having the benefit of consultation with engineers in other branches of the public service or carrying out existing agreements with the Reclamation Service: * * *

Act June 25, 1910 (36 Stat., 858): SEC. 13. That the Secretary of the Interior be, and he is hereby, authorized, in his discretion, to reserve from location, entry, sale, allotment, or other appropriation any lands within any Indian reservation, valuable for power or reservoir sites, or which may be necessary for use in connection with any irrigation project heretofore or hereafter to be authorized by Congress: *Provided*, That if no irrigation project shall be authorized prior to the opening of any Indian reservation containing such power or reservoir sites the Secretary of the Interior may, in his discretion, reserve such sites pending future legislation by Congress for their disposition, and he shall report to Congress all reservations made in conformity with this act.

SEC. 14. That the Secretary of the Interior, after notice and hearing, is hereby authorized to cancel trust patents issued to Indian allottees for allotments within any power or reservoir site, and for allotments or such portions of allotments as are located upon or include lands set aside, reserved, or required within any Indian reservation for irrigation purposes under authority of Congress: *Provided*, That any Indian allottee whose allotment shall be so canceled shall be reimbursed for all improvements on his canceled allotment, out of any moneys available for the construction of the irrigation project for which the said power or reservoir site may be set aside: *Provided further*, That any Indian allottee whose allotment, or part thereof, is so canceled shall be allotted land of equal value within the area subject to irrigation by any such project.

* * * * *

SEC. 17. * * * And whenever it shall appear to the President that lands on any Indian reservation subject to allotment by authority of law have been or may be brought within any irrigation project, he may cause allotments of such irrigable lands to be made to the Indians entitled thereto in such areas as may be for their best interest not to exceed, however, forty acres to any one Indian, and such irrigable land shall be held to be equal in quantity to twice the number of acres of nonirrigable agricultural land and four times the number of acres of nonirrigable grazing lands: *Provided*, That the remaining area to which any Indian may be entitled under existing law after he shall have received his proportion of irrigable land on the basis of equalization herein established may be allotted to him from nonirrigable agricultural or grazing lands: *Provided further*, That where a treaty or act of Congress setting apart such reservation provides for allotments in severalty in quantity greater or less than that herein authorized, the President shall cause allotments on such reservation to be made in quantity as specified in such treaty or act subject, however, to the basis of equalization between irrigable and nonirrigable lands established herein, but in such cases allotments may be made in quantity as specified in this act, with the consent of the Indians expressed in such manner as the President in his discretion may require.

That where any Indian entitled to allotment under existing laws shall make settlement upon any surveyed or unsurveyed lands of the United States not otherwise appropriated, he or she shall be entitled, upon application to the local land office for the district in which the lands are located, to have the same allotted to him or her and to his or her children in manner as provided by law for allotments to Indians residing upon reservations, and such allotments to Indians on the public domain as herein provided shall be made in such areas as the President may deem proper, not to exceed, however, forty acres of irrigable land or eighty acres of nonirrigable agricultural land or one hundred and sixty acres of nonirrigable grazing land to any one Indian; and when such settlement is made upon unsurveyed lands the grant to such Indians shall be adjusted upon the survey of the lands so as to conform thereto, and patent shall be issued to them for such lands in the manner and with the restrictions provided in the act of which this is amendatory. And the fees to which the officers of such local land offices would have been entitled had such lands been entered under the general laws for the disposition of the public lands shall be paid to them from any moneys in the Treasury of the United States not otherwise appropriated, upon a statement of an account in their behalf for such fees by the Commissioner of the General Land Office, and a certification of such account to the Secretary of the Treasury by the Secretary of the Interior.

Act March 4, 1911 (36 Stat., 1253): That the head of the department having jurisdiction over the lands be, and he hereby is, authorized and empowered, under general regulations to be fixed by him, to grant an easement for rights of way, for a period not exceeding fifty years from the date of the issuance of such grant, over, across, and upon the public lands, national forests, and reservations of the United States for electrical poles and lines for the transmission and distribution of electrical power, and for poles and lines for telephone and telegraph purposes, to the extent of twenty feet on each side of the center line of such electrical, telephone, and telegraph lines and poles, to any citizen, association, or corporation of the United States, where it is intended by such to exercise the right of way herein granted for any one or more of the purposes herein named: *Provided*, That such right of way shall be allowed within or through any national park, national forest, military, Indian, or any other reservation only upon the approval of the chief officer of the department under whose supervision or control such reservation falls, and upon a finding by him that the same is not incompatible with the public interest: *Provided*, That all or any part of such right of way may be forfeited and annulled by declaration of the head of the department having jurisdiction over the lands for nonuse for a period of two years or for abandonment.

That any citizen, association, or corporation of the United States to whom there has heretofore been issued a permit for any of the purposes specified herein under any existing law, may obtain the benefit of this act upon the same terms and conditions as shall be required of citizens, associations, or corporations hereafter making application under the provisions of this statute.

Act June 30, 1913 (38 Stat., 80): * * * That superintendents and acting superintendents in charge of Indian reservations, schools, irrigation and allotment projects are hereby authorized and empowered to administer the oath of office required of employees placed under their jurisdiction.

Act August 1, 1914 (38 Stat., 583): * * * *Provided further*, That the proceeds of sales of material utilized for temporary work and structures shall be covered into the appropriation made therefor and be available for the purpose of the appropriation; and for lands irrigable under any such system or project the Secretary of the Interior may fix maintenance charges which shall be paid as he may direct, such payments to be available for use in maintaining the project or system for which collected: *Provided further*, That all moneys expended heretofore or hereafter under this provision shall be reimbursable where the Indians have adequate funds to repay the Government, such reimbursement to be made under such rules and regulations as the Secretary of the Interior may prescribe: *Provided further*, That the Secretary of the Interior is hereby authorized and directed to apportion the cost of any irrigation project constructed for Indians and made reimbursable out of tribal funds of said Indians, in accordance with the benefits received by such individual Indian so far as practicable from said irrigation project, said cost to be apportioned against such individual Indian under such rules, regulations, and conditions as the Secretary of the Interior may prescribe; and annually thereafter the Secretary of the Interior shall transmit to Congress a cost account in detail of all moneys, from whatever source derived, expended on each such irrigation project for the preceding fiscal year, including a résumé of previous expenditures, which shall show the number of Indians on the reservations where the land is irrigated, irrigable area under ditch, irrigable area under project (approximate), irrigable area cultivated by Indians, irrigable area cultivated by lessees, amount expended on construction to June thirtieth of the preceding fiscal year, amount necessary to complete, and cost per acre when completed (estimated), value of land when irrigated, and such other detailed information as may be requisite for a thorough understanding of the conditions on each system or project: *Provided further*, That in addition to what is herein required there shall be submitted to Congress on the first Monday in December, nineteen hundred and fourteen, as to the Uintah, Shoshone, Flathead, Blackfeet, and Fort Peck Reclamation projects, a report showing the status of the water rights of the Indians and the method of financing said projects, together with such other information as the Secretary of the Interior may deem necessary for a full and complete understanding of all the facts and conditions in connection therewith.

Act May 18, 1916 (39 Stat. L., 128): That whenever it shall appear to the satisfaction of the Secretary of the Interior that the allotted lands of any Indian are arid but susceptible of irrigation, and that the allottee, by reason of old age or other disability, can not personally occupy or improve his allotment or any portion thereof, such lands or such portion thereof may be leased for a period not exceeding ten years, under such terms, rules, and regulations as may be prescribed by the Secretary of the Interior.

Act June 30, 1919 (41 Stat. L., 3): SEC. 26. That the Secretary of the Interior be, and hereby is, authorized and empowered, under general regulations to be fixed by him and under such terms and conditions as he may prescribe, not inconsistent with the terms of this section, to lease to citizens of the United States or to any association of such persons or to any corporation organized under the laws of the United States or to any State or Territory thereof, any part of the unallotted lands within any Indian reservation within the States of Arizona, California, Idaho, Montana, Nevada, New Mexico, Oregon, Washington, or Wyoming, heretofore withdrawn from entry under the mining laws for the purpose of mining for deposits of gold, silver, copper, and other valuable metalliferous minerals, which leases shall be irrevocable, except as herein provided, but which may be declared null and void upon breach of any of their terms.

That after the passage and approval of this section, unallotted lands, or such portion thereof as the Secretary of the Interior shall determine, within Indian reservations heretofore withheld from disposition under the mining laws, may be declared by the Secretary of the Interior to be subject to exploration for the discovery of deposits of gold, silver, copper, and other valuable metalliferous minerals by citizens of the United States, and after such declaration mining claims may be located by such citizens in the same manner as mining claims are located under the mining laws of the United States: *Provided*, That the locators of all such mining claims, or their heirs, successors, or assigns, shall have a preference right to apply to the Secretary of the Interior for a lease, under the terms and conditions of this section, within one year after the date of the location of any mining claim, and any such locator who shall fail to apply for a lease within one year from the date of location shall forfeit all rights to such mining claim: *Provided further*, That duplicate copies of the location notice shall be filed within sixty days with the superintendent in charge of the reservation on which the mining claim is located, and that application for a lease under this section may be filed with such superintendent for transmission through official channels to the Secretary of the Interior: *And provided further*, That lands containing springs, water holes, or other bodies of water needed or used by the Indians for watering live stock, irrigation, or water-power purposes, shall not be designated by the Secretary of the Interior as subject to entry under this section.

That leases under this section shall be for a period of tweny years, with the preferential right in the lessee to renew the same for successive periods of ten years upon such reasonable terms and conditions as may be prescribed by the Secretary of the Interior, unless otherwise provided by law at the time of the expiration of such periods: *Provided*, That the lessee may, in the discretion of the Secretary of the Interior, be permitted at any time to make written relinquishment of all rights under such a lease and upon acceptance thereof be thereby relieved of all future obligations under said lease.

That in addition to the areas of mineral land to be included in leases under this section the Secretary of the Interior, in his discretion, may grant to the lessee the right to use, during the life of the lease, subject to the payment of an annual rental of not less than $1 per acre, a tract of unoccupied land not exceeding forty acres in area for camp sites, milling, smelting, and refining works, and for other purposes connected with and necessary to the proper development and use of the deposits covered by the lease.

That the Secretary of the Interior, in his discretion, in making any lease under this section, may reserve to the United States the right to lease for a term not exceeding that of the mineral lease, the surface of the lands embraced within such lease under existing law or laws hereinafter enacted, in so far as said surface is not necessary for use of the lessee in extracting and removing the deposits therein: *Provided*, That the said secretary, during the life of the lease, is hereby authorized to issue such permits for easements herein provided to be reserved.

That any successor in interest or assignee of any lease granted under this section, whether by voluntary transfer, judicial sale, foreclosure sale, or otherwise, shall be subject to all the conditions of the lease under which such rights are held and also subject to all the provisions and conditions of this section to the same extent as though such successor or assign were the original lessee hereunder.

That any lease granted under this section may be forfeited and canceled by appropriate proceedings in the United States district court for the district in which said property or some part thereof is situated whenever the lessee, after reasonable notice in writing, as prescribed in the lease, shall fail to comply with the terms of this section or with such conditions not inconsistent herewith as may be specifically recited in the lease.

That for the privilege of mining or extracting the mineral deposits in the ground covered by the lease the lessee shall pay to the United States, for the benefit of the Indians, a royalty which shall not be less than 5 per centum of the net value of the output of the minerals at the mine, due and payable at the end of each month succeeding that of the extraction of the minerals from the mine, and an annual rental, payable at the date of such lease and annually thereafter on the area covered by such lease, at the rate of not less than 25 cents per acre for the first calendar year thereafter; not less than 50 cents per acre for the second, third, fourth, and fifth years, respectively; and not less than $1 per acre for each and every year thereafter during the continuance of the lease, except that such rental for any year shall be credited against the royalties as they accrue for that year.

That in addition to the payment of the royalties and rentals as herein provided the lessee shall expend annually not less than $100 in development work for each mining claim located or leased in the same manner as an annual expenditure for labor or improvements is required to be made under the mining laws of the United States: *Provided*, That the lessee shall also agree to pay all damages occasioned by reason of his mining operations to the land or allotment of any Indian or to the crops or improvements thereon: *And provided further*, That no timber shall be cut upon the reservation by the lessee except for mining purposes and then only after first obtaining a permit from the superintendent of the reservation and upon payment of the fair value thereof.

That the Secretary of the Interior is hereby authorized to examine the books and accounts of lessees. and to acquire them to submit statements, representations, or reports, including information as to cost of mining, all of which statements, representations, or reports so required shall be upon oath, unless otherwise specified, and in such form and upon such blanks as the Secretary of the Interior may require; and any person making any false statement, representation, or report under oath shall be subject to punishment as for perjury.

That all moneys received from royalties and rentals under the provisions of this section shall be deposited in the Treasury of the United States to the credit of the Indians belonging and having tribal rights on the reservation where the leased land is located, which moneys shall be at all times subject to appropriation by Congress for their benefit, unless otherwise provided by treaty or agreement ratified by Congress: *Provided*, That such moneys shall be subject to the laws authorizing the pro rata distribution of Indian tribal funds.

That the Secretary of the Interior is hereby authorized to perform any and all acts and to make such rules and regulations not inconsistent with this section as may be necessary and proper for the protection of the interests of the Indians and for the purpose of carrying the provisions of this section into full force and effect: *Provided*, That nothing in this section shall be construed or held to affect the right of the States or other local authority to exercise any rights which they may have to levy and collect taxes upon improvements, output of mines, or other rights, property, or assets of any lessee.

That mining locations, under the terms of this section, may be made on unallotted lands within Indian reservations by Indians who have heretofore or may hereafter be declared by the Secretary of the Interior to be competent to manage their own affairs; and the said Secretary is hereby authorized and empowered to lease such lands to such Indians in accordance with the provisions of this section: *Provided*, That the Secretary of the Interior be, and he is hereby, authorized to permit other Indians to make locations and obtain leases under the provisions of this section, under such rules and regulations as he may prescribe in regard to the working, developing, disposition, and selling of the products, and the disposition of the proceeds thereof of any such mine by such Indians.

SEC. 27. That hereafter no public lands of the United States shall be withdrawn by Executive order, proclamation, or otherwise, for or as an Indian reservation except by act of Congress.

RECLAMATION, OTHER THAN INDIAN.[1]

Act July 26, 1866 (14 Stat. L., 251): An act granting the right of way to ditch and canal owners over the public lands, and for other purposes.

Be it enacted by the Senate and House of Representatives of the United States of America in Congress assembled, That the mineral lands of the public domain, both surveyed and unsurveyed, are hereby declared to be free and open to exploration and occupation by all citizens of the United States, and those who have declared their

[1] This should not be construed as a compilation of all reclamation acts, or of acts pertaining thereto, but simply a reprint of those acts relating to rights-of-way and reclamation matters generally, deemed pertinent to Indian irrigation work.

intention to become citizens, subject to such regulations as may be prescribed by law, and subject also to the local customs or rules of miners in the several mining districts, so far as the same may not be in conflict with the laws of the United States. * * *

SEC. 5. *And be it further enacted*, That as a further condition of sale, in the absence of necessary legislation by Congress, the local legislature of any State or Territory may provide rules for working mines involving easements, drainage, and other necessary means to their complete development; and those conditions shall be fully expressed in the patent. * * *

SEC. 9. *And be it further enacted*, That whenever, by priority of possession, rights to the use of water for mining, agricultural, manufacturing, or other purposes, have vested and accrued, and the same are recognized and acknowledged by the local customs, laws, and the decisions of courts, the possessors and owners of such vested rights shall be maintained and protected in the same; and the right of way for the construction of ditches and canals for the purposes aforesaid is hereby acknowledged and confirmed: *Provided, however*, That whenever, after the passage of this act, any person or persons shall, in the construction of any ditch or canal, injure or damage the possession of any settler on the public domain, the party committing such injury or damage shall be liable to the party injured for such injury or damage.

Act October 2, 1888 (25 Stat. L., 526): For the purpose of investigating the extent to which the arid region of the United States can be redeemed by irrigation, and the segregation of the irrigable lands in such arid region, and for the selection of sites for reservoirs and other hydraulic works necessary for the storage and utilization of water for irrigation and the prevention of floods and overflows, and to make the necessary maps, including the pay of employees in field and in office, the cost of all instruments, apparatus, and materials, and all other necessary expenses connected therewith, the work to be performed by the Geological Survey, under the direction of the Secretary of the Interior, the sum of one hundred thousand dollars or so much thereof as may be necessary. And the director of the Geological Survey, under the supervision of the Secretary of the Interior, shall make a report to Congress on the first Monday in December of each year, showing in detail how the said money has been expended, the amount used for actual survey and engineer work in the field in locating sites for reservoirs and an itemized account of the expenditures under this appropriation. And all the lands which may hereafter be designated or selected by such United States surveys for sites for reservoirs, ditches, or canals for irrigation purposes and all the lands made susceptible of irrigation by such reservoirs, ditches, or canals are from this time henceforth hereby reserved from sale as the property of the United States, and shall not be subject after the passage of this act, to entry, settlement, or occupation until further provided by law: *Provided*, That the President may at any time in his discretion by proclamation open any portion or all of the lands reserved by this provision to settlement under the homestead laws.

Act August 30, 1890 (26 Stat. L., 391): * * * and so much of the act of October second, eighteen hundred and eighty-eight, entitled,

"An act making appropriations for sundry civil expenses of the Government for the fiscal year ending June thirtieth, eighteen hundred and eighty-nine, and for other purposes," as provides for the withdrawal of the public lands from entry, occupation, and settlement, is hereby repealed, and all entries made or claims initiated in good faith and valid but for said act, shall be recognized and may be perfected in the same manner as if said law had not been enacted, except that reservoir sites heretofore located or selected shall remain segregated and reserved from entry or settlement as provided by said act, until othrwise provided by law, and reservoir sites hereafter located or selected on public lands shall in like manner be reserved from the date of the location or selection thereof.

No person who shall after the passage of this act, enter upon any of the public lands with a view to occupation, entry, or settlement under any of the land laws shall be permitted to acquire title to more than three hundred and twenty acres in the aggregate, under all of said laws, but this limitation shall not operate to curtail the right of any person who has heretofore made entry or settlement on the public lands, or whose occupation, entry, or settlement, is validated by this act: *Provided*, That in all patents for lands hereafter taken up under any of the land laws of the United States or on entries or claims validated by this act west of the one hundredth meridian, it shall be expressed that there is reserved from the lands in said patent described, a right of way thereon for ditches or canals constructed by the authority of the United States.

RECLAMATION.

Act March 3, 1891 (26 Stat. L., 1096): SEC. 4. That at the time of filing the declaration hereinbefore required the party shall also file a map of said land, which shall exhibit a plan showing the mode of contemplated irrigation, and which plan shall be sufficient to thoroughly irrigate and reclaim said land, and prepare it to raise ordinary agricultural crops, and shall also show the source of the water to be used for irrigation and reclamation. Persons entering or proposing to enter separate sections, or fractional parts of sections, of desert lands may associate together in the construction of canals and ditches for irrigating and reclaiming all of said tracts, and may file a joint map or maps showing their plan of internal improvements.

SEC. 5. That no land shall be patented to any person under this act unless he or his assignors shall have expended in the necessary irrigation, reclamation, and cultivation thereof, by means of main canals and branch ditches, and in permanent improvements upon the land, and in the purchase of water rights for the irrigation of the same, at least three dollars per acre of whole tract reclaimed and patented in the manner following: Within one year after making entry for such tract of desert land as aforesaid the party so entering shall expend not less than one dollar per acre for the purposes aforesaid. And he shall in like manner expend the sum of one dollar per acre during the second and also during the third year thereafter, until the full sum of three dollars per acre is so expended. Said party shall file during each year with the register proof, by the affidavits of two or more credible witnesses, that the full sum of one dollar per acre has been expended in such necessary improvements during such year, and the manner in which expended, and at the expiration of the third year a map or plan showing the character and extent of such improvements. If any party who has made such application shall fail during any year to file the testimony aforesaid the lands shall revert to the United States, and the twenty-five cents advanced payment shall be forfeited to the United States, and the entry shall be canceled. Nothing herein contained shall prevent a claimant from making his final entry and receiving his patent at an earlier date than hereinbefore prescribed, provided that he then makes the required proof of reclamation to the aggregate extent of three dollars per acre: *Provided*, That proof be further required of the cultivation of one-eighth of the land.

SEC. 18. That the right of way through the public lands and reservations of the United States is hereby granted to any canal or ditch company formed for the purpose of irrigation and duly organized under the laws of any State or Territory, which shall have filed, or may hereafter file with the Secretary of the Interior, a copy of its articles of incorporation, and due proofs of its organization under the same, to the extent of the ground occupied by the water of the reservoir and of the canal and its laterals, and fifty feet on each side of the marginal limits thereof; also the right to take, from the public lands adjacent to the line of the canal or ditch, material, earth, and stone necessary for the construction of such canal or ditch: *Provided*, That no such right of way shall be so located as to interfere with the proper occupation by the Government of any such reservation, and all maps of location shall be subject to the approval of the department of the Government having jurisdiction of such reservation, and the privilege herein granted shall not be construed to interfere with the control of water for irrigation and other purposes under authority of the respective States or Territories.

SEC. 19. That any canal or ditch company desiring to secure the benefits of this act shall, within twelve months after the location of ten miles of its canal, if the same be upon surveyed lands, and if upon unsurveyed lands within twelve months after the survey thereof by the United States, file with the register of the land office for the district where such land is located a map of its canal or ditch and reservoir; and upon the approval thereof by the Secretary of the Interior the same shall be noted upon the plats in said office, and thereafter all such lands over which such rights of way shall pass shall be disposed of subject to such right of way. Whenever any person or corporation, in the construction of any canal, ditch, or reservoir injures or damages the possession of any settler on the public domain, the party committing such injury or damage shall be liable to the party injured for such injury or damage.

SEC. 20. That the provisions of this act shall apply to all canals, ditches, or reservoirs heretofore or hereafter constructed, whether constructed by corporations, individuals, or associations of individuals, on the filing of the certificates and maps herein provided for. If such ditch, canal, or reservoir has been or shall be constructed by an individual or association of individuals, it shall be sufficient for such individual or association of individuals to file with the Secretary of the Interior and with the register of the land office where said land is located, a map of the line of such canal, ditch, or reservoir, as in case of a corporation, with the name of the individual owner or owners thereof, together with the articles of association, if any there be. Plats heretofore filed shall have the benefits of this act from the date of their filing, as though filed under it: *Provided*, That if any section of said canal or ditch shall not be completed within five years after the location of said section, the rights herein granted shall be forfeited as to any uncompleted section of said canal, ditch, or reservoir to the extent that the same is not completed at the date of the forfeiture.

SEC. 21. That nothing in this act shall authorize such canal or ditch company to occupy such right of way except for the purpose of said canal or ditch, and then only so far as may be necessary for the construction, maintenance, and care of said canal or ditch.

Act August 18, 1894 (28 Stat. L., 422): SEC. 4. That to aid the public-land States in the reclamation of the desert lands therein, and the settlement, cultivation, and sale thereof in small tracts to actual settlers, the Secretary of the Interior, with the approval of the President, be, and hereby is, authorized and empowered, upon proper application of the State to contract and agree, from time to time, with each of the States in which there may be situated desert lands as defined by the act entitled "An act to provide for the sale of desert lands in certain States and Territories," approved March third, eighteen hundred and seventy-seven, and the act amendatory thereof, approved March third, eighteen hundred and ninety-one, binding the United States to donate, grant, and patent to the State free of cost for survey or price such desert lands, not exceeding one million acres in each State, as the State may cause to be irrigated, reclaimed, occupied, and not less than twenty acres of each one hundred and sixty acre tract cultivated by actual settlers, within ten years next after the passage of this act, as thoroughly as is required of citizens who may enter under the said desert-land law.

Before the application of any State is allowed or any contract or agreement is executed or any segregation of any of the land from the public domain is ordered by the Secretary of the Interior, the State shall file a map of the said land proposed to be irrigated, which shall exhibit a plan showing the mode of the contemplated irrigation, and which plan shall be sufficient to thoroughly irrigate and reclaim said land and prepare it to raise ordinary agricultural crops and shall also show the source of the water to be used for irrigation and reclamation, and the Secretary of the Interior may make necessary regulations for the reservation of the lands applied for by the State to date from the date of the filing of the map and plan of irrigation, but such reservation shall be of no force whatever if such map and plan of irrigation shall not be approved. That any State contracting under this section is hereby authorized to make all necessary contract to cause the said lands to be reclaimed, and to induce their settlement and cultivation in accordance with and subject to the provisions of this section; but the State shall not be authorized to lease any of said lands or to use or dispose of the same in any way whatever, except to secure their reclamation, cultivation, and settlement.

As fast as any State may furnish satisfactory proof, according to such rules and regulations as may be prescribed by the Secretary of the Interior, that any of said lands are irrigated, reclaimed, and occupied by actual settlers, patents shall be issued to the State or its assigns for said lands so reclaimed and settled: *Provided*, That said States shall not sell or dispose of more than one hundred and sixty acres of said lands to any one person, and any surplus of money derived by any State from the sale of said lands in excess of the cost of their reclamation shall be held as a trust fund for and be applied to the reclamation of other desert lands in such State. That to enable the Secretary of the Interior to examine any of the lands that may be selected under the provisions of this section, there is hereby appropriated out of any moneys in the Treasury, not otherwise appropriated, one thousand dollars.

Act June 17, 1902 (32 Stat. L., 388): An act appropriating the receipts from the sale and disposal of public lands in certain States and Territories to the construction of irrigation works for the reclamation of arid lands.

Be it enacted by the Senate and House of Representatives of the United States of America in Congress assembled, That all moneys received from the sale and disposal of public lands in Arizona, California, Colorado, Idaho, Kansas, Montana, Nebraska, Nevada, New Mexico, North Dakota, Oklahoma, Oregon, South Dakota, Utah, Washington, and Wyoming, beginning with the fiscal year ending June thirtieth, nineteen hundred and one, including the surplus of fees and commissions in excess of allowances to registers and receivers, and excepting the five per centum of the proceeds of the sales of public lands in the above States set aside by law for educational and other purposes, shall be and the same are hereby, reserved, set aside, and appropriated as a special fund in the Treasury to be known as the "reclamation fund," to be used in the examination and survey for and the construction and maintenance of irrigation works for the storage, diversion, and development of waters for the reclamation of arid and semiarid lands in the said States and Territories, and for the payment of all other expenditures provided for in this act: *Provided*, That in case the receipts from the sale and disposal of public lands other than those realized from the sale and disposal of lands referred to in this section are insufficient to meet the requirements for the support of agricultural colleges in the several States and Territories, under the act of August thirtieth, eighteen hundred and ninety, entitled "An act to apply a portion of the proceeds of the public lands to the more complete endowment and support of the colleges for the benefit of agriculture and the mechanic arts, established under the provisions of an act of Congress approved July second, eighteen hundred and sixty-two," the deficiency, if any, in the sum necessary for the support of the said colleges shall be provided for from any moneys in the Treasury not otherwise appropriated.

SEC. 2. That the Secretary of the Interior is hereby authorized and directed to make examinations and surveys for, and to locate and construct, as herein provided, irrigation works for the storage, diversion, and development of waters, including artesian wells, and to report to Congress at the beginning of each regular session as to the results of such examinations and surveys, giving estimates of cost of all contemplated works, the quantity and location of the lands which can be irrigated therefrom, and all facts relative to the practicability of each irrigation project; also the cost of works in process of construction as well as those which have been completed.

SEC. 3. That the Secretary of the Interior shall, before giving the public notice provided for in section four of this act, withdraw from public entry the lands required for any irrigation works contemplated under the provisions of this act, and shall restore to public entry any of the lands so withdrawn when, in his judgment, such lands are not required for the purposes of this act; and the Secretary of the Interior is hereby authorized, at or immediately prior to the time of beginning the suveys for any contemplated irrigation works, to withdraw from entry, except under the homestead laws, any public lands believed to be susceptible of irrigation from said works: *Provided*, That all lands entered and entries made under the homestead laws within areas so withdrawn during such withdrawal shall be subject to all the provisions, limitations, charges, terms, and conditions of this act; that said surveys shall be prosecuted diligently to completion, and upon the completion thereof, and of the necessary maps, plans, and estimates of cost, the Secretary of the Interior shall determine whether or not said project is practicable and advisable, and if determined to be impracticable or unadvisable he shall thereupon restore said lands to entry; that public lands which it is proposed to irrigate by means of any contemplated works shall be subject to entry only under the provisions of the homestead laws in tracts of not less than forty nor more than one hundred and sixty acres, and shall be subject to the limitations, charges, terms, and conditions herein provided: *Provided*, That the commutation provisions of the homestead laws shall not apply to entries made under this act.

SEC. 4. That upon the determination by the Secretary of the Interior that any irrigation project is practicable, he may cause to be let contracts for the construction of the same, in such portions or sections as it may be practicable to construct and complete as parts of the whole project, providing the necessary funds for such portions or sections are available in the reclamation fund, and thereupon he shall give public notice of the lands irrigable under such project, and limit of area per entry, which limit shall represent the acreage which, in the opinion of the Secretary, may be reasonably required for the support of a family upon the lands in question; also of the charges which shall be made per acre upon the said entries, and upon lands in private ownership which may be irrigated by the waters of the said irrigation project, and the number of annual installments, not exceeding ten, in which such charges shall be paid and the time when such payments shall commence. The said charges shall be determined with a view of returning to the reclamation fund the estimated cost of construction of the project, and shall be apportioned equitably: *Provided*, That in all construction work eight hours shall constitute a day's work, and no Mongolian labor shall be employed thereon.

SEC. 5. That the entryman upon lands to be irrigated by such works shall, in addition to compliance with the homestead laws, reclaim at least one-half of the total irrigable area of his entry for agricultural purposes, and before receiving patent for the lands covered by his entry shall pay to the Government the charges apportioned against such tract, as provided in section four. No right to the use of water for land in private ownership shall be sold for a tract exceeding one hundred and sixty acres to any one landowner, and no such sale shall be made to any landowner unless he be an actual bona fide resident on such land, or occupant thereof residing in the neighborhood of said land, and no such right shall permanently attach until all payments therefor are made. The annual installments shall be paid to the receiver of the local land office of the district in which the land is situated, and a failure to make any two payments when due shall render the entry subject to cancellation, with the forfeiture of all rights under this act, as well as of any moneys already paid thereon. All moneys received from the above sources shall be paid into the reclamation fund. Registers and receivers shall be allowed the usual commissions on all moneys paid for lands entered under this act.

SEC. 6. That the Secretary of the Interior is hereby authorized and directed to use the reclamation fund for the operation and maintenance of all reservoirs and irrigation works constructed under the provisions of this act: *Provided*, That when the payments required by this act are made for the major portion of the lands irrigated from the waters of any of the works herein provided for, then the management and operation of such irrigation works shall pass to the owners of the lands irrigated thereby, to be maintained at their expense under such form of organization and under such rules and regulations as may be acceptable to the Secretary of the Interior: *Provided*, That the title to and the management and operation of the reservoirs and the works necessary for their protection and operation shall remain in the Government until otherwise provided by Congress.

SEC. 7. That where in carrying out the provisions of this act it becomes necessary to acquire any rights or property, the Secretary of the Interior is hereby authorized to acquire the same for the United States, by purchase or by condemnation under judicial process, and to pay from the reclamation fund the sums which may be needed for that purpose, and it shall be the duty of the Attorney General of the United States upon every application of the Secretary of the Interior, under this act, to cause proceedings to be commenced for condemnation within thirty days from the receipt of the application at the Department of Justice.

SEC. 8. That nothing in this act shall be construed as affecting or intended to affect or to in any way interfere with the laws of any State or Territory relating to the control, appropriation, use, or distribution of water used in irrigation, or any vested right acquired thereunder, and the Secretary of the Interior, in carrying out the provisions of this act, shall proceed in conformity with such laws, and nothing herein shall in any way affect any right of any State or of the Federal Government or of any landowner, appropriator, or user of water in, to, or from any interstate stream or the waters thereof: *Provided*, That the right to the use of water acquired under the provisions of this act shall be appurtenant to the land irrigated, and beneficial use shall be the basis, the measure, and the limit of the right.

SEC. 9. That it is hereby declared to be the duty of the Secretary of the Interior in carrying out the provisions of this act, so far as the same may be practicable and subject to the existence of feasible irrigation projects, to expend the major portion of the funds arising from the sale of public lands within each State and Territory hereinbefore named for the benefit of arid and semiarid lands within the limits of such State or Territory: *Provided*, That the Secretary may temporarily use such portion of said funds for the benefit of arid or semiarid lands in any particular State or Territory hereinbefore named as he may deem advisable, but when so used the excess shall be restored to the fund as soon as practicable, to the end that ultimately, and in any event, within each ten-year period after the passage of this act, the expenditures for the benefit of the said States and Territories shall be equalized according to the proportions and subject to the conditions as to practicability and feasibility aforesaid.

SEC. 10. That the Secretary of the Interior is hereby authorized to perform any and all acts and to make such rules and regulations as may be necessary and proper for the purpose of carrying the provisions of this act into full force and effect.

Act June 21, 1906 (34 Stat. L., 386): An act to regulate the construction of dams across navigable waters.

Be it enacted by the Senate and House of Representatives of the United States of America in Congress assembled, That when, hereafter, authority is granted by Congress to any persons to construct and maintain a dam for water power or other purposes across any of the navigable waters of the United States, such dams shall not be built or commenced until the plans and specifications for its construction, together with such drawings of the proposed construction and such map of the proposed location as may be required for a full understanding of the subject, have been submitted to the Secretary of War and Chief of Engineers for their approval, or until they shall have approved such plans and specifications and the location of such dam and accessory works; and when the plans for any dam to be constructed under the provisions of this act have been approved by the Chief of Engineers and by the Secretary of War it shall not be lawful to deviate from such plans either before or after completion of the structure unless the modification of such plans has previously been submitted to and received the approval of the Chief of Engineers and of the Secretary of War: *Provided*, That in approving said plans and location such conditions and stipulations may be imposed as the Chief of Engineers and the Secretary of War may deem necessary to protect the present and future interests of the United States, which may include the condition that such persons shall construct, maintain, and operate, without expense to the United States, in connection with said dam and appurtenant works, a lock or locks, booms, sluices, or any other structure which the Secretary of War and the Chief of Engineers at any time may deem necessary in the interests of navigation, in accordance with such plans as they may approve, and also that whenever Congress shall authorize the construction of a lock, or other structures for navigation purposes, in connection with such dam, the person owning such dam shall convey to the United States, free of cost, title to such land as may be required for such constructions and approaches, and shall grant to the United States a free use of water power for building and operating such constructions.

SEC. 2. That the right is hereby reserved to the United States to construct, maintain, and operate, in connection with any dam built under the provisions of this act, a suitable lock or locks, or any other structure for navigation purposes, and at all times to control the said dam and the level of the pool caused by said dam to such an extent as may be necessary to provide proper facilities for navigation.

SEC. 3. That the person, company, or corporation building, maintaining, or operating any dam and appurtenant works under the provisions of this act shall be liable for any damage that may be inflicted thereby upon private property, either by overflow or otherwise. The persons owning or operating any such dam shall maintain, at their own expense, such lights and other signals thereon and such fishways as the Secretary of Commerce and Labor shall prescribe.

SEC. 4. That all rights acquired under this act shall cease and be determined if the person, company, or corporation acquiring such rights shall, at any time, fail to comply with any of the provisions and requirements of the act, or with any of the stipulations and conditions that may be prescribed as aforesaid by the Chief of Engineers and the Secretary of War.

SEC. 5. That any person who shall fail or refuse to comply with the lawful order of the Secretary of War and the Chief of Engineers, made in accordance with the provisions of this act, shall be deemed guilty of a violation of this act, and any persons who shall be guilty of a violation of this act shall be deemed guilty of a misdemeanor, and on conviction thereof shall be punished by a fine not exceeding five thousand dollars, and every month such persons shall remain in default shall be deemed a new offense and subject such persons to additional penalties therefor; and in addition to the penalties above described the Secretary of War and the Chief of Engineers may, upon refusal of the persons owning or controlling any such dam and accessory works to comply with any lawful order issued by the Secretary of War or Chief of Engineers in regard thereto, cause the removal of such dam and accessory works as an obstruction to navigation at the expense of the persons owning or controlling such dam, and suit for such expense may be brought in the name of the United States against such persons, and recovery had for such expense in any court of competent jurisdiction; and the removal of any structures erected or maintained in violation of the provisions of this act or the order or direction of the Secretary of War or Chief of Engineers made in pursuance thereof may be enforced by injunction, mandamus, or other summary process, upon application to the circuit court in the district in which such structure may, in whole or in part, exist, and proper proceedings to this end may be instituted under the direction of the Attorney General of the United States at the request of the Chief of Engineers or the Secretary of War; and in case of any litigation arising from any obstruction or alleged obstruction to navigation created by the construction of any dam under this act, the cause or question arising may be tried before the circuit court of the United States in any district in which any portion of said obstruction or dam touches.

SEC. 6. That whenever Congress shall hereafter by law authorize the construction of any dam across any of the navigable waters of the United States, and no time for the commencement and completion of such dam is named in said act, the authority thereby granted shall cease and be null and void unless the actual construction of the dam authorized in such act be commenced within one year and completed within three years from the date of the passage of such act.

SEC. 7. That the right to alter, amend, or repeal this act is hereby expressly reserved as to any and all dams which may be constructed in accordance with the provisions of this act, and the United States shall incur no liability for the alteration, amendment, or repeal thereof to the owner or owners or any other persons interested in any dam which shall have been constructed in accordance with its provisions.

SEC. 8. That the word "persons" as used in this act shall be construed to import both the singular and the plural, as the case demands, and shall include corporations, companies, and associations.

Act March 28, 1908 (35 Stat. L., 52): *Be it enacted by the Senate and House of Representatives of the United States of America in Congress assembled*, That from and after the passage of this act the right to make entry of desert lands under the provisions of the act approved March third, eighteen hundred and seventy-seven, entitled "An act to provide for the sale of desert lands in certain States and Territories," as amended by the act approved March third, eighteen hundred and ninety-one, entitled "An act to repeal timber culture laws, and for other purposes," shall be restricted to surveyed public lands of the character contemplated by said acts, and no such entries of unsurveyed lands shall be allowed or made of record: *Provided, however*, That any individual qualified to make entry of desert lands under said acts who has, prior to survey, taken possession of a tract of unsurveyed desert land not exceeding in area three hundred and twenty acres in compact form, and has reclaimed or has in good faith commenced the work of reclaiming the same, shall have the preference right to make entry of such tract under said acts, in conformity with the public land surveys, within ninety days after the filing of the approved plat of survey in the district land office.

SEC. 2. That from and after the date of the passage of this act no assignment of an entry made under said acts shall be allowed or recognized, except it be to an individual who is shown to be qualified to make entry under said acts of the land covered by the assigned entry, and such assignments may include all or part of an entry; but no assignment to or for the benefit of any corporation or association shall be authorized or recognized.

SEC. 3. That any entryman under the above acts who shall show to the satisfaction of the Commissioner of the General Land Office that he has in good faith complied with the terms, requirements, and provisions of said acts, but that because of some unavoidable delay in the construction of the irrigating works, intended to convey water to the said lands, he is, without fault on his part, unable to make proof of the reclamation and cultivation of said land, as required by said acts, shall, upon filing his corroborated affidavit with the land office in which said land is located, setting forth said facts, be allowed an additional period of not to exceed three years, within the discretion of the Commissioner of the General Land Office, within which to furnish proof as required by said acts of the completion of such work.

Act February 13, 1911 (36 Stat. L., 902): *Be it enacted by the Senate and House of Representatives of the United States of America in Congress assembled*, That the Secretary of the Interior may, in his discretion, withdraw any public notice heretofore issued under section four of the reclamation act of June seventeenth, nineteen hundred and two, and he may agree to such modifications of water-right applications heretofore duly filed or contracts with water users' associations and others, entered into prior to the passage of this act, as he may deem advisable, or he may consent to the abrogation of such water-right applications and contracts, and proceed in all respects as if no such notice had been given.

Act August 9, 1912 (37 Stat. L., 265): An act providing for patents on reclamation entries, and for other purposes.

Be it enacted by the Senate and House of Representatives of the United States of America in Congress assembled, That any homestead entryman under the act of June seventeenth, nineteen hundred and two, known as the reclamation act, including entrymen on ceded Indian lands, may, at any time after having complied with the provisions of law applicable to such lands as to residence, reclamation and cultivation, submit proof of such residence, reclamation and cultivation, which proof, if found regular and satisfactory, shall entitle the entryman to a patent, and all purchasers of water-right certificates on reclamation projects shall be entitled to a final water-right certificate upon proof of the cultivation and reclamation of the land to which the certificate applies, to the extent required by the reclamation act for homestead entrymen: *Provided*, That no such patent or certificate shall issue until all sums due the United States on account of such land or water right at the time of issuance of patent or certificate have been paid.

SEC. 2. That every patent and water-right certificate issued under this act shall expressly reserve to the United States a prior lien on the land patented or for which water right is certified, together with all water rights appurtenant or belonging thereto, superior to all other liens, claims or demands whatsoever for the payment of all sums due or to become due to the United States or its successors in control of the irrigation project in connection with such lands and water rights.

Upon default of payment of any amount so due title to the land shall pass to the United States free of all encumbrance, subject to the right of the defaulting debtor or any mortgagee, lien holder, judgment debtor, or subsequent purchaser to redeem the land within one year after the notice of such default shall have been given by payment of all moneys due, with eight per centum interest and cost. And the United States, at its option, acting through the Secretary of the Interior, may cause land to be sold at any time after such failure to redeem, and from the proceeds of the sale there shall be paid into the reclamation fund all moneys due, with interest as herein provided, and costs. The balance of the proceeds, if any, shall be the property of the defaulting debtor or his assignee: *Provided*, That in case of sale after failure to redeem under this section the United States shall be authorized to bid in such land at not more than the amount in default, including interest and costs.

SEC. 3. That upon full and final payment being made of all amounts due on account of the building and betterment charges to the United States or its successors in control of the project, the United States or its successors, as the case may be, shall issue upon request a certificate certifying that payment of the building and betterment charges in full has been made and that the lien upon the land has been so far satisfied and is no longer of any force or effect except the lien for annual charges for operation and maintenance: *Provided*, That no person shall at any one time or in any manner, except as hereinafter otherwise provided, acquire, own, or hold irrigable land for which entry or water-right application shall have been made under the said reclamation act of June seventeenth, nineteen hundred and two, and acts supplementary thereto and amendatory thereof, before final payment in full of all installments of building and betterment charges shall have been made on account of such land in excess of one farm unit as fixed by the Secretary of the Interior as the limit of area per entry of public land or per single ownership of private land for which a water right may be purchased, respectively, nor in any case in excess of one hundred and sixty acres, nor shall water be furnished under said acts nor a water right sold or recognized for such excess; but any such excess land acquired at any time in good faith by descent, by will, or by foreclosure of any lien may be held for two years and no longer after its acquisition; and every excess holding prohibited as aforesaid shall be forfeited to the United States by proceedings instituted by the Attorney General for that purpose in any court of competent jurisdiction; and this proviso shall be recited in every patent and water-right certificate issued by the United States under the provisions of this act.

SEC. 4. That the Secretary of the Interior is hereby authorized to designate such bonded fiscal agents or officers of the Reclamation Service as he may deem advisable on each reclamation project, to whom shall be paid all sums due on reclamation entries or water rights, and the officials so designated shall keep a record for the information of the public of the sums paid and the amount due at any time on account of any entry made or water right purchased under the reclamation act; and the Secretary of the Interior shall make provision for furnishing copies of duly authenicated records of entries upon payment of reasonable fees, which copies shall be admissable in evidence, as are copies authenicated under section eight hundred and eighty-eight of the Revised Statutes.

SEC. 5. That jurisdiction of suits by the United States for the enforcement of the provisions of this act is hereby conferred on the United States district courts of the districts in which the lands are situated.

Act August 13, 1914 (38 Stat. L., 686): An act extending the period of payment under reclamation projects, and for other purposes.

Be it enacted by the Senate and House of Representatives of the United States of America in Congress assembled, That any person whose lands hereafter become subject to the terms and conditions of the act approved June seventeenth, nineteen hundred and two, entitled "An act appropriating the receipts from the sale and disposal of public lands in certain States and Territories to the construction of irrigation works for the reclamation of arid lands," and acts amendatory thereof or supplementary thereto, hereafter to be referred to as the reclamation law, and any person who hereafter makes entry thereunder shall at the time of making water-right application or entry, as the case may be, pay into the reclamation fund five per centum of the construction charge fixed for his land as an initial installment, and shall pay the balance of said charge in fifteen annual installments, the first five of which shall be five percentum of the construction charge and the remainder shall each be seven per centum until the whole amount shall have been paid. The first of the annual installments shall become due and payable on December first of the fifth calendar year after the initial installment: *Provided*, That any water-right applicant or entryman may, if he so elects, pay the whole or any part of the construction charges owing by him within any shorter period: *Provided further*, That entry may be made whenever water is available, as announced by the Secretary of the Interior, and the initial payment be made when the charge per acre is established.

ACT SHALL APPLY TO EXISTING PROJECTS.

SEC. 2. That any person whose land or entry has heretofore become subject to the terms and conditions of the reclamation law shall pay the construction charge, or the portion of the construction charge remaining unpaid, in twenty annual installments, the first of which shall become due and payable on December first of the year in which the public notice affecting his land is issued under this act, and subsequent installments on December first of each year thereafter. The first four of such installments shall each be two per centum, the next two installments shall each be four percentum, and the next fourteen each six per centum of the total construction charge, or the portion of the construction charge unpaid at the beginning of such installments.

PENALTIES.

SEC. 3. That if any water-right applicant or entryman shall fail to pay any installment of his construction charges when due, there shall be added to the amount unpaid a penalty of one per centum thereof, and there shall be added a like penalty of one per centum of the amount unpaid on the first day of each month thereafter so long as such default shall continue. If any such applicant or entryman shall be one year in default in the payment of any installment of the construction charges and penalties, or any part thereof, his water-right application, and if he be a homestead entryman his entry also, shall be subject to cancellation, and all payments made by him forfeited to the reclamation fund, but no homestead entry shall be subject to contest because of such default: *Provided*, That if the Secretary of the Interior shall so elect, he may cause suit or action to be brought for the recovery of the amount in default and penalties; but if suit or action be brought, the right to declare a cancellation and forfeiture shall be suspended pending such suit or action.

INCREASE OF CHARGES.

SEC. 4. That no increase in the construction charges shall hereafter be made, after the same have been fixed by public notice, except by agreement between the Secretary of the Interior and a majority of the water-right applicants and entrymen to be affected by such increase, whereupon all water-right applicants and entrymen in the area proposed to be affected by the increased charge shall become subject thereto. Such increased charge shall be added to the construction charge and payment thereof distributed over the remaining unpaid installments of construction charges: *Provided*, That the Secretary of the Interior, in his discretion, may agree that such increased construction charge shall be paid in additional annual installments, each of which shall be at least equal to the amount of the largest installment as fixed for the project by the public notice theretofore issued. And such additional installments of the increased construction charge, as so agreed upon, shall become due and payable on December first of each year subsequent to the year when the final installment of the construction charge under such public notice is due and payable: *Provided further*, That all such increased construction charges shall be subject to the same conditions, penalties, and suit or action as provided in section three of this act.

OPERATIONS AND MAINTENANCE.

SEC. 5. That in addition to the construction charge, every water-right applicant, entryman, or landowner under or upon a reclamation project shall also pay, whenever water service is available for the irrigation of his land, an operation and maintenance charge based upon the total cost of operation and maintenance of the project, or each separate unit thereof, and such charge shall be made for each acre-foot of water delivered; but each acre of irrigable land, whether irrigated or not, shall be charged with a minimum operation and maintenance charge based upon the charge for delivery of not less than one acre-foot of water: *Provided*, That, whenever any legally organized water users' association or irrigation district shall so request, the Secretary of the Interior is hereby authorized, in his discretion, to transfer to such water users' association or irrigation district the care, operation, and maintenance of all or any part of the project works subject to such rules and regulations as he may prescribe. If the total amount of operation and maintenance charges and penalties collected for any one irrigation season on any project shall exceed the cost of operation and maintenance of the project during that irrigation season, the balance shall be applied to a reduction of the charge on the project for the next irrigation season, and any deficit incurred may likewise be added to the charge for the next irrigation season.

PENALTIES.

SEC. 6. That all operation and maintenance charges shall become due and payable on the date fixed for each project by the Secretary of the Interior, and if such charge is paid on or before the date when due there shall be a discount of five per centum of such charge; but if such charge is unpaid on the first day of the third calendar month thereafter, a penalty of one per centum of the amount unpaid shall be added thereto, and thereafter an additional penalty of one per centum of the amount unpaid shall be added on the first day of each calendar month if such charge and penalties shall remain unpaid, and no water shall be delivered to the lands of any water-right applicant or entryman who shall be in arrears for more than one calendar year for the payment of any charge for operation and maintenance, or any annual construction charge and penalties. If any water-right applicant or entryman shall be one year in arrears in the payment of any charge for operation and maintenance and penalties, or any part thereof, his water-right application, and if he be a homestead entryman his entry also, shall be subject to cancellation, and all payments made by him forfeited to the reclamation fund, but no homestead entry shall be subject to contest because of such arrears. In the discretion of the Secretary of the Interior suit or action may be brought for the amounts in default and penalties in like manner as provided in section three of this act.

FISCAL AGENT.

SEC. 7. That the Secretary of the Interior is hereby authorized, in his discretion, to designate and appoint, under such rules and regulations as he may prescribe, the legally organized water users' association or irrigation district, under any reclamation project, as the fiscal agent of the United States to collect the annual payments on the construction charge of the project and the annual charges for operation and maintenance and all penalties: *Provided*, That no water-right applicant or entryman shall be entitled to credit for any payment thus made until the same shall have been paid over to an officer designated by the Secretary of the Interior to receive the same.

RECLAMATION REQUIREMENTS,

SEC. 8. That the Secretary of the Interior is hereby authorized to make general rules and regulations governing the use of water in the irrigation of the lands within any project, and may require the reclamation for agricultural purposes and the cultivation of one-fourth the irrigable area under each water-right application or entry within three full irrigation seasons after the filing of water-right application or entry, and the reclamation for agricultural purposes and the cultivation of one-half the irrigable area within five full irrigation seasons after the filing of water-right application or entry, and shall provide for continued compliance with such requirements. Failure on the part of any water-right application or entryman to comply with such requirements shall render his application or entry subject to cancellation.

LANDS NOT SUBJECT TO RECLAMATION ACT.

SEC. 9. That in all cases where application for water right for lands in private ownership or lands held under entries not subject to the reclamation law shall not be made within one year after the passage of this act, or within one year after notice issued in pursuance of section four of the reclamation act, in cases where such notice has not heretofore been issued, the construction charges for such land shall be increased five per centum each year until such application is made and an initial installment is paid.

WITHDRAW LANDS SUBJECT TO ENTRY.

SEC. 10. That the act of Congress approved February eighteenth, nineteen hundred and eleven, entitled "An act to amend section five of the act of Congress of June twenty-fifth, nineteen hundred and ten, entitled 'An act to authorize advances to the reclamation fund and for the issuance and disposal of certificates of indebtedness in reimbursement therefor, and for other purposes,'" be, and the same hereby is, amended so as to read as follows:

"SEC. 5. That no entry shall be hereafter made and no entryman shall be permitted to go upon lands reserved for irrigation purposes until the Secretary of the Interior shall have established the unit of acreage per entry, and water is ready to be delivered for the land in such unit or some part thereof, and such fact has been announced by the Secretary of the Interior: *Provided*, That where entries made prior to June twenty-fifth, nineteen hundred and ten, have been or may be relinquished in whole or in part the lands so relinquished shall be subject to settlement and entry under the reclamation law."

WATER SERVICE.

SEC. 11. That whenever water is available and it is impracticable to apportion operation and maintenance charges as provided in section five of this act, the Secretary of the Interior may, prior to giving public notice of the construction charge per acre upon land under any project, furnish water to any entryman or private landowner thereunder until such notice is given, making a reasonable charge therefor, and such charges shall be subject to the same penalties and to the provisions for cancellation and collection as herein provided for other operation and maintenance charges.

ADMISSION OF PRIVATE LANDOWNERS TO NEW PROJECTS.

SEC. 12. That before any contract is let or work begun for the construction of any reclamation project hereafter adopted the Secretary of the Interior shall require the owners of private lands thereunder to agree to dispose of all lands in excess of the area which he shall deem sufficient for the support of a family upon the land in question, upon such terms and at not to exceed such price as the Secretary of the Interior may designate; and if any landowner shall refuse to agree to the requirements fixed by the Secretary of the Interior, his land shall not be included within the project if adopted for construction.

DISPOSITION OF EXCESS FARM UNITS.

SEC. 13. That all entries under reclamation projects containing more than one farm unit shall be reduced in area and conformed to a single farm unit within two years after making proof of residence, improvement, and cultivation, or within two years after the issuance of a farm-unit plat for the project, if the same issues subsequent to the making of such proof: *Provided*, That such proof is made within four years from the date as announced by the Secretary of the Interior, that water is available for delivery for the land. Any entryman failing within the period herein provided to dispose of the excess of his entry above one farm unit, in the manner provided by law, and to conform his entry to a single farm unit shall render his entry subject to cancellation as to the excess above one farm unit: *Provided*, That upon compliance with the provisions of law such entryman shall be entitled to receive a patent for that part of his entry which conforms to one farm unit as established for the project: *Provided further*, That no person shall hold by assignment more than one farm unit prior to final payment of all charges for all the land held by him subject to the reclamation law, except operation and maintenance charges not then due.

ACCEPTANCE OF THIS ACT.

SEC. 14. That any person whose land or entry has heretofore become subject to the reclamation law, who desires to secure the benefits of the extension of the period of payments provided by this act shall, within six months after the issuance of the first public notice hereunder affecting his land or entry, notify the Secretary of the Interior, in the manner to be prescribed by said Secretary, of his acceptance of all the terms and conditions of this act, and thereafter his lands or entry shall be subject to all of the provisions of this act.

SEC. 15. That the Secretary of the Interior is hereby authorized to perform any and all acts and to make such rules and regulations as may be necessary and proper for the purpose of carrying the provisions of this act into full force and effect.

SEC. 16. That from and after July first, nineteen hundred and fifteen, expenditures shall not be made for carrying out the purposes of the reclamation law except out of appropriations made annually by Congress therefor, and the Secretary of the Interior shall, for the fiscal year nineteen hundred and sixteen, and annually thereafter, in the regular Book of Estimates, submit to Congress estimates of the amount of money necessary to be expended for carrying out any or all of the purposes authorized by the reclamation law, including the extension and completion of existing projects and units thereof and the construction of new projects. The annual appropriations made hereunder by Congress for such purposes shall be paid out of the reclamation fund provided for by the reclamation law.

O

Lightning Source UK Ltd.
Milton Keynes UK
UKHW010304220119
335963UK00013B/1003/P